Psychology as a Natural Science

Psychology as a Natural Science

SECOND EDITION OF PSYCHOLOGY: A CONCISE INTRODUCTION TO THE FUNDAMENTALS OF BEHAVIOR

Charles W. Telford
James M. Sawrey

San Jose State College

BROOKS/COLE PUBLISHING COMPANY
MONTEREY, CALIFORNIA

A Division of Wadsworth Publishing Company, Inc.
Belmont, California

 The first edition of this book was published under the title *Psychology: A Concise Introduction to the Fundamentals of Behavior.*

L.C. Cat. Card No.: 70-167898
ISBN 0-8185-0019-0
Printed in the United States of America

1 2 3 4 5 6 7 8 9 10—76 75 74 73 72

This book was edited by Micky Stay and designed by Linda Marcetti. It was typeset at Continental Graphics, Los Angeles, California, and printed and bound at Kingsport Press, Kingsport, Tennessee.

Figure Sources

Figure 1-2. From left to right: (A) Courtesy of Dr. C. E. Schwerdt and Dr. R. C. Williams, Virus Laboratory, University of California at Berkeley. (B) From "Cyto- and histo-chemistry of the liver" by Max Wachstein. In Ch. Rouiller (Ed.), *The Liver,* Vol. I. Copyright 1963 by Academic Press, Inc., New York. Reprinted by permission. (C) From A. E. Walker, "Nervous System, Surgery of," *Encyclopedia Britannica,* Vol. 16, p. 248. Reprinted by permission of A. E. Walker, M.D. (D) Publicity still from Ingmar Bergman's *Wild Strawberries.* Courtesy of Janus Films, distributor of the film in 16mm and 35mm. (E) Photo courtesy of United Press International.

Figure 2-11. From D. B. Lindsley, "Attention, Consciousness, Sleep, and Wakefulness." In J. Field (Ed.), *Handbook of Physiology,* Section I, Neurophysiology, Vol. III, pp. 1553-1593. Reprinted by permission of the author and the American Physiological Society.

Figure 2-12. From Rudd, *Arch. Entwech.,* CXVIII, 1929. Reprinted by permission of the publisher, Cambridge University Press, New York.

Figure 3-8. Photo courtesy of The Bettman Archive, Inc.

Figure 4-6. Photo courtesy of The Bettman Archive, Inc.

Figure 5-4. "Skinner box." Courtesy of Ralph Gerbrands & Co., Arlington, Massachusetts. Portrait courtesy of B. F. Skinner, Department of Psychology, Harvard University, Cambridge, Mass.

Table 5-2. All material from Sawrey, J. M., and Telford, C. W., *Educational Psychology,* 3rd ed., 1968 is reprinted by permission of Allyn and Bacon, Inc., Boston, Mass.

Figure 5-6. Photo courtesy of David Krech, Department of Psychology, University of California at Berkeley.

Figure 6-1. Photo courtesy of United Press International.

Figure 8-2. Publicity still from Ingmar Bergman's *Wild Strawberries.* Courtesy of Janus Films, distributor of the film in 16mm and 35mm.

Figure 10-3. Photo courtesy of United Press International.

Figure 11-1. From Meryman, J. J., "Magnitude of startle response as a function of hunger and fear." Unpublished master's thesis, State University of Iowa, 1952. Reprinted by permission of the author.

Figure 11-2. Photo courtesy of Jules H. Masserman, M.D., The Medical School, Northwestern University, Chicago, Illinois.

Figure 12-2. From left to right: (A) Photo courtesy of United Press International. (B) Photo courtesy of United Press International. (C) Publicity still from Ingmar Bergman's *Wild Strawberries.* Courtesy of Janus Films, distributor of the film in 16mm and 35mm.

Figure 12-3. Photo courtesy of United Press International.

Figure 12-4. Adapted from photograph entitled *March on Washington* by Ritchie. Reprinted by permission of Globe Photos, Inc.

Preface

This book is designed to treat the basic subject matter of psychology as a natural science and to introduce the methods of psychological investigation to beginning students of psychology. This concise treatment of the core subject matter of psychology should provide both a basic framework for the understanding of human behavior and a foundation for the study of other aspects of psychology.

This second edition emphasizes psychology as a natural science more so than did the first edition. The principal changes in the format of this edition are the elimination of separate chapters on development, personality, social processes, emotions, and adjustment and the expansion of material on basic psychological processes. The new format includes an introductory chapter, one on physiological processes, two on attentional-perceptual processes, three on learning and memory, two on motivation, one on ideational processes, and one on the measurement of abilities. The concluding chapter is designed to introduce the reader to the areas of personal and social behavior that are likely to be covered in later psychology courses. In addition, the Appendix provides a basic introduction to statistics.

We have tried to keep this book short so that it might be used in a one-quarter or one-semester course dealing with basic psychological concepts and methods. If supplementary material is desired, numerous sources, such as Brooks/Cole's *Basic Concepts in Psychology Series*, are available.

Anyone who writes a text in general psychology is indebted to innumerable individuals. Every instructor has learned from his own teachers, from his colleagues, and, most of all, from his interaction with his students. We are grateful to all who have so influenced us, as well as to the authors whose works are cited formally in the text. For their critical reviews of the manuscript, we extend our appreciation to Edward L. Walker, J. David Birch, Melvin Manis, and Charles M. Butter, all of the University of Michigan, and to Robert Hicks of San Jose State College and Jon L. Williams of Kenyon College. Our wives, Aldene E. Telford and Una Mae Sawrey, have encouraged our efforts, criticized the manuscript, and tolerated our neglect of other duties sufficiently to warrant special mention.

Charles W. Telford
James M. Sawrey

Contents

1. THE SUBJECT MATTER OF PSYCHOLOGY 1

Psychology's Philosophical Heritage 2
Psychology's Physiological Roots 4
Psychology as a Separate Discipline 6
Definition of Psychology 7
The Relation of Psychology to Other Sciences 9
Psychology as a Biosocial Science 10
The Interdisciplinary Nature of Modern Psychology 10
Psychological Terminology 11

Derivation of Terms 11
The Important Distinction between Processes and Things 11

The Sources of Psychological Data 14
Psychology as a Science 15
The Components of Scientific Methodology 19

The Philosophical Basis of Science 19
Scientific Methodology (Research Design) 21

Scientific Technology 22
The Role of Measurement in Science 29

Summary 32
Suggested Readings 33

2. *THE BIOLOGICAL BASIS OF HUMAN BEHAVIOR* 35

Embryonic Development 36
Development of the Nervous System 36
The Cellular Elements 38
Cellular Differentiation and Specialization 39

The Receptors 39
The Effectors 39
The Connectors—Neurons 41

Subdivisions of the Nervous System 44

The Cerebral Cortex 48

Coding within the Nervous System 55
Patterns of "Spontaneous" Neural Activity (EEGs) 57
Stability and Adaptability in Neural Growth and Function 59

Peripheral Influences on Neural Growth 59
Visual Fixity and Adaptability 60
Plasticity and Variability in the Somesthetic Motor Areas 63

The Endocrine System 64
Summary 69
Suggested Readings 71

3. *PERCEPTUAL PROCESSES: I. GENERAL ASPECTS* 73

The Irritability of Organisms 75
Stimuli 76
The Encoding of Information 77
Sensory Thresholds 78

Weber's Law Relative to Differential Thresholds 79

Sensory Adaptation 79

The Neurophysiology of Sensory Adaptation 80

The Attentional-Perceptual System 81

Components of Attention 82
Determinants of Attention 85
Divided Attention 89

Perceiving 89

Determinants of Perception 91
Perceptual Organization 94
Perceptual Constancy 95
Illusory Experiences 99
Perception without Learning 103
Social Perception 106
Perception and Personality 106

Man's Performance Capacities 108
Summary 108
Suggested Readings 109

4. *PERCEPTUAL PROCESSES: II. A MORE ANALYTICAL VIEW* 111

Vision 112

Visual Stimuli 112
The Dimensions of Visual Stimuli 113
The Visual Process 115
Color Vision 118
Afterimages (Successive Contrast) 122
Visual Perception of Distance 124
The Integration of Visual Cues 128

Hearing 129

Some Physical-Experiential Correlates 130
The Auditory Receptors 133
Auditory Theory 134
The Neural Processing of Auditory Input 137

The Cutaneous Senses 139

Thermal Sensitivity 140
Touch, or Light Pressure 142
Pain Sensitivity 143

Kinesthetic Sensitivity 144

Neural Coding 145

Labyrinthine Sensitivity—The Sense of Balance 145
Taste 148
Olfaction 152
The Organic Senses 153
Summary 154
Suggested Readings 155

5. *ELEMENTARY LEARNING* *157*

The Nature of Learning *158*
The Scope and Importance of Learning *159*
Circumstances for Learning *161*

Classical Conditioning 162
Instrumental Conditioning 164
Classical and Instrumental Conditioning Compared 164
Escape Training 165
Avoidance Training 166
Positive-Reward Training 166
Successive Approximation 168
Trial and Error 169

Some Aspects of Conditioning *170*

Stimulus Generalization 170
Extinction and Spontaneous Recovery 172
Higher-Order Conditioning 175
Discrimination 176
Reinforcement 177
Further Aspects of Conditioning 182
The Extensive Nature of Conditioning 183

The Physiological Basis of Learning *184*
Gross Cortical Functions in Learning and Retention *185*
The Neural Locus of Learning *187*
Some Anatomical and Biochemical Accompaniments of Learning *188*

The Growth of Neural Processes 189

Some Molecular Approaches *190*
Summary *192*
Suggested Readings *193*

6. *LEARNING: THEORY AND PROCESS* *195*

Learning through Imitation *195*

Conditioning in Imitation 197
Role of Reinforcement in Imitation 199

Insight *201*
The Study of the Acquisition of Skill *202*

Measuring the Progress of Learning 203
Distribution of Practice 205
Meaningfulness as "Association Value" 207
Additional Factors in Learning 209
Transfer of Learning 212

Theories of Learning 215
Summary 218
Suggested Readings 219

7. *RETENTION AND FORGETTING* 221

Evidence of Retention 222

Repeated Performances 222
Relearning as Evidence of Retention 223
Delayed Reaction as Evidence of Retention 224

Measurement of Retention 225
The Course of Forgetting 227
Factors Affecting Retention 228

Rate of Original Learning 228
Level of Original Learning 229
Meaningfulness of Material 231
Influence of Intention 233
Recall during Practice 234
Motor versus Ideational Materials 235

Dynamic Factors in Remembering 235

Tip-of-the-Tongue Phenomenon (TOT) 236
Distortion in Remembering or Recall 236
Stimulus Conditions and Recall 237
Ego Involvement 238

Theories of Forgetting 239

Passive Decay and Organic Factors 239
Interference Theory 240
Motivated Forgetting 243
The Perseveration-Consolidation Hypothesis 244
Two-Process Theory 245

Summary 246
Suggested Readings 247

8. *IDEATIONAL PROCESSES* 249

Reasoning 250

The Motivation of Reasoning 251
Recognition of the Problem 252
Preparation 253
Formulation of Possible Solutions 253
Incubation 254

Illumination 255
Verification 255
The Limitations of "Steps in Reasoning" 255
Factors Influencing Reasoning 256
Decision Making without Reasoning 259

Conceptual Development 259

The Sensorimotor Period (Birth to 2 Years) 260
The Preoperational Period (2 to 7 Years) 260
The Concrete Operational Period (7 to 11 Years) 261
The Formal-Thought Operational Period (11 to 15 Years) 261

Concept Acquisition 261

Concept Formation as Rule Learning 262

Language and Concepts 263
Thinking as a Physiological Process 264

Ideation as Neural Activity 265
Ideation as Neuromuscular Activity 266

Creativity 267

Definitions of Creativity 268
The Characteristics of Creative People 268
The Parents of Creative Children 270
Conditions Conducive to Creativity 270

Dreams 271

Daydreams (Autistic Thinking) 275
Pathological Thinking 276
Imagining 277
Summary 278
Suggested Readings 279

9. *MEASUREMENT OF ABILITIES* 281

Validity 281

Statistical Validity 282

Reliability 283

Objectivity 285

Intelligence 286

Early Measurement of Intelligence 286
Individual Intelligence Tests 288
Distribution of Intelligence 291

Creativity 294

Factors Associated with Ability *297*

Sex and Ability 297
Race and Ability 298
Nature-Nurture Revisited 299
Socioeconomic Status and Ability 302

Constancy of IQ *303*

Variation and Age 304
IQs that Vary 305
Changes in Level of Measured Intelligence 306
Relative Constancy 308

Special Abilities *309*

Mechanical Ability 309
Musical Ability 310
Artistic Ability 310

Summary *311*
Suggested Readings *312*

10. MOTIVATION: BASIC PROCESSES *313*

Historical Considerations *314*
Instincts *315*
The Concept of Drive *317*

The Nature of Drive Theory 318
Drive or Drives? 318

The Bases for Motivation *319*

Needs of the Organism 320
Homeostasis 321
Stimulation 322
Hunger and Thirst 325
Noxious Stimulation 328
Sex 329
Other Stimuli as Sources of Variation in Drive 330
Emotion and Motivation 332

Summary *333*
Suggested Readings *334*

11. MOTIVATION: COMPLEX PROCESSES *337*

Fear *338*

Arousal, Activation, or Drive Effects of Fear 338
Fear Reduction as Reinforcement 341

Fear and Human Behavior 342
Early Experience and Fear 343
The Persistence of Fear 344
Relatively Constant Anxiety 345
Anxiety and Human Behavior 348

Language 349

Language and Arousal 349
Exhortation as a Source of Arousal 349

Motives 351

Money-Seeking Behavior 352
Affectional Responses 353
Sexually Oriented Behavior 354
Prestige-Oriented Behavior 355
The Achievement Motive 356

Summary 357
Suggested Readings 358

12. *PERSONAL AND SOCIAL BEHAVIOR* 359

Frustration 359

Frustration by Delay 360
Frustration by Thwarting 361

Conflict 363

Varieties of Conflict Situations 364

Habits of Adjustment 366
Personality 367

The Determinants of Personality 369
Environmental Influences on Personality 373
Personality Abnormalities 376

Social Processes 378
The Nature of Culture 378
Roles 381

Sex Roles 382
Conformity and Nonconformity 382

Group Functions 386
Alienation 387

The Social-Action Movement as a Search for Identity 389
Summary 392
Suggested Readings 393

APPENDIX: STATISTICS 395

Descriptive Statistics 395

Frequency Distributions and their Representations 396
Measures of Variation 401
Correlation 403

Statistical Inference 406

REFERENCES 409

AUTHOR INDEX 445

SUBJECT INDEX 451

Psychology as a Natural Science

1

The Subject Matter of Psychology

In modern Western cultures people learn as children that activity can be divided into that which is inanimate and that which is animate (Piaget, 1930; Hallowell, 1964). By contrast, primitive man does not make this distinction. Instead, he attributes all observed activity to hidden—generally willful—powers or forces. Thus contemporary primitives believe, as our forebears did, that something wills the rain to fall or the sun to shine. The primitive notion that hidden forces animate all events finds expression in the belief that the obvious physical person who can be seen and touched is animated by an immaterial duplicate. According to this dualistic concept, the hidden "man within the man" directs and controls the behavior of the physical being. When a man behaves in a strange way, a primitive explanation is that his body is controlled by evil spirits. Sleep, comas, trances, and death are all believed to be caused by the separation of the physical and the immaterial beings.

Over a long period of time such dualistic and animistic explanations of human behavior have yielded to more naturalistic explanations, although the transition from animism to naturalism is only partially completed today. The following three sections give a brief description of the historical development of the naturalistic approach to human behavior—the approach that characterizes contemporary psychology.

PSYCHOLOGY'S PHILOSOPHICAL HERITAGE

Psychology as a natural science emerged from a fusion of the new experimental physiology of the nineteenth century with certain philosophical movements. The philosophical contributions date largely from Plato (427?–347 B.C.) and Aristotle (384–322 B.C.). Much later the psychological concepts offered by these men were developed more fully by John Locke (1632–1704) and by René Descartes (1596–1650).

Before the nineteenth century, psychology was an integral part of philosophy, and most systematic speculations concerning psychological problems were made by philosophers. The teachings and writings of Socrates (470?–399 B.C.), Plato, and Aristotle had shifted the primary concern of Greek philosophy from the nature of the physical universe to the nature of man. This shift brought many psychological problems to the fore.

Plato, among his other observations, noted two principles involved in memory: association by contiguity and association by similarity. He suggested that someone's personal possession, perhaps a lyre or a garment, "forms in the mind's eye" an image of its owner because the object and the person have been repeatedly experienced together in the past. Plato also indicated that seeing one object tends to call another to mind because the two things are alike (Warren, 1921).

In a survey of the knowledge of his time, Aristotle investigated mental as well as physical phenomena and noted that thoughts follow each other more or less regularly. He listed similarity, contrast, and contiguity as three types of relationships that provide connecting links in a chain of thought. Aristotle said that the mind receives the imprint of an experience just as wax receives the mark of a ring placed on it; the persistence of such an impression constitutes memory. For Aristotle memory appeared to be the possession of a potentially revivable experience. His conceptions of learning and memory constituted a great stride toward a naturalistic explanation of mental life: he pointed out clearly that the sequences of ideational (thought) processes are not fortuitous but occur in accordance with discernible principles. He also believed that the same definite principles are involved in purposive thinking as in the spontaneous flow of thought (Warren, 1921; Boring, 1950).

It was nearly 1700 years after Aristotle that the next significant developments toward a naturalistic conception of human experience were made.

In France the philosopher Descartes developed a mechanistic conception of the behavior of lower animals. Descartes held that animal and human bodies were machines. Although he believed that man's behavior was partially governed by an immaterial soul (acting on the pineal gland, near the center of the head), he contended that lower animals were pure automata, completely subject to the principles of physics. Although Descartes religious scruples prevented him from interpreting human behavior in a completely naturalistic way, his mechanistic view of animal behavior helped lay the foundation for the development of physiological psychology and the eventual objective treatment of human behavior. When men were no longer content to explain behavior in terms of hidden powers and evil spirits, they began to take dead creatures apart to see what made them work.

In England the school of association returned to the principle of association as the key to the understanding of mental life. John Locke originated the phrase *association of ideas* and is generally considered to be most representative of the associationists. According to Locke, all knowledge comes through the senses. There is nothing in the mind that was not first in sensory experience. Ideas are linked together and are recalled according to the principles of association. Locke borrowed the *tabula rasa* (blank tablet) concept of the mind from Aristotle and made it the starting point for all his psychological theories. The contributions of Locke and the other English associationists were important for two reasons. First, they made what was probably the first attempt to provide a thorough, systematic, naturalistic explanation of mental activity. Second, their principles of association are still relevant to psychology and are incorporated in many contemporary principles, or laws, of learning. For example, the Pavlovian mechanism of conditioning (discussed in Chapter 5) can accurately be described as association by contiguity. The English school of associationism continued into the nineteenth century and fused with physiology to engender the new psychology.

PSYCHOLOGY'S PHYSIOLOGICAL ROOTS

The physiological developments that eventually came to form part of the new psychology began in ancient Greece, just as did the philosophical contributions. Hippocrates (460–370 B.C.) and Galen (129–199 A.D.) tried to break away from the mysticism and magic that dominated the medicine of their day and replace them with a more naturalistic approach. In discussing epilepsy, Hippocrates denied that it was a sacred disease, as tradition dictated. He maintained that all diseases arise from natural causes and cannot be ascribed to gods or to evil spirits (Hippocrates, translated 1869).

Galen, another Greek physician, advanced the development of a naturalistic conception of mental as well as physical illness when he asserted that the mind was located in the brain. According to him, dementia (mental illness) and imbecility (mental deficiency) result from rarefaction and reduction in the amount of "animal spirits" and from changes in the temperature and humidity of the brain. Galen, who distinguished between sensory and motor nerves, transected the spinal cord and localized some of its motor functions. His writings represented the height of the development of medicine for the next 1300 years (Boring, 1950).

Centuries later, in the early 1800s, great progress was made in the field of physiology. In 1811 Sir Charles Bell and François Magendie, working independently, discovered that the sensory fibers of a mixed spinal nerve enter the spinal cord at the posterior (dorsal) root, whereas the motor fibers of the same nerve leave the cord by the anterior (ventral) root. This discovery separated the nerve into sensory and motor functions. In 1826 Johannes Müller developed his concept of specific nerve energies. He held that sensory quality (coldness, warmness, sweetness, sourness, tone, color, and so on) is solely a function of the sensory mechanism; thus he opposed the traditional belief that the sensory nerves are merely conductors of absolute properties of stimulating bodies. Müller argued that there were five different kinds of sensory nerves, one for each of the five senses, and that each kind of sensory nerve had its own specific energy (Boring, 1950). Today it is recognized that the specificity of sensory experience is in the cortical reception area of the brain and in the patterns of nerve impulses received rather than in the specific nature of the peripheral sensory nerves. Actually, Müller had recognized this possibility: he had said that it was not known whether the peculiar "energy" of each kind of sensory nerve was seated in the nerve itself or in the part of the spinal cord or brain with which it was connected (Boring, 1950).

Also in the early nineteenth century, the electrical nature of the nerve impulse was established. By 1850 Helmholtz had measured the rate of transmission of the nervous impulse and had thus demonstrated that one aspect of thought was not instantaneous and was open to experimental investigation if man could only devise the necessary means.

At about the same time German physiologists initiated the modern field of psychophysics. Ernst Weber had noted that many visual and auditory stimuli had to be changed a proportional amount for the difference to be detectable to the human organism. Thus if two tones with frequencies of 100 and 103 could barely be distinguished, then two tones of 500 and 515 could also barely be distinguished. This proportional relationship came to be known as Weber's law or Weber's fraction. Gustav Fechner noted that Weber's law described the amount of stimulus change that was just noticeably different and applied the name *jnd*, or *just noticeable difference*. He took it as his unit of measurement and assumed that all jnd's are equal. Thus the intensity of a sensation could be measured by determining the number of jnd's it is above the limen (the lowest stimulus intensity that can be experienced). By convention, a difference that can be correctly perceived 75 percent of the time (half the distance between chance, or 50 percent, and perfect discrimination, or 100 percent) is taken as a jnd. Fechner's important contribution was neither his measurement of sensation nor the laws that he conceived; rather, it was his development of a new approach to measurement. His so-called psychophysical methods, particularly the method employing jnd's, have stood the test of time and have proven applicable to a wide variety of psychological problems.

Other nineteenth-century developments that contributed to psychology but were not directly concerned in its founding were Broca's localization of a brain center for speech at the base of the third frontal convolution of the left cerebral hemisphere; Fritsch and Hitzig's discovery of the localization of motor function in the cerebral cortex and the later discovery of the localization of the cortical centers for vision, hearing, and touch; experimental studies of the sensory processes (vision, hearing, and the cutaneous senses); investigations of the "personal equation" (differences in reaction time) by astronomers; work with hypnotism; and study of the psychoneuroses (minor mental illnesses). The concept of specific cortical localizations of function developed by Broca, Fritsch, and Hitzig has been considerably modified by later works, as is shown in Chapter 2.

PSYCHOLOGY AS A SEPARATE DISCIPLINE

Modern experimental psychology dates from the establishment of the first psychological laboratory by Wilhelm Wundt in 1879 at Leipzig, Germany. Wundt is the first man who, without reservation, can properly be called a psychologist (Boring, 1950). The psychology of Wundt was devoted almost entirely to the problems of human sensation and perception. However, before the end of the nineteenth century the realm of psychology had expanded to include the higher mental processes of memory and learning. Sigmund Freud's contributions, starting in the same century and continuing well into the twentieth, dramatically focused attention on problems of motivation, particularly unconscious motivation. Charles Darwin's evolutionary concepts, introduced in the mid-nineteenth century, directed interest in psychology to the functions of mental activity and to the possibility of extrapolation from the study of one species to the study of another.

Psychology as an independent discipline, as undertaken by Wundt, was concerned with the generalized, normal, adult human subject. Since Wundt's time psychologists have become interested in the unique individual as well as in the generalized man, in the abnormal as well as in the normal, and in individuals of all ages, from conception to death.

Figure 1-1. Wilhelm Wundt, founder of the first psychological laboratory.

Psychologists have also directed their attention toward the behavior of lower animals. Since such processes as learning, motivation, and perception can also be observed in the lower animals, it is often advantageous to study these animals rather than man. The basic nature of these mechanisms is often clearer when it is seen in simpler forms.

Whereas interest at first focused narrowly on the scientific and academic understanding of man, it has since expanded to include practical problems in law, education, medicine, politics, and business and industry. There is hardly an aspect of life that has not felt the impact of twentieth-century psychology.

DEFINITION OF PSYCHOLOGY

Although psychology as a science is less than a hundred years old, the word itself goes back to ancient Greece, where it meant a discourse about, or discussion of, the soul. Today psychology is commonly defined as the science of human behavior or as the science of the experiences and activities of humans. The term has gone through several interim definitions: it has successively been defined as the science of the mind, the science of mental activity, the science of consciousness, and the science of conscious experience. These changing definitions to some extent reflect the changing nature of the interests and preoccupations of the people who have called themselves psychologists.

Part of the reason why psychologists have continually redefined psychology has been their desire to live up to the standards of science. They have conceived of scientific observations as more impartial, more precise, more objective, and more subject to verification than ordinary everyday observations. Thus over the years psychology has shifted from introspective to objective observations and measurements. At the same time new techniques, especially the use of electronic equipment, have made possible the objective investigation of many aspects of behavior and experience that were previously considered to be purely personal and subjective, such as events in the brain.

Behavior, as psychologists think of it, can be either open to view or concealed. Naturally, covert behavior is harder to grasp and generally harder to study than overt behavior. Table 1-1 presents a tentative classification of human activities into these two categories. Like all such classifications, those in the table have some limitations. For example, we have listed oral and written language as overt, symbolic, communicative activity, but, in fact, language serves expressive and manipulative as well as communicative functions. Language is used to

Figure 1-2. Humans may be viewed at various levels of organization: a minute cluster of poliomyelitis virus particles (magnified 70,000 times); liver tissue (magnified 350 times); a human brain, exposed during an operation; a person; an aggregate of people. Psychology's focus is on one human or organism, functioning as an integrated system.

communicate information, to express one's feelings, and to control other people. Thus language could be listed under all three of these overt categories. The principal purpose of Table 1-1 is to indicate the breadth of the terms *activities* and *behavior* as they are used in psychology. Behavior includes much more than gross movements, such as walking. It includes such relatively subtle activities as perceiving, thinking, conceiving, and feeling. Psychology is concerned with all the activities of the total person.

THE RELATION OF PSYCHOLOGY TO OTHER SCIENCES

Biophysicists, biochemists, cytologists, anatomists, geneticists, physiologists, psychologists, anthropologists, sociologists, political scientists, economists, and historians all study humans. Physicists and chemists study the electronic, atomic, and molecular components of the cells of the body. Cytologists are concerned with a slightly larger unit and study the structure of the individual cells that make up the tissue of the body; histologists, in turn, study the aggregations of cells that make up the tissues of the body; anatomists study the gross

Table 1-1. Overt and covert human behavior.

Overt activities	Locomotor activities	
	Manipulatory activities	
	Symbolic activities (Communication)	Artistic communication Oral language Written language Symbolic gestures Facial movements Symbolic postures
	Expressive movements	Artistic expression Overt components of feelings and emotions
Covert activities	Perceptual activities (Perception)	Cognitive processes
	Ideational activities (Thought)	Cognitive processes
	Emotions and feelings (Affection)	

structures of the human body. These people all study the same structures, but they do so from various vantage points. The basic unit in psychology is one human, or organism, functioning as an integrated system; social science is primarily concerned with groups, or aggregates of people.

PSYCHOLOGY AS A BIOSOCIAL SCIENCE

Traditionally the various sciences were considered to be separate and distinct disciplines. Each was defined and delimited to emphasize its distinctiveness. However, when certain ones expanded and came to overlap areas of adjoining fields, transitional or interdisciplinary sciences developed. Today biophysics and biochemistry bridge the gap between the physical and the biological sciences. Also, in a somewhat analogous way, psychology is a bridge between biology and the social sciences and may be regarded as a biosocial science. Man is born a biological organism, but he also becomes a social being.

Psychology, in certain contexts, views a person as a biological organism. The special fields of physiological and comparative psychology investigate man and the lower organisms using many of the techniques of the biological sciences. The psychologist draws heavily from the traditional biological disciplines and even from the hybrid disciplines of biophysics and biochemistry for information that may help him understand the activities of the total human.

Since man grows up in a social environment, he can no more escape the effects of society than the fish can escape the effects of the watery environment into which it is born. Consequently, psychologists—social psychologists—study the social influences impinging on the individual. They use techniques of social science to learn about the effects on a person of such social forces as his family, his church, his state, and his peers. As a biosocial scientist the psychologist brings together information from the biological and social sciences as well as from his own investigations in his effort to develop an understanding of the total behavior of man.

THE INTERDISCIPLINARY NATURE OF MODERN PSYCHOLOGY

Psychology, like most other fields of study, is not particularly concerned with the extent to which an investigation stays within the formally defined borders of the discipline. Most fields of psychology overlap, borrow from, and, in turn, contribute to other fields of study. Physiological psychology both borrows from and contributes to physiology, endocrinology, biochemistry, biophysics, and general biology. Educational psychology overlaps education, sociology, and other academic areas to a lesser extent. At its edges social psychology blurs into sociology, anthropology, political science, and economics. Industrial psychology encompasses the study of business and industry and impinges on economics and sociology. New areas of joint concern to several disciplines develop almost yearly, and combinations of previously separate fields appear on the academic horizon. One such field of considerable current interest is psycholinguistics. Psychologists, linguists, sociologists, anthropologists, educators, and philosophers are all working cooperatively in this area, with considerable cross-fertilization occurring among the fields.

PSYCHOLOGICAL TERMINOLOGY

Derivation of Terms

Psychological vocabulary has developed in two ways. (1) It has developed by the formulation of new terms to refer specifically to psychological concepts. *Phi-phenomenon* (the illusion of movement generated by stationary stimuli) is an example of a term that has specific limited meaning within the field of psychology. The only problem posed by such a term for the beginning psychology student is that he must acquire a new vocabulary. (2) Psychological terms are also borrowed from the vernacular. Many psychological terms are words in common usage, although psychologists have modified their meanings, restricted their connotations, and thereby avoided inventing new terms. Terminology derived from everyday language causes trouble, for scientific constructs (fully developed scientific concepts) are never identical with the meanings commonly ascribed to such terms. Many students initially assume that, because words are familiar to them, the usual meanings are adequate for psychological purposes. But when someone uses *intelligence, personality, character,* or *creativity* as a psychological term, he uses the word differently from the way it is used in common discourse. Thus the student of psychology must learn a new, restricted set of meanings for familiar words.

The Important Distinction between Processes and Things

In discussing psychological activities or processes, it is often advantageous to use verbal nouns, such as *sensing, dreaming,* and *thinking,* rather than strongly substantive nouns, such as *sensations, dreams,* and *thoughts.* The difficulties that arise from *reifying* psychological processes (regarding them as material things) are illustrated by such questions as: Where are one's thoughts when one is not thinking them? Where are one's memories when one is not remembering them? Many students, without reflecting on the implications of these questions, will reply: "They are in the unconscious." "They are in a latent state in the mind." "They are in the brain." Even while answering in these ways, the students may feel that there is something wrong, tricky, or unfair about the questions.

Most people see what is wrong when the same kind of question is asked about more overt processes: Where does your run go when you stop running? Where does your talk go when you stop talking? Where does your respiration go when you stop respiring? Obviously these questions, like their predecessors, contain false assumptions. Although such words as *thought* and *talk* are nouns, they do not refer to objects or things; they refer to transitory processes. The only sense in which they can be said to exist during periods of inactivity is this: the potentiality for their reenactment persists. A typical sleeping dog is potentially a barking dog; that is, it will bark when properly stimulated.

Nouns are sometimes used to refer to hypothetical psychological *entities* within the person. Thus memory is considered to be the thing within the person that remembers, reason is the entity that reasons, and imagination does the imagining. The meaninglessness of this circular reasoning becomes obvious when we talk about the run as doing the running, the talk as doing the talking, and the digestion as doing the digesting. When the fallacy involved in using a reified entity to account for an activity becomes clear, students often ask "What is it, then, that reasons, remembers, and imagines?" It is simply the person who reasons, remembers, perceives, and imagines, just as it is the person who runs, sings, and engages in a thousand other activities.

If percepts, sensations, images, and ideas do not exist as things, then, on a higher conceptual level, does consciousness exist? As an entity it does not; but, as a term referring to a broad range of processes, it does. An analysis of the term *consciousness* may be helpful. On the simplest experiential levels a person sees, hears, tastes, smells, and has a wide variety of elementary sensory experiences. When we wish to indicate that a person is doing any or all of these activities, we say he is *sensing.* A person also dreams, fantasizes, recalls, imagines, and reasons. The generic term used to cover this range of processes is *thinking.* In a third area, a person loves, hates, grieves, fears, likes, and dislikes. The general term covering this entire category is *feeling.* When a still more generic term is needed to indicate that a person is perceiving, thinking, and/or feeling, we say he is *conscious*. When stated in these terms, it is clear that as activities all these processes exist. No one questions that these words have real referents. However, it is difficult to keep from reifying these higher-level processes when words like *thought* or *consciousness* are used. Table 1-2 summarizes these relationships.

The one *material thing*, or being, that is always explicitly or implicitly involved in discussing psychological processes is the person, the individual, or the organism. Thus vision really refers to a person seeing, grief means a person is grieving, and so forth. When we say a person loses consciousness, we mean that all conscious processes cease; when we say he regains consciousness, we mean that these processes resume.

Consistently maintaining a person-activity frame of reference precludes the necessity and minimizes the temptation to postulate a mind to "contain" conscious experiences and a subconscious mind as a "repository" for inactive

Table 1-2. Terms that refer to experiential processes.

The simple term	*The more generic term*	*The most generic term*
Seeing (vision)	Sensing (sensation) or Perceiving (perception)	Experiencing (awareness) or Being conscious (consciousness)
Hearing (audition)		
Tasting (gustation)		
Smelling (olfaction)		
Remembering (memory)	Thinking (thought) or Ideating (idea)	
Dreaming (dream)		
Imagining (image)		
Reasoning (reason)		
Loving (love)	Emoting (emotion) or Feeling (likes and dislikes)	
Hating (hate)		
Fearing (fear)		

percepts, ideas, and emotions. Such a person-activity approach denies neither the reality nor the usefulness of the distinction between conscious and unconscious *processes.* It is obvious that we are conscious of experiences in varying degrees, ranging from the most highly attentive awareness through lesser degrees to the level of complete unawareness (unconsciousness).

We will use the term *mind* sparingly in our discussions because it is a term commonly used as a reification of *mental processes* and/or response potentialities. The "mind" reified as an entity tends to be used as an explanatory concept (a place where experiences reside). We conceive of the mind as the sum total of one's psychological activities and/or potentialities for response. As an active process, the mind includes the entire repertoire of experiential processes. As a persisting thing, mind refers to the individual's potentialities for response. In terms of its origins, the mind consists of one's inherited potentialities as they have been actualized through experience. Mind is thus the product of one's heredity interacting with the experiences of his lifetime expressed in terms of his present behavior. Such a conception makes mind—like consciousness, emotion, thought, and percept—a descriptive rather than an explanatory term. When a person is tempted to use the mind as an entity to account for activity, he should try substituting the terms *person* or *individual* in its place. If this substitution does not make the statement either meaningless or circular, the term is probably being used legitimately. If any statement becomes meaningless with the substitution, the proposition as stated probably involves a substitution of a name for an explanation.

THE SOURCES OF PSYCHOLOGICAL DATA

Prescientific psychology was based on casual observation and unverified theorizing. It consisted of incidental observations of behavior in uncontrolled natural settings. It is typified by anecdotal accounts of the behavior of oneself or others. The following reasons explain why data obtained in this way are notoriously unreliable:

1. An observer typically does not distinguish between his observations and his inferences. For example, an observer sees a father's physical punishment of his child as indicative of the former's hatred and rejection of his son. However, on inquiry, the father is found to love his son and considers his punishment to constitute the appropriate way to make sure that the child will grow up to be a good and responsible citizen.

2. An observer is usually not acquainted with the behavioral norms of the class, species, or age of the organism he is observing. Such a person may see a child's ability to talk at 15 months as evidence of unusual precocity, whereas it is quite within the normal range.
3. An observer is usually ignorant of the past experience of the subject and of the way in which the subject acquired the observed behavior. The observer who sees the mentally retarded offspring of musical parents playing two selections on the piano quite well may believe that the child has inherited a special musical aptitude. In reality, the young pianist's mother, a music teacher, may have spent an hour each day over a period of several years painstakingly teaching the child to play these two pieces.
4. An observer is often an interested party. The parent is looking for and hoping to find evidence of intellectual superiority, creativity, or artistic promise in his child. Perception is always selective, and one's wishes function as selective devices.
5. An ordinary observer is not statistically minded. The observer seldom bothers to determine if the observed behavior is typical of a particular child or of all children. He notices and is impressed by the unusual occurrence that supports his belief and fails to note and remember the much more frequent instances that do not support his preconceptions. Charles Darwin (1896) tells us that he always carried in his pocket a notebook in which he made notes of observations that seemed inconsistent with his doctrine of evolution. He observed that he was inclined to disregard and forget such instances, whereas he very readily noticed and remembered cases that seemed consistent with his theory. Most observers are not so careful in their observations and their inferences.

When psychology advanced beyond uncontrolled observations and beyond the anecdotal level, it took the first tentative steps toward the development of an appropriate scientific methodology.

PSYCHOLOGY AS A SCIENCE

To the man on the street, science is machines, laboratories, and white-gowned men peering through microscopes or telescopes. In actuality, however, science is basically a fairly simple set of assumptions and of rules of procedure for guiding the activities and thinking of its practitioners.

In many ways, scientific method is only refined common sense; it is neither mysterious nor esoteric. A scientist starts with a problem or question. He has—or develops—relevant ideas or hunches (hypotheses) as possible solutions. He then devises and engages in activities (experiments or gathers relevant data) to prove or disprove the validity of proposed solutions. For maximum usefulness, he checks the validity of his hypotheses in ways that anyone else with proper skills can also check for himself (verifiability). An everyday occurrence can be used to demonstrate a common-sense use of the simple basic components of scientific methodology.

A man driving along a freeway detects a new noise apparently emanating from his car and asks "What's causing it?" Several ideas (hypotheses) come to him. "Maybe it's really a noise from the car that just pulled up alongside mine." To check this possibility, he slows down and permits the other car to move out of his range of hearing. The noise continues, so he discards this hypothesis. "Maybe the noise is from the rough surface of the lane in which I'm traveling." He changes to a lane with a smoother surface. If the noise continues, he develops other hunches: "It could be a vibration rattle caused by the fast speed or strong wind, or maybe a vibration from the engine caused by a defective spark plug." Driving more slowly, changing the direction of travel, or turning off the engine and coasting for a distance may prove or disprove these hypotheses. The disappearance of the noise (the dependent variable) when one of the possible causes (independent variables) is eliminated is considered proof that that cause was indeed producing the noise (verification).

Of course, because of inadequate information, the driver may be unable to generate the appropriate hypothesis (or the right question) or to manipulate the effective variables; thus he may never arrive at an answer to his question. The causation may be too complex for his controls to be effective. Maybe the noise is the result of a combination of an imbalance in a tire, the rough surface of the road, and a loose tie rod. That is, variables may act singly or in combination.

The driver, like the scientist, is attempting to discover the relationship among variables. Both start with an experience (observation of an event); both ask "Why?"; both assume that the observed event is caused and that the cause can be discovered (an orderly universe).

The scientist, unlike the driver, often goes beyond an answer to his immediate question. He looks for extrapolations and generalizations from the one observation. As a result of his systematic observations of a series of regular sequences of events (cause and effect), he develops generalized statements of experiential events (laws). Scientific laws so generated are not prescriptive like legal statutes; rather, they constitute brief, shorthand (often mathematical) statements of regularly occurring patterns of experience. These patterns become generalized descriptions of cause-and-effect relationships, which come to be used in anticipatory and predictive ways.

The methods and concepts of science constitute only one way of studying experience. Literature, art, and music deal with human experience for different purposes and within a different framework. These disciplines are not concerned with a dispassionate, orderly disclosing of the underlying causes of human events, as is science. Rather, they are concerned with expressing feelings, emotions, and concepts for pure personal enjoyment or for cathartic purposes or for sharing them with others. Understanding in an artistic sense can be very different from scientific understanding. Understanding art often involves feeling with the artist or his portrayal.

The feeling level of understanding is also invoked when a person in distress says that only a person who has suffered similarly can "really" understand him. In this sense only the person who has been a disadvantaged black man in the United States can understand the blacks, only the woman who has borne a child can understand childbirth, and only the person who has experienced a toothache can understand its pain. On a "how-it-feels" level of understanding, these propositions are undoubtedly true. However, the dentist who has never had a toothache; the obstetrician who has never given birth; and persons such as Alexis de Tocqueville (1945), Gunnar Myrdal (1944), or Charles Silberman (1964), who are not black but have spent years studying the race problems in the United States, have a much better understanding of the phenomena on a what-causes-what and what-must-be-done-to-change-the-sequence-of-events (scientific) level than do those who have suffered these experiences. The cancer sufferer is not the best person to prescribe his own treatment (scientific understanding), even though he knows much more about how it feels to have cancer (affective understanding) than does his physician.

The psychologist-scientist postulates that the same experiences portrayed so passionately in art, music, and literature can also profitably be studied in a dispassionate, orderly, what-causes-what way. Science is basically descriptive of sequences of events. It is concerned with what is and does not extrapolate to what should be. The theological, ethical, and moral question of how man ought to behave is not answerable by purely scientific investigation.

The dispassionateness and objectivity of science are not characteristic of the individual scientist but are the outcomes of the methods devised to make explicit the assumptions, procedures, and data that validate or invalidate his conclusions, inferences, and interpretations. The scientific method makes techniques and data accessible to critical evaluation by other qualified workers. Its methods and data are made public so that discrepancies in results, procedures, and interpretations can be openly discussed, debated, replicated, and verified or disproven.

Psychology, as the systematic study of human conduct, deals with man as a social being, as an individual self, and as a biological system. Man is all these things, and viewing him from one of these vantage points does not deny the reality, significance, or legitimacy of the others.

We have indicated that the scientific method is only one way of viewing and dealing with experience. The artistic feeling and moralistic judgmental frames of reference are equally valid. Thus the "nothing-but" criticism often leveled at science and scientists is fallacious. When elation and love, as emotions, are related to hormonal, neurological, and metabolic processes and when their origins are traced to innate physiological and acquired habits and attitudes, these experiences are not stripped of any of their subjective, esthetic, or moralistic values. Discovering that the peaks of ecstasy and the satisfactions of quiet contemplation are basically physiological processes does not reduce these experiences to "nothing but" mundane animal-level activities. Identifying the experiential with the organic can just as well be considered an elevation or even deification of physiological processes as a reduction of the experiential to lower-level organic processes.

Just as the psychologist, as scientist at different times, studies man as a social being, or as a personal self, or as a biological organism, he also plays several different roles in his own life. At times he views and studies people and processes as a relatively objective, descriptive psychologist-scientist. At other times he perceives these same processes and activities as esthetic experiences or as occasions for ethical judgmental decisions. Since man is one self and not several completely compartmentalized selves, his roles overlap and interact. When a scientist steps outside his area of expertise, he becomes a layman and renders esthetic and ethical judgments with no more authority and with no greater insight than the nonscientist. However, his rights and obligations to function in these additional roles are essentially the same as those of any other citizen. (For a discussion of the nature and causes of the current discontent with science and technology, see Telford & Sawrey, 1971, pp. 382–388.)

THE COMPONENTS OF SCIENTIFIC METHODOLOGY

We have already suggested that the scientific method involves three different functional levels, which we shall now discuss more fully. The first of these is the theoretical or philosophical level, which is considered most completely under the designation "the philosophy of science" (Madden, 1960; Nagel, 1961). The second is the level of research design, which includes the procedural steps involved in scientific investigation (observation, noting regularities, hypothesis, deduction, further observations, and so on). The general features of research design are common to all scientific procedures, although, in terms of specifics, they vary from field to field (Cochran & Cox, 1957). The third, the technological level, involves devising, adapting, and using particular devices, materials, and instruments to make observations more accurate, more objective, and more quantitative and, at times, even to make them possible. On this level scientists have an infinite variety of equipment, including the electron microscope, the telescope, earth satellites, atom "smashers," and the electroencephalograph, as well as such relatively simple devices as mazes, problem boxes, puzzles, tests, and rating and scaling devices for investigations of human behavior.

The various scientific disciplines vary tremendously on the technological level. But the general features of experimental design are quite universal, and, on the philosophical level, there is practically unanimity. The theoretical framework and the more general features of experimental design are, in essence, the same for all fields of scientific endeavor.

The Philosophical Basis of Science

The philosophical level of science is concerned with the basic assumptions or implied postulates that underlie scientific methodology and explanation. Many scientists do not particularly concern themselves with these assumptions; they simply take them for granted and proceed on the methodological and technological levels to get their work done. Many scientists function on a commonsense level, assuming that these basic assumptions are self-evident truths.

One of the basic philosophical assumptions of science is that the universe is orderly and predictable. It is assumed that there are basic uniformities and regularities in the universe and that beneath the haphazard events, capricious occurrences, and confusions of external manifestations, there exist basic phenomena, constellations of events, and regular relationships. Another assumption of science is that the underlying uniformities of the universe (the laws of nature) can be discovered and understood and, when known, can be turned to man's advantage.

The concept of causality is another philosophical assumption of scientific endeavor. It is assumed that the regularities of events in the universe stand in a cause-and-effect relationship to each other. Scientists who concern themselves with the problem of causality differ in their conception of the nature of the causal relationship, but that it does exist in some form is a basic assumption.

Some workers believe that science operates on a purely descriptive level and that it is not necessary to postulate an inherent or necessary relationship between cause and effect. They claim that science simply deals with concomitant variations. People subscribing to such a belief contend that in science we observe and tabulate sequences of events; we note uniformities of order of events and, on the basis of such verified sequences, build up expectancies and make predictions. As the result of repeated confirmation of our expectancies and predictions, there develops a belief in a necessary and intrinsic functional connection between cause and effect. The event that regularly precedes the other is the cause, and the event that always follows is the effect. Causality is the postulated inherent relationship between the two events.

The British philosopher David Hume (1777) insisted that the widespread conception of a necessary relationship between those events called cause and effect is nothing more than psychological expectation resulting from repeated association by contiguity. Karl Pearson (1911), among others, has contended that science merely describes sequences of events, establishes uniformities of such sequences, makes predictions, and, in a practical way, acts so as to take advantage of these sequences of events. He believed that speculations as to what produces these events are beyond the realm of science. Irrespective of the particular conception held concerning the nature of the cause-and-effect relationship, all scientists assume causality as a fundamental tenet.

Scientific psychology accepts the two basic assumptions of an orderly universe and causality as they apply to man. Present-day psychology assumes that man is a part of nature and that his behavior is an orderly sequence of events, operating according to cause-and-effect relationships and subject to scientific investigation, as is the rest of the universe. A man's behavior has antecedents that can be known and understood. Every thought, feeling, emotion, sensation, and overt act of an individual is assumed to have its antecedents and consequences; it is the task of psychology to discover, systematize, and, whenever possible, quantify these cause-and-effect relationships.

The basic assumptions of science, because of their very nature, are not subject to proof. They are stated as universals and therefore can never be proven. For example, to prove that every human activity has its cause, every act of every person in the universe would have to be proven to have such causes. In terms of its fundamental postulates, science is *a way of looking at the universe.* It is an attempt to order the events of the universe in a given way. However, it is only one way of describing or conceiving of the universe. The validity of the assumptions of science can be measured only in terms of their usefulness—that is, by a purely pragmatic test. As long as the assumptions and methods of science are fruitful and productive, they will persist. They are modified or discarded only because alternative ones have been shown to be more productive. The scientist has considerable confidence in his methods, but he is always ready to question his knowledge and his theories.

Scientific Methodology (Research Design)

The second functional level of science is that of general research design. The essential features of scientific methodology are common to all the sciences, but the specific means of realizing them vary greatly from one field to another and from one problem to another. At this point, we will only indicate the general purposes of research design, irrespective of its specifics, and pass over the many ways in which these purposes are realized.

In the ideal research design, circumstances are such that all conditions (or variables) that seem likely to influence the variable to be measured (the dependent variable) are controlled, except the one condition that is systematically varied (the independent variable). The effects of varying the independent variable (the postulated effect) are determined.

The following are some ideal characteristics of research design:

1. *Control of conditions.* In the physical sciences, conditions such as the nature of the materials used, temperature, barometric pressure, humidity, and relative movement can be fairly easily controlled, although this matter, too, is relative.

For example, it has been suggested that to indicate the length of a piece of wood "exactly," some 60 known variables would have to be controlled, among the more obvious of which are temperature, humidity, age (it is disintegrating), and place (moving or stationary). Of course, most of the variations involved are of no practical significance if the wood is going to be used to make the side of an apple box; however, if we need a stick measured down to a millionth of a millimeter, the variations become very relevant.

To control variables in psychology, we resort to such devices as control groups, subjects serving as their own controls, and the statistical control of variables. The problem of adequate controls is always a difficult one.

2. *Objectivity.* This problem is harder for psychology than it is for many other fields. Psychology has difficulty in objectively defining its concepts, such as intelligence or learning; its independent variables, such as anxiety or stress; its dependent variables, such as fatigue or creativity. Psychology uses many testing, rating, and ranking devices that are quite subjective. Much research effort in the field is expended in attempts to make possible greater objectivity in investigation.

3. *Verifiability of results.* Ideally, research should be such that it can be independently repeated and verified by any competent worker. It is the verifiability of scientific research—its independence from individual prejudices and wishes—that is one of its distinguishing characteristics.

Scientific Technology

There are at least four journals currently published that are devoted entirely to the topic of scientific instruments: *Journal of Scientific Instruments, Instrumentation, Instruments and Automation,* and *Review of Scientific Instruments.* The fact that so much is published about instrumentation indicates its tremendous importance in modern scientific investigations and applications.

In practice, the research-design level and the technological level interact. The control of conditions possible on the research-design level is often determined by the availability of specific pieces of equipment. For example, in equating groups so as to control intelligence level, we need valid intelligence tests. Conversely, technological advances often make possible the investigation of many variables previously not accessible; the electroencephalograph has made it possible to study many aspects of brain function.

The methods and techniques used to investigate human behavior are produced by combinations of experimental design and technology. Some of these methods are largely prescientific, whereas some conform quite well to the requirements of scientific investigation. Some methods provide useful data as the result of activities that are largely service oriented (as are clinical psychology and counseling). The first tentative steps in the development of scientific psychological design (beyond free, uncontrolled observation) consisted of systematic field observations.

Systematic field observations. Systematic observations of people (in practice, usually children), under natural conditions, can be very informative. Certain techniques can make field observations more reliable and significant:

1. The observer can be trained. (Instruction and training in observation can greatly increase the reliability of observation and reduce the sources of error previously listed.)
2. The observer can study one particular type of behavior at a time. (Instead of observing a group of children to see what they do, he can observe, for example, the number of social contacts made by a particular child in a given situation over a specified period of time. Social contacts may be further broken down into the following types of behavior: parallel activities with others, cooperative play with others, antagonistic responses to others, or withdrawal behavior.)
3. The observed behavior can be defined as objectively as possible. (Aggressive acts, for example, can be defined in terms of specific things that the child does or does not do.)
4. The observer can make provisions for recording and analyzing the data as completely and as quantitatively as possible. (This technique may involve the use of stopwatches to obtain the actual time spent in certain activities or the tabulation of the number of acts of a specified type.)
5. More than one observer can be used. (Thus a check can be made for agreements and disagreements among independent observers to increase the reliability of observation.)
6. Observation for limited periods of time (time sampling) on successive occasions may prove more fruitful than single long periods of observation.
7. The use of one-way vision screens can eliminate the contaminating influence of the observer's presence as a distracting factor when he is observing free activity.
8. Motion pictures and tape recordings can be used either to supplement or to replace first-hand observation.

With proper safeguards, observations of free activity can be a useful method of investigation (Butler & Rice, 1963).

Sometimes the experimenter becomes a participant-observer in the situation under investigation. In the clinic the clinician may become both active participant and observer. The cultural anthropologist or social psychologist may live as a member of the community or group whose activities are being studied. The participant-observer, as compared with the nonparticipant-observer, has the advantage of intimacy of contact and increased understanding of the meaning and feelings involved in the personal relations. However, there is always the problem of determining the extent to which the observed behaviors are elicited or influenced by the presence and personal characteristics of the investigator. The use of multiple rotating observers may help, but studies made by participant-observers require special controls on the behavioral variables under study. It should be noted that the problem of the influence of the act and process of observation is not confined to the social scientist; the atomic physicist has the same problem.

The questionnaire as a source of data. Since it is so much easier to ask people what they do, think, or feel on a printed form than it is to observe, test, or interview them, the questionnaire has often been used for research purposes in psychology. Although the questionnaire does save time and money, it has the following limitations:

1. It is difficult to elicit frank and truthful responses on a printed form. Many people simply will not fill out a questionnaire; others do not take them seriously. It is impossible to determine the degree of frankness elicited by a printed form alone.
2. When less than 100 percent of a group respond, there is a strong possibility that the people responding are a select group, and normally the nature and extent of the bias represented by the respondents are unknown.
3. Without a great many preliminary tryouts, it is very difficult to tell to what extent replies are influenced by such things as the form of the questions, the order of the questions, the nature of the instructions given, and the apparent social desirability of certain answers.

Despite these limitations, the questionnaire can be used quite successfully in certain types of investigation (Moser, 1958). As compared with the interview, the questionnaire is more objective. It reduces the personal influence of the interviewer and may be the only practical method when large numbers of people are involved.

The clinical, or case-study, method. The clinical method is not primarily a research method but a set of procedures for the diagnosis and treatment of people with behavior problems. Clinical procedures are not designed to discover general trends, laws, or relationships. Rather, they are concerned with a unique individual who is in trouble; interest is focused on the immediate, practical question of how best to help him. The starting point of a clinical investigation is an individual who needs and/or seeks help, and the procedure ideally ends with his better adjustment.

The essential features of scientific procedures can be present in the clinical study of a child. Such a study starts with the observation of behavior that is troublesome or baffling either to the child himself or to others. The child seems to need help. The clinician who studies the case makes some inferences as to the probable nature or causes of the difficulty (he forms a hypothesis). He gathers data from records, test performances, developmental history, and interviews that support, question, or disprove the hypothesis. When an acceptable hypothesis is developed, certain deductions are made as to probable treatment. The outcomes of treatment are ideally the test of the validity of the original hypothesis and the deductions made from it.

An outline of the clinical, or case-study, method as applied to a schoolchild might be somewhat as follows:

1. Observations of behavior by a teacher, parent, or the child himself that suggest that the individual has behavior problems and needs help (initial observation and inference).
2. Interview with a counselor or clinician and agreement to work with the child (additional observation with apparent support of the original inference).
3. Study of the individual and his problem, involving the following:
    a. Present status as indicated by school achievements, psychometric-test performances, medical examination, peer evaluations, family situation, direct interview, and observation of the child in school, on the playground, and in his home.
    b. Past history as revealed by the child's developmental history, medical reports, school records, and family history.
4. Analysis of the additional data in the light of the original or new hypothesis. This analysis usually consists of:
    a. Looking for behavioral consistency (Does the deviant behavior occur in all or only in certain situations?);
    b. Looking for behavioral patterns (Even inconsistency of behavior may be a meaningful pattern.);
    c. Looking for possible motives.
5. Planning a treatment program on the basis of the most probable hypothesis.
6. Following up the outcomes of treatment to determine the degree to which they support or question the hypothesis.

Although clinical methods are rather poor devices for the testing of hypotheses, they do constitute fruitful sources of new hypotheses, which may then be tested by the better-controlled experimental methods.

Controlled experimentation. It is only in controlled experimental investigations that the ideals of research methodology are approached. Since the essential features of scientific research have already been discussed, we will, by means of a sequence of related studies, detail its salient features more specifically. We begin with a detailed example of experimental research.

Many totally blind individuals believe that they possess a "facial vision." They say they are able to sense obstacles in their paths and that the identifying cues stimulate the face. An interesting series of research studies has tested these hypotheses as well as several others that developed as the studies progressed. We shall trace this sequence of research studies as an example of psychological hypothesis-testing.

> *Hypothesis:* The blind possess an "obstacle sense."
>
> *Procedure and results:* Under controlled conditions in the laboratory, 34 totally blind persons were systematically tested for their ability to perceive obstacles in their paths. Some of the blind subjects could not perceive the obstacles at all, whereas others were able to perceive the obstacles at varying distances. Seven of the 34 subjects did not possess the obstacle sense as determined by the number of collisions with the obstacles and the number of false perceptions of the obstacles. About four-fifths of the students (27 out of the 34) were able to perceive obstacles to a significant degree.
>
> *Conclusion:* Most, but not all, totally blind individuals can detect objects in their pathways (Worchel, Mauney, & Andrews, 1950).

Some of the subjects possessing an obstacle sense believed that they were getting cues from the skin of the face; others felt that auditory cues were the relevant ones.

> *Hypothesis:* Stimulation of the exposed skin of the face is a necessary condition for obstacle perception.
>
> *Procedure and results:* A group of totally blind individuals who had previously demonstrated that they could detect obstacles in their pathways were retested for obstacle perception while wearing closely fitted facial masks. These people could sense obstacles just as well when masked as with the face exposed.
>
> *Conclusion:* Stimulation of the exposed face is not a necessary condition for obstacle perception (Supa, Cotzin, & Dallenbach, 1944).
>
> *Hypothesis:* The sensory cues for obstacle perception are auditory.

Procedure and results: Plugs were placed in the ears of the totally blind individuals who were normally able to perceive obstacles in their pathways. Their success in perceiving obstacles dropped to the chance level. Walking on a carpet in stocking feet greatly reduced but did not entirely eliminate obstacle perception by blind subjects. Drowning out sounds by means of a sound screen while leaving the areas of the skin exposed to sound and air stimulation eliminated the blind subjects' ability to perceive obstacles.

Conclusion: Under normal conditions, auditory stimulation is both a necessary and sufficient condition for the perception of obstacles by the blind (Worchel & Dallenbach, 1947).

If auditory stimulation is the necessary and sufficient condition for obstacle perception by the blind, totally *deaf and blind subjects* should be incapable of such perception.

Hypothesis: Totally deaf and blind subjects do not possess an obstacle sense.

Procedure and results: Ten totally deaf and blind subjects were tested and found incapable of detecting obstacles in their paths.

Conclusion: Auditory perception is necessary for the blind to sense obstacles in their paths (Worchel et al., 1950).

Since not all blind subjects have the obstacle sense, perhaps such perception is simply more difficult for people who are both blind and deaf to learn. They may still be capable of acquiring it.

Hypothesis: Deaf and blind people, if given intensive training, can develop the ability to perceive obstacles in their paths.

Procedure and results: Deaf-blind individuals incapable of obstacle perception were given prolonged and intensive training in obstacle perception. No improvement in obstacle perception was obtained.

Conclusion: Deaf-blind subjects seem to be incapable of developing the obstacle sense (Worchel & Dallenbach, 1947). This conclusion indicates that the essential cues for obstacle perception by the blind are auditory.

If the obstacle sense is learned, blind subjects *lacking the obstacle sense* should be able to develop it with systematic practice.

Hypothesis: Systematic practice will make it possible for adult blind subjects lacking the obstacle sense to acquire it.

Procedure and results: Blind subjects lacking the obstacle sense were given systematic training in obstacle perception and were able to develop it. Striking improvement was achieved in even a short training session of 30 to 60 trials. In a total of 210 training trials, all subjects acquired considerable proficiency.

Conclusion: Obstacle perception is learned and can be developed with systematic practice by adult blind subjects lacking this ability (Worchel et al., 1950; Worchel & Mauney, 1951).

If the obstacle sense is acquired, blindfolded subjects with normal vision should be capable of developing it.

Hypothesis: Normal people can develop the obstacle sense if given systematic training.

Procedure and results: Normal adult subjects were given systematic training in obstacle perception while blindfolded. All the subjects made significant progress in obstacle perception with vision eliminated.

Conclusion: With sufficient practice, subjects with normal vision are able to develop the obstacle sense, which is apparently acquired incidentally by a majority of the blind (Ammons, Worchel, & Dallenbach, 1953; Worchel & Mauney, 1951).

If echo reception is a necessary condition for the perception of obstacles by the blind, higher frequencies should be especially important because of the better resolution of the echoes of high-frequency vibrations when reflected from small objects. Bats emitting and detecting the echoes from extremely high frequencies are able to avoid very small obstacles such as fine wires because of the superior resolution of those high frequencies (Griffin & Galambos, 1942).

Hypothesis: High-frequency vibrations are necessary for obstacle perception via echo reception by blind subjects.

Procedure and results: Using tones of various pitches as sources of sound for echo reception by blind subjects in obstacle-perception tests, it was found that sound frequencies above 10,000 cycles at normal walking speeds are necessary for obstacle perception.

Conclusion: Relatively high sound frequencies are required as cues for normal obstacle perception by blind subjects (Cotzin & Dallenbach, 1950).

Thus we started with the belief—based on incidental observation and anecdotal report—that totally blind individuals can sense obstacles in their paths and that this sensing represented a kind of supernominal sensory capacity or extrasensory capacity of some sort. We have seen how experimenters attacked the problem in a systematic, scientific way, how they worked through a series of successive hypotheses (questions put to nature), how experimental investigations verified or disproved the hypotheses, how the researchers made deductions from the findings (extrapolations from the data), and how they formulated these deductions into additional hypotheses. In short, we have seen how a number of psychologists developed a fairly clear understanding of the nature and origin of the obstacle sense of the blind.

Lest we oversimplify the matter, we should mention that some blind subjects can utilize cutaneous and olfactory cues for object detection when auditory cues are not available. Such cues are quite inefficient as compared with echo reception and so are relatively unimportant (Ammons et al., 1953).

These experimental designs have made maximum use of experimental controls. However, where experimental controls are not possible, various types of statistical controls are possible. The use of partial correlations, the analysis of variance, and factor analysis all involve some degree of statistical evaluation of the effects of several variables when more than one is operative at once. This procedure makes it possible to measure, to some degree, the effect of the variable when the others are held constant by statistical means. Interested students will find more complete discussions of research methodology in Bachrach (1962), Cochran and Cox (1957), and Minium (1970).

The Role of Measurement in Science

The psychologist, as scientist, devises and uses methods and techniques for a more accurate description and more complete understanding of human experience and conduct. He seeks to discover the order of experiences, to generalize these orderly relationships on the highest level possible, and to communicate his findings to others in the most useful and economical way. The generalized, orderly patterns of experience take the form of shorthand and, preferably, quantitative statements of relationships. Cause-and-effect relationships, which are one way of conceptualizing these patterns, are sometimes stated quantitatively as scientific laws. Such laws are, in the last analysis, statistical and probabilistic in character. Scientific laws are tools for predicting the statistical probabilities of future experience in the light of past experience.

Whenever we discover that relationships between events (experiences) exist, we must ascertain the *extent* of those relationships. As soon as we raise the question of extent or degree of relationships, we become statistical.

The terms *statistics, formulas,* and *equations* are anxiety arousing for many people. However, general ideas made quantitative and more precise by statistics are familiar to all and are involved in our daily lives. For example, when the

evening newscaster reports that the range of temperatures in our city for this date over the past 20 years has been from 45 to 70 degrees, he is giving a statistical measure of variability. If he wished to be more technically informative, he could have said that the mean (arithmetic average) temperature over the past 20 years for this date is 59 with a standard deviation of 5 degrees. To the statistically sophisticated, this figure means that the sum of the 20 mean daily temperatures divided by 20 (the arithmetic average) is 59 and that approximately 67 percent of the 20 values fall between 59 minus 5 degrees (one standard deviation) and 59 plus 5 degrees, or 54 and 64 degrees. This statistic seems much more complicated than the range (the difference between the highest and the lowest value), but it is more dependable (reliable) and more frequently used.

In the evening paper we may also read that the *median* income per family in the United States last year was $7890. Most people know that the median, like the mean, is a kind of average, but they do not always realize that they are not the same. The median is the midpoint—the point above and below which lies an equal number of cases or values.

Why do we use the median for income and the mean for temperatures? The curve (graphical representation) of income distributions is typically very skewed (lopsided). A large percentage of the population is found at the low end of the distribution, with a relatively few individuals far out at the high end of the distribution with very large incomes. The total income of the few extremely wealthy may exceed that of the bulk of the extremely poor. For example, King Ibn Saud of Saudi Arabia, who died in 1968, was one of the richest men in the world. He had an income in excess of $300 million a year in a country whose median per capita income was estimated in 1968 to be $125 a year (Simpson, 1968). Thus, in computing a mean, adding Saud's 300-plus millions to the total of the rest of the population would give it a weight equal to that of more than 2.4 million people out of a total population of 6 million. Consequently the median is a more representative value of the income of the *typical* citizen than is the mean.

When we read that family income and educational level are *correlated,* we are dealing with another statistical concept. If two variables are correlated, they vary together either directly or inversely. If they increase and decrease together, they vary directly and are positively correlated (the extremes are 0 to + 1.00); if one decreases as the other increases, they vary inversely, and the correlation is negative (from 0 to − 1.00). The size of the correlation indicates the degree of relationship. Zero is no relationship and 1.00 (either − or +) is a perfect relationship between the two variables.

When we read that there was a *statistically significant* increase in the educational level of blacks in the United States last year, we are dealing with another statistical concept. For example, if in 1970 the mean educational level of blacks was 10.5 and in 1971 it was 10.75, the question is raised about the significance of this difference. If these values were obtained by a sampling of populations rather than on 100 percent of the population, what is the probability that this difference is not so small as to be insignificant and is simply due to chance factors? It may disappear entirely on successive samples. A *standard error of the difference* between the two means will indicate whether the .25 difference is sufficiently large, in view of the number of cases involved and their variability (as indicated by the size of their standard deviations), to be dependable (reliable). If the *standard error* of the difference, when computed according to a prescribed formula, is small as compared with the difference between the means by an order of three or more, the difference is considered to be highly significant statistically. For example, if the standard error of the difference referred to above were found to be .06, the difference of .25 would be statistically significant, since .25 is more than three times .06.

Statistical significance should be differentiated from *practical* significance. For example, knowing that the mean Scholastic Aptitude (intelligence) Test score of Jewish children in the United States exceeds that of non-Jewish white children does not mean that a given child's Jewishness is the best indication of his probable educational achievements. The scholastic aptitude or educational level of a given child's parents or siblings or, if available, the child's own prior educational achievements or Scholastic Aptitude Test scores, are much better indices *for individual predictions* than ethnic origin, despite the existence of statistically significant ethnic-group mean differences. Even with statistically significant mean differences, a sizable percentage of the low group can exceed the mean of the high group and vice versa. Statistical values are not self-interpreting but are significant only in the context of their specific applications. (For a practical and entertaining discussion of this topic, see *How to Lie with Statistics,* by Darrell Huff (1954).)

A reading and understanding of common statistical terms are required of every informed citizen. Additional information on these topics will be found in the Appendix and in such books as Minium (1970).

SUMMARY

Primitive cultures explain behavior by postulating a second being—an inner man dwelling within the outer man—who perceives, desires, remembers, and thinks. The inner man also acts on the outer man and causes him to act.

Experimental psychology derives from the rational approach of the Greek philosophers to the problems of human behavior; the systematic development of the principle of associationism by the English school; the physiological mechanisms proposed by Descartes; and the relating of physiological processes to human behavior, made possible by the German physiologists.

Psychology as a natural science emerged from a fusion of certain philosophical movements with the new experimental physiology of the nineteenth century. The German physiologists Weber, Fechner, and Helmholtz demonstrated how the sense organs and the nervous system work. The British philosophical school of associationism (Locke) insisted that all knowledge comes through the senses and thus indicated the importance of the sense organs. The convergence of these two movements produced psychology as an experimental science.

As the science of human behavior, psychology defines behavior very broadly. Behavior includes covert activities (perceptual, ideational, emotional processes) as well as overt behavior (locomotor, manipulatory, expressive, and symbolic activities). Psychology studies many processes that cannot be directly observed (covert) as well as those that can be directly and objectively perceived (overt). Psychology differs from physiology in being relatively more molar and is differentiated from sociology and other social sciences in being more molecular or atomistic. Originally, psychology concerned itself largely with the conscious experiences of normal, relatively sophisticated, humans. Today, every one of these restrictive adjectives has been removed. Scientific psychology seeks generalized answers to questions concerning man as a prototype; it also seeks usable answers to important questions concerning a particular person. Answers to psychological questions concerning men in general are predominantly normative and theoretical statements concerning processes. Answers to questions concerning an individual are particularistic and utilitarian and provide a workable basis for action.

Psychology derives part of its vocabulary from the vernacular. It also develops its own nomenclature. Because of the popular tendency to reify psychological processes, it helps to use verbal nouns rather than nonverbal noun forms of reference (*perceiving* rather than *perception, reasoning* rather than *reason,* and so on).

Psychology asks questions of nature and then uses the methods of science to find answers and to test the soundness of the answers. Whereas the experimental method changes conditions in order to observe their consequences, the psychologist also tries to unravel and measure existing relationships by field studies of existing relationships and interactions between individuals, groups, and processes. He uses controlled field observations, questionnaires, case studies, and clinical investigations together with statistical—particularly correlational—aids in such investigations. These techniques make it possible for the psychologist to study what man has not yet learned or is not able to control for experimental purposes.

The observational methods of psychology differ from those of the layman in being more rigorous, more objective, more verifiable, more foolproof, and less subject to distortion by the unconscious biases (the hopes and fears) of the observer. The scientific method involves philosophical assumptions, research design, and technology.

SUGGESTED READINGS

Anderson, B. F. *The psychology experiment.* Belmont, Calif.: Brooks/Cole, 1966. This paperback provides a good discussion of the scientific method as applied to psychology. The first half of the book is particularly relevant to the subject matter of this chapter. The last half contains a good discussion of elementary statistical concepts.

Bachrach, A. J. *Psychological research: An introduction.* New York: Random House, 1962. This book provides a short but very good discussion of the principles of scientific methods as they relate to psychology.

Boring, E. G. *A history of experimental psychology.* New York: Appleton-Century-Crofts, 1950. This rather large volume is probably the best discussion of the history of psychology now available. Although the beginning student may find it a bit difficult, the first half of the book provides a good supplement to the historical portion of this chapter.

English, H. B., & English, A. C. *A comprehensive dictionary of psychological and psychoanalytical terms.* New York: McKay, 1958. This book contains helpful discussions of psychological terms, arranged alphabetically.

Sanford, F. H., & Capaldi, E. J. (Eds.) *Advancing psychological science*, Vol. 1. *Philosophies, methods, and approaches*. Belmont, Calif.: Brooks/Cole, 1964. This paperback contains a good selection of readings to supplement this chapter.

Walker, E. L. *Psychology as a natural and social science*. Belmont, Calif.: Brooks/Cole, 1968. This paperback provides one of the best available discussions of psychology as a science.

2

The Biological Basis of Human Behavior

We have indicated that psychology grew out of a fusion of philosophy and physiology. William James, who was probably the greatest American psychologist, was also a philosopher, a physiologist, and an anatomist. His background and interests consequently brought about a fusion of philosophy and physiology in American psychology paralleling that which had occurred in its European antecedents. He espoused one of the cardinal tenets of modern-day psychology—namely, that mental activity is also physiological activity. Specifically, in 1892 James said "The immediate condition of a state of consciousness is an activity of some sort in the cerebral hemispheres." The cerebral hemispheres are the two halves of the cerebrum, or largest subdivision of the brain. They are considered to be of critical importance in most psychological processes.

James further pointed out that, in association, the associative connections are not formed between objects or disembodied ideas but between processes in the brain. He insisted that the laws of association were really laws of "neural habit" and that the fundamental principle of association could be stated as follows: "When two elementary brain processes have been active together or in immediate succession, one of them, on recurring, tends to propagate its excitement into the other" (1892, p. 256). Discussing habit, he said "An acquired habit, from the physiological point of view, is nothing but a new pathway of discharge formed in the brain, by which certain incoming currents ever after tend to escape" (1892, p. 134). Although James' conceptions now seem oversimplified, modern psychologists still believe that mental processes have a physiological basis.

Physiological-response "machinery" of the human body consists of the sense organs (receptors), the nervous system (connectors), and the muscles and glands (effectors). The endocrine glands serve as a secondary integrating system along with the nervous system. These systems are sustained by the various physiological and biochemical processes involved in respiration, circulation, digestion, metabolism, and elimination.

EMBRYONIC DEVELOPMENT

The human organism begins with the fertilization of an egg by a spermatozoon. After fertilization the number of cells in the developing embryo increases dramatically. Soon three classes of cells can be distinguished. Ectodermal and endodermal cells, respectively, make up the outer and inner embryonic layers, and mesodermal cells constitute an intermediate layer. These three layers of embryonic cells further differentiate into the many tissues and organs making up the body. Ultimately several hundred kinds of cells can be distinguished in an adult human. As a result of this cell differentiation, each kind of cell becomes structurally and functionally specialized for its own unique purposes. Although many aspects of this differentiation are not fully understood, experimental embryology has shown that interaction between kinds of cells plays an important part in this differentiation.

DEVELOPMENT OF THE NERVOUS SYSTEM

The nervous system and most of the receptor (sense) cells develop from the embryonic ectoderm. The vertebrate nervous system develops from the neural plate, which is a thickened plate of ectodermal cells along the middorsal (back) line of the embryo. The more rapid growth of the marginal as compared with the more centrally located cells and the infolding of the neural plate form a neural groove. A continuation of this groove forms the neural tube, which detaches itself from the surrounding cells and, through a thickening of its walls, develops into the brain and spinal cord (the central nervous system). The head (rostral) end of the neural tube expands more rapidly and more unevenly than does the tail (caudal) portion. The rostral portion develops into the brain, the caudal part becomes the spinal cord, and the central cavity of the tube persists as the ventricles (central fluid-filled cavities) of the brain and the central canal of the spinal cord.

The motor (peripheral) nerve cells (neurons) grow out from the embryonic cells of the neural tube to innervate the muscles of the body. The sensory (afferent) neurons develop from the neural crest, a group of cells that separate from the neural plate to form a longitudinal band of cells paralleling the neural tube. From these cells arise the sensory neurons of most of the cranial and spinal nerves. The cell bodies of these neurons form sensory ganglia outside the central nervous system; one outgrowth (the dendrite) grows out to the appropriate sense organ, and another outgrowth from the cell's body (an axon) grows into the brain or spinal cord.

The neurons of the autonomic nervous system also develop from the embryonic cells of the neural crest. These cells migrate to various locations, mostly in the viscera (internal portions) of the body, to form sympathetic ganglia and send fibers back into the central nervous system and out to the smooth (involuntary) muscles and glands of the body.

These developing peripheral neurons send out long processes—their axons and dendrites—that in many cases grow to great lengths and form connections

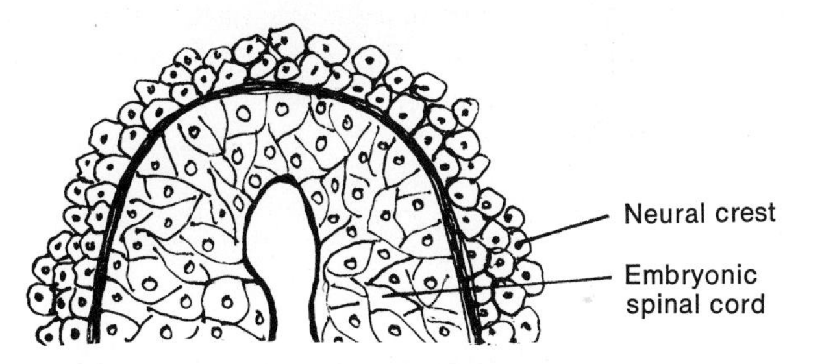

Figure 2-1. Cross section of a portion of the early spinal cord (neural tube) and the neural crest cells.

with other neurons and/or muscles and glands. The direction of growth of these processes and the other neurons or effectors (muscles and glands) on which they terminate appear to be constant in all individuals of the same species (Jacobson, 1969).

THE CELLULAR ELEMENTS

All living organisms are made up of cells, but cells can exist as separate entities. Bacteria, amoeba, and many other primitive forms of life consist of single cells. However, the higher organisms, such as man, are made up of billions of cells differentiated and specialized to form tissues and organs. In the one-celled organisms, the single cell possesses the properties of irritability (the capacity for responding to environmental changes), conductivity (the capacity for transmitting the effects of stimulation), and contractility (the capacity for changing shape in such a way as to move the organism or body part), as well as metabolism and reproductivity. In the multicellular organisms, groups of cells become specialized for certain of these functions. Figure 2-2 is a diagram of a typical cell.

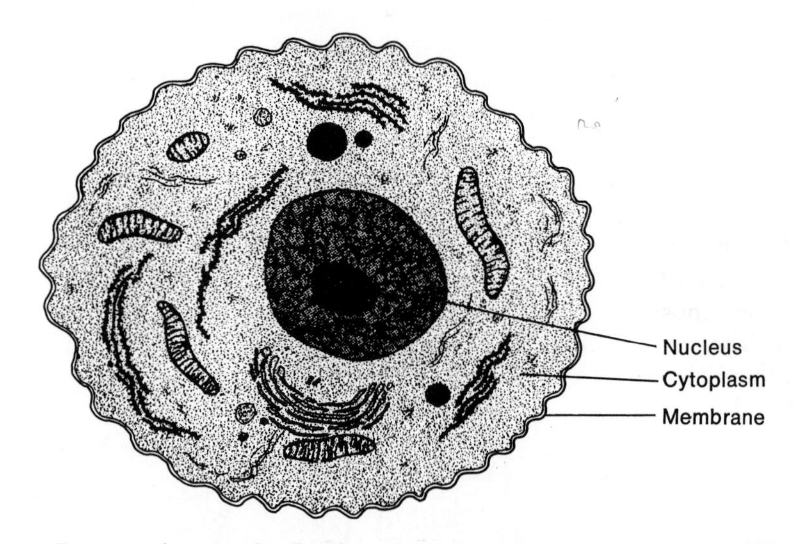

Figure 2-2. Diagram of a typical cell. The unlabeled cellular inclusions consist of a wide variety of granules and other minute structures involved in the various chemical and metabolic activities taking place in the cytoplasm.

The nucleus of the cell is the center for the control of the metabolic activities of the cytoplasm and the reproduction of additional cells. Both these processes involve the most important constituents of the nucleus: the chromosomes and their components, the genes. The genes consist of a complex chemical substance, DNA, whose varied structure carries the genetic code, which in turn is carried through messenger RNA to the sites where proteins are fabricated from amino acids and the various organs of the body are formed. The nucleus is the vital center of the cell. When it is destroyed, the cell dies. Many cells can survive and regenerate following loss of parts of the cell membrane and the cytoplasm.

CELLULAR DIFFERENTIATION AND SPECIALIZATION

Initially all cells of the organism possess all the properties we have listed. However, as the organism develops, various groups of cells undergo differentiation and become highly specialized in their functions. The nerve cell (neuron) differentiates in structure and function, becoming highly specialized for conduction and, to a lesser degree, for irritability. The sense organs (receptors) become highly irritable and are responsive to very low levels of energy change (stimuli). Glandular cells become differentiated for secretion, and muscle cells become extremely contractile.

The Receptors

The receptors of man and the other higher organisms are specialized to respond to thermal, mechanical, chemical, and light stimuli. The thermal receptors are in the skin. The mechanical receptors are involved in hearing, balance, the kinesthetic sense (sense of movement and position), and touch. The chemical receptors are those for taste and smell. The light receptors are in the retina of the eye. The receptors for pain, located in many organs, respond to a wide variety of thermal, mechanical, and chemical stimuli. Receptor processes are discussed more fully in the next two chapters.

The Effectors

Muscles and glands constitute the effectors. There are three varieties of muscles, which differ in structure and to some degree in function. The most primi-

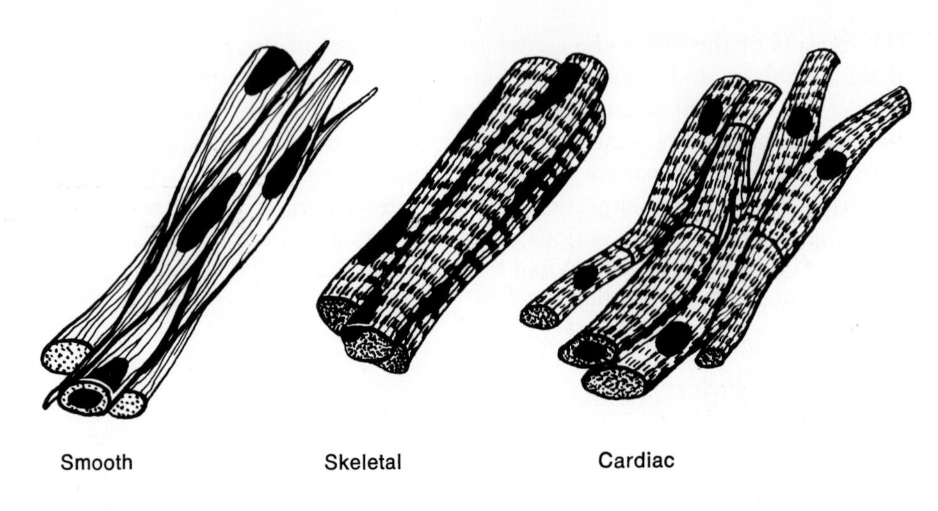

Figure 2-3. The three types of muscles. Note the peripherally located nuclei and distinct cross striations on the striated muscles and the centrally located single-nucleated cardiac and smooth muscles. The cardiac fibers branch and connect with one another.

tive and least differentiated muscle is composed of nonstriated, or smooth, muscle cells. Since we have no direct control over these muscles, they are also known as involuntary. They are found principally in the internal regions of the body and are involved in the control of respiration, circulation, digestion, and elimination. The voluntary muscles make up the second variety. Under a microscope the individual muscle cells of this type show alternating light and dark bands—hence the term *striated*, or striped. Because they attach to the bones of the skeleton of the body, they are also called skeletal muscles; moreover, they are involved in the execution of purposive voluntary acts and are thus called voluntary. The cardiac (heart) muscle, the third variety, constitutes an intermediate category, the fibers of which have a special type of cross striation; their control is involuntary.

The glands secrete chemical substances that influence growth and development, participate in many physiological processes, and have considerable effect on many of the behavioral characteristics of the individual. The two major classes of glands are the duct (exocrine) and the ductless (endocrine). The duct glands are so called because they have ducts or tubes leading from them to the cavities into which they empty their secretions, whereas the ductless glands secrete hormones directly into the bloodstream. The blood carries the endocrine secretions to the various organs of the body, where they have profound effects on growth and activity.

The Connectors—Neurons

The nervous system consists of many billions of neurons arranged in an orderly but infinitely complex network. This network serves as the principal mediating link between the organism and its environment. A neuron, like any typical cell, consists of a body, a nucleus, and a membrane. However, extending out from the cell body are axons and dendrites, which may vary from a fraction of a millimeter to several feet in length. The dendrites constitute the receiving ends of the neuron and are excited by receptor processes in the sense organs or by the activity of other neurons. The axon extends from the cell body to the dendrites of other neurons or to effectors, which it in turn excites. Thus the nerve impulse usually originates in a dendrite, passes over the cell body, out along the axon, and activates either an effector (muscle or gland) or another neuron. A neuron may have only one but usually has many dendrites extending out from the cell body like the branches of a tree. On the other hand, the axon is typically single; it is longer than the dendrites and branches less. The long axon may send off occasional branches and often has several short branches (terminal end brush) near the end.

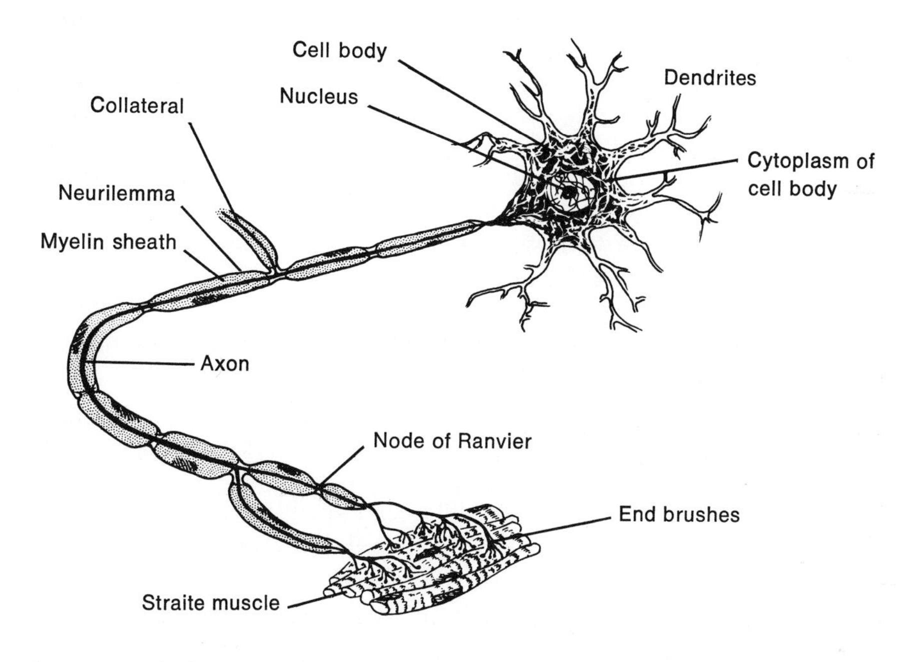

Figure 2-4. The basic structure of a motor neuron.

Neurons may have either one or two coverings. The thin membrane on the outside is the neurilemma, and the fatty, glistening white sheath between the fiber and the neurilemma is the myelin sheath. The neurilemma is found almost exclusively on the neuronal fibers of the peripheral nerves (those outside the brain and spinal cord). It seems to be necessary for the regeneration of injured or severed fibers. This fact explains why the neuronal fibers of the peripheral nerves can regenerate, whereas those within the central nervous system cannot.

The myelin sheath is found on some but not all fibers both inside and outside the central nervous system. The myelin sheath is generally found on the larger axons, whereas the smaller ones are unmyelinated. The sheath is interrupted at regular intervals by constrictions called nodes of Ranvier. The interrupted myelin sheath appears to provide a far more rapid means of transmission of the neural impulse traveling from node to node than is possible in an unmyelinated fiber.

Types of neurons. Neurons come in a nearly infinite variety of shapes and sizes. They have been given various names and classified in various ways, but for our purposes a threefold functional classification is most useful. Thus we will speak of (1) afferent neurons, (2) efferent neurons, and (3) interneurons. Afferent, or sensory, neurons conduct impulses from receptors to other neurons. Many of the afferent neurons differ from the typical neurons in having a single dendrite with few branches except near its end (the dendrite is thus structurally like a typical axon). The second type of neuron is the efferent, or motor, neuron. Motor neurons always connect other neurons with effectors. The third type of neuron, the interneuron, or association neuron, serves as a connecting link between two other neurons. Interneurons are found entirely within the central nervous system.

The nerve impulse. The primary function of neurons is the transmission of nerve impulses, which are electrochemical in nature. When a stimulus activates a neuron, it initiates a complex series of electrochemical changes that pass along the neuron. The activity passing along the neuron is like that of a fuse or a trail of gunpowder. The intensity of the stimulus, like the temperature of the igniting agent, must exceed a certain point (the threshold) in order to start the chain reaction. If the neuron responds at all, the intensity of the resulting nerve impulses is determined by the size and condition of the neuron and is independent of the nature and strength of the stimulus. The energy release involved in the passage of a nerve impulse can be likened to the discharge of a cartridge. If the impact on the cartridge is sufficient to fire it, the force of the discharge is determined by the amount and nature of the explosive it contains and is independent of the nature and force of the blow that initiates the activity.

When a neuron is stimulated, the amplitude and speed of the nerve impulse are independent of the strength of the stimulus. The impulse travels out along the axon to its endings on or near the dendrites or cell body of another neuron. The points of transmission of impulses from one neuron to another are known as *synapses.* Impulses are transmitted from one neuron to another at the synapse possibly by the release of a chemical substance from tiny vesicles or sacs in the axon endings. After a response a neuron is inexcitable for a short time (the refractory period). The arrival of a nerve impulse at the axon endings releases the chemical substance, which has either an excitatory or an inhibitory effect on the dendrite or cell body beyond the synapse. The interplay of excitatory and inhibitory activities on the neuron determines its pattern of activity.

A neuron can transmit "information" only in the form of impulses, and, because of the all-or-none characteristic of neural activity, all an axon can do is fire or not fire. Patterns of stimuli are presumably coded and transmitted within the

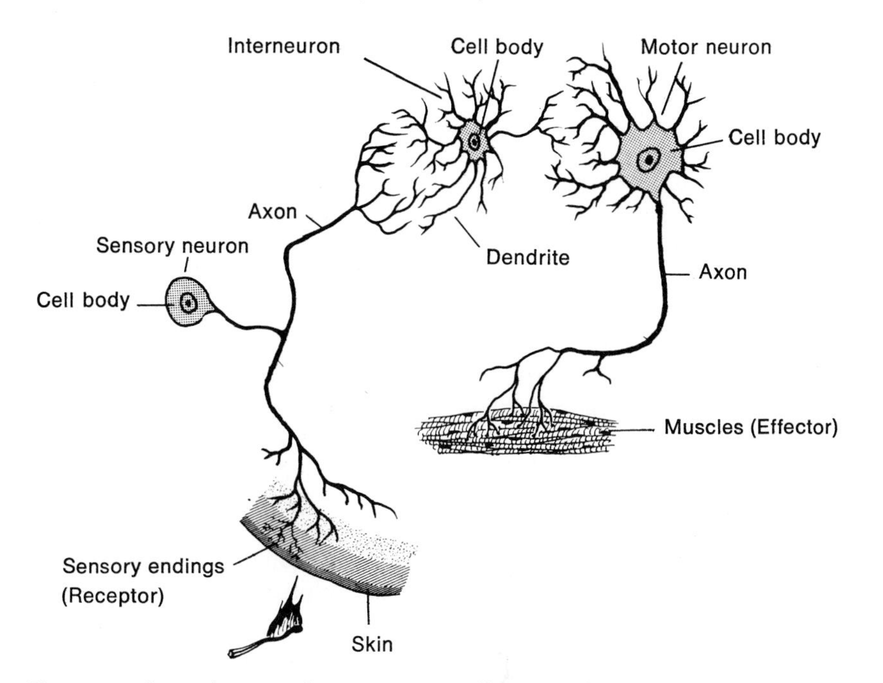

Figure 2-5. A simple circuit from receptor to effector involving three types of neurons.

nervous system as exceedingly complex organizations of neural discharges, each component of which has a simple binary (on or off) characteristic. The coding involved in the transmission of information from stimulus input to perceptual, ideational, or motor output occurs at several levels. There is good evidence that some of this coding occurs in the receptor itself. It also takes place at various levels within the nervous system (Stevens, 1970; Robinson, 1968; Gouras, 1970; Phillips & Olds, 1969). If the binary (off-on) characteristic of neural activity within each neuron seems too simple a base for encoding all the information transmitted within the human nervous system, it is well to recall that this system is used in many electronic computers and forms the basis for many of the information theories that have been developed (Quastler, 1955; MacRae, 1970; Levine, 1970).

It should be mentioned that, in addition to firing or not firing, individual neurons can vary in rates of transmission of impulses: the fibers with larger diameters transmit faster than do those with smaller ones. Within the limits set by the length of the refractory period, time intervals between successive impulses within each neuron can vary widely. This variable can be important in information encoding.

SUBDIVISIONS OF THE NERVOUS SYSTEM

Anatomically, the nervous system can be divided into the central nervous system, which consists of the brain and spinal cord, and the peripheral nervous system, which consists of the autonomic nervous system as well as the cranial and spinal nerves and the ganglia (groups of cell bodies) and plexuses (networks of interlacing nerves and fibers) associated with them. The 12 pairs of cranial nerves and the 31 pairs of spinal nerves connect the brain and spinal cord with the receptors and effectors located principally in the outer regions of the body. Some of the cranial nerves are purely motor, some are purely sensory, and others are mixed. All the spinal nerves are mixed, containing both sensory and motor fibers.

Whereas the regular cranial and spinal nerves are concerned primarily with adjustments of the organism to the external world, the autonomic nervous system is more concerned with the internal adjustments of the organism. Unlike the other divisions of the peripheral nervous system, the autonomic system is purely motor. It is subdivided into the sympathetic and parasympathetic systems. The sympathetic outflow originates in the thoracic and lumbar (middle) regions of the spinal cord. The parasympathetic division originates in the cranial (upper) and sacral (lower) sections of the spinal cord. Many, but not all, of the visceral effectors (smooth muscles and glands) of the body receive nerve fibers from both the sympathetic and the parasympathetic divisions. These fibers from the two subdivisions of the autonomic nervous system are largely, although not completely, antagonistic in their effects. That is, when one stimulates, the other inhibits, and vice versa.

Table 2-1 indicates the principal anatomical subdivisions of the nervous system. Although such a sectioning can be done and certain functions can be assigned predominantly to the various anatomical areas, the individual parts seldom, if ever, function in isolation. The central nervous system and the peripheral nervous system (the spinal, cranial, and autonomic nerves) never function independently. All the connections between incoming sensory and outgoing motor impulses are made within the brain or spinal cord.

The uneven development of the head end of the neural tube (mentioned earlier) forms the various subdivisions of the brain. The first differentiations of these subdivisions are three bulblike swellings, the embryonic forebrain (prosencephalon), the midbrain (mesencephalon), and the hindbrain (rhombencephalon). The remainder of the neural tube becomes the spinal end. The spinal cord, or adult derivative from the long caudal portion of the neural tube, largely retains its embryonic tubular form. The functions of the spinal cord are of two types. One of these is reflex. Even after the spinal cord is severed from the brain, as in paraplegia, muscular and autonomic responses to bodily stimuli occur. Thirty-one pairs of spinal nerves connect the spinal cord with most of the sensory surfaces and muscles of the trunk. A large number of ascending and descending nerve tracts are found within the spinal cord that serve as connecting links between the brain and the peripheral sensory and motor neurons —the second function of the cord.

The hindbrain (rhombencephalon) develops into three adult structures: the medulla oblongata, the pons, and the cerebellum. The medulla oblongata is essentially a continuation of the spinal cord and contains all the ascending and descending fiber tracts interconnecting the brain–spinal cord and a number of important nuclei. Several cranial nerves enter or exit from the medulla. In addition, many vital vegetative functions, such as respiration, circulation, and digestion, are controlled or partially regulated via the medulla. The pons is a further upward extension of the brainstem (technically, all the brain structures

Table 2-1. Principal anatomical subdivisions of the nervous system.

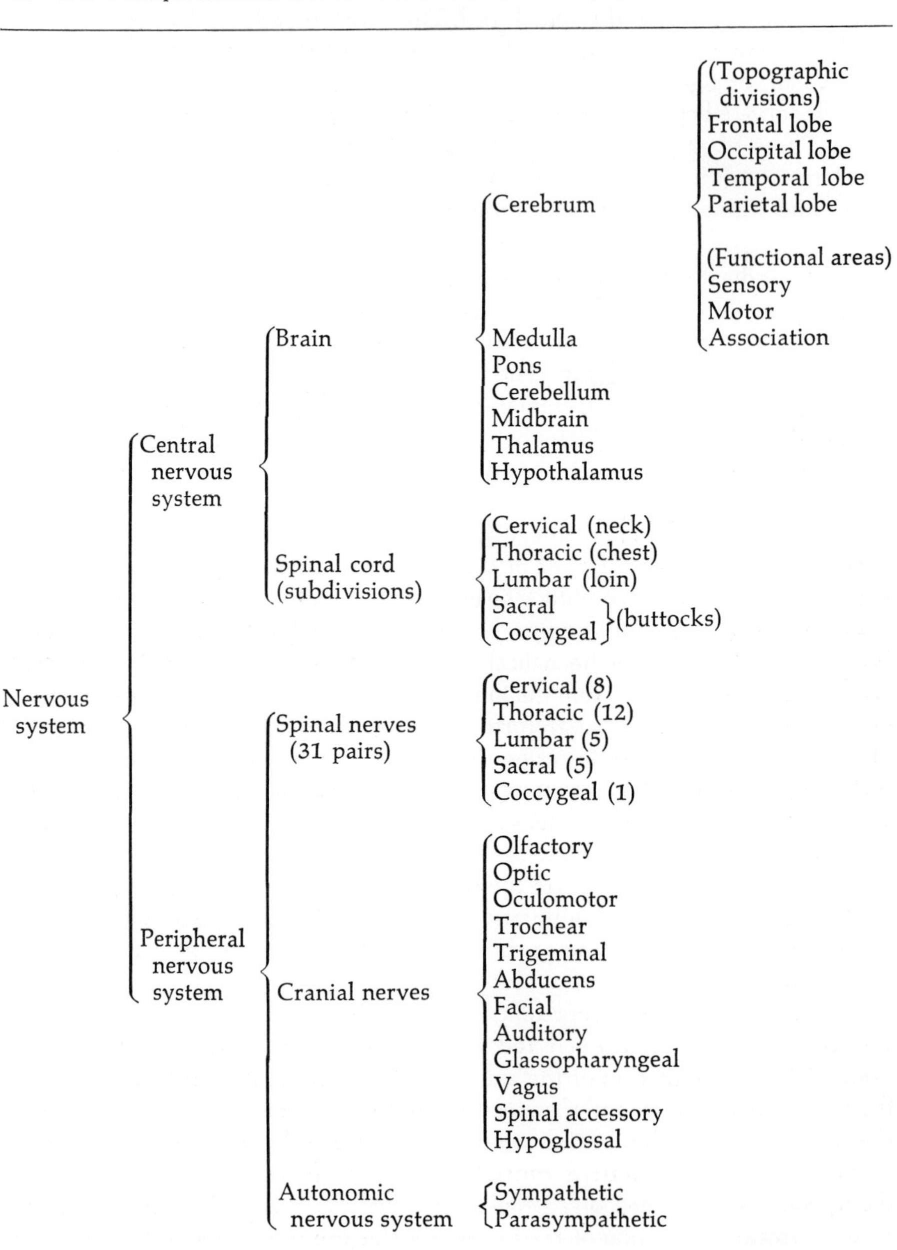

Nervous system	Central nervous system	Brain	Cerebrum	(Topographic divisions)
				Frontal lobe
				Occipital lobe
				Temporal lobe
				Parietal lobe
				(Functional areas)
				Sensory
				Motor
				Association
			Medulla	
			Pons	
			Cerebellum	
			Midbrain	
			Thalamus	
			Hypothalamus	
		Spinal cord (subdivisions)	Cervical (neck)	
			Thoracic (chest)	
			Lumbar (loin)	
			Sacral	(buttocks)
			Coccygeal	(buttocks)
	Peripheral nervous system	Spinal nerves (31 pairs)	Cervical (8)	
			Thoracic (12)	
			Lumbar (5)	
			Sacral (5)	
			Coccygeal (1)	
		Cranial nerves	Olfactory	
			Optic	
			Oculomotor	
			Trochear	
			Trigeminal	
			Abducens	
			Facial	
			Auditory	
			Glassopharyngeal	
			Vagus	
			Spinal accessory	
			Hypoglossal	
		Autonomic nervous system	Sympathetic	
			Parasympathetic	

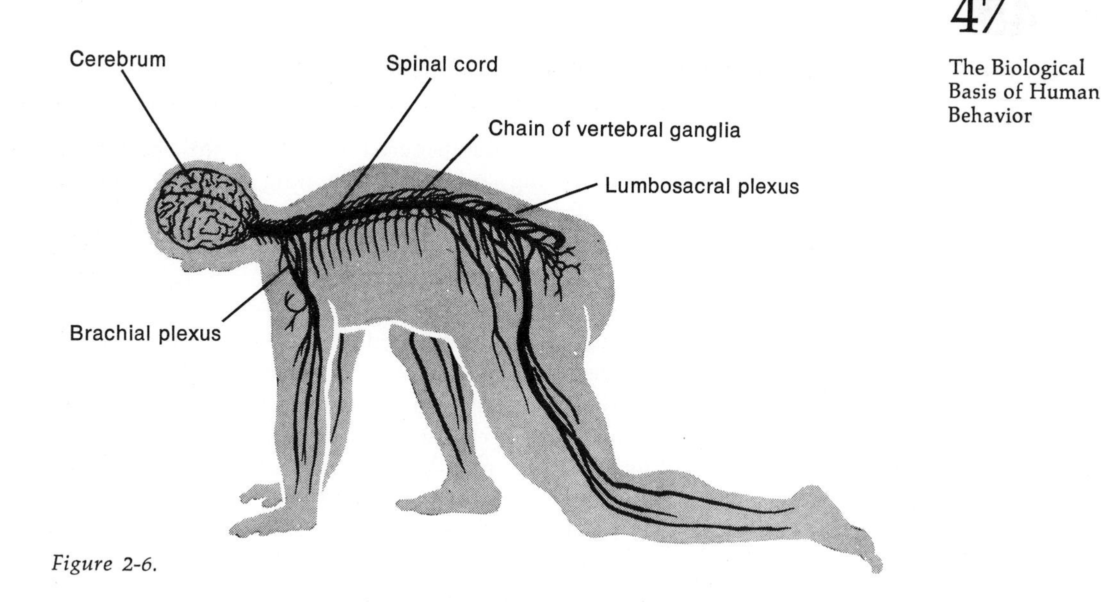

Figure 2-6.

between the spinal cord and the cortices of the cerebrum and the cerebellum). Like the medulla and the midbrain, the pons contains ascending and descending nerve tracts and many additional nuclei. The name *pons* (bridge) refers to the fact that it contains a large bundle of nerve fibers interconnecting the brainstem and the cerebellum. The cerebellum is the second largest subdivision of the mammalian brain (the cerebrum is the largest). Although the cerebellum is primarily concerned with the regulation of motor coordination and the maintenance of balance, it also receives nerve fibers from the auditory, visual, and other sensory systems and sends fibers to several other brainstem structures.

The embryonic midbrain (mesencephalon) remains comparatively simple in the adult. It consists of a basically tubular structure like the spinal cord and contains ascending and descending nerve tracts and various nuclei, some of which are associated with the optic and auditory nerves.

The adult derivatives of the forebrain are the cerebral cortex (the outer portions of the cerebrum, which comprises the large anterior part of the brain), the basal ganglia (a group of nuclei forming the central part of the cerebrum), the rhinencephalon (literally the nose-brain but now known to have a diversity of fuctions), the thalamus (a group of nuclei in the center of the brain), and the hypothalamus (a group of small nuclei crucially involved in the functioning of the autonomic nervous system). Because of the importance of the cerebral cortex, we shall discuss it more extensively.

The Cerebral Cortex

Man's cerebral cortex has long been considered the seat of the "higher" psychological functions (remembering, thinking, reasoning, talking), which are the special prerogatives of humans. The cerebral cortex is estimated to contain 9 billion neurons interconnected to form the most complex structure we know.

Because the size of the brain—particularly the cerebrum—increases as we move up the animal scale, it has often been suggested that the size of the brain may be a valid index of intelligence level. Although relative brain size may have some phylogenetic (evolutionary) significance, it has little value as an index of the intelligence of individuals except for those belonging to a few clinical types. Extremely small-headed (and small-brained) individuals (microcephalics) are severely mentally retarded. However, people with extremely large heads (hydrocephalics) are not intellectually gifted; as a matter of fact, the more extreme cases are also mentally deficient. Except for microcephaly, hydrocephaly, and a few other relatively rare clinical types, the gross size of the human brain has not proven to be a useful index of any insignificant intellectual or personality variable. The brain weights of persons rated as geniuses have varied from 1200 to more than 2000 grams (Lassek, 1957; Munn, 1966).

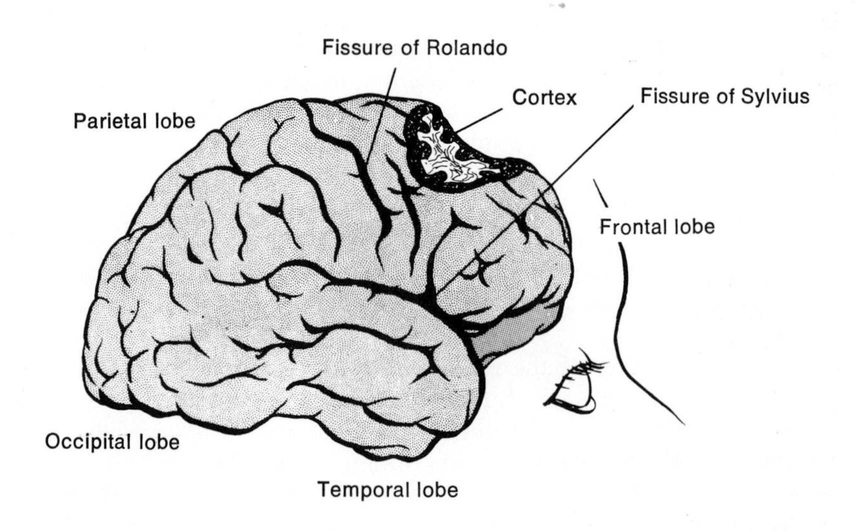

Figure 2-7. Fissures and lobes of the cerebral cortex. The cerebal cortex is the outer layer of the cerebrum.

Sensory functions of the cortex. One essential prerequisite of most, if not all, conscious sensory experience is the reception of nerve impulses in the projective areas of the cortex. These areas have been identified by tracing the sensory-nerve tracts to their termination in the cerebrum; by recording the electrical activity evoked in the cortex when the sense organs are stimulated; by electrically stimulating the surface of the cortex in conscious subjects undergoing brain operations and determining the areas that give rise to various sensory experiences; and by observing the behavior af animals stimulated similarly.

The sensory projection area from the somesthetic (skin and kinesthetic) senses occupies a strip of cortex immediately behind the fissure of Rolando, the deep fissure extending from above the region of the ear up to the central region of the cortex. Stimulation of this area in conscious subjects evokes such statements as "My foot feels warm," "My leg feels as if it is moving," and "It feels as if something is touching my face." Thus the subject typically reports sensations of warmth, cold, contact, movement, tingling, or numbness in some particular body part. When the somesthetic cortical area of a dog is similarly stimulated, the dog will vigorously scratch various areas of the body depending on the cortical area stimulated. The sensory experiences evoked by artificial stimulation of the sensory cortex are not identical with those produced by normal sensory stimulation: the person never feels that he is actually touching an external object or that he is actually moving the body part (Penfield, 1958). Such electrically aroused experiences are always attributed to the side of the body opposite the stimulated side of the brain. Thus we have a fairly complete projection of the external surface of the body within the cortical sensory projection area of the brain.

The relationship between extent of skin area stimulated and cortical projection area is not close. Those body regions having high sensitivity to differential cutaneous stimulation have a large proportional representation, whereas those parts of the body that are relatively insensitive have proportionately small areas of cortical projection. This relationship is often shown graphically by drawing a homunculus, a man in which the body parts are drawn in proportion to their cutaneous sensory cortical representation. An adaptation of such a homunculus is shown in Figure 2-8.

This same figure also represents fairly accurately the relationship between the musculature of the body and the relative size of its neural representation in the main motor cortex (to be discussed in a later section). The same general areas of the body that have high cutaneous sensitivity also have high degrees of mobility and large proportional cortical representations; regions of low cuta-

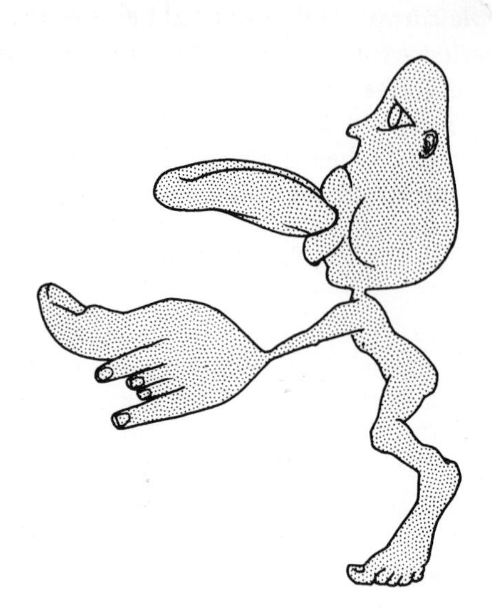

Figure 2-8. A homunculus whose body parts are drawn in proportion to amount of sensory cortical representation.

neous discrimination have small cortical representations and correspondingly low capacity for making differential motor responses. The hands and fingers and the tongue and lips have many small muscles and are capable of making a large number of finely adjusted and highly differentiated movements. The musculature of the trunk, on the other hand, consists principally of large flat muscles that control only gross movements of the body such as bending and turning. The differential mobility of these body parts is reflected in the respective sizes of their representation in the motor cortex.

The sensory projection areas for vision are in the most posterior part of the occipital lobe. Like the sensory areas of the skin, there is a point-to-point projection of retinal areas of the eye to the corresponding areas of the visual cortex. However, unlike the sensory tracts for the somesthetic senses, which all cross from one side to the other, only half of the optic-nerve fibers coming from the retina of an eye cross before their termination in the cortex. Nerves from the two eyes meet at the optic chiasma at the base of the brain; the fibers coming from the lateral (outside) half of each retina do not cross but terminate on the same side of the brain, whereas the fibers from the medial (inside) half of each retina cross and project to the visual cortex of the opposite side. With such an arrangement, the patterns of nerve impulses set up in the right half of each retina are received in the right side of the brain; those from the left half of each retina go to the left side of the visual cortex.

Electrical stimulation of the visual cortex results in visual experiences, such as flashing or moving lights, and various color experiences. The colors are often seen as whirling or moving. Similar visual experiences are reported by some epileptics whose seizures originate in the occipital lobe (Penfield, 1958). (Epileptic seizures involve the apparent spontaneous firing of large numbers of cortical neurons, often starting in a localized area of the brain.)

Auditory impulses from the ear go to the temporal lobe of the cerebral cortex. Although the majority of the auditory nerve fibers cross and terminate on the opposite side of the brain, some do not cross. Thus each ear is represented in both temporal lobes. When the auditory cortex in a conscious subject is stimulated electrically, the subject reports hearing buzzing, chirping, ringing, clicking, or rumbling, usually from the side opposite the stimulated side of the cortex. Subjects thus stimulated never report hearing words or music. Epileptic seizures that originate in the temporal lobes are often preceded by similar auditory experiences—an "auditory aura."

We are less certain of the location of the cortical projection areas for olfaction (smell), gustation (taste), and pain than we are of those for vision, audition, and the other somesthetic senses (warmth, cold, touch, and movement). Because taste and smell are intimately fused in experience, and because the receptors of both are located in the oropharyngeal area, the two were formerly thought to terminate in the same area of the cerebral cortex. However, in its evolutionary and embryological development, taste is more closely associated with the skin senses than with smell. Recent studies have shown that the nerve tracts for taste follow those from the skin of the face and mouth to the cerebral cortex. It also seems clear that the cortical projection area for taste overlaps that of the face and mouth at the base of the fissure of Rolando and that the cortical projection area for smell is in an adjacent area. The proximity of these areas accounts for the fact that pressure from a tumor in the mouth or nose usually results in olfactogustatory hallucinatory experiences rather than solely gustatory or olfactory experiences.

Although sensation of pain originates in skin tissues, as do other cutaneous sensations, and although nerve fibers carrying impulses from the pain receptors follow the same general pathways as do the other cutaneous senses to the thalamus, the cortical representation of pain seems to be different from that of the other cutaneous senses. One puzzling thing is that electrical stimulation of the surface of the cortex of conscious subjects has regularly evoked experiences of cold, warm, contact, and movement but never pain. This finding led to the speculation that awareness of pain is mediated by centers below the cortex. Since severing nerve tracts leading to and from the frontal areas of the cortex gives relief from intractable pain, the frontal lobes seem to play some role in the experience of pain. However, following such operations, patients report that they still "feel" the pain but that it no longer bothers them. Their reports, along with the fact that such operations reduce the emotional components of phobias (abnormal fears), obsessions (pathological beliefs), and chronic anxieties without eliminating their ideational components (the patient still believes his delusions), indicate that, although the emotional accompaniment of the total experience is reduced or eliminated by severing nerve tracts to the frontal lobes, the pain sensation itself continues.

Motor areas of the cortex. The motor cortex is a relatively narrow strip of cortical tissue immediately in front of the fissure of Rolando and parallel to the somesthetic area posterior to this fissure. (See Figure 2-9). Electrical stimulation of the motor cortex produces contraction of the muscles of the opposite side of the body. When the uppermost region of the motor cortex is stimulated, the muscles of the toes or foot of the opposite side of the body are forced to contract. When a conscious subject is so stimulated, he is unable to prevent the movements of the affected body part. He feels as though something is forcing the response.

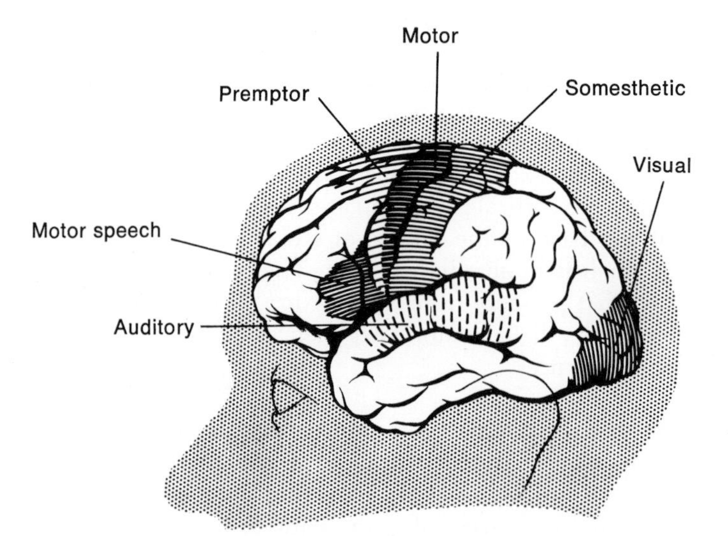

Figure 2-9. Sensory projection areas of the cortex.

Although the somesthetic nerve tracts and the voluntary motor pathways all cross to the side opposite that of their origin, the cortical projection areas for speech seem to be unique. This function involves structures in the midline of the body, and, although traditional belief has related the location of the speech center to handedness, the most complete recent studies indicate that the cortical areas for speech are predominantly on the left side of the brain regardless of the individual's handedness (Penfield & Roberts, 1959). These studies find no difference in the frequency of speech disturbances after injury or operation on the left cerebral hemisphere between people who are right- or left-handed. It seems that the left hemisphere is dominant for speech, regardless of handedness, with the possible exception of those individuals who suffer cerebral injuries early in life. The cortical areas involved in speech are in the region where the frontal, parietal, and temporal lobes come together behind the Rolandic fissure.

Associative functions of the cerebral cortex. Practically all areas outside the motor and sensory areas of the cerebral cortex at one time were called "silent areas" and were assumed to serve associative functions. Aphasia or dysphasia is considered to involve a disturbance of the associative aspects of speech—as contrasted with disturbances of the purely motor activities of lips, tongue, and throat in such a way as to produce paralysis or motor incoordinations of written or oral speech.

Aphasia. Aphasia is a disturbance of the ideational components of any or all aspects of language. Different types of aphasias have long been recognized. Difficulties in understanding the written or spoken word are called sensory aphasia, and difficulties in speaking or writing are called motor aphasia. Researchers describe additional types and give them differentiating names. In sensory aphasia the individual is not blind and his sensory acuity may be normal, but he does not comprehend what he sees. He does not know its meaning. If the comprehension of oral speech is the primary deficiency, the individual may understand written but not spoken words. In motor aphasia the individual may comprehend the written and spoken word but cannot say or write what he wants to. He may say something that is either meaningless or inappropriate and at the same time recognize its meaninglessness or inappropriateness.

Electrical stimulation of the motor-speech area of either side of the brain may produce vocalization or an interference with the motor control of speech that is in progress. The vocalization produced by electrical stimulation is typically a sustained or interrupted vowel sound. No intelligible word has been induced

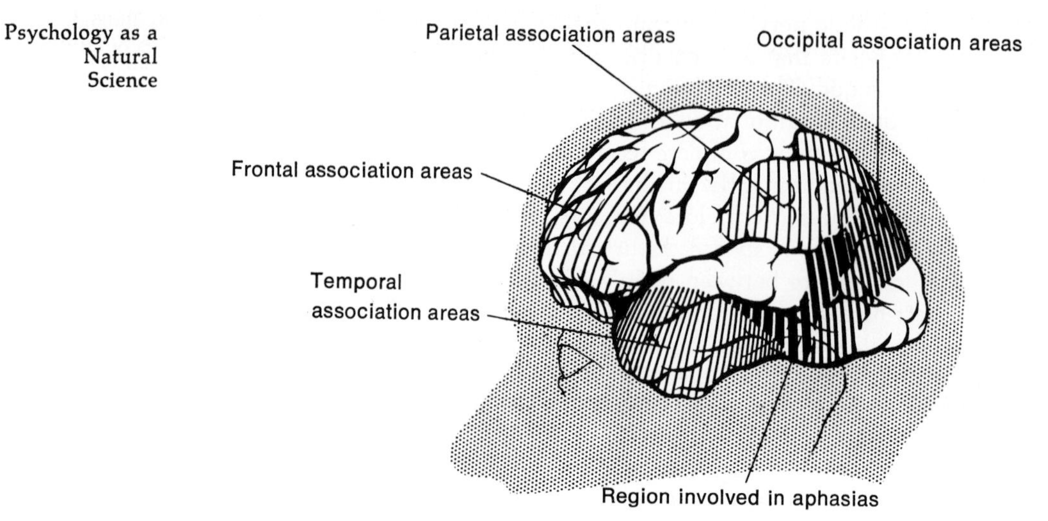

Figure 2-10. Association areas of the cortex.

by such cortical stimulation. Vocalization results from stimulation of the cortical areas involved in lip, jaw, and tongue. Vocalization occurs with equal frequency on stimulation of either the dominant or nondominant motor areas. Electrical stimulation of these same areas on the left hemisphere (and, on rare occasions, of the dominant right hemisphere) while the patient is speaking may produce total arrest, hesitations, slurring or distortions of sound, or repetition of words and syllables. Stimulation of the left speech areas in most subjects also results in the confusion of numbers in counting, an inability to name familiar objects, the misnaming of well-known objects, and difficulties in reading and writing (aphasic symptoms). These studies indicate that the purely motor responses involved in simple vocalization have bilateral cortical representation but that the left cerebral hemisphere is dominant in the complex language functions. The disturbance of these language processes has usually been classified as aphasic. Aphasia is primarily a disorder of the associative components of language.

There may be similar difficulties in writing. In practice, "pure" forms of aphasia practically never exist. The patient is labeled in terms of the area of language that is dominantly affected, but an aphasic is rarely, if ever, unaffected in other departments of language (Penfield & Roberts, 1959).

Electrical stimulation of association areas. Experiences of an ideational sort have been reported by persons undergoing stimulation of the cerebral cortex. The experiences have been described as dream states, flashbacks, and familiar memories. Most often they consist of the recall of experiences from one's earlier life. The subjects regularly report that the experiences are more vivid than voluntary recollections of the same or similar events. These induced experiences are not "still pictures." People move, talk, and laugh, and the events move forward as in the actual occurrences. Removal of the electrical stimulation stops the experience as abruptly as it initiates it. Sometimes, by interrupting the stimulation and then reapplying the electrode at the same point, the same events will be reexperienced.

Such ideational responses are evoked by stimulation of the temporal cortex and a small area of the adjacent parietal lobe. They have also been produced by stimulation of the tissues immediately under the temporal lobe, after surgical removal of this area. Such associative responses have never been produced by stimulation of any other areas of the cortex (Penfield & Jasper, 1954; Penfield & Roberts, 1959).

These results indicate that the temporal cortex and related structures are somehow critically involved in the retention and recall of past experiences, but the results do not indicate how. Memories, as such, are certainly not "stored" in this or any other part of the brain. These areas may be the more accessible portions of a complex series of neural processes involved in retention and recall. For example, the processes involved in the recall of visual and auditory experiences may be at considerable distance from the point of electrical stimulation. They may be adjacent to the sensory projection areas for these senses. The stimulated portion of the cortex may simply serve as a mechanism for "scanning" and "reassembling" patterns of past experiences, the residues of which are elsewhere. Although the reactivation of ideational processes by electrical stimulation raises more questions than it answers, it does support many traditional conceptions of the role of the cerebral cortex in higher mental processes, such as learning, recalling, and reasoning.

CODING WITHIN THE NERVOUS SYSTEM

We have previously indicated that patterns of stimulation are encoded in the sense organs and at various levels within the nervous system. Yet experimental evidence supporting this belief was not obtained until techniques were developed for studying the connections and activities of individual nerve cells. By means of microdissection techniques and the use of microelectrodes, it has been demonstrated that there is considerable neuronal specificity involved in the coding of sensory input within the nervous system. The use of implanted electrodes makes it possible to both stimulate and record the neural activity in selected parts of the brain. By combining behavior and behavioral changes with recordings of the activities of relevant neural mechanisms, many relationships between neural mechanisms on the one hand and differential responses and learning on the other have been demonstrated.

The evidence for neuronal coding of various stimulus variables has been accumulating over a long period. This coding of sensory input has been demonstrated to occur at various levels all the way from the receptor cells to the cortex (Gouras, 1970; Pomeranz & Chung, 1970; Hyvärinen, Sakata, Talbot, & Mountcastle, 1968; Konishi, 1969). Motivational and exploratory activities have been correlated with specific midbrain, hypothalamic, and limbic-system neuronal activity (Phillips & Olds, 1969; Smith & Coons, 1970; Komisaruk & Olds, 1968). Evidence that learning and the development of differential responses involve electrical coding in the cortex has been repeatedly demonstrated (Fox & Rudell, 1968; John, Shimakochi, & Bartlett, 1969; Fetz, 1969; Jacobson, 1969; Begleiter & Platz, 1969). These studies have demonstrated the development of specific neural activity to a novel stimulus via generalization. The evidence seems to indicate that, in learning specific responses, a unique pattern of neural activity is established in the nervous system. This pattern is somehow "stored" in the nervous system and can be reactivated by appropriate stimuli.

The existence of specific neuronal activities and interconnections underlying relatively unmodifiable reflex and instinctive behavior in the lower animals has been well documented (Sperry, 1951; Jacobson, 1969). For example, Sperry, in a series of studies on the regeneration of neural connections in lower vertebrates, showed that visual perception and motor coordinations could best be explained in terms of highly specific cellular interconnections that were invariant and appeared to be unaffected by experience. Recently there has been some speculation and research on the possible anatomical, physiological, or biochemical differences in those neural components or interconnections between the modifiable and relatively unmodifiable systems. One suggestion is that the difference may be related to differences in the synapses. The current consensus is that the agent of transmission at the synapses is chemical. However, purely electrical synapses have been found in invertebrates (Furshpan & Potter, 1959).

It has been shown that following repetitive stimulation, chemically mediated potentials change, whereas electrically mediated synaptic potentials do not (Kennedy, Selverston, & Remler, 1969). This finding has given rise to the possibility that the difference between modifiable and unmodifiable neural systems may be related to their chemical and electrical synaptic mediators.

PATTERNS OF "SPONTANEOUS" NEURAL ACTIVITY (EEGs)

The central nervous system is an active mechanism long before birth and does not cease its functioning until death. This continuing activity is not entirely the result of the continuing stream of sensory impulses feeding into it; it is partly caused by the regular autonomous, synchronous activity of groups of neurons producing the so-called brain waves or EEGs (electroencephalograms).

It has been known since 1874 that electrical activity is a component of the functioning of the neural tissue of living animals. In 1924 Berger demonstrated a spontaneous rhythm of the brain that varies with certain internal and external changes in environment and shows certain characteristic deviations in the presence of certain brain disorders. Each cell seems to act as a low-power generator, and groups of cells synchronize their activities to generate sufficient power to be recorded through the intact skull. The electrical activities of these groups of neurons can be classified in a spectrum of frequencies, or waves, from 1 to 60 a second. The dominant adult frequency is 8 to 13 a second, which produces the "alpha waves."

EEG activity is not restricted to the cortex and is apparently a general property of aggregations of nerve cells. It has been found in the isolated nervous ganglia (groups of cell bodies) of caterpillars and water beetles and in the isolated brainstem of goldfish.

The EEG shows maximum amplitude and regularity when the eyes are closed, when the individual is relaxed, and when mental activity is at a minimum. The alpha rhythm disappears or is "desynchronized" if the person opens his eyes or attends to an object in his visual field. Ideational activity, such as mental arithmetic and any form of sensory stimulation to which the person attends, abolishes the wave pattern. Emotional tension, apprehension, and anxiety also decrease alpha activity. The EEG pattern changes during sleep. In the lower animals the EEG during sleep is indistinguishable from that present in an

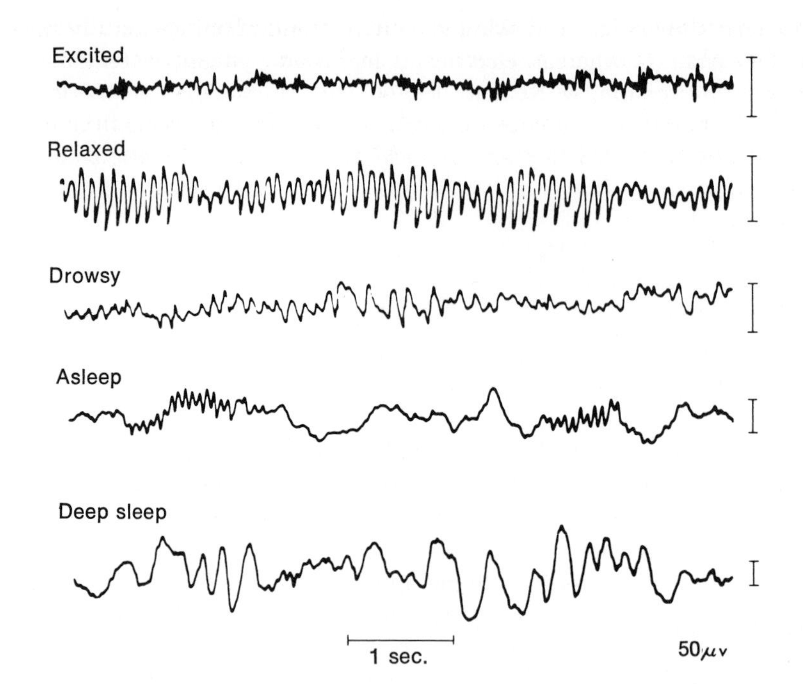

Figure 2-11. Normal EEG records characteristic of different stages on the sleep-wakefulness continuum.

animal decerebrated by transection of the brainstem. EEG abnormalities occur in epilepsy and in brain injury. For this reason, the EEG is used in the diagnosis and localization of the pathological areas in these conditions.

Study of EEG activity gives us a picture of the living brain as incessantly active. Even when physical, ideational, and emotional activities are at the lowest ebb, rhythms of electrical activity are sweeping through the brain continuously. The neural activity induced by sensory stimulation, ideational activity, and motor activity is superimposed on and sometimes interferes with, but at other times summates with, the spontaneous activities already in progress. The usual effect of interjected activities is to desynchronize or interrupt inherent cortical rhythms. However, if a light flickering approximately ten times a second is flashed into the eyes, instead of being abolished, the EEG summates with the effects of the periodic photic stimulation and in some 3 to 4 percent of the cases builds up and shows cortical EEG activity indistinguishable from that usually considered to be typical of clinical epilepsy. With continued stimulation, these people report sensations of color, movement, strange feelings, faintness, confusion, dizziness, and anxiety. Some even become unresponsive to external stimulation. In other individuals the limbs jerk in rhythm with the flashes of light. If the rate of the photic stimulation is gradually increased from ten times a second, the alpha rhythm can be paced so that, instead of becoming desynchronized, it will, within limits of from 8 to 20 cycles a second, wax and wane in time with the visual stimulation (Glaser, 1963).

STABILITY AND ADAPTABILITY IN NEURAL GROWTH AND FUNCTION

The picture we have hitherto presented of anatomical, physiological, and biochemical factors controlling the development and growth of the human organism is too static to do justice to the considerable adaptive characteristics of that organism.

Peripheral Influences on Neural Growth

There is considerable evidence that there are peripheral influences on neural development. Sense organs and muscles exert some sort of influence on the central nervous structure so that appropriate nerve fibers grow out to them. For example, it has been known since 1907 that limbs grafted onto such animals as the salamander will receive a normal nerve supply and function normally. If developing limbs are severed and moved backward or forward from their previous position, they receive normal nervous innervation. They receive nerve fibers just the same as they would in their normal location. Extra limbs grafted onto an animal become innervated and function as they would in the location from which they were removed. If they are grafted in a new location or in the old position with the direction of the limb reversed so that the leg is pointed in the opposite direction, the limb will receive a nerve supply, but it will function in the way appropriate to its former orientation. Thus the grafted limb may move in reverse, compared with the other limbs. If connections of leg muscles are reversed prior to receiving their nerve supply, the muscles will function in a manner appropriate to their former connection. Flexors still act when flexors would normally act, even though the contraction of the muscle may now result in extension. The patterns of action in the grafted limb are the same regardless of its orientation, even though its activities may be dysfunctional in its reversed position. There is no evidence of any readjustment with time. The inappropriate movements seem to continue indefinitely.

If the normal nerve supply to a limb is blocked and prevented from growing out to the appropriate muscles, other nerves may grow out from the spinal cord, make connections with the muscles, and enable the limb to function in a normal fashion. Under some conditions nerves will even grow into the limb from the opposite side of the spinal cord. Similarly, if sense organs in early stages of development are transplanted to other parts of the body, nerves will grow into them.

It is clear that peripheral sense organs and muscles to some degree control the direction and extent of growth of nerve fibers within the central nervous system. If budding limbs are removed from a tadpole, the dorsal ganglia, which normally send nerves to those organs, develop in only a rudimentary way. Grafting additional limbs onto the developing frog results in increased size of the dorsal ganglia. Muscles and sense organs somehow attract nerve supplies with central connections appropriate to the various kinds of muscles and receptors. If the lower section of the spinal cord is severed and rotated, the generating nerve fibers tend to reconnect with their corresponding tract locations in the rotated segment (Sperry, 1951). Electrical, physical, and chemical influences have all been thought at various times to guide nerve fibers to their destinations.

Once the basic patterns are established, they cannot be changed. For example, if, in older animals, we cross the nerves to extensor and flexor muscles and permit them to regenerate, we reverse the pattern of movement (Morgan, 1965).

Visual Fixity and Adaptability

Because the retina of the eye is relatively accessible, several studies have been made of the regeneration of the optic nerve after it has been severed. Since there is a regular projection of retinal area on the visual receptive areas of the brain, interest in these studies has focused on the problem of the way in which the optic fibers form their central connections. It was shown in 1926 that the optic nerve of a grafted amphibian (frog) eye is capable of reestablishing appropriate functional connections in the brain.

In the 1940s it was further demonstrated that it is possible to rotate the eyeball on its axis, leaving the optic nerve intact. When the eye heals in this position,

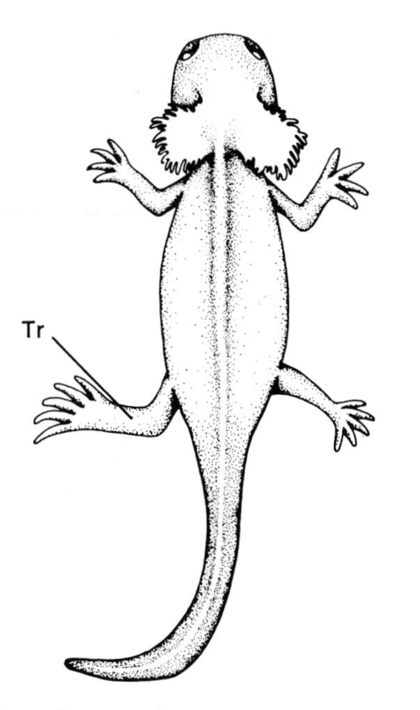

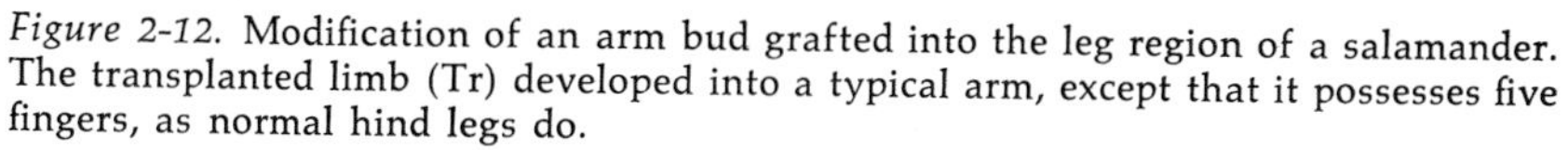

Figure 2-12. Modification of an arm bud grafted into the leg region of a salamander. The transplanted limb (Tr) developed into a typical arm, except that it possesses five fingers, as normal hind legs do.

the visual responses become reversed. Pursuit or striking movements are directed toward the corresponding places opposite those in which the objects are located. These maladaptive movements apparently continue indefinitely without modification. Rotation of the eye with severance of the optic nerve results in an orderly restoration of the original functional relations between retinal areas and brain centers. However, this restoration again results in the animal's making systematically reversed visuomotor reactions. The maladaptive reactions persist without correction. Sometimes, in performing such operations, the blood supply to the retina is impaired, and the retina degenerates, disintegrates, and is absorbed. In a few months new optic-nerve fibers develop and make central connections in the same orderly way and with the same reversal of visuomotor activities. Other types of rearrangements can be made of the amphibian eye with various distortions of adaptive movements resulting. The neuronal connections are made in a definite prefixed manner with no evidence that the maladaptive responses are modified by experience. Each retinal point seems to have a corresponding area in the brain and invariably makes connections with this area (Sperry, 1951, 1958).

Similar results have also been found when analogous experiments are made with the vestibular nerves of the ear and with the transplantation of skin flaps. In the latter the transplantation is done with the nerves intact. In these cases, localizing responses and reflex responses are misdirected so as to be appropriate to their previous locations.

The above results indicate the permanent relationships of function to structural neural pathways in a relatively low order of animals—the amphibians. What about the higher animals, including man? Since learning is much more important in the life adjustments of the higher animals, it is possible that the fixity and invariability of function found in the lower orders may not hold for the higher animal forms. Experimental studies bear out this expectation.

In man we may not surgically rotate the eyeball in its socket, but by means of a lens we can invert or otherwise distort the retinal image to produce comparable visual effects. In several studies since the first such report in the nineteenth century, subjects have worn lenses that inverted the retinal images. It has been consistently found that, although the visually perceived world looked upside-down for a while, reasonably normal adjustments came to be made to the inverted images. Removal of the inverting lens resulted once again in reversals, which were soon corrected (Stratton, 1897; Ewert, 1930).

More recent studies indicate that human subjects can adjust rapidly to consistent distortion of the visual image, provided that they are permitted to move about and act in a more or less normal way. For example, subjects who were permitted to walk around while wearing distorting goggles made much more rapid adjustments to the distortion than did subjects who traversed the same pathways sitting in a wheelchair. Under conditions of active movements, adult subjects were able to achieve fairly adequate adjustments in a few hours, whereas subjects passively put through essentially the same activities achieved virtually no adaptation (Held & Freedman, 1963). It appears that actions, together with their sensory consequences, provide essential sources of information for learning to adjust to distortions of the visual image. These and similar studies have shown that amphibians do not make adjustments to inversions or other distortions of the apparent direction of source of visual stimulation, that rats make minimal adjustments, that other species of mammals make some adjustments, and that man makes the most adjustments (Held & Bossom, 1961).

Plasticity and Variability in the Somesthetic Motor Areas

Although the somesthetic sensory cortex and the motor area immediately anterior to it are organized so that the various bodily regions are represented in an orderly and constant fashion, there is considerable overlap of sensory and motor areas. If all the stimulated cortical points producing somesthetic sensations are plotted, between 20 and 25 percent of them are in front of the fissure of Rolando, the primary motor area. Similarly, almost an equal proportion of motor area overlaps the general sensory area posterior to the Rolandic fissure.

In addition to the primary sensory and motor areas, secondary areas in the cat, monkey, and man have been discovered. The secondary areas are almost exclusively those of the extremities—the legs and feet, the arms and hands. These secondary sensory and motor areas are close together. Yet their functions are not clear. The removal of these areas produces no obvious sensory or motor disturbance after the first few days following the operation, but there is no question of their existence.

The hypothesized point-to-point relationship of body part to cortical area in the sensory and motor cortex is an oversimplification. Under deep anesthesia the cortical point activated by stimulation of a spot on the skin is quite restricted. Similarly, stimulation of a cortical point in the motor area produces a limited muscular contraction. However, similar stimulation in a conscious subject, with only local anesthesia, produces whole areas rather than points of activity in the sensory cortex and patterns of movements rather than isolated muscular contractions. Typical patterns of movement are flexion or extension of a joint, movements of the eyes and face, swallowing, gagging, or vocalization. Many of these movements are complex, requiring the cooperative action of several muscle groups. In some ways, movements rather than muscles may be spatially represented in the motor cortex.

As a matter of fact, the relationship of cortical point to motor movement is not anatomically stable. The motor response evoked by stimulation of a given cortical point is altered by the preceding stimulation of an adjacent area. If the surface of the motor cortex is repeatedly stimulated by an electrode advancing step by step, the initial response will continue to follow each stimulation until the electrode is considerably outside the area of what was formerly the limit for that response. Indeed, by means of this step-by-step movement of the electrode, a given response can even be produced in an area that normally produces the opposite response. For example, flexion can be produced by an area that normally produces extension. A response such as finger flexion can also move step by step to an area where stimulation previously produced wrist movement. After a period of rest these areas return to their original state and function.

Variability of response can result from the immediately preceding activity of the involved body part. For example, stimulation of a given motor area will produce flexion of the leg if the leg is in extension or extension if the limb is flexed.

The effects of electrical stimulation also vary with the rate of stimulation. Repetitive stimulation of the so-called face cortical motor area produces facial movements if the rate of stimulation is more than 10 or 12 shocks a second; stimulation rates of less than 10 shocks a second result in movements of the tongue. Even under relatively constant conditions, stimulation of a given point in the motor cortex may produce a particular movement one time, a slightly different movement another time, and no movement a third time (Penfield & Roberts, 1959).

THE ENDOCRINE SYSTEM

Although the nervous system is the principal integrative system of the body, the secretions of endocrine glands also have integrating and coordinating functions. Table 2-2 provides an incomplete summary of the principal hormones secreted by the endocrine glands and the primary effects of these hormones on development and behavior. This table shows that most of the endocrine glands secrete several hormones. Many of the hormones supplement each other, and several hormonal agents have regulative effects on other glands in the system. The pituitary gland is notable in that it produces several such regulative agents. The endocrine system supplements and interacts with the nervous system. One example of this relationship is found in the interaction of the adrenal medulla and the autonomic nervous system (which innervates the internal organs). Stimulation of the sympathetic (middle) division of the autonomic nervous system has many of the same bodily effects as does the secretion of the adrenal medulla (adrenalin and noradrenalin). The secretion of the adrenal medulla is largely controlled by the activity of the sympathetic division of the nervous system. The adrenal medulla and the autonomic nervous system are particularly active in certain emotional states.

For example, when a stimulus evokes fear, nerve impulses over the sympathetic division of the autonomic nervous system spread widely throughout the body, thereby increasing the rate and amplitude of pulse and respiration and elevating blood pressure. These impulses produce decreased secretion of most of the digestive glands and reduce the motility of the gastrointestinal tract. They also produce an outpouring of secretions from the adrenal medulla. These secretions pass into the bloodstream and are transported to all parts of the body, where they mediate many of the effects resulting from sympathetic neural activity.

It is interesting to note that the sympathetic nerve fibers and the secretory cells of the adrenal medulla have a common embryonic origin. In the early stages of the development of the embryo, a chain of embryonic nerve cells (neuroblasts) forms just outside the neural tube. The neural tube, a long cylindrical structure that will later be enclosed by the spinal column, is the forerunner of the central nervous system. Some of the neuroblasts outside the neural tube send their axons into the tube; their dendrites grow out to various sense organs and become the sensory nerves. Others of the same group of cells develop into neurons of the autonomic nervous system. A third group of these neuroblasts migrates outward and comes to rest over the top poles of the kidneys, where it develops into the secretory cells of the adrenal medulla. These cells are innervated by a single set of fibers from within the central nervous system. In other words, there is only a single neuron between the central nervous system and the effector in the case of the adrenal medulla, whereas there are two such fibers in other glands and smooth muscles. Thus the secretory cells of the adrenal medulla develop from the embryonic analog of the second set of nerve fibers found in the rest of the autonomic nervous system. It is perhaps more than coincidental that one of the chemical transmitter agents synthesized in and discharged from the axons of certain synapses in the autonomic nervous system is noradrenalin, one of the secretions of the adrenal medulla.

We have been discussing the relationship of the nervous and hormonal factors. In many cases there is such a continuous interaction among stimulus, central neural, hormonal, and experiential (learned) factors that these all may have essentially equivalent behavioral effects. Some of these equivalences can be demonstrated in certain components of mammalian maternal behavior. For example, in mammals such as the rat, maternal behavior involves nest building, retrieving young animals that wander outside the nest, and nursing the young. Each of these components is influenced by *all* the above-mentioned factors. Let us consider nest building in particular.

Table 2-2. Endocrine gland system.

Gland	*Hormones*	*Major functions*
Thyroid	Thyroxin	Regulates metabolism. Stimulates heart action. Extreme deficiency in infancy produces cretinism and in adults myxaedena.
Parathyroid	Parathormone	Maintains proper calcium and phosphorus level in the blood. Deficiency produces tetanus and finally death.
Adrenal cortex	Many components, which may be grouped into: (1) Cortisone, (2) Androgens, (3) Estrogens	(1) Influences water balance, carbohydrate metabolism, sodium and potassium balance. (2) Promotes development of male sexual characteristics. (3) Promotes development of female sexuality.
Adrenal medulla	Epinephrine (adrenalin)	Increases heart action, vascular constriction, relaxation of gastrointestinal musculature, clotting of blood, and blood-sugar level.
	Norepinephrine (noradrenalin)	Contracts small blood vessels and increases blood pressure. (Epinephrine and norepinephrine both act with and reinforce the action of the sympathetic nervous system in emotion-arousing emergency situations.)
Sex glands		
Male gonads (testes)	Androgenic hormones (several, best known is testosterone)	Involved in sexual arousal and in the development of male secondary sex characteristics.
Female gonads (ovaries)	Estrogenic hormones (several, such as estrodial, estone, equalin, and stilbestral)	Produces estrus, sexual receptivity, and development of female secondary sex characteristics.
	Progesterone	Prepares uterus for implantation and nutrition of the embryo. Deficiency produces miscarriage.

Gland	*Hormones*	*Major functions*
Placenta	Placental-gonadotropin	Suppresses production of pituitary gonadotropin and prevents ovulation.
	(1) progesterone, (2) estrogen	(1) Late in pregnancy takes over function of corpus luteum. (2) Involved in milk production.
Pancreas (islets of Langerhans)	Insulin	Controls sugar metabolism and storage. Deficiency produces diabetes mellitus. Excess produces feelings of hunger, muscular twitchings, and convulsions.
Pituitary (anterior)	A large number; some of the best known are: (1) growth hormone, (2) adrenocorticotropic (ACTH), (3) thyrotropic, (4) diabetogenic, (5) pancreatropic, (6) gonadotropins, (7) lactogenic	(1) Regulates bone growth and protein storage. Deficiency produces dwarfism; excess produces gigantism. (2) Stimulates adrenal cortical secretion. Deficiency produces atrophy of the adrenal cortex. (3) Stimulates thyroid secretion. (4) Promotes conversion of fats and proteins to carbohydrates. (5) Reduces insulin secretion. (6) Promotes development of sperm and interstitial cells in males and ovarian follicles and corpus luteum in females. (7) Stimulates secretion of milk in mammals. Induces maternal behavior in some animals.
Pituitary (posterior)	(1) antidiuretic, (2) pitressin, (3) oxytocin	(1) Regulates excretion of water through the kidneys. (2) Increases blood pressure by contracting arterial muscles. (3) Stimulates smooth muscles of arteries, gall bladder, intestines, and uterus.

Normal rats often do some nest building. However, during pregnancy there is a great increase in this activity, which begins some time before, and continues until well after, the young are born. Nest building in mature nonpregnant females is also related to the estrus cycle, being lowest when sexual receptivity is high and highest midway between estral periods, when the female rat is not sexually receptive.

Some of the environmental and hormonal determinants of nest building in rats are as follows: Environmental *temperature* operates clearly as a stimulus factor. Nest building varies inversely with temperature. At temperatures of

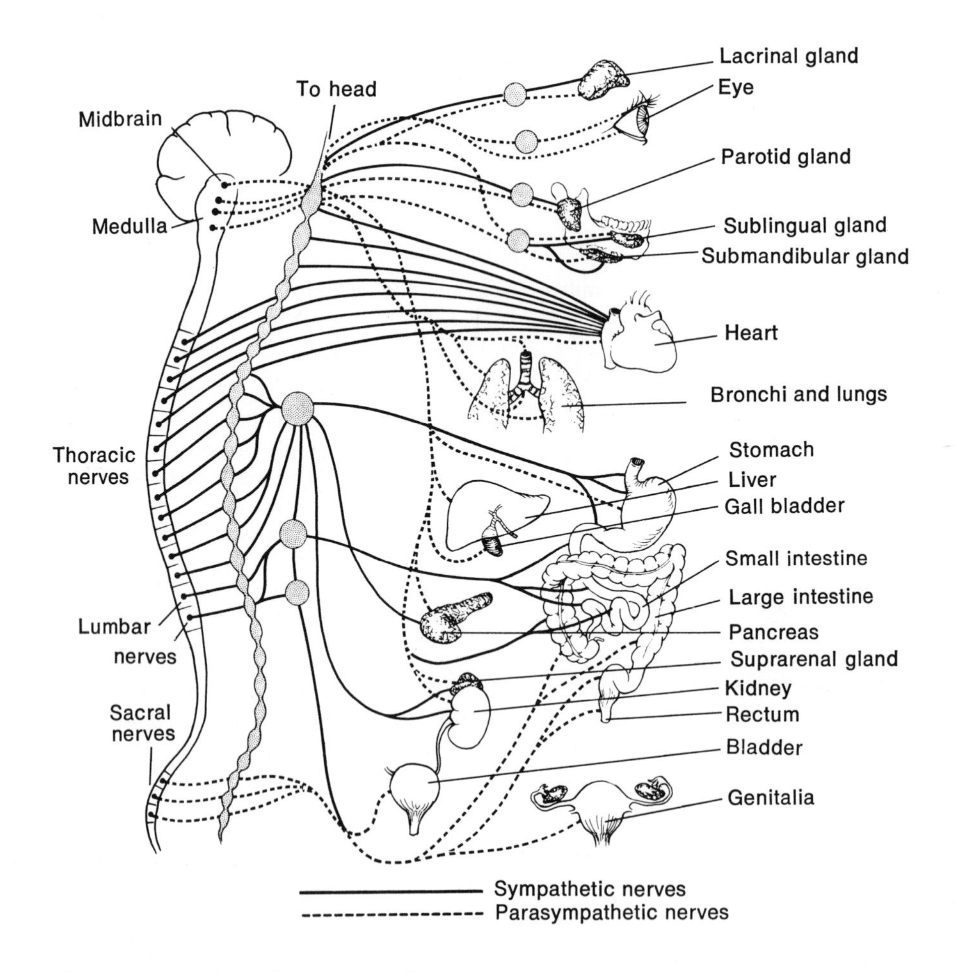

Figure 2-13. Autonomic nervous system.

85–90°F. very little nest building occurs, whereas at temperatures of 50–60°F. many substantial, well-built nests are constructed. At a given constant external temperature, only small, loosely built nests are constructed when the animals live in a single, well-lighted cage; but they build much more substantial nests if *a separate, small dark room* is provided within the larger living cage. Thyroidectomy substantially increases nest building and the injection of thyroid extract reduces nest building. Removal of the pituitary gland has a similar result. The effect of removal of either of these glands builds up gradually following the operations, until nest building is approximately double the normal rate about three weeks after the glands are removed. These *hormones* affect the general metabolic rate of the animal and thus may be indirectly related to temperature regulation. Gonadal hormones are also involved in the regulation of nest-building behavior in rats. In nonpregnant animals the injection of progesterone produces a striking increase in nest building. Yet there is still another factor that influences nest-building behavior: the mere *presence of young rats* in the nest of a virgin female rat will stimulate increased nest building.

The effect of *learning* on maternal behavior is less easily documented for female rats than for primates, but there is some evidence that it is probably operative to some extent even among rodents (Wehmer, 1965). Monkeys raised in isolation and deprived of social contacts with other animals until adulthood are very deficient in maternal behavior (Harlow & Harlow, 1966). The ablation of certain brain areas results in the disappearance of normal maternal behavior. It seems, then, that, in addition to central neural processes, endocrine hormones, and environmental stimuli, learning must be involved in nest building as well as in other similar behavior.

SUMMARY

A basic assumption of psychology is that all mental activity has a physiological basis. The two principal integrative systems of the body are the nervous system and the endocrine system. These systems interact continuously.

The nervous system is composed of neurons. A neuron consists of a cell body, a nucleus, a membrane, and one or more processes extending out from the cell body. Those processes that are stimulated by sense organs or by other neurons and conduct nerve impulses toward the cell body are known as dendrites. Those processes that conduct nerve impulses away from the cell body are called axons. Nerve processes may have two, one, or no sheaths, or coverings.

Neurons are classified functionally as sensory, motor, and association. Sensory neurons conduct nerve impulses from sense organs to the central nervous system; motor neurons conduct impulses from the central nervous system to effectors (muscles or glands); association neurons serve as connecting links between two other neurons.

The nerve impulse consists of a complex set of electrochemical reactions that pass along a neuron when it is activated. The impulse is an all-or-nothing affair like a gunshot, inasmuch as it is either triggered off or it is not. Immediately following the passage of a nerve impulse, the neuron is inexcitable. The absolute refractory period that immediately follows the passage of an impulse is followed by a relative refractory period during which the neuron will respond, but only to abnormally intense stimuli. This phase, in turn, is followed by a period of supernormal excitability and then by normal excitability.

The synapse is the place where two neurons come into functional relationship with each other. The effective agent acting at the synapse is sometimes, if not always, a chemical substance. Two such chemical agents are acetylcholine and norepinephrine.

The entire nervous system is divided into the central nervous system (the brain and the spinal cord) and the peripheral nervous system (the spinal nerves, the cranial nerves, and the autonomic nervous system). The principal subdivisions of the brain are the medulla, pons, cerebellum, midbrain, thalamus, hypothalamus, and cerebrum. The medulla is a vital center for the control and regulation of many of the visceral or vegetative processes that are necessary for life. The pons is the bridge between the cerebellum and the brainstem. The cerebellum is a center for the integration and coordination of the proprioceptive (kinesthetic and balance) functions of the body. The midbrain contains nuclei for auditory and visual reflexes. The thalamus consists primarily of relay centers (nuclei) for most of the sensory pathways going to the cerebral cortex. The hypothalamus controls or regulates a large number of vital functions somewhat in the way the medulla does.

The cerebrum is the largest subdivision of the human brain. The functional areas of the cerebral cortex (outside layer) are sensory, motor, and association.

The sensory projection area for vision is located in the occipital lobe (back part of the brain); the center for hearing is in the temporal lobe in the region above the ear; the somesthetic area (cutaneous and kinesthetic) is just behind the fissure of Rolando. The main motor cortical area parallels the somesthetic area just in front of the fissure of Rolando in the posterior part of the frontal lobe. The remaining parts of the cortex are considered to be primarily association areas.

The autonomic nervous system either controls or regulates most of the visceral organs of the body. Each of its two subdivisions (the sympathetic and the parasympathetic) independently innervates most of the smooth muscles and glands of the body and operates antagonistically to the other. The autonomic nervous system is particularly active during emotions. Function and structure interact in neural activity. Both fixity and plasticity are characteristic of neural growth and function. The nervous system is *continuously* active, and the activation of neural processes redirects the flow of activities already in progress. The relation of sensory surfaces and effector organs to brain processes seems to be best described in terms of related anatomical areas rather than related anatomical points.

The endocrine system is the second major integrative system of the body. The various endocrine glands supplement and interact with each other. Consequently, the endocrines must be viewed as an integrated system rather than as a collection of independent glands.

Neural, hormonal, situational, and experiential factors all can be shown to be involved in the activation, control, and regulation of many types of behavior.

SUGGESTED READINGS

Butter, C. M. *Neuropsychology: The study of brain and behavior.* Belmont, Calif.: Brooks/Cole, 1968. This paperback book provides a short discussion of the neural basis of human behavior.

Louttit, R. T. *Advancing psychological science,* Vol. 4. *Research in physiological psychology.* Belmont, Calif.: Brooks/Cole, 1965. This paperback contains a good selection of original research articles on physiological psychology.

Sheer, D. (Ed.) *Electrical stimulation of the brain.* Austin, Texas: Hogg Foundation and University of Texas Press, 1961. This book is recommended for the student who wishes more complete information on this fascinating topic.

Stevens, C. F. *Neurophysiology: A primer.* New York: Wiley, 1966. This volume is a good introduction to neurophysiology.

Thompson, R. F. *Foundations of physiological psychology.* New York: Harper, 1967. This book is an advanced text for the student who wishes to delve more extensively into physiological psychology.

Perceptual Processes: I. General Aspects

Most of the rest of this book will be devoted to a discussion of *psychological processes*. These processes are not isolated from one another and can be separated only for purposes of expediency. The psychological processes are conventionally labeled attention, sensation, perception, learning, memory, thought, affection, and motivation. These processes are mutually interdependent, and a complete understanding of any one involves some understanding of all the others. The organism is a unitary system, and a human is actively attending, sensing, perceiving, learning, feeling, striving, retaining, recalling, thinking, and behaving simultaneously.

Sensory processing involves the translation of environmental energy into experiences of meaningful awareness, which, in turn, makes possible reports of experiences and adjustments of the organism. In other words, sensory-perceptual processes can be conceptualized as the input component of a communication system. Attention makes certain components of the informational input more explicit at the expense of others. Attentional and perceptual processes involve learning and memory (acquired meanings), which are partial determinants of the informational components that are attended to and the perceptual categories to which the sensory inputs are relegated. Perceptual processes change the individual. These changes constitute learning, and their persistence constitutes memory. Memory and retrieval processes are involved in thinking. Thus attention, sensation, perception, learning, memory, recall, and thought all constitute an interacting continuum of sensory-cognitive processes.

Affective experiences (feelings and emotions) are treated as if they were not a part of the cognitive continuum. However, most experiences, either because of innate organic mechanisms or as a result of learning, have affective components or accompaniments.

In this and the following chapter we shall discuss the sensoriperceptual system, keeping in mind that these processes are separated artificially and only for expository purposes. There are many ways of conceptualizing sensoriperceptual processes. One way is on a purely input-output level with no reference to the intervening physiological (sensory, neural, motor) components. One of the most popular current concepts of this type is that of information processing. In this conceptual system, electronic data processing and computer models are the physical analogs of the human perceptual-cognitive system. At any point in the entire process, information-processing analogs may be concerned with the "informative" content of the stimulus or the experience and/or with responses. That is, they may not be concerned with the specific physiological mechanisms involved in the information flow and/or transformation. Perceptual responses are considered to go through a number of stages (processes). The processes in each stage are limited by the capacities and characteristics of the information-handling "channels," the informational content of the input, and the nature (temporary state and prior experiences) of the individual perceiver. Although such an approach to perception is not opposed to specification of the neurological-physiological nature of the processing machine, it is not dependent on such information.

However, for more than a hundred years investigators have studied sensoriperceptual processes largely from a physical and physiological standpoint. These investigations have been concerned with the physical characteristics of the stimulus; the events occurring in the receptors that initiate neural impulses; and the different pathways, synapses, and nerve centers involved in the transmission of inputs to the cortex and beyond. We shall use the data-processing analogs where we consider them appropriate and relate these processes to their physiological correlates insofar as the latter have been determined.

A fundamental problem in sensory experience is how patterns of stimulation are coded in the nervous system. Since man can differentiate literally millons of different stimulus characteristics, these differences must somehow be coded in the sensory receptors and the nervous system. Prescientific conceptions of perception assumed that a given stimulus somehow impresses itself on the mind in an exact replica of the external stimulus. Johannes Müller (1838) noted that pressure on the eyeball, a sharp blow on the head, and stimulations of light on the retina all evoked *visual* experiences. He decided that it is not stimulus characteristics that determine sensory *quality* (visual, auditory, and so on) but rather the receptors and/or nerves activated.

Studies since then have demonstrated that the fundamental difference in gross sensory quality is determined by *where* the nerve impulses go. However, this is only the simplest level of sensory differentiation. Although there are some subdifferentiations based on spatially differentiated neural reception areas, differential patterns of discharges in the receptor and nerve cells and the activities of specific categories of neurons are apparently the primary bases for coding perceptual experience.

THE IRRITABILITY OF ORGANISMS

Sensory experiences are initiated by environmental events (stimuli) impinging on the organism. In the higher forms of life, stimuli arouse the organism by initiating nerve impulses in sense organs. The fundamental property of protoplasm that makes sensory experience possible is irritability. One-celled organisms (*Protozoa*) respond to some elementary forms of stimulation; by contrast, animals high on the evolutionary scale develop highly specialized sensory equipment. Slight sensitivity to light (photosensitivity) exists in the amoeba, whereas a tremendous variety of visual experiences emerges in higher animals. The first step in the development of the vertebrate eye and its related structures is the appearance of a light-sensitive spot in such animals as the earthworm and the medusa. This elementary receptor makes these organisms more sensitive to light than is the amoeba, and it also makes them differentially responsive to light-stimulus variables. Although the light-sensitive spot on an earthworm is a far simpler structure than the complex vertebrate retina, the two are basically similar in function.

The receptors for taste and smell in the higher animals have developed from the primitive, general chemical receptors still found on the body surfaces of many lower animal species. The ear developed from primitive vibration receptors, which certain fish still have along their sides. Of course, in addition to ears, man still possesses cutaneous (skin) receptors that respond to vibrations of very high intensities.

Thus it is believed that sensory experience starts with irritability and that specialized receptor functions develop phylogenetically out of the primitive irritability of the protozoa. In this evolutionary process a diffuse general sensitivity becomes differentiated into specific sensory functions activated by particular stimuli. This differentiation makes possible qualitatively different sensory experiences. The various sense organs of the human body can best be perceived as protoplasmic cells and tissues that become especially sensitive to certain forms of energy while remaining relatively insensitive to other forms of energy.

STIMULI

Stimuli have been defined as those forms of energy change that initiate activity in sense organs. Technically, stimuli must arouse activity in the sense organs and be external to either the nervous system or the receptor, although the definition is not always so restricted. Stimuli may be external (*exteroceptive*) or internal (*interoceptive*) or result from previous motor responses of the organism (*proprioceptive*). Visual, auditory, cutaneous, and olfactory (smell) experiences are exteroceptive in origin; gustation (taste), organic sensory experiences such as hunger, thirst, and sexual arousal, and various internal sensory visceral experiences are introceptive in origin; kinesthetic experiences and those experiences associated with balance and equilibrium, which are stimulated by movements of the body or by changes in tension on the muscles of the body, are proprioceptive in origin.

The terms *stimulus, situation,* and *environment* constitute a continuum of increasing complexity. Although *situation* and *stimulus* are often used synonymously, they really differ in complexity. *Situation* refers to the entire combination of circumstances affecting a person at any one time—the complete pattern of stimulation to which he is responding. A stimulus, on the other hand, is one particular part of a situation abstracted by an observer. A person is always responding to a situation and never to a particular stimulus. When we say that a stimulus "initiates" activity in a sense organ, we do not mean that it arouses a previously inactive organism; we mean that it redirects or modifies the direction or nature of the stream of activities that is already in progress. A person's behavior is never the result of a single stimulus, but the stimulus-response relationship is a convenient and useful abstraction for classifying, discussing, and conceptualizing certain aspects of experience and behavior.

The energy impinging on the receptor surface contains potential "information" about external and internal events. In the receptor the information in the stimulus energy is translated into chains and patterns of nerve impulses, which are transmitted to the central nervous system. The conversion of stimulus energy into neural impulses is called energy *transduction*, and the translation of stimulus information into patterns of impulses is *stimulus encoding*.

Transduction in the auditory, cutaneous, and kinesthetic receptors involves a series of mechanical steps. In vision, photochemical processes intervene between the light stimulus and the generation of nerve impulses. The processes involved in the conversion of chemical stimuli into nerve impulses in olfaction and gustation are still unclear.

THE ENCODING OF INFORMATION

The patterning of nerve impulses involved in the encoding of stimulus variables undoubtedly includes several levels. We have previously indicated that the differential sensitivity of the various receptors to specific types and ranges of energy changes provides an initial sorting out of information at the sense-organ level. In addition to gross sensory encoding in terms of the sensory system involved (visual, auditory, cutaneous, and so on), some sensory systems make further differentiations at the receptor level. Three types of cones, each responsive to a limited range of wavelengths, provide for the encoding of visual information in terms of hue. Although there is also some degree of receptor specificity in the other senses, the encoding of sensory quality is not entirely a matter of receptor specificity. At various "higher" levels along the nervous pathways, the nerve fibers from receptor cells converge on other neurons. These higher-order neurons have inputs from various receptor cells and are excited or inhibited by their differential inputs. For example, some third-order (ganglion) cells in the retina are excited by impulses from green and inhibited by impulses from red receptor cells. Encoding in terms of perceptual categories involving many dimensions, such as color, shape, size, movement, and use, certainly occurs at various levels from receptor or cerebral cortex, and the systems involved must be very complex. It seems clear that neural coding of various stimulus characteristics is the result of inherent structural organization.

However, additional neural coding develops as the result of experience. For example, it has been shown that specific cortical association areas of the brain show distinctive neural discharges of certain cells when a cat responds in terms of a previously learned numerical designation such as 1, 2, or 3. These responses are independent of the sense modality (such as vision) involved (Thompson, Mayers, Robertson, & Patterson, 1970). In a certain sense, we know more about how these differentiations come about and function behaviorally than we do about the physiological mechanisms involved. At the present time we have several conceptual systems of the encoding process. They are hypothetical constructs that are consistent with what is known about the sensory-neurological systems involved and seem to account for the behavioral phenomena.

SENSORY THRESHOLDS

Many of the stimulus properties of environmental objects can be best understood in terms of thresholds. The intensity of energy acting on a sense organ must exceed a certain minimum to be experienced. The lowest intensity required to produce sensory experience is the *absolute sensory threshold*. Sensory thresholds are not constant; they vary tremendously from person to person and within the same person, depending on many factors, such as previous stimulation. Despite these variations, the following mean threshold values have been obtained for the sense organs of touch, hearing, and vision (von Fieandt, 1966):

The most sensitive contact receptor	1/10,000 erg/sec.
Auditory receptors at middle frequencies	1/10,000,000 erg/sec.
Visual receptors (green light)	1/100,000,000 erg/sec.

(The erg/second is the energy required to move a mass of one milligram vertically a distance of one centimeter in one second.) These values indicate both the large differences among the senses and the relatively minute amounts of energy involved.

The *differential threshold* is the smallest change in intensity of stimulation that can be sensed. Time, as well as relative stimulus intensities, influences differential thresholds. For example, rapid stimulus change may be readily perceived, whereas the same change occurring gradually over a longer period of time may not be noticed at all.

Weber's Law Relative to Differential Thresholds

One of the earliest contributions to experimental psychology showed that differential thresholds are roughly proportional to stimulus intensities. That is, the change in stimulus intensity required to be perceptible is proportional to its previous intensity. If the original intensity was very low, small absolute change may be noticeable; when the original intensity was high, a much greater absolute change is required to exceed the threshold. Weber considered the ratio of the required change to the original intensity constant for any given sense but different for the various senses. Weber's law can be written

$$\frac{\Delta s}{s} = C,$$

where s is the stimulus intensity, Δs is the increase in intensity required for detection, and C, the Weber fraction, is a constant. For visual intensity, C is about 1/100; for sound, 1/3; for smell, 1/4; and for pressure, 1/5 (Wheeler, 1940).

Weber's law has been evaluated and criticized, and it may not hold for the extreme intensities. But, within certain limits, it holds reasonably well as a description of differential threshold relationships.

SENSORY ADAPTATION

The crucial importance of time in the perception of stimulus-intensity differences illustrates the phenomenon of adaptation. Adaptation refers to the diminution or complete cessation of response to a long-continued constant stimulus. For example, when a person enters a chemistry laboratory, he is aware of a decided odor; but, after working in the room for some time, he no longer notices it. If he leaves the room for some time and then returns, he is again aware of the smell. Similar adaptation is made to such common stimuli as room temperature or darkness. There are limits to the adaptation process, and the senses differ greatly in the rate and degree of adaptation attained, yet adaptation seems to be a universal phenomenon.

The Neurophysiology of Sensory Adaptation

As was previously pointed out, all receptors have threshold values that must be reached before neural excitation results. When above-threshold stimulus values are reached, a series of impulses is generated in the receptors; the propagated nerve impulses then pass out over the sensory neuron. The number of nerve impulses transmitted per unit of time depends on the strength of the stimulus and its duration. A stimulus just above threshold initiates very few impulses per second, the number constantly declines, and the impulses soon cease. Strong stimuli result in a high frequency of impulses, and, if the stimulus is maintained at constant strength, the frequency drops regularly and will either level off at a very low rate or cease entirely. This phenomenon is not primarily due to fatigue, for, if the stimulus is momentarily removed and then reapplied, there is another burst of activity, and the slowing process is repeated.

If electrical recordings are made from the sensory neurons of the footpad of a cat when a light glass disc is placed against the foot, a burst of nerve impulses is recorded at a frequency of about ten a second. The frequency of discharge declines very rapidly and drops to zero at the end of 2 seconds. Pressure exerted on the disc evokes a second series of impulses, which again comes to an end in a short time. Removal of the disc initiates an additional burst of impulses. Such adaptation seems to be a universal sensory phenomenon. However, the senses differ tremendously in their rates of sensory adaptation. Figure 3-1 graphically shows variations in the rate of decline of nerve-impulse transmission in neurons activated by various types of receptors over a 6-second interval. This figure also shows that adaptation is immediate and complete following direct electrical stimulation of a nerve fiber. In this case, the neuron gives only one discharge and then will respond again only if the electrical contact is broken and applied again. By contrast, adaptation is slowest in a muscle spindle, where kinesthetic receptors are involved in the maintenance of muscular tone and bodily posture. The advantage of slow adaptation in this sense is obvious.

Adaptation phenomena indicate that a stimulus applied with absolute constancy eventually ceases to operate as a stimulus. A stimulus must involve change in order for it to arouse activity in sense organs. Thus a stimulus is best defined as a *change in the energy sources* impinging on the sense organs that is of sufficient magnitude and rapidity to produce a response.

THE ATTENTIONAL-PERCEPTUAL SYSTEM

The attentional-perceptual system acts much as a limited-capacity communication system. Only a limited amount of sensory input (quantity of information) can be handled at a given time. However, it is obvious that the information "tuned out" is not discarded at random but is determined by some inherent stimuli—organism relationships (intensity, size, form, movement, contrast, and repetitiveness), temporary states of the organism (momentary expectancies and emotional states), or acquired interests, attitudes, and perceptual probabilities.

For example, the limited-channel characteristic of the attentional-perceptual system is involved when a person tries to deal with two competing messages he is receiving simultaneously. In such a situation, there is a limit at which his performance breaks down. Subjects reporting messages heard through one ear may be unable to report the content of competing or different messages presented at the same time to the other ear. The fact that similar results are obtained when one message is visual and the other is auditory indicates that it is not the peripheral sensory channel that is overloaded. Neither is the channel limitation motor, for it still exists when alternate or successive motor responses are given to each message. The channel limitation must be, at least partly, central. This view is in keeping with the general belief that, although the attentional response has peripheral components such as sense-organ adjustments, increased muscular tension, postural adjustments (leaning toward the source of the stimulus), and respiratory changes, the basic physiologically limiting component is within the brain.

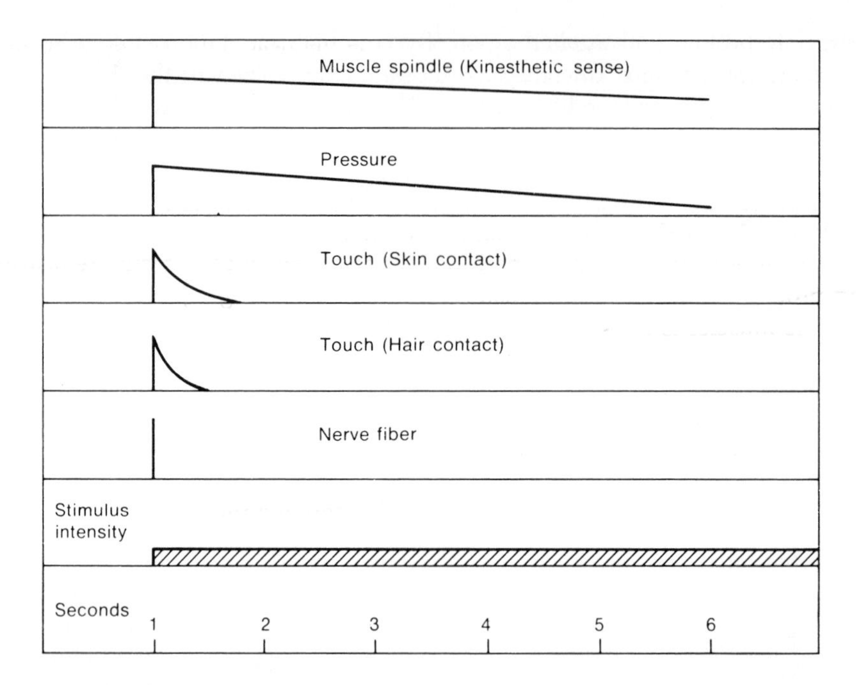

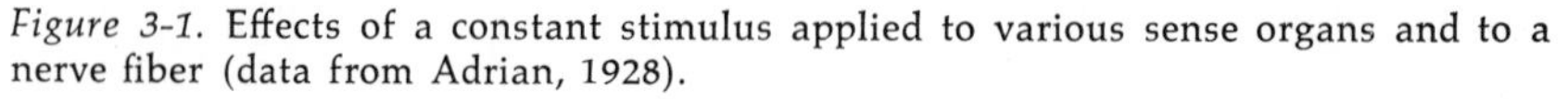

Figure 3-1. Effects of a constant stimulus applied to various sense organs and to a nerve fiber (data from Adrian, 1928).

Components of Attention

If we consider the process of attending to be a persisting response that selectively prepares the individual to act or to perceive, it becomes appropriate to ask what attending consists of behaviorally. Five different behavioral components of attention can be differentiated: (1) sense-organ orientation, (2) postural adjustment, (3) increased muscular tension, (4) changes in visceral functioning, and (5) central-nervous-system activities.

Sense-organ adjustments. When attending to visual stimuli, the eyes are turned so as to focus the image on the fovea of the retina for most effective perception. When we see a number of people all looking at some object, we assume that they are attending to that object. Advertisers have photographed the eye movements of people viewing advertising displays and used the length and number of eye fixations as an index of the attention value of the different components of the displays.

When attending to a sound, the person turns his head so as to place his ears in the best position for the reception of the sound. This is particularly obvious when the sound is not clearly audible. The horse and the dog prick up their ears. Some animals turn their ears in the direction of the source of the sound. We have lost our abilities to prick up and turn our ears, so we have to turn the head or cup the hands behind the ears when listening attentively. Two small muscles in the middle ear adjust the tension on the stapes and the tympanic membrane according to the intensity of sound so as to facilitate hearing and protect the delicate mechanism of the ear from being injured. Contraction of these muscles is induced by strong acoustical stimulation and by the anticipation of a loud sound (Djupesland, 1965). These adjustments are a part of the attentive process.

The receptors in the skin, the taste buds in the tongue, and the olfactory area of the nose cannot be moved. However, either moving the hand over an object or moving the object about in the hand when we are attending to cutaneous stimulation increases the effectiveness of the stimulus and thus serves the same function as receptor adjustments do. Moving food about in the mouth and pressing it against the roof of the mouth bring the substance more directly in contact with the taste cells and facilitate its perception. "Sniffing" forces a gaseous substance into the olfactory area and increases its stimulating properties. All these adjustments of sense organs serve to increase the effectiveness of the relevant stimuli.

Whereas various sense-organ adjustments increase the potency of the relevant stimuli, concomitant reactions occur that mute or block out competing stimuli. When listening intently to a concert or when taking a hearing test, we close our eyes, sit very still, and either breathe shallowly or hold our breath for an instant in order to block out visual stimuli and to minimize the noise caused by our body movements and the sounds of our own breathing.

Postural adjustments. Postural adjustments are made when one leans forward toward the source of a sound and when a sprinter or swimmer crouches, waiting for a starting gun. The "pointing" of the bird dog and the stance of the cat watching a bird are examples of attentive postural adjustments in lower animals. Much "mind reading" is really "muscle reading" in which the reader interprets the small involuntary movements and postural adjustments made as the subject concentrates his thoughts on (attends to) some object in the room.

Increased muscular tension. Changes in muscular tension, which are part of the attentive response, may be either gross or subtle. Increased muscular tension is involved in leaning toward the stimulus to which the individual is attending, but it may also be present without gross postural adjustment. When a person has been attending steadily for some time and then ceases to do so, he relaxes and settles down in his chair as muscular tension decreases. The distracting effects of competing stimuli are often countered by increased muscular tension. For example, if the force with which typists strike their typewriter keys is recorded as efforts are made to distract them, the records show that efficiency is maintained only by an increase in energy expenditure. A considerable part of this increase in energy output seems attributable to heightened muscular tension.

Visceral changes. Visceral changes as a part of the attentive process are neither marked nor obvious. However, attention involves slight changes in pulse and in blood pressure. The most easily observed of these changes are shallow breathing during a period of keen attention and holding the breath for short intervals when attention is at its height. The fact that a person commonly draws a deep breath immediately upon relaxing, following a period of attentiveness, indicates that an excess of carbon dioxide has accumulated.

Activities of the central nervous system. There are neural correlates of attention. However, it is not known whether they represent the central core of the process or are simply the neural correlates of the peripheral receptor, motor, and visceral components.

Regular changes in the rhythmic electrical activity of the cerebral cortex occur during attention. Brain waves recorded by an electroencephalograph (EEGs) are either flattened out or desynchronized. During attention, the reticular system* discharges diffusely to the cerebral cortex. The arousal effect, or priming effect, of the reticular system on the other parts of the central nervous system may constitute the neural substrate of attending. The fact that the reticular formation has inhibitory as well as activating functions may account for the selective nature of attention, which requires that the reaction to competing stimuli be modulated or suppressed. Electrical stimulation of the reticular formation in a cat or monkey alerts the animal and produces a concomitant disturbance of the alpha rhythm, comparable to that which occurs during

*The reticular system is a neural structure in the brainstem, the activities of which affect the general arousal level of the individual. The system is activated by sensory input and by ideational activity.

attention in man. This fact supports the notion that activity in the reticular system is indeed a neural substrate of attention.

Investigators have also found that the speed of reaction in monkeys is increased during electrical stimulation of the reticular system (Fuster, 1958). The activity of certain points in the auditory cortex in response to an auditory stimulus has been shown to be contingent on the cat's turning its head toward the source of sound, looking at it, and appearing to listen. Such evidence indicates that the activity of the neural processes presumably responsible for attention determines whether or not a given stimulus is adequate to arouse activity in certain cortical areas (Hubel, Henson, Rupert, & Galambos, 1959).

There is evidence of neural inhibition of sensory input at the level of the brainstem. In studies of cats, recording electrodes have been implanted in the cochlear nuclei, which are in the brainstem and serve as the reception nuclei for impulses from the cochlea. From the cochlear nuclei, auditory impulses go on up to the thalamus and to the cerebral cortex. Clicks near the cat's ear normally can be recorded from the electrodes. However, if these clicks are sounded while the cat is sniffing a fish odor, or while the cat is watching mice, no activity is recorded. When the extraneous attention-provoking stimuli are removed, the responses of the cochlear nuclei return (Hernandez-Péon, Scherrer, & Jauvet, 1956). Thus there must be a neural mechanism that selectively blocks one kind of sensory input when the cat is attending to another. Other research has shown that electrical stimulation of a certain part of the reticular formation has a similar inhibitory effect on sound-produced impulses in the cochlear nuclei (Munn, 1966). This finding suggests that the inhibition of competing stimuli as well as the perception of relevant stimuli may be mediated by activities of the reticular system.

Determinants of Attention

It is customary to divide the determinants of attention into two groups: (1) the external, objective, or innate factors, and (2) the internal, subjective, or acquired factors. We prefer to use the terms *innate* and *acquired* to designate these two classes to avoid the misleading notion that attention is determined *either* from without *or* from within. Every response is the product of the interaction of stimuli and organism; a response can never be determined by either alone. The fact that an environmental force functions as a stimulus depends on the specialized sensitivity of the organism. Stimulus variables such

as rate of change, intensity, size, duration, and extent are determinants of attention only because the organism is differentially sensitive to these variables. When a person attends, his response is the product of the interaction of (1) what he is as a consequence of inherited and acquired factors, *and* (2) the stimuli impinging on his sense organs.

Innate (objective, external) determinants of attention. *Intensity* of stimulation is the most obvious determinant of attention. The bright flash of light, the blaring loudspeaker, the intensely painful stimulus, the sharp odor, the highly concentrated gustatory stimulus—all have an attention-provoking potency greater than that of comparable stimuli that are less intense. In a study of the percentage of pedestrians stopping to view a window display, 10 percent stopped when the display was illuminated at 15 footcandles, 15 percent stopped when the illumination was increased to 50 footcandles, and, when the illumination was increased to 110 footcandles, 21 percent of the pedestrians stopped to look at the display. Although the number of pedestrians who stopped at the lighted window increased as the intensity of the illumination increased, the two increases were not proportional to each other (Burtt, 1938).

Size, or *extensity*, is another factor determining attention. Advertisers vie with one another in the size of their displays, since they recognize that, other things being equal, larger signs have an advantage over smaller ones. Larger advertisements cost more than small ones, so the advertiser is interested in the relationship between the size of an advertisement and its relative effectiveness. Studies have shown that, as a rough rule of thumb, the effectiveness of an advertisement increases as the square root of its area increases. In other words, increasing the size of an advertisement from half a page to a full page will not double its effectiveness; it will take a two-page spread to double the effectiveness of a display occupying half a page. One study that attempted to quantify the amount of attention evoked by a newspaper advertisement found that the size of the advertisement had to be increased approximately 35 times to increase the amount of attention 8 times (Strong, 1915).

Definite form or *distinct outline* is more effective than indefinite form or indistinct outline in attracting attention.

Color also seems to have some attention-provoking potency. Sears Roebuck and Company discovered many years ago that the colored pages in their catalog had much greater advertising potency than did comparable pages in black and white. Although some of the effectiveness of color may be due to associations acquired through experience, there is evidence that hue has some innate efficacy in attracting attention.

A moving pattern is a more effective stimulus than the same pattern when it is stationary. The high cost of producing and maintaining moving advertising signs is more than compensated for by their effectiveness. One advertiser discovered that seven times as many people stopped to watch a window display on a rotating pedestal than stopped when the same display was stationary. The movement of a leaf catches our attention, whereas the stationary ones remain unnoticed.

Repetition has limited effectiveness as a determinant of attention. The sound or the visual display that is not noticed on the first presentation may be attended to on the second or third exposure, but continued repetition will result in sensory adaptation—a diminished responsiveness to the same stimulus. Advertisers are concerned with the diminishing returns resulting from the sensory adaptation that sets in following repeated exposure to the same advertisement. Rhyme, rhythm, and music have been found to decrease the rate of sensory adaptation caused by constant repetition. Consequently, many advertisements make use of rhymes, rhythms, and alliteration, as well as music, in order to prolong their effectiveness.

Acquired determinants of attention. Those attention-provoking factors that depend on learning for their effectiveness are not so easily classified as are the innately determined factors. The acquired determinants consist of habits of attending—habits the individual has developed in the course of his lifetime. Although we have no specific research to document the idea, habits of attention and inattention are probably acquired, strengthened, and weakened, just as are other response tendencies. The learned aspects of attention consist of the meanings, interests, hopes, and fears of the individuals, as manifested in his response readinesses, which predispose him to attend to certain stimuli and to disregard others.

A somewhat arbitrary dichotomy of acquired determinants of attention classifies them as temporary or permanent. *Temporary determinants* are relevant to a particular occasion. (1) A person who is searching for a small blue book has a temporary set to notice books, especially small books, and more especially small blue books. His heightened sensitivity to this class of objects is induced by the immediate situation and persists only until the book is found or the search is abandoned. (2) An individual is more likely to detect threatening stimuli around him when he is angry than when he is calm. The fear-aroused person is sensitized to attend to stimuli that we would disregard under other circumstances. (3) A hungry person is particularly attracted to stimuli that have acquired relevance to eating. (4) The homesick individual may overreact to anything that reminds him of home.

A person's occupational and avocational interests consist, in part, of a *relatively permanent tendency* to notice certain categories of objects. An automobile mechanic may be able to tell you quite a bit about the car that he just serviced but nothing in particular about the man who drove it. On the other hand, a physician might have noticed the slightly jaundiced face of the driver but failed to notice anything about the car. Similarly, a botanist who specializes in research on a minute species of plant will notice such plants readily, although they are completely disregarded by the layman.

It is obvious that the permanence of attentional tendencies is relative. The permanent determinants of attention are only gradually acquired. They are also continuously modified, strengthened, or weakened throughout one's lifetime. Temporary interests may increase in strength and permanence or wax and wane over the course of time.

Since no two people have identical repertoires of interests, each person has a unique set of acquired attentional tendencies. Thus it is much more difficult to use acquired factors of attention in appeals to the public than is the case in the use of the innate determinants. Intensity, size, color, form, movement, and repetition can be manipulated with results that are reasonably predictable, because people are considerably alike in innate reactions to these stimulus variables. But, because of the infinite variability of human experiences, the range of acquired interests that are relevant to public appeals is less predictable. However, when types of public messages are varied according to the age, sex, religious interests, political affiliations, and occupational or avocational interests of the prospective buyers, the acquired determinants of attention become the most important variables.

When one uses such discrete classes as innate and acquired, there are always some factors that do not fall clearly into either category. *Novelty* and *change,* for instance, are important determinants of attention, but they are neither clearly innate nor learned. In one sense, when we list the determinants of attention, we are also enumerating the determinants of responses in general. It will be recalled that when we attempted to define a stimulus, we had to include change as a characteristic. As a factor in the determination of attention, change is an essential component of all the other determinants. In addition to the factors of extent and rate of change, deviation from an expected or customary stimulus dimension or pattern (such as intensity, size, color, form, or rate of movement) functions as the most significant acquired variable. Novelty, strangeness, unusualness, unexpectedness—these factors transcend the innate-acquired dichotomy. These terms refer to changes in patterns of stimulation within a context of one's past experience.

Divided Attention

If two streams of speech are presented simultaneously, one to each ear, a listener can normally separate them and, with effort, follow one and ignore the other. However, if the two streams are both important to him, he may be able to get the gist of both of them. This does not mean that he is able to attend to and perceive both simultaneously; it means that an individual is normally able to miss much of what is said without losing the overall meaning of the speech. Language has a great deal of formal structure and redundancy. When the messages contain a lot of expected word sequences, familiar phrases, and other predictable components, the listener can get the general meaning of the message by tuning in only a few key components. We hear and read words and larger units as they should be for the speech schema we have acquired, even though the actual stimulus patterns or the components attended to only flirt with the complete message. With minimal attention to a stimulus pattern, a component not precisely perceived may still provide fragmentary cues that restrict perceptual alternatives to those consistent with the minimal sensory information. People perceive words and sentences not because they recognize the individual sounds, words, or phrases, but because they recognize the general sense of the message. Thus, when a listener is following two streams of speech simultaneously, he is shifting attention from one to the other so as to pick up the most relevant cues from each and to interpolate sufficiently to follow the essential meanings of both.

PERCEIVING

Some theorists have suggested that perception involves the selection of the most appropriate stored hypothesis evoked by the sensory input. The selection of alternative hypotheses has sometimes been conceptualized in terms of "stimulus-detection theory." That is, the individual selects from alternative interpretations or hypotheses the one with the greatest probability of being "correct." Prior experiential frequencies have developed "likelihood ratios" for alternatives, and the human organism, functioning in some respects like a computer, comes up with the hypothesis with the greatest likelihood ratio, or greatest probability of being right.

There is considerable evidence that perceptual input is processed and stored so as to develop probabilities when various alternatives are possible but not equally probable. For example, in a two-choice discrimination-learning problem in which the subject indicates whether he predicts a light will next appear on his left or on his right and then finds his choice to be correct according to a fixed probability (such as 60 percent left and 40 percent right), adults tend to match their responses to the rate of actual occurrence of the rewards. (The rewards in this situation were verbal expressions of approval.) In other words, over a series of trials, the subject's response-choice proportions tend to approach reinforcement (reward) probabilities. This finding seems to involve an internalization of objective probabilities that find their outlet in similar behavior contingencies. However, the maximum "payoff" is obtained not by matching reward and choice probabilities but by predicting on all trials the most frequently occurring response-reward contingency and responding accordingly (Estes, 1964; Pecan & Schvaneveldt, 1970). It seems that learners can be shifted from matching to maximizing behavior when a gambling rather than a problem-solving approach to the situation is induced. When the subject perceives the situation as a problem having a solution, he tries to be correct on each trial, and "matching" behavior occurs. However, when he views the situation as a gamble in which he can be successful without winning on each trial, he consistently makes the response with the greatest probability of a payoff and thus maximizes his reinforcements.

If perception involves the selection of the most appropriate stored hypothesis, perceptual-response probabilities must be of the maximizing rather than the matching type, as described above. That is, the perceptual mechanism acts as if it contained a statistical decision-maker that takes into account sensory input as well as many nonsensory factors, such as relative frequency of prior occurrences and the consequences of selecting the various hypotheses in the past (Abrahamson & Levitt, 1969). This principle is the basic concept in Bayesian statistical inference (Edwards, Lindman, & Savage, 1963) and suggests that man in some respects responds according to Bayesian principles.

The acquisition of language is one of the best examples of the internalization of stimulus and reinforcement contingencies and is a special case of the general problem of the organization of behavior patterns and sequences. In language acquisition, the child generates rules and makes many of the interpolations necessary for his perception of oral and written language. In accordance with these rules, he makes his own transformations by generating new verbal combinations and extrapolations. Rules are implicit in the structure of all language, and every normal adult "knows" these rules in the sense that he can use them

Figure 3-2. A case of reduced cues.

freely. The normal 6-year-old child has, in this sense, learned the rules governing the use of his native language. Although it is clear that physical maturation, intellectual ability, and learning interact, the mechanisms of language acquisition are still in dispute. For alternative explanations, see Lenneberg (1969), Chomsky (1965), Skinner (1957), and Kintsch (1970). We shall return to this topic in Chapter 8.

Determinants of Perception

Attending and perceiving share many of the same determinants. Those stimulus characteristics that we listed earlier as innate determinants of attention constitute the *sensory component of perception.* The acquired determinants of attention constitute the *meaning component of perception*. In addition to sensory input and acquired meaning, the motivational states and expectancies of an individual are also determinants of his perception.

We have previously stated that perception is often preceded by a definite readiness or expectancy to perceive a given stimulus. Such a readiness is a *perceptual set.* If a picture is projected on a screen for a short time after (1) some subjects have been instructed to observe the number of people in the picture, (2) other subjects have been asked to observe the way the people are dressed, and (3) still other subjects have been requested to notice what the people are doing, the subjects' reports about the picture are definitely related to their previous instructions. Thus they clearly bring a particular perceptual set to the picture. When an ambiguous figure, such as Figure 3-3, is shown to a person and he is told that he will see a vase, he will almost always do so. If he is told that he will see two silhouetted faces, that is what he will usually see.

Sometimes the context induces perceptual sets that determine one's interpretation of stimulus patterns. When a person is searching for a valuable coin he has lost, he is inclined to see every shining object as the lost article. When he is anxiously awaiting the arrival of a friend, he may "see" the friend several times before he actually appears.

The act of reading is a good example of perception involving responses to reduced cues influenced by context. The individual learning to read by the alphabet method first learns to recognize each letter. He then learns to recognize larger and larger groups of letters making up syllables and words. Finally, he learns to recognize entire phrases and short sentences without being aware of either the individual letters constituting the words or the individual words making up the phrases and sentences. The fluent reader perceives larger units of print on the basis of a relatively few visual cues. The upper contours of the printed line can be shown to constitute the dominant cues, as is evidenced by

Figure 3-3. A case of ambiguous design.

the facility with which printed material can be read when only the upper half of the line is exposed as compared with the greater difficulty of reading with only the lower half exposed. The importance of contextual meanings in determining perception can be demonstrated by systematically omitting certain words and letters from a paragraph and asking fluent readers to read it. Such people will read the paragraph in terms of its general meaning and are unaware of the absence of several words and the presence of many misspelled words. If a general point is developed throughout the paragraph but a negative word is introduced into one sentence, most people will overlook the negative and read it as consistent with the overall meaning of the rest of the paragraph.

The tendency to overlook misspelled and omitted words when reading meaningful written material is known as the proofreader's illusion. Authors are prone to this illusion when proofreading their own material. The proofreader's illusion is an example of a tendency to perceive the world as we believe it to be rather than as it is represented by the specific patterns of stimulation impinging on our sense organs.

A person's motivational and emotional state influences perception. The hungry man is more likely to perceive food and food-related articles than is the satiated one. Men and women who existed on a semistarvation diet for long periods of time in concentration and prisoner-of-war camps eventually organized their entire lives around the themes of food and eating. Hungry subjects, as compared with nonhungry subjects, have been shown to see ambiguous figures as food more often, to see food objects as larger in size, and to recognize food-related words more readily (Wispe & Drambarean, 1953).

Children from slum areas, as well as other people who were hypnotized and told that they were poor, overestimated the size of coins much more than did children from prosperous homes or other people who were hypnotized and told that they were rich (Bruner & Goodman, 1947; Ashley, Harper, & Runyon, 1951). Such studies indicate that perception is influenced by one's sense of relative values. One assumption on which projective tests like the Rorschach are based is that one's feelings, emotions, beliefs, and general frame of reference influence perception. In such tests a person is shown ambiguous or relatively unstructured stimulus material, such as inkblots, and is asked to tell what he "sees" in the pictures. Those who analyze Rorschach tests consider the responses to represent a person's projection of his own attitudes, feelings, and emotions. Figure 3-4 is an illustration of the type of stimulus material used in such studies of the projective component of perception.

Figure 3-4. An inkblot of the type used in the Rorschach test.

Perceptual Organization

Our everyday perceptual world consists of organized patterns and coherent units. One of the most basic of these experiential patterns is the figure-ground relationship. Practically every complex experience tends to be organized into a dominant portion, or figure, and an unimportant portion, or background. The figure has more structure, is more clearly defined and localized, and stands out sharply from the rest of the total percept.

The component parts of a total perceptual experience tend to organize themselves according to certain principles. Some of these principles are proximity (nearness), similarity, and closure. Other things being equal, objects that are close together tend to form subgroups or patterns within a larger complex, and, in general, objects that are alike or have something in common also tend to form subgroups. (See Figure 3-5.) Closure as an organizational principle refers to the tendency to perceive partial objects as wholes and incomplete objects as completed. This phenomenon is partly a matter of responding to minimal cues. Figure 3-2 was an example of an incomplete object that is per-

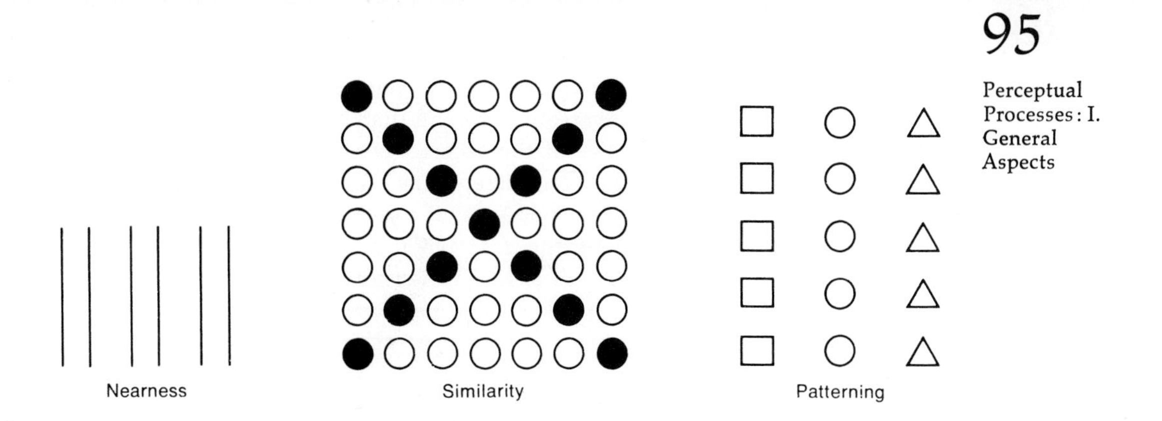

Figure 3-5. Three principles of organization.

ceived as complete. These principles of perceptual organization are a part of a general perceptual tendency to order one's world into consistent and stable patterns and categories. Such ordering makes possible maximum predictability and thus maximum economy of effort in dealing with one's world.

Perceptual Constancy

Perceptual objects seem to retain "true" characteristics despite marked changes in the sensory input from them. People perceive objects as having constant size, shape, color, and so forth, despite tremendous changes in the pattern of raw sensory data. This tendency is known as perceptual constancy.

Size constancy. Size constancy refers to the tendency for objects to be perceived as having a constant size, irrespective of their distance from the eyes

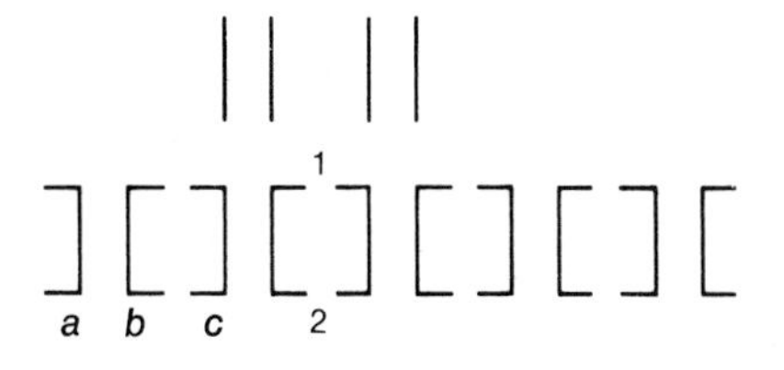

Figure 3-6. Although lines *a* and *b* are closer together than lines *b* and *c*, perceptual closure of gaps, such as 1 and 2, makes a viewer likely to group lines *b* and *c* as parts of a common rectangle.

and the size of their image on the retinas of the viewer. Of course, the size of the retinal image varies inversely with the distance at which the object is viewed. If perception of the size of the object were directly related to the size of the retinal image, a rod 100 centimeters (cm.) long at a distance of 50 cm. should look just as long as a rod of 600 cm. at a distance of 300 cm. (see Figure 3-7). This actually seems to be the case when all cues other than rods are removed from the subjects' visual fields. When all cues to distance are eliminated, the size constancy breaks down and perceptual size corresponds to the size of the retinal image (Holway & Boring, 1941).

Of course, size constancy is not the result of a series of conscious, rational judgments. Perceptual habits develop as the result of learning that goes on incidentally and largely without an individual's awareness. We learn that an automobile is moving away from us, not shrinking, as its retinal image shrinks. We may become partially aware of some of these habitual ways of seeing things when we look at familiar objects from the top of a skyscraper or from an airplane. When viewing familiar objects from these positions, the transfer of learning is incomplete, and full-size houses and cars look like toys. Part of the disturbance of size constancy may arise from the absence of many of the distance cues that are normally present when viewing these same objects from more usual positions. For example, the absence of customary distance cues is responsible for a person's mistaking the glint on his eyeglasses for a light in the sky. Similarly, tiny particles moving in the viteous or aqueous humor of the eyes are sometimes perceived as objects moving in the sky. When a familiar object suddenly becomes visible immediately in front of one out of a dense fog, it may momentarily seem several times its normal size, because indistinct

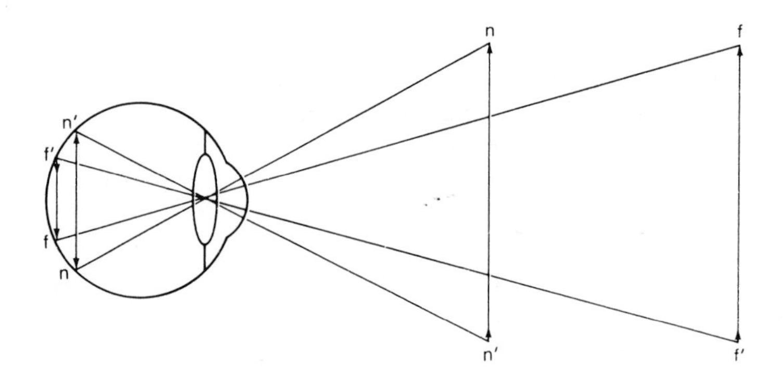

Figure 3-7. Far rod (f) looks smaller to the viewer than near rod (n), unless cues indicate the distances of the rods.

outline is normally a cue for distance. Furthermore, the image of the fog-shrouded object on the retina is very large. An object as far away as the indistinctness of outline indicates, producing such a large retinal image, would be tremendous. As other cues operate, the illusion of size is dispelled.

Shape constancy. With every shift in position of the eyes with reference to a visually perceived object, the shape of the retinal image changes. Despite the constantly changing shape of the retinal image, the object is perceived as maintaining a constant shape. A dime, seen edgewise, is still believed to be round. One of the first things that must be learned in mechanical drawing and in painting is that the shape of objects varies according to the vantage point from which they are viewed. To look "right," a figure must be drawn as the image is projected on the retina.

Not all visual shapes maintain perceptual constancy. If a square table, on which a round spotlight is focused, is tilted, the shape of the lighted area changes from round to oval, whereas the tabletop maintains its perceptual squareness. Perceptual constancy is dependent on the frame of reference in which the perception occurs. For example, if all but the surface of the square table is blacked out, so that the visual field is limited to this area, the tabletop seems to change shape, just as does the spot of light. Perceptual shape constancy means that an object is perceived as having a permanent and invariable shape when it is moving or being moved.

Color and brightness constancies. Perceptual colors of known objects remain constant even when the circumstances are such that hues are not perceptible. The red rose in the garden is still perceived as red in the evening when its color would be indistinguishable if its identity were not already known.

If a lump of coal and a white sheet of paper are gradually differentially illuminated until the paper is darker than the coal, with the background remaining constant, the coal will still seem to be the darker. If a person were to look at a portion of each object through tubes, not knowing which was which, the brightness-constancy effect would, of course, disappear.

Studies of the relationship of hue and brightness constancy have shown that, the more objects there are in the visual field, the greater is the degree of perceived hue and brightness constancy. Conversely, the more homogeneous the visual field and the more impoverished the perceptual field, the more hue and brightness are perceived to change with the physical variables (von Fieandt, 1966). As we mentioned in the preceding paragraph, perceptual constancy is

Figure 3-8. A man viewed from this unusual angle seems to have shoes far out of proportion to his body. This photograph was taken in Aberdeen, Scotland, in 1880.

absent when one views only a portion of an object through a tube. Perceptual constancy thus seems to be not a response to specific cues but rather a set of relationships. The richer, the more highly articulated, and the more customary the perceptual frame of reference, the greater is the degree of perceptual constancy.

The distorted-room illusion. An interesting series of studies related to perceptual constancy has been performed by Ames and his co-workers at the Institute for Associated Research in Hanover, N. H. One of these studies involves the distorted-room demonstration. The floor of the distorted room slopes up to the right of the observer; the rear wall recedes from right to left; and the windows are of different sizes, but all are trapezoidal so as to follow the slope of the floor and the recession of the back wall. When viewed with one eye from a small window, the room appears completely normal: the floor seems level, the rear wall appears to be at right angles to the line of sight and to the side walls, and the windows are apparently rectangular and of the same size.

If one person stands in the far-left-hand corner of the room and another person of equal height stands in the far-right-hand corner, which is really closer to the observer, the person in the left corner appears much smaller than the person in the right corner. In this situation the viewer's shape-constancy assumption concerning the room predominates over that of size constancy concerning human figures.

If the observer takes a long stick and tries to touch various parts of the distorted room, he is quite unsuccessful in judging respective directions and distances. With practice, he becomes more successful. If he enters the room, its distortions immediately become apparent. With additional experience, the room comes more and more to assume its true shape, even when viewed with one eye from the previous vantage point. The perceptual response to the same stimulus pattern on his retina has changed.

Such experiences demonstrate that the object perceived is neither a stimulus-determined revelation of an external reality nor the projection of a purely mentalistic "something" into the external world. Perception involves the relating of relevant past experiences to stimulus patterns impinging on the sense organs (Ittelson, 1960).

Illusory Experiences

Illusions are percepts that are grossly false. Yet there is no sharp distinction between ordinary perceptual experiences and illusions. If illusions consist in experiencing the world as something other than it really is, then all perceptual experience is partially illusory. We have indicated repeatedly that perception always involves the transformation of sensory input by the internally stored memories of previous experiences with similar patterns of stimulation. Experiences commonly called illusory are those perceptual experiences that are proved by additional checking to have been inconsistent with more complete information. Thus the illusions of distance and area illustrated in Figure 3-9 can be verified by measuring distances and calculating areas. Why are the results of these perceptually based measuring and calculating operations accepted as more real than are the free perceptions that they are used to verify? The reason is that past experience has convinced us that such measurements lead to greater consistencies and more useful outcomes than does dependence on unverified general impressions.

Although many of the common illusions of length, direction, and area (spatial illusion) have never been completely explained, some of the causative factors are known. Gregory (1968), Leibowitz, Brislin, Perlmutter, and Hennessy

(1969), and Stacey and Pike (1970) have shown that illusions involve the same principles as ordinary perception. Specifically, Gregory contends that illusions arise from the same information-processing mechanisms that are involved in our comprehension of the larger visible world. All these authors believe that perceptual development includes the formation of an internal size-scaling component. This size-scaling mechanism contains a size-constancy element, which indicates that like-sized objects, lines, or areas producing different-sized retinal images must be different distances away. Conversely, the like-sized retinal images of objects perceived as closer will register as smaller compared with those judged to be farther away. Thus in the Ponzo illusion the perceptually closer identical lines or rectangles are perceived as smaller than the perceptually more distant ones. Similarly, two-dimensional figures arranged like components of three-dimensional figures produce perceptual distortions according to indicated perspective, even when the perceiver does not see the figure with depth.

Some analogies may make the general concept clearer. Gregory (1968) uses the size-weight illusion as analogous to the visual illusions shown in Figure 3-9. In this illusion two objects of the same weight but of differing size are perceived as differing in weight when hefted. The larger of the two is regularly perceived as the lighter. The weight of the two is perceived not only according

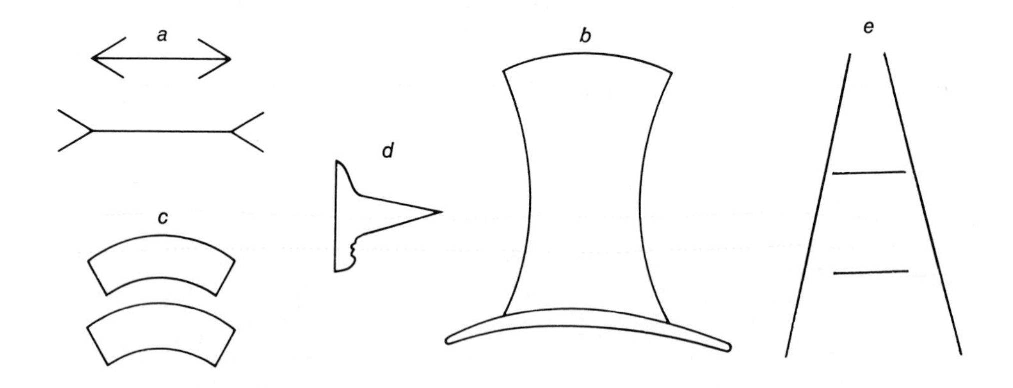

Figure 3-9. Illusions of area and distance. In (a) the two horizontal lines are of the same length, and in (c) the two areas are identical. However, in both cases the lower figure seems larger. In (b) the width of the brim is equal to the height of the hat, although the latter seems much larger. In (d) the elongated nose looks longer than the height of the face, but the two are equal. The illusion in (e) is known as the Ponzo, or railway lines, illusion. In this case the apparently more distant of the two rectangles seems larger, but the two are identical in area.

to the pressure exerted cutaneously and kinesthetically but also according to the expected weight of the object as indicated by its visually perceived size. The larger size suggests greater weight with a resulting greater force being exerted, and this perception results in the person's making magnified movements in hefting such as would occur if the larger one actually were heavier. The illusion persists even in the face of objective evidence (weighing) that the two are of the same weight. The perceptual expectancy (hypothesis) that the larger object is the heavier persists and accounts for the perceptual distortion despite the person's "knowing" that the weights are the same.

I (C. W. T.) recall an illusion in which the same kind of mechanism was involved. One morning while I was hurrying to school along a largely deserted sidewalk, a human figure suddenly loomed up immediately in front of me out of the dense fog. For a short fraction of a second the figure seemed a giant—several times man-size. This momentary illusion was undoubtedly the result of the indistinctness of color and outline, the absence of sharp detail, and similar factors registering "great distance." However, the physical proximity of the person produced a large retinal image. The size-constancy hypothesis, combined with the great-distance cues, produced the perceptual distortion of size; a man producing the given size of retinal image from a great distance would be a giant (see Figure 3-8).

A vertical line looks longer than a horizontal line of equal length. This illusion can be understood as the result of vertical lines in linear perspective providing progressively diminished retinal-image length with increasing distance from the viewer; horizontal lines do so to a lesser degree. The vertical line registering greater distance is perceived as physically longer than the horizontal line of the same length closer up. In the railway-lines (Ponzo) illusion (Figure 3-9d), two stick rectangles of identical sizes superimposed on a real or simulated railroad track will result in the farther one looking distinctly larger. In the Muller-Lyer illusion (Figure 3-9a), the arrows could represent a three-dimensional figure, such as a sawhorse, seen in three dimensions. In the acute-angled figure the legs will be going away from the observer (greater distance); in the obtuse-angled figure they will be going toward him (closer). The same-sized more-distant-appearing lines are perceived as longer than the closer-appearing lines of the same length.

Visual perception involves responding to cues provided by retinal images in terms of previously acquired information about objects and their characteristics. Gregory (1968) suggests that we can consider perception as the selection of the most appropriate stored hypothesis according to the current sensory input. The depth-cue scaling that results in the perceptual distortions of the visual illusions represents this adjustment made in terms of the available information. Receding and converging lines in the retinal image are ordinarily associated with distance and cue the organism to correct for the retinal image associated with distance of distant objects (size constancy). When a cue falsely indicates depth, the observer corrects for the assumed distance and makes an overestimation of size.

Most of the familiar illusions of length, direction, and area are fairly universal in man, and some can be demonstrated to operate in the lower animals. For example, if a chicken is taught to always peck grains of wheat from the larger of two areas and is then presented with grains of wheat on the two areas in Figure 3-9, the animals will peck from the lower of the two figures—the one that looks larger to humans but is actually identical in area to the one above it.

Illusions of movement. Some illusions of movement result from the absence of customary cues or from the operation of unusual combinations of cues. A person in a train may be sure that his train is moving when it is really the train on the next track that is moving. Illusory reversals of the direction of movements can occur as an aftereffect of actual motion. When one's fast-moving train stops at the station, the station and the stationary train viewed from the window may seem to be moving in the direction opposite the train's previous movement. After a person views a waterfall and then shifts his gaze to the rocks nearby, the rocks may seem to be moving in an upward direction (the waterfall illusion). When a spiral is rotated, it seems to expand or to contract, depending on the direction of rotation. When such rotation ceases, the spiral seems to display the opposite effect. Many similar illusions of movement can be produced. Although explanations in terms of eye movements and fading afterimages have been proposed to account for these illusions, no explanation has been found to be completely satisfactory.

The phi-phenomenon. A particular form of the illusion of movement that results from the appropriately timed projection of a series of still pictures on a screen is known as the *phi-phenomenon.* This illusion has been studied quantitatively in the laboratory. Let us suppose that two lights a few inches apart are flashed on one after the other with appropriate time intervals between. Under these circumstances one sees a single light moving back and forth between the locations of the two lights (see Figure 3-10). If a barrier is interposed between the two lights, the light seems to jump the barrier as it moves back and forth (Figure 3-10b). If three bars of light are used, as in Figure 3-10c, and the flashing of the light in the vertical bar is followed by the flashing of the two horizontal bars, the vertical bar will seem to split and become the two

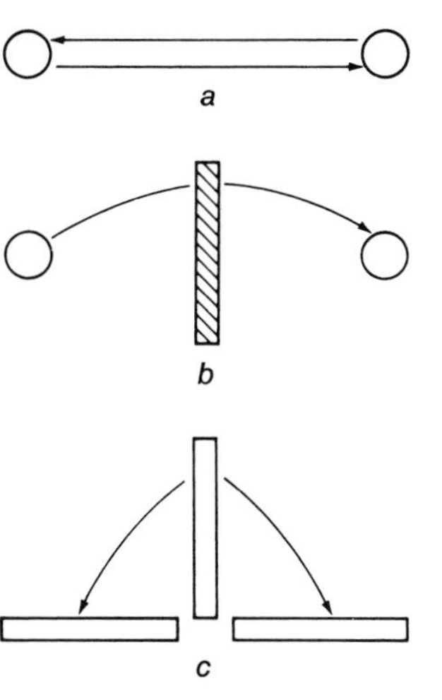

Figure 3-10. The phi-phenomenon.

horizontal bars. A large number of illusions of movement can be produced by varying the spacing, intensities, and time relationships of the lights. Such illusions of apparent movement make possible the many animated electric signs used in advertising displays. Apparent movement can be achieved when two sounds are produced from different locations with their relative intensities and their time relations appropriately adjusted. The sound will seem to move from place to place. Light taps on adjacent parts of the skin can produce an experience of something brushing back and forth across the skin between the two stimulated points. Illusions of movement are not confined to vision.

Illusions based on personal meaning. Some illusions are caused by hopes, fears, and high levels of expectation. A fearful child perceives the shrubbery blown against the window as a burglar attempting to open the window. A timid, superstitious boy perceives a wind-blown garment on the clothesline at night as a ghost. Such illusory experiences are determined primarily by personal meanings attached to objects and differ only in degree from the perceptual constancies that derive from the contextual meanings and expectancies of the perceiver.

Perception without Learning

In the past, the question of whether perception is innate (nativism) or learned (empiricism) was posed in absolute terms, but today the question concerns itself with which aspects of perception are innate and which are the outcome of learning. Perception is the organism's maintenance of contact with its environment and is essential to its adaptation and survival. It would seem that, for many animal species to survive, certain components of perception must be manifest at birth. This is particularly true in the lower animals in which adaptive behavior is largely innate.

The evidence that visual discrimination of distance is unlearned is quite convincing. Rats raised from birth to 100 days of age in complete darkness, except for a few seconds of dim illumination each day, were able to discriminate different distances between a jumping platform on which they were placed and a platform containing food at varying distances away (Lashley & Russell, 1934).

The most extensive studies on this question involve the avoidance of a "visual cliff"—a falling-off place or drop-off of the ground (Gibson & Walk, 1960; Gibson, 1969, 1970). (See Figure 3-11.) In these studies an apparatus providing a simulated drop-off downward was constructed that eliminated all cues to the existence of the cliff except the visual ones. A wide variety of animals, including rodents, birds, cats (even lions, tigers, and snow leopards), sheep, goats, dogs, and, of course, primates (monkeys and man) have been studied with this apparatus. The studies show that visual-cliff avoidance develops very early and in some animal species certainly without learning. Chicks, sheep, and goats avoid the cliff a few hours after birth. Rats reared to various ages in the dark avoid the cliff at first testing. Human infants avoid the cliff as early as they can crawl, and monkeys show evidence of differential responses at 3 days of age. It seems that perception of a safe surface in contrast to a drop-off appears early in life and that little, if any, learning is required for its appearance.

"Looming" is another type of space perception that seems to involve a large innate component. Looming refers to the increasing magnification of the retinal image of an approaching object. When an object such as a baseball is perceived as coming directly toward a subject, humans and most other animals duck, dodge, move backward, flinch, flatten out, or otherwise show alarm. A series of studies has been carried out involving the continuously accelerated magnification or diminution of the picture or shadow of an object projected on a large translucent screen in front of the experimental animal. In such an artificial looming situation, nothing actually approaches the animal, but the "optical information" is that of an object approaching or receding at a uniform speed. Subjects studied in this situation have been as varied as crabs, chicks, kittens, monkeys, and humans (Gibson, 1970). Crabs responded to magnification by running backward, flinching, or flattening out; chicks by running or crouching; kittens struggled and made aversive head movements; infant monkeys leaped to the rear of the cage and made alarm cries; and human infants blinked at 3 weeks of age with evidenced attempted head withdrawal as early as 2 weeks (White, 1969; Gibson, 1970).

Investigations also indicate the innateness of some degree of size constancy. Perceptual size constancy has been demonstrated in fish, ducklings, kittens, young rats, monkeys, chimpanzees, and human infants (Freeman, 1968; Gibson, 1970). Since evidence of size constancy is found in human infants as young as 2 months of age, the importance of learning seems to be minimal.

In perception, patterns of stimulation provide information to appropriately tuned organisms. Innate mechanisms provide a means for animals to detect information needed for spatial orientation and for avoiding obstacles and pitfalls.

Figure 3-11. The visual-cliff apparatus used to test the sensory development of a puppy or other small animal. The animal is placed on a slightly raised narrow board. Under a sheet of clear plate glass, there is a steep drop on one side and a shallow drop on the other. Results are based on which way the animal turns in repeated trials (Gibson & Walk, 1960; Walk, 1965; Scott, 1968).

Social Perception

Social perception begins with the infant's differentation between people and objects. People soon come to constitute those patterns of simulation that move about, remove irritants, and provide food, warmth, and contact. People become prepotent stimuli because of their nurturing functions. Very early the configuration of the human face comes to identify a human to an infant. Because all people are not equally significant in the child's life, he soon learns to differentiate between classes of people (men and women, boys and girls, adults and children) on the basis of the more precise perception of size, dress, and facial features. This differentiation is carried still further when the child learns to recognize a specific person.

Almost from the moment of birth, the infant begins to attach meanings to gestures, postures, facial expressions, and vocal inflections. As the result of the processes of social learning, subtle details of facial expressions, tone of voice, and even muscular tension come to signify to the child that the other person is happy or sad, pleased or displeased, friendly or threatening. With the development of language, words become the most meaningful and precise form of social stimulation. The recognition of the cognitive and affective significance of the spoken and written word comes to be an important type of social perception.

Perception and Personality

We have indicated that stimulus and sense-organ characteristics, as well as a broad background of meanings, motives, emotions, and purposes that the individual brings to a situation, all help determine perception. It is clear that the personality of the individual also enters into his perceptual processes. Conversely, the sum total of one's perceptual experiences enters into the development and organization of his personality. The nature and pattern of his personality, in turn, exert a profound influence on his perceptual processes.

A series of studies performed by Witkin and his associates (1964) illustrates the relationship between personality traits and perceptual styles. These studies have shown that people differ markedly in the extent to which their perceptions in ambiguous situations are determined predominantly by external stimulus patterns as compared with internal factors, such as maintaining an active internal "set" that resists the influence of the external stimulus pattern. The individuals whose percepts are largely internally controlled are designated as "field independent," and those people whose perception is predominantly stimulus controlled are called "field dependent." Perceptually, field-dependent people are relatively more dominated by a situation. They have greater difficulty in keeping specific stimulus items isolated from the background, are less able to maintain their own bodies upright in a "tilted-room" situation, and are less able to discover simple figures hidden in the designs of an "embedded-figures" test than are field-independent individuals.

In the realm of personality, field-independent, as contrasted with field-dependent, people are more able to withstand the pressures of their social environment, are less anxious, have higher levels of self-esteem, and think of themselves as more adequate. The personality organization of field-independent children is more complex and shows greater independence in a variety of social situations compared with more field-dependent peers. The degree of field dependence found in children decreases with age, which indicates that perceptual development involves a shift toward more internal controls.

It should not be inferred from this discussion that the most extreme degrees of inner-directed perception are characteristic of the most mature individuals. The percepts of the psychotic individual are predominantly determined by inner-directed perceptual processes. The external world of such people is perceived largely in terms of the individual's projected unconscious motives. The paranoid individual interprets all perceived events within the framework of his unique delusional system. An individual who believes that an international ring of gangsters is trying to kill him interprets everything he sees and hears within this frame of reference. The two people conversing on the corner are gang members plotting his capture; their glances in his direction are evidence that they are talking about him; their failure to look at him is evidence that they are being especially careful not to tip him off beforehand. The percepts of such deluded individuals are dominated by their own unique set of meanings.

The most adequate perception would seem to require a dynamic interaction between internal and external factors. Both a completely situation-dominated world and a completely inner-dictated perceptual world are restricted and inappropriate. Adequate perception requires a rich background of experientially derived meanings that have sufficient flexibility to change with the situational context. Appropriate perception must remain situation-bound, but it is also modifiable as the meaning of a situation changes. Only a person whose personality is sufficiently flexible to permit a dynamic interaction between the inner and outer determinants of perception is truly free—free to react spontaneously and appropriately to changing situations.

MAN'S PERFORMANCE CAPACITIES

We indicated earlier that perceptual, ideational, and motor performances are interrelated and have much in common. Skilled motor activities, like perceptual processes, are adaptive mechanisms; both are organized spatially and temporally with reference to certain ends. Perceptual and motor processes are intertwined in the sense that ongoing motor activities are continually monitored and guided by perceptual components. The kinesthetic, vestibular, cutaneous, visual, and even auditory feedback combines with the environmental consequences of motor acts to provide constant informational feedback, which, in turn, operates to perpetuate, eliminate, or modify response patterns.

The feedback from the motor performance adds the intrinsic sensory input to the environmental consequences of the action and becomes a part of the total informational load of the system. Man's motor-performance capacities, like his attentional-perceptual capacities, are limited and can become overloaded.

Technological advances such as supersonic and space travel place new demands on man's information-processing and motor-performance capacities. These demands have made it imperative that design engineers, psychologists, and others concern themselves with man's informational and motor-performance potentials. The monitoring of control information from instrumental panels and other sources and the speed, accuracy, and complexity of responses required must be kept within man's information and performance limitations. In addition, they must also be designed and arranged so as to make maximum use of man's potentials in these areas. There is a specialty within psychology known as Human Factors Psychology, which deals largely with these problems (Fitts & Posner, 1967; Chapanis, 1965).

SUMMARY

Attention is a preparatory adjustment that facilitates perceptual clearness and efficient motor activity. Attending is a highly selective process that accentuates certain sensory elements and either mutes or blocks out other components of sensory input. Both stimulus characteristics and the personal characteristics of the perceiver cause sensory data to be filtered. The five behavioral components of attention are sense-organ orientation, postural adjustments, increased muscular tension, changes in visceral functioning, and central-nervous-system activities.

The innate determinants of attention are intensity of stimulation; size, or extensity, of the stimulus pattern; definite form; color; movement; and repetition. The acquired determinants of attention consist of the temporary and permanent interests as well as the temporary emotional states of an organism.

Some principles of perceptual organization are figure-ground relationships, proximity, similarity, and closure. The organization of the individual's perceptual world consists of the development of a set of reasonably consistent and stable patterns and categories of experience that provide an element of predictability and economy of effort. One manifestation of this orderly predictability of one's perceptual world is perceptual constancy.

Illusions are grossly false percepts. Some illusions arise from the perceiver's inability to isolate the relevant variables to be compared. Other illusions are caused by an absence or unusual combination of perceptual cues; still others derive principally from the perceiver's unique pattern of hopes, fears, and expectancies.

The organism seems to be innately provided with a mechanism for sensing qualities of the perceptual world. In addition, the perceiver has some primitive organization tendencies that, together with maturational processes, provide the foundation for the vast accumulation of specific meanings that go to make up each individual's perceptual world.

SUGGESTED READINGS

Dember, W. N. *Psychology of perception.* New York: Holt, 1960. This volume presents a more advanced discussion of this topic. It is a good basic text.

Forgus, R. H. *Perception: The basic process in cognitive development.* New York: McGraw-Hill, 1966. This is a good recent text on perception. It deals with the broader conceptual problems.

Leibowitz, H. W. *Visual perception*. New York: Macmillan, 1965. This volume provides a thorough discussion of vision.

Weintraub, D. J., & Walker, E. L. *Perception*. Belmont, Calif.: Brooks/Cole, 1967. This is a brief but thorough discussion of perception (paperback). A good selection of readings is also included.

4

Perceptual Processes: II. A More Analytical View

Chapter 3 dealt with the more general aspects of the attentional-perceptual processes. Attention was conceptualized as the selective processing of a sensory input. It seems that informational "messages" are processed one at a time. Consequently, an individual cannot attend to two different sensory inputs requiring independent discrimination at precisely the same moment.

Perception consists in encoding the attentionally screened sensory input in terms of a number of attributes or dimensions. Some of these dimensions are stimulus-related characteristics such as intensity, color, size, and shape. Other perceptual-encoding attributes are the products of the individual's experiential history. In this chapter we shall consider the various dimensions of sensory input and the kinds of perceptually relevant information involved in the processing of information.

VISION

To the average person, vision is a relatively simple process: seeing is a matter of opening one's eyes and looking. However, to the student of vision, the visual processes are exceedingly complex; despite more than a century of intensive investigation, they are still not fully understood.

In vision, a distorted image of a segment of the external world is focused on the retina of the eye by the cornea and the lens. This is the first step in a complex set of processes involving the interaction of various stimulus attributes with relevant stored information, resulting in visual perception.

Visual Stimuli

An adequate stimulus for vision consists of certain electromagnetic frequencies emanating from bodies such as the sun or reflected from the surfaces of other objects in one's visual field. Electromagnetic radiations may, for some purposes, be considered as *quanta* (a quantum is a discrete unit of energy); for other purposes, electromagnetic radiation is conceived of as a wave motion possessing such characteristics as (1) wavelength; (2) amplitude, or pressure; and (3) homogeneity, or purity. For our purposes, light can best be described as wave motions comprising that part of the electromagnetic spectrum that falls between wavelengths of 380 to 760 nanometers (a nanometer is a millionth of a millimeter). The visible wavelengths occupy only a small portion of the entire range of known electromagnetic frequencies, as shown graphically in Figure 4-1. The range of frequencies represented in this figure indicates that the human organism is immersed in a universe of energy sources and manifestations and is sensitive to only a relatively small fraction of them. In addition to the small band of wavelengths to which the eye is responsive, the skin is sensitive to certain of the infrared range immediately adjacent to the visible range. Infrared rays stimulate the warm receptors in the skin and are experienced as warmth. Several other of the known electromagnetic radiations affect body tissue, but without the immediate awareness of the affected individual. Ultraviolet rays, X rays, and, possibly, cosmic rays can injure and destroy tissue.

Except for light and infrared rays, we know of the existence and nature of electromagnetic radiation only indirectly. When an X ray affects a photographic plate, we can see its effect on the film, but we do not see the ray

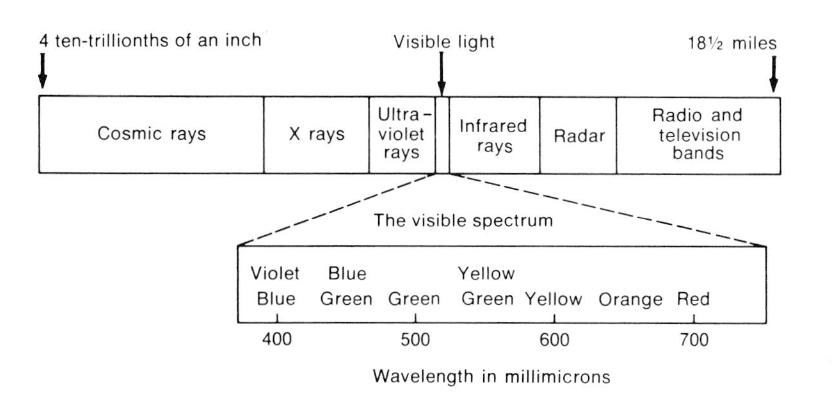

Figure 4-1. The electromagnetic spectrum.

itself. By means of appropriate instrumentation, the various extrasensory frequencies can be "translated" into auditory or visual sensory experiences. For example, radio and television programs, which are broadcast in a frequency range to which humans are insensitive, are converted into sound and visible light by common electronic receivers.

The Dimensions of Visual Stimuli

All visual stimuli have two, and many have three, dimensions of interest: wavelength, luminosity, and homogeneity. Within limits, each of these dimensions can vary independently. One dimension, illustrated by Figure 4-2, is wavelength. This same dimension can also be stated in terms of vibration frequency. The expansion of the visible spectrum in Figure 4-1 shows that, as the wavelength of the stimulus varies from approximately 440 to 750 nanometers, the sensations produced normally range from violet through blue, green, and yellow to red, with all the intermediate mixtures between these colors. Thus the *hue,* or *color tone, is determined primarily by wavelength.*

A second dimension of every light stimulus is luminosity. The luminosity of a visual stimulus is related primarily to the intensity of the light wave. The intensity of the wave can be physically represented as the wave amplitude, as shown in Figure 4-2. *The experiential dimension of brightness is determined principally by the amplitude of the light wave.*

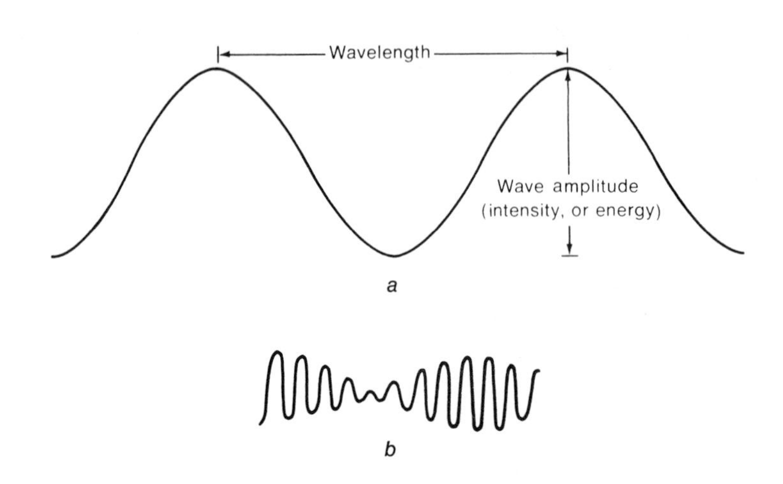

Figure 4-2. A simple wave form, demonstrating the meaning of wavelength (hue) and wave amplitude (brightness). (b) A more complex wave, showing a mixture of wavelength components.

Saturation, the third dimension of a color stimulus, *is determined by the wavelength complexity of the pattern striking the eye.* When the light stimulus consists of a single frequency or a small range of frequencies, the color is highly saturated and will be experienced as a very deep and pure color. Since white light consists of a mixture of all wavelengths, its addition to a color stimulus will decrease the saturation of that color (see Figure 4-3). The addition of other frequencies to a homogeneous light will also decrease the saturation of the original color by increasing the stimulus complexity.

Every color stimulus can be described in terms of these three dimensions. Each chromatic stimulus has a certain hue ranging from one end of the spectrum to the other. In addition, there are some extraspectral colors—the purples and some reds—that are not found in the spectrum but can be produced by mixing spectral colors, the reds and violets. Each visual stimulus can also be assigned a given brightness value ranging from extremely bright to extremely dark. In other words, every color sample can be matched in brightness by a point on a brightness scale ranging from white, through various shades of gray, to black. Similarly, every color sample can be assigned a saturation value depending on the homogeneity of the wavelengths. These values can range from completely saturated to the least perceptible color tone. Figure 4-3 is a conventional diagrammatic representation of these three dimensions.

It should be mentioned that there is no one-to-one relationship between these three stimulus and perceptual variables. Experientially, the effects of wavelength, amplitude, and homogeneity interact. Apparent hue and saturation vary with brightness. At both extremely high and extremely low intensities, colors lose in both hue and saturation. The relative brightnesses of colors of different hues change with variations in the intensity of illumination. Furthermore, phenomenal, or experiential, vision is also determined by many factors other than these stimulus variables.

The Visual Process

Light rays reflected from environmental objects are focused on the retina of the eye by the cornea and the lens as an optical system. This process forms a spatial representation of the visual field on the retina. However, the person does not see the visual image on his retina; he sees with the aid of the retinal image. The retinal image is the first part of a complex set of processes that intervene between stimulation and perceptual-motor response. The pattern of

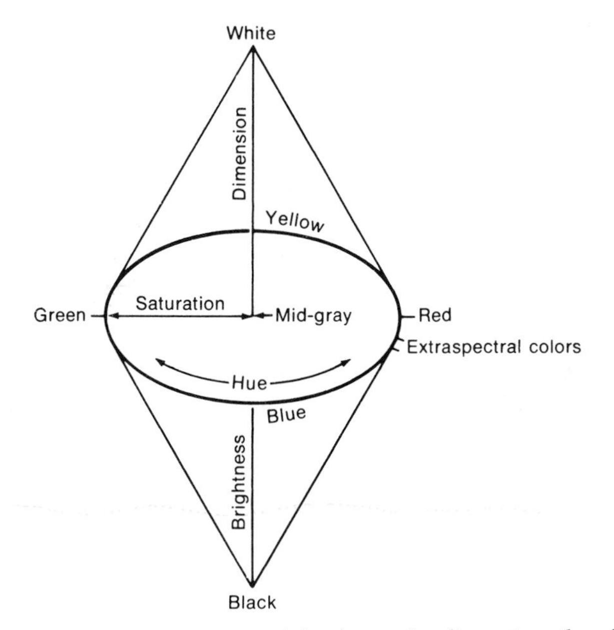

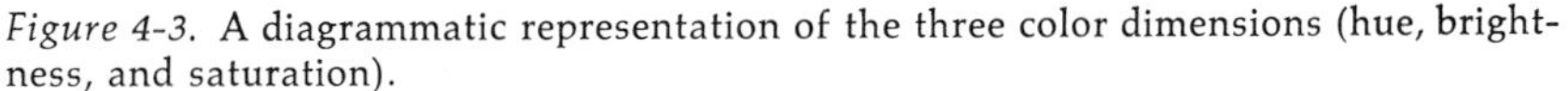
Figure 4-3. A diagrammatic representation of the three color dimensions (hue, brightness, and saturation).

stimulation provides "information" that the nervous system is able to pick up, code in various ways and at various levels, and finally find an outlet for in perceptual-motor ways. The organism uses this information in learning, retaining, thinking, and guiding its movements.

Within the retina the pattern of stimulation is converted into volleys of patterned neural activity. The transformation of the visual image into nerve impulses involves photochemical reactions within the retinal receptor cells—the rods and cones. However, the retina is more than just the equivalent of a photographic emulsion; it performs a considerable amount of processing or coding.

In the vertebrate retina the cell bodies are arranged in three layers. The outermost layer (the one farthest from the front of the eye) contains the true receptor cells, the rods and cones, which contain light-absorbing pigments. The next (middle) layer includes the bipolar cells, which conduct impulses from the rods and cones to the cells of the third layer. This middle layer also includes additional cells, some of which are involved in the lateral transmission of impulses from one part of the retina to another. The third layer contains the ganglion cells, whose axons form the optic nerve. Since the optic nerve is the only connection between the retina and the brain, it carries within its patterns of nerve impulses the total informational output from the retina.

Studies of the neural activity within the nerve cells of the retina indicate that the retina has numerous analytical properties and that many visual variables are differentially coded in this structure. A given ganglion cell receives impulses from a group of receptor cells from a limited area—its receptive field. Some ganglion cells have been shown to respond differentially, according to whether the centers of their receptive fields were darker than, lighter than, or of the same intensity as their outer zones. Moreover, some ganglion cells have been found to be directionally selective, being excited by stimuli moving in one direction across their receptive fields and inhibited by motion in the opposite direction. There is evidence that the human visual system contains different classes of size detectors, each maximally sensitive to visual targets with sizes within a particular range (Pantle & Sekuler, 1968).

One of the brain centers where the optic tracts make synaptic connections is in the thalamus (the lateral geniculate). This center may provide additional coding of visual input. One study has shown that the thalamus in the rabbit signals the direction of movements more precisely than does its retinal counterpart, which, as we have already shown, has some direction-selective cells that are able to indicate an object moving in a particular direction. Workers have now established the existence of cells within the visual area of the thalamus that specify the direction of movement still more precisely. In this same area cells that respond differentially to long and short wavelengths have been found in the cat (Pearlman & Daw, 1970). These studies indicate that the neural coding of visual impulses may take place at various levels within the nervous system, including the visual cortex.

In the cat visual cortex neurons have been found that are activated when the two eyes are stimulated by equal stimuli in two slightly noncorresponding areas of the retina. These neurons are considered to be involved in binocular depth perception. Data indicate that the same types of binocular disparity detectors are present in the human visual system (Tiorentini & Maffei, 1970).

Hirsch and Spinelli (1970) have identified and studied visual cortical areas with elongated receptive fields that respond to elongated stimuli with the same orientation. These workers devised a means of rearing kittens under experimental circumstances: each animal's total visual experience consisted of viewing with one eye a white field containing black vertical lines and simultaneously with the other eye the same field containing horizontal lines. Studies of these animals between 10 and 12 weeks of age showed that, instead of the elongated fields being activated by both eyes, as in normally reared animals, nearly all (21 out of 23) the elongated fields were activated by one eye only. Moreover, in 20 of these monocular units, the receptive-field orientation corresponded to the orientation of the lines to which the eye was exposed during rearing. There was also a complete absence of the diagonally oriented fields found in normal animals. Such studies indicate that the horizontal and vertical indicating structures are anatomically distinct and that visual experience modifies the functioning of these mechanisms.

An image falling on the retina exerts an influence on millions of receptors. Visual perception is the process of "making sense" out of the spatial and temporal patterns of retinal excitation. We have already indicated that visual information is initially coded in terms of patterns of active and inactive cells in the retina. Receptor fields of cells are also arranged in such a way that differential patterns of impulses from them can indicate such things as shape, orientation, and movement of the stimulus patterns. Some further coding of visual information probably occurs in the visual area of the thalamus. In addition, the cortical cells respond to visual neural input with considerable selectivity. In this way the visual cortex further codes its sensory input so as to make still more explicit such things as lines, contours, directionality, and movement, as well as complex shapes and the more general perceptual and conceptual meanings (Thompson, Mayers, Robertson, & Patterson, 1970). Part of this neuronal specificity is predetermined by inherent structural characteristics, but neural coding also develops as a result of experience (learning).

Color Vision

Another important problem of vision is that of the differential coding of color. It has been recognized for more than a hundred years that the gross differential coding of color takes place in the retina. Anatomists and physiologists a century ago observed that animals that move about freely at night have many rods (long cylindrically shaped cells) and few or no cones (shorter and more conically shaped cells) in their retinas, whereas the retinas of animals active only in daylight contain many cones and sometimes lack rods entirely. These scientists deduced that rods are highly sensitive cells and function when light is dim, and cones are stimulated only by relatively bright light. It was also discovered that animals with few or no cones in their retinas were color-blind, whereas animals with many cones had color vision. From this finding it was deduced that the cones mediate color vision and function only in relatively bright light. In dim light only the rods are stimulated; colors are not discriminated, and the world is seen only in shades of gray.

Since the retina, in a very limited sense, functions like a photographic plate, it was assumed very early that there are photosensitive substances in the rods and cones, the activities of which are intermediaries in the initiation of nerve impulses in the optic nerve. All these observations and deductions have been verified many times. The photochemical substances in the visual receptors have been identified, and considerable progress has been made in our understanding of color vision.

The prevailing conception of color vision holds that, in addition to the rods, which subserve twilight vision and contain a specific photochemical substance (rhodopsin), the retina also contains three kinds of cone photoreceptors, each containing a different selective photochemical substance. These three types of photoreceptors absorb wavelengths of light differentially; one is most sensitive in the blue region, another in the green region, and a third near the red region (violet) of the visible spectrum. Each cone is, in turn, associated with its own specific nerve-fiber system, the activities of which are correlated with each of these three fundamental color sensations: red, green, and blue. All chromatic (color) sensations are considered as compounds of the varying levels and patterns of activity in these three systems. Colors that are intermediate between the three fundamental ones are considered to result from the blending or interaction of impulses from the three types of cones (Rushton, 1962).

The cones are also linked together functionally as "opponents," so that the simultaneous and equal excitation of opponents cancels each other as in the mixing of complementary colors. Mixtures of all wavelengths, as in white light, produce simultaneous excitation of all three types of cells, and no color is seen.

Thus a good deal of the processing of color information takes place in the retina. The color-perception systems of animals with color vision contain cells that are excited by one wavelength and inhibited by another (opponents). These spectrally opponent cells are found both in the retina and in the visual nuclei of the thalamus (Gouras, 1970; Pearlman & Daw, 1970). These cells usually receive impulses from two of the three, and sometimes from all three, types of cone mechanisms. It seems that such trichromatic interaction also occurs in the visual projection area of the cortex.

In addition, spectrally "nonopponent" cells have been found in the visual thalamus. Cells of this type show either increases or decreases in activity to all wavelengths and are thought to be involved in mediating achromatic (colorless) experiences. Thus it seems that opponent cells are analyzing and signaling color information, since they give differential responses to different wavelengths; the nonopponent cells, which respond similarly to all wavelengths, are thought to transmit achromatic information (DeValois & Jacobs, 1968).

The rods and cones of the retina are differentiated both structurally and functionally. The rods are long and narrow; the cones are short and fat. However, this structural distinction does not apply in the fovea, which is packed full of cells that function like cones but that are long and narrow like rods. In general, each cone connects with an individual bipolar cell, whereas the thinner rods connect with more than one and, in the extreme periphery of the retina, with as many as 400, bipolar cells. A third difference between the rods and cones is their distribution in the retina. In the center of the fovea there is a small area, subtending an angle of about 1.5°, that contains only cones. Moving out from the fovea, the density of cones declines until, in the peripheral regions, there are few, if any. The distribution of rods, on the other hand, is almost the reverse. Moving toward the periphery from the rod-free area of the fovea, the number of rods increases as the number of cones decreases. It is estimated that the human retina contains about 6.5 million cones and 120 million rods.

Because of the differential distribution of rods and cones in the retina, visual acuity, with good illumination, decreases from the fovea to the periphery. Color sensitivity also varies from the fovea and the immediately surrounding area, where all hues can be perceived, to the periphery of the retina, where no hues are perceived (total color blindness), with a zone of variable width in between in which the blues and the yellows but not the reds and the greens are perceived (red-green color blindness). The boundaries of these color zones are not precisely defined but vary with the intensity of the stimulus. One is not aware of the change in the hue of objects as the visual image moves from one color zone to another any more than he is aware of the blind spot (perceptual constancy). Because the rods have lower thresholds than do the cones, the periphery of the retina is more sensitive to very faint illumination than are the fovea and the immediately surrounding area.

Color blindness. Color-blind people are usually classified as total or red-green blind, with some further subdivision of the latter according to whether their insensitivity is greater for either red or green. However, there is considerable evidence that color blindness comes in all gradations ranging from the complete absence of color vision through red-green and red or green blindness, through various degrees of color weakness, to normal and, possibly, to superior

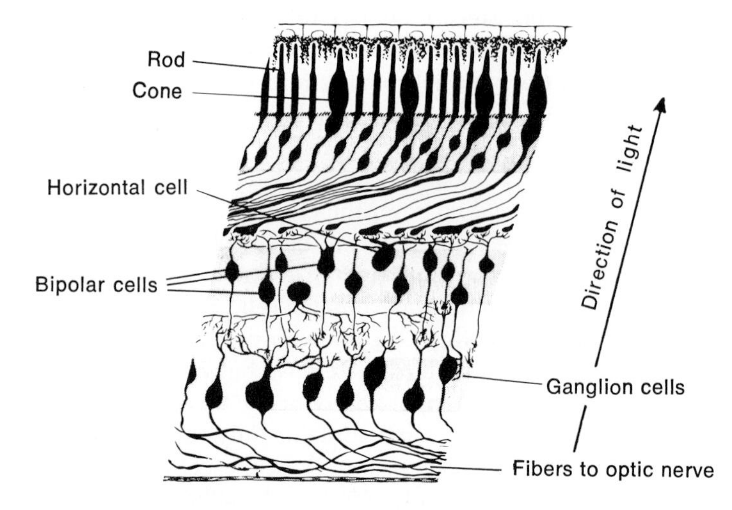

Figure 4-4. The rods and cones, at the surface of the retina, respond to certain wavelengths of electromagnetic radiation and set up impulses in the nerve cells beneath them. These impulses travel to the visual sensory areas of the cortex.

color vision. The rare people who are completely color-blind see the world in black, white, and various shades of gray—in the way that normal people experience a black-and-white motion picture. Red-green color blindness is the most common type. It is usually inherited as a sex-linked characteristic. Some 5 percent of human males and less than half of 1 percent of human females are affected. The red-green blind have difficulty distinguishing between green and red; they usually fail to differentiate them from poorly saturated yellows or browns.

Totally color-blind individuals are presumed to have nonfunctional cones in their retinas and should therefore, according to the duplicity theory, be blind in the center of the fovea. This seems to be the case. This fact apparently explains the nystagmus (rapid involuntary eye movements) commonly seen in the totally color-blind. Nystagmus may keep the point of visual fixation from falling in the center of the fovea, which is presumably blind.

Color mixture. Color mixture may be either additive or subtractive. Additive mixture involves the combination of different wavelength components into a single radiation or stimulus. This combination can be made by casting overlapping beams of colored lights on an achromatic (white) background. A laboratory device for producing additive color mixture consists of a color wheel that rotates colored discs interlocked with each other in such a way that the visible sectors can be varied at will. When the color wheel is rotated with sufficient speed, the radiations from the colored discs fuse, just as do the overlapping colored lights. Actually, the mixing achieved with the color wheel really takes place in the eye. When the wheel rotates, a given part of the retina is alternately stimulated by the two colors. When the interval between the stimulation of a given retinal area by the two colors is sufficiently short, the retinal effect is the equivalent of simultaneous stimulation by both colors. Results obtained when mixing colors with the color wheel agree with those produced by the direct mixture of lights, indicating that, in the retina, the effect of one light adds to that of the other.

The mixture of pigments illustrates color mixing by subtraction. Pigment surfaces absorb certain wavelengths and reflect others, and the hue of an object is determined by the wavelengths reflected. The wavelengths absorbed and reflected are not sharply defined, so that the light reflected is not monochromatic; it contains a mixture of wavelengths. A blue pigment reflects blue light but also some frequencies in the green range; a yellow pigment also reflects some green. When the two are mixed, the yellow pigment absorbs the blue and the blue pigment absorbs the yellow, thus leaving reflected only the light waves that produce a green sensation. Pigment mixtures in which hues cancel each other are called subtractive. A mixture of all hues by the subtractive method produces black, and a mixture of all wavelengths by the additive method produces white. Because experimenters have better control over the stimulus when mixing lights of different hues additively than when mixing pigments subtractively, our discussion will refer to additive mixtures.

Laws of color mixture.

1. Every hue has its complement—a hue that, when mixed with it in the proper proportions, produces gray. Complementary colors cancel each other when mixed in equal proportions.
2. If the mixed complementary colors are not equal, an unsaturated hue of the stronger component will be produced.
3. When noncomplementary colors are mixed, a hue intermediate between the two is produced.
4. The brightness of a mixture of colors is the average of the brightness of the components.

Figure 4-5 will help clarify these relationships. Complementary colors are placed opposite each other on the color wheel. When any two colors are mixed in equal proportions, the result is a hue halfway between them on the color wheel, with a loss in saturation proportional to the distance between them. For example, the mixture of complementary colors that are the maximum distance apart will give complete loss of saturation—gray or white.

Afterimages (Successive Contrast)

If a person looks at a small yellow square for some time and holds his eyes still, there is a gradual loss of saturation: it looks somewhat faded out. This phenomenon is simple sensory adaptation. If the eyes are now shifted to a neutral gray background, a blue square of the same size and shape will appear on the gray background. This phenomenon is the *negative afterimage.* If a black square is used in place of a colored one, the afterimage will be white or, at least, light. If the fixated square is light, the afterimage will be dark. Everyone has probably been aware of these poststimulation phenomena. If a person looks out a window with the sun shining through it for a few seconds and then

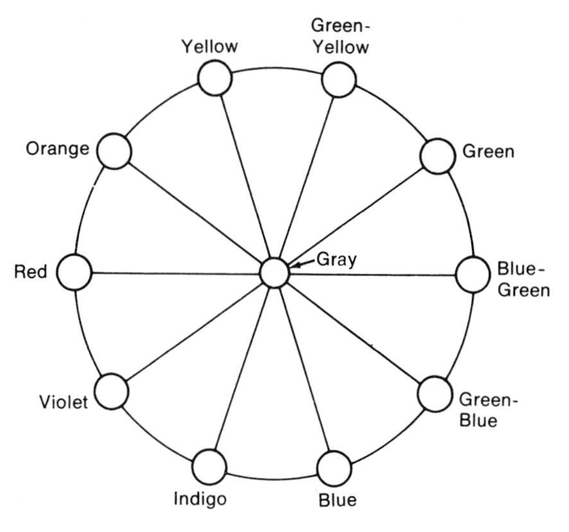

Figure 4-5. A color wheel.

glances about the room, he may see a very vivid reverse picture of the window wherever he looks. Similarly, fixating on the center of a stained-glass window for 30 seconds and then staring at a blank wall will cause all the details of the stained window to appear with the hues and brightness reversed. The complements of the colors and the reversal of the brightnesses will be seen.

Color mixing can be achieved by means of negative afterimages. If the afterimage is seen against a colored background, the resultant experience will be a mixture of the afterimage with that of the background color. If the background and the stimulus color are of the same hue, the color of the background will simply lose in saturation—that is, it will appear to fade out in the area occupied by the afterimage. If the saturation of the background and the afterimage could be properly equated, the afterimage would appear gray—representing a complete loss of saturation. If the background hue is complementary to the stimulus color, there will be an increase in saturation of the afterimage. If the stimulus and background colors are neither the same nor complements, the resultant hue will be intermediate between the color of the afterimage and the color of the background. The result of viewing an afterimage against a colored background can be predicted from the laws of color mixture. It must be kept in mind that it is the afterimage and not the stimulus color that is mixed with the hue of background. For example, the afterimage of blue is its complement, yellow. The yellow afterimage seen against yellow will simply increase the saturation of the yellow and not change its hue. The yellow afterimage seen against its complement, blue, will tend to cancel the background color, producing either a gray or an unsaturated blue, depending on the relative saturations of the afterimage and the background. In all these cases the brightness of the resultant visual experience will be intermediate between the brightness of the afterimage and that of the background, in accordance with the laws stated above.

Afterimages are also positive. They are not readily observable, but they are responsible for certain experiences with which we are all familiar. The experience of regular, smooth, continuous movement produced by the projection of a series of still pictures on a screen is made possible by the existence of the positive afterimage, or aftersensation. The positive afterimage is the persistence of the visual experience for a short interval after the removal of the stimulus. The activity in the retina acts as though it had an element of momentum so that it "coasts" a bit and continues to respond for a fraction of a second following the removal of the stimulus. Thus, if a second image is projected on the retina before the response to the previous stimulation has subsided (before the positive afterimage has disappeared), the visual effect is the same as that of continuous stimulation of the retina. The timing of successive projections in the motion picture is critical. If it is too slow, either individual still pictures or a flickering is experienced. Only when the interval between successive projections is less than the duration of the positive afterimage will fusion occur. Color mixing by means of a color wheel, as described in the previous section, depends on the existence of the positive afterimage.

Visual Perception of Distance

We indicated in Chapter 3 that perceptual size constancy was partially dependent on the perception of distance. At that time we related distance perception to the size of the retinal image. Yet there are many additional factors involved in visual perception of distance: linear perspective, aerial perspective, interposition, gradients of texture, differential lights and shadows, the brightness and saturation of colors, the position with respect to the horizon, apparent rate and direction of motion, retinal disparity, strains of accommodation, and strains of convergence.

Linear perspective refers to the apparent distant convergence of parallel lines. When a child draws the borders of a path, a road, or some railroad tracks parallel, as he knows them to be, they do not look right. Eventually he learns that parallel lines perceptually come closer and closer together as they move toward the horizon and at some point seem to come together. This phenomenon is a result of the diminishing size of the retinal image with increasing distance from the viewer.

Aerial perspective refers to cues of distance related to the atmosphere. The distinctness of visually perceived objects diminishes as their distance increases; the outline of distant objects is indistinct; distant objects appear hazy and slightly bluish. These effects are due to diffraction of light waves by the atmosphere and the presence of various particles in the air.

Interposition, as a cue to visual depth, refers to the fact that closer objects may be interposed between the viewer and more distant objects, obscuring the view of the more distant objects. The rancher who cannot tell whether the cow in the distant field is on the near or far side of the fence moves until a fence post is in line with the cow. If the fence post is still visible, he knows the cow is on the far side of the fence; if the cow obscures the sight of the post, it is on the near side.

Figure 4-6. Linear perspective of stacked lumber creates a strange view. Photo is from early lumbering days on the Pacific Coast.

Gradients of texture refer to the fact that the texture of a flat surface loses its distinctness with increasing distance from the viewer. The size of the retinal image of the individual components of the texture also decreases. Like linear perspective, this cue can be reduced to other factors—atmospheric conditions, aerial perspective, and the relative distinctness of lights, shadows, and outlines. The atmospheric conditions contributing to aerial perspective result in a decreasing distinctness of the variations producing the appearance of texture. If the texture is produced by particles of varying heights, the differential lights and shadows will be increasingly less obvious, and the size of the retinal images corresponding to the variations constituting the texture become smaller with greater distances.

The distinctness of *patterns of light and shade* becomes less obvious with increasing distance from the viewer. This change results from a combination of aerial-perceptive factors and variations in size of retinal images.

The *brightness of lights and saturation of colors* also affect the perception of distance. In general, lights lose in brightness and colors appear less saturated with increased distance from the viewer. A combination of apparent brightness and size of retinal image is responsible for an interesting illusion that can be produced in the laboratory. Two balloons are placed in fixed positions about a foot apart. Their relative sizes and brightnesses can be regulated by the experimenter. When the size and brightness of the balloons are the same, the observer sees two spheres of equal size and at equal distances from him. If the brightness of the two balloons remains constant and one is made larger, it will be seen as nearer. If the relative sizes of the two balloons are varied continuously, they appear to move nearer and farther through space. When size remains constant and the relative brightnesses of the balloons are systematically varied, they similarly seem to move nearer or farther away. Brightness and size can supplement each other and exaggerate the extent of illusory movement, or they can act in opposition to each other. Percepts are not photographic reproductions of "what is out there" but are more of the nature of the most reasonable or likely interpretation of "what is going on out there" based on past experience (Ittelson, 1960).

The position of an object with reference to the horizon also affects perceptual size. If a person sits in a dark room with three spots of light of equal size and brightness visible, one near the floor, one near eye level, and a third on the ceiling, they will appear to be at varying distances from the viewer when they are all equidistant from him. The light on the floor will appear to be the closest, the one on the ceiling the farthest away, and the one at eye level will appear to be at an intermediate distance. At the same time, and less clearly, the light on the ceiling will seem to be dimmer and smaller than the others. The one at eye level will seem to be intermediate in size and brightness, and the light on the floor will appear to be the brightest and largest.

Apparent rate and direction of movement occasionally provide visual cues to distance. When you are riding on a train, distant objects appear to move in the same direction that you are moving; those objects at intermediate distances appear to remain fixed in their relative positions; those nearest to you appear to move in a direction opposite to that of the train. When objects are moving at a constant rate, the apparent rate of motion decreases with increasing distance. The car whizzing past very close to us seems to be going much faster than one going at the same rate a mile away. When the rate of motion is known, the objects apparently moving faster are judged to be closer than comparable objects seen at a distance. Differential sizes of retinal images, as well as other factors, contribute to the apparent rate of motion as a cue to the perception of distance.

Retinal disparity and strains of convergence are *binocular* factors providing cues to the perception of distance. They depend on the functioning of the two eyes for their effectiveness, whereas those factors discussed previously operate monocularly. Retinal disparity refers to the difference in the images received by the two eyes due to the centers of the eyes being separated by approximately 2.4 inches. If one holds a book upright at arm's length with its spine toward the middle of his face, and if he first closes one eye and then the other, the book will seem to shift position because of the difference in the two images. If one looks closely, he will notice that when only the right eye is open, he can see the right but not the left side of the book. With only the left eye open, he sees only the left side of the book. When the book is viewed with both eyes open, he does not see two books. The two images fuse, with both sides of the book being seen simultaneously in perspective. If the object is moved closer to or farther from the eyes, the difference between the two images increases or decreases accordingly. The closer the object is to the eyes, the greater the retinal disparity. Thus as the disparity in the images produced on the retina increases, the closer the object is judged to be.

Three-dimensional still and motion pictures make use of the principle of retinal disparity. Pairs of pictures are used to produce 3-D effects. The pictures are taken with two lenses a short distance apart, analogous to two eyes. To achieve the 3-D effect when the two pictures are viewed, the picture taken by the lens on the right must be seen by the right eye, and the picture taken by the left

lens must be seen by the left eye. When this is done, the pictures fuse into a single image depth.

Strains of accommodation refer to the adjustment of the curvature of the lens of the eye according to its distance from the object. For near objects the ciliary muscle, which regulates the tension on the lens, contracts, which diminishes the tension on the lens and permits it to bulge (increase its curvature), due to its own elasticity. For far objects the ciliary muscle relaxes and the lens flattens. The kinesthetic receptors on the ciliary muscles register the degree of tension exerted by these muscles and provide a cue to the distance from the object fixated. Strains of accommodation are significant cues for near objects only. Beyond 5 or 6 feet accommodation is relatively unimportant.

Strains of convergence, like those of accommodation, are registered by the kinesthetic sense endings in the muscles that turn the eyes. Since the eyes are about 2½ inches apart, in order for both eyes to fixate on a given spot, the eyes must turn in toward each other as the spot moves closer to the eyes. As the point fixated moves farther from the viewer, the axes of the eyes become more parallel. Beyond 30 or 40 feet the axes of the eyes are nearly parallel, and strains of convergence become insignificant cues to distance. The available evidence indicates that strains of accommodation and convergence contribute relatively little, if any, to the perception of distance, retinal disparity being by far the dominant binocular factor (McDermott, 1969).

Although retinal disparity can greatly increase the third-dimension effect in pictures, as demonstrated by viewing the same pictures with and without a stereoscope (Viewmaster), monocular depth perception is quite accurate. Monocularization has been found to produce little behavioral disturbance in any animals, including predators whose lives depend on accurate distance perception (Walk, 1968). Chicks, ducklings, and rats respond to the visual-cliff situation monocularly, much as they do with binocular vision. Human infants of various ages are able to discriminate depth monocularly provided the discrimination is not too fine—that is, less than about 5 inches (Walk, 1968).

The Integration of Visual Cues

It should not be inferred from our discussion that the use of these various cues in perceiving the distance of an object is a matter of rational analysis by a viewer. The individual does not stop to say to himself that he observes (1) a certain distinctness of outline, (2) a convergence of parallel lines, (3) a given size of retinal image, (4) a gradient of texture, (5) patterns of light and shadow, (6) a disparity of the two visual images, and (7) a given degree of tension in the muscles of the eye. What really happens is that, as he perceives an object, he perceives it to be a certain distance away. Psychologists have attempted to parcel out the various components of the total perceptual experience in order to study them. But in experience they are *fused* with color, brightness, form, and other contextual and experiential factors that contribute to the total perceptual experience.

HEARING

The stimuli for hearing consist of waves in a material media, normally the air. Sound waves are composed of successive phases of condensation and rarefaction of the air molecules, caused by the pushes and pulls of a vibrating surface. Every sounding body sets up vibration patterns that are transmitted through the air to the ear. Liquids and solids, as well as the air, can conduct sound waves. When we click our teeth or chew celery, the sounds reach the inner ear by bone conduction, which makes them much more audible to us than they are to others. In fact, the vibrations set up in the air and conducted to the ear in normal hearing reach the receptor of the inner ear via the liquids of the cochlea. The cochlea is a snail-shaped structure in the inner ear that contains the auditory receptors. The inner ear consists of liquid-filled chambers. Bone conduction is also involved in hearing one's own voice. More of the low-frequency components are lost in air-conducted than in bone-conducted sounds. Consequently, one's own bone-conducted speech sounds much more powerful and dynamic than do the purer air-conducted sound waves heard by a second person or by the speaker himself via a recording. A recording of one's own voice often strikes the individual as thin and lacking in quality. We can hear our own voices as others hear them only via a recording. For this reason, listening to a recording of one's voice is commonly a part of speech-correction methods. People can more readily detect undesirable speech characteristics and small changes in quality from listening to successive recordings than by simply listening to themselves speak (von Békésy, 1960, 1966).

Liquids and some solids are more efficient conductors of sound than is the air. Sound travels about four times as fast in water as in air and much faster in solids than in either of these. Many a swimmer has experienced the terrific intensity of sounds produced when some practical joker knocks two rocks together underwater while the swimmer's head is immersed. Many hearing aids attach to the mastoid bones behind the ear and facilitate hearing by amplifying sounds and transmitting them to the inner ear by bone conduction. Although air is the dominant transmitting agent for normal hearing, the conduction of sound waves by both liquid and solids is quite common and has considerable practical significance.

Some Physical-Experiential Correlates

In hearing, as in vision, adequate stimuli can be represented as sinusoidal waves with three major dimensions that are primarily responsible for three corresponding experiential variables: pitch, loudness, and timbre.

1. The experiential variable largely determined by vibration frequency is *pitch*. The greater the vibration frequency, the higher the pitch. The range of the human voice and that of the piano are much shorter than the range of normal hearing. The average piano keyboard has a range of about 27 to 4200 cycles per second (cps). (A cycle is a double vibration.) The range of the human voice is about 50 to 10,000 cps.

2. *Loudness* is primarily dependent on wave amplitude. Thus loudness is analogous to brightness inasmuch as they are both related to wave amplitude. A tone of a given pitch can vary in loudness from barely audible to painfully loud. Zero on the decibel scale is usually the absolute threshold for hearing. Painfully loud sounds start at about 130 decibels. Normal conversation registers around 60, and a low whisper has a decibel value of about 10. In terms of the physical energy required to produce a barely audible tone, the ear is most sensitive in the frequency range of 2000 to 4000 cps. Higher and lower tones require much more physical energy to make them audible.

3. The *timbre*, or quality, of a tone is determined by the complexity of the sound wave. In some ways auditory quality is analogous to the saturation of colors, since both are determined primarily by the homogeneity or complexity of the vibration frequency. Just as colored light is seldom monochromatic and fully saturated, tones are seldom produced by a single frequency. Most vibrating bodies, such as violin strings, produce tones consisting of a fundamental tone, which results from the string vibrating as a whole, plus several overtones with frequencies that are multiples of the frequency of the fundamental. The overtones are additional vibrations of portions of the vibrating string. Pure tone can

be produced by electrically operated oscillators. The tones produced by tuning forks are also quite pure, but practically all musical instruments produce tones that are rich in overtones and thus have a characteristic timbre. A pure tone is not very "interesting" musically. Each type of musical instrument, as well as each individual instrument, has its own peculiar quality; this quality is determined by its own pattern of overtones, which are produced by its unique resonating properties.

It is possible to demonstrate the relationship between tone quality and vibration-frequency complexity by repeatedly playing the same note on three instruments, such as a violin, a piano, and a clarinet, when the instruments are all in perfect tune (vibration frequencies are the same) and with loudness equated (wave amplitudes are equalized) with more and more of the overtones filtered out with each repetition. The notes played on the three instruments sound more and more alike until, when only the fundamental tones are left, they sound identical.

The human ear is sensitive to vibration frequencies of from about 20 to 20,000 cps. There is considerable variation in the limits of hearing. Some people can hear at sound frequencies below 20 cps, and many cannot hear frequencies as high as 20,000. With increasing age the individual's sensitivity to the higher frequencies declines. One study found that people in their forties experienced a decline of about 160 cps per year in their upper limits of hearing for tones at a fixed level of intensity (von Békésy, 1960, 1966).

Fortunately, the frequencies up to 3000 cps are the most important for understanding speech. It is at the higher frequencies that hearing losses become most marked with advancing age and with the impairment due to exposure to loud noise. Because permanent hearing loss can result from repeated or continuous exposure to high noise levels, there is widespread concern about the noisy environment of modern man.

Many lower animals are sensitive to frequencies far beyond the range of human hearing. "Silent" whistles are available that produce sound frequencies beyond the human range but that are audible to dogs. Porpoises and cats can hear sounds ranging from 30 to 70,000 cps. Bats emit sounds in the 40,000–60,000-cps range and can hear sounds up to 100,000 cps (Marler, 1967). By means of echoes from such vibration frequencies, they are able to avoid objects in flight. The higher frequencies make the echolocation of objects very accurate. It has been shown that the echolocation abilities of blind humans depend largely on the higher frequencies.

In addition to the fundamental tone and the overtones mentioned above as present in most sounds, there are additional sources of tonal complexity, including *beats, difference tones,* and *summation tones.* If two tones differing in vibration frequency by only a few cps are sounded together, a single tone with periodic beats in it will be heard. The number of beats per second corresponds to the difference between frequencies of the two tones. For example, if one tone is 100 cps and the other is 102 cps, the single tone produced will wax and wane in intensity (beat) two times a second.

When the differences between the two tones sounding simultaneously are small, the number of beats is related to the difference between the vibration frequencies of the tones. As the difference between two tones is increased, the beats get faster. In an intermediate range of frequency (differing 6–20 cps), the individual beats are not recognizable, and only a roughness in the tone is heard. Finally, as the frequency difference between the two tones reaches and exceeds a certain critical point (usually 40–60 cps), the two tones are perceived as two; moreover, a third tone that corresponds in pitch to the difference in cps between the other two is heard. This third tone is a difference tone. Two tones of 1000 and 1100 cps, respectively, sounding together will produce a difference tone of 100 cps. In addition to beats and difference tones, sum-

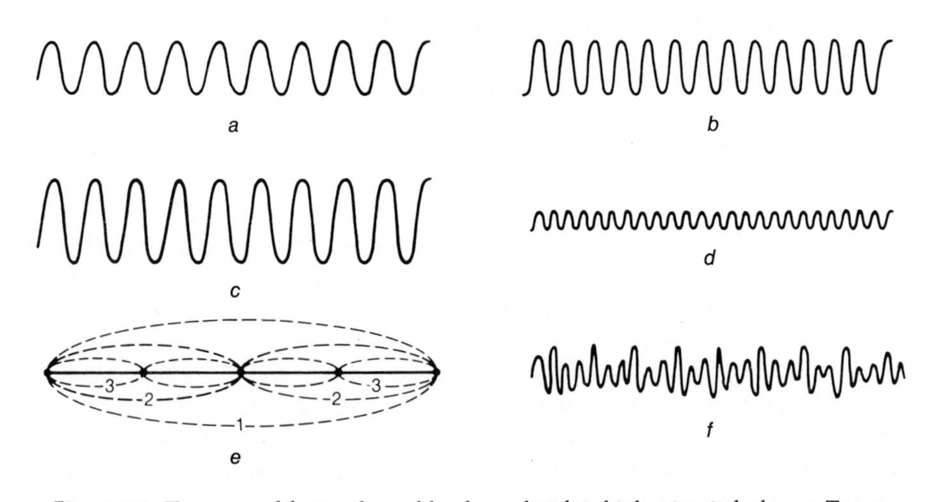

Figure 4-7. Tones *a* and *b* are of equal loudness, but *b* is higher in pitch than *a*. Tones *a* and *c* are of the same pitch, but *c* is louder than *a*. Tone *d* is higher in pitch than *a*, *b*, or *c* but is weaker. Sound wave *e* represents the vibration of (1) a string as a whole, producing a "fundamental tone," and (2) and (3), parts of the string that produce overtones, or "upper partials." Wave *f* is a diagrammatic representation of a complex human voice consisting of many individual components.

mation tones are also produced. The pitch of the summation tone is equal to that produced by a vibration frequency equal to the sum of the frequencies of the two primary tones. The summation tone produced by a 1000-cps and a 2000-cps tone sounding together will be 3000 cps. Summation tones are often hard to perceive, as they will often coincide in frequency with an overtone of the primary tone. Combination tones can become very complex, since they may correspond to all the sums and differences of the fundamental tones and the partial tones.

The Auditory Receptors

The ear has an outer, middle, and inner portion. The outer ear consists of the pinna, the part of the ear that is externally observable, and the ear canal, or external auditory meatus. The tympanic membrane, or eardrum, forms a partition between the outer and the middle ear. The middle ear consists of an air-filled chamber spanned by three tiny bones or ossicles, the malleus (hammer), incus (anvil), and stapes (stirrup). The middle ear connects with the throat through the eustachian tube, thus permitting air to reach the middle ear and equalize the pressure on each side of the tympanic membrane. When the air pressure is not equal on both sides of the tympanic membrane, the increase in tension interferes with its normal movements. If the pressure is extreme, it may become painful. Yawning and swallowing open the eustachian tube and admit air into or out of the middle ear. Thus chewing gum and yawning during sudden changes in elevation help ward off possible discomfort and temporary impairment of hearing.

The inner ear consists of two liquid-filled cavities. One of these, the cochlea, contains the receptors for hearing. The other subdivision of the inner ear consists of the semicircular canals (and related structures), which have to do with balance, not hearing. The cochlea is a snail-shaped, fluid-filled structure coiled around itself approximately two-and-a-half times. Projecting into the fluid from the side of the cochlea is a complex structure, the basilar membrane, containing hair cells that respond to vibrations in the fluids of the inner ear. The activity of the hair cells initiates impulses in the nerve endings, which discharge to the brain by way of the auditory nerve.

The relationship of these structures to each other will be clarified by tracing the connections between an auditory stimulus and the brain. Vibrations in the air between 20 and 20,000 cps are collected to a slight degree by the pinna and pass down the ear canal, where they strike the eardrum and cause it to vibrate in unison with the pattern of vibrations in the air. The pattern of vibrations of the eardrum is mechanically transmitted across the middle ear by the malleus, incus, and stapes, which are connected with each other and to the inner side of the eardrum and to the oval window. The oval window is an opening in the bony partition separating the middle and the inner ear. The opening is covered by a thin membrane (see Figure 4-8). The movements of the three ossicles are transmitted to the fluids of the inner ear via the membrane of the oval window, which forms part of the partition between the middle and the inner ear. The vibrations in the fluids of the inner ear (the cochlea) selectively activate the hair cells of the basilar membrane. The activity of these receptors, in turn, initiates nerve impulses that pass out along the auditory nerve and finally reach the auditory sensory center in the temporal lobe of the cortex. As a result, the person hears.

Auditory Theory

Theories of hearing have been concerned with the problem of how stimulation of the auditory receptors in the inner ear can produce the estimated 340,000 different pitches and intensities of pure tones that the average human is able to differentiate. Theories of hearing have been predominantly either place theories or frequency theories in terms of primary emphasis, although recent evidence suggests that some type of combination place-frequency conception may be most accurate.

Place theory. The place theory of hearing holds that pitch is the result of the stimulation of a given point or region of the basilar membrane. The evidence that there is a relationship between the functioning of given regions of the basilar membrane and the pitch of the resulting auditory experience is quite overwhelming. Electrical recordings show that the portion of the basilar membrane nearest the base of the cochlea responds maximally to high-frequency tones; the region near the apex of the basilar membrane responds to tones of low frequency; tones of intervening frequencies activate intermediate areas. Animals exposed over long periods to loud sounds of constant pitch become deaf to these frequencies. Examination of the basilar membranes of such animals after death shows degenerative changes in these structures. The location of the damaged areas is related systematically to the pitch of the stimulating tones. Portions of the basilar membrane have been destroyed by drilling through the cochlear wall. Good correlations have been obtained between the location of the lesions in the cochlea and changes in the threshold of stimula-

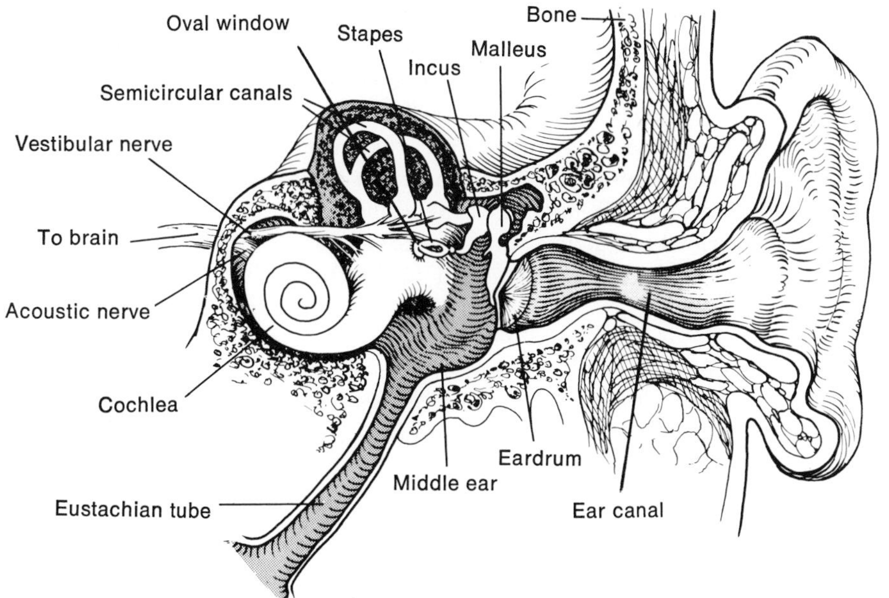

Figure 4-8. Cross section of a human ear.

tion with different vibration frequencies (Bredberg, Lindeman, Ader, & West, 1970). An occupational disorder known as "boilermaker's deafness" is the condition of individuals exposed to loud noises over long periods of time who have become deaf to tones of the same pitch as that of the noise. At autopsy, degenerative changes are found in localized regions of the basilar membrane. Postmortem examination of the internal ears of subjects experiencing high-tone deafness shows atrophy of either the basal part of the basilar membrane or of the nerves supplying this part of the cochlea (Best & Taylor, 1955).

In addition to the evidence just cited indicating a relationship of pitch to place of stimulation in the cochlea, the structure of the basilar membrane makes it admirably suited to function as an acoustic frequency analyzer. The basilar membrane is narrowest at the cochlear base, where the vibrations enter, and it is widest at the apex. The membrane also varies in mass and stiffness throughout its length, which makes it more selective in its responsiveness to differences in pitch.

The best available evidence indicates that the basilar membrane does not respond to acoustic stimulation by sympathetic vibrations like a series of simple resonators. Actually, when the ear is stimulated by a tone, a wavelike motion passes along the cochlea. This motion produces a bulge in the basilar membrane. At the basal end of the cochlea, where the basilar membrane is stiffest, the wave in the cochlea causes relatively little bulge in the basilar membrane. As it travels up the cochlea to points of greater flexibility in the basilar membrane, the bulge increases. Thereafter the energy of the wave is dissipated and it rapidly dies out. The exact pattern and extent of travel of the wave depend on the frequency of the acoustic stimulus. It is this difference in travel for various frequencies that enables the basilar membrane to function as a frequency analyzer; this function forms the basis, at least in part, for pitch perception.

The mechanisms responsible for differences in loudness have been less completely worked out. However, loudness is apparently correlated with the total amount of basilar membrane activity produced by tonal stimulation.

Frequency, or telephone, theory. The frequency theory assumes that the ear operates much like the telephone. When you speak into the telephone, the vibrations of your speech activate the telephone diaphragm to vibrate with the same frequencies as those contained in your voice. These vibrations are then converted into electrical impulses, which are transmitted at the same frequencies as those contained in your speech. Thus the electrical impulses reflect the frequency patterns of the original sound. In a similar fashion, a tone of 1000 cps striking the ear sets up neural impulses of 1000 cps in the auditory nerve that transmits them to the brain.

We know that a nerve fiber cannot transmit more than about 1000 nerve impulses per second. The frequency theory has difficulty in explaining the fact that we can hear tones with frequencies 20 times this high. This problem has been met by assuming that above a certain frequency neurons operate in "squads," which are synchronized to produce volleys of impulses that exceed the rate of firing of the individual neurons. In this way the frequency theory, plus the hypothesis of nerve fibers functioning in squads on the volley principle, might explain neural transmission at a rate beyond the capability of any individual neuron (Marsh, Worden, & Smith, 1970).

A place-frequency theory. It is known that impulses in the individual fibers of the auditory nerve follow the frequency of an acoustic stimulus up to about 1000 cps and then, by volleying, keep up reasonably well to about 4000 cps. (Volleying means that individual nerve fibers skip some cycles of the stimulus and respond to every second or third vibration cycle. No one fiber follows the stimulus cycles, but together they do so by staggering their responses). At higher frequencies such following breaks down. Thus the frequency principle seems to account for pitch perception at the lower but not at the higher frequencies. On the other hand, the cochlear-bulge conception of the place theory seems to account for the analysis of high tones much better than it does for low tones. At the low frequencies more and more of the basilar membrane is stimulated, until, below a certain point, virtually all of the membrane is activated. Yet the human ear can distinguish such tones. The areas of excitation produced by high frequencies are much more limited and differentiated. The difficulties encountered by both the frequency and place theories have led to the discard of both in their pure form in favor of some type of combination place-frequency, or duplex, theory (Morgan, 1965). At low frequencies, where auditory-nerve-impulse frequency follows the stimulus frequency quite accurately, the frequency explanation seems to be adequate. At the higher frequencies, where activity in the auditory nerve fails to reflect pitch in terms of impulse frequency, a place theory of the "traveling-bulge" type is generally accepted.

The Neural Processing of Auditory Input

Tone frequency is represented in a spatial manner at all levels within the auditory system, all the way from the basilar membrane to the auditory area of the cerebral cortex. In other words, there is a topographic arrangement of nerve cells at all levels from the cochlea to the cerebral cortex, and these cells are tuned to a limited range of frequencies. At progressively higher levels within the auditory neural system the tuning becomes increasingly sharp—that is, the range of frequencies to which a given cell responds becomes increasingly narrow. The coding of auditory intensity also involves some topographical elements. As the intensity of a tone increases, the range of frequencies exciting a given cell broadens. Some cells have "best intensities" as well as "best frequencies." They cease firing at intensity levels either below or above certain critical points (Rose, Greenwood, Goldberg, & Hind, 1963).

Auditory perception of distance. Auditory, compared with visual, perception of distance is poor. There is also a relatively small number of sensory cues involved. The most obvious cue is the intensity of sound: relative intensity can serve as a cue to the distance of familiar sounds. Accordingly, a band leader can produce the illusion of the band's marching away from the listener if he has the orchestra first play very loud and then gradually decrease in intensity until it can barely be heard.

At best, auditory perception of distance is poor. It is almost impossible to perceive the distance of a relatively pure, unfamiliar tone. (The purer the tone, the less the quality of sound will vary with the distance.) When there is a conflict between the auditory and visual cues to the source of a sound, the visual usually predominate, as one finds at a drive-in movie.

Auditory perception of direction. Auditory perception of the direction of sound is more complex and more accurate than is auditory perception of distance. A simple demonstration will show that the essential prerequisite to the auditory perception of the direction of sound is the differential stimulation of the two ears. If a blindfolded person is seated in the center of a room and a sound is produced from a constant distance but from varying directions, he can judge the direction quite accurately except when the source of the sound is in the median plane of his body. That is, if the source of the sound is straight ahead or behind, he is totally unable to judge its direction. As soon as the source of the sound is moved to the right or to the left of the median plane, the individual can correctly identify its direction.

If a tube is inserted into each ear canal and then run up over the head and connected with a trumpet-shaped artificial pinna (outer ear), the sound normally picked up by each ear will be heard by the other. When wearing such an apparatus with the eyes closed, a person hears a sound from the left as coming from the right, and vice versa. A blindfolded person wearing such an apparatus will attempt to avoid someone whose footsteps seem about to pass him on the right by stepping into the path of the person. One subject wore such a device for 18 days, and the confusion persisted the entire time (Young, 1928). The principal effect of wearing the pseudophone, as the experimenter called it, was to increase the dominance of the visual cues when vision and hearing were both operating. At first there was a tendency to make double localizations, the correct one being visually cued and the false one produced by the transposed auditory cues. From the first, the visual cues tended to dominate, and, as the experiment progressed, the auditory cues came to be more and more neglected. It seems clear that differential stimulation of the two ears is necessary for auditory perception of the direction of sound. It has been shown that the sound waves striking the two ears can differ in amplitude (loudness), in purity (quality), in phase (rarefaction or condensation), and in time of arrival at the two ears (the sound strikes the closer ear first). The difference in intensity of sound as heard in the two ears is produced principally because of their differing distances from the sound source. Since one ear is, at most, only a few inches farther from the sound source than the other, the difference in intensity in the two ears is very small. The closer the source of the sound, the greater the difference will be. The differential intensities in the two ears when the source of sound is as far as a hundred feet are probably indistinguishable.

Differences in quality of sounds heard in the two ears are probably more important than are intensity differences. The head produces a "sound shadow" on the side opposite that of the source of the sound. The shadow effect of the head increases with the shortness of the wavelength of the sound component. Thus the fundamental and low-frequency components of a complex tone will be heard more by the farther ear than will the high-frequency upper components. As a result, a sound coming from one side of the head will be richer in quality on the closer ear. This difference in the quality of the sound as received in the two ears operates as a cue to direction. The sound shadow provided by the head may reduce the intensity as well.

Phase difference refers to the fact that the sound waves may arrive at one ear in condensation and at the other in rarefaction. There has been considerable experimental work and theoretical discussion on the reality of phase difference as an auditory cue. The consensus seems to be that phase differences somehow do function in the auditory perception of the direction of the source of sounds.

Time differences in reception of the onset and the termination of interrupted tones may also be cues to the direction of sound. The onset and termination of a sound will affect the closer ear before they affect the farther ear.

As in the visual perception of distance, the listener does not stop to analyze how he locates a given sound. He just hears the sound as coming from a certain direction and distance as a part of the total auditory percept. Even though the subject is not aware of the relevant cues and, by careful analysis of his own experience, is unable to become aware of them, experimental manipulation of the various factors demonstrates their importance. Without these differential cues, the listener is helpless in localizing sounds.

THE CUTANEOUS SENSES

The traditional sense of touch is not one but four senses—cold, warmth, pressure, and pain. If one takes a metal stylus that is cooled below a critical point and systematically explores an area of the skin, he can make a map of the places where a person feels a cold sensation. Then, with a stylus heated to above skin temperature, the same skin area can be remapped, locating the points at which the subject feels warmth. The two maps thus obtained are not the same. Different spots in the skin mediate cold and warmth experiences. The same is true for pain and light pressure (touch). It seems that different spots in the skin respond to distinctive stimuli and mediate four different qualities of cutaneous experience.

If there are four different qualities of cutaneous experience, it seems logical to expect that there are four corresponding types of receptors in the skin. After a great deal of investigative effort, this idea has been rejected. Quite a variety of sense endings have been identified in the skin: free nerve endings not associated with any specialized sensory cells, hair follicles served by nerve endings, and various types of more elaborate encapsulated end organs.

Some correlations have been found between the relative sensitivity of different skin areas and the regional distribution of different types of end organs. However, microscopic examination of the portion of the skin where the subject experiences a given type of sensation fails to identify distinctive types of sense endings uniformly associated with the four cutaneous sensory experiences. The results of biopsies have shown that free nerve endings may mediate any cutaneous sensory quality and that, with certain exceptions, one cannot tell the type of receptor by its structure. It seems clear that free nerve endings can serve as receptors for all four cutaneous sensations and that encapsulated end organs are sometimes the receptors for cold and for warmth. Apparently certain encapsulated end organs may mediate pressure sensations, whereas pain is mediated by no organs other than free nerve endings. Thus researchers have had to look for more complex mechanisms than a simple direct relationship between four sensory experiences and four types of receptors.

Thermal Sensitivity

To define adequate stimuli for the thermal senses (coldness and warmth), it is necessary to invoke the concept of the "physiological zero." Physiological zero is that temperature for which the skin is adapted at a given time; it is neither cold nor warm but neutral. Temperatures above physiological zero stimulate the sense endings for warmth, and temperatures below physiological zero stimulate the cold receptors. As is true of all the senses, the extent and rapidity of change must exceed a critical point (threshold) to operate as a stimulus. Physiological zero is not a fixed value but depends on the previous conditions of stimulation. A simple demonstration will show the meaning and significance of this concept.

The right hand is placed in a vessel of water that is definitely warm (above a particular physiological zero), and the left hand is placed in a similar vessel of water that is decidedly cold (below the physiological zero). Both hands are kept in the water for some time. The temperature of the water is kept constant. Under these conditions the apparent temperatures of the two vessels of water will shift toward neutrality. If the temperatures are not too extreme, and the hands are kept immersed sufficiently long, adaptation will become complete and neither temperature will be experienced. If both hands are then placed in water that is at a temperature intermediate between those of the two original vessels, the new temperature will feel cold to the right hand and warm to the left hand. The physiological zero of the right hand has been shifted upward, and that of the left hand has shifted down. The new, intermediate temperature activates the cold receptors in the one hand and the warmth receptors in the other.

Paradoxical thermal sensations. Although adequate stimuli for cold and warmth cutaneous receptors are temperatures that are respectively below and above the physiological zero of the body, some cold receptors will respond to stimuli *above* this point, and some warm sense endings will respond to temperatures *below* the physiological zero. Thermal experiences thus evoked are called paradoxical. This phenomenon is not really paradoxical, for it is in keeping with the law of specific nerve energies, discussed earlier. The response of the cold receptor to a stimulus above the physiological zero of the body results in a cold sensation in accordance with this law. Similarly, the warm sensation produced by the stimulation of a warmth receptor by a cold stimulus is in keeping with this law.

Paradoxical cold and warm sensations are examples of the cross-sensory effects found in a variety of senses. Both forms of thermal sensitivity interact, and this interaction can occur at various levels within the system (Hartley, 1969, p. 339; Wall, 1960; Granit, 1955, p. 53).

"Hot" and "biting cold" involve *a combination of elementary cutaneous sensations.* Hot is apparently a combination of either warmth and pain or warmth, paradoxical cold, and pain. As the temperatures stimulating the skin increase with the hot area, the pain element predominates more and more. Biting cold apparently stems from combinations of either cold and pain or cold, paradoxical warmth, and pain. With increasingly lower temperatures, short of freezing the tissues, the pain element increases. Very intense cold and hot, in both of which pain is predominant, may be momentarily confused when the subject is ignorant of the source of the stimulation. Figure 4-9 may help clarify these relationships.

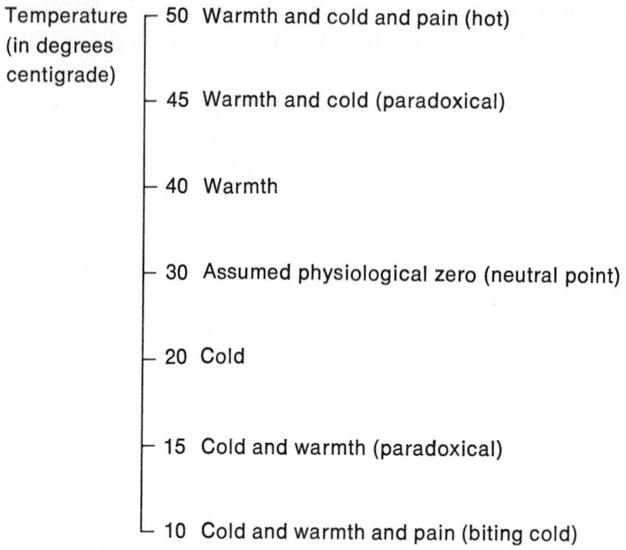

Temperature (in degrees centigrade)

- 50 Warmth and cold and pain (hot)
- 45 Warmth and cold (paradoxical)
- 40 Warmth
- 30 Assumed physiological zero (neutral point)
- 20 Cold
- 15 Cold and warmth (paradoxical)
- 10 Cold and warmth and pain (biting cold)

Figure 4-9. Diagram relating thermal sensations to temperatures. The placement of the various thresholds of sensation on this scale is arbitrary.

Many thermal experiences involve touch and deep pressure in addition to cold, warmth, and pain. For example, a strong, cold wind blowing against one's face will stimulate the cold, warmth, pain, and touch receptors and, if the pressure is great enough, the kinesthetic sense endings located in the muscles, tendons, and joint surfaces.

The number of thermal "spots" found in the skin will vary with the temperature of the stimulus relative to physiological zero, the duration of the stimulus, the size of the stimulator tip, and the concomitant mechanical pressure. However, with these variables held constant, the number of cold and warm spots found varies considerably in different parts of the body. The number of cold spots per square centimeter may vary from 19 on the upper lip to 2 or 3 on the sole of the foot. The range for the warmth spots is from 2 to 0.2 (Geldard, 1953). These values indicate the relatively small number of warm, as compared with cold, receptors.

Touch, or Light Pressure

Inequalities of pressure, or pressure gradients, seem to be the essential factor in stimulation of touch receptors. Unequal pressure causes deformation of the skin surface, and this deformation seems to be needed to stimulate these sense endings. When pressure is uniformly distributed on the skin, no deformation occurs and no touch sensation is experienced. If a finger is put into a beaker of mercury and held there, a touch sensation is experienced only at the surface of the mercury, where the skin is deformed as a result of the unequal pressures above and below this boundary. If a person stands perfectly still in quiet, tepid water, he is aware of a contact ring around his body at the surface of the water. He is not aware of the much greater uniform pressure on the skin below the surface. Of course, when uniform pressures become sufficiently intense, pain, kinesthetic, and possibly other sensations register the pressures.

A sense ending for touch is located at the base of the hairs on the body. A slight bending of the hair is sufficient to stimulate the receptor at its base and produce a contact experience. If the surface of the skin around the hair follicle is viewed under a magnifying glass when the hair is bent or moved, the skin will be seen to be deformed there also.

The sensitivity of the skin to touch varies widely in different regions of the body. The minimal pressure required to elicit a sensation of touch ranges from 2 grams per square millimeter on the lips and fingertips to between 25 and 30 grams on the abdomen and the sole of the foot. "Local sign," the recognition of the body location of the point stimulated, varies in accuracy in the various parts of the body, as does the "two-point" threshold, which is the minimal distance that must separate two stimulated points for them to be sensed as two. The two-point threshold varies from about 2 millimeters on the tip of the tongue, the lips, and the fingertips to between 50 and 60 millimeters on the middle of the back and on the thigh. Cutaneous sensitivity and the accuracy of local sign are highest—and the size of the two-point threshold is smallest—in the parts of the body that are the most differentially mobile. The tongue, lips, and fingers contain a large number of small muscles and therefore can make a great many finely differentiated responses. The thigh and the back, on the other hand, have a relatively small number of large muscles and are capable of executing only a small number of gross movements. These latter parts of the body are relatively insensitive to cutaneous stimulation and have poor local-sign thresholds and very large two-point thresholds. There are many more pressure spots than either cold or warm spots on the surface of the body.

Pain Sensitivity

Compared with the other cutaneous receptors, the sense endings for pain are the least selective. They respond to a wide variety of chemical, thermal, and mechanical stimuli. Sufficiently intense stimuli of almost any kind will evoke pain. The pain thus produced is the result of excessively intense sound-, pressure-, or temperature-stimulating pain receptors. This relationship can be demonstrated by severing the nerve tracts carrying the pain impulses from a given area. Pressures and thermal stimuli above the level sufficient to arouse pain prior to the operation no longer evoke pain, although they still evoke thermal and tactile sensations.

All painful stimuli seem to have one thing in common—namely, they injure or tend to injure body tissue. However, all the agents that injure tissue do not evoke pain. X-ray and ultraviolet radiation, as well as some other agents, can make one ill, seriously injure tissue, and even kill a person without arousing pain directly.

Pain-arousing stimuli often evoke reflex responses that serve to withdraw the body part from the noxious stimulus. Such reflexes have considerable prepotency over other types of reflex activities. Most parts of the body are freely supplied with pain receptors. A few special structures such as tooth pulp and the lining of some of the blood vessels contain no receptors except pain, whereas the brain itself and a small part of the skin on the inside of the cheek opposite the second lower molar tooth are insensitive to pain in most people. A few individuals are congenitally insensitive to pain. Some of them have been found to be either neurologically damaged or severely mentally retarded. However, a few cases are otherwise normal but apparently lack sensitivity to pain (Sternbach, 1963).

KINESTHETIC SENSITIVITY

In addition to registering the position, direction, and extent of movement, the kinesthetic receptors are involved in the maintenance of normal muscular tone and body posture. Kinesthetic sensitivity has been studied relatively little. Kinesthetic receptors are not readily accessible, their stimuli are difficult to control, and they function largely without awareness. The average person becomes aware of the existence and importance of kinesthetic receptors only if he suffers their loss or serious disturbance. In a disorder known as locomotor ataxia, there occurs a progressive degeneration of the sensory nerve tracts carrying kinesthetic nerve impulses in the spinal cord. The resulting symptoms include loss of one's sense of the direction and extent of movements of the body parts involved.

The kinesthetic sense endings are located in the muscle spindles, the tendons, and the joint surfaces. They are stimulated by any change in tension on these respective body parts. These changes in tensions are normally produced by muscular contractions, which means that every muscular contraction and every tension change in the muscle are not only responses but also serve as stimuli to activate the kinesthetic sense endings in the muscle and its related tendons and joints. The kinesthetic sense is also known as the motor sense and as the sense of movement. One differentiating characteristic of kinesthetic functioning is its slow rate of adaptation, which has an obvious utility in the maintenance of bodily posture and muscular tone.

Neural Coding

The coding of cutaneous and kinesthetic impulses seems to involve spatial representation, nerve-impulse frequency, and cell specificity. There is a spatial representation of the body surface from which these impulses originate at all levels, from the periphery to the cerebral cortex. This representation is in terms of body area rather than sense modality (cutaneous vs. kinesthetic). Nerve-impulse frequency is related to stimulus intensity. There is also some cell specificity related to sense modality. In the thalamus (an intermediate nerve center), nerve cells have been isolated that respond only to skin stimulation, deep pressure, or joint movements. Some cells respond to both mechanical and painful stimuli, and others respond only to one of these stimuli (Thompson, 1967).

LABYRINTHINE SENSITIVITY— THE SENSE OF BALANCE

The receptors involved in kinesthetic sense and in the sense of balance, or the labyrinthine sense, are grouped together as proprioceptors. The two senses are alike in that they are both stimulated by the action of the body itself. In contrast to the intermittent action of the exteroceptors, proprioceptive stimulation is continually active, guiding every body movement. One is seldom aware of the function of either the kinesthetic or the labyrinthine sense.

The labyrinthine sense takes its name from its location within the membranous chambers of the ear: the cochlea, the vestibule with its two subdivisions, the semicircular canals, the utricle, and the saccule. (The cochlear division is concerned with hearing and has already been discussed. We are now concerned with the nonauditory parts of the inner ear.) The semicircular canals consist of three looped semicircular structures lying in three perpendicular planes (like the walls that meet in the corner of a room). They are known as the anterior, posterior, and horizontal canals. One end of each of the three semicircular canals is expanded to form an ampulla, which contains specific receptors. The saccule and the utricle contain receptors similar to those found in the ampulla of the semicircular canals. The entire labyrinth is filled with fluid. The receptors in the semicircular canals and in the utricle and saccule are stimulated by changes in rate of movement of the head and by gravitational forces. These receptors are hair cells. The utricle and saccule contain a gelatinous mass and small bonelike particles called otoliths, which move under the influence of rotational, linear, or gravitational forces and thus act on the hair cells.

A demonstration and an analogy will provide a simplified version of what is involved in the functioning of these sense organs. Imagine a person sitting in a chair that can be rotated in a controlled fashion something like a barber's chair. The subject is blindfolded and required to keep his head still. He then is told that he will be rotated in either a clockwise or counterclockwise direction and will be asked to report periodically on whether or not he is moving and, if so, in which direction. If we start rotating the person clockwise, he will indicate correctly that he is being rotated. As long as the rate of rotation is being accelerated, the person is able to report movement and the direction correctly.

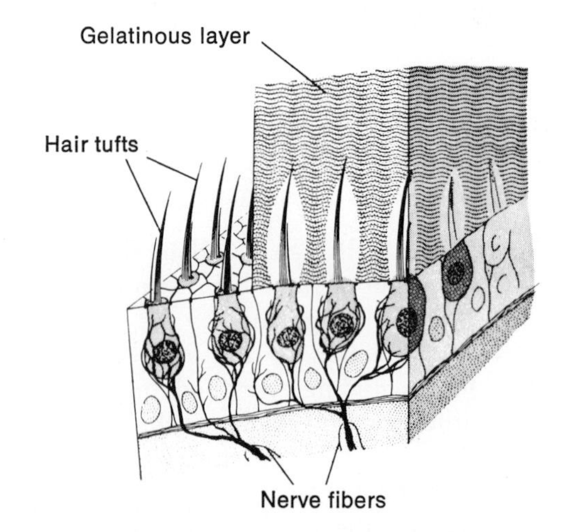

Figure 4-10. Labyrinthine receptors are hair cells that are responsive to mechanical stimuli arising from rotational, linear, or gravitational forces.

However, if we rotate the individual at a constant rate for some time, he will eventually report that he is no longer moving. So long as he does not receive other cues, he will insist that he is still. If the rate of rotation is then slowed, he will report that he is starting to rotate again but in a counterclockwise direction. He will continue to perceive rotation in the counterclockwise direction as long as the deceleration continues.

Analogous experiences can be obtained from riding in a very smooth-running, windowless elevator. A person in the elevator is aware of the movement at the start, but, as long as the rate of ascent or descent remains constant, he is not sure whether or not he is moving. He only becomes aware of movement again when the elevator slows up preparatory to stopping.

These examples indicate that the effective stimulation of the vestibular sense is not movement as such but rather *changes in rate or direction of movement.* Changes in rate of movement stimulate the hair cells in the semicircular canals, utricle, and saccule and mediate nerve impulses that provide information concerning changes in orientation of the body in space. These changes also produce a series of reflex adjustments of head and body movements designed to maintain one's balance and equilibrium. There is evidence that some of the vestibular receptors constitute static receptors that function continuously, presumably in response to the effect of gravity, and provide continuous information concerning one's orientation in space (Morgan, 1965). These labyrinthine static receptors, like the kinesthetic sense endings, adapt very slowly.

Undoubtedly much of the disorientation that astronauts experience in space flights is due to the absence of normal orienting cues from the vestibular system. Motion sickness is caused primarily, but not solely, by excessive stimulation of the semicircular canals. Many individuals who are deaf because of destruction of the auditory nerve also suffer loss of the vestibular sense. Such people are quite deficient in maintaining balance. When they attempt to stand perfectly still, they sway excessively. With the eyes closed, they may sway so much that they seem almost on the verge of falling before they right themselves. Deaf children with vestibular impairment have to be especially careful when riding on devices such as rapidly rotating merry-go-rounds, as they do not make the normal reflex responses involved in leaning inward to compensate for the centrifugal force of their circular motion that tends to throw them off. In diving, they also become more easily disoriented than are comparable individuals with intact vestibular sense; when they are underwater, they cannot tell which direction is up and which is down.

Experimenters and observers have found it very difficult to isolate the functions of the vestibular sense from those of several other senses that are also involved in the maintenance of balance and equilibrium and in maintaining one's orientation in space. For example, in such a relatively simple process as maintaining the upright posture while standing still, vestibular, visual, kinesthetic, and cutaneous sensory cues may all be involved. When functioning normally, the vestibular mechanisms are capable of registering bodily or head angular movements as small as 0.12° per second (Kimble & Garmezy, 1963). Without vestibular cues, body or head movements must be much larger to be perceptible or to initiate compensatory motor adjustments. However, when a person is trying to maintain a stationary stance, and his visual field begins to move, he "knows" that his head or body is moving and makes appropriate compensatory movements to keep the visual field stationary. When head and body movements exceed the threshold of the kinesthetic senses, body sway and head movements are registered in terms of changes in tension on the muscles, tendons, and joints. Finally, with increasing body sway or head movement, changes in cutaneous stimulation from contact with one's clothing provide additional cues. Many interesting and important illusions of position and movement result from unusual combinations of vestibular, cutaneous, and visual cues (Clark & Graybiel, 1966).

TASTE

The receptors for taste are specialized epithelial cells grouped together to form the taste buds, located principally in the sides of the papillae (projections) on the tongue. In the fetus and in young children, the taste buds are found on the inner surface of the cheek, on the soft palate in the roof of the mouth, and in the pharynx and larynx, as well as in the tongue. As the individual gets older, the distribution of the taste buds becomes more restricted, the number of functional taste buds per square area declines, and the threshold for gustatory stimulation regularly increases. These changes in the distribution, number, and sensitivity of the taste buds undoubtedly are partially responsible for the loss of appetite and changes in food preferences that often occur in old age.

Each taste bud is an onion-shaped structure consisting of a number of taste cells clustered together. At the upper end of each cell is a slender hairlike process. These processes from all the individual taste cells making up a taste bud come close together and are contained in a slight depression in the skin on the tongue surface.

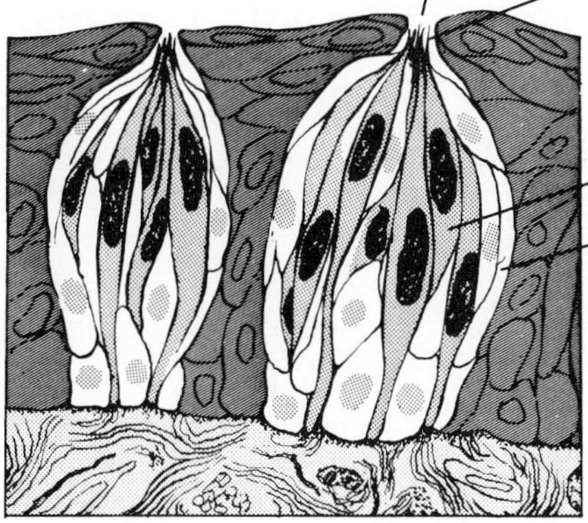

Figure 4-11. Cross section of taste buds.

Adequate stimuli for taste consist of substances in solution. Perfectly dry substances are incapable of acting as stimuli. If the surface of the tongue is wiped perfectly dry, and dry sugar is placed on it, no sensation is produced until saliva or a drop of water dissolves some of the sugar. Although the taste of a substance is probably related to its chemical makeup, no complete pattern of such relationships has yet been worked out.

On the basis of subjective judgments and rather limited objective experimental evidence, it is generally assumed that there are four fundamental taste qualities: salty, sweet, sour, and bitter. (See Morgan, 1965, p. 112 for a discussion of this evidence.) The many taste differentiations presumably result from combinations of these four qualities at varying intensities, together with additional olfactory, cutaneous, and kinesthetic components. However, the relationship between these fundamental taste qualities and their effective stimuli is still unclear. Evidence from neurological studies indicates that the activity of a variety of receptor surfaces and/or nerve cells may be involved in producing each of these individual taste qualities.

The most uniform relationship between chemical composition of the stimulus and taste quality is for sour. The hydrogen ion of acids so regularly elicits sour that there seems to be little question about its importance. However, the fact that relative sourness is not always related to hydrogen-ion concentration and the additional fact that not all acids are sour indicate that factors other than acidity (as indicated by hydrogen-ion concentration) are also involved.

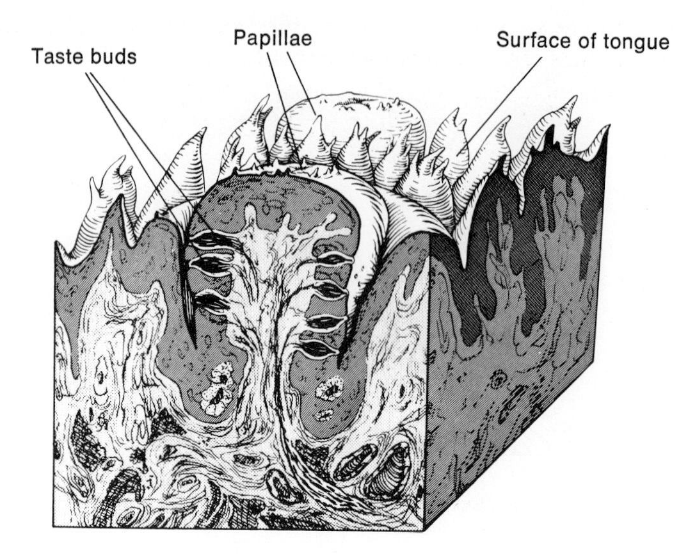

Figure 4-12. Cross section of a papilla on the tongue, showing the location of taste buds.

A typical salt is common table salt (NaCl). Although most of the salty-tasting substances are halogens (chlorine, iodine, bromine), many nitrates and sulphates that are chemically quite different also evoke a salty taste.

Bitterness is most commonly evoked by chemical substances known as alkaloids, but many substances chemically unrelated to the alkaloids are also bitter. A similar statement applies to sweet—most, but not all, of the substances designated as sugars by chemical makeup are sweet, but several substances, such as saccharine, are chemically unrelated to the sugars but are also sweet.

The search for specific receptor cells that mediate each of the four elementary taste qualities has failed to disclose any simple one-to-one relationship. Studies of the relationship between stimuli for taste qualities and sense endings have involved the recording of the electrical responses produced in individual nerve fibers when a series of stimuli adequate for evoking the four taste qualities is applied to the receptors under study. Such studies show that individual receptors have different sensitivities to different stimuli and that the relationship between sensory structures and the four sense qualities is not simple (Pfaffmann, 1959). It seems that a sensory quality must depend on the *pattern of activity* in sets of nerve fibers, rather than on the activity of a single unique type of receptor or nerve fiber. For example, one study recorded impulses from nine different taste fibers that were stimulated by five standard taste solutions. Only two of the nine fibers were in any sense selective. Some fibers responded to more than one type of stimulus but were more sensitive to one than to the others. Some fibers responded about equally to several of the solutions (Pfaffmann, 1959). The coding of taste quality seems to be rather complex even at the receptor level (Frank & Pfaffmann, 1969). One area of the thalamus responds quite exclusively to taste stimulation, but some other "taste" cells also respond to tactile stimulation. This finding may be of some significance, since most taste substances also provide tactile stimulation. The location of the cortical projection area for taste is uncertain, and it has been suggested that the nerve tracts for taste may terminate subcortically (Thompson, 1967, p. 280).

The different areas of the tongue are differentially sensitive to the four taste qualities. The tip of the tongue is particularly sensitive to sweet, the rear to bitter, and the sides to sour. The entire tongue surface seems to be about equally sensitive to salt.

About 30 percent of the population cannot taste phenylthiocarbamide (PTC), a substance that tastes bitter to most people. This "taste blindness" seems to follow the Mendelian ratio of a simple recessive hereditary factor. The disability is specific for PTC and a few closely related substances and does not extend to other bitter substances.

Most tastes experienced in the normal process of eating are really a fusion of gustatory qualities with experiences from several other sense modalities. Olfac-

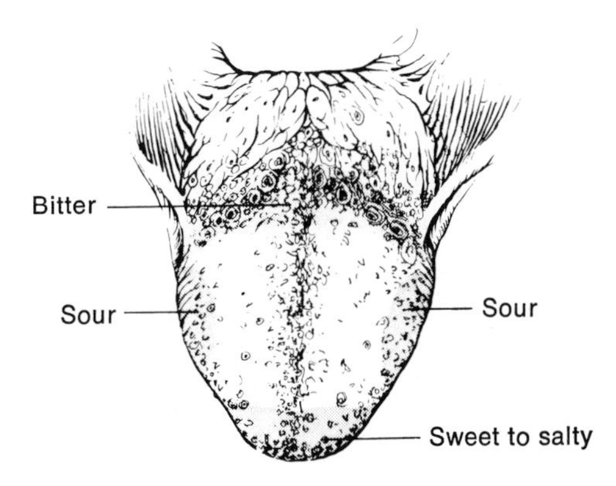

Figure 4-13. Sensitivity to taste qualities, as mapped on the tongue.

tion contributes considerably to most "tastes." Those foods that you cannot taste when you have a cold never are tasted in a strict sense—cold inflames and covers the olfactory area of the nose with a thick mucus that prevents one from smelling. The nasal congestion of a cold does not affect gustation as such. However, the loss of the olfactory component is experienced as a deficiency of taste. In addition to a relatively small gustatory component, the "taste" of vanilla ice cream consists of the sweet taste of sugar, odor from the vanilla flavoring, the sensation of cold, and the awareness of texture. We tend to lump all these elements together as taste.

OLFACTION

The receptors for smell are bipolar cells in the olfactory area of the nose. The olfactory area, which is about the size of a dime, is situated in the upper part of the nasal passages, somewhat above the direct pathway between the nostrils and the pharynx. A vigorous sniff forces inspired air toward the olfactory membrane and increases the intensity of stimulation. Adaptation to most odors takes place quite rapidly.

The whole olfactory area is covered with mucus. Because the receptors, which are hair cells, are covered with mucus, it seems that the odorous substances must be in solution to stimulate the olfactory receptors. Moducules of gas of an odorous substance in solution seem to constitute adequate stimuli for the olfactory sense endings.

No satisfactory classification of elementary olfactory sensory qualities has yet appeared. The number of classes proposed has ranged from four to nine, but no meaningful relationship between chemical makeup of adequate stimuli and olfactory sensory quality has been worked out.

Some individuals are completely anosmic—they can smell nothing. Partial anosmia, or smell blindness for certain substances, has been reported. Smell blindness, like taste blindness, is rather specific for a small number of substances. Because the nasal and mouth cavities communicate with each other, gases released in the mouth in the act of eating readily diffuse into the nose and stimulate the olfactory receptors. This process produces the intimate fusion of taste and smell previously mentioned.

The neural coding of olfactory impulses seems to be similar to that of taste. If stimulation is sufficiently intense, each olfactory nerve cell responds to

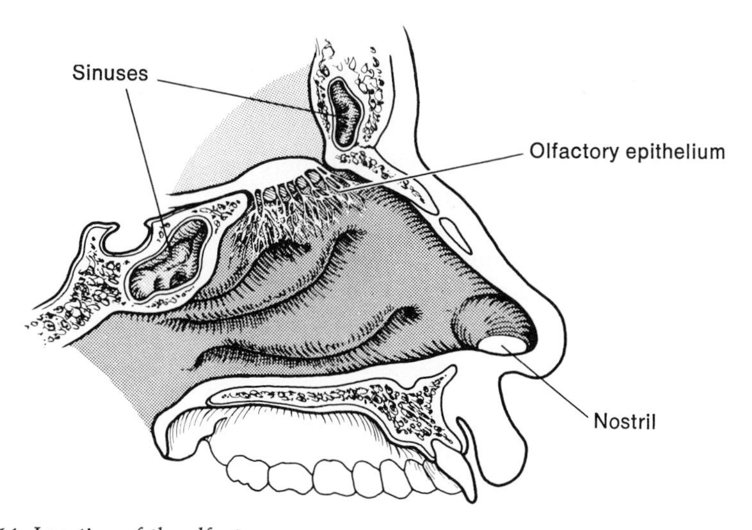

Figure 4-14. Location of the olfactory area.

almost any kind of olfactory stimulation. When the stimuli are near threshold level, units often respond to only one class of stimulus. Nerve impulses from olfactory receptors go to several structures in the brain. However, the course of the main sensory tract is uncertain, as is the location of the cortical projection area (Morgan, 1965).

THE ORGANIC SENSES

Gustation, olfaction, and the organic sense are classed as interoceptive senses because they are all found in the internal portions of the body. Embryologically, the nose and mouth are parts of the primitive gut from which the gastrointestinal system and its related structures are derived. The nose and mouth are therefore considered to be internal parts of the body.

The organic sense is an ill-defined, miscellaneous group of receptors in the viscera of the body. These receptors provide an organism with some information concerning the state of its internal organs. It seems probable that some of the organic receptors are either similar or identical to some of the exteroceptors. There are sense endings in the throat and stomach that mediate a dim awareness of cold and warmth. In addition, pain receptors are widely distributed throughout the internal organs of the body. Distention of the internal tissues seems to be the most usual stimulus for visceral pain. Distention of the gastrointestinal tract mediates a feeling of fullness, discomfort, and pain. The extreme tensions exerted by the accumulation of pus in the appendix produce the excruciating pain of appendicitis. When it is irritated chemically or mechanically, the inflamed stomach wall of gastric ulcers and gastritis mediates pain. The reports of subjects who have undergone abdominal operations while conscious indicate that cutting, burning, and pinching the visceral organs do not produce pain (Best & Taylor, 1955). Hunger, thirst, and sexual experiences are probably combinations of affective, ideational, and interoceptive sensory elements. The vague feeling of well-being or illness that arises principally from the internal organs of the body probably consists of unidentified sensory and feeling components.

Compared with the exteroceptive sensory experiences, the organic sensations are ill defined. Whereas external cutaneous sensations have fairly accurate local signs, internal sensory experiences are poorly localized. Many internal pains are felt as originating in some external body part and are called "referred pains." In angina pectoris, the pain produced by muscular spasms in the heart is experienced in the shoulder and down the left arm. In this phenomenon there is a fairly uniform relationship between the injured internal part and its place of reference. In other cases the places to which the pain is referred are unpredictable.

SUMMARY

Adequate stimuli for vision are electromagnetic wavelengths ranging from 380 to 760 nanometers. The hue, brightness, and saturation of colors are determined principally by the length, amplitude, and homogeneity of the light waves constituting the visual stimulus. The rods and cones of the retina are the visual receptors. The rods mediate achromatic (colorless) vision, and the cones mediate chromatic (color) vision.

Auditory stimuli consist of vibration frequencies between 20 cps and 20,000 cps. The pitch, loudness, and quality of a tone are determined principally by the wavelength (or vibration frequency), the amplitude, and the homogeneity of the waves.

Cold, warmth, pressure, and pain are the four cutaneous senses. Cold receptors respond to temperatures below the physiological zero of the body. The receptors for warmth are stimulated by temperatures above the physiological zero.

The physiological zero is that temperature to which the skin is adapted at a particular time.

A deformation of the surface of the skin is an adequate stimulus for touch. The skin of the tongue, lips, and fingertips is most sensitive to contact stimuli, whereas the middle of the back and the thigh are the least sensitive body areas. Painful stimuli, which may be chemical, thermal, or mechanical, tend to injure tissue.

The kinesthetic receptors are located in the joint surfaces, muscles, and tendons. They are stimulated by changes in tension of these organs. The labyrinthine sense organs are located in the semicircular canals and vestibule (utricle and saccule) of the inner ear. They are stimulated by changes in rate of movement of the body or the head and by the force of gravity. The labyrinthine sense is important in the maintenance of balance and in maintaining one's orientation in space.

Sweet, sour, bitter, and salty are the four elementary gustatory sense qualities. The receptors for taste are specialized cells in the taste buds, which are located principally, but not exclusively, on the tongue. There are some general but no universal relationships between taste qualities and the chemical makeup of adequate stimuli for each.

The olfactory receptors occupy a small area in the upper part of the nose. They are stimulated by gaseous substances in solution in the mucus covering the sense cells. The number of elementary olfactory sensations is unknown. Taste and smell are intimately related experiences.

Organic sensory experiences include hunger, thirst, certain coital responses, internal pains, and a wide variety of ill-defined, vague experiences arising from internal organs of the body. They are characterized by being poorly localized and indefinite in nature. When pains arising internally seem to be located in external organs of the body, they are called referred pains.

SUGGESTED READINGS

Alpern, M., Lawrence, M., & Wolsk, D. *Sensory processes*. Belmont, Calif.: Brooks/Cole, 1967. This paperback provides a good, short but complete discussion of sensory processes.

Békésy, G. V. von. *Experiments in hearing.* New York: McGraw-Hill, 1960. This is an advanced book on hearing by the leading current investigator. He was awarded a Nobel Prize for the investigations reported in this volume.

Butter, C. M. *Neuropsychology: The study of brain and behavior.* Belmont, Calif.: Brooks/Cole, 1968. This book offers a good discussion of the neurophysiology of the senses.

Gregory, R. W. *Eye and brain: The psychology of seeing.* New York: McGraw-Hill, 1966. This book is one of the best sources on the nature of vision.

Mueller, C. G. *Sensory psychology.* Englewood Cliffs, N. J.: Prentice-Hall, 1965. This book contains a very complete discussion of the same topics covered by this chapter.

5

Elementary Learning

The behaviors that are of greatest concern to psychologists are those that are learned—that is, acquired and modified through experience. The study of learning itself is the study of the procedures and processes involved in the acquisition or modification of behavior.

Humans are continuously stimulated from both internal and external sources, and they are constantly responding to this complex stimulation. Learning is going on in this constant interaction between stimulation and response. The challenge facing investigators is how to study learning. If it is investigated in the usual situations in which it occurs in everyday life, the complexity of both stimuli and responses is so great that many meaningful patterns and principles are next to impossible to isolate. Only by controlling a stimulus situation as much as possible and by observing and recording a response can the relationship between the two become clearer. Therefore most investigations of learning are conducted in the laboratory, where many of the confounding factors encountered in the usual everyday situation are controlled.

When human subjects are used in investigations of learning, they are rigidly selected on some definite basis, stimulation is controlled as much as possible, and the predesignated responses are systematically observed and recorded. Even under the best of laboratory conditions, however, there are many factors in studying human learning that are difficult or impossible to control. For example, it is difficult to study the effects of fear on human learning in a laboratory. If a situation is made genuinely fearful, a human will remove himself from the situation and will no longer cooperate in the study. Man is an extremely complex organism; this complexity—coupled with the investigator's humane concern—makes man a difficult subject to investigate experimentally.

Thus psychologists frequently use lower forms of animals as subjects in their laboratory investigations of learning. Physiological techniques, such as ablation (tissue removal) and electrical stimulation of the brain, can be used effectively in studies involving lower animals. Moreover, the genetic background and early experience of lower animals can be controlled and manipulated with considerable precision. Psychologists who study the behavior of rats, monkeys, and other animals contend that such investigations of learning in lower animals may yield principles that are characteristic of human learning. They also maintain that basic principles of learning are more readily discernible in the comparatively simple responses of laboratory animals because more precise experimental controls can be employed with animals than are possible with humans. Results of laboratory investigations of learning using animals as subjects have indeed often been confirmed by later investigations of human behavior. The greater latitude permitted in the laboratory control of animals—together with their relative simplicity when compared with man—makes them valuable subjects in the experimental investigation of learning.

THE NATURE OF LEARNING

Learning is a process that is *inferred* from changes in performance under specified conditions; it cannot be directly observed. Because it is supposed to relate both to stimulation and to response, it can be termed an *intervening variable.* Learning is that process that is inferred to happen when one's response to a particular stimulus changes in a unique or particular way as a result of experience.

All changes in behavior deriving from experience cannot be said to result from this intervening variable called learning. Some changes in behavior are the result of other processes and events. Changes in response pattern may result from temporary or permanent organic impairment, such as a broken leg or the destruction of brain tissue by injury or lesion. Other changes in behavior may derive from alterations in biochemical conditions of the organism. Fatigue and hyperthyroidism would be examples of such conditions. Some changes in response are the result of inherent growth processes (maturation) and are relatively independent of learning.

Although learned behavior is usually described as being relatively permanent, this description is not very satisfactory unless we impose some limitations on it. A human should not be thought of as static; he is always undergoing changes of one kind or another. When a person learns, he does not acquire a "thing" that is retained intact until it is lost (forgotten). Changes produced by experience themselves continually undergo modification. Every subsequent experience probably has some effect on previous modifications and acquisitions of behavior. The products of learning are thus not static entities that remain unchanged throughout life; they are only relatively stable or permanent.

Relatively permanent changes in behavior that result from experience but cannot be accounted for by maturation, injury, or physiological alteration of the organisms are usually designated as having been learned. When learning is viewed in such a broad manner, it is easy to understand why so much of the behavior of humans is said to derive from learning. Learning will occur in a great variety of situations. Therefore various learning situations are conventionally referred to by their descriptive labels: verbal learning, motor learning, cognitive learning, perceptual learning, social learning, and various others. These labels are, at least in part, descriptive of the various dominant conditions under which learning takes place. It is tempting to refer to these circumstances as different *kinds* of learning, which has indeed been done by a number of psychologists. However, learning is treated in this book as a process that may occur under a variety of circumstances and in numerous situations. The labels will be used only as descriptive ones to identify the general nature of the conditions in which learning occurs.

THE SCOPE AND IMPORTANCE OF LEARNING

Learning in its broadest sense may be coextensive with life itself. It has been established that all the more highly organized forms of animal life learn. It has even been demonstrated that paramecia, with practice, will reduce the time required for them to turn around in a capillary tube (Day & Bentley, 1911). Shortening of the time for the performance of this task is a change in behavior resulting from experience, and, although the change is rather short-lived, we are inclined to call it learning. Planaria (very simple flatworms with a primitive nervous system) also have been used as subjects in investigations of learning (Thompson & McConnell, 1955). Research with these simple organisms (McConnell, Jacobson, & Kimble, 1959; Halas, James, & Knutson, 1962), indicates that they do learn (Jacobson, 1963). The list of animals other than man that have been used in laboratory investigations of learning is extensive. Mice, rats, cats, dogs, and monkeys are frequently employed, but other animals, such as fruit flies, cockroaches, goldfish, chickens, and pigeons also have been used.

The importance of learning in the various species is extremely variable. In some of the species, learning plays a vital role; in others it has little or no significance. Among the lower animals, learned activities constitute a relatively small and not very important part of the animal's total behavioral repertoire. Protozoa are born as essentially mature organisms, capable of performing almost all the acts they will ever be able to perform. They have practically no period of infancy, a very limited capacity for learning, and a short period of retention; products of learning are of little or no importance in their lives. Most of the responses that they will ever use appear to be instinctive and function quite adequately from birth.

As the phylogenetic scale is ascended, the period of infancy, the capacity for learning, the length of retention, and the importance of learning in the life of the organism steadily increase, and the fixity of innate behavior shows a corresponding decrease. Man, possibly the highest form of animal life, has the least-established instinctive behavior at the time of birth. He has the longest period of infancy, the greatest capacity for learning, and a long period of retention; moreover, acquired responses constitute the bulk of his repertoire.

Learning begins early in the life of the individual and continues until death. It is probable that prenatal environment is so constant that learning before birth is negligible, although there is experimental evidence that a fetus can be conditioned. Learning is pervasive in the life of man and enters into nearly every facet of his existence. He learns to make gross and fine responses of his neuromuscular system (motor learning); he acquires knowledge and meanings (ideational or cognitive learning); and he acquires likes and dislikes (emotional learning). Although these learned responses are labeled after the most dominant feature of the learning situation and its outcomes, none of them occurs in

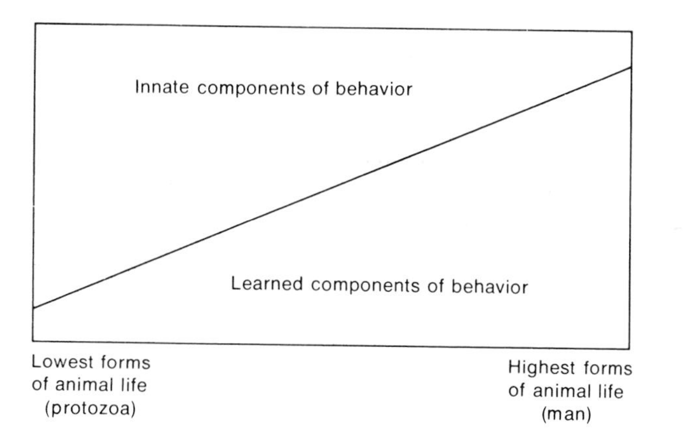

Figure 5-1. Learned and innate components of behavior and form of animal life.

isolation from the others. Everything that is learned has motor, ideational, and affective components in varying degrees. A person learns to do something (motor learning), gains knowledge about how it is to be done (cognitive learning), and forms attitudes toward the particular situation (affective or emotional learning). A person is a unit, and, when a person responds, it is the total person who responds. The various learning categories are never discrete and are designated largely for descriptive purposes.

Man learns manual skills, verbal skills, and graphic skills. Through learning he acquires knowledge, meanings, fears, attitudes, beliefs, ideals, personality characteristics, frames of reference, prejudices, values, and self-knowledge. Learning produces such an imposing array of characteristics that knowledge about learning becomes imperative in understanding man's behavior.

CIRCUMSTANCES FOR LEARNING

In the following section we will discuss a number of procedures that have become standard in laboratory investigations of learning. These procedures and circumstances are not exhaustive of all of the possible situations in which learning has been investigated, but they do represent the basic designs of experimental investigation to date.

Classical Conditioning

Conditioning procedures were first developed in the experimental laboratories of the Russian physiologist Pavlov (1927). He trained dogs to salivate to an auditory stimulus by procedures that have come to be known as *classical conditioning*. Pavlov sounded a tuning fork shortly before he presented food to a dog. After a number of such presentations, the dog salivated to the sound of the tuning fork, even when the sound was not followed by food. Pavlov was a careful researcher who kept meticulous records of his procedures. He controlled the intensity of the sound and the length of time before presenting the food; he counted the number of drops of saliva secreted; he measured the length of time it took for the first salivation to appear; and he counted the number of times the sequence had to be repeated before salivation without the food occurred.

Classical conditioning involves several components of considerable importance. To carry out the procedure, one must employ a stimulus that reliably produces a response. Such a stimulus is called an *unconditioned stimulus* (US), and the response that it evokes is termed an *unconditioned response* (UR). (In Pavlov's work, the US was meat powder placed on the dog's tongue. It produced the UR of salivation.) Another stimulus, called the *conditioned stimulus* (CS), must be added that does not initially produce the unconditioned response under investigation. (In Pavlov's initial work the CS was the sound of the tuning fork.) It is typically presented shortly before the US, although they may be presented simultaneously. The UR then occurs following the presentation of

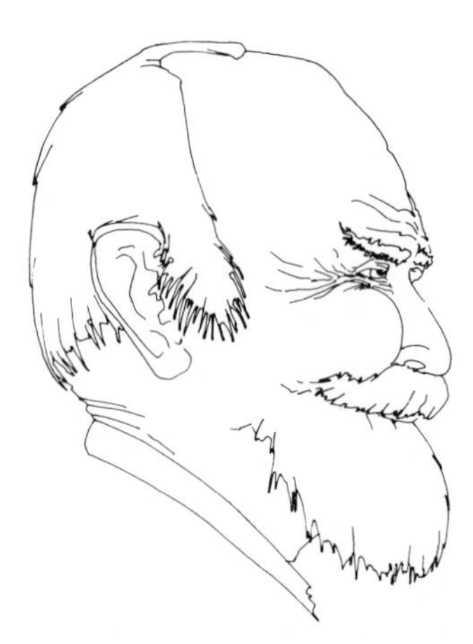

Figure 5-2. Ivan Petrovich Pavlov, pioneer in the study of conditioned responses.

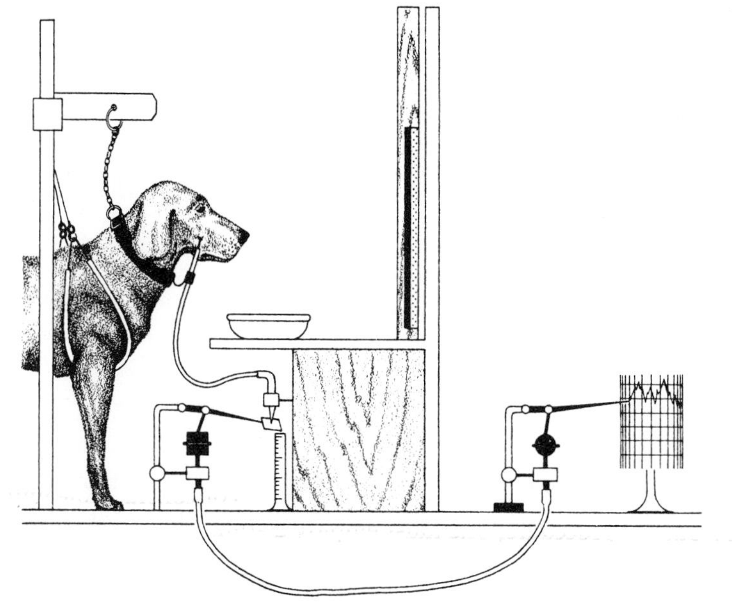

Figure 5-3. Pavlov's conditioning apparatus.

both the CS and the US. After repeated pairings of the stimuli, which are followed by the occurrence of the UR, the CS—the stimulus that did not initially evoke the UR—becomes effective in eliciting a response that is highly similar to or nearly identical with the UR. Such a response is called a *conditioned response* (CR). (In Pavlov's conditioning of dogs, the CR was salivation on the presentation of the sound.)

Since the early reports of Pavlov's experiment, conditioning has been demonstrated with a great number of organisms and a wide variety of conditioned stimuli. Conditioning of protozoa, worms, fish, reptiles, chickens, rats, sheep, dogs, monkeys, and men has been reported in psychological literature (Hilgard & Marquis, 1940). Conditioning investigations with humans have been extensive. A great deal of work has been done in the United States on the conditioning of the eye-wink reflex. The CS in such situations is an auditory or visual signal, and the US typically is a puff of air in the eye (Kimble, 1961).

If a buzzer is sounded regularly just before an infant is fed for the first three to six days of its life, crying and general activity will come to cease at the sound of the buzzer, and mouth opening and sucking movements will occur. Since the cerebral cortex is believed not to be functioning for some time after

Table 5-1. Essential features of classical conditioning. Initially the US elicits the UR. The CS is then paired with the US, and the UR is elicited. This step is repeated a number of times. Eventually the CS elicits a response highly similar to the UR. This response is the CR.

1.	US	elicits	UR
2.	CS and US	elicit	UR
3.	CS and US	elicit	UR
	CS and US	elicit	UR
	CS and US	elicit	UR
	CS and US	elicit	UR
	CS and US	elicit	UR
N.	CS	elicits	CR

birth, this response indicates the possibility that some conditioning may occur subcortically (Marquis, 1930). The pupil of the eye has been conditioned to contract and dilate on command (Hudgins, 1933); various other autonomic responses have also been conditioned. The Russians have been active in research on conditioning (Razran, 1961, 1965), and American research using classical-conditioning procedures has been energetic and fruitful (Prokasy, 1965).

Instrumental Conditioning

A widely used set of procedures for establishing conditioned responses in an experimental laboratory has been designated *instrumental conditioning.* The basic varieties of instrumental conditioning are (1) escape training, (2) avoidance training, and (3) positive-reward training. The methods employed in these situations differ from those in classical conditioning but also have much in common with them.

Classical and Instrumental Conditioning Compared

In classical conditioning the CS can be much more clearly specified than in instrumental conditioning. The CS in classical conditioning may be a distinct sound, such as a buzzer, or it may be a distinct visual, cutaneous, or olfactory stimulus. In instrumental conditioning the CS may be the entire complex of the experimental situation (for example, Skinner box or runway), without any discrete stimulus to act as a distinctive cue. In classical conditioning the trials are discrete and controlled by the experimenter; in instrumental conditioning the trials are more under the control of the experimental subject, who may initiate a trial (for example, press a lever) without regard to interval between trials.

In instrumental conditioning, reinforcers (rewards or punishments) are deliberately presented only after the to-be-conditioned response has occurred. In the classical-conditioning situation, the organism can do nothing to ensure or prevent the occurrence of the reinforcement. The term *instrumental conditioning* refers to the fact that the response is instrumental in procuring or perpetuating a reward of some kind or in avoiding or diminishing punishment. An instrumental response typically results in one of the following: (1) reducing or escaping noxious stimulation, (2) avoiding some noxious stimulus, (3) securing a positive reinforcement such as food or water, or (4) effecting some state of affairs previously associated with (1), (2), or (3). The consequence of the conditioned response is said to reinforce the response; for this reason the consequences are called *reinforcers*, and obtaining them is termed *reinforcement*.

In Pavlov's (1927) classical-conditioning procedure, meat powder on the dog's tongue was the reinforcement for the salivary response as well as the US for it. In this classical procedure the response employed is a well-established one that regularly occurs upon presentation of the US. In instrumental conditioning, on the other hand, there is originally no particular connection between the US and the response that is to be conditioned. The principal unconditioned stimulus is frequently complex and difficult to identify. Sometimes it is discrete and readily identifiable, as when electric shock or some other form of noxious stimulus is employed. But in some instrumental situations it may be a combination of discrete stimuli that constitutes the US complex (for example, the consequences of food and water deprivation). The stimuli provided by the experimental apparatus and various other internal and external stimuli may combine to form the effective stimulus for producing the activity that leads to the UR. This entire discussion should become more meaningful after these procedures are examined more thoroughly.

Escape Training

In escape training the organism is placed in a situation in which it receives a noxious stimulus that can only be terminated by performance of a particular act, such as running off the electrically charged portion of a grid, pressing a bar, attacking another animal or object, or anything else previously designated by the experimenter as the appropriate response. In such situations the noxious stimulus is the unconditioned stimulus that produces unconditioned responses of increased body tension, jumping, crouching, running, and so on. The particular response that is to become successful is awaited, and, when it occurs, the noxious stimulus is terminated. The experimental animal learns to escape the noxious stimulus and, upon its reapplication, makes the particular responses that have been reinforced. In a situation in which escape from an electrically charged grid is employed, the animal soon learns to run to the uncharged portion of the grid. Its running is instrumental in terminating the electric stimulation; the reduction in its pain is the reinforcer; and running directly off the charged portion of the grid is designated the conditioned response.

Avoidance Training

If the conditioning situation is so arranged that a signal (*stimulus*) of some kind is presented a short time before the onset of the noxious stimulus, an experimental animal will come to respond by avoiding the noxious stimulus entirely. The procedure is the same as that employed in escape training, except that a CR is added to the situation. The animal at first will run off the charged portion of the grid when the current comes on. It eventually will learn to run off the grid when a light or buzzer is presented preceding the shock. In this situation the CS is the light or buzzer, the US is the electric current, the UR is running when the shock is experienced, and the CR is running when the light or buzzer occurs, or avoidance of the shock.

Organisms can learn to perform a wide variety of responses on cue when such procedures are employed, and many learning situations can be interpreted as containing elements of avoidance. One may learn to study to avoid the chagrin of failure, acquire appropriate behavior to avoid social ostracism, and eat to avoid the unpleasant consequence called hunger.

Positive-Reward Training

Rewarding a desired performance is a common technique that differs from escape or avoidance training in some important ways. In positive-reward training the situation is complex and the discovery of the appropriate response is more difficult. Positive-reward training is used in the study of learning when animals are reinforced by food for traversing a maze, when children are given candy for appropriate behavior, when adults are praised for their accomplishments, or when a rat is reinforced by food in a Skinner box. A Skinner box is a small cage with a lever in it. When the lever is pressed, a piece of food or a drop of water is released into a container where the animal can get it. The apparatus was designed for laboratory investigations of animal learning by the noted behaviorist B. F. Skinner. The name *Skinner box* has become a generic term to identify almost any experimental box wherein an animal is trained to perform a particular act to receive a reinforcer.

If a rat deprived of food for 22 hours is placed in a box containing a bar that must be pressed before food can be obtained, it will engage in a variety of behaviors, including self-grooming, moving about, sniffing, and climbing. In the course of these activities, it may press the bar that makes food attainable. Eventually it comes to press the bar with great proficiency. The US is complex and rather ill defined in this situation, but the discrete stimuli constituting it no doubt derive from hunger and from the experimental apparatus itself. The URs are those of grooming and movements that represent the general activity of the animal. From among the responses elicited by the stimulus situation, that of bar pressing results in reinforcement, and bar pressing thus becomes the CR.

Positive-reward training is an effective training procedure. It may be interpreted as a complex form of escape or avoidance, or it may be regarded as a

B. F. Skinner

Figure 5-4. A Skinner box. When an animal is kept in such a chamber, automatic records can be made of its responses, as well as of the scheduling of stimuli and rewards. In a typical study the measured response is pressing a lever and the reward is a food pellet.

positive-reinforcement situation. If the hungry animal is allowed to consume food after reaching the goal box in a maze or after pressing the bar in a Skinner box, hunger contractions diminish, and the animal escapes from the noxious internal stimuli produced by deprivation. An animal may be viewed as eating to terminate hunger or avoid the occurrence of hunger, or eating may be viewed as a positive reward. In other words, the goal of its behavior may be viewed as obtaining and eating food, or it may be seen as avoiding or escaping noxious stimulation.

By reinforcing appropriate or desired responses, parents and teachers guide and direct the social and academic behavior of the children under their management.

Successive Approximation

Sometimes, complex responses are desired that are not likely to occur very frequently or at all under the conditions in which training must take place. For example, if we wanted to condition a rat to press a bar in an experimental box with its left forepaw, it would probably take a long time for this response ever to occur and be reinforced. However, if we start to reinforce the animal's behavior at various stages of the appropriate response or when it makes approximations of correct response, we can condition it very shortly.

When the rat is placed in the experimental situation, we will reinforce it with a food pellet whenever it approaches the bar and food cup; after a few such reinforcements, we will reinforce its behavior only when it begins to stand up near the lever; then we will reinforce it only when it presses the lever. When this bar-pressing response is fairly well established, we will reinforce it only when it presses the bar toward the end on the right; this procedure moves the animal out toward the end of the bar, where its left paw will be nearest to the bar. Then we will reinforce it only when it presses the bar with its left paw. It will soon press the bar consistently with its left paw. Such procedures result in "shaping" the animal's behavior. *Successive approximations* of the appropriate response have been reinforced until the final correct response is achieved.

Responses that are seemingly irrelevant to the situation at hand can be reinforced to produce behavior that appears superstitious. Thus a pigeon can be reinforced when it turns away from the feeder box after pecking. By allowing the bird to turn farther and farther each time before reinforcement, it will finally make a complete circle between pecks. Such behavior, if we did not know its origins in reinforcement, would indeed appear to be comparable to human superstitious behavior. The big difference, of course, is that we know the relevant reinforcement history of the pigeon. If we knew the relevant reinforcement history of people who behave superstitiously, their behavior might be equally understandable. By using methods of successive approximation, intricate and complicated behaviors can be developed in various animals and in man. These methods have been employed successfully by animal trainers for training various animals to perform remarkable tricks.

Such methods are used whenever refined skills are to be developed. If we want a person to learn to operate a typewriter at the rate of 60 words a minute, we do not wait until he can do so before we reinforce him. Rather, he is reinforced for expressing interest in learning to type, for mastering the keyboard, for gaining in speed and accuracy over a broad range of speeds, and so on. It is highly unlikely that a person would ever learn to type at 60 words a minute without reinforcement for successive approximations of the desired speed.

We undoubtedly shape one another's behavior in many situations by reinforcing those behaviors of which we approve and failing to reinforce those of which we do not approve. The reinforcers in such situations could be the signs of approval and acceptance that we provide one another by smiling, nodding, agreeing.

Trial and Error

In situations in which the environment is not so rigidly controlled as it is in the experimental laboratory, the nature of the learning process sometimes becomes rather obscure. If the behavior to be learned is complex and the stimulus situation is ambiguous and confusing, the term *trial and error* is sometimes used to describe the behavior. This process is highly comparable to what has been described as positive-reward training. In both situations the organism is *motivated.* The source of motivation may range from the need for food or some other biological consideration to the desire for prestige or love and acceptance, but, in any case, *a problem exists.* The problem is attacked in a *variable manner.* The randomness of attack may vary from being blind and apparently irrational to being logical in applying previous knowledge to this new situation. Approaches to the problem are tried on a more or less selective basis until one of them is *successful* (is *reinforced*). *Extraneous responses are eliminated,* and the successful, or reinforced, responses are *refined or integrated* into a smoothly running, unified process, whether it be pressing a bar or solving a mathematical problem.

SOME ASPECTS OF CONDITIONING

Several significant phenomena of conditioning that are important to an understanding of learning have been discovered in the laboratory. A tremendous amount of research has been done using conditioning as an experimental procedure, and, in presenting the salient aspects of conditioning phenomena in abbreviated form, it is necessary to be highly selective in terms of both phenomena presented and research cited.

Stimulus Generalization

An individual trained to respond to a given stimulus will later respond not only to the particular stimulus employed in training but to a variety of similar stimuli as well (Mednick & Freedman, 1960). Empirical evidence attesting to the existence of such *stimulus generalization* has grown to rather large proportions and derives from research in a number of areas (Razran, 1961). In an early demonstration of generalization in conditioning, a pet rat was presented to a child. When he reached for it, a loud sound was produced that caused the child to start, whimper, and withdraw from the animal. The experience was repeated several times, until the child would cry and withdraw from the rat when it was presented without the loud noise. The child was conditioned to fear the rat. The CS was the rat; the US was the loud noise; the UR was crying to the loud noise; and the CR was crying at the sight of the rat. Later investigation showed that the child now responded with fear to the presentation of a rabbit, a cat, a pup, and even a fur muff. He reacted to any object having the characteristic of furriness in much the same way as he did to the rat to which he had been specifically conditioned (Watson & Raynor, 1920).

The general procedure for investigating stimulus generalization is illustrated in the preceding example. An individual is conditioned to respond to a particular stimulus. After the desired response has become well established to the CS, tests for stimulus generalization are instituted. Stimuli varying in degree of similarity to the initial CS are presented, and the response to them

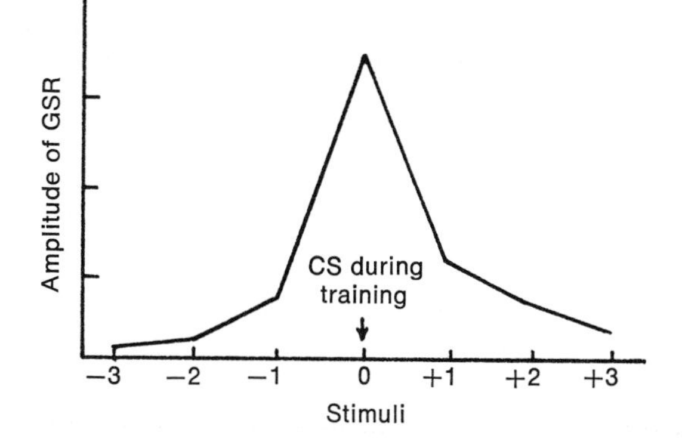

Figure 5-5. Gradient of generalization. Zero denotes the tone to which the galvanic skin response (GSR) was conditioned. The numbers +1, +2, and +3 represent test tones of increasingly higher pitch; −1, −2, and −3 represent tones of lower pitch. The amount of generalization decreases as the difference between the test tone and the training tone increases (adapted from Hovland, 1937).

is measured and recorded in some fashion. Stimulus generalization is said to have occurred to the extent that stimuli similar to the CS elicit the conditioned response. The strength of the response or the regularity with which it can be elicited to stimuli of varying degrees of similarity or proximity to the initial CS is used as a measure of the extent of generalization. By plotting degree of similarity and response strength, a gradient of stimulus generalization can be noted. Research results indicate that the degree of closeness or similarity between the original CS and the test stimulus is positively correlated with response strength. That is, the greater the similarity, the greater the tendency for the test stimulus to produce the conditioned response; the greater the discrepancy between the two stimuli, the less the strength of responding to the test stimulus.

Stimulus generalization has been demonstrated to occur with a variety of CSs. Generalization from the original CS has occurred after training to respond to a particular pitch (Hovland, 1937), to a particular light intensity (Bass, 1958), to a sound of a particular intensity (Miller & Greene, 1954), to a particular-sized object (Grice & Saltz, 1950), and to particular words (Razran, 1961).

A child who receives a painful "shot" from the family doctor may develop a fear of white-clad figures or, more specifically, white-clad male figures. He may become conditioned to other stimuli present at the time of his treatment, and generalization from these stimuli may occur, too. We are probably being conditioned in some way by every one of life's situations, and stimulus generalization probably follows most such conditioning experiences. The development of attitudes, prejudices, biases, and conceptual meanings may occur largely on the basis of conditioning and subsequent stimulus generalization. It is important to recognize that the effects of conditioning are not limited to the stimulus situation in which conditioning initially occurred. Generalization makes other related stimuli effective in eliciting the responses that were initially conditioned.

Extinction and Spontaneous Recovery

Once a conditioned response has become established, it may be desirable to eliminate it. As a matter of fact, in experimental investigations of learning, one of the means of testing the strength of the learning is to measure its resistance to attempts to eliminate it. One way to eliminate a subject's response is for

Table 5-2. Extinction and spontaneous recovery. A CR is well established (1). When it is not reinforced (2–4), it disappears (5–7). Some time elapses with no trials (8), and the CR recurs when the CS is presented (9). Continued extinction trials completely extinguish the responses (10–11) (after Sawrey & Telford, 1968).

(Conditioning)	1.	CS ——→ CR ——→ Reinforcement (Well established)
(Extinction trials)	2.	CS ——→ CR
	3.	CS ——→ CR
	4.	CS ——→ CR
		CS ——→ CR
		CS ——→ CR
(Extinction)	5.	CS ——→ No response
	6.	CS ——→ No response
		CS ——→ No response
		CS ——→ No response
	7.	CS ——→ No response
	8.	Time lapse
(Spontaneous recovery)	9.	CS ——→ CR
(Extinction)	10.	CS ——→ No response
		CS ——→ No response
		CS ——→ No response
	11.	CS ——→ No response

the subject to learn to make a new response to the stimulus. Thus a child who has learned to fear a rat can be taught another response, such as feeding or petting it, and the old responses of fear will diminish. Such a procedure (the teaching of a new response to replace the old one) is called *counterconditioning*. However, the most unusual way of eliminating a conditioned response is to present the CS over and over without following it with the US. Under these conditions there is a progressive decrement in responding to the CS. This procedure is called *extinction*. In the extinction of a classically conditioned salivary response in a dog, if the tone is sounded (CS) and is no longer followed by meat powder on the dog's tongue (US and reinforcement), a progressive decline in amount of salivation occurs with the nonreinforced trials. If a rat has been conditioned to press a bar to obtain food, its responses can be extinguished by failing to follow the bar pressing with the presentation of food.

Parents and others in positions of authority commonly attempt to control behavior through *punishment*. Evidence from the psychology laboratory has shown that punishment is effective in the temporary suppression of a response. However, it is not so effective in weakening the response, which may be resumed very shortly. Punishment is only effective when it forces the individual to make an alternative response that can be positively reinforced.

Estes (1944), in an early investigation of the effects of punishment, used two groups of rats that had learned to press a bar to obtain food as a reward. Both groups were then given extinction trials (food was withheld). In addition, the experimental groups were given electric shock through the floor of the Skinner box on the first few extinction trials. There was a temporary suppression of response rate, but the response was not weakened, for at the end of the experiment the experimental animals (punished) had made as many responses as the nonpunished animals. The phenomenon of the punished subjects emitting more responses during the postpunishment extinction phase (compensatory recovery) has not been found by some other investigators (Boe, 1964), and relatively permanent effects of punishment have been reported (Boe & Church, 1967). It has been demonstrated that the strength and duration of the suppression effect of punishment are dependent on its intensity and duration as well as the amount of deprivation (Karsh, 1962; Azrin, Holz, & Hake, 1963). Boe and Church (1968) have compiled an interesting collection of research articles on punishment and its effects.

It thus appears that the effect of punishment on responses is to suppress rather than eliminate them. The response eventually may reappear when the punishment has ceased and the motivation to commit the response becomes high enough. Punishment of a harsh nature produces maladaptive behavior and in severe conflict situations may produce ulcers (Sawrey, Conger, & Turrell, 1956; Sawrey & Sawrey, 1968).

Punishment does not serve as a guide to different behavior; it merely indicates that the current behavior is inappropriate. The punished individual may exhibit even more undesirable responses following punishment unless a clear alternative is provided—preferably, an alternative that can be rewarded. Punishment may lead to the dislike or fear of those administering it. When punishment is administered for failure at a task, the task may become disliked. Thus the consequences of punishment are unfavorable. Although punishment may be informative if it is not too severe, it is important to provide alternative behaviors that can be given positive reinforcement.

Unless some extinction procedure is instituted, conditioned responses are well retained. A conditioned pecking response in pigeons was maintained for 4 years (Skinner, 1950), and a conditioned human eyelid reaction was retained for 20 weeks (Hilgard & Campbell, 1936). In general, the most effective means of extinguishing a conditioned response is to present a great number of nonreinforced trials in a short period of time. If the conditioned response is periodically reinforced, it becomes highly resistant to extinction. (This fact may account for the maintenance of some conditioned responses that seem to be useless or even detrimental to the organism.)

An apparently extinguished response may recur after some time has elapsed since the last extinction trial. This effect is termed *spontaneous recovery* and is quite characteristic of learned behavior after a series of extinction trials followed by rest or distraction. If extinction procedures are carried on after spontaneous recovery has occurred, spontaneous recovery gradually decreases, and eventually the response fails to recur.

The recurrence of well-established responses that apparently have been extinguished is a rather common phenomenon in the experimental laboratory. After having been reinforced for pressing a bar to obtain food, a rat will press the bar repeatedly. If reinforcement (food) is later removed from the situation, the rat will cease pressing the bar. However, if the rat is removed from the situation and later placed back in it, it is likely to resume bar pressing for a time or two. Such behavior is to be expected in the general progress of behavioral change. In the process of developing a new response to an old stimulus, spontaneous recovery of the old response is a predictable phenomenon.

Higher-Order Conditioning

After a previously neutral stimulus has become effective in eliciting a designated response through conditioning, that stimulus, the CS, can now be used as a US in further conditioning. By pairing this former CS (now being used as a US because it *does* elicit the response) with another stimulus that has never been associated with the original US, the new stimulus will also become effective in evoking the conditioned response. A report from Pavlov's laboratory (1927) illustrates this phenomenon of *higher-order* conditioning. A dog was conditioned to salivate to the sound of a metronome. This response became well established and occurred although meat powder on the tongue no longer followed it. A black square was then placed before the animal for a short time before the metronome started to beat. After nine such training trials, the dog salivated when the black square was placed in front of it without the beating of the metronome. The black square had never been directly associated with the original effective US, the meat powder, yet the square was now effective in eliciting the CR. In another investigation (Finch & Culler, 1934) a tone was used as a CS and paired with shock to the dog's leg as a US to produce leg withdrawal. After the tone became established as a sufficient stimulus to produce leg withdrawal by itself, it was paired with a squirt of water to the nose. This second CS shortly became effective in producing the withdrawal response, although it had never been directly associated with shock to the leg. (This result can be called successful *second-order* conditioning.) Eventually a bell and a fan were introduced as effective stimuli in evoking the CR.

Conditioning higher than second order is difficult to establish in the laboratory. Many psychologists believe that the orders of conditioned responses acquired under conditions of everyday life may be rather great. They may be dependent on the occasional subsequent pairing of the original CS with the US. For example, a child learns what an orange is by tasting and eating it. By pairing the orange with the spoken word *orange*, he learns the meaning of the spoken word and subsequently may learn the meaning of the written word by having it paired with the spoken word. By pairing a meaningful spoken or written word with a new word that is a synonym, meaning may be acquired for many orders of stimulus pairings. During the course of cumulative learning while a child is maturing, higher-order conditioning becomes rather important. Although there is more involved in *complex learning* than simple conditioning and higher-order conditioning, elements of conditioning are probably present in every learning experience. Experimental demonstrations of higher-order conditioning in the laboratory are difficult because, when reinforcement is not presented, experimental extinction occurs. The original CS must be periodically reinforced while attempting to establish higher-order conditioning. Otherwise the response will extinguish, and the CS will not become effective as a US in the attempt to bring about higher-order conditioning.

Discrimination

Learning to make discriminations among stimuli is essential for learning to respond to a particular stimulus situation. Stimulus generalization has been demonstrated to occur reliably in both lower animals and men. An organism conditioned to respond to a light, a tone, or an odor usually will respond to other closely related visual, auditory, or olfactory stimuli. Reducing the range of effective generalization can be accomplished by *differential conditioning*, presenting stimuli in the same sensory modality that are "close" to the conditioned stimulus but reinforcing responses to the CS only. Eventually the organism responds only to the stimulus that is reinforced. It has learned to discriminate the appropriate stimulus from related stimuli. Such discriminations are learned when a rat is reinforced for its behavior when a black stimulus is present, and not when a gray or white one is present, or when it is reinforced for running into a goal box with a square door rather than one with a rectangular or circular opening.

Discrimination training goes on all the time. We learn to discriminate among sounds, light intensities, odors, degrees of temperature, and so on. By using reinforcement selectively (reinforcing one and only one stimulus), it is possible to investigate various characteristics of sensory functioning. The smallest difference in pitch, loudness, light intensity, weight, color, temperature, or pressure that an individual can detect can thus be determined. This smallest difference to which an organism responds is the *just noticeable difference* (jnd) employed as a unit of psychophysical measurement.

If the difference between reinforced and nonreinforced stimuli is reduced to the point at which discrimination is no longer possible, and the individual is forced to decide which response is correct when the wrong choice will result in punishment, he may become very disturbed. Such a procedure has been employed to produce experimental neurosis, in which an organism's behavior becomes disorganized and ineffective.

Reinforcement

The role of reinforcement (rewarding and punishing) in learning situations has long been recognized. Deliberate rewards for desired behaviors and punishments for disapproved behaviors have long been used to control children and animals. Thorndike (1911) formally stated the utility of rewards and punishments in the control of behavior in his "law of effect," which stated in essence that those responses that are accompanied or followed by satisfaction to the organism tend to be repeated and those that result in discomfort or dissatisfaction for the organism tend not to be repeated. The precise manner in which reinforcement produces its behavioral consequences is not clearly understood, although various theories have been advanced. Without regard to theoretical considerations of how reinforcement affects the organism or whether reinforcement is essential for learning, we can safely say that the most efficient means now available for controlling what will be learned is through reinforcement.

A great variety of objects, events, and circumstances has been found to function effectively in influencing the probability of response recurrence in a learning situation. Food when hungry, water when thirsty, companionship, approval, praise, blame, tokens, electric shock, fear, and the reduction of fear all have reinforcing properties. Experimental investigations of the role and function of reinforcement are being conducted in psychological laboratories throughout the world.

Partial reinforcement. The rate at which learning occurs, what is learned, and the resistance of what is learned to extinction are, at least in part, functions of the particular *schedule of reinforcements* employed: reinforcement may be given every time a response occurs, every so many responses, every so often on a determined time schedule, every so often on a variable time schedule, or in various other fashions. The quickest and simplest way to condition a given response is to reinforce it every time it occurs. However, it is possible for learning to occur as if every trial were being reinforced, if every other trial or every third trial is reinforced. Learning may occur when only 1/192 of the desired responses is followed by deliberate reinforcement (Skinner, 1938). Schedules of reinforcement have been investigated extensively by Skinner and his associates (Skinner, 1938; Ferster & Skinner, 1957), and each schedule of reinforcement appears to hold its own unique consequences for performance.

Reinforcement may be administered very simply on a *fixed-interval* schedule. Fixed-interval schedules are followed in the issuance of weekly or monthly paychecks, the issuance of report cards to schoolchildren, and in many other situations. In essence, this procedure involves the administering of reinforcements that are spaced an equal amount of time from each other. A subject in such a situation is reinforced every so many seconds, minutes, or hours, as the conditions of the experiment dictate. The rate of responding (as long as one response follows the prescribed period of time) is irrelevant to the schedule of reinforcement. When training on a fixed-interval schedule has been carried out for a considerable period of time, response rate is not very steady. It tends to decrease immediately following reinforcement and increases only near the end of the fixed time interval.

When the interval between reinforcements is not constant but is randomly varied, the schedule is referred to as a *variable-interval* schedule. A beggar whose patrons appear irregularly could be said to receive money rewards on a variable-interval schedule. The subject may be reinforced for his behavior two or three times very close together; on the other hand, a considerable amount of time may be allowed to elapse between reinforcements. The rate of responding on a variable-interval schedule will be high or low, depending on the length of the intervals employed. If the intervals are long, responding will be at a relatively low, steady rate, and, if the intervals are relatively short, high rates of responding will develop. The rate of responding is typically higher on this kind of schedule than it is on the fixed-interval one, but the main feature of this kind of schedule is the steadiness of the rate of responding it produces.

Reinforcement may be presented after *a given number of responses.* If the number of responses between each reinforcement is always the same (for example, one response or three responses), reinforcement is on a *fixed-ratio* schedule. A fixed-ratio reinforcement schedule results in a higher rate of responding than does a fixed-interval schedule. By starting at a low ratio of reinforcement (two or three responses between reinforcements) and moving up by gradual increments, behavior can be maintained on very high ratios such as 500:1 (500 nonreinforced responses for every reinforced one) or even 1000:1 (Ferster & Skinner, 1957).

A *variable-ratio* schedule of reinforcements, in which responses are reinforced randomly around some average ratio, has proven to be a very effective means of reinforcement. Sometimes the reinforcement occurs after two responses in a row, and sometimes it will occur after a large number of responses. Such a procedure results in a steady rate of performance at a high level.

Each of the partial-reinforcement schedules yields characteristic differences in responding. When reinforcement occurs at random intervals, learning is manifested by a reduction in the variability of behavior. Acquisition of a response with partial reinforcement (reinforcement on some but not all trials) requires more trials but fewer reinforcements than does acquisition with continuous reinforcement (Kanfer, 1954). The behavior of both children and adults under intermittent reinforcement conditions closely resembles the behavior of lower animals on similar schedules (Long, Hammack, & Campbell, 1959). The various schedules can be used in combinations for the effective control of acquisitions and performances of various kinds.

When responses are acquired under conditions of partial reinforcement, they are often much more resistant to extinction than when they are acquired under constant reinforcement. Various theories have been advanced to account for this fact. It may be that when an organism is not reinforced for every response during acquisition, it begins to expect that a reinforcer will not always be forthcoming and will persist in its behavior. Whatever the reasons for this resistance to extinction for responses acquired under partial reinforcement, it is a fortunate circumstance because, for a wide range of animal and human behaviors, reinforcement is impossible following every response. Thus most learning occurs under conditions of partial reinforcement, and learned behavior is relatively persistent over time. The learning of fears and other emotional responses may come about under partial-reinforcement conditions, however, and be extremely resistant to extinction.

Amount of reinforcement. When amount of reinforcement is conceived of as a quantitative variable in an experimental situation, it can be controlled in terms of weight, volume, or number. The subject in the experiment can be given a certain amount of food, water, or electric shock, and the magnitude of the reinforcement can be measured in some manner.

Amount of reinforcement can also be treated as a qualitative variable rather than a quantitative one. Quality of reinforcement is much more difficult to control, in that quality is a personal as opposed to a physical measure. Do two pieces of candy that are liked by a child constitute a greater or lesser reinforcement than one that is relished? The answer to this question will vary from child to child and circumstance to circumstance. Quality is much harder to manipulate and measure than is quantity. Even quantitative identity may vary from person to person and from one circumstance to the next. For example, a dime to the hungry child who knows he can obtain an ice-cream cone with it has more value for reinforcement than a dime to a child who is not hungry or who does not know that it can be used to procure an ice-cream cone. The same physical amount of something may have different reinforcement effects for different recipients. In general, quantitative and qualitative increases in amount of reinforcement are followed by increases in performance (Rock, 1935; Hutt, 1954). The same general relationship seems to hold for the amount of negative as well as positive reinforcement (Kimble, 1961).

Absolute amount of reinforcement may not be an important variable in some learning situations. When learning or performance is controlled primarily by reinforcements other than those obviously being manipulated, the probability that the amount will be an important variable is not very high. For example, when reinforcement serves primarily an informational function, and the continuation of behavior is determined primarily by the knowledge of whether or not one is proceeding correctly, the amount of immediate reinforcement would not be expected to be an important variable in performance. If the reinforcement merely acts as an indicator that the response was right or appropriate, *any* reinforcement provides complete knowledge of correctness or appropriateness, and reinforcement operates in an all-or-none fashion. However, when obtaining a reinforcer is the principal motivation for learning or performance, as in many instances of animal learning, one would expect that the relationship between amount of reinforcement and level of performance would generally be positive.

Delay of reinforcement. Reinforcements apparently have their maximum effect when they follow as closely as possible the responses that they are to perpetuate. Experimental investigations of learning in rats have demonstrated that, if effects of secondary reinforcement are controlled, the effectiveness of reinforcement diminishes rapidly as the period of delay increases. Primary reinforcement for learning has practically no effect with rats if the period of delay is more than 10 seconds (Grice, 1948; Spence, 1947). However, the ability to profit from delayed reinforcement probably increases as the phylogenetic scale is ascended. The effects of delay of punishment are about the same as the effects of delay of reward, in that there is a delay-of-punishment gradient that has the same general characteristics as the delay-of-positive-reinforcement gradient: the longer the delay following the response, the less the effectiveness (Kamin, 1959; Weinberger, 1965).

The delay of reinforcement acts similarly to decrease its effectiveness in humans as well as in lower animals. Research on delay of punishment with children has indicated that delayed punishment is less effective than immediate punishment as a deterrent to forbidden behavior (Walters & Demkow, 1963; Walters, Parks, & Cane, 1965).

In one investigation of delay of reinforcement with humans (Greenspoon & Foreman, 1956), reinforcement was administered (1) with no delay, (2) 20 seconds after the response, and (3) 30 seconds after the response. The task was the drawing of a 3-inch straight line while blindfolded. The verbal expressions "right," "short," and "long" were used as reinforcers. Four groups of subjects were used, one group for each period of delay and a control group receiving no reinforcement. The results indicate that increasing the length of the interval of delay reduced the rate of learning to perform the task. However, even the 30-second delay was found to be superior to no reinforcement at all.

With young children reinforcements must follow responses very closely, or they will become relatively ineffective for learning and performance. With older, more mature individuals, reinforcements can be more remote and still be effective in the guidance of learning activities.

Secondary reinforcement. Stimuli that are effective in establishing higher-order conditioning have acquired value as reinforcers. They are called *secondary reinforcers* because they have *acquired* reinforcing value through their association with a finally effective stimulus. The following is an example of a secondary reinforcement in classical conditioning. A dog may learn to salivate upon presentation of a black card, even though the card itself has never been paired with meat powder but only with a conditioned stimulus—the beat of a metronome. In this case the metronome beat acts as the reinforcer for salivation to the card.

The effectiveness of secondary reinforcement in instrumental conditioning has been demonstrated by training chimpanzees to put a poker chip in a vending apparatus that automatically releases a grape (Wolfe, 1936; Cowles, 1937). Thus the poker chips became associated with the grapes and themselves became reinforcers in teaching the chimps to lift a lever and to pull a small sliding tray by means of a cord. The animals would work for these tokens, which could not be exchanged for food until a later time. The tokens were effective reinforcers for the acquisition of several other complex habits.

The click made by the food mechanism in a Skinner box has been demonstrated to develop secondary reinforcing properties for rats. The bar-pressing response is reinforced each time it occurs by a pellet of food that is accompanied by a click. After the bar pressing has become firmly established, if both the food and the click are withheld, a typical curve of extinction can be plotted from the performance of the animal. However, if only the food is eliminated and the click is allowed to occur, bar pressing can be maintained for a long time, and extinction occurs at a much slower rate.

If a stimulus is employed as a secondary reinforcer in a number of situations, it is likely that that stimulus will become a generalized secondary reinforcer and be effective as a reinforcement for behavior whenever and wherever it is employed. By reinforcing behavior in animals when they are exposed to a black stimulus and withholding it when they are exposed to a white one, it has been demonstrated that black stimuli will serve as reinforcers for subsequent learning and performance (Saltzman, 1949). Similarly, verbal expressions (such as "good") or a smile can become effective reinforcers for the behavior of children. Experimental evidence supports the hypothesis of generalized secondary reinforcers (D'Amato, 1955; Wike & Barrientos, 1958), but it is difficult to demonstrate with laboratory animals (Myers & Trapold, 1966).

Because of the wide degree of generalization of the effects of secondary reinforcers, it is possible to develop "chains" of responses by a single reinforcement at the end of the response chain. This procedure becomes possible because of the operation of secondary reinforcers that sustain the learned behavior as the goal is approached. Secondary reinforcers such as money, praise, and prestige are of unquestionable importance in directing the learning and behavior of adult humans. These secondary reinforcers are utilized over a broad range of behaviors and are extremely potent as reinforcers of human learning.

Further Aspects of Conditioning

There are some important aspects of conditioning that have not yet been mentioned in the course of our discussion.

Interstimulus interval is the time that elapses from the onset of the CS to the onset of the US. The quest for the most effective interstimulus intervals has been fruitful. The most effective interval for some classical conditioning (for example, eyelid conditioning) has been found to be 0.5 second. Because of the great amount of work done with eyelid conditioning, this figure has been commonly accepted as *the* optional interstimulus interval. Unfortunately, the situation is not that simple. In other arrangements for conditioning (for example, avoidance), other intervals have been found to be more effective, and interstimulus intervals of 5, 10, or even 20 seconds have been found to be the most effective under certain circumstances. The optimal length of the interstimulus interval is a function of the response, the organism, the methods employed, the intensity of the stimuli, and possibly other variables as well. However, for many classical conditioning situations, 0.5 second appears to be the most effective interval.

The *intensity* and *duration* of both the CS and the US have been found to be relevant variables in regard to the ease with which conditioned responses can be established. In general, the more intense, complex, or distinctive the stimuli, the more readily conditioning occurs.

Various *temporal relationships* of stimuli can be employed with varying degrees of efficiency, depending on the situation. (1) The CS may come on simultaneously with the US and terminate with it. (This procedure is termed *simultaneous conditioning*.) (2) The CS onset may precede the onset of the US by a given amount of time and remain on until both are terminated together (*delay conditioning*). (3) The CS may come on and then terminate before the onset of the US (*trace conditioning*). (4) If the US precedes the CS and terminates before the onset of the CS (*backward conditioning*), conditioned responses are extremely difficult to establish. The most frequently and probably the most effectively employed temporal arrangement is that of delay conditioning.

The Extensive Nature of Conditioning

Conditioning of one kind or another is probably going on continuously throughout our lives. Although simple conditioning does not account for the entirety of learning, it probably is basic to most acquisitions. If a broad view is taken, conditioning no doubt is involved in most situations in life. Most of our ordinary fears are probably acquired by the same basic process as were those of the child in Watson and Raynor's (1920) experiment who was taught to fear furry objects.

Many of the responses that we make may be interpreted as resulting from conditioning. It has been demonstrated that, by reinforcing the use of certain words or certain expressions, their frequency of use is increased. By reinforcing certain behaviors and not others, we can shape behavior in a variety of ways. Behavior-modification techniques modeled after those of conditioning have been employed successfully in a great variety of psychotherapeutic situations (Rachman & Eysenck, 1966).

In addition to routine habits and fears, many complex responses may result from the cumulative effects of conditioning in previous situations. Much of our awareness of "emotional climate" and our feelings of comfort or discomfort in social situations derives from our past conditioning and learning history. Hundreds of minor associations gradually build up in us certain unverbalized and often unrecognized responses, such as feelings of relaxation or tension, anxiety or pleasant expectancy. These responses are elicited when situations arise that have stimulus components in common with previous situations wherein conditioning occurred. The cumulative effect of these incidental associations may be more important than any single experience, no matter how dramatic, in the formulation of complex patterns of response. When a man observes that a situation is one of "tenseness and hostility" or of "warmth and pleasantness," his judgment derives from his own prior conditioning. Our feelings of security, self-confidence, and general well-being similarly derive from the kinds of learning experiences we have had.

THE PHYSIOLOGICAL BASIS OF LEARNING

One of the basic assumptions of psychology is that learning, retention, and recall are basically physiological processes. The general notion is that (1) *learning* involves changes in the nervous system, (2) *retention* is primarily the persistence of these neural modifications, and (3) *recall* involves the reactivation of the neural "engrams" (the residue of the modifications that took place during learning). Evidence for the physiological basis of learning is partly derived from general observations, but it is also derived from clinical case studies and from experimentation.

Casual observations of the temporary or permanent amnesias following brain contusions, concussions, and more serious brain injuries indicate, even to the untrained observer, that the products of learning can be either disrupted or erased by brain injury. Innumerable clinical observations of the loss of specific habits and associations as the result of medically verified brain injuries have been recorded. Marked reduction in one's ability to learn following widespread brain injury has been clearly demonstrated, as in certain cases of cerebral palsy. Thousands of research studies have been made involving the removal or inactivation of portions of the brain prior to or after learning a wide variety of habits. We now have available a bewildering array of rather specific data concerning the effects of such operations on various aspects of learning, retention, and relearning. From these studies we know a great deal about what areas of the brain are involved in certain kinds of learning.

GROSS CORTICAL FUNCTIONS IN LEARNING AND RETENTION

Associative processes other than language have been studied principally in the lower animals. By associative processes, or functions, we mean the acquisition, retention, and use of learned-reaction tendencies. Studies of the function of the cortex in such higher mental processes have been concerned primarily with the specificity of the cortical areas involved. In other words, is the learning of a specific process the function of a certain part of the brain, or is it a function of the entire brain or the entire cerebral cortex? Before we present some of the experimental evidence on this question, we might say that some processes have been found to be quite specifically related to cortical areas, although others seem to have little if any localization. Language, in humans, and visual-form perception, even in the lower animals, involve specific localized brain areas with some limited substitution of one nerve center for another being possible. On the other hand, maze learning in rats seems to have little or no localization of function. All areas of the cortex appear to function interchangeably in maze learning and retention. In general, there seems to be greater specificity of function for the various parts of the cortex as we ascend the animal scale.

The classical studies of the role of the cortex in the maze learning of rats were done more than 40 years ago (Lashley, 1929). The general procedure in these studies was to destroy portions of the cortex before and after learning and to assess the effects of the extent and location of the lesion on learning and retention. Mazes of three levels of difficulty and lesions ranging in extent from zero to 90 percent of the cortex and involving practically all regions of the cortex were involved. Lashley's most significant findings were:

1. For the simplest maze, lesions involving less than 50 percent of the cortex did not affect the rate of learning, whereas larger lesions had a deleterious effect on learning. The correlation between size of cortical lesion and impairment of learning rate was only 0.20. The correlations were 0.58 for a maze of intermediate difficulty and 0.75 for the most difficult one. The reduction in rate of learning was proportional to the size of the cerebral lesions. The relationship is also proportional to the difficulty of the learning problem.

2. The location of the cortical lesion was not important in determining the reduction in rate of learning. The detrimental effect of cortical lesions on maze learning was determined by the extent of the lesion and was independent of its location. All areas of the rat's cortex seem equally involved in maze learning.

3. Retention of the maze habits was affected in the same way as was the original learning. That is, lesions involving more than one-third of the cortex were required to disturb retention of the simplest maze habit. The more difficult a maze, the greater the loss of the maze habit subsequent to cortical lesions. Furthermore, as with the original learning, there was no relationship between the location of a lesion and the amount of impairment.

4. The deficits produced by a lesion of a given size were greater for retention than for the original learning. Cortical lesions did more harm to the retention of habits already learned than to the ability to learn a new maze habit.

Subsequent studies have shown that maze-bright rats show less of a deficit in the retention of maze habits subsequent to cortical lesions than do maze-dull rats (Eriksen, 1939). As we stated above, there seems to be no specific localization of function in maze learning in rats. The reason for this lack of specificity may be found in the fact that all parts of the cortex appear to contribute equally and interchangeably to the acquisition and retention of the maze habit. Since maze learning involves a number of sense modalities (visual, cutaneous, olfactory, kinesthetic), the various senses may function alternatively in learning and performance. In contrast to maze learning, visual-discrimination habits are fairly specifically localized. There are, however, limited possibilities for vicarious functioning, since other areas of the cortex can take over visual-discrimination functions normally mediated by a particular cortical region. Experiments with a variety of animals (rats, cats, monkeys) have shown that if they are trained to make a simple two-choice discrimination between a light and a dark stimulus, the habit is completely lost when the visual area of the cortex is removed. These animals are not blind and can reacquire the visual-discrimination habit in about the same number of trials as was required for the original learning. If the visual cortex is removed prior to learning, the discrimination can be acquired in about the same time required to learn it with the visual area intact. The visual area of the cortex seems to be crucially involved in visual learning when it is intact. However, in its absence some other areas function equally well (Smith, 1937; Morgan, 1965).

The learning and retention of a visual-discrimination habit are somewhat different when the discrimination is a difficult one. When the difference between the light and the dark stimuli is very small and the animal has to learn to make a fine discrimination, relearning the discrimination after removal of the visual cortex is much more difficult than learning it with the cortex intact. In one study, removing the cortex of an animal that had learned a difficult successive-discrimination habit (in which the animal went to the left when it saw a dark card and to the right when it saw a light one) eliminated the habit and rendered the animal incapable of relearning it (Thompson & Malin, 1961; Morgan, 1965).

Form discrimination is a still more complex and difficult form of learning, and the visual cortex is essential for this function. When it is completely removed, animals are unable to make any form discriminations. In the learning of form-discrimination habits, a small part of the visual cortex seems to function about as well as the entire area. In the rat no area of the cortex other than the visual seems to be involved in form discrimination, whereas in the monkey several other cortical areas are normally involved.

Thus, in the lower animals, some habits show no evidence of cortical localization, whereas others show various degrees of specialization of function. We have no comparable data on humans. However, it seems that as we ascend the animal scale there is an increase in the extent of localization of function in the cerebrum and probably fewer vicarious functions. Even on the human level, functions such as language and motor skills can be reacquired, through intensive training, following their loss due to brain injury.

Interest in the physiological basis of learning has shifted recently from the gross brain structures that are involved in learning or are critical for learning. Interest today is directed to more analytical problems, such as where the learning takes place in the receptor–sensory-nerve–central-nervous-system–motor-nerve–effector–activity circuit.

THE NEURAL LOCUS OF LEARNING

The evidence to be presented in this section should make it clear that the location of the physiological changes constituting learning is in the central nervous system. More particularly, it seems to be in the primary-sensory and motor areas or in the related association areas. The sensory and motor areas or some neural centers functionally related to both apparently must function simultaneously or in close succession for learning to take place.

The evidence for these conclusions comes from research findings such as the following: In simple conditioning, an electrical stimulus can be substituted for either an original unconditioned stimulus or a substitute conditioned stimulus at various points in the receptor-effector circuit in order to determine which segments, if any, of the neural pathway are not necessary for learning. For example, if the sound of a buzzer regularly accompanies or precedes an electric shock applied to the foot pad of a dog, the dog will soon withdraw its foot at the sound of the buzzer. The buzzer has become a CS and produces foot withdrawal, just as the original electric shock did as a US. Can artificial electrical stimulation of the nerve tracts and centers involved in auditory stimulation be substituted for the buzzer in conditioning? Apparently it can. If electrical stimulation is applied anywhere from the peripheral sense organ to the auditory area of the cortex along with the US (shock to the foot), typical conditioned learning occurs. If electrical stimulation of the auditory nerve, the auditory nucleus in the medulla, or the auditory cortex is paired with repeated shocks to the foot, such stimulation will eventually produce foot withdrawal. Apparently the stimulation of almost any site in the brain can come to function as a CS in learning (Nielsen, Knight, & Porter, 1962).

Electrical stimulation of appropriate brain areas can also serve as the *unconditioned* stimulus in associative learning. The US is the stimulus that is originally effective in producing a given response; that is, electrical shock to the foot produces foot withdrawal. Electrical stimulation of the appropriate spot in the motor area of the cortex can replace the shock to the foot and produce similar foot withdrawal. If the stimulation of the motor cortex is repeatedly accompanied by the ringing of a bell, the sound of the bell by itself will eventually produce foot withdrawal (Thompson, 1967).

Other studies show that electrical stimulation of a brain area related to vision will evoke responses that were originally conditioned to photic stimulation (Kitai, 1966). Similar effects have been obtained with other sensory systems. Researchers have paralyzed an entire motor system from the cerebral motor cortex down to the muscle and have found that this paralysis does not prevent conditioning. The neural locus of conditioning seems to be in the sensory brain areas or the motor areas or somewhere between the two—probably the latter (Morgan, 1965).

SOME ANATOMICAL AND BIOCHEMICAL ACCOMPANIMENTS OF LEARNING

Another problem of considerable current interest is exactly what changes occur in the nervous system when learning occurs. Past speculations concerning the nature of these changes that underlie learning have included the following possibilities: (1) changes in synaptic resistance, (2) the growth of neural processes, and (3) modifications of the rate of passage of the discharge of nerve impulses so as to synchronize or desynchronize their relationships. The current hypothesis is that RNA and DNA and other chemical substances may play roles in the learning process.

The Growth of Neural Processes

Although the notion that the neurons of the brain may grow with use is an old one, the fact that correlations between intelligence and size of the human head are negligible led to the general idea being discarded. However, recent studies indicate that there may be relationships between the bulk of neural tissue in the brain and the functional level of the animal, although these correlations are too small to be reflected in the measurements usually made. The absence of a correlation between gross size of the skull and the intellectual level of humans may be partially the result of the operation of certain developmental and medical conditions that have nothing to do with the size and function of the brain and the further fact that neural growth changes incident to learning are relatively small. Some studies almost a century ago indicated that when fine measures were made in autopsy of the cortical visual areas of congenitally blind subjects, these areas were found to be thinner and less well developed than were the corresponding areas of comparable sighted subjects. Recent experimental studies have used the lower animals (principally rats) as subjects, in which case control groups can be employed and environmental experiences systematically varied to see if measurable changes take place in the brain as a consequence of learning. Rats have been raised alone in small metal-walled cages, with a minimum of environmental stimulation and handling. Their littermates were raised in large cages with many exercise wheels, ladders, tunnels, boxes, and other objects about and were allowed to explore new territory each day. Two significant differences were found in autopsy of the brains of the two groups. The rats raised in the enriched environment had larger brains and larger amounts of two of the enzymes involved in nerve-impulse transmission (cholinesterase and acetylcholinesterase). The differences were not large, but they have since been found quite consistently in several experiments (Rosenzweig, Bennett, & Krech, 1964).

The internal structure of the brains of cats raised in the dark also differs from that of their littermates raised normally. The brains of the animals raised normally—in the light—have more nerve-cell branchings than do the brains

Figure 5-6. An enriched environment. This "educationally active" cage is located in a noisy well-lighted laboratory. These rats are reported to develop larger, deeper, and heavier cortexes than do littermates that are raised in small cages in a quiet and dimly lit room (Krech, 1968).

of their littermates raised in the dark. It seems that experience does induce structural and chemical changes in the brain, particularly in the cerebral cortex. The areas of the cortex showing the greatest changes incident to experience are those areas functionally related to the type of training given the animals. Chronic electrical stimulation of the brain has also increased total brain weight, as well as total cholinesterase and acetylcholinesterase activity in the brains of experimental animals (Pryor, Otis, & Uyeno, 1966).

SOME MOLECULAR APPROACHES

In addition to the anatomical and biochemical approach to the problem of the physical basis of learning and retention, a more molecular approach has also been made. This approach has usually taken the form of trying to relate learning, retention, and recall to DNA–RNA molecular patterns. The linear sequences of amino-acid bases in DNA are believed to constitute the genetic code; for a number of reasons, a similar linear sequence in either DNA or RNA has been posited as an experiential and memory code: (1) Since at least six types of RNA have been identified, DNA and RNA could well be involved in more than just the genetic code. (2) RNA is produced in the nerve cells at a rate that varies with the extent of neuronal activity. (3) The RNA content of the nerve cells ranks with the highest of all the cells in the body. (4) The nerve cells belonging to the sensory system of an animal deprived of that sense (a blind or deaf animal) are impoverished in both protein and RNA. (5) Stimulation of the cortex of cats also produces a change in the RNA in the stimulated areas (Gaito, 1963).

Another interesting line of experiments may have some relevance to the possible role of RNA and DNA in learning and retention. If flatworms (planaria) learn a simple habit and then are cut in the middle, both the tail and head sections will regenerate and both the regenerated animals retain the acquired response. When the two sections of a trained animal regenerate in the presence of ribonuclease (an enzyme that destroys RNA), the animal regenerated from the head normally retains the previous learning, but the animal regenerated from the tail shows no retention of the learned response. The experimenters suggest that the ribonuclease does not affect the intact neural tissue of the head but does interfere with the new nerve tissue regenerating from the tail portions of the transected worms (Corning & John, 1961).

A further study supports the general notion that some chemical mediators are involved in learning. Planaria were fed pieces of other planaria that had previously been conditioned. Animals ingesting pieces of previously conditioned earthworms subsequently learned the same responses more rapidly than did planaria that had ingested naïve planaria (Jacobson, 1963). Other studies have failed to replicate these findings, so perhaps we will not be grinding up old professors and feeding them to students after all (Hatry, Keith-Lee, & Morton, 1964).

Some clinical studies have reported memory improvement following the administration of RNA to senile patients suffering memory impairment (Gaito, 1963). Additional reports—(1) that the injections of chemical substances differing only slightly in their molecular structure have opposite effects on learning and (2) that transfer of learning can be induced by the administration of brain extracts from trained to untrained animals—have resulted in a large number of studies that have experimentally tried to facilitate learning by intravenous RNA injections, intraperitoneal RNA injections, and by injections of RNA directly into the brain. To date some 25 or 30 studies have failed to find any positive effects from such treatments (Byrne et al., 1966; Luttges,

Johnson, Buck, Holand, & McGaugh, 1966). These negative findings indicate that additional RNA from external sources does not facilitate learning, but it does not prove that RNA, as formed or modified at the site of learning, may not be involved.

The possibility that the molecular basis of learning may be discovered is still being actively pursued, but evidence in support of this possibility is indirect, and the arguments for it are primarily theoretical.

SUMMARY

Learning occurs in a variety of circumstances. This fact does not constitute valid evidence that there are as many kinds of learning as there are circumstances in which it occurs. Learning is an intervening variable, the existence of which is inferred from performance. Measures of learning are, in reality, measures of performance from which we make the inference of learning. Learning is a process that cannot be directly measured or observed. Relatively permanent changes in behavior that cannot be accounted for by maturation, injury, or physiological alteration of the organism but that result from experience are usually designated as having been learned. Learning is pervasive throughout the higher forms of animal life.

Two learning situations, those of classical and instrumental conditioning, represent basic or elementary arrangements wherein learning occurs. The components of the classical-conditioning situation are essentially the same as those of instrumental conditioning. That is, there is a CS, a US, a UR, and eventually a CR. The identification of these components is not accomplished with equal ease in the two situations, and the arrangements have some important differences as well as similarities. Instrumental conditioning usually involves escape, avoidance, or positive-reward training. Positive-reward training and so-called trial-and-error learning have a great deal in common.

Stimulus generalization, higher-order conditioning, reinforcement, extinction, and spontaneous recovery are important phenomena of conditioning.

By reinforcing successive approximations of desired behavior, complex behaviors can be developed in both animals and men. Conditioning procedures can be employed to teach fine discriminations as well as to determine the limits of discriminability. The role of reinforcement in learning is a complex matter with a long history of experimental investigation behind it. Learning and performance vary with the schedules of reinforcement employed. Fixed-interval, fixed-ratio, variable-interval, and variable-ratio reinforcement schedules each have unique effects on learning, performance, and extinction. The parameters of reinforcement (in terms of amount), the functions of delay, and the nature of secondary reinforcement have been the subjects of much experimental investigation.

Conditioning and learning are probably coextensive with life and living. Most situations from which we learn involve components of conditioning.

Studies concerning the physiological basis of learning have been concerned with both the gross anatomical critical points or structures involved in learning and with the biochemical and biophysical changes occurring during the learning-retention process. There is a tremendous amount of evidence that learning basically involves anatomical, physiological, neural, biochemical, and molecular processes, but just how these processes are involved is still undetermined.

SUGGESTED READINGS

Ban, T. *Conditioning and psychiatry.* Chicago: Aldine, 1964. Part IV of this book discusses the use of conditioning methods in psychiatry.

Kimble, G. A. *Hilgard and Marquis' conditioning and learning.* (2nd ed.) New York: Appleton-Century-Crofts, 1961. This book is an advanced treatment of conditioning and learning. It is the second edition of a classic in its field.

Smith, W. I., & Moore, J. W. *Conditioning and instrumental learning.* New York: McGraw-Hill, 1966. This short paperback text provides an excellent self-instruction program on principles of conditioning.

Staats, A. *Human learning.* New York: Holt, 1964. This good collection of studies extends conditioning principles to complex behavior.

Walker, E. L. *Conditioning and instrumental learning.* Belmont, Calif.: Brooks/Cole, 1967. This very readable paperback treats the topics of the title and discusses some issues of learning theory.

6

Learning: Theory and Process

The elements of conditioning are not so obvious in everyday learning situations as they are in laboratory experiments and demonstrations. In our daily lives an acquired response may be composed of a complex series of ideational and overt responses that lead to the solution of a problem. This chapter will discuss ways in which we acquire subtle and complex responses through *imitation* and *insight*. It will also discuss learning theories as well as some important variables that affect the learning process.

LEARNING THROUGH IMITATION

Imitation refers to copying specific ways of acting or behaving. The concept of imitation in psychological theory has a long history. At an earlier time, imitativeness was considered to be an innate, instinctive tendency. *Imitation* was then employed as an *explanation* for the phenomenon of learning through observation. Such explanations were largely abandoned as the doctrine of instinct fell into psychological disrepute. Imitation is now used *descriptively*. That is, when learning through observation is apparent, the individual is said to be imitating the observed behavior. It is intended to describe the circumstances wherein learning occurred. The important questions for psychologists are why and how organisms first come to imitate and what the role of imitation is in their subsequent learning.

Imitation appears to be a product of learning as well as a means of facilitating further learning. The essential feature of imitation is observation of another organism's response. What the imitator usually does is not to duplicate the exact behavior of the observed model but to attain the same result in somewhat the same fashion.

The mere fact that people tend to do some things alike cannot be interpreted as evidence that a process of imitation exists, because: (1) We should expect uniformities in behavior to occur simply on the basis of common neurophysiological equipment. We all start and blink our eyes when a sudden loud sound is heard, not because we have observed others registering surprise but apparently because this reaction is a uniform inherent response. (2) Most of us conform to many complex patterns of social behavior because such behaviors have been deliberately taught us through the manipulation of rewards and punishments. For example, we wear clothing because of family and social coercion. (3) We may conform to common ways of doing things because we find them to be the most economical in terms of time and energy. Thus we may all follow the same route from one classroom to the next simply because we find it to be the shortest and most direct. Such behaviors—those emanating from common biological structure and from rewards and punishments, as well as those commonly found to be most effective—are simply parallel, or matched, and do not involve imitation.

Even when we act just as we have seen others acting, we are not necessarily imitating their behavior. The actions of others may simply be directing our attention to certain stimuli, and the fact that our response is similar to someone else's is only incidental. For example, if we observe someone drinking at a fountain, we may do so, too. In most instances, our reason for drinking is that we are thirsty. Observing another person enhances the effectiveness of stimuli that are already present, but the effective stimulus could just as well have been the sight of a water glass or the sound of the word *water* or *thirsty*. Imitation is not involved when an observation of another's behavior simply enhances the effectiveness of stimuli to which we would ordinarily respond.

Several factors that produce uniformities of behavior do not necessarily involve imitation but *may* do so. To deviate very far from the behavior of the social group often invites criticism, social ostracism, or even expulsion from the group, whereas conformity to group-behavior patterns is reinforced by acceptance and continued or increased friendship within the group. A general tendency to imitate may develop from the operations of reinforcements for behavior. We learn that by doing what others do, we can avoid the painful consequences of group disapproval and perhaps gain the pleasurable consequences of group approval. Thus, as a result of the operation of positive and negative social reinforcements, we may purposely attempt to imitate others' behavior to attain desirable goals.

The use of the performance of another person as a model is seldom blind, routine, or wholesale. When we purposefully imitate, we do so on a highly selective basis: we want to improve our chances of attaining a goal or avoiding an unpleasant circumstance. Experiments have shown that people who are attractive, rewarding, prestigious, competent, and powerful are more likely to be selected as models than are people who lack these qualities (Bandura, 1962). The following informal behavioral observations are consistent with empirical findings in this regard: The aspiring young society woman does not imitate the dress, hairdo, and mannerisms of a go-go dancer but may copy those of prominent women in a group to which she would like to belong. In the same way a young boy may copy the speech and mannerisms of his hero rather than those of his more numerous and immediate associates, and, if the boy is a basketball player, he may imitate an accomplished professional rather than a friend who is no better than he. In such instances, imitation is not an end in itself; that is, it is not simply a tendency to copy blindly the actions of others. Rather, it is an effective means of attaining prestige and acceptance as well as of developing motor and social skills. Such imitation can decrease the time, effort, and risk that trial-and-error behavior would require. It provides a shortcut to the actual, overt experiences that result in effective behavior.

Conditioning in Imitation

Some imitation can be understood in terms of classical-conditioning procedures. Such conditioned responding may result from the contiguity of stimuli. (Indeed, perhaps learning occurs whenever two stimuli occur contiguously, as in the classical-conditioning situation.) One of the difficulties of experimentally demonstrating that learning occurs by contiguity alone stems from the fact that learning must be inferred from performance. It is quite possible that learning may occur but not result in immediate performance. In such a situation an experimenter may need to introduce some incentive to elicit the designated behavior from which learning can then be inferred. Thus learning may occur as a consequence of stimulus contiguity, but performance may be dependent on reinforcement (Bandura, 1965).

Much of the imitation shown by animals is probably acquired as the result of the contiguity of stimuli and their sensory consequences. For example, a calf in the pasture hears a loud sound, is startled, and runs. The calf's mother hears the same sound and runs at the same time. The calf perceives the sight and sound of its mother and other running cattle in close temporal proximity to the loud sound. If this pattern of events occurs a number of times, the sight and sound of cattle running may become a conditioned stimulus for running. After several repetitions, the calf may run whenever it hears or sees other cattle running, whether or not there is a loud sound. If this is the case, it has acquired its behavior from the contiguity of stimulus events in the same way that organisms acquire behavior in other conditioning situations.

The same general pattern is followed in some of the conditioning of a young child. For example, a mother is holding an infant in her arms when a loud sound startles mother and child. The increased tension of the mother's muscles is felt by the child at the same time that he hears the mother catch her breath or cry out. The child may also observe a frightened expression on the mother's face. Later these responses (gasp, outcry, facial expression) may come to be conditioned stimuli that produce the startle, or fear reaction, in the child. The child will thus imitate the emotional response of the mother, of other adults, or of people in general.

Imitative behavior in rats has been investigated experimentally by training rats to "follow" leader rats to receive positive reinforcement (Miller & Dollard, 1941). The experimental subjects were rewarded only if they followed their leaders, and they developed strong tendencies to follow (Church, 1957). Imitative behavior can be demonstrated in rats when the situation allows for a variety of other responses to be made (Stimbert, Schaffer, & Grimsley, 1966). In addition, children reinforced for imitating specific behaviors of a model are reported to develop tendencies to imitate not only those behaviors but other nonreinforced responses made by the model as well (Baer & Sherman, 1964). The facts that imitation is a learned response and that components of classical and instrumental conditioning are involved in its acquisition have been well established in the experimental laboratory. Much imitative behavior is acquired through conditioning, through employing reinforcements for the copier's behavior, or through allowing the copier to observe the reinforcement of a model.

Role of Reinforcement in Imitation

Reinforcement operates in acquisition of imitative behavior in the same way it does in other learning situations in which it is employed. Investigations of human and animal behavior have attested to the effectiveness of a variety of reinforcers in eliciting and maintaining imitative behavior. Imitative learning has been shown to be affected by various patterns and schedules of reinforcement, as is learning in other instrumental-conditioning situations (Lanzetta & Kanareff, 1961; Skinner, 1958).

Much imitative behavior may be acquired in day-to-day activities. Thus the role of social rewards and punishments in the acquisition of imitative behavior is an important one. Bandura (1962) has reported an extensive series of research studies in which he has demonstrated various factors influencing the effectiveness of social reinforcement with children. As we noted previously, people who are attractive, rewarding, prestigious, competent, and powerful were found to elicit more imitation than models who lack these qualities.

Social rewards and punishments are part of the culture in which children grow up and mature into adults. Some social reinforcers are rather subtle or indirect, whereas others are obvious and direct, occurring as a consequence of imitation or of deviation from the pattern of others' behavior. Out of a child's experience with social reinforcement, there develops an intricate set of tendencies to imitate, or to do the opposite of what certain other people or classes of people are observed to do. Culture has been conceptualized as a human maze with a built-in system of rewards and punishments (Sawrey & Telford, 1968). Successfully learning the cultural maze involves, in part, imitating the things that other people do. This imitation makes it possible to obtain food, drink, warmth, affection, prestige, and security more effectively than does blind trial and error. That is, the intricacies of learning socially appropriate behavior can be bypassed through observing the behavior of others and copying it.

In many life situations, imitative tendencies are rewarded and nonimitation is punished. More often than not, a child is rewarded for imitating or copying activities in which others engage. In our culture he is rewarded by approval

Figure 6-1. Imitation in skill acquisition. Thousands of Japanese children, who are not selected on the basis of special ability, learn to play the violin through positive reinforcement for the imitation of adult models. The children's mothers are asked to take up the violin at the same time they do, and their parents are encouraged to expose them from infancy to recordings of great violinists. A lesson stops when a child loses interest. (Dr. Shinichi Suzuki pioneered this program. He is the founder and president of Talent Education of Matsumoto, Japan.)

for using his spoon rather than his fingers when eating, for making sounds like those of others (talking) rather than babbling, and for making affectionate responses (hugging and kissing). As he matures, he finds that activities in which others engage are followed by pleasant consequences. Thus he may try foods that other people eat. He may learn, by copying his friends, that swimming, skating, and dancing are pleasant. On the other hand, departure from established social patterns may bring him rejection and reproof as punishments. As a result of the operation of positive and negative social reinforcers, he may develop a general tendency to conform. In this broad sense, imitation operates as a conservative process—a process that conserves accepted patterns of behavior. Of course, when imitation of the behavior of the majority is positively reinforced, people may find it difficult to break away or to be different; their individuality may thus be stifled. However, if people are positively reinforced for forms of nonconformity—that is, for creative endeavor, for innovation, and for making contributions to their culture—then they may go beyond the kind of simple conformity that produces mediocre performances.

INSIGHT

Learning situations can be so arranged that learning appears to occur suddenly. Such instances are referred to as *insightful learning*. Suddenly coming upon the solution to a problem after not having been able to solve it previously is commonly reported.

The classic demonstration of insightful learning was reported by Wolfgang Köhler (1925). A particularly intelligent chimp, Sultan, with whom Köhler was investigating problem solving, learned to solve a problem involving the use of tools. Two joinable sticks were placed inside Sultan's cage, and a banana was placed outside the cage at such a distance that it could be retrieved only by joining the two sticks. Sultan tried unsuccessfully to obtain the food with first one stick and then the other. After a time he abandoned his attempts at retrieval and sat with his back to the food. Some time elapsed, and then he picked up a stick in each hand in such a manner that they formed a straight line. Observing this, the chimpanzee thrust the end of the smaller stick into the hollow end of the larger, turned toward the food, and retrieved it. This behavior was repeated on several occasions.

Learning by insight is probably synonymous with the human phenomenon of "getting the idea," or suddenly "understanding" the problem. It has been termed the "Aha!" experience. The perception of the relationships around the stimuli has been emphasized in the analysis of such a situation. The "understanding" is said to derive from the perception of the relationships involved in the entire situation.

It can be seen from the description of the chimpanzee's behavior in solving the stick problem that he tried trial and error in his unsuccessful attempts to retrieve the banana. The sudden appearance of a solution in this and many comparable situations probably results from implicit trial and error and observation of the situation plus actual overt trials of one kind or another. Insight, then, is a product of learning rather than a unique means of learning.

Like trial and error and imitation, insightful learning is descriptive of the circumstances in which learning and performance occur. Problems can be so arranged that a solution will appear suddenly, or they can be arranged so that the solution appears gradually out of the positive and negative reinforcements of various responses. If an animal of very limited intelligence is confronted with a very difficult problem, overt trial and error is the fundamental approach to the problem. If an animal of high intelligence is presented with a very simple problem, learning appears to occur suddenly, by "insight."

Most demonstrations of insightful learning have involved problems in which the requisites of the solution are all observable to the subject. Such demonstrations—generally involving puzzles or tools—have been accomplished with children and with lower animals. When the entire problem situation can be perceived, it is likely that covert or implicit trials are employed in problem solution. For example, in putting together a jigsaw puzzle, children soon learn, with a little trial-and-error behavior, that large pieces do not fit into small spaces. They start to employ more covert or implicit trials as they develop skill in this kind of problem solution. With practice in form, size, and color discrimination, a child should have an increasing number of "Aha!" experiences as he continues to engage in such tasks.

Insight—the sudden perception of relationships—is thus not independent of the previous experience of the organism. Past experience with similar problems has been shown to increase the probability that relationships will be perceived and applied in the solution of new problems (Birch, 1945).

THE STUDY OF THE ACQUISITION OF SKILL

Much learning has to do with acquiring skill of one kind or another. Pressing a bar in a Skinner box, avoiding or escaping electric shock, running a maze, hitting a baseball, riding a bicycle, using language effectively, thinking logically, reading, writing, and performing psychological experiments are all skills that develop through learning.

The acquisition of these skills can be investigated without any particular concern for the immediate application of the knowledge gained to practical problems of education, business, or social living; the same phenomena can also be investigated to gain rather immediate, practical benefits—for example, to improve certain kinds of skills. Frequently scientific investigations are carried out for the sole purpose of adding to existing knowledge, without any real concern for the practical applicability of the results. Nevertheless the results turn out to be of practical utility. Conversely, research that is done to answer practical questions or to solve immediate problems may turn out to be a basic contribution to psychology as a science. Such results tend to obscure the line drawn between "pure" and "applied" science.

Measuring the Progress of Learning

We mentioned previously that learning cannot be measured directly but can only be inferred from performance. When one wishes to know something of the course or rate of learning, he must find some way to measure performance. There are several kinds of conventional measures.

If a person wishes to know how long it takes the average college student to memorize a given poem or list of nonsense syllables, he can simply direct subjects to learn the list or poem as rapidly as possible. The *criterion* for having learned is usually the subject's ability to recite one time perfectly what is learned. The measure taken would, in this case, be the amount of *time* elapsing between starting to study a written item and being able to recite it perfectly. This measure of learning is relatively crude and tells nothing about the *course* of acquisition during the required period of time. A comparable measure of learning can be made by keeping track of the *number of trials* (number of repetitions) required before perfect performance can be made. Such measures determine the differences in speed of acquisition between two known but differing groups of individuals.

The amount of skill possessed at any given time can be used as a measure to determine the amount of skill gained per unit of practice. Such is the case in learning to operate a typewriter. One can measure the speed of someone's typing after the person has typed so many lines or pages or has spent so much time in practice. Speed can be plotted against units of practice, and one can draw a curve of progress over so much time or so much practice. A hypothetical *learning curve* for gain in typewriting skill is presented in Figure 6-2.

In some situations, such as maze learning, one can maintain a record of the number of errors committed on each trial. Such *error scores* reflect the progress of learning by the reduction of the number of errors per trial. When the task can be performed without error, the learning *criterion* has been reached. When

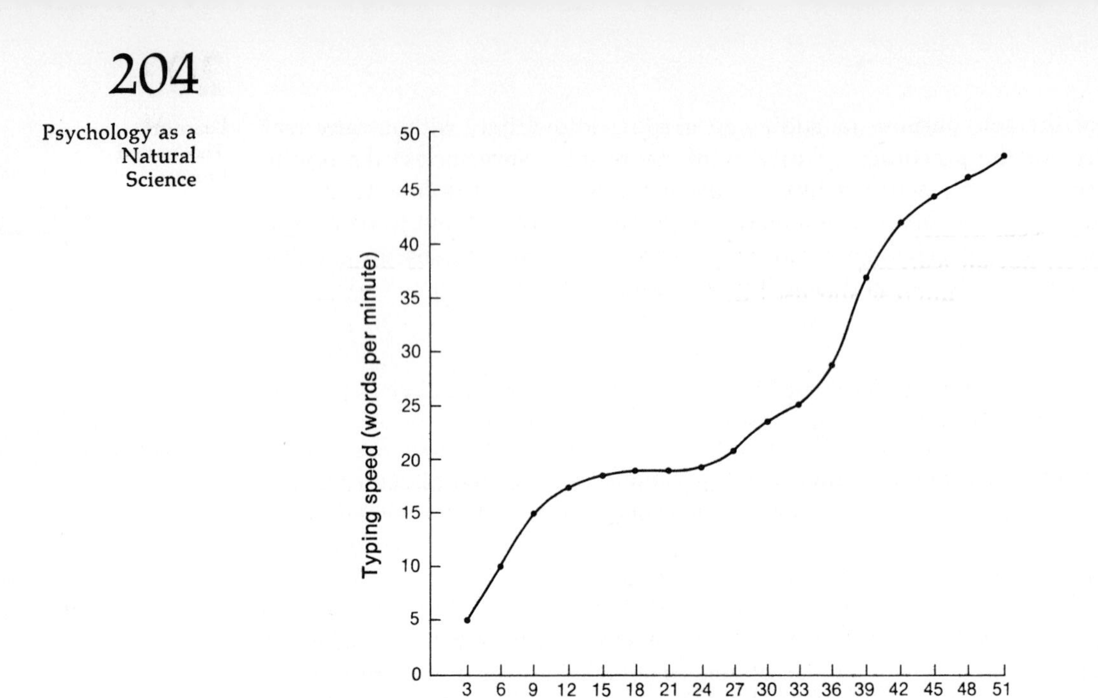

Figure 6-2. A hypothetical learning curve for gain in typewriting skill.

the number of errors is plotted against the number of trials, the resulting curve starts out high and gradually decreases (Figure 6-3). It can be observed from the curve in Figure 6-3 that the course of learning does not run smoothly. Variation in the number of errors from trial to trial is typical and has many causes, including motivation and attention as well as variations in the conditions of performance.

Another frequent measure of learning is the rate of responding. Such a measure is taken when a record is maintained of the number of bar presses a rat makes in a Skinner box over a given period of time. Changes in *rate* of bar pressing indicate the *course* of learning.

When skill is plotted against amount of practice, there is likely to be rapid progress from a small to a moderate amount of skill during the earliest period (the first 15 hours of practice in Figure 6-2). After this initial rapid increase in performance, many hours of practice may result in little progress (practice hours 18 to 27, Figure 6-2). This period is called a *plateau* in learning because improvement levels off and the curve reaches a flattened area. With continued practice further gains are made until, finally, a level of optimum performance may be reached.

Plateaus occur in most curves that depict the course of the acquisition of skills. However, not all learning curves contain plateaus. If the learner maintains a constant level of interest and uses the same procedure throughout the task—and the task is well within his limits of ability—he may avoid the learning plateau entirely. It is doubtful, under the ordinary circumstances of day-to-day living, that many of us ever really perform fully to the point of our physiological limits. After all, records of performances of one kind or another are broken nearly every day. Under ordinary circumstances most of us are not sufficiently motivated to reach our physiological limits because we do not have to in order to receive the kinds of satisfactions that we seek.

Distribution of Practice

The question of how one should space his efforts for most effective learning is an interesting one, from the standpoint of both scientific curiosity and prac-

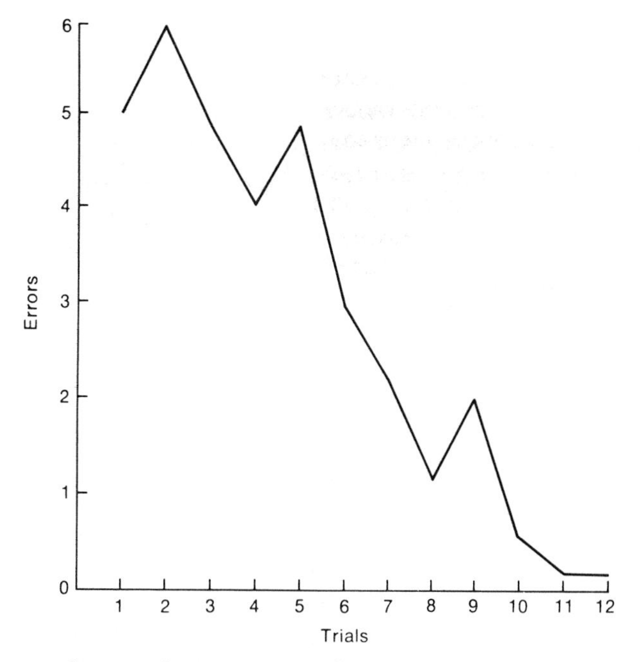

Figure 6-3. Reduction of errors over trials in learning a simple maze. (Entering a wrong alley is considered an error.)

tical concern. Should we have short practice sessions with frequent rest periods? Should we start to practice and stick to the task until it is mastered, with as little intervening rest and distraction as possible? Should learning trials be *massed,* or should they be *spaced* at some particular interval? Will five hours of massed practice result in the same level of performance as five one-hour periods of practice separated by half-hour rest periods?

Kimble (1949) required five different groups of subjects to print the alphabet upside down and backward. Each group was allowed 20 trials of 30 seconds each. The period between trials (intertrial interval) was either 0, 5, 10, 15, or 30 seconds. The results showed that after the first 10 trials the advantage of spacing the trials increased proportionately as the length of the rest period increased. Intertrial intervals of greater than 30 seconds were not investigated, so it is not known whether there would have been an even greater advantage with longer intervals. Other investigators have found that rats learn a simple maze with fewer trials if the trials are spaced 12 hours apart rather than 6 hours apart (Warden, 1923) and when one trial is given every three days as opposed to one each day (Ulrich, 1915).

Experimental evidence indicates that for many sensorimotor skills and verbal materials, spaced practice is superior to massed practice. However, when learning involves a high degree of problem solving, the advantage of spacing tends to disappear. In studies of concept learning and problem solving, in which the correct response and patterns of responses must be derived from a number of possibilities, massed practice proves to be better than the spacing of practice periods (Erickson, 1942; Riley, 1952). It has been reported (Kendler, Greenberg, & Richman, 1952) that when problem solving requires shifts in methods of attack from one problem to another, spaced practice may be an advantage because inappropriate "mental sets" are more likely to develop under conditions of massed than distributed practice.

Massing practice and spacing practice have different effects for different levels of ability. Studies of the effects of massed versus spaced practice on grade-school children of high, medium, and low intelligence found that the advantage of spaced practice was greater for those of low intelligence than for those of medium or high intelligence (Madsen, 1963). Essentially the same results have been obtained using strains of rats known to differ in maze-learning ability (McGaugh, Jennings, & Thomson, 1962).

The beneficial effects of spaced practice have been demonstrated under a wide variety of conditions in numerous learning situations. In general, spaced practice has been found to be superior to massed practice in the learning of meaningful and meaningless material, in school learning situations, in both human and animal maze learning, in the learning of code-substitution tasks, and in the acquisition of sensorimotor skills. One notable exception to this generalization is that massed practice appears to be more effective than spaced practice in certain complex learning and problem-solving situations.

The most effective scheduling of practice and rest will vary from task to task and from individual to individual. In general, however, periods of practice should be relatively frequent and long enough so that the entire series of appropriate responses can be learned, but not so long that fatigue becomes a factor, causing interest and attention to wane.

Meaningfulness as "Association Value"

The more meaningful the material to be learned, the more readily learning will occur. This generalization, long held by psychologists and laymen alike, is given support by a host of research results. However, the difficulty involved in invoking "meaningfulness of material" to account for differences in the ease with which various materials are learned has been that the meaning of the word *meaning* is elusive. Early psychological definitions of meaning were lacking in the conciseness essential for the purposes of scientific investigation. *Meaningfulness* gradually became more meaningful as psychologists began to employ word association as a technique. In the use of word association, a subject is given a word as a stimulus and asked to respond with whatever associations he might have with that word. One can view the operational meaning of a word as the associative responses to that word. Meaningfulness can then be quantified by using the number of associative responses to the stimulus word.

Glaze (1928) determined the "association value" of various nonsense syllables (combinations of letters that do not form a word) by presenting them to subjects who were asked to respond with any association that the syllable brought to mind. If all subjects responded with an association, it was assigned an association value of 100 percent; if the syllable evoked responses from only two-thirds of the subjects, it was given an association value of 66 percent.

Association value, determined by the number of subjects reporting associations, by the number of associations reported in a given time, or by combination of subjects' ratings of the meaningfulness of the stimulus word, was made an operational definition of meaning. Hull (1933) explicitly defined *meaning* as association value. Despite the fact that differing methods were employed in deriving indices of meaning, the meaningfulness scores obtained for the various syllables are highly similar (Noble, Stockwell, & Pryer, 1957).

Associative meaning is not a simple unitary dimension; it includes a variety of factors that also influence rate of learning. Pronounceability and association value are positively related (Underwood & Schulz, 1960). Association value is also related to the frequency of occurrence, which in turn is related to emotionality as indicated by the subject's ratings of the item on a pleasant-unpleasant scale (Noble, 1958). Words and concepts may have *connotative meaning*, which is ascribed three major dimensions: evaluation (good-bad), potency (strong-weak), and activity (active-passive) (Osgood & Suci, 1955). All these factors, in addition to number of associations, operate to influence the course of learning.

The three lists in Table 6-1 are composed of units of unequal associative meaning. The first list is composed of three-letter nonsense syllables. The second list contains words with the same letters as those of the first list, and the third list contains words that may all be associated with school. In comparing the number of repetitions, or amount of time required for the average person to learn each of these lists, it is found that the list of nonsense syllables requires the most repetitions (10–12), the three-letter words next (3–4), and the list of related words least (1–2). The ease of learning these lists is directly related to their meaningfulness. This generalization holds for serial learning (as in the learning of the lists), paired-associate learning (as in the learning of foreign words paired with their English equivalents), and the learning of complex or extensive verbal material (mastery of content).

Table 6-1. Lists of words with varying degrees of meaningfulness.

wne	for	teacher
yrd	sun	chalk
dna	the	write
sah	red	blackboard
yob	cob	examination
boc	boy	read
der	has	grade
eht	and	pass
nus	dry	fail
rof	new	repeat

In addition to association value per se, the pattern, organization, or form of the material to be learned is involved in meaningfulness. It has been demonstrated that subjects require twice as much time to learn 200 words of prose as they do the same number of words of poetry (Lyon, 1914) and that logical arrangements of materials facilitate learning (Bruner, 1963). The patterning and organization of the material seem to make it more meaningful and thus easier to learn. The experimental literature on the concept of meaning is extensive and continues to expand (Creelman, 1966).

Additional Factors in Learning

Attitude, or set. An important factor influencing the rate of learning has to do with the attitude, or set, of the learner. If the learner intends to learn—is *interested* in the task—learning proceeds at a more rapid pace than if there is little or no desire or intention to learn. Dozens of experiments and hundreds of incidental observations have demonstrated the enormous advantage of an active, aggressive attitude and a high level of attention and concentration, as contrasted with a passive, listless attitude and its accompanying low level of concentration. A student who repeated a list of 13 nonsense syllables over and over without any particular instructions to learn required about 100 repetitions before he mastered the list. The same student learned comparable lists with one-tenth the number of repetitions when he was instructed to learn (MacDougal & Smith, 1919). Sanford (1917) reports that over a period of 25 years he had read the "Order for Daily Morning Prayer" of the Episcopal Church at least 5000 times but was unable to recall the prayer without prompting. It seems clear that *intention to learn* and *attention to the task* are essential for efficient learning.

Knowledge of results. Knowledge of the results of practice operates to facilitate learning and performance in at least two ways. (1) It provides *information* so that the learner can identify his errors and successes more readily. This information assists him in eliminating errors and directs his attention to those facets of his behavior that result in improvement or success. (2) It is *motivational* in that knowledge of how he is progressing toward a goal helps him maintain active interest in the task at hand and results in enhanced performance.

Whole versus part methods of learning. If a learning task is relatively long or involved, would it be better to attempt to learn the required material as a unit or to divide it into smaller portions? The answer to this question cannot be stated in a concise fashion that would cover all individuals and tasks. Early researchers recommended the "whole" method as being superior, but this blanket recommendation is subject to several restrictions (McGeoch & Irion, 1953). It has been shown that the more intelligent the subjects, the more likely they are to be able to use the "whole" method to advantage. Older students also seem to be able to profit more from the "whole" procedure than do younger ones. Furthermore, it has been demonstrated that the effectiveness of the "whole" method is greater under conditions of distributed, as opposed to massed, practice and that practice with the "whole" method increases its effectiveness.

Both methods appear to have advantages and disadvantages for learning, although the "whole" method tends to work better than the "part" method with meaningful material. Most material taken as a whole is more meaningful than when it is divided into segments. The meaningfulness and organization of the material are left intact with the "whole" method, and the additional task of learning the proper order of the parts is avoided. On the other hand, when a person learns a discrete part of the total material to be learned, he has clear evidence that progress is being made and thus tends to maintain his motivation to learn. In that most people have had practice with the "part" method, its familiarity may have some advantages.

It is likely that advantages accrue from a combination of "whole" and "part" learning. After a complete task is studied enough to give it meaning and some perceived continuity, attention may then be directed to its more difficult parts. Large and meaningful parts can be studied and then pieced together for further study by the whole method. The relative efficiency of the two methods will depend somewhat on the individual, previous learning practices, and the nature of the material to be learned. No hard and fast rule will cover all the variables, but for many learning situations there are advantages that derive from the "whole" method.

Attempts to recall. In studying ideational or verbal material, it is possible to read and reread the material until learning is complete. However, studies have shown that, after initial study or reading, a considerable portion of time may be effectively devoted to attempted recall. It has also been demonstrated that the sooner recall attempts are made after initial reading, the shorter the learning process (Skaggs & Grossman, 1930).

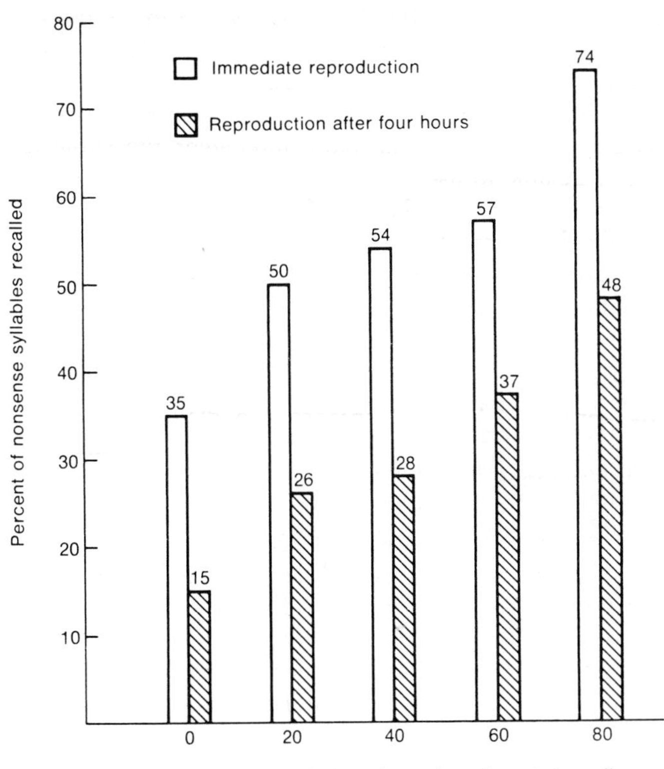

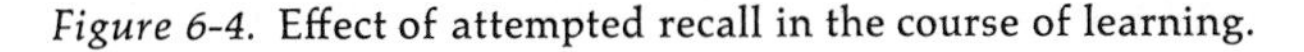
Figure 6-4. Effect of attempted recall in the course of learning.

A comprehensive study involving the learning of both nonsense syllables and short biographies by fourth-grade, sixth-grade, and eighth-grade students has become a classic reference in this area. The results of this investigation show that, as the relative amount of time spent in recall increases from 0 to 80 percent, the amount of material learned increases. When 80 percent of the time is spent in recitation, the recall scores are more than twice as large as those obtained when the entire time is devoted to reading and rereading (Gates, 1917).

The advantages of attempting recall as one studies probably accrue from some factors that were previously discussed. Attempting recall (1) provides knowledge of progress, (2) directs attention to the task and actively involves the learner in the situation, and (3) provides practice of the very thing one must do when learning is complete. By contrast, reading and rereading material do not afford much practice in recalling the material. If recall is the goal of learning, recall should be practiced.

Repetitions. How many times will one have to go over some material to learn it? How long will one have to practice in order to learn? Research evidence is unclear as to the function of repetition in learning. Thorndike (1931) concluded, after performing an elaborate set of experiments designed to determine the role of repetition in learning, that repetition in and of itself has no selective power and cannot account for learning. The generality of this conclusion still seems reasonable.

Repetition without intent to learn, without knowledge of results, and without reinforcement probably has little effect on learning. Repetition apparently makes possible the operation of other factors that are more directly responsible for changes in behavior. Repetition may be important when only a fraction of the stimulus situation becomes conditioned on any given trial. In such a case repetitions would be required to produce sufficient learning for adequate performance.

Transfer of Learning

"Transfer" refers to the effect of previous learning on subsequent learning. Having learned *X*, will it be easier or harder for one to learn*Y*? Research on transfer deals with the extent to which acquisition of skill, knowledge, understanding, and attitudes in one situation affects such acquisition in other situations. Transfer does occur. If it did not, all the learning that takes place would be of no use beyond the situation wherein it first occurred.

An early view held that students could acquire *mental discipline* through study. This view was based on the theory that man's mind is composed of various *faculties*, such as memory, reasoning, will, and attention. According to *faculty psychology*, these mental faculties could be strengthened and improved, much as a muscle is strengthened by exercise and practice. A faculty of mind, properly trained, was held to function equally well in all situations, even though training had been in a particular situation. Such a view of human functioning has been demonstrated to be lacking in validity, but vestiges of the theory persist. One hears an occasional reference to "strengthening the mind and sharpening its faculties."

William James (1890) found that practice in memorizing materials of a given writer was not of particular help in subsequently memorizing the writings of another author. James concluded that the power of retention was not affected by training and that improvement in memory as the result of practice was not due to any improvement in *retentiveness* but was the result of improvement in the *method* of memorizing. Investigations such as James' tended to discredit the mental-discipline doctrine, and a great number of studies were performed that were interpreted as evidence against the doctrine.

Transfer theory. As a result of the research questioning the whole doctrine of mental discipline, Thorndike and Woodworth (1901) concluded: "Improvement in any single mental function need not improve the ability in functions commonly called by the same name. It may injure it. Improvement in any single mental function rarely brings about equal improvement in any other function, no matter how similar, for the working of every mental function-group is conditioned by the nature of the data in each particular case. . . . There is no inner necessity for improvement of one function to improve others closely similar to it, due to definite factors, the operation of which the training may or may not secure." Thorndike (1903) later stated these conclusions more concisely in his theory of *identical elements:* "A change in one function alters any other only insofar as the two functions have as factors identical elements." The identities that he cited included methods, general principles, attitudes, and ideas about aims. Such transfer has been demonstrated in a variety of research situations.

It has been contended that transfer is not a function of identical elements in two situations, but that insight into the situation in all its *relationships* is essential in securing general training. Köhler (1929) taught subjects (chickens, chimpanzees, and a 3-year-old child) that food could be obtained by going to one of two stimuli, one of which was light gray and the other dark gray. The food was invariably obtained by going to the dark-gray stimulus. After learning was complete (the chickens required 400–600 trials, the child 45), a gray stimulus darker than either of the two original ones was substituted for the light-gray one. The chickens went to the new stimulus on 70 percent of the test trials and to the original positive stimulus on 30 percent of the trials. The child invariably went to the new darker stimulus. It is contended that the subjects did not respond to an identical stimulus in the two situations but that they responded to the relationship "darker of two." This sort of evidence was interpreted to mean that insight into relationships was the real means of securing general transfer. However, if the concept "darker of two" is considered to be an identical component in the two tasks, Köhler's results could be interpreted in terms of identical-elements theory. Although such a liberal use of the term *identical elements* was objectionable to some theorists, it was acceptable to Thorndike.

The transfer of discrimination learned on one set of stimuli to new pairs of stimuli is called *transposition*. Researchers have found that the amount of transfer decreases as the difference between training and test stimuli becomes larger. Spence (1937) has accounted for transposition phenomena in terms of the generalization of excitation and inhibition from the original positive and negative stimuli. Such a formulation, although extremely useful, will have to be expanded in order to account for some of the aspects of transposition (Ellis, 1965).

The enhancement of transfer effects. Research has shown that there are ways by which transfer effects can be enhanced. A simple design for a transfer experiment is shown in Table 6-2.

Transfer effects may be either positive (facilitation) or negative (interference). It is difficult to make a definitive statement as to the conditions under which each type of effect will occur; however, a reasonably accurate generalization can be made. In general, when the task requires that an old response be made to a new stimulus, the effects will be positive; when a new response to an old stimulus is required, the effects will be negative. An example of a positive transfer effect is the use of skills learned in school (old response) to outside-of-school situations (new stimuli). Negative effects would derive from having to stop (new response) rather than start when a traffic light is green (old stimulus).

Woodrow (1927), in an experiment with college students, demonstrated that transfer effects could be enhanced by certain procedures. A control group was tested only at the beginning and end of the experiment. A practice group, in addition, devoted three hours to memorizing poetry and nonsense syllables. A training group divided the same amount of time equally between instruction and exercise in "proper methods of memorizing." Subsequent tests of memory span and memorization of verbal materials of various kinds showed that the training group was better than the other two groups on every test. Undirected drill or practice produced little or no transfer, whereas directed training with the same materials produced consistently large and positive transfer effects. This and other investigations have demonstrated that transfer can be enhanced if practice is directed toward effective training for transfer. Transfer of training does not occur automatically as a function of identity. Thus active search

Table 6-2. Design for an experiment in transfer.

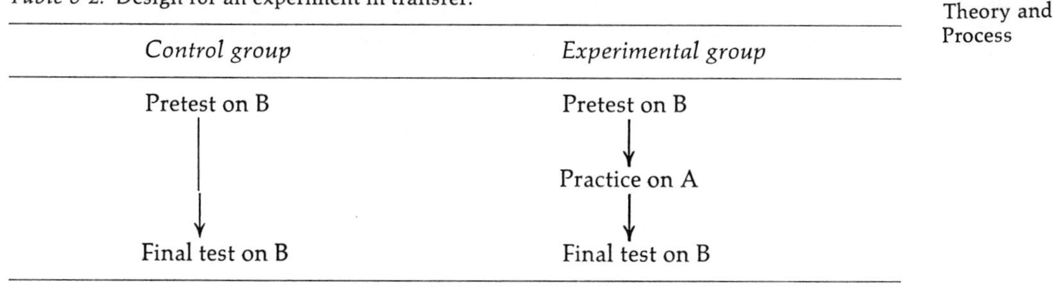

Control group	*Experimental group*
Pretest on B	Pretest on B
↓	↓
	Practice on A
	↓
Final test on B	Final test on B

for principles, relationships, and similarities, as well as an intent, or set, to transfer what is learned, should be encouraged by those who direct or manage learning activities.

Learning to learn. The concept of learning to learn (Harlow, 1949) has been derived as a result of the observation that problems or tasks of increasing levels of difficulty can be solved by providing the subject with a sequence of tasks of increasing complexity. By progressively increasing task difficulty in training, problems can be solved that could not be solved by subjects directly trained only on the complex task itself (Harlow & Harlow, 1949; Duncan, 1958). In such training situations, the subject learns how to attack the problem and, as a result of his successes on earlier tasks, develops an interest in learning. Originality training, provided by reinforcement for giving original responses to stimuli, has been shown to enhance the originality of responses in subsequent situations (Maltzman, 1960). The importance of previous learning (learning to learn) and the transfer of "set" to learn have been emphasized in the acquisition of new knowledge and in learning from programmed instruction (Gagné, 1962).

THEORIES OF LEARNING

The psychologist, like other scientists, builds theories that enable him to better understand diverse phenomena and to make predictions about the matters of concern to him. A theory provides a general point of view—a frame of reference within which one is able to think productively about the phenomena of concern. Furthermore, a theory provides a set of generalizations from which testable predictions can be made. Thus it provides a guide for scientific investigation (research) that will tend to confirm or deny the theory's truth and utility. Several general theories of learning have been formulated that tend to serve these functions. Sahakian (1970) has described both general and limited theories of learning in an abbreviated and readable fashion.

When competing theories exist within any field of investigation, there is a tendency to discount the validity of knowledge within that field. However, the existence of competing theories does not imply that the research and knowledge in the field are faulty; rather, it reflects differences in how empirical data are interpreted. Two theorists may look at the same empirical results and interpret them differently. Neither denies the existence or the validity of the data derived from replicable, scientific investigations. They both accept the same kinds of data, but they try to make sense out of them within differing frames of reference.

General theories of learning can be roughly divided into two kinds, those that are termed *stimulus-response* theories and those that are termed *cognitive* theories.

Stimulus-response theorists emphasize the importance of associations between stimuli and responses that develop as the result of experience. The association, or link, between a stimulus and a response is said to occur as the result of learning. S-R theorists are inclined to follow the reductionist model provided by the physical scientists. That is, they are eager to analyze learning situations, to divide learning phenomena into small elements, and to investigate the simplest possible S-R relationships in order to better understand the more complex total phenomena. Such theorists are thus said to be *atomistic* or *molecular* in their scientific approach.

Cognitive theorists generally believe that the reductionist approach to learning loses the essential character of the phenomenon. They prefer to attempt to describe and understand a whole complex-learning situation. They maintain that the whole is not equal to the sum of its parts and prefer to view a learning situation as one whole, complete phenomenon. Such an approach has been called a *molar* one.

S-R theorists make little or no reference to central or brain processes in the integration of simple responses into complex ones. Instead, they place heavy emphasis on the overt, observable behavior of the organism. They tend to view overt responses as the integrators and mediators of behavior. Because of this emphasis on observable responses and their role in learning, S-R theories are said to be *peripheral*. Cognitive theorists have been designated as *central* as opposed to peripheral in their orientation because they readily invoke central or brain processes as the integrators of behavior.

S-R theorists analyze the behavior of a rat running through a maze to an unseen goal box in terms of conditioned responses to the stimuli of the maze that produce running as a response. The muscular responses provide stimuli to which further running becomes conditioned, and so on until the goal is reached. On the other hand, cognitive theorists prefer to interpret the same behavior in terms of central processes. The animal is said to run in the maze because it has an "expectancy" of food.

Theorists disagree as to what is learned. S-R theorists emphasize the acquisition of habits of responding. For them, habits, or responses to stimuli, are what is learned. Cognitive theorists contend that knowledge, or cognitive structures, is what is learned and that behavior is derived from a knowledge of what leads to what. Cognitive theorists are inclined to account for problem solving in terms of cognitive restructuring, or insight, whereas S-R theorists tend to emphasize transfer of previous experience and trial and error in the solution of problems.

The general learning theories of Hull (1951) and Tolman (1932) are representative of S-R and cognitive theories, respectively. The long-raging theoretical controversy between these positions has not come to an end, but many of the differences in general theory have been moderated. The great body of findings relative to learning has served to provide an empirical base for the consideration of the phenomena of learning. Research over the past few years has tended to be guided more by existing data than by existing theoretical considerations.

The current trend in the construction of learning theory appears to be away from the building of omnibus, general theories and toward the building of miniature theories to account for particular phenomena of learning. This trend has been evident for the past decade or more. The development of miniature theories has probably stemmed from the complexity of learning itself. A single general theory to account for all learning phenomena may simply not be feasible at present, although miniature theories can and do help to clarify what is happening in particular situations. Someday, learning theorists may be engaged in the integration of miniature theories into a complex of theories that will provide a general theoretical base for the study of learning —a theoretical base to match its broad empirical base.

SUMMARY

Imitation is both a product of learning and a means of facilitating further learning. Imitation is a behavior that is learned in the same manner that other behaviors are learned by both men and lower animals. It can be used to reduce trial-and-error behavior and thus short-circuit the learning process. Insight is considered a product of learning rather than a unique learning process.

Learning frequently is measured by the amount of time required to learn, by the number of trials before a performance criterion of one perfect repetition is reached, by the reduction of the number of errors over trials, or by the rate of responding. Measurements of the progress of learning can be plotted on a graph to yield curves of learning. Many, but not all, learning curves show a leveling off after initial rapid progress. This relatively level portion of the curve is termed a *plateau.*

There are a number of factors to be considered in the acquisition of skills of one kind or another: the nature of the material to be learned, the most appropriate distribution of practice and rest, and the meaningfulness of the material to be learned. Other factors affecting the rate of learning are the motivation—the attitude and interest—of the learner, the extensiveness and immediacy of knowledge of results of practice, the method of practice employed, and the frequency with which recall is attempted.

Transfer of learning from one task to other related tasks has been the topic of a great deal of research. The broad utility of much that is learned is dependent on effective transfer of principles, identities, attitudes, and skills. Transfer
of a great deal of research. The broad utility of much that is learned is depen-
the adherents of the mental-discipline doctrine. However, if one desires to learn something, he shows good sense to study it rather than something related to it and then to depend on transfer's taking care of the situation.

Although there is some difference of opinion about what is transferred and how transfer takes place, there is no question that it does occur. In general, when an old response is to be made to a new stimulus, the transfer effect will be positive; when a new response is to be made to an old stimulus, the effect will be negative. The kind of material involved, the type of training, the motivation, the techniques of learning, the intelligence, and a number of other factors affect transfer.

Theories of learning have been developed to explain what happens when learning occurs and to provide a point of view or frame of reference in investigating learning phenomena. Two principal families of theory are the *stimulus-response* theories and the *cognitive* theories. Current emphasis in learning tends to be on the development of miniature theories to explain learning in definite, circumscribed situations.

SUGGESTED READINGS

Bandura A., & Walters, R. H. *Social learning and personality development.* New York: Holt, Rinehart & Winston, 1963. The role of imitation in social learning is treated in this short, readable book.

Ellis, H. C. *The transfer of learning.* New York: Macmillan, 1965. An excellent review of empirical findings on transfer is provided in this paperback book.

Hill, W. F. *Learning: A survey of psychological interpretations.* San Francisco: Chandler, 1963. This paperback presents a very readable introduction to learning theories.

Logan, F. A., & Wagner, A. R. *Reward and punishment.* Boston: Allyn and Bacon, 1965. This book provides an excellent advanced treatment of the role of reward and punishment in behavior.

Staats, A. W., & Staats, C. K. *Complex human behavior.* New York: Holt, Rinehart & Winston, 1963. The authors present a systematic extension of learning principles to complex behavioral phenomena.

Retention and Forgetting

Memory and learning are complementary aspects of the same general process. If there were no retention of the results of previous practice, each learning trial would result in the same behavior as the first one; there could be no learning without the hold-over effects of previous experience. Learning refers to modifications (presumably neural) resulting from experience; memory is the term applied to the persistence of such modifications. Psychologists separate memory and learning so that learning can be broken down into more readily discernible components for purposes of investigation and discussion.

A memory of an experience may be negligible, partial, or rather complete. The variables affecting retention are essentially the same as those that affect acquisition; thus the factors that facilitate learning also facilitate retention.

EVIDENCE OF RETENTION

Whenever anything is learned, there must be a change of some kind in the nervous system. The precise nature of these changes is not known, but they have been referred to as the *memory trace*.

In view of our lack of information as to what actually takes place in the nervous system when we learn, some investigators prefer to make no assumptions about neural traces. They are content with the simple observation that, as practice continues, there is an increasing probability that a given stimulus will be followed by a given response. This probability is referred to as *associative strength*, which is investigated without speculations about neural traces.

Repeated Performances

A person learning a poem or list of nonsense syllables to a criterion of three perfect repetitions is asked to repeat the poem or list one minute after the cessation of practice and is able to do so. The results of practice have been retained at least for a minute. Such retention is commonly observed. Retention of some learned materials after the elapse of periods of time involving days or even weeks is not uncommon.

Rats that have learned to run a maze or solve simple discrimination problems have been observed performing a learned task perfectly after a month with no intervening practice. Still higher organisms may retain such habits for very long periods of time—weeks, months, or even years. Certain motor skills, once acquired, appear to be retained for life. For example, having once learned to ride a bicycle, people find they can ride after half a century without practice.

If an organism is able to repeat a performance after an intervening period without practice, the repetition is evidence of retention of the results of learning. However, such evidence does not tell us a great deal. Either an individual can still ride a bicycle or he cannot, can still recite a poem or he cannot, or can still solve a problem or he cannot. The criterion of being able to perform the task tells us nothing of the *amount* of a learned task that is retained by those who are unable to perform whatever task is required.

Relearning as Evidence of Retention

Retention is not always sufficient to result in perfect performance of previously learned material. If we determine *how much* material has been retained, we will have a more subtle measure than that provided when the criterion for retention is simply being able to repeat the performance. To get an indication of amount retained, we can keep track of the number of trials or the amount of time it takes to learn to do something to a given criterion; then, after a period of no practice, during which some forgetting occurs, we can have the subject relearn the task to the same criterion of performance as before. If we now compare the number of trials or amount of time it takes to relearn the task with the number of trials or amount of time it took to learn it initially, we can determine the proportion of material retained to material forgotten. For example, a rat may initially require 20 trials to learn a maze to a criterion of three successive repetitions without error and may relearn the same maze some time later in 5 trials. The difference in number of trials between learning and relearning is 15. This figure constitutes 75 percent of the number of trials originally required, and we conclude that 75 percent of the task was retained. Stated in terms of forgetting, the rat had forgotten 25 percent of the task. There was a *saving* of 75 percent in relearning. This method is termed the *savings method* of measuring retention. By this method experimenters have shown that rats save an average of 90 percent on relearning a maze after two weeks and 73 percent after eight weeks (Tsai, 1924).

Titchener (1923), a famous psychologist, reported savings in time to relearn 200 lines of Milton's hymn "Morning of Christ's Nativity" after original learning 46 years previously; Worcester (1923) found a 40 percent savings in time to relearn a prose selection after a period of 5 years; Ebbinghaus (1885) reported savings in time to relearn stanzas of "Don Juan" after 22 years.

Savings in the amount of time and in the number of repetitions required for relearning have occurred when subjects had not learned material to the point of recall, and even when no attempt was made originally to learn the material. This phenomenon is well illustrated by a prolonged investigation by a psychologist who used his son as a subject (Burtt, 1941). The psychologist read certain Greek passages aloud to his son when the child was between the ages of 15 months and 36 months. Years later he required the child to memorize them, as well as some passages to which the child had never been exposed. Some of the passages were memorized after 7 years and others after 12 years. The average number of repetitions needed to learn the old material was 317 and to learn the new passages 435. There was a saving of 27 percent, even though there was no intent to learn, and learning to the point of recall was never initially established. The materials learned after 12 years yielded only a small saving over new material, but in each instance the repetitions required were fewer than those required for new passages of equal difficulty.

Delayed Reaction as Evidence of Retention

When a subject responds to a stimulus that has come and gone, we assume that the response depends on some kind of internal process that represents the absent transitory stimulus. Such an internal process has been designated a *symbolic process* (Hunter, 1913). Investigations of the ability of animals to respond to a stimulus after it has stopped have indicated that for certain of the lower animals to respond correctly, the period of delay must be very short and the directional orientation of their bodies must not be changed. Rats and dogs did not respond correctly in a situation in which one of three compartments (the one in which a light occurred) was to be approached for food, unless the organism kept its head turned toward the compartment where the stimulus had occurred. Children and raccoons, on the other hand, were able to respond correctly in such a situation after considerable delay and without maintaining a constant directional posture (Hunter, 1913). Subsequent investigations have indicated that rats and dogs can perform such tasks in simplified situations (Munn, 1950). Primates have been shown to exhibit recall after considerable periods of delay. In such situations the subject is allowed to observe food being placed under one of two cups. The subject is then removed from the situation; later he is brought back to test his ability to recall the cup under which food was placed. Such demonstrations have shown successful recall after periods of hours (Tinklepaugh, 1928; Harlow, Uhling, & Maslow, 1932).

The period of delay after which recall can occur tends to increase from lower mammals to humans. It also tends to increase in humans from infancy to adulthood. As language develops in children, they become more and more capable of recall after delay. Language perhaps provides the symbolic representation necessary for recall after long periods. However, we should not discount the fact that recall after delay is not independent of immediate stimulation. Some stimulus events are essential in activating the symbolic representations to which the subject overtly responds.

MEASUREMENT OF RETENTION

When we say that someone has forgotten the answer to a question, we are not necessarily saying that he will not recall the answer under different circumstances. Thus popular use of the word *forgetting* takes into account the effect of various factors on the process of remembering.

Several different measures are available to determine the amount of retention of learned material. (Naturally, an obtained score is a function of the particular measure employed.) One method for measuring the amount of retention in humans is to ask them questions about material they have studied; measures of this nature are known as *methods of recall.* The subject is expected to recall, with no further stimuli, the correct answer to such questions as "In what year did Columbus discover America?" Similarly, the subject is asked to draw a simple geometric form to which he has been exposed. He is expected to reproduce the figure without further hints or cues. Such a recall method measures whether or not a subject can, at a given moment, produce the correct response. If he can, he is said to have *recalled* the answer; if he cannot, he is said to have *forgotten* it. Recall methods yield the lowest scores of all the measures of retention that can be employed. We cannot always recall all the things we know.

If a *recognition method* of measuring retention is employed, it will yield a somewhat higher score than do methods of recall. It is well known that it is usually easier to recognize a familiar melody than to recall it. Students who are asked to recall answers to specific questions do not answer as many questions on a test correctly as do students who are asked to pick the correct answer from among four alternatives provided. A question on a multiple-choice test is a measure of retention that employs the recognition method.

The recognition method can be used in the laboratory by showing the subject in an experiment a group of 20 photographs. After a time we can remove the pictures and mix them with another 20 photographs that have not been seen by the subject. His task then is to sort out those pictures that he has previously seen. If he picks them all correctly, there is no difficulty in saying that his score is 100 (or, if he gets them all wrong, that his score is zero). However, if there are scores between zero and 100, one must correct for chance success by employing the following correction formula:

$$\text{Recognition score} = 100\left[\frac{\text{right} - \text{wrong}}{\text{total}}\right]$$

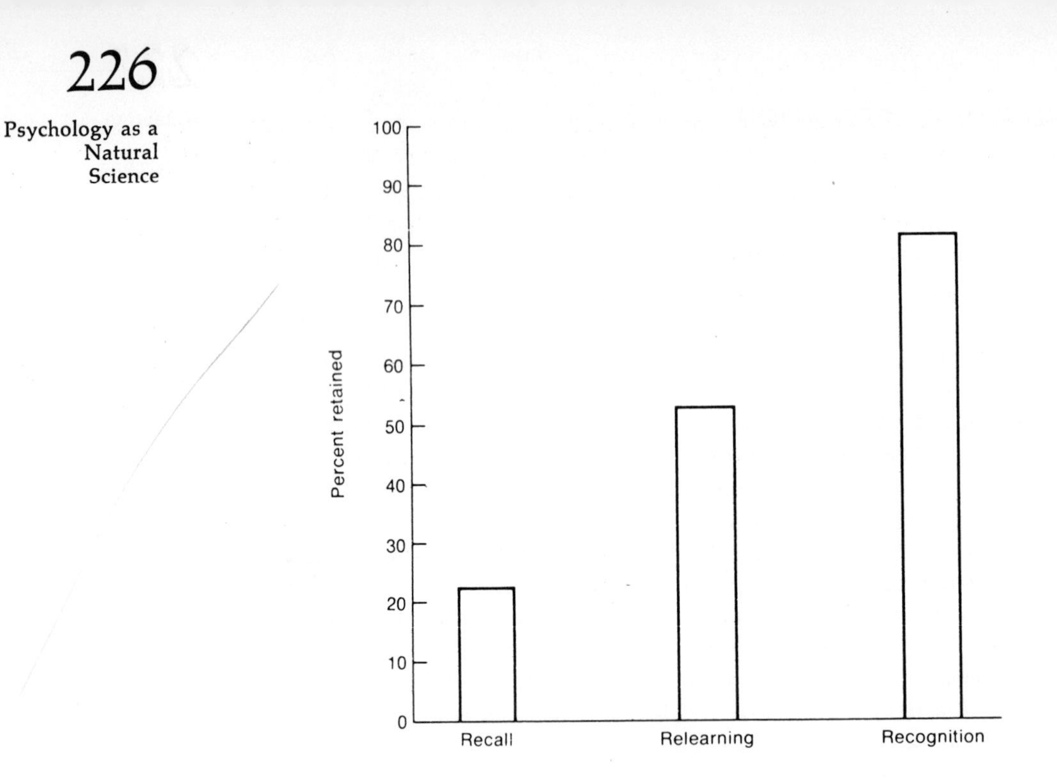

Figure 7-1. Retention of nonsense syllables as a function of method of measurement one day following learning (after Luh, 1922).

This formula is needed because the subject could select half the pictures correctly by chance. Thus, using this formula, one can see that if the subject selected 15 of the 20 pictures correctly, he would get a score of 50, even though he selected 75 percent of the pictures correctly.

A third method of measuring learning is the *method of relearning.* A subject learns something to a given criterion (one perfect repetition), forgetting occurs, and then he relearns the same material to the same criterion. The measurements in this case are the number of trials or the amount of time required for initial learning and the number of trials or amount of time required for relearning. The percent of retention can then be calculated by this simple formula:

$$100\left[\frac{\text{initial trials} - \text{relearning trials}}{\text{initial trials}}\right] = \%\ \text{saving.}$$

Scores obtained by using the relearning method are called *savings scores.*

All three methods of measuring retention (recall, recognition, and relearning) are useful. In comparing investigations of retention, it is imperative to know what methods of measurement were used. Only those investigations using the same method should be directly compared. Depending on the method, the same performance may result in a retention score of zero, 50 percent, or 90 percent.

THE COURSE OF FORGETTING

The German psychologist Ebbinghaus was the first person to study the quantitative aspects of forgetting. Toward the end of the nineteenth century he plotted the first "curve of retention." In such a curve, the amount retained is plotted against time. There is usually a rapid initial drop, with a steadily decreasing rate of fall as time passes, indicating that forgetting takes place rapidly immediately after practice and then more slowly as time passes. Ebbinghaus' studies were limited in that he used only himself as a subject. He learned and relearned lists of nonsense syllables to obtain his data. Since his time, hundreds of studies of the course of retention have been made. Whereas most of them have not found forgetting to be so rapid as Ebbinghaus did, the extent

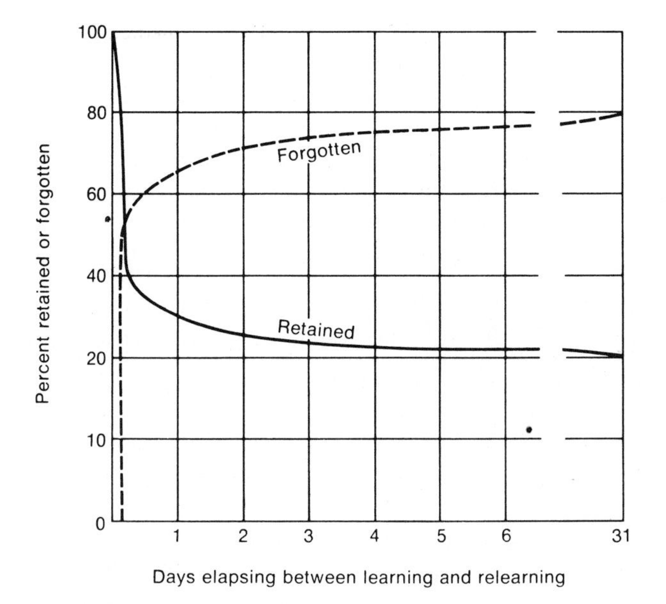

Figure 7-2. Curves of forgetting and retention for nonsense syllables (data from Ebbinghaus, 1885).

to which the curves retain the same general shape described by his pioneering work is surprising. After an extensive review of these experimental studies, McGeoch and Irion (1952) said: "It may be concluded that, over a wide range of conditions, the course of retention may be represented by a curve which has its most rapid fall during the time immediately after the cessation of practice and which declines more and more with increasing interval."

If the curve of forgetting is a negatively accelerated one, in which forgetting is first very rapid and then slower and slower as time passes, does it ever level out entirely and become a straight line before reaching zero? In other words, is forgetting ever complete? Although we have no systematic experimental studies on this point, there are some incidental observations and limited quantitative evidence that suggest the possibility that nothing is completely forgotten—if we mean that there is no residual effect of the original learning.

The degree of retention at any given time will vary greatly with the way in which we measure it. If, some time after a subject has learned some material to a given level, we measure retention, we may find that the person is unable to recall any of it and is even unable to recognize the material as familiar when it is again presented. But, if the material is relearned to the same level as that of the original learning, we may find a saving in the time needed to relearn the material compared with the time needed for the original learning. In other words, there will often be some retention measured by the method of relearning when none is measured by the methods of recall or recognition.

FACTORS AFFECTING RETENTION

A number of factors affect the amount of retention. Some of these factors have to do with the nature of the material to be learned or the skill to be acquired; others have to do with the course of acquisition or with the kind of practice employed in learning.

Rate of Original Learning

Variations of the general statement "It takes him a long time to learn, but once he gets it, he remembers it a long time" are frequently heard. Parents say this about their children, and students say it about themselves or their classmates. It is usually implied that if learning occurs with ease or rapidity, then what is learned is quickly forgotten. Practically all the studies of the relationship between speed of acquisition and tenacity of retention indicate that this popular notion is false. In general, "when learning is rapid, forgetting will be slow, and when learning is slow, forgetting will be rapid" (Underwood, 1949). It is quite possible that a highly motivated slow learner may superficially appear to retain learned materials better because he persists longer in practice and tends to learn far beyond that which is necessary for the normal learner.

Although there are many variables to control in trying to get a reliable index of the relationship between rate of original learning and tenacity of retention, the best of the studies indicate that fast learners retain more of practically any type of material than slow learners do. This finding seems to be true irrespective of the measure of retention—whether relearning, recall, or recognition.

More intelligent, mature, and experienced learners may learn more rapidly and retain more because of the simple fact that learning and remembering are two aspects of intelligence. In other words, they are related components of intelligence, and one does not cause the other. If we are dealing with two components of a unitary process, rather than two discrete processes, then any separation of learning and remembering must be arbitrary. We are probably really taking different sets of measurements along the same continuum when we measure learning and remembering, the difference being in the greater length of time involved in the measurements of retention. Our measure of learning is taken after each trial, or repetition, whereas our measure of retention is taken some time after the end of practice. Learning as a change in what is remembered from trial to trial is examined and discussed in detail by Kintsch (1970).

Level of Original Learning

If forgetting sets in rapidly when learning stops, then recall after a long time interval depends on a subject's learning the material well—that is, beyond the point at which he can just barely recall it. After an extensive review of the studies dealing with level of learning, McGeoch and Irion (1952) concluded that memory is better for those things that have been learned far beyond the point at which they are barely recalled. In the area of perceptual and motor skills, it has been found that retention is positively related to the level of original skill development (Ammons, Farr, Block, Newmann, Dey, Marion, & Ammons, 1958). Thus some overlearning is necessary for good retention and recall after a period of time. By *overlearning* we mean carrying practice beyond the point at which recall is just barely possible.

The problem of overlearning was one of the earliest attacked by experimental psychologists. For example, Ebbinghaus (1885) found a linear (straight-line) relationship between savings in time in relearning after 24 hours and the original number of repetitions when these repetitions were varied from zero to 64. In this experiment each repetition in the original learning saved 12.7 seconds in relearning time 24 hours later. This value was practically the same whether the repetition was the first or the sixty-fourth. Although this particular value applied only to Ebbinghaus and the conditions of his experiment, his general finding shows good agreement with later studies on the relation of degree of original learning to savings in relearning at a later time.

A later study found that with large amounts of overlearning, a law of diminishing returns sets in, so that each additional repetition yields a smaller amount of saving in time in retention (Luh, 1922). One study used degrees of learning of 100, 150, and 200 percent—100 percent standing for the number of repetitions required to learn the material to the level of one errorless reproduction, 150 and 200 percent representing that number of trials increased by half and doubled. This study shows that the amount of material retained increased as the number of repetitions throughout the range used increased, but the increase between 100 and 150 percent was much greater than that between 150 and 200 percent (Krueger, 1929). This finding indicates a diminishing return from

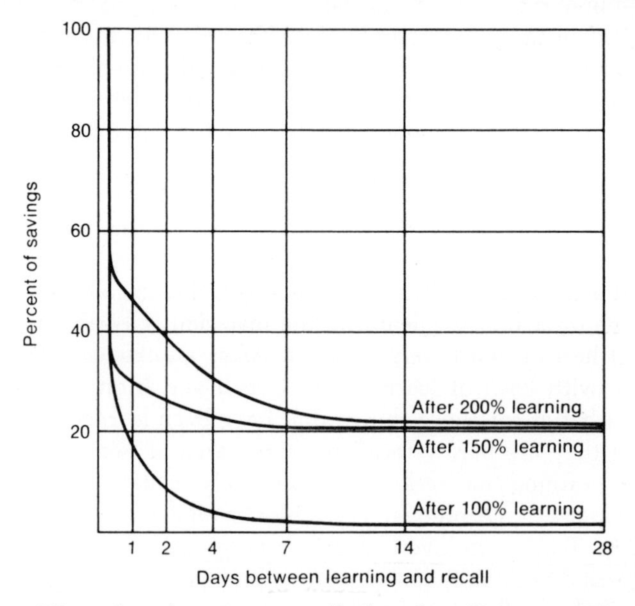

Figure 7-3. Effect of overlearning on recall (data from Krueger, 1929).

high degrees of overlearning. More recent research confirms these findings in other situations and indicates that the type of material learned is also a relevant variable (Postman, 1962).

A similar study of motor learning (finger-maze learning) shows a positive relationship between number of repetitions in the original learning and measures of retention after intervals of time varying from 1 to 14 days. Analysis of the results likewise shows diminishing returns at the higher numbers of repetitions (Krueger, 1930).

Overlearning is related to the question of distributed versus massed practice. When overlearning is obtained by continued massed repetitions beyond those necessary to barely learn, retention will be less than when the repetitions are spaced over a period of time. One way to accomplish this spacing is to learn the material to a satisfactory level and then to relearn it to the same level in periodic reviews. These relearnings amount to distributed practice and yield higher retention then does massed practice.

One rather extensive experiment was carried out to determine the influence of reviews systematically spaced at varying intervals after reading a selection. Several thousand children were divided into groups judged to be equal by the experimenters and were given 4-minute review tests at varying intervals after the original reading to determine the effect of early reviews on retention. The data show that, when a single review is given, the more closely the review follows the original learning, the greater the amount retained (Spitzer, 1939). This result indicates that reviews soon after original learning may prevent the rapid forgetting that characteristically takes place immediately after practice. For example, one of the groups of children, which had a review test soon after the single reading, forgot only 2 percent after one day and 17 percent after a week, whereas the groups without a review forgot 44 percent after one day and 67 percent after a week. Thus retention can be kept at a high level through properly spaced reviews. In general, it seems that reviews at increasingly longer intervals will produce maximum retention for the same time expenditure.

Meaningfulness of Material

Poetry is retained better than comparable prose. Prose is retained better than lists of unrelated meaningful words. Lists of meaningful words are retained better than lists of nonsense syllables. Clearly, these differences in retention relate to the presence of internal associations, to the organization of the material learned, and to the relevance of the material to the learner. The retention of individual nonsense syllables is related to their association values, which are indicated by the percentage of people associating words or phrases with the given syllables.

Most studies of forgetting have dealt with the loss of specific items of verbatim material previously learned to a given level. The general trend of such studies has been to indicate a great loss in the retention of memorized material in a comparatively short time. Not much attention has been given to the retention of general concepts and ideas or to the possible applications of previous learning to new situations. These broader problems may be more important than the detailed, specific instances, examples, and individual "facts" from which they are distilled.

Most of the studies attempting to measure the retention of some of these more general outcomes have found surprisingly good retention when compared with the findings of the more conventional classic studies. One study found that, whereas only 23 percent of the specific terminology learned in courses in biology was remembered a year later, the students' ability to interpret new data in the light of the course content and to apply the general principles learned had actually increased (Tyler, 1943). Part of this increase, of course, may represent transfer from other courses studied in the interim.

A similar study, with seventh-graders, showed a much greater retention of their increased ability to explain scientific phenomena than their recall of the specific facts of the course content (Ward & Davis, 1938). In still another study, 86 percent of the essential ideas of three stories were reproduced correctly after eight hours, but only 23 percent of the nonessential items were recalled (Newman, 1939). All studies agree in showing more permanent retention of general concepts, broad meanings, and interpretations than of the specific, verbatim, factual material usually studied in classical experiments on memory (Tyler, 1934; McDougall, 1958).

The better retention of general concepts and broad principles is probably related to the meaningfulness of such materials. Broad concepts are, by definition, meaningful; specific, verbatim material, however, may be learned by rote without any genuine understanding.

The meaningfulness-retention relationship is an extremely difficult topic to investigate. When we designate some material as "meaningful," we imply that

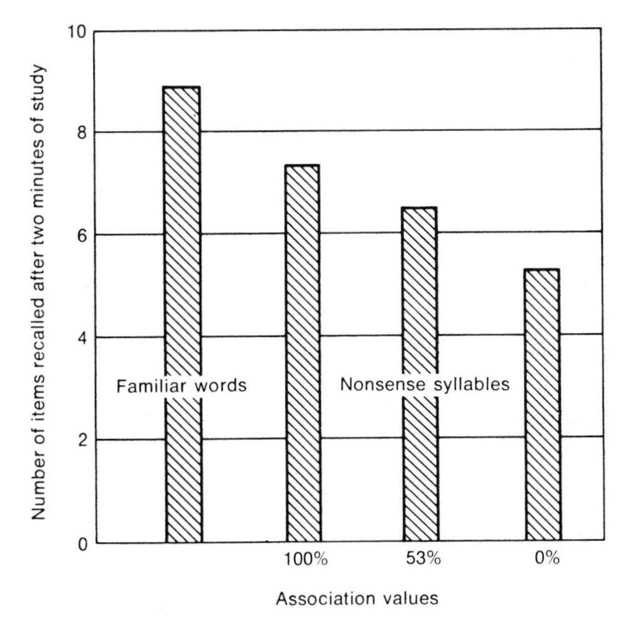

Figure 7-4. Effect of meaningfulness on retention (data from McGeoch, 1930).

previous learning has occurred to make it meaningful. It is difficult to control for meaningfulness and to get precise information as to its function in retention. For instance, investigators have asked whether nonsense material would be retained equally well when compared with meaningful material if both were learned to the same level. This question has not been given any decisive answer. One study reported better recall of carefully explained solutions to a problem than of arbitrary solutions taught without understanding (Katona, 1940). However, when the study was repeated by other investigators, the earlier finding was not confirmed (Hilgard, Irvine, & Whipple, 1953). From a practical point of view, meaningful material seems better retained than nonsense material. Thus other factors, such as the level of initial learning, may contribute to the superior retention of meaningful material.

Influence of Intention

The learner's "set" (intention), while learning, affects the retention of material as well as the rate of original learning. When students repeated a list of words both with and without intending to learn, the difference in favor of the students who had the intent to learn was greater after an interval of 48 hours

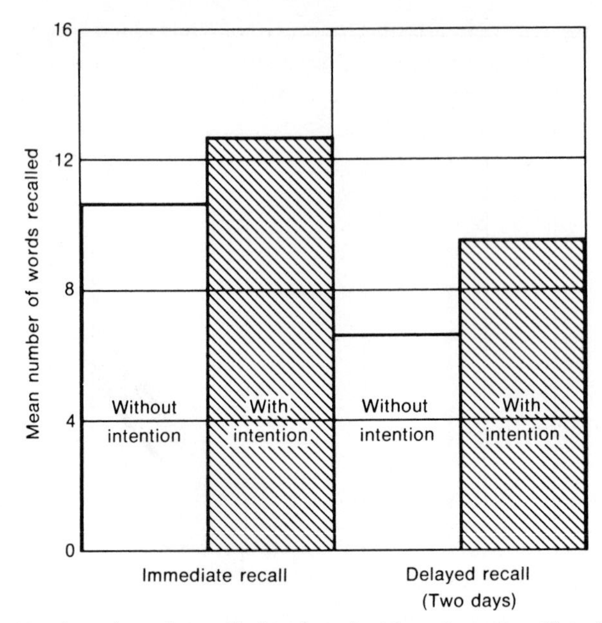

Figure 7-5. Number of words recalled with and without intention (data from Peterson, 1916).

than it was immediately after the reading (Peterson, 1916). When a subject learns with a set for recall after a given interval—for example, for an exam a week later—favorable results are found (Thisted & Remmers, 1932). Recall is less if a test comes either sooner or later than the subject expects (Geyer, 1930). Although intention is probably not the only factor involved in the experiments cited above, the set or expectancy of the learner does influence both rate of learning and tenacity of retention.

Recall during Practice

The generalization that it is good to spend a significant proportion of study or practice time attempting recall or recitation is supported by experiments with laboratory learning, as well as by experiments with school learning. In the laboratory it has been shown that as much as 80 percent of study time can be devoted to recitation with beneficial results for both acquisition and retention of nonsense syllables and biographies (Gates, 1917). The same general results have been found using the learning of French vocabulary (Seibert, 1932) and for spelling and arithmetic (Forlano, 1936).

Reading interspersed with attempted recall or reproduction produces better retention than do simple reading and rereading. This advantage is probably a result of the subject's maintaining both motivation and attention, as well as practicing the thing he will want to do when learning is complete. When a subject reads material knowing that he is going to attempt recall, his attitude is more conducive to rapid acquisition than when he knows that the reading is going to be followed by more reading. When he reads with interspersed, active self-testing, he is much better set for permanent retention. When a person attempts recall, he is practicing recall, whereas when he reads repeatedly, he is practicing reading. The former—not the latter—is what he actually wants to be able to do.

Motor versus Ideational Materials

Probably no task learned or practiced by human subjects can be considered purely motor. In the acquisition of any motor skill there are no doubt verbal components and ideational accompaniments. In comparing retention of verbal material to retention of motor performance, there is thus always some contamination. However, investigations do indicate that motor responses are well retained in animals and men. Skinner (1950) found target-pecking responses in pigeons to be retained after 4½ years. A pursuit motor skill (following a moving target with a stylus) in humans was found to be better 7 days after practice had ceased, whereas a verbal task was poorer after that period (Leavitt & Schlosberg, 1944).

Everyone is familiar with the relatively good retention of motor skills over long periods of time. The loss of typing skill has been found to be very small after 6 months without practice (Towne, 1922). In one case, an interval of more than 2 years without practice resulted in a loss of about one-third of original performance and very little additional loss in a 4½-year period (Swift, 1906). In all cases studied by Swift, relearning of typing skills was very rapid. In typing instruction a great deal of overlearning takes place. In general, the better retention of motor skills, as compared with ideational material, seems due to intensive practice in the one as compared with the other (McGeoch & Melton, 1929).

DYNAMIC FACTORS IN REMEMBERING

It becomes obvious from the examination of one's own experience that remembering is not a simple restatement of what was previously learned. Our memories for events are imperfect, frequently distorted, and better at some times than at others. These variations have been of concern to experimental investigators who work with such problems as how information is stored, processed, and retrieved by the individual.

Tip-of-the-Tongue Phenomenon (TOT)

Everyone has had the experience of trying at a particular moment to recall a specific name or word and being unable to do so. The person is certain that he knows the word or name and is distraught by his inability to recall it. He will say that it is on the tip of his tongue. The fact that the word really is known is demonstrated by the person's eventual successful recall or recognition of the elusive word.

People in the "tip-of-the-tongue" (TOT) state seem to search actively for the appropriate word, to produce words that are incorrect, and then to discard the incorrect words. This phenomenon has been experimentally investigated (Brown & McNeill, 1966). In the investigation, college students were read the definitions of words infrequently used in the English language—words that were likely to be in the recognition vocabulary of the subjects but not in their active recall vocabulary. A word such as *sampan* might fall into this category for a given subject. Whenever a subject felt that he knew a word but was unable to recall it, he was questioned relative to the words he did recall in his attempt to recall the appropriate one. It was demonstrated that the words that were recalled while attempting to recall the correct one (target word) had certain characteristics in common with the target word. Although some words recalled were similar in *meaning* to the target word, most recalled words were similar in *sound* to the correct one. The subjects certainly did not merely recall words at random until the correct one was recognized. They often could indicate how many syllables were in the target word and often could identify the first letter of the word. Recall is thus not a simple all-or-none reproductive process.

Distortion in Remembering or Recall

If a subject reads some material or sees an object, and then is asked at a later date to recall the material or to describe what he saw, two types of changes in the material recalled are found to occur (in addition to the subject's simply being able to recall less and less).

1. The first of these changes has been called *distintegration,* which involves a loss of the finer details, contrasted with less loss of the larger, more dominant features. The object, figure, word, or concept loses some of its distinctive characteristics and becomes more generalized in nature. It tends to be remembered as a type of item rather than as a particular item. This change often takes the form of a shift toward increasing simplicity and symmetry.

2. The second dynamic change involved in forgetting material is called *assimilation,* which involves selection and retention of certain aspects, features, or items, plus the addition of features not present in the original material. Selection, elimination, and addition tend to produce a more familiar figure that is better understood by the subject. Either the original perception was imperfect or the original experience undergoes a reworking and reduction to a form, type, or category that can be dealt with more readily and satisfyingly by the learner and also acquires the specific characteristics of a particular object. There is evidence that reproductions of figures made after greater elapsed time do not show more striking distortions than ones made almost immediately after initial exposure (Hebb & Foord, 1945; Riley, 1962).

From the above facts, we should expect that experiences that fit into one's already existing frame of reference will be remembered better than those that do not. Studies directed specifically at this problem indicate that our expectation has been borne out by the experimental results.

One study that dealt with the retention of political views that are in or out of harmony with one's frame of reference indicates much better retention of the former (Edwards, 1942). Similarly, it has been shown that material considered to be "acceptable" to the learner—in the sense that it is consistent with the learner's values, beliefs, and modes of conduct—is much better retained than is material judged to be neutral in this regard. Neutral material, in turn, was found to be retained better than material judged to be "unacceptable"—that is, out of harmony with the learner's attitudes, beliefs, and ways of acting (Sharp, 1938). The results of these studies indicate that forgetting and retention are dynamically related to the learner's motives, expectancies, and general frame of reference and are not simple functions of the particular technique of learning or of the number of repetitions, the distribution of repetitions, and the meaningfulness and other similar characteristics of the material learned.

Stimulus Conditions and Recall

Everything is learned in a particular setting. Information or skill always has a certain context within which it is acquired. Recall of previously learned material is dependent on the presentation of an adequate stimulus. Since, to some extent, the desired response is conditioned to all the stimuli present during the original learning, altering the environmental, or contextual, conditions decreases the likelihood that the response will be reinstated. Our inability to recall something at a given time or in a particular situation stems from a lack of the proper stimulus to evoke recall rather than from a lack of retention.

When students learned words in a given context and later tried to recall them either in the particular context or out of it, there was decidedly better recall in the familiar contextual setting (Pan, 1926). It has been demonstrated that relearning is facilitated by the maintenance of even the same-colored backgrounds for the stimulus materials as those present during the original learning (Weiss & Margolius, 1954). From present evidence we can conclude that the recall of material is influenced by the presence or absence of any environmental factor associated with the original learning.

Ego Involvement

In general, rate and permanence of learning are positively related to degree of ego involvement and active participation in the activities to be learned. For example, the students in a home-economics class were learning pattern design. Half the girls were trained in pattern-design techniques by being given specific directions for each step of the work; they were required to adhere to specific methods. The other half of the girls were given no specific directions as to methods to be followed; they were allowed to talk over possible plans and try whatever they liked. At the end of the project, it was found that the girls in the second group had produced much better results and had reacted more favorably to the work of the project and the course. In addition, tests given at the end of the course and repeated a year later showed much better retention of the acquired skills and subject matter of the project by the girls who had been permitted to plan and manage the details for themselves (Cranor, 1931). Whether the improvement in learning and retention was due to better understanding by the girls and greater meaningfulness of the work or due to the increased motivation deriving from the social discussion and ego involvement, or to all these factors, we do not know. The results indicate that improved retention is related to greater involvement in the planning and training process, although we are not sure whether ego involvement or greater meaningfulness of the material should be credited.

Ego involvement was probably the principal variable involved in the following experiment. Students were urged to learn as much as they could of materials presented but were told that their learning scores were inconsequential as indices of their abilities and that they would in no way be held responsible for their records. This group showed relatively poor retention. A comparable group of students learned the same material but with the opposite instructions. This second group showed not only an increased rate of learning but better relative retention when tested at various time intervals after the learning (Brown & Lewin, as reported by Davis, 1935).

Recall in ego-involved situations is probably a function of the subject's set for recall, as well as of his personality (Alper, 1952). To make reliable predictions about the relationship between recall and ego involvement, we must develop better measures of personality factors than are currently available.

THEORIES OF FORGETTING

Various theories have been offered to explain the numerous factors operative in forgetting and remembering. Each can account plausibly for some of the observed data of forgetting.

Passive Decay and Organic Factors

At one time it was thought that forgetting was solely the result of the organic changes incidental to life itself. Since the body cells continually undergo metabolic changes involving the inevitable loss and replacement of the material basis of the organism, it seemed logical that those organic changes thought to form the basis of learning would gradually be lost with the passage of time. Thus a *passive decay* of the memory trace due to time or disuse was thought to account for loss of retention.

Learning and retention have an organic basis. Brain injury or the operative or experimental removal of brain tissue is known to have often preceded the loss of ability to learn and the loss of previously acquired skills, haibts, and information. Furthermore, the decline in capacity for learning and the memory losses that occur in old age are presumably the result of organic deterioration accompanying senescence. It seems probable that forgetting is partially due to such organic changes, but to date we have been unable to determine just how much forgetting is the result of these factors. Considerable evidence has accumulated that indicates that factors other than organic change are largely responsible for forgetting.

Recent investigations of the organic basis of memory have resulted from the proposals of Hydén (1959) and Hydén and Egyhâzi (1963) that ribonucleic acid (RNA) may be the complex molecule that serves as a mediator for memory. The work of McConnell and his associates (McConnell, 1966; Zelman, Kabot, Jacobson, & McConnell, 1963) with planaria has caused a great deal of interest in RNA involvement in memory. They reported that injections of RNA taken from planaria that had been conditioned to contract to a light increased the conditionability of other planaria for the same task. These results have been difficult to replicate in other laboratories (Bennett & Calvin, 1964), as have similar results obtained using rats as subjects (Jacobson, Babich, Bribash, & Jacobson, 1965). The organic basis for memory remains an intriguing subject for investigation. Although there is little information currently available on the topic, it appears to be a very active area for future research.

Interference Theory

Interference theory emphasizes the role of competing responses in forgetting. McGeoch (1942) proposed that forgetting was produced by the subsequent learning of responses that interfered with those already learned(retroactive interference); if something were learned, and there were no subsequent learning, there would be no forgetting. The claim that forgetting is a sole function of subsequent learning has been challenged by a number of investigators (Bugelski, 1948). Previously learned material also has been shown to have an interfering effect on the recall of subsequently learned material. This latter situation has been termed *proactive interference.*

Retroactive interference. One factor that has an influence on the retention or forgetting of previous acquisitions is the amount and nature of experience intervening between original learning and the subsequent effort to recall. Let us take a hypothetical example. Suppose we have three equated groups of subjects who have learned the same material to the same level and in the same way and who are then measured for the retention of the material at a later time. Suppose the only difference among the groups is how they have spent the time between the original learning and our measurement of the amount they have retained. Let us assume that Group *A* spent the entire time between learning and recall in sleep. (We will pass over the question of just how we would assure ourselves that they all spent the entire time sleeping.) Group *B* spent their time awake but resting. Group *C* spent the entire period studying some other material. Under these circumstances, retention would probably be best with Group *A* (asleep), second best with Group *B* (resting), and poorest with Group *C* (studying). It seems that when activity is at a minimum, as during sleep, forgetting is at a minimum. As the amount of activity increases, the amount forgotten increases.

If we carry our hypothetical experiment one step farther, we can demonstrate another factor influencing the extent to which subsequent experience exerts an interfering or disruptive effect on previously learned material. Suppose we have three groups of experimental subjects, all having learned the same material to the same level and in the same way, and allow three hours to intervene before attempting recall and reproduction of the previously learned material. All the groups will spend two of the three hours in rest and one hour in study. The only difference among the three groups is which one of the three hours is used for study. Group *A* will use the first hour (the one immediately following the learning of the original material) for study. Group *B* will use the second hour for study. Group *C* will use the third hour. The order of events for the three hours between learning and recall for the three groups, then, will be as follows: Group *A*, study-rest-rest; Group *B*, rest-study-rest; Group *C*, rest-rest-study. It will be found that retention is poorest with Group *A*, next poorest with Group *C*, and best with Group *B*. It seems that subsequent experience has a maximum interfering effect on previously learned material when it immediately follows the original learning. The deleterious effect is less when the subsequent study immediately precedes attempted recall. The inhibitory effect of subsequent experience is at a minimum when it is immediately adjacent to neither the original learning nor the attempted recall. The results of this hypothetical experiment are given empirical support by the research of Postman and Alper (1946).

Another question related to retroactive interference is that of *similarity*. The hypothesis has been advanced that the greater the similarity of the interpolated task to the original learning, the greater the interference with the remembering of the original material; as the similarity decreases, a decrease in the amount of interference is obtained. This speculation has become known as the Skaggs-Robinson hypothesis (Robinson, 1927). Theoretical questions have arisen as to what constitutes similarity and what is the difference between maximum similarity and identity (Osgood, 1956). Similarity of interpolated material to the originally learned material presents problems in research, as does response similarity (Bugelski & Cadwallader, 1956). These questions have received a great deal of attention from researchers. The general observation that as similarity of the interpolated task to the original task increases, interference in recall increases up to the point of identity seems to hold fairly well. When identity is reached, the intervening task is merely another learning trial that facilitates recall of the original material.

In investigations of retroactive interference, one assumes that loss of retention is due to a number of factors other than that of the deliberately imposed task in the control group. Investigators have used different interpolated tasks as they have employed the retroactive-interference paradigm. These variables make it difficult, if not impossible, to compare retroactive-interference effects from study to study (Slamecka & Ceraso, 1960).

Experiments with the lower animals indicate that cockroaches made inactive by immobilization following learning retained more than those permitted to remain active. The inactive animals showed some loss of retention during the first 2 hours after learning, but practically no additional loss during the next 6 hours (as long a period as the study covered), whereas the active group continued to show progressive loss of habits as further time elapsed (Minami and

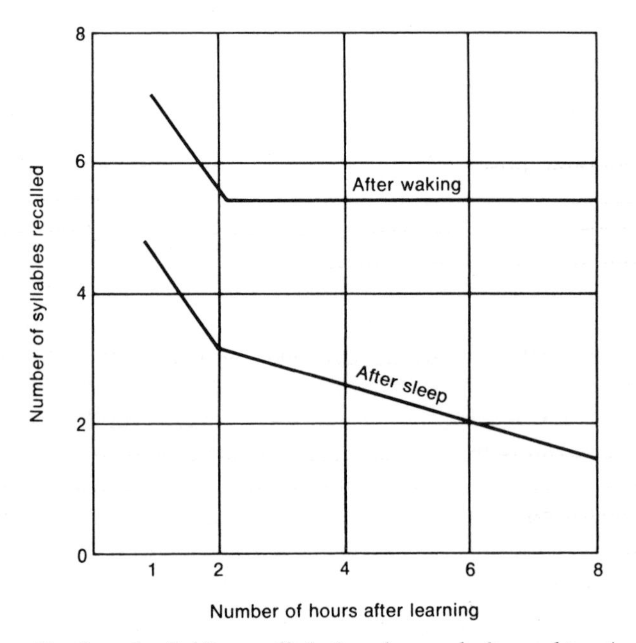

Figure 7-6. Number of syllables recalled after sleep and after waking. Average of two subjects (data from Jenkins & Dallenbach, 1924).

Dallenbach, 1946). It seems pretty well established that the amount and kind of subsequent activity are important determinants of retention or forgetting.

Proactive interference. Although *proactive interference* has not received the investigative attention that retroactive interference has, there is evidence that much forgetting that takes place may be the result of such a process (Postman, 1962). Proactive interference is the interference of that which was previously learned with the recall of something newly learned. If a group of subjects learns Task *A*, then learns Task *B*, and subsequently recalls *B* less well than subjects who had not previously learned *A*, the loss in efficiency of recall is said to result from the interference of *A* on *B*. Underwood (1957) has shown that in the learning of lists of nonsense syllables, this phenomenon is likely to occur. The nonsense syllables one has learned in the past may make it harder for him to recall those he has recently learned.

Proactive (and retroactive) interference effects are not so apparent when material to be learned is meaningful or when learning is carried beyond the point of minimal mastery. This circumstance is fortunate for learning and retention, for, unless there were some way out of the interference phenomenon, attempting new learning would seem rather futile.

Motivated Forgetting

There is considerable observational and incidental evidence that some forgetting, or at least some inability to recall, is the result of one's not wanting to recall. The purpose or wish involved in such motivated *forgetting* is thought to operate without our being aware of it—in other words, some forgetting is unconsciously motivated. This process of wishful forgetting and inhibition of recall is known as *repression*. The general idea involved in repression is that experiences are forgotten, or are not recalled, because of their relationship to one's personal problems. The memories are unacceptable to the individual because they are self-depreciating in nature and arouse guilt or anxiety. The typical amnesia victim is thought to represent this type of forgetting. His forgetting is usually selective. If it were not, he would return to a state of infancy and have to relearn all that he had acquired during his entire lifetime. He typically can talk, write, count, and conduct the ordinary affairs of life; most of his normal skills remain intact. The things he forgets have a personal reference—his name, his home, the members of his family, and the events of his past life. Amnesia is thought to represent an escape from certain aspects of the individual's life and past that he finds displeasing.

Numerous experiments have been made to test the concept of repression. Early studies in this area had difficulty isolating the area for investigation. Among the more successful experiments designed as tests of the repression hypothesis are those of Sharp (1938) and Zellar (1951). Generally, laboratory demonstrations of repression have not been very satisfactory. The concept seems to be an elusive one when it comes to experimental investigation. However, Clemes (1964), using hypnosis, found that when he suggested that half of a list of words learned would be forgotten, "critical" words were forgotten more frequently than "control" words.

A desire to achieve makes a difference in the recall of tasks. In one situation some tasks were interrupted before they could be completed by the subject. Those subjects with high-achievement motivation recalled more of the incomplete tasks than did those with low-achievement motivation (Atkinson, 1953). Uncompleted tasks apparently represented more of a challenge to high- than to low-achievement-oriented individuals. Motivational factors no doubt are operative in remembering and forgetting, but they are difficult factors to bring under laboratory control.

The Perseveration-Consolidation Hypothesis

A form of the *perseveration-consolidation hypothesis* proposed by Müller and Pilzecker (1900) has received a great deal of attention. The general nature of this hypothesis is that the processes involved in practice continue for a time after practice has ceased. A given trial, then, is seen as initiating neural activity that persists for some time after the end of the trial. This theory assumes that if post-trial neural activity were interrupted, memory would be impaired, and that the greatest impairment in memory would come from interruptions that were closest to the end of the trial. If the interruption were to follow after a critical amount of time had passed, no impairment of memory would occur, for memory would have consolidated—the persevative neural process would have subsided.

In support of the perseveration-consolidation hypothesis, it has been shown that electroconvulsive shock (ECS) interpolated between the learning and the relearning of pairs of words disrupted memory for them. The pairs most closely followed by the ECS showed the greatest impairment (Zubin & Barrera, 1941; Williams, 1950). The same general finding has been reported with animals as subjects, with a variety of *tasks* (Duncan, 1949; Thompson & Dean, 1955;

Thomson, McGaugh, Smith, Hudspeth, & Westbrook, 1961). The research of Coons and Miller (1960) challenged the interpretation that the ECS was disrupting neural traces and thereby producing retrograde amnesia. Coons and Miller contended that fear produced by ECS may be interfering with subsequent performance. Adams and Lewis (1962) interpreted the ECS data, demonstrating that learning of fear responses such as crouching and freezing competes with the previously learned behavior in animals. Attempts have been made to put fear in opposition to the amnesic effects of ECS in an experimental design (Madsen & McGaugh, 1961) and to "partial out" the aversive and amnesic effects of ECS experimentally (Hudspeth, McGaugh, & Thomson, 1964). The researchers in these cases found some support for the perseveration-consolidation hypothesis and some support for the contention that ECS may produce aversion and fear.

Differences in the interpretation of the research on electroconvulsive shock and retrograde amnesia are reported in the psychological literature. Lewis and Maher (1965, 1966) contend that ECS produces a generalized inhibitory response that becomes conditioned to the environmental stimuli at the time of its occurrence. McGaugh and Petrinovich (1966) provide evidence that this is probably not the case. Before these issues can be resolved, more research will be necessary. Definitive statements relative to the comparative effects of the competition of responses and the interruption of perseveration cannot be made at this time.

Two-Process Theory

Investigations of memory have led to the speculation that it may involve two processes. One process in this dichotomy is postulated for *short-term memory* (STM) and another for *long-term memory* (LTM).

Short-term memory is the process involved when one looks up a telephone number in the directory and remembers it only long enough to dial it. The number is retained for a short period of time and then disappears; it is not stored for long-term retention. Short-term memory has been investigated by Peterson and Peterson (1959), and a two-process theory has been advocated to account for their findings and the results of additional research (Peterson, 1966). Other investigators (Hebb, 1949; Broadbent, 1957; Buschke, 1968) have urged the treating of short-term memory as a different phenomenon from long-term memory.

Long-term memory, according to the two-process theory, results from the transfer of short-term memory to long-term storage. Material has to remain in the short-term memory long enough to be coded and classified for long-term storage. If other material is introduced into short-term memory before this transfer can occur, the trace is destroyed or replaced and cannot be transferred to permanent storage. Long-term memory is generally said to be governed by the conventional factors of associative interference, response competition, and the like.

Melton (1963) has raised several critical questions relative to research in memory, including the fundamental question as to whether STM and LTM are really different phenomena that require different principles for explanation. Researchers are still engaged in attempts to determine whether the variables affecting short-term memory are different in kind from the variables affecting long-term memory. If, in fact, short- and long-term memory are subject to influences different in kind, a two-process theory gains support, whereas, if memory is subject to the same variety of influences on a continuum from immediate to long-term memory, a unitary process could well account for phenomena of memory and forgetting. Investigations in this area continue, but currently there is not sufficient evidence on the questions involved to make a definitive statement as to the dual or singular nature of the processes involved in short-term and long-term memory.

SUMMARY

The phenomena of memory and forgetting have long been of interest to layman and scientist alike. Ebbinghaus was the first man to investigate memory quantitatively. His early efforts contributed important knowledge about memory and its systematic investigation.

There is ample evidence for retention for both short and long periods of time and for a great variety of learned tasks. Such evidence comes from repeated performances, studies of savings in relearning, and delayed-reaction studies. Retention is a measurable phenomenon and may be measured by methods of recall or reproduction, recognition, and savings in relearning.

The course of forgetting can be measured, and, when amount retained is plotted graphically against time since learning, a "curve of retention" appears. Such a curve shows forgetting to take place rapidly immediately after practice and then more slowly as time passes. It is probable that forgetting is never really complete, but the amount of retention can vary greatly. The amount retained is a partial function of the way in which it is measured. Various factors affect the amount of retention: rate of original learning, level of original learning, meaningfulness of material, "intention" or "set," methods of learning, circumstances for remembering, and motivation.

There are several theories that attempt to account for the phenomena of remembering and forgetting. None of the theories is capable of accounting for all the results of empirical investigations. The most commonly accepted theory that probably accounts for more of the data than any other is referred to as interference theory. Interference theory includes the effects of both retroactive and proactive inhibition. The idea of passive decay of the neural trace has been largely abandoned, because it has been demonstrated that events occurring in time that interfere with memory are more important than the sheer elapse of time itself. However, in the area of short-term memory, some current investigators invoke a decay-over-time hypothesis.

Motivational theories are employed to account for forgetting under certain circumstances. Such theories may have appeal, but they are also difficult to put to laboratory test.

Perseveration-consolidation processes and short-term memory and long-term storage are areas of theory that currently receive a good deal of investigative attention.

Much is known about the course of forgetting, and the means of measurement of retention and forgetting are sophisticated. Even so, we still do not yet have enough understanding of memory processes and functions to build an adequate theory to account for all the findings of empirical research.

SUGGESTED READINGS

Bartlett, F. C. *Remembering: A study in experimental and social psychology.* Cambridge: Cambridge University Press, 1932. This classic on remembering is easy to read and presents a way of viewing the field that is in sharp contrast to that of Ebbinghaus.

Ebbinghaus, H. *Memory: A contribution to experimental psychology.* New York: Dover, 1964. The pioneering work of Ebbinghaus is presented. Students of psychology will find it a valuable and interesting volume.

Paul, I. H. Studies in remembering. In G. S. Klein (Ed.), *Psychological issues.* New York: International Universities Press, 1959. Part II of this volume deals with investigations of the reproduction of connected and extended verbal material.

Slamecka, N. J. *Human learning and memory.* New York: Oxford University Press, 1967. This book is a fine collection of articles on learning and memory. Parts I and IV present important papers on interference theory and short-term memory, respectively.

8

Ideational Processes

Man differs most from the lower animals in his ability to develop abstract concepts, to reason, and to communicate. Conceptualizing, reasoning, and communicating are all interrelated. Man abstracts such properties of objects and people as redness, roundness, and goodness to form concepts. He uses linguistic symbols to communicate these conceptualized meanings to others and to assist him in thinking about them.

In this chapter we are concerned with conceptualization and thinking. Concepts vary in breadth and degree of abstractness from the very specific ones such as dog, tree, and man at the one extreme to truth, dependability, and the fourth dimension at the other. Thinking also covers a wide range of activities. At the one extreme it includes dreaming and revery, which involve the relatively free flow of association; at the other extreme it encompasses purposive reasoning and creative problem solving. When we order ideational processes in such a continuum, we consider them all to be the same qualitatively but different principally in degree of abstractness and purposiveness. We shall begin our discussion with the controlled, purposive, and abstract end of the continuum.

Figure 8–1. The Thinker, a creation of the sculptor Francois Auguste René Rodin (The Metropolitan Museum of Art, Gift of Thomas F. Ryan, 1910).

REASONING

Reasoning is ideational problem solving. Most problem solving contains both ideational and motor components. We can conceive of problem solving as ranging all the way from "blind" motor trial-and-error efforts to purely cognitive and ideationally creative solutions, with all gradations of reasoning falling in between these two extremes.

We shall concern ourselves with problem solving that is near the ideational end of the continuum. In our discussion productivity and creativity will refer to basically the same processes and products. Two descriptions of productive thinking provide a good starting point: one is John Dewey's (1933) five stages of ideational problem solving, and the other is a description of the act of creative production provided by Wallas (1926). According to Wallas, the complete process of creative thinking involves the four stages of preparation, incubation, illumination, and verification. Dewey's five-stage description of ideational problem solving includes (1) recognition of a problem, (2) analysis

Table 8-1. A comparison of Dewey's stages in problem solving, Wallas' description of creative production, and Rossman's analysis of the process of invention.

Rossman's list	*Dewey's list*	*Wallas' list*
Observation of a need	Recognition of a problem	
Analysis of the need	Analysis of the problem	Preparation
Survey of available information	Suggestions of possible solutions	
Formulation of possible solutions		Incubation
Birth of a new invention	Testing of the selected solution	Illumination
Testing out of the new idea	Judgment of the selected solution	Verification

of the problem, (3) suggestions to possible solutions, (4) testing of the consequences of the possible solutions, and (5) judgment, or testing, of the selected solution. These two lists are sufficiently similar to justify the inference that they cover the same underlying processes. These lists are also similar to a breakdown of the inventive process proposed by Rossman (1931) as the result of his study of more than 700 productive inventors. All three lists are shown in Table 8-1. A composite list, which is more complete and more detailed than any one of the three, is provided in Table 8-2. Some of the terms used in this list are changed to conform to contemporary usage.

The Motivation of Reasoning

Motivating influences instigate and sustain all problem-solving activities. For a man faced with the threat of chronic or acute hunger, thirst, or general bodily discomfort, the sources of drive are principally organic. In a modern Western

Table 8-2. Composite list of steps in productive thinking (reasoning).

Motivation
↓
Recognition of the problem
↓
Preparation
- Analysis of the problem
- Survey of available information

↓
Formulation of possible solutions (hypotheses)
↗
Incubation
↓
Illumination
- Sudden or gradual
- Tentative acceptance of solution

↓
Verification
- Testing out of the selected solution
- Acceptance or rejection of the solution

society the anticipation of monetary rewards as symbolic status, the potential affiliative enrichment of one's life, or the anticipation of attainment of increased social acceptance or prestige as the result of successful achievement may be the principal sources of motives. Sometimes the motivation for creative thinking seems largely autonomous; it arises from within the individual as the result of his internalized ideals, values, and self-concept.

In addition to the utilitarian organic, social, and personal-conflict sources of drive, many writers today are postulating a unique drive that initiates and sustains creative activity. This drive serves both self-expressive and problem-solving functions. Studies of highly productive and creative people uniformly show that many such individuals produce, create, and invent solely because of the thrill or satisfaction of surmounting difficulties or solving problems. They seek out and welcome challenges. To explain such phenomena, many workers have postulated the existence of a unique drive, given various names such as *competence, self-actualization,* and *self-realization.* This drive is conceived of as an all-pervasive autonomous tendency to exercise and develop all of one's potentialities to their maximum. Such a drive can presumably account for problem solving and creative activity, whether such activity is of a motor, intellectual, or artistic sort.

The status of such an all-pervasive autonomous drive is still uncertain. There is no doubt that some motivation is internal and autonomous; only the question of its source and origin is in dispute. Some people believe that it is innate and primary; others think it can best be explained as acquired. The latter consider the autonomous type of motivation to be derived from external sources by a process of learning. Irrespective of its origin, many creative people are highly autonomous in their motivation.

Recognition of the Problem

In addition to motivation, problem solving assumes the existence of a problematic situation. As long as an individual is able to satisfy his motives immediately and directly, no additional learning, no creative activity, and no problem-solving behavior are necessary. Even the most highly autonomous motives require a challenge for their activation. In artistic productions activated by internal conflicts, both the motivation and its solution may operate below the level of individual awareness; however, formal problem solving requires the individual to be aware of the problem. One characteristic of creatively productive people is their "sensitivity to problems" (Guilford, 1965). The recognition of a problem requires an evaluation of the situation to determine whether or not the situation requires action. If the situation is considered to call for action to satisfy one's motives, a problem is present.

Preparation

A period of preparation follows the acceptance of the challenge of a situation requiring action. Formal problem solving and invention require an analysis of the problem. The exact nature of the difficulty is not always obvious, and some study of the situation may be required before the person is ready to move ahead.

Preparation may involve *gathering all the information available* concerning the problem. If there is published literature on the problem, it can be surveyed. The history of previous attempts at solution may provide fruitful leads or indicate hypotheses that already have been proven fruitless. Relevant information may be provided by the immediate environment. It may have to be sought out, or it may be recalled from one's store of information.

Available information must be used in novel ways in productive thinking. Thus things learned in a certain situation must be transferred and used in a new context. This process can be difficult. One of the characteristics of the creative person is his ability to perceive old elements in new relationships. The perceptual and ideational processes of creative individuals are flexible and can readily be detached from their customary settings.

Formulation of Possible Solutions

Analysis of the problem and the gathering of relevant information are followed by the *formulation of hypotheses,* the idea-generating phase of productive thinking. In this part of the creative process, divergent thinking is at a premium. A large number of possibilities from which to choose increases the probability of finding a fruitful one. A high level of adaptive flexibility allows an individual to revise or abandon his hypotheses when they prove to be inapplicable. The person who is rigid and inflexible in his approach to problems is likely to engage in futile repetition of ineffective approaches.

Incubation

Incubation may occur at almost any stage in the reasoning process. However, it is most likely to occur just before, during, or after the hypothesis-formulation phase. Table 8-2 shows it following this stage. The sudden emergence of fruitful ideas—the "Eureka!" experience—occurs sufficiently often for us to assume that something active is going on during periods of relative inactivity. Some people have postulated an "unconscious mind" that works things out for us. This theory provides an easy answer—but hardly an explanation.

The apparently spontaneous and sudden insight that occurs during periods of relaxation following intense mental activity is analogous to the experience everyone has had after unsuccessfully struggling to recall someone's name during a period of stress: the name comes to mind apparently spontaneously and without effort some time later, when one is relaxed and not trying to recall it. In such a case the set for recall somehow persists, and retrieval of the name occurs as soon as the inhibitory influences of the stressful situation are removed. When ideational activities resolve themselves into a dream, or when the solution to a problem comes to a person in a dream, the processes involved are analogous to the sudden illumination that occurs during waking periods of inactivity following strenuous efforts at problem solving.

A period of rest may permit the elimination of fatigue and the dissipation of the mental sets that keep an individual's ideational processes perseverating in such a stereotyped way that they preclude the new configurations necessary for more fruitful hypotheses. It has been shown experimentally that practice with tools in conventional ways and in familiar contexts operates against the solution of problems that require the use of these same objects in novel ways. However, the restricting effects of such practice diminish with time. Analytical studies of the advantage of spaced over massed practice in experimental studies of learning have disclosed that rest periods improve learning more by the elimination of errors than by the fixation of the correct responses. There may be some such selective influences operative during rest periods interspersed between periods of ideational activity.

Illumination

Dramatic flashes of insight, called *illumination* by Wallas, catch the eye of the general public and serve to throw an aura of mystery around the entire process of creative thinking. Although occasional sudden fruitful insights do occur, it is more common for a number of small glimmerings, vague ideas, and fortunate chance events to coalesce and form a specific solution that proves to be successful. The sudden inspiration is most often preceded by many apparently promising hypotheses that are proven to be incorrect and are discarded. Productive thinking involves a great deal of trial and error, just as does the learning of most motor habits.

The "something new" that emerges in reasoning may come either by large spectacular leaps or by small accretions; however, in either case, the final product represents the emergence of a new pattern of experience. An insight brings together into a coherent pattern elements and bits of experience that were formerly parts of diverse configurations and were embedded in relatively unrelated contexts.

Verification

The act of insight, or illumination, carries with it a conviction of its correctness. Then follows a process of critical evaluation, which results in verification and final acceptance, disproof and rejection, or modification. If evaluation results in confirmation, the problem is solved and the activity ceases. If the hypothesis is disproven, it is discarded or revised, and the process is repeated with new suggestions replacing the discarded hypotheses.

The Limitations of "Steps in Reasoning"

The separation of reasoning into discrete stages greatly oversimplifies and overformalizes the process. The stages of reasoning are interrelated components, rather than discrete steps that regularly follow each other in a staircase sequence. In many cases a person may go back and forth within a given segment of the sequence many times before he moves forward to the next. Later stages are foreshadowed in earlier ones. When blocked at one point, a person may return and redo or build more completely the earlier components.

After going completely through the process and failing to verify what seemed to be fruitful hypotheses, an individual may go back and reexamine his original conception of the problem. Maybe he did not really understand the nature of the problem. Maybe he is trying to answer the wrong question. Of course, he may reexamine the original problem at any time. He may likewise be continually obtaining additional information to assist him in arriving at a satisfactory solution. He may be reading, talking, recalling, and obtaining additional experience that has relevance to his problem throughout the sequence of steps. These activities may go on concomitantly with the formulation and evaluation of possible solutions.

The formulation of possible solutions occurs before complete information is obtained. As soon as the individual formulates and understands the problem, possible solutions come to him. Some of them are quickly discarded, but others are retained to the verification stage. All during the process of preparation, hypothetical solutions will be entertained. The obtaining of more information may lead to their prompt rejection, revision, or retention for later testing. At any time, from the recognition of the problem through the period of incubation, sudden or gradual, complete or partial, appropriate or inappropriate insights may occur. Evaluation is going on continually from beginning to end of the process. In short, stages overlap each other and have fuzzy boundaries, and the reasoning individual may go back and forth within the sequence.

Factors Influencing Reasoning

The factors that influence reason also, to some degree, affect all forms of thinking. Although our discussion will focus primarily on the more formal reasoning processes, we will also make some reference to other forms of ideation.

Relevant information. *Relevant information* is essential to problem solving. Ideational problem solving assumes the presence of "ideas" with which to think. Since reasoning involves the use of concepts, the reasoner must possess relevant concepts and be able to bring them to bear on the problem at hand. Concepts are abstracted meanings distilled from perceptual experiences. In reasoning, the problem at hand must activate meanings that have been sufficiently abstracted and detached from their original contexts to make their transfer to the immediate problem possible.

Reasoning assumes the acquisition, retention, abstraction, and recall of relevant concepts. An individual's thinking is always limited by the extent, completeness, accuracy, appropriateness, and availability of his concepts and information.

Mental set. Problem solving assumes the ability to make and maintain a preparatory adjustment that facilitates a particular kind of action or act—a set. However, stereotyped and rigid sets may preclude the flexibility that successful solutions and creative thinking require. The selective function of mental set is evident in associative responses made under different instruction-induced sets. If people are read a list of words and are told to respond by writing the first word that comes to mind after hearing each word, they will give a wide variety of associations. If they are told to respond by writing the name of an article of the same class as the spoken word, not only is the range of written words greatly restricted, but the associations aroused by the same words under the more restrictive directions are much more limited. If the subjects are instructed to respond by giving the opposite of each word, the range of associations aroused by the words is still more restricted. Naturally, the instructions they receive not only determine the range of words that they write but also serve to funnel and direct the associative processes. In a similar way, the set induced by a person's understanding of a problem screens and channels the flow of available information and concepts relevant to the problem at hand.

Just as appropriate sets facilitate solutions, inappropriate ones can work against problem solving. For example, if a series of problems is solved by one method, and then a problem is given that is superficially similar to the others but is insolvable by the same method, the probability of successful solution is much less than if this problem had been given first: the successful solution of the series of problems by the one method induces a set that channels subsequent efforts into this same path. There are innumerable puzzles, conundrums, and "brain teasers" whose difficulty arises from induced sets and assumptions that militate against successful solution.

Many of the problems conventionally used in laboratory studies of reasoning and insight involve the use of tools and other objects in unusual ways and thus require the individual to break away from the stereotyping effects of conventional frames of reference. One such problem consists of providing a person with nothing but a pair of pliers to assist him in tying together the ends of two strings suspended from the ceiling. The strings are too far apart for him to reach either while holding onto the other. The solution is to tie the pliers to one string and then to set them swinging on the end of the string as a pendulum. Holding onto one string, the subject can then catch the pliers when their pendular motion brings them—and the string—within reach. The difficulty of the problem arises from the fixity of the concept of pliers as tools to squeeze, turn, or hold objects and the difficulty of developing a new concept of pliers as a pendulum bob. In one such experiment subjects were given preliminary practice using tools in conventional ways; other comparable subjects were given equal amounts of practice using the same tools in novel ways—using pliers to prop up a board and using an unbent paper clip as a hook, for example. In the subsequent solution of tasks requiring the use of tools in unconventional ways, the group whose previous use had been conventional scored 61 percent successful, but the group whose practice involved novel uses scored 98 percent successful (Duncker, 1945).

Emotional bias. Reasoning is never a formal, logical process. The emotional biases of the individual may determine the outcomes of his reasoning processes as much as the available information. There is a decided tendency for people to believe things they wish to believe. This type of thinking is referred to as autistic. Whereas reasoning is usually considered the opposite of autistic ideation, there are some autistic elements present. In ordinary thinking, people accept the outcomes of reasoning as much because of the attractiveness of conclusions as by the logic of the ideational processes. For example, compare the following two syllogisms:

1. All x's are y's.
   All z's are y's.
   Therefore all z's are x's.

2. All Communists are radicals.
   All labor leaders are radicals.
   Therefore all labor leaders are Communists.

Which conclusion follows logically? Neither. Both conclusions are unwarranted in terms of what is given. However, when these syllogisms were presented to individuals who believed that all labor leaders are Communists, many more of them accepted the reasoning in (2) than in (1), although the two problems are exactly the same in form (Morton, 1942). When a logically false conclusion matches a strong emotional bias, it is more readily accepted than is an identically false conclusion expressed in terms of neutral x's and y's. Straightforward, logical reasoning is particularly difficult in the area of religion and politics, because prejudicial attitudes and emotional biases are so prevalent in these fields.

Decision Making without Reasoning

The processes of productive thinking, as we have described them, take time. However, many problems in everyday life certainly are not solved by successive steps of reasoning. The solutions to innumerable problems are provided on an authoritarian basis by social customs and by legal codes and norms. Although many of these solutions have a rational basis, the codified decisions are not arrived at anew by each individual every time he makes a decision based on them. There is nothing creative or intellectually productive involved in the individual's conforming behavior. Only a small part of one's decisions is the product of formal reasoning.

Each individual's unique pattern of percepts, concepts, ideals, and value systems constitutes a kind of decision-making mechanism that processes information provided from sensory and memorial sources. The larger and more stereotyped the individual's repertoire of perceptual and conceptual categories, the greater the number of ready-made solutions to life's problems they offer. Such decision making does not involve reasoning. The cumulative experiences of one's lifetime provide a tremendous number of automatic, ready-made answers to such questions as: What is this object? How should I feel and act about this class of objects? What kind of proposition am I hearing or reading? Is it scientific? humanistic? altruistic? democratic? sacrilegious? conservative? radical? liberal? moderate? extreme? prejudicial? self-seeking? Communistic? autocratic? Is the statement to be accepted, approved, believed, and acted upon?

The rigidly conscientious individual has internalized a stereotyped set of ideals and values that function quite autonomously and identify acts, ideas, and beliefs as good or bad in an almost reflex and absolute way. On the other hand, more rational individuals possessed of an "open" set of moral principles must evaluate conduct in terms of probable consequences. The rational person must make unique decisions based on his own set of values and principles, the requirements of the immediate situation, and the probable personal and social consequences of alternative courses of action. The morality of such a person involves problem solving.

CONCEPTUAL DEVELOPMENT

Concepts are acquired through a complex set of processes, including perception, discrimination, generalization, and transposition. The child, through his increased ability to discriminate and to generalize, develops perceptual and conceptual schema and rules. In doing so, he becomes increasingly emancipated from the immediate stimulus aspects of his environment and is able to deal with his world in a more conceptual way.

Many workers claim that conceptual development in the child proceeds in a sequential and invariant order. For a child to arrive at stage *B* in his development, he must have reached and passed through stage *A*. That is, the order is fixed. Piaget is by far the most prestigious figure sponsoring the notion of stage-dependent cognitive development. According to him, intellectual development goes through four stages from birth to maturity: the sensorimotor period, the preoperational period, the concrete operational period, and the formal-thought operational period (Piaget, 1960, 1968; Inhelder & Piaget, 1958; Flavell, 1963).

The Sensorimotor Period (Birth to 2 Years)

During this period the child organizes his perceptual world, from which his concepts will later emerge. He differentiates between himself and the rest of the world. He establishes some awareness of time and space and of the permanence and stability of objects. At the end of this period he is still dominated by the physical aspects of his environment; that is, he is still a perceptually dominated being.

The Preoperational Period (2 to 7 Years)

During this period the child begins to function symbolically. He is able to distinguish between a name and what that name stands for. With the beginnings of symbolic thought, language plays an increasingly more important role. The child in this period can conceptualize in terms of a single dimension but is unable to classify objects in terms of several dimensions simultaneously. Because of this inability to handle multiple characteristics of objects, the child is operating in terms of what Piaget calls preconcepts. Children in this period begin to utilize numbers and to order things quantitatively. They are beginning to abstract.

The Concrete Operational Period
(7 to 11 Years)

In this period, according to Piaget, the child begins to think in logical terms. He is able to treat objects as alike even though they are diverse in many respects. He also develops considerable ability to handle number concepts as well as concepts for representational thinking. Moreover, he is evolving a conceptual system with some coherence and stability, which emancipates him from the perceptual dominance of his immediate environment.

The Formal-Thought Operational Period
(11 to 15 Years)

During this period the child takes the final steps toward true abstract thinking and conceptualization. He can make inferences, evolve abstract concepts, and develop and evaluate hypotheses. Since he can now handle multiple variables in a systematic way, he can organize and think scientifically.

CONCEPT ACQUISITION

The experimental analog of the child's concept acquisition consists in presenting a learner with stimulus objects varying along such dimensions as color, size, shape, and number. One dimension is arbitrarily chosen as the basis for classification, and the task of the learner is to discover the relevant dimension and classify the objects in terms of this dimension. For example, the stimulus objects of various sizes, shapes, materials, and colors are to be sorted according to color. Feedback is provided so that the subject can determine the appropriateness of his tentative groupings. When the subject is able to either verbalize the basis for the proper classification or consistently sort the objects or similar ones according to color and disregard the irrelevant dimensions, he is judged to have developed and properly identified the concept.

A subject presented with the varied materials in a concept development and identification problem does not choose randomly. Among other things, he is influenced by certain stimulus variables. For example, subjects regularly find it easier to learn concepts on the basis of the more concrete or "thing" classes as contrasted with the more abstract form, color, size, or number dimensions

(Heidbreder, 1949). Perceptual distinctiveness and ease of verbal coding also facilitate concept identification (Heidbreder, 1949; Shepp & Zeaman, 1966; Baum, 1954).

Increasing the number of relevant cues also facilitates concept identification; increasing the number of irrelevant dimensions makes the problem more difficult. For example, if the objects in one category are not only red but also square and large, whereas those in the alternate category are blue, triangular, and small, the coding can be done in terms of color, shape, *or* size or any combination of these characteristics. Obviously these possibilities simplify the problem. Increasing the number of irrelevant dimensions makes it more difficult, largely because it increases the number of hypotheses from which a selection must be made (Bourne, 1966).

Concept learning is often seen as a searching or hypothesis-testing process. Concept identification as hypothesis testing should be largely an all-or-none phenomenon. According to such a conception, the learner would consciously formulate plans and then systematically test each one. When the correct hypothesis is discovered, the problem is solved and the principle can be verbally formulated. However, evidence indicates that although some subjects do so, many do not. That is, some subjects learn to make proper classifications and respond consistently but are never able to formulate and verbalize their solutions (Hull, 1920). Many college students, after mastering a concept to the point of errorless performances and successfully applying the newly learned solution to new materials, were still unable to verbalize correctly the rules they were employing (Phelan, 1968). This situation is also found in rule learning of a somewhat different sort.

Concept Formation as Rule Learning

As in the simple cases mentioned above, the rule learning involved in concept development may be quite simple: all *A* items are red; all *B* items are blue; all living things reproduce themselves; all nonliving things do not. However, many concepts involve multiple dimensions, and the rules may have many conditions. In the simplest concept-identification situation, partitions between categories are made on the basis of a single unqualified dimension, as indicated above. However, on a higher level, categorization may involve combinations of two or more attributes, such as (1) *A* items are both red and round; or (2) *A* items are either red or square or both; or (3) *A* items are either red and square or blue and round. The solution to problems involving such combinations and alternatives requires the development of fairly complex rules. A person consciously or unconsciously acquires and uses many such rules during his lifetime.

Another slightly different type of rule learning involves the discovery and generalization of recurring patterns or cycles of experience. For example, when the child learns to count, he develops the concept of cycles of events in terms of *equal* and *next*. When he learns to count by fives or learns about number systems on bases other than ten, he identifies the cyclic intervals and is able to extrapolate the process indefinitely. Learning to count involves rule identification and rule utilization.

Language acquisition and performance are probably the best examples of the development of complex perceptual-motor patterns involving the generation and utilization of rules without their conscious formulation. There are many rules involved in the use of language. One set of rules is the grammar of the language; other rules dictate word order. It is clear that the child learns these rules in the normal developmental way and utilizes them without being aware of their existence. We suggested earlier that the normal child of 6 has already learned these rules, and every normal person "knows" these rules in the sense that he can use them freely.

Verbal rule-following behavior, once developed, facilitates the learning of "nonsense" verbal material that is grammatically organized (Miller, 1962; Kintsch, 1970). Acquisition of the rules of a language also facilitates the perception, learning, and use of additional language components. The rule-following component of language makes it possible for a person to extrapolate, generate, and comprehend novel linguistic components and sequences.

LANGUAGE AND CONCEPTS

Humans have linguistic symbol (words) associated with most of their concepts. Attaching linguistic symbols to concepts helps acquire and transfer those concepts. Children and the lower animals develop concepts without verbal labels. Many lower animals can develop the concept of "triangularity" or "roundness," as evidenced by their ability to learn to use these characteristics as cues in responding. For example, they can learn to always select a pathway marked by a circle in preference to an alternative marked by any other shape, irrespective of the size, color, or other differentiating characteristics of the circle. The animal is able to differentiate and abstract the one variable of circularity and use it as the relevant cue in a variety of situations. Young children learn to categorize and display evidence of the use of concepts before they develop speech. The early speech of the child is largely a motor, rather than an intellectual, activity.

However, words can facilitate all aspects of concept acquisition. When the word *square* is heard each time the shape is seen, an additional differentiating cue is added to the visual ones. The constant repetition of the word when the one variable "squareness" is present assists in its abstraction. Having abstracted the meaning, the word serves as a symbol and helps in its generalization. Language can assist in these ways because it serves as a mediator. Words as symbols operate as response or object surrogates. They can mediate meanings, feelings, and motivational power, just as the original perceptual experiences do. The mediating function of language can be demonstrated in ordinary conditioning experiments. For example, if an electric shock to a person's foot (unconditioned stimulus) is regularly accompanied by the visual stimulus of the printed word *urn* (conditioned stimulus), the sight of the printed word will eventually evoke the same galvanic skin response (a change in the electrical conductivity of the skin) originally produced by the electric shock. The galvanic skin response (conditioned response) to the word *urn* can also be mediated by *earn* and by *vase*. In the first case the mediation (transfer) is by means of their common sounds; in the latter the transfer is by means of the common meanings of the two words. Every person acquires an intricate set of associational matrices based on linguistic mediators. The following is a small section of such a matrix:

```
                            run — dance
                           /
gate — gait — walk ——— path — road — route — root — pig — pretty
    \
     door — house — step — steppes — Russia — rushes — plant — flower — flour
                         \
                          stairs — walk
                                \
                                 stare — look — hear
```

THINKING AS A PHYSIOLOGICAL PROCESS

In Chapter 1 we indicated that modern-day psychology assumes that all perception, learning, retention, recall, and thinking have physiological bases. We also stated that these processes are all interrelated and interact with one another. The primary perceptual processes modify, or change, the individual physiologically. This modification primarily occurs in the nervous system. The "registration" and "fixation" of the primary perceptual or secondary ideational experience consist of the implantation and persistence of a neural trace, or engram. This modification of the individual's reaction potential as the result of experience constitutes learning, and the persistence of this modification constitutes memory (retention). In the memory phase of the process, the engram of the original perceptual or ideational experience is latent but potentially available for evocation. This phase is referred to as the period of trace storage. In ideation, the engram is revived either by appropriate sensory stimulation or by prior ideational activity. This final process in the acquisition-storage-retrieval sequence is called trace evocation or trace retrieval. The physiological basis of ideation refers to what takes place in the organism during trace evocation and the subsequent functioning of these retrieved engrams in thinking.

Ideation as Neural Activity

There are two conceptions of the physiological nature of thought. One is a central, or neural, conception. The second is a central-peripheral, or neural-motor, theory. According to the neural hypothesis, thinking consists solely of neural activity. Ideation consists of patterns of neural activity—principally or exclusively brain activity. This conception comes closest to the statement commonly made that "we think with our brains." According to this view, the brain is the "seat" of thinking, and thinking entails the reactivation of the neural segment of a sensory-neural or sensory-neural-motor sequence that functioned in the original experiential-learning process.

No definitive evidence is available to prove that ideation is confined to activity of the nervous system. However, two types of evidence are relevant to this question.

1. The fact that learning can occur in the absence of any evidence of overt response gives support to the central, or neural, conception. When the motor nerves to the leg are severed or paralyzed by drugs and a tone is repeatedly paired with an electric shock, a flexion response to the tone can be evoked when the motor nerve regenerates or the effects of the paralyzing drug wear off (Beck & Doty, 1957). If the neural engram constituting learning can be established without involving the motor component, it seems reasonable to infer that the ideational counterpart of the activity also would be purely neural.

One human subject was administered gradually increasing amounts of curare (a drug that is supposed to paralyze the muscles without affecting the central nervous system) until paralysis was judged to be complete. The electroencephalograms (EEGs) taken throughout the period remained normal, and the subject subsequently reported that he was fully conscious and was able to think quite normally even when he was completely paralyzed (Smith, Brown, Toman, & Goodman, 1947).

2. The arousal of memories by the electrical stimulation of the cortical areas of conscious subjects also supports the hypothesis that thinking is purely neural brain activity. The trouble with all such evidence is that it is impossible to prove that *no effector responses* are taking place during the learning and thinking. Although no observable overt activity is taking place, it does not necessarily mean that there is a complete absence of covert responses.

Since verbal activities can function in symbolic ways and operate as behavioral surrogates, it is always possible that language—even subvocal language—may provide a response substitute for gross motor activity.

Ideation as Neuromuscular Activity

Ever since electronic equipment was devised to amplify and record the changes in electric potential associated with muscular contraction, it has been possible to demonstrate that slight muscular activity accompanies some ideation. Thoughts of lifting a weight with the right hand are correlated with action currents in the biceps muscles of the right arm. When a person imagines that he is walking down the street, periodic volleys of impulses can be recorded from the muscles of the legs. If the person imagines that he is looking up at a tall building, action currents indicate that there is slight activity in the muscles of the neck and eyes that would be involved in actually performing this act (Jacobson, 1932). When a person recalls his previous visual inspection of an object, his eye movements during recall are similar to those he made when originally viewing the object (Totten, 1935). Records of eye movements made during both the reading and the recall of a passage are very similar (Ewert, 1933). Such findings show that the recall of previous experiences has motor components or accompaniments. But what about abstract concepts? What is the motor counterpart of abstract thinking? What physical activity would correspond to *three* or *square root* as thoughts? Since these concepts are abstract and are handled by means of spoken or written symbols, thinking in these terms may be "subvocal talking," "implicit language activity," or "talking to oneself." Experimental studies have shown that verbalization while solving problems facilitates their solution (Gagné & Smith, 1962). Incidental observations also lend some support to this hypothesis. Many people, when working on a difficult problem, talk to themselves. If they are alone, they may even talk out loud. Young children tend to vocalize their thoughts, but, as they get older, they learn to suppress such overt manifestations. However, in senility, many individuals revert to talking to themselves.

Thinking is often associated with activities of the speech mechanisms, just as it is with the activity of other muscle groups (Jacobson, 1932). What about the ideation of deaf-mutes? Action currents are obtained from the muscles of the hands of deaf-mutes during thought. When doing mental arithmetic, more than 80 percent of deaf-mutes showed muscularly induced action currents in the hands, whereas only 30 percent of hearing subjects showed such records. (Muscular activities in the hands of a hearing subject may represent tentative writing movements.) The magnitude of the action currents from the hands was four times larger for the deaf-mutes than for the hearing subjects (Max, 1937).

Although such observations and experimental findings are interesting and show that much ideation has motor accompaniments or components, they do not prove that the motor activities are essential parts of thinking. It is quite possible that these motor activities are only secondary or incidental to ideation. That is, ideation may still be basically central neural activity. The question of whether ideation is purely neural or neuromuscular cannot be answered at the present time. The trend of thinking on the problem has shifted over the past 20 years from the neuromuscular hypothesis to a preference for the neural hypothesis.

CREATIVITY

Since the 1950s there has been a resurgence of interest in the problems of productive thinking—that is, creativity. Perhaps one pragmatic reason for this interest is that modern technology has less need of man as a physical source of energy and more need of his creative talents; much of the manual labor and routine problem solving previously done by man can be done better and much more efficiently by machines. Social, political, and industrial progress is largely dependent on the creativity of man. Current research on creativity is concerned with definitions and criteria of creativity, the distinguishing characteristics of highly creative individuals, and specification of the conditions that are conducive to creative productivity.

Definitions of Creativity

Definitions of creativity tend to be either personal and phenomenological, on the one hand, or social and utilitarian, on the other. Those individuals emphasizing the personal frame of reference define as creative all behavior that is novel or unique to the particular individual, without regard to its social novelty or utility. However, most workers insist that a creative product, in addition to being novel to the individual, must also be socially unique and useful. Within a cultural frame of reference, creative products must be original both to the individual and to society, and, in addition, they must be useful (Guilford, 1965).

The Characteristics of Creative People

Studies of creative adults have consisted largely of investigations of the personal characteristics, developmental histories, and intellectual processes of individuals who are judged by others in their own fields of work to be highly creative. Highly creative children have been identified by means of tests developed for this purpose. Most of the tests of creativity in children are modifications of similar tests devised for and validated on adult subjects. Although these tests have a certain face validity, there have been no longitudinal studies of individuals who scored high on such tests as children.

A few examples will make clearer the nature of some of the tests of creativity currently in use. A series of tests made by Getzels and Jackson (1962) is fairly typical. These five tests are (1) a Test of Definitions, (2) a Use of Things Test, (3) a Hidden Shapes Test, (4) a Fables Test, and (5) a Make Up Problems Test. In the Definitions Test, the subject is required to give as many definitions as possible for some fairly common words, such as *bolt* and *sack*. The responses are scored according to the number and range of different categories represented by the definitions. In the Use of Things Test, the person is instructed to give as many uses as possible for such common objects as a brick or a toothpick. Responses are scored on the basis of the number and the originality of the uses listed. In the Hidden Shapes Test, the subject is shown a series of geometric figures printed on cards and is asked to find a figure hidden in the larger pattern. In the Fables Test, the subject is required to add three different endings to an incomplete fable. One ending is to be moralistic, one humorous, and one sad. These endings are scored in terms of their relative appropriateness and originality. In the Make Up Problems Test, the subject is provided a paragraph of information and is required to make up as many mathematical problems as possible, using the information provided. The score depends on the number, appropriateness, complexity, and originality of the problems. Batteries containing as many as 25 different kinds of tasks have been used (Torrance, 1962). These tasks all call for the production of many items, each a divergent and unique response that requires the types of ideation theoretically necessary for creative thinking.

Studies of highly creative adults have shown certain characteristics to be common to divergent occupational groups. On the Allport-Vernon-Lindzey Scale of Values, physicists, writers, artists, architects, and mathematicians scored high on the theoretical and esthetic scales and low on the religious, social, and economic scales. Scientists, mathematicians, creative writers, artists, and architects all preferred more complex, asymmetrical figures, were more highly imaginative, and enjoyed esthetic qualities more than did a less creative but otherwise comparable group. Highly creative people in these fields have a high degree of intelligence, emotional stability, personal dominance, and forcefulness of opinion. They are challenged by the unknown, by contradictions, and by apparent disorder. In personal relationships they are somewhat detached and distant. They prefer to deal with things and abstractions rather than with people. They also appear to be self-sufficient and self-directing in their work. Creative individuals are more interested in broad concepts and meanings than in specific details, in the immediately practical, or in the small matters of everyday life (MacKinnon, 1962). Highly creative people seem to be able to tolerate ambiguities, conflicting motives, and the tensions arising from these circumstances better than the average individual. They also seem to enjoy intense, sustained, and vigorous effort.

Children designated as highly creative on the basis of test scores show an interesting pattern of traits. When Getzels and Jackson (1962) compared a "high-IQ" with a "highly creative" group of children, they found some marked differences between the two. The personal traits preferred for themselves by the high-IQ group were those that they believed to be both predictive of adult success and highly favored by teachers. The highly creative children valued quite different personal characteristics. They were just as aware of and in agreement with the other group as to the characteristics highly valued by society and by teachers. However, unlike the high-IQ children, they did not want these characteristics for themselves and were not highly success oriented in terms of conventional norms.

On projective tests the highly creative children scored significantly higher in the use of stimulus-free themes, unexpected endings, humor, incongruities, and playfulness. They had more themes of violence in their stories and displayed a disparagement of conventional success and conformity. In occupational preferences they were much more diffuse and unconventional (adventurer, inventor, explorer) than the high-IQ children. Of the preferential choices of the high-IQ children, 75 percent were in the five conventional professions of medicine, law, education, engineering, and science.

The Parents of Creative Children

The parents of the highly creative children, as compared with the parents of the high-IQ children, were found to be more secure and to have less education. They were less concerned about and less sure of the correctness of their child-rearing practices, put less pressure on their children to do well scholastically, and differed in the types of companions they preferred for their children. On the whole, the families of the highly creative children were not highly child centered or closely knit. A good deal of individual freedom was permitted, and certain risks were accepted.

Conditions Conducive to Creativity

Rogers (1959, 1963) has suggested that two conditions are favorable to creative activity: "psychological safety" and "psychological freedom." Psychological safety requires acceptance that is not conditional on conformity. Creative activity is, by definition, deviant behavior. When acceptance and positive valuation of an individual depend on his conformity, creative behavior will be devalued and deviant ideas will be discouraged. According to Rogers, a "good" society will provide a wide variety of socially approved roles for its citizens and will have considerable flexibility in its acceptance of the deviant individual. In such a nonthreatening social environment, the creative individual should experience little anxiety, and his principal sources of motivation should derive from the positive satisfactions of exploration and discovery, rather than from the reduction of anxiety. In an acceptant social atmosphere, Rogers maintains, the creative individual can be comfortable and need not waste time and energy protecting himself. He can be divergent without being defensive and can be a nonconformist without fear of social disapproval.

Psychological safety makes psychological freedom possible, according to Rogers. Some of the characteristics of the person who is psychologically free are:

1. Without fear of ridicule, the creative person is able to accept himself for what he is.
2. He can give at least symbolic expression to his impulses and thoughts without having to repress, distort, or hide them.
3. He can handle percepts, concepts, and words playfully and in unusual ways without feeling guilty.
4. He sees the mysterious and the unknown as challenges to be met or as games to be played.

Experimental studies have demonstrated that originality can be increased by instruction, encouragement, and rewards of a specific nature, just as more general cultural acceptance, encouragement, and reinforcement are thought to increase creativity in general (Mearns, 1958; Maltzman, 1960; Mednick, 1962; Covington & Crutchfield, 1965; Torrance, 1962).

DREAMS

Dreams, which consist of ideational activities during sleep, are characterized by their relative lack of motivation and purpose, their apparent spontaneity, and their mostly internal origin. They differ from waking ideational activities in their apparent unreality and their relative lack of consistency. Some dreams, however, are stimulus related and illusory: a sleeping person hears a scraping sound and dreams that he is outdoors shoveling snow off the sidewalk. A low, rhythmic sound in the distance becomes the beating of a bass drum in a band. To cite a personal recollection, one of the authors awoke one morning from a dream in which he was out shooting ducks. When he was fully awake, he recognized that the terrific bombardment taking place in the dream was the sound of an alarm clock going off. A French psychologist of the last century reported that, whenever his knees got cold while he was asleep, he would dream that he was riding in a particular type of horse-drawn carriage in which his knees always got cold. At least portions of such dreams are illusions—misinterpretations of actual stimuli.

Most of the content of dreams is hallucinatory. Hallucinatory experiences are ideational processes mistaken for perceptual experiences. Dreams are typically taken for reality while they are going on. The proof of the hallucinatory nature of the dream comes on awakening, when the dream is recognized as inconsistent with the broader context of experience provided by one's waking experiences. The dream does not dovetail in time and place with what preceded and what follows it. The bizarre and "impossible" events that occurred in the dream are seen as inconsistent with one's past and present perceptual experiences.

Occasionally dream content is related to the immediately preceding event of one's life. There have been reports of fortunate individuals who have gone to sleep after working very hard on a problem without success, only to arrive at the solution in their dreams. However, experimental attempts to influence dream content systematically have produced only nonspecific, rather than specific, content-related effects on dreams. For example, following the viewing of films of violence, dreams were longer, more vivid, and more emotional than were dreams following nonviolent films (Foulkes, 1966). Yet there seemed to be no relationship between the specific content of the films and the subsequent dreams or between the effective tones (pleasantness or unpleasantness) of the two. The effect of the films seemed to be nonspecific.

Prior to the 1950s, studies of the content of dreams depended for material on delayed recall or accidental awakenings from dreams. Most of the available data were of an anecdotal sort and were subject to all sorts of biases. In the 1950s it was discovered that dreaming is characterized by a particular patterning of electrical activity (EEG) of the brain and by rapid movements of the eyeballs. The characteristic eye movements of dreaming were similar to those that might be made if the dreamer were "watching" the pictorial content of the dream. When awakened during these periods of characteristic EEG and eyeball activity, the person would regularly report that he had been awakened from a dream, which he was able to describe quite completely.

With these indices of dreaming, experimenters could awaken a subject at appropriate times and collect relatively complete samples of his dream experiences. These objective indices of dreaming made it possible to establish the amount of time devoted to dreaming, to determine the patterns of dream activity, and to study systematically the effect of various factors on the duration and content of dreams. Using these criteria, it is also possible to distinguish different phases of sleep.

Studies using these improved methods have disclosed that there is far more ideational activity going on during sleep than had previously been suspected. It has been known for a long time that the brain is a continuously active organ, as indicated by EEG activity, which starts before birth and continues until death. (EEG activity is discussed in Chapter 2.) Recent studies have shown that there is a regularly recurring, cyclic pattern of four different states of EEG activity spanning the typical night's sleep. These four states of EEG activity

Figure 8-2. Dr. Isak Borg (Victor Sjörström) dreams of the days of his youth in Ingmar Bergman's film *Wild Strawberries.* Some students may find the relationship of dreams to works of art an intriguing topic.

are correlated with changes in sensitivity to external stimulation, with motility during sleep, and—most significantly for our purposes—with the extent and type of dream activity. Apparently we actually spend more than one-fourth of a typical 6- to 7-hour sleep period dreaming. The periods of dreaming are also much longer than had previously been thought; they are seldom less than 10 minutes long and may last for as long as an hour. It has been shown that acting out, while awake, the events that took place in the dream takes about the same time as the duration of the dream, as indicated by the EEG and eye-movement records. Contrary to previous opinion, dreaming is not compressed in time.

Comparisons of groups of people who claim they seldom or never dream with those who claim that they dream often indicate that these groups do not differ significantly in their actual dream frequency or duration. The difference is in their ability to recall dreams some time after the dreaming takes place (Foulkes, 1966).

The rhythms of the phases of sleep and patterns of dreaming are highly regular and predictable for any given individual. Moreover, the timing and frequency of episodes of dreaming are quite similar from one night to the next. This regularity suggests that situational and experiential factors do not affect dream patterns much. *Selective sleep deprivation* (awakening the subject whenever the records show he is starting to dream so as to reduce the amount of dreaming by from 70 to 90 percent) leads to *larger amounts of dreaming on "recovery" nights.* Recovery-night dreaming time may be elevated as much as 50 percent. Control nights, with an equal number of awakenings that do not interrupt dreaming, fail to increase subsequent dreaming. It seems that a dream deficit accumulated one night is made up by increased dreaming activity on the following night.

Some subjects who had their dreaming time reduced by 65 to 75 percent for five consecutive nights developed high levels of anxiety, unusual increase in appetite, and difficulty in concentration (Dement, 1960). Two subjects who were deprived of an estimated 95 percent of their normal dreaming activity—one for 15 and one for 16 consecutive nights—underwent dramatic changes in personality after the fourteenth consecutive deprivation night. One of the subjects became so paranoid in his suspicions of others that the experiment was terminated because of fear that the subject might develop into a full-blown psychotic. Both subjects returned to normal behavior following the first recovery night, during which they dreamed nearly half of the time, a value far in excess of their normal amounts (Kales, 1964; Foulkes, 1966).

These studies indicate that dreaming may serve functions other than the free play of ideational processes. The fact that an individual can incur dream deficits that are made up by subsequent increased dreaming is compatible with Freud's notion that dreams provide a mechanism for the release of potentially harmful *tensions* that are unable to find expression during waking experience. Freud saw dreams as the symbolic manifestation of repressed experiences. He believed that, because of the prohibition and taboos imposed by society and by one's own conscience, many wishes and impulses are inhibited and repressed in ordinary waking experience. During sleep, the repressing and inhibiting mechanisms (the censor) are less active (the censor is less vigilant), and the repressed impulses manifest themselves in dreams. Because the censoring mechanisms are not entirely inactive during sleep, the repressed tendencies cannot reveal themselves in their obvious *manifest* forms and so they do so in disguised, symbolic ways (*latent forms*). Since many of the social taboos are directly or indirectly related to sex, Freud considered most dreams to be sexual in nature. Since these behavioral tendencies were conceived of in terms of tensions, or pressures, it was believed that dreams provided a harmless means of discharging the tensions that these repressed desires and impulses generated in the unconscious.

Freud's explanations in terms of reified processes do little more than restate the problem, and the apparent support that they receive from the experimental studies of dream deprivation has alternative explanations. William Dement, who performed the experiments on sleep deprivation, has reproduced most of the symptoms of dream deprivation in normal cats as well as in cats with all the brain structures above the pons removed. He is now inclined to believe that the dream-deprivation effects are to be explained in terms of some kinds of *specific biological functions* rather than for the psychological reasons specified by the "safety-valve" psychoanalytic theory (Foulkes, 1966).

DAYDREAMS (AUTISTIC THINKING)

Autistic thinking is wishful thinking. Reverie and daydreams often take the form of autistic ideation, in which fantasies portray reality in wish-fulfilling ways rather than in terms of objective reality. Much of the average person's daydreaming is casual ideation related to immediate, concrete situations, transient problems, and interests. Such daydreaming is closely tied to reality and is not autistic. Much fantasy of this type contributes to problem solving and is socially and personally useful. However, a considerable portion of daytime reverie is autistic.

Autistic thinking may be either casual and unsystematic or defensive and systematic. Systematic daydreams take characteristic forms sufficiently often for them to be given names. The two most common are the "conquering-hero" and the "suffering-hero" types. The nature of these forms is indicated by their names.

The average individual also participates vicariously in daydreams that are fabricated for him by others. Such prefabricated daydreams constitute the fictions supplied by novels, short stories, radio, stage shows, movies, and television. In stories of romance, adventure, and achievement, the reader or viewer vicariously lives adventurously and romantically or becomes accomplished and highly esteemed. The fact that much popular fiction is known as "escape literature" is evidence of its wish-fulfilling nature. Much of the pathological ideation of psychotic, particularly schizophrenic, individuals is autistic. There are also other forms of pathological thinking.

PATHOLOGICAL THINKING

Pathological thinking is grossly distorted ideation that is accepted as valid and authentic by the individual. In ordinary daydreaming, the individual differentiates between the fantasies and the realities of his life, whereas in the more extreme forms of pathological ideation (delusions), this distinction is not made.

The paranoid individual's systematized delusion of persecution or of grandeur are classical examples of pathological thinking. Such individuals defend their beliefs with great ingenuity. The supports for their contentions are clothed in all the appearances of logic and reason. For example, a paranoid who believes that people are trying to kill him will reason that the individuals claiming to be his relatives are really disguised private detectives trying to trick him into betraying himself. His relatives have really all been killed by these impostors and conspirators. Thus a paranoid individual reasons quite consistently within the confines of his delusional system.

Some pathological thinking is characterized by superficialities in its associative connections and by discontinuities of thought. The following is an example of such thinking, where the transitions from thought are mediated by association based on superficial similarities in the sounds or meanings of words.

> I am the President of the United States. I will be the last President. I will not be present because I am not a resident of Pennsylvania. Pennsylvania in Transylvania. Transcontinental trains are the best kind. In trains when it rains. Rains in April bring May flowers. Flour makes bread. Cast your bread upon the water. Blood is thicker than water. I am of royal blood. Red blood, black blood, black power. I am the most powerful except for policemen and police dogs. The German shepherd was the best dog this year.

Where discontinuities are dominant features, the thinking is disjointed and becomes almost random. The speech of such a person becomes a "word salad." The person starts to say something, but, before more than a few words or a phrase is uttered, he drops it and starts to say something else. The result is that nothing comprehensible is said:

> America discovers Columbus on May day. America is not made of granite but of two dozen eggs. Wire wheels have bungalows and solid granite tops. The fourth of February in the year 1977 with a Ford sports car. I am marrying a bungalow in June. It will have thick upholstering and wire wheels. It will have two dozen eggs and many other things. This bungalow will not be of granite but of solid stone. It will roll down hills but will not gather moss. In not more than five minutes it will be grass.

There is evidence that even the most jumbled and apparently chaotic speech and thought of psychotic individuals has meaning. Such ideation and speech may contain many private meanings and symbols that are meaningful to the individual and that he is trying to communicate. When the pathological thought is characterized by a constant change in direction or by superficial associations, the disorganized ideation is the consequence of the individual's inability to maintain a given "mental set" for any period of time. Such a person starts to say something, but some ideational or perceptual element reminds him of something else and redirects his train of thought. If one does not listen carefully to what he is saying, it seems to make sense. However, when one listens carefully and tries to follow his thoughts, what he says means nothing. Trying to stop him and point out his inconsistencies or lack of coherence is futile, for he pays no attention.

Other less pathological forms of ideation are *fixed ideas* (the perseveration of ideas), *obsessions,* and *circumstantiality.* A fixed idea is a specific trend of thought that persistently recurs and dominates the thinking of the individual. An obsession refers to a persistent idea that the individual recognizes as irrational but that he is unable to dispel. Circumstantiality in ideation and speech is characterized by the inclusion of innumerable tedious and irrevelant details. The following is an example of circumstantiality:

> It happened on Wednesday—last Wednesday. I know it was last Wednesday for that was the day Mr. Knight brought me the note. Mr. Knight is my neighbor on the west. My other neighbors are . . . . Mr. Knight works for James Hardware and on Wednesday he brought me a note from his wife. She and I have always been good friends. We visit back and forth a lot. Mr. Knight brought me the note at five minutes after eight. I know it was five minutes after eight for I had put my egg on to boil just as the clock struck eight and had just taken it off when he came. . . .

In circumstantiality there is an impartial and unselective recall and reproduction of past events. The individual is unable to discriminate between important and unimportant, significant and insignificant events in recall. This type of ideation is characteristic of certain psychotic individuals. It is, however, shared by many otherwise normal people.

IMAGINING

Imagining, as an ideational category, overlaps several others. It may range from the free, uncontrolled type that merges into reverie and autistic thinking, or it may be purposive and controlled and thus overlap ideational problem solving and reasoning. Imagination is sometimes dichotomized as *reproductive* and *productive*. Reproductive imagination is largely synonymous with recall. However, recall in reproductive imagining is never truly an exact reproduction of perceptual experience. There are always omissions, additions, confusions, and transpositions in reproducing perceptual experiences. Productive imagining may consist of a recombination in only slightly new ways of the experiential components derived from perception, or it may involve the selective use of extremely divergent elements in unusual ways for problem solving and for highly original and creative purposes. If we conceive of the materials of imagination as deriving from perceptual experience, the most productive and creative ideational activities still make use of and are limited by the past experiences of the individual.

SUMMARY

Thinking is a form of covert activity. It involves the manipulation of symbols and concepts that operate as the surrogates of perceptual experiences. The forms of thinking are dreams, daydreams, recalling, imagining, and reasoning.

Reasoning is ideational problem solving. The steps or components of the complete reasoning process include motivation, recognition of the problem, preparation (analysis of the problem and survey of available information), formulation of possible solutions (hypotheses), incubation, illumination (either sudden or gradual), and verification (acceptance, rejection, or modification). Factors influencing the course of reasoning include one's store of available information, one's mental set, one's emotional biases, and one's available strategies.

Concept acquisition involves discrimination, abstraction, and generalization. A concept is a learned response to the common properties of a variety of stimuli and constitutes a form of adaptive and useful categorizing. Concepts differ in degree of abstractness. Many of the lower animals can develop concepts, but only man has the capacity to use words to symbolize concepts. Language and thinking are intimately related.

Ideation as a physiological process has been considered to be either purely neural (we think with our brain) or as neuromuscular (we think with our whole body). Although there is no definitive evidence in support of either conception, present-day thinking tends to subscribe to the neural, or central, conception.

There is currently considerable interest in the nature of, and conditions that are conducive to, creative thinking. Highly creative individuals have been found to differ in many significant ways from less creative persons. These differences include family background, motivations, value systems, and interests.

Dreams are relatively free ideational activity going on during sleep. Some of them are illusory, but most dreams are hallucinatory experiences. A person normally dreams in excess of one-fourth of a typical night's sleep. Periods of dreaming may exceed an hour in length and are not greatly condensed in time, as was previously believed. Artificial reduction in dreaming time on one night produces increased dreaming on the following night. Prolonged reduction in dreaming time may result in dramatic personality changes and even some psychotic symptoms.

Some daydreaming is tied to reality and is useful to the individual. However, much daydreaming is wishful thinking and is consequently called autistic. The "conquering-hero" and "suffering-hero" types of daydreams are autistic in nature. Many daydreams are prefabricated for us in fiction. The autistic ideation of psychotic individuals is a form of pathological thinking. The ideational components of delusional systems, fixed ideas, obsessions, and circumstantiality are other forms of pathological ideation. Thinking that seems meaningless and pathological to someone else may be meaningful to the individual.

SUGGESTED READINGS

Anderson, R. C., & Ausubel, D. P. *Readings in the psychology of cognition.* New York: Holt, 1965. This volume consists of a wide variety of original articles, many of which relate to thinking.

Inhelder, B., & Piaget, J. *The growth of logical thinking from childhood to adolescence.* New York: Basic Books, 1958. This book traces the development of thinking from early childhood to adolescence.

Manis, M. *Cognitive processes.* Belmont, Calif.: Brooks/Cole, 1966. Cognitive processes cover much more than thinking. However, the last half of this paperback covers the topics of thinking, problem solving, and creativity very well.

Torrance, E. P. *Guiding creative talent.* Englewood Cliffs, N. J.: Prentice-Hall, 1962. This book deals with the problem of identifying and encouraging creativity in the school-age child.

9

Measurement of Abilities

The use of various kinds of tests as tools in psychological investigations of interests, attitudes, social and personal adjustment, intelligence, and achievement is a well-established practice. If such measurement is to be performed for purposes of psychological investigation, we must pay close attention to those attributes we are measuring and to the characteristics of the measuring instrument we employ.

VALIDITY

Perhaps the most important criterion of a good measuring instrument is its validity. Validity can be defined as *the extent to which an instrument measures that which it purports to measure.* On the surface this criterion may appear to be obvious, but it is not always so. If a teacher gave an arithmetic test to measure his students' knowledge of history, the instrument would be inappropriate and would violate the criterion of validity. A more subtle violation would be the use of an arithmetic test too advanced for the students.

This illustration demonstrates that validity is specific. An instrument possesses validity for a particular purpose. An arithmetic test may be a valid measure of arithmetic skills, but this fact does not enhance its validity for measuring knowledge of history or for measuring arithmetic skill at a different level. Thus an instrument can be highly valid for one purpose and grossly lacking in validity for another.

The above-mentioned example illustrates the concept of validity but not the kinds of errors involving validity that are made. A common practice is to measure some particular subject matter with a test that is worded in such a way so as to become a test of reading ability rather than of knowledge of subject matter. Those who can read the questions sufficiently well can also answer them; poorer readers cannot understand the questions and obviously cannot answer them appropriately. In the construction of test items, the use of vocabulary that is too complicated for many students may have nearly the same results. The test may be a better indicator of intelligence than of knowledge of subject matter because vocabulary is the best single measure of intelligence currently available.

The validity of many tests that are used for the selection of employees in various industries has been challenged recently. Another highly suspect area is tests of intelligence standardized on predominantly white, middle-class Americans but applied to other ethnic or socioeconomic groups.

Statistical Validity

Validity can be determined statistically in several ways. One difficulty lies in finding an outside criterion with which to correlate test scores. Coefficients obtained from correlating a test with some outside criterion are called *coefficients of validity*. The higher the correlation, the greater the validity of the instrument. This postulation, of course, is based on the assumption that the criterion measures may be accepted as measurement standards. School marks can be used as a criterion with which to correlate test results, based on the assumption that marks assigned, in the long run, will actually be reflective of achievement in the course. Thus those who get the better marks in a course should score higher on a test on that subject matter. The teacher, here, is taken to be an *expert judge*. When those pupils whom the teacher considers to be the highest achievers in class get the higher grades on a test, the test has a high validity.

If the validity of a given test has already been established, the test can be used as a criterion, and other tests may then be validated in terms of their relationship to it. This method is used when an outstanding test in the field has already been developed. For example, group-intelligence tests currently depend for their validity on their agreement with individual measures of intelligence.

The validity of a test may be attested to by its administration to groups of different ability levels. If a reading test is to be administered to all fourth-graders, and the pupils have been divided into reading groups on the basis of the teacher's experience with these students, it would be expected that the poorest reading group would score lower than the group designated as the best reading group. There should be a statistically significant difference between the scores of the groups in favor of the "better" group.

Test validity is difficult to establish. Establishment of validity criteria for examinations presents great difficulty at best. When the examination is not carefully constructed and administered, the question of validity becomes even more difficult to answer. Students who are emotionally aroused or frightened by test situations are difficult persons from whom to procure valid measures of any kind. Validity is the first and chief concern of the test constructor, and every effort should be given to assure the use of the most valid instruments possible in the measurement of achievement and ability.

RELIABILITY

In the measuring of ability or achievement, the necessity of using an instrument that yields consistent results is rather apparent. Such consistency results in *reliability*. Reliability may be defined as *the extent to which an instrument measures consistently whatever it does measure*. Some clarification may be necessary to differentiate between the concepts of validity and reliability. A test may be highly reliable for a given purpose—that is, it may yield consistent results when applied—yet be low in validity for that purpose. The test may be a quite consistent measure of what it does measure without effectively measuring that which it is supposed to measure. Contrariwise, it cannot efficiently measure what it purports to measure and not measure consistently that which it does measure. A test may be reliable for a purpose without being valid for that purpose, but it cannot be valid for a purpose without being reliable at the same time. For example, when one uses a government-inspected scale to determine his weight, he can get off and on the scale a great number of times and he will always weigh the same number of pounds. This scale provides a reliable and valid measure of his weight. If the poundage read from the scale is taken to be indicative of his intelligence, it is still a highly reliable measure, but it suffers because of lack of validity. The scale as a measure of weight is both reliable and valid; as a measure of intellect it is reliable, but its validity is very low. Assuming relative constancy of intelligence, any valid measure of it would have to be consistent (reliable).

Reliability is a statistical concept. Little can be told about the reliability of a test by examining the test items themselves. To determine the reliability of a test, it must be administered to an appropriate group of people under appropriate circumstances. Reliability is expressed by a correlation coefficient, which is designated a *reliability coefficient*.

Reliability coefficients can be obtained by correlating the results of the same test administered to the same subjects on two different occasions. If the test scores of the individuals remain nearly the same or if individuals do not vary in rank on the test, the correlation and the reliability will be high. This method is called the *test-retest method*. It is subject to errors that may arise from the particular sample of tasks chosen for the test and to variations because of memory and practice effect.

Two tests can be constructed as equivalent forms. The specific questions in the test are different, but the same sorts of questions are asked about the same areas. With two forms of the same test, each pupil can take one test first and then the other. The correlation between the two forms will provide an appropriate reliability coefficient. This method of *equivalent forms* is a sound way to estimate the reliability of achievement tests.

Economy in time and effort frequently dictates that a single test be divided into two parts for scoring purposes. Thus there may be obtained a measure of internal consistency from correlating the scores on the two parts—one score obtained from the odd-numbered questions and another from the even-numbered questions. This method is the *split-half method*. Because of the simplicity of the procedures involved, the shortcomings of this method have not discouraged its use. The greatest limitation of this method is its lack of meaning on tests in which speed is an important factor. The speed factor will tend to inflate estimates of reliability based on the split-half procedure. The inflation of the estimate of reliability is proportional to the preponderance of the speed factor.

Kuder and Richardson (1937) have devised several methods of computing reliability coefficients that do not call for splitting of the test in two halves and calculating the coefficient of correlation. The limitations relative to speed factors that artificially inflate these reliability coefficients are the same as those for the split-half method.

The coefficient of reliability is difficult to interpret. The coefficients reflect the methods in their computation, the variability of the groups, the interval between tests, the characteristics of the particular groups employed, and other factors. Kelley (1927), however, has suggested the following minimal requirements for reliability coefficients of a single grade:

0.50 for determining the status of a group in a subject or group of subjects;

0.90 for differentiating the achievement of a group in two or more scholastic lines;

0.94 for differentiating the status of individuals in the same subject or group of subjects;

0.96 for differentiating individuals in two or more scholastic lines.

Objectivity

Objectivity is an aspect of reliability. When test scores are not affected by the scorer's bias or personal judgment, the test is said to be objective. Obviously, if a test is scored by the same reader on several occasions and is scored differently each time, or if the test is scored by several readers, each of whom gets a different score, the test could hardly be said to be highly reliable. If highly objective items are selected for a test, there will be little or no disagreement as to what constitutes the correct answer.

Answers to objective test items are typically short, and the question is worded so that only one answer fulfills the requirements of the question. If the test is such that it can be scored without involving the bias or judgment of the scorer, regardless of who scores the tests, the results should be the same except for chance errors that might occur. If the questions cannot be scored objectively, reliability suffers.

INTELLIGENCE

Psychologists and laymen alike recognize that some people have greater understanding and are shrewder, quicker to learn, more skillful, or more adaptable than others. A number of factors differentiate the very bright from the very dull and thereby pertain to the concept of intelligence.

Intelligence is a complex quality possessed in varying amounts by all people, and psychologists have developed many instruments to measure it. These instruments (often written tests) measure a person's level of current functioning in a variety of areas. This level of current functioning is frequently taken as an index of intellectual capacity or potential intellectual capacity.

Much of the confusion surrounding the effectiveness, and even the desirability, of measures of intelligence might have been avoided if psychologists had earlier pointed out that a test of intelligence is *a measure of current performance* and, as such, may or may not be useful in the prediction of future performance. Hilgard and Atkinson (1967) have offered a practical definition of intelligence as simply that which an intelligence test measures.

Tests have been skillfully constructed that can differentiate the bright from the dull. Although these tests have been developed from somewhat differing theoretical approaches, their results are highly correlated and are assumed to measure something in common. The high correlation between various tests of intelligence and their effectiveness in differentiating levels of performance in a variety of areas indicates their usefulness for a number of selective and predictive purposes.

Early Measurement of Intelligence

Historically, intelligence was measured solely to discover which children in the public schools had insufficient capacity to profit from the usual type of instruction. With this question in mind, the French government asked the psychologist Alfred Binet to serve on a commission in 1904. The task assigned to the commission was to devise an instrument that would be more valid than the judgment of teachers to segregate these children for placement in special classes. The government realized that the teachers' judgment would be affected by parents, by personal prejudice, and by many other influences. Binet felt that a graded set of psychological tests could be devised that would indicate the degree of each child's intelligence. He and an associate named Simon constructed some tests and used them with schoolchildren in an attempt to determine each child's mental development. If a given schoolchild could perform no better than children known to be feebleminded, obviously he, too, was feebleminded. Binet and Simon obtained data on normal schoolchildren, and thus they were able to tell by the number of tests passed how a given child compared with other children. If a 6-year-old child could do only those tasks usually performed by a 4-year-old, the child was said to be retarded by two years.

Later Binet and Simon revised the tests and arranged the items in age groupings with definite tests for the various age levels. If a given item was passed by a majority of 7-year-olds and failed by most 6-year-olds, but nearly all 8-year-olds passed it, that item was included in the test for 7-year-olds. Binet and Simon thus developed the concept of *mental age* (MA). If a child of 10 passed the tests commonly passed by an 8-year-old, the child was said to have an MA of 8. If a child of 7 passed the tests commonly passed by an 8-year-old, the child was said to have an MA of 8. The concept of mental age gave an indication of intelligence level achieved without regard to chronological age, but it gave no indication of how bright or dull the individual was, because a child of 10 with an MA of 8 is not very bright, whereas a child of 6 with an MA of 8 is quite bright.

These tests were brought to the United States, translated into English, and modified somewhat, and norms were constructed for Americans. They soon became widely used. From these early efforts have grown a vast field of knowledge and a considerable number of different tests designed to measure individual intelligence. The testing of soldiers during World War I afforded opportunities for practical experiments on a large scale and gave impetus to the development of group tests.

People engaged in the education of children will soon find instances when the measurement of intelligence becomes imperative to academic planning. However, since we cannot measure intelligence directly, we must currently accept evidence of having learned as indicative of potential ability to learn. If we can understand the child's intelligence-test performance as it is now in comparison with other children's, we can, perhaps, use it to predict what his performance will be like in comparison with others in the future.

Individual Intelligence Tests

Intelligence tests have been designed for use in assessing ability to learn, to think abstractly, or to adapt to life's situations. They are in fact used as measures of current performance ability, and their results have proved to be predictive indices of academic and intellectual achievement. As we have indicated, a number of individual tests of intelligence have been developed. We shall describe some of the more prominent ones.

The Stanford-Binet tests. The Stanford-Binet tests (Terman & Merrill, 1937, 1960) have been widely used in intelligence testing. They are administered by a trained examiner to one person at a time in a face-to-face situation. The test consists of groups of questions corresponding to various age levels, starting with 2 years and running up through the superior-adult level. At the lower age levels of the test, there are six test items (questions to answer or tasks to perform) at each level, with age breaks every six months. In other words, there are six items for age 2, six for age 2½, six for age 3, and so forth. In addition to the basic mental age, which is determined by the highest age level at which the subject satisfactorily passes all the test items for that age, each question answered correctly or each task properly performed contributes one month of mental age (MA). For example, if a child satisfactorily passes all the 3-year items but passes only four of the items at the 3½-year level, his basic MA is 3 years. In addition, he is given one month of mental age for each item passed at age levels beyond his basic mental age. (The examiner continues to administer the test until that age level is reached at which the child can answer none of the items correctly.) If this same child passed all the 3-year items, four of the 3½-year items, two of the 4-year items, and none of the 4½-year items, the examiner would stop administering the test and calculate the mental age. The MA would be 36 months for the basic mental age, plus four months for items passed at the 3½-year level, plus two months for the items passed at the 4-year level. The total is 3½ years', or 42 months', mental age. This MA indicates that the child has reached a point of intellectual development comparable to that of the child of 3½ years of age.

Mental age by itself does not tell us much about the rate of intellectual growth of the child. The usefulness of this concept by itself is rather limited. It can readily be seen that there are remarkable differences in intellectual development between the 5-year-old child with an MA of 3½ and the 2½-year-old child with an MA of 3½. It was this discrepancy that gave rise to the concept of the intelligence quotient (IQ). It was recognized that chronological age (CA—actual age since birth) was an important variable in the understanding of the significance of mental age. The intelligence quotient takes this variable into account. The Stanford-Binet IQ is a ratio between mental age and chronological age: IQ = MA/CA × 100. Thus a person with an MA of 3½ and a CA of 3½ would have an IQ of 100, which represents the level of intellectual development typical for people of that age. The 5-year-old with an MA of 3½ would have an IQ of 42/60 × 100, or IQ = 70, and the 2½-year-old with an MA of 3½ would have an IQ of 42/30 × 100, or IQ = 140. Average IQ is attained when CA and MA are equal. Discrepancies between the two produce IQ deviations from this theoretical average. Most people score within a few IQ points of 100. Extreme deviations are unusual.

After age 5 the Stanford-Binet test provides six test items for each age level one year apart rather than half a year apart. Each of these items is assigned a value of two months of mental age. IQs for adults are calculated using a maximum CA of 15. (The author of the Stanford-Binet believed that MA ceased growth at age 16 but, because the rate of growth from 13 to 16 was slower than that at lower ages, decided to use 15 as a corrected CA divisor for adults.) A maximum mental age of 22 years and 10 months can be obtained on the test, thus providing for the measurement of adults with superior ability. For an adult with a mental age of 22 years and 10 months, MA = 274 months, CA = 180 months, IQ = 152.

It usually takes about an hour to administer a Stanford-Binet test. Skills are required for administering the test and for interpreting the results. Special care must be taken to see that physical, motivational, and emotional conditions are such as to result in the best possible performance on the test. Form L-M, the most recent revision of the Stanford-Binet, includes a method of computing the IQ from tables. For this form the IQ really becomes a form of standard score with a fixed mean of 100 and a standard deviation of 16 for each age level. This IQ is a deviation IQ used earlier in the Wechsler tests. The tables run through age 18, and the test is not recommended for use with adults.

Wechsler-Bellevue and Wechsler Adult Intelligence Scales. The Wechsler-Bellevue and Wechsler Adult Intelligence Scales are designed to measure adult intelligence. Wechsler objected strongly to the MA method of computing intelligence scores because of its basic premise that there is a perfect positive correlation between chronological and mental age. According to Wechsler, this assumption did not prove to be the case. As measured, the rate of growth of intellect is not the same from age 9 to 10 as it is from 12 to 13. IQ as an index of relative brightness, as a result, varied from age to age; no individual test of intelligence standardized on adults was available. The Wechsler tests avoided the MA concept and provided a test of individual intelligence standardized for adults.

The Wechsler tests do not include different tests for each age level. The Wechsler-Bellevue test (Wechsler, 1939) was designed to be used with individuals from ages 10 to 60 and the Wechsler Adult Intelligence Scale (Wechsler, 1955) with people from 16 to 64. (The earlier test is now considered obsolete.) Test items in each of the several subtests are arranged in order of ascending difficulty, and each person tested goes as far in each category as he can until he begins to miss consecutive items consistently. The raw scores obtained on the individual subtests are weighted according to their relative contribution to total intelligence.

The total weighted score can be converted directly to IQ by consulting the Wechsler tables. The Wechsler IQ is a relative index of intelligence. It is not the same as an IQ computed by the MA method. The average Wechsler IQ is 100, the same as on the Binet test. Deviations from 100 are computed in terms of standard deviation. These IQs, which are indices of relative brightness, should be more constant than MA-obtained IQs.

Wechsler's instrument included tests of information, comprehension, digit span, arithmetic similarities, vocabulary, picture arrangement, picture completion, block design, object assembly, and digit symbol. These subtests are broken down into two groups identified as verbal and performance. A verbal IQ, a performance IQ, and a full-scale IQ can be obtained. Administration of the Wechsler Adult Intelligence Scale usually requires more than an hour, and trained examiners are required for proper testing and interpretation.

Wechsler Intelligence Scale for Children. The Wechsler Intelligence Scale for Children (WISC) is not just an additional part of the Wechsler-Bellevue scales but is a distinct test that is standardized independently. It is designed to be used with individuals from 5 to 15 (Wechsler, 1949). The organization, content, and methods of this test are not unlike the W-B scales. The MA concept is again abandoned, and the deviation intelligence quotient is used. The standard deviation of IQs is kept identical from year to year. Thus a child's obtained IQ does not vary unless his actual test performance, as compared with his peers', varies. The IQs obtained from the WISC represent his relative intelligence rating at his age. The mean IQ for any given age group is 100, with a standard deviation of 15 IQ points. As with other individual measures of intelligence, specially trained examiners are required for its administration and interpretation.

Group measures of ability. Because of the necessity for measuring the intelligence of large numbers of people, tests were devised that could be administered to a great many people at the same time. Giving individual intelligence tests to all the draftees of World War I would have been an impossible task. For that matter, the task of testing each child in the public schools in a given city would take so much time and energy as to be impractical. Group tests of intelligence can be administered to many people simultaneously and are largely verbal in nature. They are of the paper-and-pencil variety, and most of them are designed for people who can read. The tests probably measure the linguistic abilities of the person taking the test with greater thoroughness than they measure other abilities involved in individual intelligence.

Distribution of Intelligence

Measures of intelligence, like measures of other characteristics of individuals, are distributed in the population according to a "normal curve." The average IQ of the population is approximately 100, and the number of people scoring close to this figure is great. There is a decrease in the number of people with increasingly higher or lower IQs.

The distribution of IQ measures in the population is partially a function of the particular test used, because the standard deviation of Wechsler IQs is 15 and that for Stanford-Binet IQs is 16. Thus roughly 68 percent of the population will score between 85 and 115 on the Wechsler, and the same percentage will score between 84 and 116 on the Stanford-Binet. The standard deviation on some of the paper-and-pencil tests of intelligence is less than 15, and more people score closer to the mean on these tests than on the others. Figure 9-1 represents the distribution of IQs when the mean is 100 and the standard deviation is 15. Individuals scoring at the higher and lower IQ levels become fewer as the distance from the mean increases.

The mentally retarded. *Mental retardation* is a term used to describe the intellectual level of those scoring at the low end of the distribution of intelligence. It refers to significantly subaverage intellectual functioning and is characterized by inadequacy in adaptive behavior (Kidd, 1964). Individual differences among the mentally retarded are great, and to attribute uniformity to them because of the common label *mentally retarded* would be misleading. Mental retardation is not a unitary thing; neither is it a disease. It has diverse

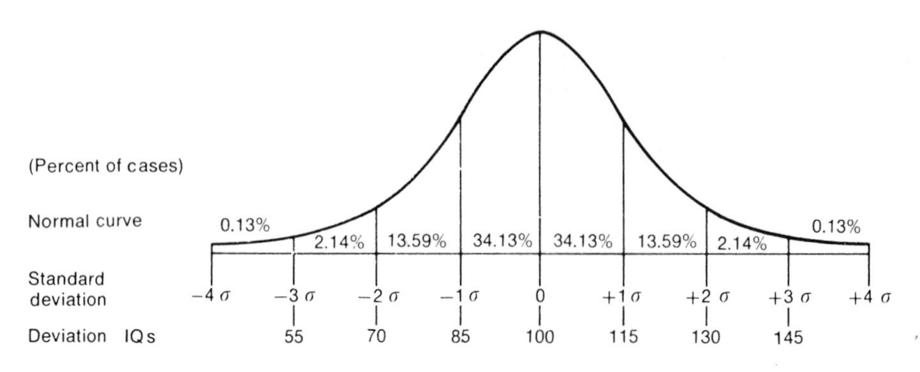

Figure 9-1. Normal distribution of IQs.

causes and physical accompaniments and embraces a rather wide range of intellectual levels.

It has been estimated that between 2 and 3 percent of the population can be classified as mentally retarded. The difficulties of determining the precise percentage result from differing means of diagnosis, detection, and classification. Terminology has changed over the years and currently lacks uniformity, although the classification and terminology proposed by the American Association on Mental Deficiency (AAMD) have been widely employed in the United States since about 1960.

Many factors are involved in the causation of mental retardation. Some mental retardation is produced by *endogenous* factors. That is, the causes may be considered primarily of a hereditary nature. Other retardation may be the result of *exogenous* factors. That is, the causes may stem from injury, disease, toxins, or cultural disadvantage. The etiology of mental retardation is complex, with endogenous and exogenous factors being interactive. It is known that genetic factors, prenatal environmental conditions, accidents at the time of birth, and various postnatal injuries, diseases, diet factors, and general cultural factors may all work as causes of retardation.

Variability in performance by the mentally retarded is to be expected. In terms of intellectual attainment, some generalizations can be made that may contribute to the understanding of the limitations and capabilities of those designated as retarded. Retardates designated as "mild," "moron," or "educable" can be expected to become capable of intellectual behavior characteristic of an 11-year-old of normal ability, or eventually achieve at about the level of the ordinary sixth-grader. The next lower level, designated as "moderate," "imbecile," or "trainable," eventually should be able to attain an intellectual development roughly comparable to that of a 6-year-old. The lowest designated group ("severe," "idiot," or "custodial") does not exceed the intellectual development common to 4-year-old children.

The mentally retarded can and do learn. Their education and training require a great deal of effort and patience and have received considerable attention from educators and psychologists. Much can be done to provide the higher levels of mental retardates with vocational, personal, and social skills necessary for functioning as relatively independent persons or, at least, to help them live more independently within sheltered environments.

The intellectually superior. The intellectually superior, also referred to as the "very bright," or the "gifted," are those with the highest levels of intellectual ability. This group constitutes approximately the top 3 percent of the population. Investigations of the characteristics of the gifted are numerous. One of the best known and most extensive of these investigations was started in 1921 by Terman and his associates and continues to the present time. The latest report on this project represents a follow-up of the children tested during their earlier active years (Terman & Oden, 1959). The original subjects of the investigation are now in the middle years of adulthood. This investigation involved 1500 children who scored at IQ 140 or above when tested. Approximately 10 children out of every 1000 in the public schools score this high. The Terman investigations have yielded a great deal of information relative to this group, and many studies by other investigators report essentially comparable results.

The early evidence from these investigations served to demonstrate the falsity of a stereotype of the intellectually gifted (weak, frail, bespectacled, bookish, and poorly socialized). Children in Terman's gifted group were reported to be superior to normal children in height, weight, and general physical development (Burks, Jensen, & Terman, 1930). Gifted children have been found to be of better-than-average bodily development (Witty, 1930), to have superior neuromuscular capacity (Monahan & Hollingworth, 1927), and to have fewer physical defects (Jones, 1925).

The gifted tend to excel in the academic aspects of education. This statement holds true whether their achievement is assessed by the grades assigned to their schoolwork or by achievement tests (Witty, 1940). Gifted children typically display a very strong liking for school and are active in the various sponsored clubs, organizations, and special-interest groups. They enjoy sports and games and rate them highly as school activities.

There appears to be agreement among the early investigators that the gifted, as a selected group, differ in a favorable direction from unselected children on personality traits and character development. However, the gifted tend to come disproportionately from better social and cultural backgrounds, which may be a strong contributive factor to their better personal and social adjustment (Bonsall & Stefflre, 1955). Intellectually superior children, in relatively high proportions, have parents with a good education and fathers with prestigious occupations. The homes from which the intellectually superior come can be described as more intellectually stimulating, less autocratic, and more encouraging of education and achievement than the average.

The general characteristics of gifted children tend to be maintained into adult life. That is, gifted adults maintain their superiority in those areas in which they are reported to be superior as children.

CREATIVITY

Theorists have long pondered the correlation of intelligence and creativity. According to some, beyond a certain IQ level, intelligence does not appear to be an important factor in creativity. Developers of tests of creative thinking for elementary school children rather consistently report little relationship between scores on such measures and scores on tests of intelligence (Torrance, 1962). Investigators using other populations and different criteria for creativity also report low correlations between measures of creativity and intelligence. (Barron, 1957, 1968; Getzels & Jackson, 1962). However, the correlation between IQ and creativity obtained in an extensive investigation of a carefully chosen sample of 7648 15-year-old-boys and girls in Project Talent (Shaycoft et al., 1963) was reported to be 0.67. This figure becomes 0.80 when corrected for attenuation (McNemar, 1964). It would appear that early speculation that the relationship between IQ and creativity was slight may have been exaggerated and may have produced considerable confusion. Certain kinds of creativity are no doubt highly dependent on intelligence, whereas creativity in other areas may not be. A high level of intellect is certainly essential for the production of cultural, scientific, and technological innovation.

In an attempt to identify children who will later become creative adults, a number of tests have been developed (Torrance, 1966). A serious problem in the construction of such instruments is that of validity. Test questions that tend to evoke novel or unusual responses or solutions may or may not be indicative of later creative endeavors (Harvey, Hoffmeister, Coates, & White, 1970). Terman and Oden's (1959) follow-up studies of gifted children at adulthood have indicated that the highly intelligent tend to be highly productive as adults. However, these individuals were not necessarily creative, either as children or adults.

Creative thinking has been designated as "divergent," as contrasted with "convergent" thinking, which is measured by the usual intelligence tests (Guilford, 1959). Convergent thinking is required when one is given a body of facts and is required logically to either construct or select the one correct solution to the problem. Divergent thinking is required when one is confronted with a problem that has many possible solutions. In such a situation one must employ many intellectual functions, including fluency, originality, and integration (Guilford & Merrifield, 1960). The individual must isolate one possibility after another and try to fit them to the problem at hand in some reasonable fashion until the most appropriate solution is discovered. Measures of various aspects of creative thinking have been developed.

There have been many investigations in which people identified as highly creative by some criterion have been contrasted with equally intelligent people on personality characteristics as they are conventionally measured. Torrance (1962) lists 84 characteristics that have been found to differentiate highly creative persons from less creative ones. MacKinnon and his associates at the University of California Institute for Personality Assessment and Research (IPAR) report characteristic patterns of scores on the Strong Vocational Interest Blank. The more creative persons tend to rate high on scales for architects, author-journalists, and psychologists and on specialization levels. They tend to rate low on scales for purchasing agents, bankers, farmers, carpenters, veterinarians, policemen, and morticians (Barron, 1968). These findings have been interpreted as indicating that the more highly creative persons are more concerned with meanings, implications, and symbolic equivalents of things and ideas and less interested in small details and the practical aspects of life (MacKinnon, 1960).

Highly creative groups of males have been reported to score higher ("more feminine") on tests of masculinity-femininity than do less creative males. This finding held true despite the fact that these men did not appear to be effeminate in either manner or appearance (MacKinnon, 1960). The creative individual appears to be more open in his expression of emotion and range of interests, more sensitive, and more aware of himself and others. These characteristics are frequently regarded as "feminine" in our culture. The same general picture is given further support by the report that the highest values obtained by creative individuals on the Allport-Vernon-Lindzey Scale of Values were on the theoretical and esthetic scales (MacKinnon, 1960). Esthetic values are frequently considered effeminate in our culture.

Torrance (1962) reports, from an investigation of the needs of highly creative adults, that the more highly creative person tends to enjoy intense, sustained, and vigorous effort in surmounting obstacles and that he needs to "prove his personal worth and dramatize and display his ideas." These needs are counterbalanced by needs of self-awareness, awareness of the feelings of others, and intellectualization. The creative person is aware of his own experiences and those of others and is desirous of organizing and seeing meaning in them.

Reports of investigations of the personalities of highly creative children (Getzels & Jackson, 1962; Torrance, 1962) indicate some rather distinct characteristics. Teachers and peers agree that creative children, especially boys, have wild and silly ideas. The work of creative children is characterized by the production of unusual and humorous ideas as well as by playfulness, relaxation, and lack of rigidity. The same general factors seem to be characteristic of creative adolescents. Getzels and Jackson (1962) emphasize the importance of humor in the life of the creative adolescent and indicate that they seem to enjoy the risks of uncertainty of the unknown more than people with high IQs do. Such enjoyment was deduced from the fact that 62 percent of the creative group chose unconventional occupations, such as adventurer, inventor, or writer, whereas only 16 percent of the highly intelligent group chose these areas.

Highly creative children are likely to have personality characteristics that may not endear them to a teacher. Their senses of humor may not always be exercised in the most proper ways. They may be overly energetic, highly independent, somewhat rebellious, and emotionally expressive. These characteristics can become a source of annoyance to the busy teacher, and, unless he is fully appreciative of the potential of these children, he may be tempted to overcontrol the situation and suppress the expression and exercise of creative talent.

FACTORS ASSOCIATED WITH ABILITY

Several factors are reputed to have some correlation with intelligence. It has been a common opinion that sex influences intelligence, and usually a superiority has been ascribed to the male. Racial differences in intelligence have been considered, and, in our culture, even if unexpressed, there seems to be a belief in the superiority of groups of certain national origins over others. Different occupations and different economic positions have been associated with different intellectual levels. We shall consider some of these variables and their relationship to IQ.

Sex and Ability

More men than women attain national recognition and eminence. This fact, among others, has led to a presumption of masculine intellectual superiority. However, this presumption is not supported by psychological measurements. Tests of general intelligence tend to yield scores for boys and girls that are not signficantly different in average total score. There is some evidence of more variability of ability in the male than in the female, which would provide a greater number of very dull as well as very bright boys. The results of school achievement, if regarded as relative measurements of ability, do not indicate the superiority of boys over girls because, on the contrary, girls tend to get better grades throughout grade school, high school, and college.

The differences in ability that do exist between boys and girls are small and cannot be reflected in measurements of general ability. The two sexes do score differently on many special tests. If abilities are broken down into those that are primarily verbal and those that are primarily spatial relations, and tests are administered that tend to measure one ability and not the other, we find girls superior to boys in tests emphasizing language and verbal memory (Hobson, 1947; Meyer & Bendig, 1961). This superiority is apparent rather early in life, in that girls learn to talk at an earlier age than do boys. Perhaps some of the jokes about the verbal fluency of the female have some basis in fact. It is possible that the language superiority of the female stems from an earlier physiological maturation. This superiority, however, is maintained throughout life.

Boys commonly exceed girls on tests of arithmetic or other mathematical ability. This difference in favor of the male is not one that is apparent early in life, as is the linguistic ability of the female. Initially, little girls learn to count and form number concepts earlier than little boys. It is not until they are near adolescence that the numerical ability of boys tends to gain and maintain its superiority over that of girls. The gain in arithmetic ability for the boys seems to be rather constant through the elementary school until they eventually surpass the girls. There may be some cultural basis for this superiority, in that boys are encouraged early to deal with money and with measurements—perhaps as the result of their eventual roles of family providers.

The difference between boys and girls, as demonstrated by these findings, is not sufficient to account for the superiority of the male in adult achievement. The lack of adult achievement on the part of the female in comparison to the male is probably a product of biology and culture. Childbearing restricts the female's activities, and, all in all, more opportunities are provided by our culture for the male than for the female.

Race and Ability

The problems in determining differences in intelligence among races are even more complicated than those of the measuring of differences between the sexes. In the first place, the identification of race is extremely difficult. It is a relatively easy job to separate sexes into male and female, but the problem of segregating groups into "pure" races is not easy at all. Anthropologists have systems of observation and measurement for the identification of races, but to find enough individuals of common background that fit various racial types is a problem of the first magnitude. If, for example, only those people who immigrated to the United States and have lived here long enough to have "absorbed" our culture are used in racial studies, we have to contend with the sampling error produced by selective immigration. Not all Swedes or Italians or Chinese come to the United States. Only a few come, and the factors that caused the Swedish, for example, to give up their ties in Sweden and immigrate to the United States were probably not the same factors that caused the immigration of other groups. If we try to measure the intelligence of groups of different national origin in their own country, we encounter differences in culture and differences in learning experiences, motivation, and language. All these elements make comparative studies of intelligence and race or national origin rather unreliable.

The problem of analyzing the intelligence of blacks in the United States has received a good deal of attention. Black children in the United States, as a group, do not score so high on tests as do white children, although there is a large overlap in the test scores of the two groups. At present we do not know to what extent the different levels of performance are a reflection of differences in educational and economic opportunity. If we equated for all the operative variables and could do so accurately, we would be able to formulate some meaningful conclusions one way or another (Alper & Boring, 1944).

With the large overlap in scores in these studies, as well as in studies of other races, membership in one race or another is not a useful indicator of intellectual capacity; that is, a person of race *X* is not necessarily brighter than a person of race Y. The brightest people in any racial group common to the United States will test higher than the majority of the other groups. We must use criteria other than either race or national origin for the evaluation of the intelligence of any individual.

Nature-Nurture Revisited

The questions of the relative heritability of intelligence and the validity of inferring the causes of cross-cultural differences from measures of heritability were raised anew in the late 1960s. Jensen (1968, 1969) derived heritability values from the statistical analysis of intelligence-test scores and claimed that these values were sufficiently high to indicate that intelligence is overwhelmingly the result of genetic inheritance rather than environmental influences. He also contended that compensatory educational programs such as Operation Headstart had failed to reduce the educational deficits of disadvantaged children, particularly blacks, because these children were incapable of higher levels of conceptual learning as a result of their genetic limitation.

Predictably, the appearance of Jensen's articles evoked many critical reactions. Interested individuals will find the McCord and Demerath (1968), Thoday and Gibson (1970), and Bodmer and Cavalli-Sforza (1970) responses among the better objective evaluations. We shall summarize the research findings that cause us to question the Jensen genetic interpretation of the origin of racial differences.

1. Heritability values are based on individual differences within a specific group and have nothing to do with mean differences between groups. There-

fore the percentage of heritability based on the variances within one population cannot be extrapolated to other populations or to differences between populations. The values obtained from one population or subpopulation may differ markedly from those from another. A heritability figure is not a value that can be applied to a trait in general but only to a trait as found in a particular population and under a particular set of environmental circumstances.

2. The ranges of environmental and genetic variations in the groups and environs investigated are also critical variables in determining heritability values. A given behavioral characteristic may be uninfluenced by environmental variations within a particular range but be extremely sensitive to changes outside that range. For example, Cooper and Zubek (1958) found that the large difference between "bright" and "dull" strains of rats disappeared entirely when the rats were reared either in a very restricted or a very enriched environment. Large genetically determined differences in rates of learning present under one set of environmental circumstances disappear entirely under different conditions.

3. A given environmental change may exert marked effects at one stage of development but have relatively little influence during other developmental periods—the critical-period phenomenon. A child born without a functional thyroid gland (a potential cretin) but administered a small amount of thyroxin from birth can develop into a mentally normal adult instead of a low-grade mentally retarded individual. However, the same amount of thyroxin will have no appreciable effect on mental level when it is administered to an adult cretin. Bloom (1964) and others believe that the first four years of a child's life constitute a critical period for mental development and that environmental enrichment or impoverishment has a much greater effect during this period than in later life.

4. The overall difference between the mean intelligence-tests scores of blacks and whites in the United States is about one standard deviation, or 15 IQ points (Jensen, 1968). Jensen believes that this difference cannot be accounted for in terms of environmental differences. However, it has been shown that environmental differences, commonly encountered in contemporary society, can produce *larger* differences. The mean difference between the IQs of identical twins reared under contrasting "favorable" and "unfavorable" conditions is about 20 points (Newman, Freeman, & Holinger, 1937; Bloom, 1964). Siblings reared apart under similar conditions differ by approximately the same amount (Sontag, Baker, & Nelson, 1958). Bloom (1964) believes that 20 points is a conservative estimate of the effects of extreme social environments on

measured intelligence. Thus it seems that the social, economic, educational, and color-related caste differences between blacks and whites in the United States *can* account for the black-white intelligence-test-score differences and do not necessitate the postulation of intellectually related genetic differences.

5. Jensen and others confuse the heritability of a trait within a population with the hereditary origin of a difference between two populations. These factors are not the same and are not necessarily related. Some extreme examples will make this point clear. The genetic variability of pure strains (such as identical twins) is zero, and the heritability values obtained within such strains is also zero. All variations within strains stem from environment. However, if the contrasting strains have been selectively bred and developed for differing specific behavioral characteristics, such as maze "brightness" and "dullness," the differences between the two populations, reared under the same environments, are entirely hereditary. Heritability values are zero, but group differences are entirely hereditary. The origin of differences between two populations has no necessary relationship to the heritability within the populations and cannot be inferred from it.

6. The fact that a large percentage of the variance of a trait within a population is attributed to hereditary factors does not preclude the production of significant group changes due to changing environmental variables. Estimates of variance in height due to genetic factors run as high as 90 percent. However, major illness or inadequate diet during critical growth periods can significantly effect adult height. In the early years of the twentieth century, children born in the United States after their immigrant parents had resided here for four or more years were considerably taller than their siblings born and reared partly or completely in Europe (Boas, 1911). The second- and third-generation American-born children of pure Japanese extraction are several inches taller than their parents or grandparents born and reared in Japan (Tanner, 1955).

7. Available evidence suggests that if all relevant environmental variables could be equated, the black-white difference in intelligence-test scores would disappear:

a. The first intelligence test (Army Alpha) administered to a nationwide sample showed that the average score of Northern World War I Army recruits was considerably above that of Southern blacks. The median scores of blacks in Pennsylvania, New York, Illinois, and Ohio were above those of white recruits in Mississippi, Kentucky, Arkansas, and Georgia. However, these latter differences were small and based on small numbers of cases, and they attracted little attention when first reported (Yerkes, 1921).

b. The superiority of Northern as compared with Southern blacks, found consistently in the early studies, was shown not to be a result of selective migration of the superior individuals to the North (Klineberg, 1935; Lee, 1951).

c. The children of black migrants from the South showed increases in intelligence-test scores directly proportionate to length of residence in the North (Klineberg, 1935; Lee, 1951). Earlier studies had found a similar relationship between the Army Alpha test scores of foreign-born immigrants and length of residence in the United States (Brigham, 1923).

d. If a battery of tests ranging from heavily culturally loaded ones at the one extreme, through those less culturally related, to relatively culture-free tests at the other extreme, are administered to blacks, American Indians, and whites, the relative superiority of the whites diminishes as the cultural component of the tests decreases (Telford, 1938).

e. The more closely the socioeconomic and educational backgrounds of black and white comparison groups are equated, the smaller the test-score differences become (McCord & Demerath, 1968).

f. When groups are equated in such specific areas as proportion of broken homes, time spent with children in education-related activities, and "housing crowdedness," in addition to the conventional indices of socioeconomic and educational status, the customary test-score discrepancies practically disappear (Tulkin, 1968).

During the last 50 years the consensus has shifted from a preponderance in support of heredity as the major cause of the superior achievements and test-score performances of whites as compared with blacks to a small dissonant minority who still hold this belief. Current arguments in support of heredity are given by Garret (1962), Shuey (1966), and Jensen (1968, 1969). For recent, more balanced reviews of the problem, see Dreger and Miller (1960, 1968).

Socioeconomic Status and Ability

Groupings of people according to educational level or occupations are similar to those made according to intelligence. We naturally expect that a hierarchy of intellect will be established by years of attendance in school, because those who are brilliant (and therefore more successful) tend to remain in school, whereas those who are less bright (and therefore less successful) tend to leave school. Those occupations requiring more educational background are reserved for comparatively brighter people. This is not to say that intelligence is the only factor operative in determining educational level or eventual occupations, but it is an important one. Other factors, such as availability of educational institutions, economic ability, and general cultural background are also operative (Riessman, 1962). Children in rural areas in the United States typically do not score so high on intelligence tests as do urban children, and there seem to be plausible explanations for this finding in terms of selective migration to the cities, educational opportunities, and test bias in favor of urban dwellers. In Scotland, where high standards of training for rural schoolteachers are required and educational opportunities are more nearly equal, these rural and urban differences in intelligence-test scores are not found.

Children from homes of higher socioeconomic status not only have more brilliant parents but also have better opportunities for intellectual, physical, and emotional development. We have operative here favorable heredity as well as a stimulating environment that continues to favor intellectual growth.

Great overlappings in intelligence and occupations occur, but differences in average intelligence of occupational groups have been found consistently.

It would seem that, from very early in life, the home is important to the emotional, motivational, and intellectual development of the child and that educational opportunity and stimulation to develop intellectually are provided in these early years by the home and the school. A good home and school environment will provide an opportunity for each child to develop according to his potentialities.

CONSTANCY OF IQ

The question of whether or not IQ remains constant over extended periods of time is vital to educational planning. However, even if IQ did fluctuate rather remarkably, it would still be profitable to measure it in order to determine what conditions caused it to fluctuate and whether these fluctuations were predictable and perhaps controllable. One of the difficulties encountered in making studies of stability of IQ is the fallibility of tests of intelligence. Such tests are not perfect instruments, and they may not measure the same functions at different age levels. Another difficulty involved in most psychological measures is motivation. Tests of ability try to measure the best possible performance of the individual. We have little assurance, particularly with young children, that they are performing at their best level. It may be that the child is frightened, insecure, or disinterested and not trying. These factors will, of course, contribute to the variability of the intelligence quotient. It is not known how much of the variation in measured intelligence is due to real changes in intellect.

If intelligence is a potential, the development of which is affected by environment, one might assume that the earlier this potential is measured after birth and before environment can have significant effect on it, the more stable the measurement would be. Unfortunately, however, early measures of intelligence have not proven to be good predictors of later achievement on tests of intelligence (Bayley, 1940, 1960; Terman & Merrill, 1960).

Variation and Age

Many measures of infant intelligence have been developed, but the scores are not good indications of how a child will perform on tests of intelligence at the age of 6 and beyond. Some children tend to develop rather steadily, others rather rapidly, and others slowly. The net result is that more can be told of the intelligence of the child under 2 years of age by studying his parents than by studying the child himself (Bayley, 1940). As much can probably be told of the intelligence of the child before the age of 2 by studying a single parent as by studying the child (Conrad & Jones, 1940). After the age of 2, the measuring of intelligence tends to be predictive of intelligence-test scores at the age of 6 with much more accuracy than is true during the first two years of life. Using current tests, it would seem that measurement of intelligence under 5 years of age for purposes of attempting to predict eventual IQ is not too advisable.

Intelligence measurements taken after the age of 6 seem to be somewhat more stable than they are previous to this age. At least for the period between the ages of 6 and 15, intellectual growth indicated by test performance seems to be fairly steady and predictable. Correlation between test scores at age 6 and those at 15 has been found to be 0.70 (Honzik, MacFarlane, & Allen, 1948). This figure might indicate that groups of children will remain rather constant in measured intelligence over a number of years. It may be that individuals within this group will vary somewhat, and we therefore can be less certain of the constancy of a given individual's scores. The closer together in terms of time that tests are given to the child, the greater will be the relationship between the two scores. Thus a large part of the variance may be due to the changing organization of intellect rather than to the unreliability of the measuring instrument. If the test itself were grossly unreliable, we should expect that tests given close together might show as much variance in score as those given after a lapse of several years.

Intelligence-test scores appear more constant for the period of usual school attendance than for other periods in the development of the individual. This fact makes the use of tests of intelligence a most practical educational procedure and gives the educator a tool for realistically determining the levels of functioning for groups of children as well as for individuals.

IQs that Vary

If IQ were fixed and unchangeable from conception, and if our methods of measurement were perfectly reliable, we would have no problems presented by changing IQs in children. Neither of these two assumptions is true, as has already been pointed out.

Studies of factors influencing the variability of measured intelligence have made use of identical twins in different environments. For these studies, identical twins were found who had been separated at early ages and had grown up in different situations and with varying opportunities for optimal development. These studies show a rather remarkable resemblance between the intellects of the twins even after periods of prolonged separation. There was not a perfect correlation between the IQs of identical twins, but they were more nearly alike than the scores obtained in other familial relationships. Identical twins' IQs were more alike than the IQs of fraternal twins reared together and more alike than the IQs of ordinary siblings reared together.

Although studies of identical twins reared apart are few and the number of twins so studied rather limited, there still would appear to be sufficient data to indicate that part of the greater similarity in intelligence scores of identical twins is due to inheritance. Studies of degree of relationship in IQ between parents and true children and between parents and foster children have yielded evidence pertinent to this problem. Studies in California (Burks, 1928), Iowa

(Skodak & Skeels, 1944), and Minnesota (Leahy, 1935) have all reported similar results. The intellectual status of adopted children consistently resembles that of the true parents to a greater degree than it does that of the foster parents. If parental education and intelligence affect the IQ of the child through providing a more stimulating environment, we should expect a positive correlation between the child's IQ and the educational level of the foster parents. This relationship does not seem to hold, as the only significant correlation obtained in these studies was between real parents, with whom the child has not lived, and the child.

Small correlations would be expected between educational level of the foster parents and children and between occupational level and intelligence of foster children, because social agencies try to place children as often as possible in homes that will closely match the anticipated intellectual level of the child. Studies further indicate that the correlation of intelligence scores of true children and parents is consistently and significantly higher than the correlation between foster children and the parents with whom they live. These data certainly indicate that parent and child resemblances in intellectual level are greater with true parents than with foster parents, without regard to whether the child has grown up with his true parents or not (even taking into consideration the improved present-day placement practices of child-adoption agencies).

Changes in Level of Measured Intelligence

A portion of the change in level of intelligence-test performance may be attributable to environment (perhaps a larger portion than has heretofore been considered). The question that we shall now consider is one of rise or fall in intelligence-test scores, without particular regard for whether or not changes in degree of relationship in intelligence between parents and children or children and environment take place. The same three studies cited in the consideration of relationships (Burks, 1928; Skodak & Skeels, 1944; Leahy, 1935) also yield data pertinent to this problem. These studies uniformly indicate that the level of intelligence-test score is changed in a favorable direction by residence in homes of a superior socioeconomic level and homes that might generally be considered as more stable. A child reared in a home that provides not only the physical necessities for adequate living but also consistent affection, care, and general acceptance is given an excellent opportunity for development of potential intellectual strength beyond that provided for the typical child. Adopted children have a better chance of being placed in a home that provides conditions for optimal development than do ordinary children. Although the child's eventual IQ is not related to the foster parents as closely as it is to the real parents, changes in the direction of improvement do take place. The average intelligence-test score of foster children ends up very much like that of true children in comparable homes. However, the foster children showing the greatest gains were those children from the brightest true mothers, which again emphasizes the role of inheritance.

The question of the amount of change in IQ that may take place as a result of better environment cannot readily be answered. Some of the gains reported have been rather large. These studies have not gone without criticism, and

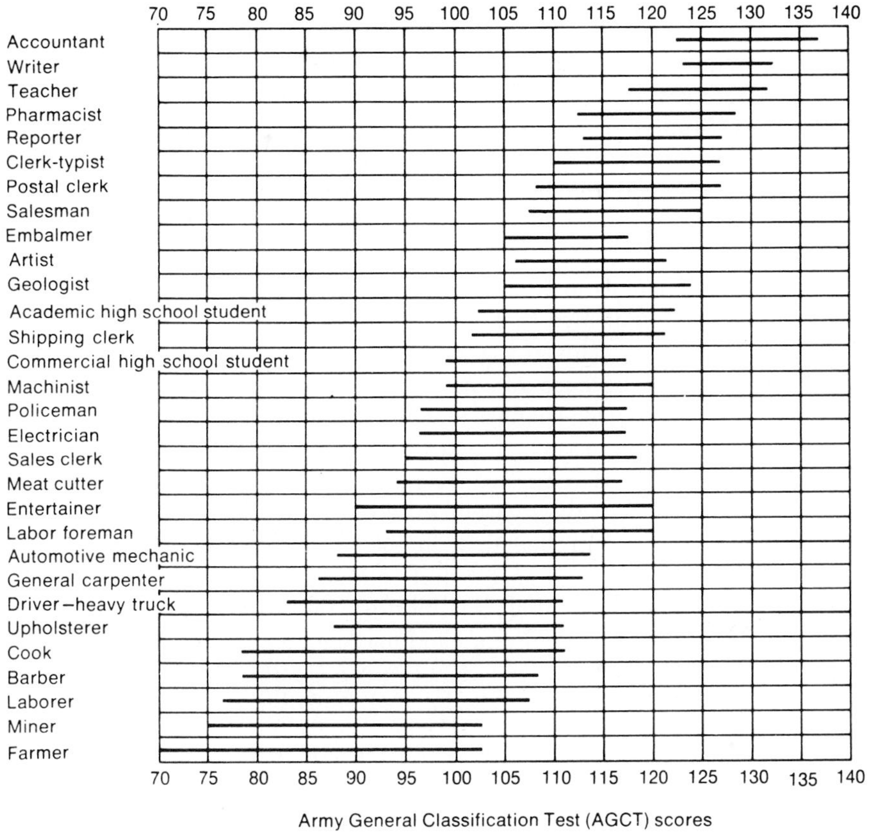

Figure 9-2. Standings of occupational groups on the Army General Classification Test of intellectual ability (data from Stewart, 1947).

those students interested in the studies and their critics should acquaint themselves with both. Differences in sampling and statistical treatment may account for differences existing among the various studies. A rise in IQ as the result of improved environment does appear to take place. Yet not all children have the same potential for improvement. The relative positions of groups of individuals seem to remain quite constant. For example, there was an increase in general test level for American soldiers between World War I and World War II, but the relative standing of occupational groups remained relatively constant (Stewart, 1947). Scores on racial groups in Hawaii (Smith, 1942) all increased over a 14-year period, but the relative standing of the various ethnic groups remained constant. These higher group scores may stem from increased educational opportunity, improved command of the English language, and increased familiarity with tests and testing, as well as from generally improved living and cultural conditions.

Conversely, studies of children in impoverished environments have shown a decrease in test scores in proportion to the amount of time spent in these environments. Studies of northern Georgia and eastern Kentucky mountain children (Asher, 1935) and canalboat and Gypsy children (Gordon, 1923) indicate that older children in these environments do not score so well on intelligence tests as do younger children.

Investigations of changes in IQ as a result of attendance in Operation Headstart programs have indicated that significant gains in score are obtained over limited periods of time (Howard & Plant, 1967). The changes that occur are difficult to interpret because of the short-term nature of such programs. Whether or not the reported changes will be maintained over time is not known. In another investigation of such changes with comparable children, significant positive change in IQ was obtained over a 6-month period (Plant, Herold, & Southern, 1967). In this investigation the interim experience provided in the experiment was more controlled than in the usual Operation Headstart program. This study represented an attempt to identify some of the experiential variables that may enhance intellectual performance. These investigations and other comparable ones are continuing and may be able to provide us with data relative to the results of such experiences over greater periods of time. Such data are badly needed and may make real contributions to understanding intellectual growth.

Relative Constancy

Despite the fact that the IQ of some people does vary from time to time, relative constancy for the vast majority of children seems to be the rule. Tests are not perfect, and testing conditions are not constant. A certain amount of variability is to be expected, but the assumption of relative constancy for the majority of people seems to be a valid one. In a large majority of cases, the average deviation from one intelligence test to another is about 5 IQ points in either direction. When deviations are greater, careful analysis should be made to determine their causes in terms of tests used, possible coaching on items, marginally successful responses, rapport established, physical health, and a number of other factors. Reports of extreme changes in IQ for groups may result from selection of subjects for study from clinic populations that may provide a greater number of cases in which IQs fluctuate more markedly than is common in the general population.

SPECIAL ABILITIES

Tests of intelligence have been found to correlate rather highly with school achievement in general and with achievement in those subject-matter areas considered essentially linguistic and abstract in particular. The correlations found between achievement in those areas considered essentially to involve spatial, mechanical, and motor abilities and intelligence have not been found to be so high. It should be remembered that the correlations, although not high, are positive. Groups of children with high IQs will exceed groups of children with low IQs in these areas as well as in the essentially linguistic ones. Because the relationship between measures of general intelligence and these areas is low, it is perhaps important to consider some of these abilities separately.

Mechanical Ability

Mechanical ability has been an area of primary concern to many persons, perhaps because of the dependence of our society on a great number of mechanical items. Mechanical ability is not to be thought of as a simple unitary capacity but rather as a complex group of functions. It is not a highly specific ability unrelated to general intelligence. Measures of mechanical ability should be used along with other measures of ability, such as intelligence tests.

Schools have long made a practice of encouraging children low in general intelligence to take courses that are essentially manipulative and mechanical in nature because these courses do not depend so highly on general intelligence as do other more linguistic courses. The assumption that because these children do not do well in the usual academic subjects, they will do well in the others should be guarded against. This theory has not proved to be the case in general, although in some cases students can better perform and find more satisfaction there than in the usual academic classroom situation.

There are many tests of mechanical ability and aptitude on the market. They measure the various aspects of mechanical ability at different levels and for different purposes. These instruments vary from those measuring the knowledge of tools and their uses to those measuring the understanding of physics and from simple dexterity tests to those designed to measure rather complex coordinative activities. Not all studies agree as to how practical these tests are, but knowledge of the abilities measured by them has been found to be useful in terms of self-planning, educational planning, and guidance.

Musical Ability

Musical ability, like mechanical ability, should not be thought of as a single simple capacity. It would seem that musical ability is dependent on the organization of many capacities and that the individuals most likely to succeed in musical endeavors are those with certain combinations of abilities. It was on this assumption that the Seashore Musical Talents Tests were designed. They measure ability to discriminate between sounds of different pitch and intensity and ability in memory, rhythm, timbre, and time. The tests seem to be more successful in determining which individuals lack sufficient ability in these areas to become successful musicians than they do in locating those individuals with sufficient ability to become successful in musical fields. Other abilities than those involved strictly in musical talent are essential to success in the field of music. Among these, general intelligence is no doubt a factor to be considered along with others. Tests of musical ability are, however, useful tools to be used in educational planning, self-direction, counseling, and guidance.

Artistic Ability

Artistic ability has been sufficiently unrelated to general ability as to receive the particular attention of those interested in trying to predict success in the field of the arts. In attempting to measure the ability of sudents to learn art, test constructors have tried to break the total product into a few fundamental parts, which, if adequately done, may indicate probable success in the field. The field of art is an extremely broad one, and the attempts to isolate basic underlying abilities have not been too successful. Tests of capacity such as the Meier Art Judgment Test with its 100 pairs of pictures, each pair to be compared for superiority on definite points, have been used along with measurement of achievement and capacity in art such as the Knauber Art Ability Test, which requires the subject to actually draw things from memory and make original drawings that are graded on a quality scale. Color, line proportions, perspective, and memory do not constitute the whole of an art object; measured superiority in these areas, however, tends to indicate aptitude for art. The same statements about the usefulness of such measures for purposes of self-direction, counseling, and guidance as were made about mechanical and musical ability can be made about artistic ability.

SUMMARY

Those who use psychological measurements are particularly concerned with the validity, reliability, and objectivity of the measuring instruments they use. If measurements are to be meaningful, their validity and reliability must be high.

Defining intelligence in a manner that would be satisfactory to all psychologists is not currently possible. Intelligence is a quality possessed in varying amounts by all people. Differing theories and tests of intelligence have been developed. The Stanford-Binet and Wechsler tests are widely used.

Intelligence is distributed in the population in a manner that can be described by a normal distribution curve. The average IQ is 100. Those deviating the greater distances from this norm are the groups designated as mentally retarded and intellectually superior, or gifted. Highly creative individuals have been given considerable investigative attention in recent years.

Several factors are associated with ability. Among these factors are sex, race, and socioeconomic status.

IQ is a relatively constant measure, although there is some variability associated with it. Severe deprivation, aging, and environmental change in the form of enrichment or cultural disadvantage may produce changes in IQ. Relative constancy of IQ for the vast majority of children, however, appears to be the rule.

Measures of special abilities, such as mechanical, musical, and artistic, have been developed and are used for purposes of prediction of success.

SUGGESTED READINGS

Cruickshank, W. M. (Ed.) *Psychology of exceptional children and youth.* (2nd ed.) Englewood Cliffs, N. J.: Prentice-Hall, 1963. Eleven authorities combined efforts to produce this volume, which contains interesting information on intelligence.

Getzels, J. W., & Jackson, P. W. *Creativity and intelligence.* New York: Wiley, 1962. Creativity and its relationship to intelligence are explored in this book. Research findings of the authors are reported from their research with children and adolescents.

Telford, C. W., & Sawrey, J. M. *The exceptional individual.* (2nd ed.) Englewood Cliffs, N. J.: Prentice-Hall, 1972. Several chapters of this text are devoted to consideration of those who deviate from the normal in intellectual functioning. The exceptionally brilliant, those who are of borderline intellect, and the mentally retarded are discussed. The chapter on creativity should be of considerable interest.

Terman, L. M., & Ogden, M. H. *The gifted child grows up.* Stanford, Calif.: Stanford University Press, 1947. These follow-up studies of children who were classified as gifted 25 years previously provide an abundance of information about the gifted.

10

Motivation: Basic Processes

Motivation is a concept frequently invoked to account for variations in behavior. If two persons of near-equal ability and opportunity achieve differently, the variation is frequently attributed to a difference in motivation.

Motivation undoubtedly is of great importance in understanding the behavior of man. Motivational phenomena include behaviors that appear to be guided by the biological functioning of the organism or the species, such as eating, drinking, avoiding pain, breathing, and reproducing. Also considered to be motivational in nature are those behaviors that appear to result from the organism's wants, wishes, desires, aversions, purposes, interests, affections, fears, angers, loves, and so on. These motivational sources of behavior may appear to be so all-inclusive as to encompass everything that man does. Indeed, it has been argued that all behavior is motivated. Whether or not this statement is true, motivation is considered an important factor in the general behavior of man.

Two important aspects of motivated behavior have been described: (1) the vigor with which a response is committed and (2) the direction of the motivated behavior. Theorists have assumed that the vigor of a response is determined by the nature of the stimulus producing the tendency to activity. This stimulus-produced tendency to engage in activity has been termed *drive, activation,* or *arousal.* The stimuli resulting from food deprivation (hunger), water deprivation (thirst), and noxious stimuli (pain) have been manipulated extensively in laboratory investigations of vigor of response, which is measured in terms of speed or force of response. The second aspect of motivated behavior has to do with the nature of the response—more specifically, with the *direction* of behavior, what the organism does as a result of being aroused by stimuli of one kind or another. Thus stimuli produced by food deprivation elicit activity by the organism. The organism learns that these aversive stimuli are reduced by eating. When subsequent food-deprivation stimuli (hunger) are experienced, the organism may seek food as its *goal.* The *need* for food gives rise to *stimuli* that arouse the organism. Arousal results in activity that produces ingestion and reduces the stimuli experienced from food deprivation. As a result, a *motive* of food seeking appears when subsequent stimulus conditions are appropriate. Thus the sight of food comes to serve as an incentive.

In this chapter we shall discuss those conditions and events that tend to arouse or activate the organism. The following chapter (Chapter 11) will be concerned principally with complex behaviors in which motivational variables are assumed to be important. A brief look at some of the ways in which psychologists have dealt with the topic of motivation may help clarify the nature of the problems involved.

HISTORICAL CONSIDERATIONS

In the belief systems of primitive man, motivation was of no concern: behavior was readily explained by postulating the existence of hidden forces. Spirits or demons were believed to possess the individual and cause him to behave in particular ways. If his behavior was socially acceptable or meritorious, a good spirit guided his behavior. If his behavior was not socially acceptable, an evil spirit, or demon, was to blame. The nature of the spirit was deduced from the nature of behavior, and the spirit determined the nature of the behavior. This primitive circularity of reasoning provided what must have seemed to be a self-evident truth. The names of these special forces changed over time, but the concept remained fairly stable. As far as the nature of the concept is concerned, it made little difference whether it was labeled a spirit, a demon, a soul, or a mind.

The postulation of immaterial entities as animating forces made scientific inquiry impossible, since the entity was believed to be responsible for behavior. Of course, "explaining" certain behavior by pointing to an immaterial entity as the responsible agent inevitably led to the postulation of still further entities to explain those agents already proposed. Eventually, the result was a group of postulated entities that were supposed to explain one another. The problem of understanding behavior was still at hand, but attention was diverted to understanding the operation and interaction of the immaterial entities.

The French philosopher Descartes tried to answer questions about motivation without reference to a "soul." He considered animals as machines and postulated fluid spirits rushing through their nerves as the dynamic agents that moved these complex machines. Although he ran into difficulty in applying this model to human behavior, he maintained that much of human behavior was mechanistic and could be accounted for by the theory. He resorted to the soul concept to account for the rational acts of man, including judgment, choice, and will. The practice of interpreting animal behavior in terms of one set of concepts and human behavior in terms of another was not discarded until Darwin's influence became widespread.

Darwin (1873) discussed the anatomical and physiological continuity between animal and human species and implied that there was also a corresponding continuity in their behavior. This theory was a radical departure from older views and had a profound influence on the study of behavior. From his time on, the study of animal behavior gradually came to be regarded as providing models for, and clues to, the understanding of the more complex, but essentially similar, behavior of humans.

INSTINCTS

The concept of "soul" had been reserved for humans, but, with the emphasis on the continuity of behavior between animals and man, theorists' appeals to that concept gradually lessened, and it was eventually replaced by the concept of "instincts." Instinct as a concept has been a part of intellectual thought for centuries (Beach, 1955). McDougall (1908) introduced the idea of instinct, with its biological implications, into psychological theorizing. He postulated instincts as the fundamental motives that moved organisms toward particular goals, or purposes. For him, an instinct was an innate biological process—an emotional impulse or striving—that predisposed the organism to notice particular stimuli and to make either approach or avoidance movements in response to them. McDougall first sought to account for all behavior with 12 instincts. He later added to his list until it finally contained 18 "native propensities" (McDougall, 1923). Included in his list were food seeking, disgust, sex, fear, curiosity, gregariousness, submission, anger, laughter, migratory propensity, and a cluster of specific body needs, such as coughing, sneezing, and elimination. He suggested ways in which instincts could be modified, compounded, and integrated in order to account for the varieties and complexities of observed behavior.

The concept of instinct was used extensively in explaining various animal and human behaviors for a short period of time (Thorndike, 1913; Watson, 1914; Dewey, 1917; Woodworth, 1918). Criticism of the doctrine began to appear in the scientific literature following a general attack on the concept of instinct by Dunlap (1919–1920). It was argued that there was no way to directly observe processes called instincts and that the concept was an easy substitute for true explanations of observed behavior. To say that an animal fights because of the instinct of pugnacity is merely to give a redundant description of the observed activity. The description would be as complete if one stated merely that the animal fights (Watson, 1925). Dunlap argued that instinct was not explanatory and that an attempt should be made to determine the relative roles of experience and innate factors involved in specific behaviors.

The experimental analysis of such complex behaviors as migration, nest building, maternal behavior, and mating that had been attributed to instinct was undertaken. Hormonal, experiential, and perceptual factors were found to be basic to these complex activities (Morgan, 1943; Beach, 1951). It was shown that nest building by rats is related to the mechanisms of temperature control and that migration in birds is related to gonadal development. Obstacle avoidance in bats was shown to be accomplished by responses to the echoes of sounds they produced in flight. Much of the mystery of some of the complex activities that had been attributed to instinct was removed, and it became obvious that the concept of instinct did not provide a complete, or even an adequate, basis for explanation. Some of the behaviors were better understood in terms of hormonal influence and perceptual and experiential factors, even though innate factors might be present. The concept of instinct has not proved to be particularly helpful in the study of human behavior and has been abandoned by most investigators. Complex, unlearned behavior patterns characteristic of a species are frequently referred to as *species-specific* behaviors. This description is more accurate than "instinct" and does not carry with it the implications of explanation that the word *instinct* has acquired. Once a variable was labeled an instinct, there developed the unfortunate tendency to abandon further investigation of that variable. This tendency led to a premature cessation of investigation of the phenomenon. Many complex behavior patterns in animals seem to involve a minimum of learning and to require only the proper stimuli for them to appear. Such behaviors have been of particular interest to ethologists (Lorenz, 1950; Tinbergen, 1961; Thorpe, 1963). It would be less than accurate to report that the complex behaviors of animals or men can now be explained. Much of human and animal behavior is difficult to understand in terms of innate qualities because the behavior may be extremely variable from individual to individual. It is also difficult to understand much complex behavior in terms of learning because but little in the way of experience may be necessary for a behavior to appear. This complex area of investigation will continue to be examined by scientists from a variety of disciplines.

The uncritical use of the word instinct has subsided, and the concept is rarely invoked in reference to man. Psychologists, in search of better explanations for the dynamics of behavior, have developed other concepts. It seemed appealing and logical to psychologists that complex behavior patterns are acquired from elementary processes. Otherwise, they would appear to be unitary and not meaningfully analyzed into component parts. The idea that stimuli are associated with various physiological functions and produce changes in the arousal, or activation, or drive, of the organism appears to be a concept with greater explanatory power than instinct and has played an important role in the development of psychological theorizing.

THE CONCEPT OF DRIVE

The theoretical reduction of sources of behavior to more fundamental biological functions has not resulted in unanimity as to the nature and function of basic processes. The task of explaining how complex behaviors can be built from such elementary functions as hunger, thirst, sex, and pain avoidance has been an imposing one. A great amount of research has been done within the general framework of drive theory. Yet there is no agreement as to the sources of drive, the stimuli giving rise to drive, or the number of drives. There is, however, a great body of literature related to these topics and to the general theory that behavior derives, in part, from the biological processes of the organism.

The Nature of Drive Theory

Drive is an intervening variable; it is not something of substance that can be seen, weighed, or felt. Drive is used as a logical connection between the conditions that establish it and the effect of those conditions on behavior. It has become customary to speak of a hunger drive, thirst drive, and sex drive. What is meant by such expressions is that stimuli deriving from food deprivation, water deprivation, or sexual stimulation are causing a change in the arousal level, or level of activation, of the organism. Drive theory holds that motivation of behavior comes from drive-establishing stimuli that release energy deriving from the metabolic processes of the organism. Drive, then, is an energizer of behavior and not a director of it. The energy released by drive stimuli is said to be directionless and may serve to activate a variety of behaviors. The apparent directionality of motivated behavior (food-deprived animals seek food) derives from learning associated with the arousing stimulus (drive stimulus). For example, a dog aroused to activity by stimuli from food deprivation learns appropriate acts to reduce the stimuli. It may cast about for food, bark, or seek out the person who usually feeds it. The behavior elicited in this situation can be as varied as the capacity of the animal to learn and the conditions for learning that have previously prevailed. Any behavior of which the animal is capable can probably be learned as the consequence of association with drive-producing stimuli.

Differing drive stimuli can be discriminated by laboratory animals. In other words, differing responses to differing drive-stimulus conditions are learned. Rats can readily learn to go to one arm of a *T* maze when they are thirsty and to the other arm when they are hungry (Bolles & Petrinovich, 1954). Moreover, rats can discriminate between different intensities of the same drive stimulus. These animals have been trained to go to one arm of a *T* maze after a short period of water deprivation and to the other arm after a longer period of water deprivation (Jenkins & Hanratty, 1949). This ability to discriminate among drive stimuli (stimuli that change the arousal or activity level of the organism) makes it possible to learn behaviors appropriate to the particular source of stimulation.

Drive or Drives?

It has been emphasized that drive is principally an activator and not a directional determinant of behavior. If drive serves an energizing function regardless of the stimuli producing it, is it logical to label as distinctive drives deriving from different stimuli? When one speaks of various "drives," one usually implies that drive exercises a directional control of behavior—that is, that hunger drive directs the organism toward the attainment of food, thirst drive toward the attainment of water, and sex drive toward sexual satisfaction. It is difficult to separate the activating function of stimuli from their functions as distinctive stimuli to which specific responses can be learned. However, if stimuli are conceived of as serving these two functions, it makes sense to separate the drive functions (arousal or activation) from directional functions for purposes of investigation. If all stimuli affect the drive level of the organism, then they serve a common function as far as activation is concerned. Drive, as such, is not considered as a determinant of behavior but simply as an energizer of the organism. Since drive derives from different stimuli, these stimuli can be referred to as *sources* of drive. Those sources of drive that appear to be rather directly biological or physiological in their effect (hunger, thirst, sex) have been most frequently designated as *primary drives.* More accurately, they should be referred to as *primary sources of drive.*

Drive is a function of changes in the stimulation of the organism. Although the organism is constantly aroused to some extent, his drive level will fluctuate with the variations in stimuli deriving from these primary sources. The hungry person will possess more drive than the sated one, and the person who is both hungry and thirsty will have a higher level of drive than the one who is just hungry. The reduction of drive stimulus, which results in learning, can come about by reducing the stimuli from any of the sources of drive.

The conception of drive as a unitary rather than a multiple construct and as an activator rather than a director of behavior is consistent with the position taken by Hull (1943). This position has been supported and expounded by a number of researchers (Hebb, 1955; Lindsley, 1957; Brown, 1961), although support for the position is by no means universal (Bolles, 1967; Berlyne, 1967).

THE BASES FOR MOTIVATION

Motivational theorists have tried to designate bases for the derivation of motivated behavior. The arousal of an organism has been said to derive from its biological needs, from its tendency to maintain relatively constant conditions of balance, and from stimulation in general. We shall examine these factors as possible bases for activation or arousal.

Needs of the Organism

The concept of need has been popular in psychological theorizing. However, the word *need* has been used in a variety of ways, frequently without adequate definition. It has been used synonymously with *drive* and interchangeably with *motive*. As a psychologically meaningful term, *need* has been impaired by this uncritical application.

Need can be used to designate absolute necessities for survival, such as food, moisture, appropriate gases for breathing, a critical range of temperature, and certain aspects of pain avoidance. These factors are essential to the biological functions of the organism. Removal of food or moisture for prolonged periods of time results in death of the individual; severe temperature is destructive to the organism; absence of appropriate gases for breathing results in death; severe pain that results from tissue destruction cannot be tolerated by the individual for very long. There is no evidence that sexual abstinence is destructive to the individual in any such imperative way; however, the necessity of sexual activity for species survival may be an adequate reason to include sex as a biological need.

The use of the word *need* to designate motives of one kind or another probably stems from value judgments about effective living. It has become popular to speak of various psychological functions as needs. However, the need to be loved, to be accepted, to understand, to achieve, to master, to express oneself, and so on, can hardly be considered necessary for biological existence. These needs are used to designate apparent motives that should be fulfilled for a person to live happily and effectively. The variety of needs thus employed will be variable and dependent on the philosophy of the individual designating the needs. As such, the list of needs can be extended to include any behavior of which the organism is capable. The meaning of *need*, when employed in such a manner, becomes vague, indefinite, variable, and lacking in the precision required for scientific investigation or communication.

If need is conceived of as a partial basis for motivated behavior, we must limit the word to its biological meaning. We assume that necessities for existence have accompanying biological mechanisms that operate to enhance the probability of the organism's obtaining the essentials for survival. That is, absence of food or water gives rise to hunger or thirst (stimuli), which effect motivation. Either arousal or increased drive produces greater activity and increases the possibility of procuring food and water. Noxious or painful stimulation acts the same way. As a result, activity level goes up, and the chances of terminating the pain through movement are enhanced. Sexual stimulation produces responses that act as stimuli and increase the possibilities of reproductive behavior. The *stimuli* produced by need deficit appear to be more imperative to concepts such as drive than do the needs themselves. The stimuli resulting from these needs are what effect the motivational state. Of course, other stimuli or other changes in stimulation than those associated with need states may have motivational properties (that is, they may have arousal effects). These stimuli will be considered in a later section of this chapter.

Certain physiological needs apparently do not give rise to stimuli that enhance the arousal of the organism as reflected in activity level. Vitamin-deficient animals do not demonstrate any increased activity as the result of an increase in deficiency. Thus, if activity is taken as a measure of drive level or arousal, its covariance with need is not very great. Not all needs are reflected in the activity level of the organism, and not all increases in arousal or drive are functions of need. Although activity level of the organism has been used as a measure of arousal, it is not clear that it does accurately reflect arousal level. Arousal may be enhanced by deprivation of a drug to which the individual has become habituated. We may say that in such instances a need for the drug has developed, but it is difficult to invoke such a line of reasoning when sustained drug use, for example, has deleterious effect on the individual. Need may be invoked in theory as a partial basis for motivated behavior but is clearly inadequate as its exclusive basis.

Homeostasis

Homeostasis refers to the tendency of the body to maintain certain rather constant conditions. This tendency is said to result from the operation of homeostatic mechanisms. Biological controls of body temperature and salt content of the body fluids are examples of such mechanisms. These biological processes maintain the required range of conditions necessary for existence. They are automatic in the sense that we are not aware of their functioning and need not consciously exert effort for them to operate. The concept of homeostasis has been employed extensively in the biological sciences and has been utilized in accounting for motivated behavior.

When the concept of homeostasis is employed in motivational theory, there is an implication that physiological disequilibrium is the basis for arousal and that the organism engages in behavior that serves to restore the state of equilibrium. In psychological theorizing, the meaning of the word *homeostasis* has been expanded to encompass a variety of behaviors. The "maintenance of constancy" in the life of the individual has come to be referred to as homeostasis. The tendency to rest following activity is said to be a homeostatic mechanism. Using the term in this way, any regulatory or compensatory behavior on the part of a person can be viewed as homeostatic.

Some psychologists have indicated that certain behaviors are difficult to interpret within a homeostatic frame of reference. Beach (1956) has pointed out the difficulties of interpreting copulation as a homeostatic process. The tension systems and subsequent behavior do not fit readily into such a model. Attempting to interpret all behavior dynamics in terms of homeostasis places a great strain on the physiological meaning of the word and results, as with the concept of need, in making the meaning of the word unclear and lacking in the conciseness essential for scientific use. It can be argued, too, that, as far as increasing understanding is concerned, we are as well off saying that an animal does thus and so as to say that it is in an ill-defined nonhomeostatic condition and, as a result, does thus and so. If we overemphasize homeostasis, we may always assume disequilibrium from an animal's behavior, and we may assume that the animal behaves as it does because of this disequilibrium. Such reasoning is quite circular unless we can demonstrate that such behavioral disequilibrium does, in fact, exist and that equilibrium is restored by the behavior. Unless the concept can be tied to other behaviors than those from which it is deduced, it cannot add much to the clarity with which behavior can be understood. Homeostasis used in a physiological sense can be tied to neural and glandular processes and may improve our understanding of physiological functioning. Although the concept may have some validity in psychological theorizing, caution should be used in attempting to spread its mantle over all behavior.

Stimulation

It is readily observable that stimulation of certain kinds results in increased activity on the part of an individual. A pinprick, sudden noise, food or water deprivation, and various other irritating stimuli are reflected in increases in activity. Some of the stimulus conditions that may act as motivational variables are well recognized; others have been discounted or ignored. Intense stimulation as an energizer has received some acceptance, but stimulation that is not intense or persistent has received little investigative attention—for good reasons. Stimuli that are not intense are difficult to isolate and measure and would be expected to have only small behavioral consequences. Both the stimuli and the responses would be elusive variables to isolate in a laboratory.

Improvements in laboratory apparatus and procedures have made it possible to conduct more sophisticated investigations of neurological functioning than was possible a few years ago. The role of the brainstem reticular formation in the activation of behavior has been the object of a great deal of investigation. The reticular formation is a dense network of neurons extending from the medulla of the lower brainstem to the thalamus of the diencephalon (Lindsley, 1957).

The reticular formation serves a two-way function. Fibers pass downward from the reticular formation into the spinal cord. These fibers carry impulses that may either inhibit or facilitate certain complex postural and muscular reactions. Other fiber systems pass upward to the basal ganglia, thalamus, hypothalamus, hippocampus, and cortex. The diffuse nature of the ascending reticular formation allows impulses from lower segments of the formation to

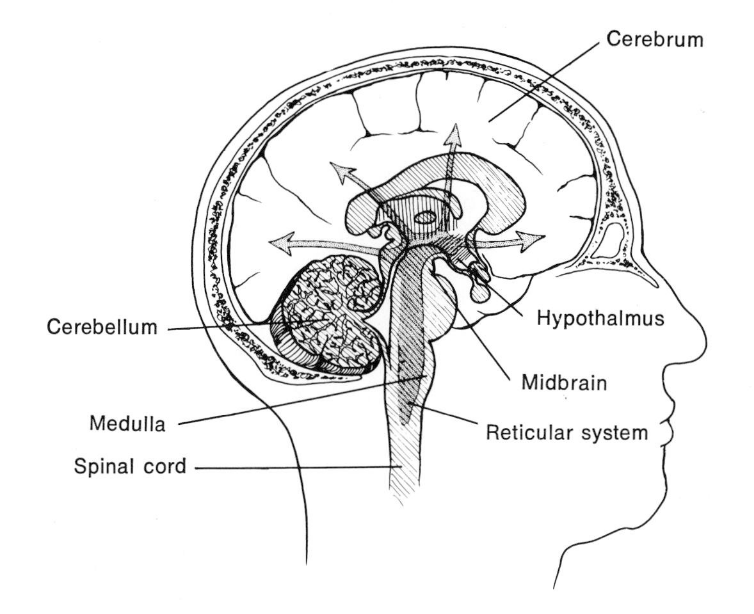

Figure 10–1. The reticular system is a diffuse and scattered area of gray nerve tissue, mixed with white in certain regions of the brainstem.

bring about widespread changes in cortical activity. As we have indicated, the wave patterns of electrical potentials recorded from the brain differ markedly between sleep and waking states. Stimulation from the ascending reticular formation has an "activation effect," which is widespread in that it can be observed at numerous points on the cortical surface. Electrical stimulation in the area of the reticular formation has been found to change the cortical brain-wave pattern from one of "sleep" to one of a "waking" or "excited" nature (Moruzzi & Magoun, 1949). Stimulation of this area results in arousal. These nonspecific activating, or arousal, effects of the ascending reticular system appear to be consistent with the construct of a general-purpose drive.

Although Lindsley (1951) had observed the broad importance of reticular-system activity for problems of emotion and motivation, Hebb (1955) first commented on the diffuse bombardment of the cortex as being synonymous with a general drive state. He further observed that the concept of drive could now assume anatomical and physiological identity. The reticular system is thought to be affected primarily by signals diverted via collaterals from the primary sensory pathways. It is also thought to be affected by impulses descending from the cortex. Lindsley (1957) has pointed out that the activity level of the reticular formation may thus be modified from within the organism or by stimulation that is peripheral to the organism. Ideational impulses from the higher cortical centers thus may serve to increase reticular activity and thereby affect arousal.

Cofer and Appley (1964), in an extensive treatment of motivation, have abandoned the conventional concept of drive and, in effect, have substituted *arousal* for it.

Arousal can be seen to be affected by both internal and external stimuli. If it is subject to ideational effects, arousal can be altered in various ways by verbal instructions as well as by self-induced ideations and directions. This kind of "self-control" would seem to be an important source of arousal regulation among humans.

If arousal were to become too intense, the bombardment of the cortex by the ascending reticular system would become excessive, and decrements in performance would result. This phenomenon could explain decrements in the performance of an "overly motivated" person, as well as the reverse situation, in which a person is not sufficiently activated to perform adequately. Optimal arousal, then, becomes imperative for optimal performance.

Olds and Milner (1954) demonstrated that electrical stimulation of the brain can function as a reinforcer for the performance of instrumental acts. They implanted electrodes in the brains of rats and administered an electrical stimulus of controlled strength and duration to the animals whenever they pressed a lever in an experimental box. With no reward other than electrical stimuli, rats would press the lever for long periods of time at high rates. The reinforcing effects of brain stimulation have been found not only in rats but in cats (Roberts, 1958) and in monkeys (Bursten & Delgado, 1958). Thus stimulation of the brain (limbic system) is rather well established as a reinforcer for instrumental behavior (Mogenson, 1964; Kling & Matsumiya, 1962).

It is difficult to determine why subcortical electrical stimulation acts as a reinforcer in view of the fact that the same intensity of stimulation may be either reinforcing or inhibiting (Roberts, 1958). Whether stimulation will be reinforcing or inhibiting depends on the training procedures, stimulation duration, and testing environment. Brown (1961) has pointed out that behavioral effects quite similar to those produced by brain stimulation have been reported with externally administered shock and other strong stimuli. He cites Masserman's (1946) studies of "experimental masochism" in cats. In these studies cats were trained to operate levers to get a blast of air in the face (the air blast ordinarily elicits violent avoidance behavior in untrained animals). It has also been found that, by introducing mild electric shock in the middle of an alley leading to food and then gradually increasing the shock intensity, rats can be trained to tolerate intensities that would otherwise cause them to cease running (Farber, 1948). An interesting biological theory of reinforcement has been advanced (Glickman & Schiff, 1967). The understanding of certain aspects of subcortical organization of reinforcement effects may be facilitated by distinguishing two arousal systems (reticular and limbic) (Routtenberg, 1968).

Hunger and Thirst

Effects on activity. Food or water deprivation results in hunger or thirst for the organism. Hunger or thirst may be conceived of as complex responses by the organism to deprivation. These complex responses may have their bases in the physiological needs of the organism and may be responses to biochemical changes occurring as the result of deficit. As responses, hunger and thirst have stimulus consequences for the organism: the hungry person is activated and learns to seek ways of dissipating the stimuli. The stimuli of hunger or thirst

Figure 10-2. In self-stimulation experiments, electrodes are implanted to stimulate small regions of the brain. A rat can stimulate itself for an instant by pressing a lever. Rates of response as high as 5000 an hour are observed, depending on the location of the electrode. One rat responded 80,000 times in a 48-hour period (Olds, 1958).

thus serve two purposes: (1) increasing the drive or arousal of the organism and (2) providing an identifiable stimulus with which appropriate behavior can become associated.

Under conditions of food deprivation for various lengths of time, changes in the organism's general activity level, as measured by amount of running in an activity wheel, have been investigated. Research has shown that increases in general activity are roughly proportional to the degree of food or water deprivation up to a given point (Finger & Reid, 1952). If food deprivation is extended beyond 72 hours for the rat, its activity level tends to go down. Increases in activity level occur not only when the animal is completely deprived for a long period of time but also when it is moved from a free to a restricted feeding schedule (Hall, Smith, Schmitze, & Hanford, 1953). Morgan and Stellar (1950), after reviewing the literature on the relationship between activity level and nutritional deficiencies, concluded that the nutritional conditions producing a decrement in general activity are those that tend to weaken the animal physically. Prolonged deprivation has a weakening effect and, consequently, produces a decrement in general level of activity.

The periodic nature of spontaneous activity has been investigated by Richter (1927). From extensive investigations, he reports 2-hour rhythms of activities in both animals and man and relates these activities to food ingestion and digestion. These activity rhythms in the white rat do not appear until about the tenth day after birth and are well established by the sixteenth day. In certain lower animals, activity rhythms are present from birth. Factors other than food ingestion and digestion may be involved in the establishment of cycles of activity, but the presence of other causal factors does not negate the effect of these vegetative processes.

Richter reports on the periodic nature of many physiological functions, including eating, drinking, urination, and defecation. The influence of water deprivation on the rate of water consumption has been demonstrated by Siegel (1947). In this study rats were placed in environments in which temperature and humidity were thermostatically regulated and other experimental variables were well controlled. Animals were tested after various periods of water deprivation to determine the amount of water they would consume in 5 minutes' time. It was found that the longer the deprivation, up to 48 hours, the greater the amount of water consumption in the 5-minute period. Findings relative to food consumption after controlled deprivation essentially parallel the results obtained in the study of water deprivation (Horenstein, 1951). Birch and Veroff (1966) have described and discussed the periodic nature of activity in a very readable fashion.

Deprivation influences not only eating and drinking behavior but also the performance of instrumental responses in the obtaining of food or water (Bass, 1958; Fredenburg, 1956). After reviewing the literature relative to deprivation and level of activity, Brown (1961) tentatively concluded that deprivation tends to enhance consummatory activities (eating, drinking) as well as the speed of acquisition and resistance to extinction of responses instrumental to consummatory activities.

Physiological correlates. Hunger and thirst as sources of variation in drive may exert their influence via several different physiological channels (Grossman, 1955). Dryness of the mouth and throat, induced by water deprivation, and the impulses arising from vigorous contractions of the empty stomach serve as ways in which hunger and thirst may become distinctive stimuli (Cannon, 1929). The stimulation of sensory receptors in the mouth and throat, produced by the presence of food or water in the mouth, together with the stimulation resulting from the subsequent swallowing, have an effect on the cessation of eating or drinking (Miller, Sampliner, & Woodrow, 1957). Grossman (1955) has demonstrated that stomach distention also plays a significant role in the control of eating. Circulating nutrients in the blood and stored nutrients in the tissues are also of importance relative to the control of eating and drinking. Neural impulses from various parts of the body (mouth, throat, stomach, intestines, and possibly other tissues) may have consequences in the central nervous system that exert a controlling influence over consummatory behavior. Appropriate stimulation of the brain results in eating and gnawing in rats (Smith, 1956); injections of hypertonic saline solution into the hypothalamus of cats increase water consumption (Miller, 1958). The effects of various changes in the organism are reflected in the brain in such a manner that the brain itself becomes an integral portion of the mechanism of hunger- and thirst-produced activity.

Noxious Stimulation

Ordinary observation leads one to conclude that various noxious stimuli have a motivational effect. General activity increases or decreases with extreme changes in temperature. Loud noises, bright lights, and strong odors bring about changes in the vigor of response, and these stimuli evoke avoidance or escape behaviors as well. The unconditioned stimulus in a classical-conditioning situation can be an aversive one. In laboratory research on the motivational effects of noxious stimuli, the experimental arrangement is typically such that the subject, by performing a previously established response or by learning a new response, can escape, avoid, or terminate a noxious stimulus. Performance measures are taken for different intensities or durations of the noxious stimulus. Air puffs delivered to the eye have been used in eyewink conditioning with human subjects. The intensity of the puff of air has been found to be positively related to the frequency of conditioned eyelid responses (Passey, 1948; Spence, 1958; Spence & Platt, 1966). Few studies of the effects of aversive stimuli on drive in humans are available. Air puffs to the eye as unconditioned stimuli have been more systematically investigated than have any other aversive stimuli.

Electric shock has also been widely used in laboratory situations as an aversive stimulus, probably because it can be readily administered under a variety of circumstances. Overt behavior produced by electric shock may not be a good measure of its motivational effects because the behavior may vary not only with the intensity of the shock but with its duration and temporal relationship to the behavior being observed. Mild shocks have been shown to facilitate learning when they follow the correct responses made in a maze (Tolman, Hall,

& Bretnall, 1932). In such cases the mild shock may have little or no motivational value and may serve only an associative (learning) function. That is, the shock serves an informational function.

Hall (1961) proposed that so-called weak punishment or shock is not really punishment at all and serves only as a stimulus that directs the organism's attention to certain other stimuli. Electric shock, depending on such experimental variables as temporal relationships, opportunities to escape, intensity, and duration, may serve either to increase drive level or to evoke competing responses and thus reduce response efficiency. If an animal's feet are given a shock to get it to run down an alley, the response of jumping or leaping may compete with the running response and decrease the efficiency with which the running response is executed.

In general, increasing the intensities of electric shock has yielded increased performance measures (Campbell & Kraeling, 1953). If the intensity of the shock does not become too great, performance on easy discriminations improves progressively with shock intensity. On difficult problems, performance is poorer with either weak or strong shocks than with shocks of a moderate intensity (Yerkes & Dodson, 1908). Easterbrook (1959) has indicated that arousal is inversely related to the number of cues the organism utilizes in performance. The optimal motivational level for problem solving appears to decrease as the difficulty of the problem increases.

In a study using air deprivation as the noxious stimulus, Broadhurst (1957) found that the speed with which rats swam underwater in a straight alley increased as the period of air deprivation, previous to their being released, increased. Since the rats were experienced underwater swimmers, the changes in performance level could be reasonably attributed to the noxious stimulus of air deprivation.

Sex

As was previously mentioned, sex does not have the imperative nature of the need for food, water, or pain avoidance. A human or other animal can live out its life without overt sexual relations and without undue suffering from this lack of sexual activity. Nevertheless, stimuli deriving from sexual stimulation do affect arousal. Indeed, the activity level of female animals in estrus is considerably higher than when they are not in estrus. Sexual arousal appears to have both internal and external controls (Beach, 1951). The internal nature of sexual arousal is indicated by the role of sex hormones in the bloodstream. Sexual receptivity and appropriate mating behavior can be made to appear in female rats through the injection of ovarian hormones. As the result of such injections, they develop mature mating patterns well in advance of the time when such behavior would ordinarily appear. Removal of ovaries from mature female rats produces a cessation of sexual activity. With subsequent injections of ovarian hormones, these animals will engage in normal sexual behavior. Hormonal injections establish mating patterns in ovariectomized rats even when removal preceded sexual maturity.

The male rat engages in incomplete sexual behavior even before maturity, whereas the female does not. Moreover, sex-gland removal results in immediate cessation of sexual responsiveness in the female, but it does not do so in the male (Beach, 1944). Removal of the sex glands has a profound influence on the activity levels of both male and female rats. Thus, if activity level is taken as a measure of drive, sex certainly contributes to general drive level.

Hormones become less significant in the control of sexual behavior as we move from lower animals to primates and man (Beach, 1956). Glandular, sensory, and experiential factors combine to determine the ease and extent of sexual arousal. The important role of experiential factors in human sexual arousal is well illustrated by the great variety of events to which sexual significance is attached. The results of sex-gland removal in the human are variable. Among a high proportion of women, sexual desire and capacity are little changed. Castration of the male may result in a gradual decrease in sexual interests; however, sexual activity may continue at about its original level for several decades. These facts indicate the extensive involvement of learning processes in the sexual arousal of humans. Whalen (1966) indicates that sexual arousal is modulated by the presence or absence of relevant stimuli and that arousability is determined by hormonal state and experience.

Other Stimuli as Sources of Variation in Drive

Direct sources of drive other than hunger, thirst, pain avoidance, and sex have been suggested by investigators who observed activities that could not be immediately accounted for by these principal sources. According to Hebb (1949), the disruption of cerebral processes constitutes emotional disturbance and has motivational, or arousal, consequences. One source of this disruption is a discrepancy between present receptor inputs and the residues of previous sensory experience of a similar nature. According to this position, any change in receptor input (novelty) should increase affective arousal. One kind of discrepancy is absence of accustomed stimulation, which has been shown to influence affective arousal. Berlyne (1960) has emphasized the role of conflict in arousal and suggested that a variety of stimuli contribute to motivational states. The absence of aversive accustomed stimulation does not appear to have arousal functions (Meier, Fashee, Wittrig, Peeler, & Huff, 1960; Hunt & Quay, 1961). Fiske and Maddi (1961) have indicated that variation in stimulation is an important source of arousal. When a novel or striking stimulus appears, the organism responds by changes in posture and sense-organ adjustments (orienting reflex), which have widespread physiological consequences that may serve an alerting function (Sokolov, 1963).

Some colors, tastes, odors, and visual patterns appear to have greater attractiveness for human infants than do others. Berlyne (1966) showed a group of patterned stimuli to infants ranging in age from 3 to 9 months. The infants most frequently focused their eyes on the more *complex* of the simultaneously displayed patterns. These and similar findings have led theorists to consider that there may be positive stimulus-seeking elements in motivated behavior. There is evidence that rats may spend more time in rooms with greater complexity than in rooms with a lesser variety of stimulus objects (Walker, 1964). Butler and Rice (1963) postulate and argue convincingly for the existence of "stimulus hunger" as a source of drive.

Curiosity, exploration, manipulation. Much activity on the part of animals has been attributed to curiosity—to a tendency to seek problems, to explore, to manipulate. The explanations for these behaviors have ranged from a postulated primary, nonhomeostatic exploratory drive, which is reduced by exploration (Harlow, 1953), to various acquired sources of motivation (Fowler, 1965).

Exploratory and manipulatory activities are apparent when it is highly unlikely that they could be directly attributed to hunger, thirst, pain avoidance, or sex (Harlow, 1953). Opportunity to explore and to manipulate has been found to be adequate reinforcement for learning (Montgomery, 1954; Butler & Harlow, 1954). Monkeys will open a window repeatedly to peer outside and see what is going on. Such behavior has been attributed to curiosity (Butler, 1953). If various mechanical devices are placed in a monkey's cage, the animal will manipulate and take them apart, and it will become more skilled with practice.

Some researchers have suggested that the satisfaction of some sort of manipulation drive constitutes the reinforcement for the performance (Harlow, Harlow, & Meyer, 1950). Whether or not the postulation of a special-purpose exploratory, curiosity, or manipulatory drive is essential to understanding these behaviors, the fact that opportunities to explore and manipulate are reinforcing is well established. Harlow has been particularly critical of attempts to interpret these activities within the frame of reference of a limited number of drives. He has indicated that young monkeys and other animals tend to maximize body contact with their mothers. They even run to artificial terry-cloth mothers and cling to them when frightened. Harlow has manipulated the experimental situation enough to indicate that this attraction of the infant for its mother does not necessarily stem from the fact that the mother has been its source of food. He indicates that body contact, or contact comfort, may be the drive that is being satisfied in such situations (Harlow, 1958).

It has also been contended that much of the inquisitive, exploratory, or manipulatory behavior of human infants may be attributable to a desire to gain new information (Berlyne, 1966; Piaget, 1952).

Variety of stimuli. It may be that the organism seeks variety in its stimulation. Unless different stimuli are encountered, a sort of boredom acts as an aversive stimulus that impels various kinds of activity and results in changes in stimulation and dissipation of the boredom. Thus certain investigatory responses, such as manipulation and exploration, which have been said to derive from curiosity, could be interpreted as learned responses that were reinforced by the reduction of monotony and boredom.

There do appear to be inherent likes and dislikes. Certain stimuli are approached, and others are avoided. The exact physiological basis of much of this behavior is not clearly understood. When one considers the variety of stimulation that appears to have a motivational effect, the possibility that *all* stimuli, both internal and external, have drive consequences must be considered. This position would include the stimulus consequences of learned behavior, innate response systems, thoughts and thought processes, language, ideas, and other internal and peripheral responses of the organism.

Emotion and Motivation

Both *emotion* and *motivation* derive from the Latin word meaning *to move*. The concepts represented by these two words have much in common, and

Figure 10-3. An intense, immediate state of arousal. After hours of anxious waiting, this miner's wife greets her husband. He survived an avalanche in which many other miners were killed.

some theorists have argued that the words refer to the same phenomenon as far as behavior is concerned. That is, they both have the effect of arousing, or alerting, the oganism. Conventionally, we have referred to intense, immediate states of arousal as emotional and to more prolonged and directed emotional states as motivational. Perhaps various arousal states could be placed on a continuum of intensity or immediacy, with those closer to the intense and immediate end of the continuum being labeled emotional and those more distant being labeled motivational. For purposes of discussion in this chapter, we have assumed that both emotion and motivation refer to dimensions of the same concept.

SUMMARY

The meaning of the concept of motivation is open to discussion. Motivational phenomena are those that appear to be activated and guided by the biological functioning of the organism and those that derive from the organism's wants, wishes, desires, aversions, purposes, affections, and emotions. Whether or not all of man's behavior is motivated, motivation is considered an important factor in his behavior. The vigor with which responses are committed and the direction responses take both have been subsumed under the heading of motivation.

Early in man's history, behavior was attributed to animating spirits, forces, or demons. As long as these agents were held responsible for behavior, scientific investigation of the motivation of man was nearly impossible. Gradually, animism began to disappear, and new concepts replaced it. Following Darwin, man began to be perceived as a part of the rest of the animal kingdom. Man's physiological continuity with other animals led to a postulation of behavioral continuity as well.

Instinct was widely used in descriptions and explanations of behavior until dissatisfaction with its lack of explanatory power developed. The concept of *drive* appeared on the scene as a more parsimonious means by which behavior might be explained. The arousal, energizing, or activation of the organism is central to the concept of motivation and has been the subject of much research.

The physiological needs of the organism are partial determinants of arousal, as are homeostatic processes and various internal and external stimuli.

Hunger, thirst, noxious stimuli, and sex are usually considered to be principal sources of stimuli that increase the activity level of men and animals. These stimuli have been investigated extensively in the laboratory; the results of such investigations have considerably advanced our knowledge of motivational phenomena.

There are various motivating stimuli besides those deriving from food deprivation, water deprivation, noxious stimuli, and sexual arousal. Any variation in stimulation may be considered as having at least potential motivational consequences.

SUGGESTED READINGS

Birch, D., & Veroff, J. *Motivation: A study of action.* Belmont, Calif.: Brooks/Cole, 1966. This paperback publication presents an overview of motivational theory and research. It is designed for the beginning student of psychology and should be informative and interesting for the reader.

Bolles, R. C., *Theory of motivation.* New York: Harper & Row, 1967. Drive theory is critically examined, and reinforcement theories are presented.

Brown, J. S., Harlow, H. F., Postman, L. J., Nowlis, V., Newcomb, T. M., & Mowrer, O. H. *Current theory and research in motivation: A symposium.* Lincoln: University of Nebraska Press, 1953. This is the first of an annual series of publications. It contains articles by leading motivational theorists and presents their differing points of view. Since 1954 this publication has been entitled *Nebraska symposium on motivation.* Each edition contains papers on motivation by a number of psychologists.

Cofer, C. N., & Appley, M. H. *Motivation: Theory and research.* New York: Wiley, 1964. An extensive treatment of the research literature is contained in this volume, which is an excellent reference book.

Teevan, R. C., & Smith, B. D. *Motivation.* New York: McGraw-Hill, 1967. This short programmed textbook for the beginning student provides a good overview of motivational phenomena.

11

Motivation: Complex Processes

We shall now consider complex energizers of behavior. Whereas basic sources of arousal or drive have their origins directly in the physiological state of the organism, complex sources of drive are more subject to the influence of learning and are more variable.

The significance of acquired sources of arousal in humans can hardly be overestimated, because so much human behavior derives from learning. People learn to attach importance to innumerable objects, events, and circumstances. The things that are important to the person are those that affect his emotional level. Given the amazing capacity of the human organism to learn, many elements can acquire motivational value. It is, of course, impossible for us to explore all sources of arousal. Therefore we shall focus our attention on only two topics that are representative of the complexity of arousal in humans: fear and language.

In this chapter we shall also consider some of man's motives. We deem motives to be complex behaviors that are directional in nature. As we suggested earlier, the direction of behavior derives largely from learning; thus motives are a complex of arousal and learned ways of behaving.

FEAR

One of the stimuli that theorists believe can innately produce fear is pain (Miller, 1951). According to such a view, fear is a complex response to painful stimuli. This complex response can, in turn, serve as a stimulus and, like other stimuli, can have motivational consequences. People learn to respond with fear in a variety of circumstances; fear can be a motivator of performance in the same sense as hunger or thirst.

That fear and anxiety have motivational effects on other responses has long been a common-sense notion. Cannon (1929) and Freud (republished 1936) focused the attention of psychologists on this phenomenon, and Mowrer (1939) formulated the notion of conditioned fear as a motivational variable with sufficient precision to make it an experimental variable in psychological research. According to Mowrer, fear, or anxiety, is an emotional reaction to stimuli that indicates the advent of pain or other noxious stimuli. This emotional reaction is acquired via classical conditioning. That is, stimuli that regularly precede or accompany painful, fear-producing stimuli eventually become capable of producing fear themselves. Fear seems to act as a general energizer of behavior. Experimental investigations of fear as an agent of arousal have been carried out in psychological laboratories with considerable success.

Arousal, Activation, or Drive Effects of Fear

Fear has long been accepted as an energizer by the layman. Stories of tremendous feats of running, lifting, or climbing under conditions of fear have become a part of our literature, and such events are reported from time to time in the newspapers. Cannon's (1929) observations of the physiological consequences of fear led him to treat it as an emergency reaction involving the mobilization of energy for use in expediting the responses evoked by the fearful situation.

Evidence that fear does result in an increased intensity of responding has been reported from the research laboratory. Brown, Kalish, and Farber (1951) investigated the effects of fear on the startle response. (The startle response is an overall bodily response to sudden stimuli; it can be elicited in small children by sudden loud noises or other sudden stimuli.) The investigators reasoned that fear should increase unlearned reaction tendencies if it is to act as a motivational variable. The startle response was chosen as a dependent variable because people had previously been observed to show exaggerated responses when they were startled. The investigators decided to test whether a loud noise that would induce the startle response, presented during the time a conditioned stimulus for fear was being presented, would enhance the startle response. Using laboratory rats as subjects, fear conditioning was accomplished by pairing the presentation of a buzzer and a light (conditioned stimuli) with an electric shock (unconditioned stimulus for fear). These events were paired for seven trials on each of four consecutive days. During this experiment the animals were placed in a confinement box with a grid floor. Each animal's mobility was reflected by mobility of the confinement box; thus any movements of the animal, including those associated with startle, were automatically recorded. (The required apparatus is known as a *stabilimeter*.) Three test trials, in addition to the seven conditioning trials, were given on each day. A test trial was one in which the conditioned stimuli (buzzer and light) were presented but the unconditioned stimulus (electric shock) was not. In place of the electric shock, a toy pistol was fired. A control group was treated in the same fashion except that the conditioned stimuli and unconditioned stimulus were presented without pairing. This procedure was used to prevent their fear from becoming conditioned to the buzzer and light.

The magnitude of the startle response (as measured by the stabilimeter) evoked by the pistol shot in the presence of the conditioned stimuli for fear increased progressively during the four days of training for the experimental animals. No such increase in startle response was observed in animals in the control group that had not been conditioned to fear the light and buzzer. During a subsequent period of extinction training, in which the conditioned stimuli were presented without the electric shock, we would expect that fear would diminish and that the amplitude of the startle response would be less. This is precisely what was found. The report of this investigation concluded that (1) the conditioned stimulus came to arouse more fear in the experimental animals than in the control animals and (2) fear functioned as a source of drive and resulted in an increase in the unlearned startle response.

Meryman (1952) conceived and executed an investigation to determine if the activation of a primary source of drive (hunger) would increase sound-induced startle responses in rats. His study was so designed that he could also determine if hunger and fear in combination would result in greater increases in sound-produced startle responses than either would alone. The apparatus employed in this investigation was a stabilimeter. Four different groups of animals were used in the experiment. One of the groups was made fearful and was deprived of food for 46 hours; another group was fear conditioned and deprived of food for only 1 hour; a third group was not made fearful but was deprived of food for 46 hours; the fourth group was not made fearful and was deprived of food for only 1 hour. Animals were placed individually in the confinement box, and the amplitudes of their startle responses to the sound of a toy pistol were recorded on three trials daily for ten days. On the third trial of each day, the groups that were to be made fearful were administered an electric shock in place of the sound of the pistol. The administration of shock was designed to produce fear associated with the stabilimeter confinement box. The box itself thus came to serve as the conditioned stimulus for fear. The nonfearful groups were not shocked at any time and should not have become so fearful as the others. Initially, that is, before any of the animals had received shock, the four groups were approximately equal in their reactions to the sound of the pistol.

The results of ten days of training and testing indicated that the startle responses of the two groups that deliberately had been made fearful were greatly increased from their initial levels. The startle response of the fearful nonhungry rats increased in amplitude, as compared with the nonfearful nonhungry rats. The fearful hungry rats showed a considerable rise in the amplitude of their responses, as compared with the nonfearful hungry rats. Fear was found to be more effective than hunger in enhancing the startle response, and fear and hunger combined were more effective than either stimulus alone. These data are depicted in Figure 11–1. An inspection of this figure will make the results of the investigation stand out more clearly. The data indicate that fear enhances the unlearned startle response, and they can be interpreted as supporting the view that learned fear may act as a source of drive.

Essentially the same general notion—that fear should act as a drive variable—was given further support in a later investigation by Meryman (1953). Human subjects were studied, and the dependent variable was the galvanic skin response (GSR), which is a measure of change in electrical conductivity of the skin. The conductivity is a function of sweat-gland activity and has been used as a measure of emotional involvement. Meryman's subjects were presented with a visual stimulus (a light), followed by a mildly painful electric shock. Thus, it was thought, they should become conditioned to respond with fear to the light. In testing, a click replaced the electric shock, and the GSR was recorded. The click was never paired with the shock, so it would be difficult to argue that the click itself was becoming a conditioned stimulus for fear. Meryman concluded that fear intensified an unlearned tendency to respond to a weak click.

The combined results of these three investigations indicate that fear causes an increase in both the startle response and the galvanic skin response. These responses may be taken as indicators of arousal, or drive level.

Fear Reduction as Reinforcement

If fear does act as a source of drive, it should be possible to demonstrate that learning can occur as the result of the reduction of fear or the reduction of the stimuli associated with it. Experimental results have indicated that fear reduction *can* be used as a reinforcer for the learning of new responses.

The reinforcing properties of fear reduction have been demonstrated by Miller (1948) in a study that has become a classic in the literature on the subject.

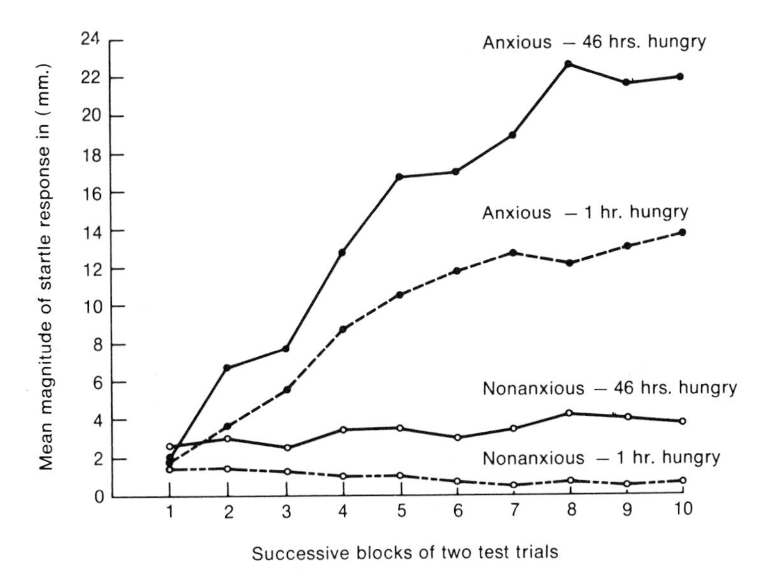

Figure 11-1. Magnitude of response by anxious and nonanxious subjects (Meryman, 1952).

Miller administered electric shock to rats placed in the white compartment of an experimental box composed of two compartments, one painted white and the other painted black. The piece of equipment is called a *shuttle box* because the animal must learn to run from one compartment to the other to escape or avoid a noxious stimulus. Miller administered shock in the white side of his experimental apparatus until his animals learned to escape through a door into the black compartment. Thus the animals learned to fear the white compartment. He then placed the rats in the white compartment with the escape door closed. A wheel was placed by the door, and the new task was to turn the wheel to open the door and escape from the white compartment. The animals were not shocked while the door was closed. They were simply placed in the white compartment in which they had been shocked. The fear generated by the stimuli of this compartment was sufficient to motivate the animals to learn to turn the wheel to escape. Furthermore, the wheel-turning response of the animals was later extinguished by not reinforcing it with the opportunity to escape. Without further administration of shock, the animals then learned to press a lever to escape to the black compartment. Escape from the white compartment, which had become fear inducing, served as reinforcement for the acquisition and maintenance of a new response. Fear reduction was interpreted as the reinforcement for escape and for subsequent wheel turning and lever pressing to escape.

Supporting this interpretation, Brown and Jacobs (1949) demonstrated that tension resulting from conflict and frustration produced by the blocked door preventing escape was not responsible for the drive Miller had attributed to fear. Following these research reports, it has generally been accepted that fear reduction may function as a reinforcer in the acquisition of new responses. It has been demonstrated that conditioned fear is related to the number of acquisition and extinction trials (Kalish, 1954; Sawrey & Sawrey, 1964). Animals exposed to more fearconditioning trials were demonstrated to be more fearful in test situations than were those animals that experienced fewer trials. Thus fear can be manipulated as an independent variable in experimentation in the same way that other sources of drive, such as hunger and thirst, can be manipulated. Various other investigations have agreed that fear reduction can be used as a reinforcer (Mowrer & Lamoreaux, 1942; Gwinn, 1951).

Fear and Human Behavior

Fear in humans is difficult to investigate experimentally in the laboratory. If an experimental situation is made genuinely fearful, the human subject will refuse to participate. Moreover, society dictates that people should not manipulate other people in such a fashion. In an obviously contrived experiment the usual human subject will be more amused, perhaps, than anything else.

Most investigations of fear and its role in behavior have been carried out with laboratory animals, since such experimental situations can be readily arranged. The task of translating animal experimental results to human behavioral equivalents is imposing. Many factors eliciting fear and many consequences of fear in animal investigations are probably similar to those of humans. Some suggestion of the behavioral consequences of human fear can no doubt be extrapolated from animal research.

Feelings of guilt (moral fear), anxiety (fear with a future referent), insecurity (fear of being inadequate), and other fears have occupied important positions in interpretations of both normal and disordered behavior. There is reason to believe that these fear reactions are acquired and function in humans in much the same manner as they do in animals.

Fear and anxiety have sufficient common elements that they may be treated in the same general fashion as far as their motivational consequences are concerned; however, some theorists have drawn distinctions between fear and anxiety (Goldstein, 1940; Jersild, 1954). The most critical distinctions made are relative to either the immediacy or the identifiability of the stimulus conditions. When a fearlike emotional reaction is provoked by a situation in which the fearful stimulus elements cannot be readily identified, the reaction is usually designated as anxiety. This label is also applied when the feared situation is not present in the immediate stimulus situation. That is, one can be anxious about being struck down by a car tomorrow or next week; by contrast, one can be fearful of a car that is bearing down on him while he is crossing the street. Acute anxiety can become quite severe and can take on the general characteristics of what is ordinarily labeled as fear. The distinction between fear and anxiety is difficult to relate to intensity of response. However, for motivational purposes, anxiety can be conceptualized as fear with a future referent.

Early Experience and Fear

Fear can be considered an inherent reaction to pain; experimental evidence indicates that fear is a learnable source of drive (Miller, 1951). Thus fear can become conditioned to a great variety of situations. Infants and children experience pain in any number of circumstances in the ordinary processes of their dependent existence. Even the most careful mothers cannot prevent their children from experiencing pain and discomfort. Hunger pangs, as painful stimuli, are experienced by every child. Children are sometimes handled roughly; they are placed in bath water that is too hot or too cold; they have digestive disturbances; they get stuck by pins and get bumps and bruises. Painful experiences coincidental to development and growth are no doubt rather numerous, and the opportunities to acquire fears through these experiences are manifold.

If an infant experiences pain or discomfort in his crib with some degree of frequency, the stimuli of the crib may come to evoke anxiety. Parents attempt to make playpens, cribs, and the like comfortable and attractive to prevent the conditioning of fear or anxiety to those facilities. However, if a child consistently experiences hunger pangs or irritation from soiled diapers in such environments, he will experience anxiety in them. This situation will result in arousal rather than contentment for him.

As the child continues to develop, the expansion of his experiential world permits greater opportunity for the occurrence of situations of a fear-conditioning nature. Older brothers or sisters who sometimes hit, pinch, poke, or bite may become the source of pain for a younger child. When the infant suffers pain at the hands of his older siblings, he can usually see them at the same time. If this situation happens with some frequency, the sight of the older sibling may itself serve as sufficient stimulus for the evocation of anxiety or fear. The acquired, or learned, nature of such fears can be appreciated when one realizes that the infant originally responds to *painful* stimuli; he later responds to the *sight* of his older brother or sister; he may learn to respond to thoughts of them with anxiety and apprehensiveness. By stimulus generalization, he may respond with fear not only to the siblings who have inflicted pain on him but to other children of the same general size or stature. Moreover, if his older brother or sister hurts him only when the mother or father is not present, the absence of the parent may become sufficient to evoke responses of fear. In this way the child actually may come to fear the absence of the parent.

The Persistence of Fear

Avoidance responses are those elicited by fear conditioned to a previously ineffective stimulus. Such responses are highly resistant to ordinary extinction procedures. Animals conditioned to avoid electric shock maintain their responses over a long period of time without receiving further shock (Solomon & Wynne, 1954). Great numbers of extinction trials must be given for a reasonable amount of extinction to occur when stimuli are complex (Kostansek & Sawrey, 1965). Fears acquired in early childhood are alleged to persist and have motivational effects in adulthood. This persistence of acquired fears has caused speculation that fear conditioning may be partially irreversible. There are several ways to view the persistent nature of acquired fear. One way is to reason that, after learning has occurred, whenever the fear-evoking stimulus is encountered, avoidance behavior is instituted quickly; as a result, the fear does not become sufficiently aroused for it to be extinguished. Also, it is possible that, when the fearful stimuli are encountered, fear is experienced, and avoidance behavior, which reduces the fear, is elicited; thus the stimulus situation (the feared situation) is not further explored. In other words, there is no chance to learn new responses to these stimuli. It is likely that there is a reciprocal relationship between fear as a response and overt avoidance behavior. That is, the feedback from overt behavior reinforces the fear, and the fear supports the overt behavior, thus both fear and overt responding are maintained at high levels. Whatever the theoretical reasons for the persistence of acquired fears, they are apparently long-lived and can act as energizers of behavior and as a basis for the development of further fear and anxiety, which can in turn serve arousal functions.

Relatively Constant Anxiety

If fear or anxiety acts as a source of arousal, those persons who have learned to respond fearfully to great numbers of situations should operate at higher drive levels than do those who maintain a rather low level of such anxiety. Generalized anxiety maintained consistently over time has been designated as "free-floating anxiety" by some psychologists. They imply that everyone has learned to respond apprehensively to some degree to many of life's situations. The specific stimuli provoking the anxiety cannot be readily identified; the person functions as though he maintains a constantly high level of anxiety. Such a person may have learned to respond with anxiety rather constantly and in such a way that his anxiety could be termed a generalized response to all or most of life's situations. Such anxiety has been referred to as "manifest," and a Manifest Anxiety Scale (MAS) has been developed for its measurement (Taylor, 1951). Scores reflect differences in a chronic emotional state, so that individuals scoring high on the scale are more anxious and should

Figure 11-2. Apparatus in which "neurotic" behavior is induced in cats. When a cat that is used to getting food from a box on cue gets a blast of air in the face instead, it retreats in fear. More air blasts will radically affect its behavior. After the blasts are discontinued, patterns of "neurotic" behavior (such as restlessness, viciousness, or apathy) persist unless treatment is given. Some therapeutic procedures have proved to be of value in reducing such maladaptive behavior (Masserman, 1967).

therefore be characterized as having a higher drive level than those scoring lower on the scale (Taylor, 1956). This test was devised for the purpose of selecting subjects who would differ in general drive level and was not designed to be a clinical or diagnostic instrument, although the items on the scale were selected by clinicians as referring to manifest anxiety as it is described psychiatrically. This test has been used in a number of experimental investigations designed to determine the relationship between drive level and performance in learning situations. Theoretically, the higher the drive level, the more readily acquisition should take place. The evidence indicates that, within limits, this contention generally appears to hold true.

In time, fear may produce response inhibition (Estes & Skinner, 1941; Amsel, 1950); animals may "freeze" and "crouch" when they are exposed to intense fear-producing situations. High anxiety levels may result in similar responses that would impede performance in learning situations. These apparent negative effects at first glance appear to conflict with the notion of fear, or anxiety, as a motivator. Amsel (1950) has interpreted such behavior as resulting from the simultaneous activation of competing or incompatible responses. That is, high levels of arousal may result in the activation of so many response tendencies that effective responding becomes inhibited. In such a view, the hypothesis that fear or anxiety acts as a source of drive is not impaired. It is possible, too, that intense fear or high anxiety may produce such biochemical disturbance and neurological disorganization that the acquired response tendencies are delayed in their emission.

Investigations of eyelid conditioning, using groups of subjects with high and low scores on the MAS, have demonstrated that anxious subjects show a greater number of conditioned responses than do nonanxious subjects (Taylor, 1951; Spence, Taylor, & Farber, 1954; Spence, 1964). Anxious subjects have been shown to exhibit greater stimulus generalization than nonanxious groups (Wenar, 1954). In more complex learning situations, anxious subjects have been found to perform less adequately than do nonanxious ones. In such situations, errors may be largely the result of interfering response tendencies. In maze learning, the greater number of errors are made by anxious subjects (Taylor & Spence, 1952; Matarazzo, Ulett, & Saslow, 1955). The number of errors for anxious subjects is positively related to the difficulty of the choice point at which they are made. These findings are in agreement with the theoretical predictions of the performance of anxious subjects in complex situations. In verbal-learning studies, anxious groups differ from nonanxious groups in the learning of a list of syllables differing in amount of intralist similarity (Montague, 1953). Anxious subjects were significantly superior in performance on the lists for which similarity was low and association value high (easy-to-learn lists). Nonanxious subjects were significantly superior in learning a list of high similarity and low association value (hard-to-learn list). When attempts were made to minimize the presence of competing response tendencies in a task, the superior performance of anxious subjects was demonstrated (Taylor & Chapman, 1955). Similarly, when an attempt was made to maximize the number of competing response tendencies by increasing the similarity among stimuli, anxious subjects were inferior in performance (Spence, 1953). A relationship between the effects of anxiety level and the effects of task complexity on learning and performance is fairly well substantiated by experimental evidence. In general, "high-anxious" subjects learn in simple situations more rapidly than do "low-anxious" subjects; with more complex tasks, the reverse is true. The achievement of high-anxious college students of the middle ranges of ability tends to be lower than that of low-anxious, very bright students. Students in the lower ranges of ability appear to do well or poorly regardless of anxiety level (Spielberger, 1962).

Anxiety and Human Behavior

The experimental evidence relative to performance and anxiety levels is in general agreement with the behavior of people under stressful conditions. If stressful conditions and consequent anxiety are not too high, performances of various kinds tend to be enhanced; however, if anxiety level goes too high, performance breaks down and irrelevant and inappropriate behavior is observed. Frequently the observation that a person's performance was not up to his usual capabilities is explained by the statement that he was trying too hard (that is, motivation, or drive, level was too high for optimal performance). College students may encounter this phenomenon when they take examinations (Gordon & Berlyne, 1954). It is not at all uncommon for athletes to perform less well than ordinarily when they want badly to win (when anxiety over a possible poor performance or a lost game becomes too high). In games requiring extensive motor coordination, it can be observed that the vigorousness of execution may increase to the detriment of overall performance. A basketball player may pass with such vigor that his teammate cannot handle the ball, or the player may shoot at the basket with such force that the ball bounces away. Hebb (1955) has indicated that optimal arousal for performance probably follows an inverted U shape when performance is plotted against level of arousal. This statement implies that both very low and very high levels of arousal should detract from optimal performance. If the anxiety level of the already highly anxious student is increased, the resulting increment to drive level may produce disorganization and a decrement in performance. Increasing the anxiety of those who are relatively low in chronic anxiety may result in an increase in drive level and the enhancing of performance.

It is probably true that people ordinarily are never completely free from anxiety. The sources of anxiety may range from vague fears about what the future has in store to concerns for what is happening at the moment. When people are relatively free from uncertainty, threat, and conflict, they are less anxious than when the courses of their lives and futures are uncertain and their frustrations and conflicts are numerous. Differences in drive level from individual to individual can be expected to vary with the degree of chronic anxiety in their lives, as well as with the anxiety produced by the immediate situation and by other basic and learned sources of drive.

LANGUAGE

Language and Arousal

Many of the child's fears may be acquired through association with language. If a mother expresses alarm immediately before the child experiences pain, expressions of alarm may come to evoke fear. Parents' verbal expressions, as well as the manner of those expressions, may come to serve as stimuli for the evocation of fear. This conditioning of fear to verbal cues serves an important role in providing the child with protective fears. Fear can be aroused by verbal means in situations in which the child has had no previous experience. The child's fear or anxiety can be aroused by the spoken word *hot* or *hurt* after he has associated these words with painful stimuli. Thus, he can learn to avoid objects that are so labeled without directly experiencing the pain these avoided stimuli would evoke. The words themselves may become anxiety arousing, and movement away from the object labeled by the word may be reinforced by the reduction of anxiety.

Words become associated with events in the life of a child. If he is frightened by an object and that object is labeled *dog,* the spoken label may come to have fear-arousing effects. Subsequently, on hearing the word *dog,* the child may respond with fear comparable to that produced by the actual sight of the animal. Furthermore, if he sees a dog, reacts with fear, and utters the word *dog* to himself, he has a double stimulus for fear—the animal and his own spoken word.

When physical punishment is administered to a child, it is frequently accompanied by scolding. The scolding associated with the punishment may cause the words used and the manner of their utterance to arouse anxiety and increase arousal. Almost any word in the language may come to evoke small amounts of anxiety in both children and adults as a result of its association with painful, frightening, or arousing events.

Exhortation as a Source of Arousal

Exhortation is frequently used to arouse people to exert greater effort. Such exhortations, when they are modest in nature, probably enhance the level of arousal and have a positive effect on performance. However, when exhortation is vigorous and impelling and anxiety is already high, arousal may have deleterious effects on performance.

Exhortations are used by athletic coaches to get players *up* for the game. At sales meetings, salesmen are exposed to "pep" talks and other more subtle means of anxiety arousal designed to increase effort and subsequent sales. Exhortation in both subtle and obvious forms is employed throughout our culture. It is used in schools to encourage achievement, in industry to increase productivity, in business to enhance sales, in sports to produce greater effort, by parents to encourage appropriate behavior in children, and among many other groups and individuals to increase arousal and the enthusiasm with which various problems and situations are approached.

Both the meaning of words and the manner of their expression may result in changes in drive level. Brown (1961) has suggested that, for verbal commands to serve strictly as learned motivating agents, they must be essentially devoid of specific content. That is, such commands as "hurry" may serve to enhance whatever behavior is going on at the moment. Other commands, such as "close the door," have a specific goal as a referent and probably do not have overall drive-increasing effects unless they are uttered in such a manner as to create emotional or motivational consequences. People tend to administer instructions and commands to themselves, and these self-administered instructions

Figure 11-3. Political leaders often employ exhortation. Fidel Castro addresses a rally in Cuba.

may have motivational consequences, much as do verbal instructions from others. Overt verbalization may not be essential to self-instruction, which probably can be given ideationally. That is, a person merely has to think about hurrying or the consequences of failure for increased drive, or arousal, to result. Such ideational functioning can provide an almost limitless source of stimulation and arousal for the individual. Although laboratory demonstrations of the arousing effects of ideation are difficult, it can be observed that thinking about certain things is sufficiently anxiety arousing to interfere with sleep. Thoughts of certain situations and events (for example, sex) have arousal consequences. The proper "frame of mind" is essential for both relaxation and effective, vigorous energy expenditure.

MOTIVES

The distinctive nature of any given stimulus can be said to serve a "cue" function. This cue function is involved in learning. A cue is that aspect of the stimulus to which responses become conditioned. When responses have been conditioned to distinctive drive stimuli, these stimuli result in behavior that appears to be goal-oriented, or purposive, in nature. Thus the food-deprived person is stimulated by hunger stimuli, which arouse the organism and provide a cue for learning.

The person stimulated by hunger learns responses that reduce this stimulus: he learns to actively seek food. We see, in this case, that food deprivation results in distinctive stimuli that provide cues to which responses become conditioned. The food-seeking and subsequent consummatory responses have become conditioned to the stimuli for hunger. Such a complex of stimulation, arousal, and learned responses is called a *motive.* The number of motives that can be acquired is limited only by learning ability and the opportunities for learning to occur. Thus a person can acquire motives for almost any object, event, or circumstance available in the environment. Motives for food, money, sex, friendship, achievement, prestige, esteem, security, and a host of more specific things are typically acquired in the course of social living. *Desires, wants, wishes,* and *interests* are words used to refer to motives. A motive has a specific goal orientation, or direction. Once acquired, motives may themselves have motivational properties. Having developed a food-seeking motive or a motive for money, one can learn to feel anxious when these objects are not available, and that anxiety serves an arousal function.

Various theorists and authors of textbooks have attempted to classify the universe of human motives in some meaningful way. As a result of these attempts, a body of literature has developed that uses behavioral classifications to delineate motives. Such classifications are rather arbitrary and are derived chiefly from opinion. Indeed, it appears that these attempts may have resulted in more confusion than clarification: there is a lot of overlap, and no single classification can be considered as discrete, for all such categories are meant to deal with complex learned responses in various circumstances. By considering motives as learned, we suggest that there is no more reason to classify them than there is to attempt to classify all responses when one is studying learning.

Man strives to attain goals, or purposes. This apparent goal-directed aspect of behavior has long been considered within the area of motivation, although it is probably more an associative, or learning, function than it is a motivational one. In the following sections we will present illustrations of the acquisition and function of motives in the determination of behavior. Certain motives are used in these illustrations because they are well known and popular, but they are not intended as classifications.

Money-Seeking Behavior

Chimpanzees can learn to work for a token reward (poker chips) that can be exchanged for food (Wolfe, 1936; Cowles, 1937). In these studies the poker chips are interpreted as having acquired secondary reinforcing value through their association with the obtaining and consuming of food. This explanation is a plausible one, and the same general explanation may account for man's acquired tendency to work for money. Obviously, people in our culture tend to learn to strive for the acquisition of money.

Brown (1953) has suggested an additional explanation that would not negate the value of the secondary-reinforcement principle but would operate along with that principle. Brown has postulated that a person, having learned that money can be used to obtain desired items and that lack of money means that certain items must be foregone, becomes anxious. The person comes to feel anxious when money is not present or when indicators, or cues, denoting the absence of money are present. Obtaining money reduces the anxiety associated with the cues denoting its absence. Money-seeking responses, while the person is anxious, are reinforced by the reduction of anxiety when money is obtained.

The money-seeking behaviors in which people engage are many and varied. People learn to perform a great number of tasks, jobs, occupations, and professions, in part at least to obtain money. The variety of behaviors defies enumeration, but the same general principles are no doubt operative in most cases.

People tend to become anxious when cues denoting the absence of money are present. Children are told "It is too expensive," "We cannot afford it," "We could do thus and so if we had enough money." Such expressions are often accompanied by tones of voice and facial expressions associated with anxiety. Through language as well as through direct experience, anxiety is aroused by insufficient funds. In some people anxiety may be aroused by the fact that they have only a meager amount to "get by" on until the next paycheck; in others anxiety may be aroused when they are about to lose one of many millions of dollars. Opening and maintaining savings accounts probably reduce such anxiety.

Of course, responses other than those of vigorous money-seeking behavior can be acquired as the result of anxiety associated with the absence or insufficiency of money. A person can escape anxiety-arousing stimuli by going to sleep, by getting drunk, or by seeking various diversions. These reactions produce a temporary reduction of anxiety and can be acquired in the same way that positive money-seeking behavior is acquired.

Affectional Responses

The social phases of the infant's environment soon become his most potent sources of stimulation. His needs are constantly ministered to by others. People bring needed warmth, food, and moisture, and they remove irritants. This association of people with drive-stimulus reduction provides an excellent conditioning situation. People are constantly associated as a CS with the reduction of the US of hunger, thrist, pain, or discomfort. The child can come to like people, to enjoy being with them, and to cooperate with them. Thus he becomes gregarious. He feels lonely (anxious) when he is deprived of human fellowship and strives to establish and maintain affectional relationships.

Having developed affectional responses toward others, the child can become anxious in the presence of cues denoting an absence of affection and can acquire behaviors that ensure or maximize probabilities that affectional relationships will be obtained. Children soon learn that, when mother and father behave in nonaffectional ways (get angry and punish), life is not very pleasant. It is unlikely that small children can understand the expressions "This is for your own good" or "This hurts me more than it hurts you."

Punishment—especially painful physical punishment—is often interpreted by the child as an indication that he is not loved. This assumption may be fairly accurate. If punishment is associated with the absence of affection and occurs following behavior that is disapproved, absence of affection can become synonymous with punishment and be anxiety arousing. Engaging in behaviors that one has learned are approved by others reduces the anxiety associated with cues indicating a lack of affection. We learn to behave courteously in our relationships with others in order to reduce anxiety over cues indicating the absence of affection.

Certain environmental cues, when not accompanied by sight and sound of the mother, may arouse fear in the young child. A child seeking and approaching his mother is reinforced by the reduction in fear provided by her presence (Dollard & Miller, 1950).

Although gregariousness, cooperation, and affection are revered in our culture, these characteristics can be developed to a personally disabling degree. An individual can become so anxious over loss of affection or over possible loss of affection that he behaves in ways that are inappropriate to the establishment and maintenance of these relationships. The person who is afraid to express an opinion, who is overly solicitous of the welfare of others, and who is overly apprehensive about offending someone can become so innocuous as to be uninteresting or boring to others.

Sexually Oriented Behavior

Certain objects in the environment acquire sexual significance for certain individuals. The sight of a pretty girl will turn men's heads and may spur them to try to make her acquaintance. Such attractions are probably developed in the same general way (secondary reinforcement and anxiety reduction) as are tendencies to seek money. If pretty girls have become associated with reduction in drive stimulation related to sex, the mere presence of a pretty girl may come to have drive-arousing functions. Thus the companionship of pretty girls is sought. Another facet of sexually oriented behavior may derive from concern for one's lack of attractiveness. Such anxiety can be diminished by friendly association with the opposite sex.

Previously neutral stimulus objects may develop sexual significance for a person because of their association with the reduction of stimuli associated with sexual arousal. Objects may acquire inordinate significance—to the point that they are nearly the exclusive stimuli a particular person associates with sexual arousal.

It is doubtful that many objects are imbued with universal symbolic sexual value. The attribution of sexual significance to objects that have some of the same general characteristics as male or female sex organs seems to derive from the fact that someone, somewhere, somehow attached sexual significance to that object or to one similar to it. If such a criterion for sexual symbolism is followed, one can attach "universal" sexual meanings to objects of all kinds, shapes, and varieties.

Prestige-Oriented Behavior

The desire to maintain or enhance one's prestige or esteem has been held to encompass a potent class of motives. Prestige-oriented behaviors have received much emphasis in attempts to account for certain social behaviors. Prestige-oriented behavior is acquired very early in life. Children learn that, if they are highly regarded, they will be treated well and will not be subjected to punishment and embarrassment. They observe that those who are highly regarded by others and are treated with affection have attributes that can be emulated. Thus children strive to do those things that will assure high regard, and they try to attain superiority in those characteristics valued by their culture. They learn that many of life's sweetest satisfactions derive from the elevation or maintenance of prestige and that there are few absolutes in their world. That is, they learn that no one is big or small, bad or good, strong or weak, sinful or virtuous—except by comparison to others. They learn to excel in order to be highly regarded.

Situations that are threatening, or even potentially threatening, to status will create anxiety. Engaging in those behaviors that are approved by the culture reduces the anxiety aroused by threatened loss of stature. One can acquire a tendency to maintain or enhance his prestige either through secondary reinforcement (as in the acquisition of money or possessions that are associated with prestige) or through anxiety arising from the absence of appropriate esteem or the potential loss of prestige. The ramification of possible prestige motives in our culture could be made as lengthy as the list of potential sex symbols.

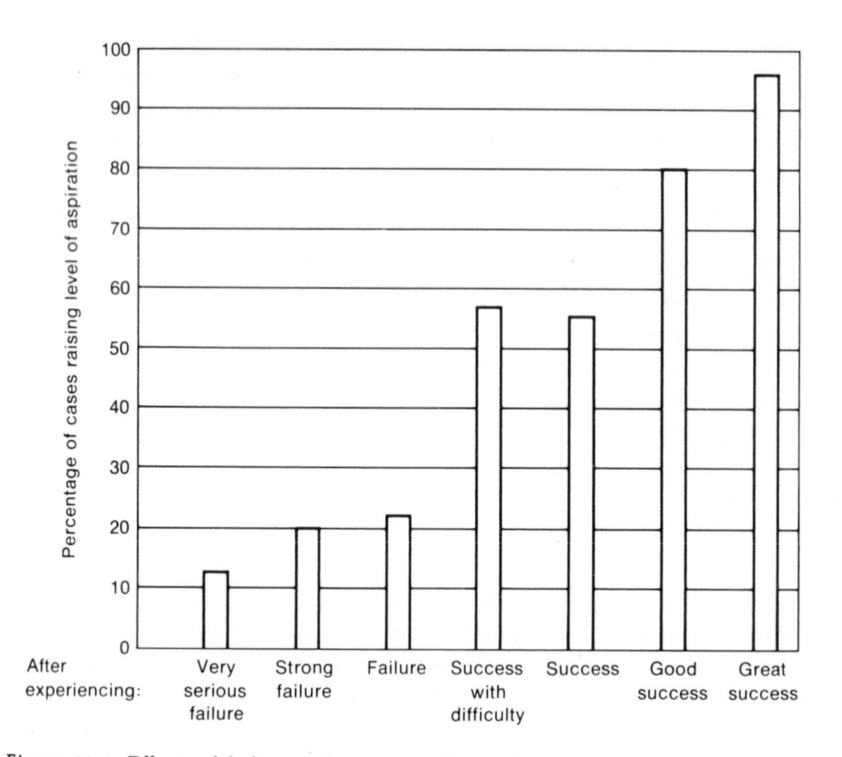

Figure 11-4. Effects of failure and success on level of aspiration (after Jucknat, 1937).

An idle social conversation can degenerate into a duel for supermacy between the participants. If a funny story is told, someone will try to top it; if a frightful experience is related, someone is certain to relate a more frightful one. The person who relates the funniest or most startling story enhances his prestige.

Prestige and affection are probably highly interdependent. To be liked is to be well regarded. In general, behaviors that result in prestige and esteem for the individual are those that enhance the probability of affection and affectional relationships.

The Achievement Motive

Motivation for achievement has received a great deal of investigative attention. Early studies, concerned with the variables that affect the level of aspiration of individuals, discerned that feelings of success or failure were dependent on the difficulty of the task for the subject (Hoppe, 1930). If tasks were much too difficult for the subject and he could not reasonably be expected to succeed, he would feel no particular sense of failure at lack of success. Conversely, if the task was much too easy and could be accomplished readily, no particular feeling of success derived from adequate performance. Investigations of the consequences of the performance of other groups on personal level of aspiration (Hilgard, Sait, & Margaret, 1940; Festinger, 1942) and the effects of failure and success on level of aspiration (Lanz, 1945; Jucknat, 1937) have also been conducted.

Achievement motivation refers to the tendency to define one's goals and aspirations according to some standard of excellence. McClelland and his associates (McClelland, Atkinson, Clark, & Lowell, 1953) developed a method of measuring achievement motivation through analysis of the stories people told when they were asked to write a short story about a picture. This method has been employed extensively in achievement-motivation research (Atkinson, 1964). Western culture is vigorously competitive, and investigations of the tendency to achieve in this culture have been numerous. Achievement motivation, as such, may be a result of various other motives acquired during the course of living. Such motives as those involving prestige, affection, and esteem are no doubt involved in the complex tendency to achieve.

SUMMARY

Both learning and motivation are pertinent to the investigation of activating stimuli. People live together and acquire behaviors common to their communities. Within a given culture, a number of stimuli acquire the capacity to elicit responses that have motivational value for most of its members.

People inherently respond with fear to painful stimuli and learn to respond fearfully to other stimuli associated with the painful stimulus. A number of research investigations demonstrate the energizing function of fear and anxiety. As a source of arousal, or as an acquired source of drive, fear and anxiety may be more pervasive factors than a cursory examination would indicate. Anxiety is experienced rather constantly, and levels of anxiety have been found to affect levels of drive. People learn to feel anxious relative to a host of situations, and their general level of arousal is affected by this fearlike reaction.

The motives of man defy enumeration. Classificatory systems of motives have been devised by many psychologists. These classifications derive principally from the opinions of theorists and are designed to be descriptive rather than explanatory.

Language and motives themselves may act as learned sources of arousal. Motivation for money, sex, prestige, affection, and achievement are representative of the wide range of possible motives.

SUGGESTED READINGS

Atkinson, J. W. *An introduction to motivation.* Princeton, N. J.: Van Nostrand, 1964. This book provides a good introduction to the background and investigations in motivation. Chapter 9 contains an excellent survey of achievement motivation.

Fiske, D. W., & Maddi, S. R. *Functions of varied experience.* Homewood, Ill.: Dorsey Press, 1961. The role of variation in stimulation is given prominence in this treatment of motivation.

Fowler, H. *Curiosity and exploratory behavior.* New York: Macmillan, 1965. This very readable paperback presents the theory and supporting evidence for curiosity and exploration.

Levine, D. (Ed.) *Nebraska symposium on motivation.* Lincoln: University of Nebraska Press, 1966. Current research and thinking relative to motivation in a variety of areas are presented.

McClelland, D. C. *The achieving society.* Princeton, N. J.: Van Nostrand, 1961. McClelland presents descriptions of achieving societies and attempts to relate these descriptions to investigations of the achievement motive. Students interested in social problems should find this book very appealing.

12

Personal and Social Behavior

Personal and social behavior has been a fascinating area of speculation and research for thousands of years. The preceding chapters have dealt with the study of psychological processes basic to these behaviors. This chapter concerns the direct investigation of personal and social behavior. Such behavior is ordinarily treated under topics like adjustment, personality, and social processes.

FRUSTRATION

Frustration can be thought of as a complex emotional response to the disruption of ongoing motivated behavior. Frustration has stimulating properties for the organism. The responses elicited by frustration are called adjustments. A response may be socially or personally desirable or undesirable. It may be socially conformant or nonconformant, or it may combine elements of both conformity and nonconformity.

The adjustments that are made in a given situation are dependent on a great many factors, including previous experience, the source of the frustration, the intensity of arousal, the strength of motivation, and the ability of the person to cope with the situation. Adjustive responses range from simple and uncomplicated to extremely complex.

Frustration can be produced by a variety of situations. The basic procedures that produce frustration can be classified as frustration by *delay*, frustration by *thwarting*, and frustration by *conflict*. Frustration by conflict has some components that differ from frustration by delay or by thwarting. Conflict will be treated somewhat more extensively than the other two procedures in a later section of this chapter.

Frustration by Delay

If a response has been regularly reinforced, and if the reinforcement is then delayed or is not available, frustration frequently ensues. The period of delay may vary in length. If the delay is momentary, there is only a slight break in the organism's ongoing behavior. This slight delay in receiving reinforcement frequently precipitates frustration. The reactions may be described as emotional, and ensuing behavior is affected (Amsel, 1958).

Delay in achieving sexual reinforcement is a prominent source of frustration among adolescents in our culture. Autosexual behavior is frowned on in our society, and sexual relations are forbidden adolescents. Certain forms of sexual activity are even punished. Ideally, the adolescent is supposed to wait until he reaches a certain age at which economic independence has been achieved and marriage and subsequent monogamous heterosexual activities are condoned. However, throughout adolescence, models for nonconventional behavior are numerous and stimulation for sexual activity is generally strong. Sexual frustration as a source of later personality problems has received a great deal of attention from clinical and personality theorists. Evidence indicates that these frustrations have important dynamic influences on personality.

The frustrating effects of delay of reinforcement for various kinds of performances have been demonstrated in the experimental laboratory, using both animals and humans as subjects (Amsel & Ward, 1954; Amsel, 1958, 1962).

Increases in response strength following the first few extinction trials in classical conditioning have been reported (Hilgard & Marquis, 1935; Hovland, 1936), as have increased activity and response intensification after periods of enforced waiting (delay) (Skinner, 1932; Brown & Gentry, 1948).

Frustration by Thwarting

Interference with motivated behavior in almost any fashion can be considered thwarting. Any time a response is prevented from occurring or motivated behavior is interfered with, frustration results. In the learning situation presented to a hungry rat in a maze, there are barriers between the animal and the food. Frustration of a minor sort probably occurs as the result of such obstructions. Minor frustrations are an inevitable part of any learning situation. Thwarting that produces frustration of a more serious nature is typically more intense or more prolonged.

Society places many rules, regulations, and restrictions on behavior. Unattainable standards set by parents frustrate children (Jost, 1941). Some thwarting of infants and children is inevitable, but we can safely say that much of it is unnecessary for the welfare and protection of the child. The unnecessary thwarting of children's activities probably stems from thwarting experienced by the parents and their own consequent frustrations.

Thwarting by personal characteristics. The person's physical characteristics can create frustrating obstacles to performance. The short college athlete can

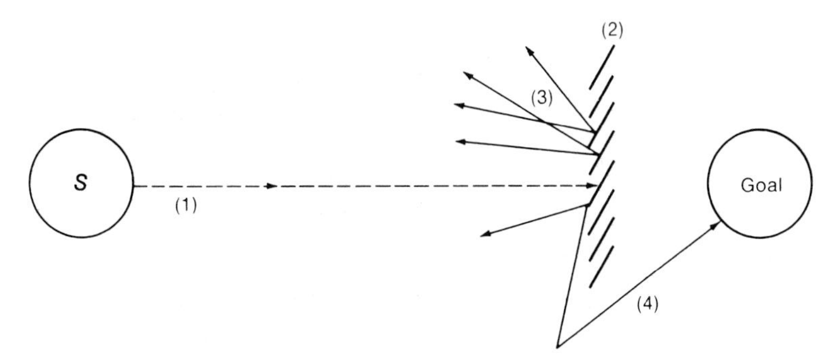

Figure 12-1. Frustration by thwarting. An organism (*S*) is motivated to approach a goal (1). It encounters a barrier (2), is thwarted, and tries various responses (3). Successful solution (4) may be discovered.

be frustrated when he tries to play basketball. The physically clumsy or inept cannot do well in games that call for physical agility. The person who is ill or handicapped cannot engage in physically strenuous activity.

Other physical characteristics may also serve as thwarting agents, not because of actual physical restriction but because of the personal or social value placed on the possession of the characteristic. It is more frustrating for a girl or woman to be physically unattractive than it is for a man to be unattractive because of the social evaluation of beauty in the female. Acne and other skin blemishes, because of their social or personal evaluation, may act as thwarting agents and prevent the establishment or the maintenance of satisfactory social relationships. Although physical charatceristics of unattractiveness may be a deterrent to effective social interaction, it is probably true that the person's own *evaluation of himself as a person* possessing these characteristics operates as the more effective barrier to socialization. Lack of self-confidence, which leads to anxiety over personal failure, can be a thwarting agent.

Social sources of thwarting. The source of much frustration is social. Other people do not always behave in ways that are conducive to the satisfaction of our motives. Other people's behavior, designed to satisfy their own motives rather than ours, may constitute a barrier to the satisfaction of our own needs. They may not let us join their group or club or society; they may prevent us from attending the college of our choice; they may stop us from marrying when we want.

Parents frustrate their children and are frustrated by them. Girlfriends thwart their boyfriends. Brothers and sisters thwart each other. Teachers frustrate students, and students frustrate teachers. The list of persons who act as thwarting agents for other persons could be extended almost indefinitely.

Further sources of thwarting. Frustration by one circumstance or another is a lifelong process. The desire to be independent and free from the restraint of living with one's parents results in frustration when independence is unattainable because of immaturity, lack of employment, or other reasons. Many people would like to travel and see the world but are thwarted by economic considerations, social circumstances, or emotional involvements. People are frustrated when they want to get a job but none is available, or when they do not possess the necessary training or experience for a desired job. A young man who wants to buy a car may find he cannot afford it. The desire for a college education may be thwarted by a number of factors. Married couples are thwarted by the inability to procure the kind of home they want in the location they find most suitable. Vacations from work cannot be arranged for the most convenient time; the activities that can be arranged for the vacation are not always those that are really desired. The furnishing or refurnishing of a home must usually be carried out within the restrictions imposed by budgetary and space considerations as well as those imposed by convention. One may want to retire but be unable to because of personal responsibility and social obligation; or he may want to work beyond retirement age but finds employment impossible because of a legal restriction or a physical infirmity.

CONFLICT

Conflict is an appropriate word to describe situations in which a person is motivated to behave in two incompatible ways. In frustration, the attainment of a motive is blocked by some barrier and must be coped with. In conflict, the individual is confronted by equally desirable or equally distasteful situations between which he must choose.

Conflicts are usually of such a nature that one motive is stronger than the other and thus takes precedence over it. Most people occasionally find themselves suffering from the demands of conflicting motives, and this situation leads to difficulties in personal adjustment.

Lewin (1935) describes conflict as a form of interaction between an individual and his environment. Lewin's system of concepts is a useful one in understanding conflicts: individuals respond to the things in their phychological environment and learn to be either attracted or repelled by them. The tendency for an object to either attract or repel serves as the basis for the person's responses toward that object. The degree to which an object elicits approaching or avoiding responses from the individual is its *valence*. Objects toward which the individual makes approaching responses are said to have *positive valence* for that individual, and objects that evoke avoiding responses have *negative valence*.

According to Lewin, a person's response to each aspect of his environment is either to approach it or retreat from it—unless a given object has zero valence. The strength of a response tendency is a function of the valence of the object and its "psychological distance." A distant goal is usually approached less strongly than is one that is similar and closer. A threat that is close at hand evokes stronger avoidance responses than does one that is not immediate or imperative.

Varieties of Conflict Situations

Four types of conflict situations may arise between the tendencies to approach and to avoid objects. Experimental investigations of these situations have supported the contention that they are valid descriptions of conflict (Brown, 1948, 1961). (1) A conflict may occur when a person wants to approach two objects or to fulfill two motives that are incompatible. This type is called an *approach-approach* conflict. (2) Similarly, conflict may arise when one wishes to avoid two threatening situations, but the avoidance of one makes the other imperative. This type is called an *avoidance-avoidance conflict.* (3) A conflict may result from a situation that has both positive and negative valence for the individual. This type is the *approach-avoidance conflict.* (4) A fourth variety, the *double approach-avoidance conflict,* arises when there are many stimulus elements evoking both approach and avoidance responses in the same situation (Hovland & Sears, 1938).

Approach-approach conflict. Approach-approach conflict occurs rather frequently and is usually readily resolved. When two alternative goals are equally or nearly equally attractive, conflict is the end result. The person would like to approach both, but if he chooses one, the other favorable alternative becomes impossible. Slight fluctuations in motives or in the environment usually cause such situations to be resolved without too much difficulty. Approach-approach conflicts are apparent when we must decide which TV program to watch, which movie to attend, what to order from a menu in a café, and when we are in other, similar situations in which the same motive would be satisfied by either decision.

More complicated approach-approach situations are those in which one motive must be satisfied at the expense of the other. Instead of which TV program will be watched, the decision here must be made between watching another hour of TV or going to bed, whether to attend a movie or save the money, or whether to go out to dinner or attend a party.

Students are sometimes forced into approach-approach conflicts when it is impossible for them to participate in a social group and do good work in school at the same time. Some social groups are so active that they interfere with study time and thus cut down the quality of schoolwork. Or, they are disdainful of academic endeavor, thus making it difficult, if not impossible, for a member to be socially acceptable and academically prepared at the same time.

Another approach-approach dilemma occurs when behavior standards are grossly different in the home and in the peer group. A child may find himself in conflict between peer-group acceptance and parental approval.

Avoidance-avoidance conflict. Avoidance-avoidance conflicts are produced when the individual must choose between two unpleasant alternatives. As he approaches one, it becomes more unattractive, and he withdraws. As he approaches the other, its negative qualities also become more and more apparent, and he withdraws. The organism's typical response to such a situation is to escape and thus avoid the whole unpleasant business.

Students frequently find themselves in avoidance-avoidance conflict situations. They want to avoid the unpleasant prospect of failure in a course or the disapproval of the instructor for being ill-prepared; at the same time, they want to avoid the drudgery of study and academic preparation. The student may vacillate for a short time, then resolve that study is absolutely necessary, and finally attempt to prepare for an assignment or for an impending test. The person finds himself easily distracted and frequently tempted to do other things. He may spend much time in daydreaming or avoid the unpleasant task by lengthy and elaborate preparations for study. His attempts to escape the entire situation may run from the devious ways just mentioned to the obvious escape of going to a movie or going to sleep.

It is hard to resolve dilemmas of the avoidance-avoidance type. In a situation like the one just described, in which a student wants to avoid study and to avoid failure at the same time, psychological distance becomes an important factor. Failure on a test or failure in a course is not so immediately imperative as the unpleasant prospect of study. The student neglects his study because it is the closer of the two unattractive alternatives. This behavior does not satisfactorily resolve the conflict, because he will still suffer anxiety over the possibilities of failure. His behavior is controlled by the strength of his motives at the moment. His motivation to avoid the whole unpleasant situation may be stronger than either the motive to avoid study or the motive to avoid failure. In this case the avoidance motive will dominate, and the individual will tend to escape the whole affair, at least for the moment. He cannot approach either undesirable activity, so he removes himself from the situation.

Approach-avoidance conflict. When a single object or situation possesses characteristics that tend to attract and to repel the individual at the same time, it has both positive and negative valence. The tendency to approach and the tendency to avoid are in conflict. Such conflict situations are relatively common. A young man who would like very much to marry a particular young lady but does not want to give up the liberties of bachelorhood is in such a situation. Someone once facetiously observed that a man may experience an approach-avoidance conflict situation in observing his mother-in-law drive his new automobile over a cliff.

Actually, such conflict situations can be serious, and they cannot be resolved by escape. If the person withdraws, his fear and tension are temporarily reduced, but he still wants to approach the favorable aspects of the situation. His motives to approach are active when he is farther from the conflict. As he approaches the situation, his fears are reactivated. A vicious circle of conflict is thus established. The person is in an almost constant state of fear and tension. When motives to approach and to avoid are nearly evenly matched, the individual may vacillate between the two motives, and tension is maintained at a high level.

Double approach-avoidance conflict. Double approach-avoidance conflict situations involve two complex stimuli. That is, each of the two stimuli elicits both approach responses and avoidance responses. (It is conventional to refer to all these situations as double approach-avoidance, even though there may be more than two complex stimulus situations involved.)

Conflict situations are frequently of a complex nature. The young lady who must choose between two attractive suitors probably is more illustrative of double approach-avoidance than of approach-approach conflict. It is likely that, although both men are extremely attractive to her, one is more talkative than the other, one is more economically secure than the other, one is taller than the other, one has a better sense of humor than the other, or one is more aggressive than the other. When the conflict is described in this manner, it becomes apparent that, although the overall picture is one of approach-approach conflict, the situation is really a double approach-avoidance conflict. The young woman can choose to remain single, or she can seek still another prospective mate. The factory worker who has an option of taking his two-week vacation to go on a trip or working and getting double pay is in a complex conflict situation. Either choice has both positive and negative aspects.

HABITS OF ADJUSTMENT

Everyone experiences thwarting in some form or other and, as a consequence, suffers frustration and conflict. We learn to respond to frustration and conflict in various ways that become routinized as they are reinforced and repeated. When they have become habitual, they are called *mechanisms*. Nothing mysterious or obscure is implied by the word *mechanism*; a mechanism is simply a learned way of responding to the total situation of our motives, frustrations, conflicts, and opportunities for adjustment. Since none of us is capable of satisfying all our motives or solving all our problems directly, we learn to solve some of them deviously, or indirectly. Direct methods of satisfying our motives differ from the indirect ways in that direct motive satisfaction is recognized as such by society and by ourselves. The behavior mechanisms that result from indirect problem solution are often dealt with in textbooks on adjustment and mental health. These mechanisms are treated under such topics as aggression, compensation, withdrawal, daydreaming, projection, rationalization, regression, and identification.

PERSONALITY

Personality refers to an individual's unique organization of relatively permanent reaction patterns and to other characteristics that influence the way other people respond to him. More than 80 different definitions of personality have been proposed. Despite this diversity, five common characteristics can be discerned: (1) an emphasis on the molar, or global, nature of personality, (2) an emphasis on the predominantly social reference of personality, (3) an emphasis on the distinctive characteristics of the individual, (4) a recognition of both its stimulus and response components, and finally (5) an emphasis on the dynamic aspect of the concept.

Personality represents the highest level of organization of an individual's cognitive, affective, and behavioral systems. As a *global* concept, it stresses the fact that an individual's traits and characteristics are integrated in such a way as to produce a degree of consistency in behavior. Although personality is sometimes analyzed into various innate, acquired, organic, and social components, these elements are really developmental sources rather than elementary components. Personality is the product of the dynamic interactions of the contributions of various developmental sources as they are fused into an integrated system.

The concept of personality gives special weight to those distinguishing characteristics of the individual that have a *social reference*. On the response side, personality consists of those habits and characteristics acquired as the result of one's social interactions, habits, and characteristics that manifest themselves principally in social situations. Briefly, personality refers to an individual's socially relevant physical and behavioral characteristics.

Personality has particular reference to the *unique characteristics of the individual.* A person's personality is not characterized by the fact that he is human, has two legs, is able to talk, and is a gregarious organism. Those things that are universal characteristics of humans are less important components of personality than are those qualities that set one individual apart from others. Personality is identified particularly in terms of how the individual deviates from the norm. The individual's personality is thus reflected in his unique organization of characteristics.

Personality has both a stimulus and a response aspect. *Persona,* the root of the word *personality,* originally referred to a theatrical mask that an actor wore to identify the part he was portraying. This root meaning is still retained when the term *personality* is used to refer to the "stimulus value" of the individual. That is, it refers to the impression one makes on other people. When we describe a person as having a pleasing and gracious personality or an irritating and obnoxious personality, we are not telling what he says or does or describing his behavior; we are registering his effect on us or on people in general. Thus personality has its *social stimulus-value aspect.*

One's personality can also be indicated by the way in which he characteristically acts in social situations. When personality is defined as the organization of behavior patterns that characterize the person as an individual, personality is conceptualized in response terms rather than in stimulus terms. When we describe a person as dominant or submissive, aggressive or withdrawn, we are describing how he characteristically responds in social situations. Thus personality also has its *social-response aspect.*

Personality as a dynamic concept places particular emphasis on *social interaction,* which involves both stimulus and response components as well as their relationships. The distinction between stimulus and response is a matter of one's point of view; the same event may be both stimulus and response. In social intercourse, one person's response can become another person's stimulus. In conversation, one person's response is what he says, but what he says is the other person's stimulus. The second person's response, in turn, becomes the first person's stimulus.

The Determinants of Personality

The unique pattern of traits that constitutes a person's character and personality develops as the result of both genetic and environmental factors. Genetic determinants manifest themselves via the organic and constitutional makeup of the individual. Environmental determinants include such factors as prenatal and infantile experiences, family constellations, and parent-child relationships. They also include the broader cultural and subcultural institutionalized influences mediated by school and church, as well as those resulting from membership in ethnic, religious, and social groups. Practically all of one's gentic inheritance, as well as the total experiential history of the individual, influences personality.

Constitutional—presumably genetic—factors. Of course, there is no direct causal relationship between one's genetic makeup and such characteristics as aggressiveness, sociability, or cooperativeness. The effect of genetic factors on personality is indirect. We respond to the world with our physiological mechanisms, the structure and functioning of which are influenced by genetic factors. Evidence concerning the effect of genetic factors on personality is derived principally from studies of the lower animals and neonatal humans.

Through processes of selective breeding, strains of animals have been developed that differ markedly in activity level and in emotionality. Natural selection and domestication have also developed strains of animals that differ widely in wildness, savageness, aggressiveness, timidity, and emotionality (Sawrey & Telford, 1963). The fact that selective breeding can produce significant differences in behavioral traits indicates that genetic factors are involved in certain components of temperament. The more emotional and more active strains of animals have been found to have larger adrenal, thyroid, and pituitary glands than do comparable nonemotional and less active strains. Wild Norway rats have larger adrenal glands than do domestic strains of the same species. The lethargy of basset hounds as contrasted with the more alert and active Salukis and German shepherds is probably related to the more active thyroids and higher metabolic rates of the latter two breeds of dogs (Rogers & Richter, 1948; Stockard, Anderson, & James, 1941). These studies indicate that heredity plays a part in endocrine-gland structure and function, which, in turn, affect the behavioral traits of the lower animals and, presumably, man.

The great differences found in human infants during the first days of life also suggest the operation of genetic factors. From their first day, some neonates show five times the activity of others. The daily amount of time devoted to crying by presumably normal infants ranges from less than one to more than four hours. Ratings made by trained observers, as well as objective measurements, show that an infant's relative levels of general activity, irritability, and fearfulness remain fairly constant during the first three years of life (Irwin, 1930; Fries & Levi, 1938). Children who cried a lot as infants and were highly active have been found to be more prone to startle reactions, to be aroused from sleep more readily by sounds, and to react more violently to frustration than do the more lethargic children (Fries & Woolf, 1953). One study of 200 randomly selected neonates showed that 12 percent of them had levels of pepsinogen sufficiently high to fall within the range of those found among adult ulcer patients (Mirsky, 1958). Adult patients who develop ulcers tend, prior to actual ulceration, to have a high rate of gastric secretion, as indicated by a high concentration of pepsinogen in the blood or urine. Pepsinogen is the substance secreted by the stomach and is the precursor of the digestive enzyme, pepsin. Although no follow-up studies of children with high pepsinogen levels have been made, it seems likely that such individuals may be the ones who are highly sensitive to emotional stimulation and, as adults, develop ulcers.

Personality and physique. There have been many attempts to relate dimensions of body structure to personality characteristics. Bone structure, muscle distribution, and general bodily conformation have been considered either to determine or to be indicative of character and personality traits. Man still entertains many of these beliefs: the big, muscular man is dominant and aggressive, the fat person is jolly and easygoing, the frail person is tense and serious. Shakespeare said in Julius Caesar:

> Let me have men about me that are fat;
> Sleek-headed men, and such as sleep o' nights.
> Yond Cassius has a lean and hungry look;
> He thinks too much: such men are dangerous.

Bodily handicaps and physical deformities have also been thought to influence personality. According to this conception, the absence of a body part or a physical defect produces feelings of inferiority, which may explain both low self-concept and poor achievement and compensatory high achievement. Alfred Adler (1929) advanced this conception vigorously. According to him, man's feelings of inferiority derive principally from organic inferiorities, and most of man's defensive behavior represents attempts to compensate for real or imaginary physical inadequacies.

Research studies regularly report a greater incidence of social withdrawal, personal unhappiness, and defensive behavior among individuals who possess physical defects than among those who are closer to the norm. Consistent but low positive correlations are also found between many dimensions of physique and various measures of personal and social adjustment. However, the assumption that there is a direct causal relationship between the two variables is questionable. It seems unlikely that observed behavioral characteristics derive directly from physical deviations. Occasionally, both behavior and bodily deviation may arise from the same genetic or prenatal cause, but more often the relationships between physique and behavior are the result of intervening social variables.

These social variables operate in the following way: a person who deviates significantly from the culturally approved norm is devalued by his associates. He is considered a less worthy individual than someone who has a more ideal physique. His devaluation is indicated by his being less sought after and less popular. He is rebuffed in his social overtures and is socially ostracized. He is also labeled as less worthy in the sense that other people expect less from him than they expect from "normal" people.

The individual who is devalued by his culture tends to accept this social judgment as valid. He internalizes the low-value judgment as he sees it reflected in the reactions of other people. This internalized cultural judgment becomes his own self-concept. The individual then tends to act in accordance with others' expectations of him as well as with his own self-expectations. The intervening variables involved in the conversion of a physical trait into a handicap are the social evaluation of the trait and the individual's acceptance and internalization of the social judgment.

Another indirect influence of physique on behavior is anxiety level. A person with a socially defined physical handicap is more vulnerable to anxiety than is the average person. He feels more threatened by the ordinary demands of his culture. When such threats produce high levels of anxiety, there occurs a decrease in the individual's ability to deal adequately and constructively with his environment. Rigid, constricted, compulsive, or impulsive and fragmented solutions to problems tend to develop. The high-anxiety levels of the deviant individual may result in a high incidence of socially unacceptable and blind-alley solutions to life's problems.

The anxious physically handicapped individual may also restrict his activities, maintain a lower level of aspiration, and persist in an unrealistically low self-definition as a defense against the threat of failure and increased anxiety. When a person has had a great deal done for him, when he has not been required to develop competence and to display initiative as much as the normal person, and when he has lived in a greatly simplified world, he has a tendency to remain in such a situation or to regress to such a condition when stresses become too great and anxiety mounts (Wenar, 1953, 1954).

The converse of this process operates with individuals whose physical deviations are in socially approved directions. Girls who are beautiful and boys who are superior in strength and "manliness" are found to be above average in social and personal adjustment (Dimock, 1937; Silverman, 1945; Sawrey & Telford, 1963, 1971).

The average person is largely unaware of the extent to which his own culture has conceptualized the ideal human physique. Traditions, folklore, and the mass media perpetuate ideal stereotypes.

Americans annually spend billions of dollars and tremendous amounts of time and effort to bring themselves as close as possible to culturally specified ideal male and female types. The use of makeup, foundation garments, shoulder pads, elevator shoes, "falsies," toupees, hair dyes, artificial eyelashes, and colored contact lenses; the bewildering array of machines, medicines, diets, and systems for either reducing or increasing weight in general or of specific body parts; facial creams and lotions whose types (foundation, vanishing, theatrical, lubricating, moisturizing, and hormonal) are limited only by the ad writer's vocabulary; cosmetic operations, silicone injections—all are evidence of a widespread concern by people who believe they have a less-than-ideal set of physical attributes.

Of course, the prevailing conception of what constitutes the ideal human form varies from culture to culture, from generation to generation within the same culture, and, to a lesser extent, from one age group to another within the same culture and generation. In certain primitive African tribes, to be desirable as a prospective bride, a girl must be big, strong, and preferably weigh at least 200 pounds. Consequently, the girls and women are fed large quantities of curdled milk to fatten them (Wood, 1872; Thomas, 1937). These women also scarify their bodies from the breasts to the pit of the stomach and on the forehead in such a way as to produce rows of small almond-shaped swellings. The members of other African tribes chip or file their front teeth to sharp points for beauty and distinction. In other tribes no young woman thinks herself beautiful until she has removed the upper incisors (Thomas, 1937). All these physical characteristics are far from the American ideal of the sylphlike female

Figure 12-2. A man in the Congo and women in Pakistan and Sweden show varying cultural conceptions of attractive attire and ornamentation.

with unblemished skin and intact, perfectly matched teeth. Among some German college students a saber cut on the cheek is considered a mark of honor, whereas the same cut on an American college boy would be only a facial disfigurement.

The hourglass figure of the 1890s was the ideal female profile of that era. It gave way to the straight, boyish figure of the 1920s, when the breasts were bound and compressed so as to diminish their apparent size. In the 1950s a fully developed breast became the ideal, which was achieved, when necessary, through wearing sponge-rubber "falsies." Parents seem to be perpetually surprised and disturbed to find that their children's conceptions of what is proper and desirable in dress and body build differ in many respects from their own.

Environmental Influences on Personality

Environmental influences on personality operate from the moment of conception. Although prenatal environment is relatively constant, marked deprivations and unusual conditions can have considerable impact on development. Inadequate diet during pregnancy can lower the infant's intellectual level and increase his proneness to rickets, anemia, bronchitis, and colds (Montague, 1950). A pregnant mother addicted to narcotics will give birth to an addicted infant who requires a program of drug withdrawal. X-ray treatment of a pregnant mother may produce serious damage to the developing fetus. When the pregnant mother is emotionally disturbed, the fetus becomes excessively active, presumably as a result of the hormonal secretions being transmitted to the fetal bloodstream through the placenta. There is evidence that effects of emotional disturbance of a pregnant mother can carry over into the child's postnatal life. Infants born to mothers experiencing severe emotional disturbances during pregnancy are reported to be hyperactive and irritable (Montague, 1950). It is difficult to separate genetic and prenatal environmental effects in such cases. However, the consensus favors the notion that both genetic and prenatal environmental factors contribute to the emotionality of infants.

Early experiences. Studies of the lower animals have demonstrated that infantile deprivation can have marked effects on personal and social development. Newly weaned rats experiencing food deprivation hoard significantly more food as adults than do littermates not subjected to such deprivation. Pups raised in isolation in kennels where they did not experience pain seem almost unable to learn to avoid painful stimulation after they attain maturity (Melzack & Scott, 1957). Monkeys raised from birth with surrogate wire-mesh mothers do not show normal affectional or affiliative behavior as adults. They are almost entirely incapable of mating, and, when the surrogate-raised females are impregnated and give birth to young, they show a complete absence of normal maternal behavior (Harlow, 1962). Puppies raised in social isolation to maturity are unable to learn to interact socially with either humans or other dogs. The evidence indicating marked behavioral effects of early experiential deprivations in the lower animals is quite convincing.

Since it is impossible to greatly manipulate the environment of human infants for experimental purposes, the investigations of the effects of infantile experiences on humans have used children living in nonmanipulated deprived environments; that is, infants in orphanages, foundling homes, and hospitals have been compared with children cared for by their mothers in their own homes (Goldfarb, 1947; Spitz, 1951; Rheingold, 1956). The alleged effects of institutional care include gradual decline in physical status, poor health, a high mortality rate, progressive intellectual decline, poor social adjustment, a high incidence of behavioral problems, and shallow affectional relationships. Most of the studies claiming to demonstrate these effects have such serious methodological limitations that they are of questionable value. One of the most serious of such limitations is the fact that children in institutions are not a representative sample of the general population: infants and young children with behavioral problems and intellectual retardation are more likely to be placed in institutions and tend to remain in institutions longer than do normal children.

One study has shown that institutional infants who were given additional "mothering" for a period of 12 weeks showed significant increases in social responsiveness as compared with a group in the same institution receiving only routine care (Rheingold, 1956). However, a year later the two groups were indistinguishable. Apparently the advantages of increased mothering were not maintained for a year. There was no evidence in either group that institutionalization had a negative influence on these particular children. A second study by the same researcher showed a superiority of institutionalized children as compared with own-home children when both groups came from high-socioeconomic-status families (Rheingold, 1961). Follow-up studies of young adults who, as children, had been evacuated from London during World War II and had been cared for in residential nursery school for an average period of three years have shown them to be quite normal. There is a notable absence of the extreme disturbances of affective relationships, social adjustment, and intellectual retardation previously reported for institutionalized children (Maas, 1963). The earlier statements to the effect that institutional care is necessarily disadvantageous to the young child are not warranted. Institutions probably vary as much as parents do. In trying to define "healthy" and "unhealthy" psychological environments for young children, perhaps we need to differentiate between loss of mother, with a resulting relative lack of handling, fondling, and caressing, and a more general perceptual or sensory deprivation.

Child-rearing practices and personality. Fashions in child-rearing practices are regularly justified in terms of their alleged effects on the personalities of the children. However, efforts to relate specific child-training practices to personality development have revealed surprisingly few stable relationships. When parental practices such as bottle versus breast feeding, regular versus demand feeding schedules, abrupt versus gradual weaning, early versus late toilet training, and punishment versus ignoring toilet accidents are related to the personality traits and general adjustment of the children later in life, no differences have been found (Sewell, 1952).

Attempts to relate global parental variables to the personality adjustment of offspring have fared somewhat better. When detailed studies of parents have been made and ratings of the "total parent" are obtained in terms of underlying parental attitudes, character structure, perception of the parental role, and general conduct toward children, a significant relationship with the children's adjustment is obtained (Newton & Newton, 1950; Behrens, 1954).

Three additional relationships between parental practices and character and personality traits of children have held up quite well in replicated research studies. (1) Parental warmth and the withdrawal of love for wrongdoing are related to strength of conscience in children. Parents who have close, warm relationships with their children and who use psychological techniques of behavior control, such as praise or reproof, isolation or intimate contact, and the bestowal or withdrawal of affection, have children with highly developed concepts of right and wrong and appropriate behavior controls. (2) Parents who use the withholding or bestowal of tangible rewards and physical punishment as their principal means of discipline have aggressive children with poorly developed consciences. (3) There is considerable evidence of a relationship between parental stress on early independence and strong achievement motivation in the child (Brown, 1965).

Society and personality. In addition to family organization and early experiences, the broader neighborhood, subculture, and general culture in which the individual is reared also influence characteristics of his personality. The patterns of behavior and standards of one's peer group become increasingly important as the child gets older. The powerful social pressures exerted by adolescent peer groups become major determinants of the behavior of teenage children. Acceptance or rejection by one's peers becomes an important determinant of the child's developing self-concept.

The school is probably second only to the family as a determinant of personality in the child. It is not only an important source of ideals and values but provides peer groups that constitute one of the child's most important subcultures.

Personality Abnormalities

What are the criteria for defining a normal personality? In a statistical sense, a normal person is average. The abnormal individual is one who deviates by more than a given amount from the mean of the group. However, when one considers the tremendous range of social systems in the world and the great variety of behavior patterns required to live in such systems, it is conceivable that certain of these systems are more "normal" in an ideal sense than others.

Thus, in a broad perspective, conformity to the standards of certain cultures could conceivably be deemed abnormal.

The abnormal individual is sometimes defined as one who deviates sufficiently from either the statistical or the ideal norm of his culture to require special care and supervision. This variation of the statistical concept defines the extreme deviate as abnormal. Sometimes abnormality is defined as deviation from an ideal standard. When a child is given a dental or medical examination, he may be pronounced "perfectly normal"; this diagnosis usually does not mean that he has the average number of dental defects and medical deviations but that he has a complete absence of these conditions.

Current conceptions of personality abnormality tend to be multidimensional and frankly limited to our culture. Elsewhere, we have conceptualized "good" personality adjustment to be an ideal combination of traits, as indicated by the person's position on theoretical scales of selective awareness, tolerance, autonomy, impulse control, and self-actualization (Sawrey & Telford, 1971).

Abnormal personalities can range from a theoretical "normal," through minor abnormalities in which there is a slight but definite impairment of the individual's adaptive capacities, through more serious deviations commonly called neuroses, through still more dramatic inappropriate behavioral outbursts and psychotic episodes, to the deteriorated, chronic psychosis. Personality disorder, or "mental illness," can be ordered according to the degree of disorganization of function. This view provides a unitary concept of mental illness as differing from normality principally in degree rather than in kind.

Historically, a personality abnormality has been referred to as "demonological possession," "madness," "lunacy," "insanity," "psychosis," and "mental illness." Today many people believe that the relatively new concept of "mental illness" has outlived its usefulness. They conceive of "mentally ill" people not as patients afflicted with certain diseases but as people making inadequate, inappropriate, and self-defeating efforts to cope with the problems of living. The mentally ill person is a human experiencing excessive anxiety or hostility; engaging in rigid, nonproductive, and autistic thinking; becoming isolated from his fellowmen; and displaying socially inappropriate behavior. His stresses exceed the power of his "normal" coping devices, so he develops special techniques in a vain attempt to maintain a tolerable state of affairs with a minimum of discomfort. Even these special techniques are essentially exaggerations and distortions of processes and techniques found in all people. Abnormal personality is viewed as an oversized, distorted picture of normal personality. The fundamental assumption of such a view is that there is a continuity between the normal and the abnormal and that the same processes are involved in the development of both normal and abnormal behavior.

SOCIAL PROCESSES

From the moment of birth, other people are the most important part of a child's world. At first they are sources of food, warmth, and comfort. Later, as the child learns that people provide more rewarding than punishing experiences, the sight and sound of other people become positively reinforcing, and social interaction itself becomes rewarding and self-perpetuating.

The social contacts of the individual gradually but constantly expand from infancy to maturity. The infant's initial social contacts are predominantly with one person—usually the mother. This interaction between two people—a dyadic relationship—is the initial center of the child's existence. The mother-child relationship normally expands to include the other members of the family. The family is the most significant primary social group in the child's life. When he moves outside his family circle, he establishes contact with other children of his own age—his peer group. On entering school, his peer group expands, and he has greater freedom in selecting his own friends and associates. In school the child encounters a new authoritarian figure, his teacher, who dispenses a new set of reinforcements and a new set of standards. Within his peer culture he progresses from the relatively unstructured play of the 5-year-old to the ritualized gang activities of the adolescent subculture.

As an adult, the individual becomes a member of many formal and informal groups and comes to play a variety of roles in these group relationships. Some of these groups, such as the family, are primary—that is, characterized by close affectional relationships. Others, such as the company, the union, the community, and the church, are secondary groups involving less personal and intimate relationships. At all stages of life, other people constitute the most important segment of a person's environment. Man is the product of, as well as an active participant in, his social environment.

THE NATURE OF CULTURE

Man is born the most helpless of all organisms. He has the longest period of infancy and dependency. As an adult he has relatively few fixed, innate

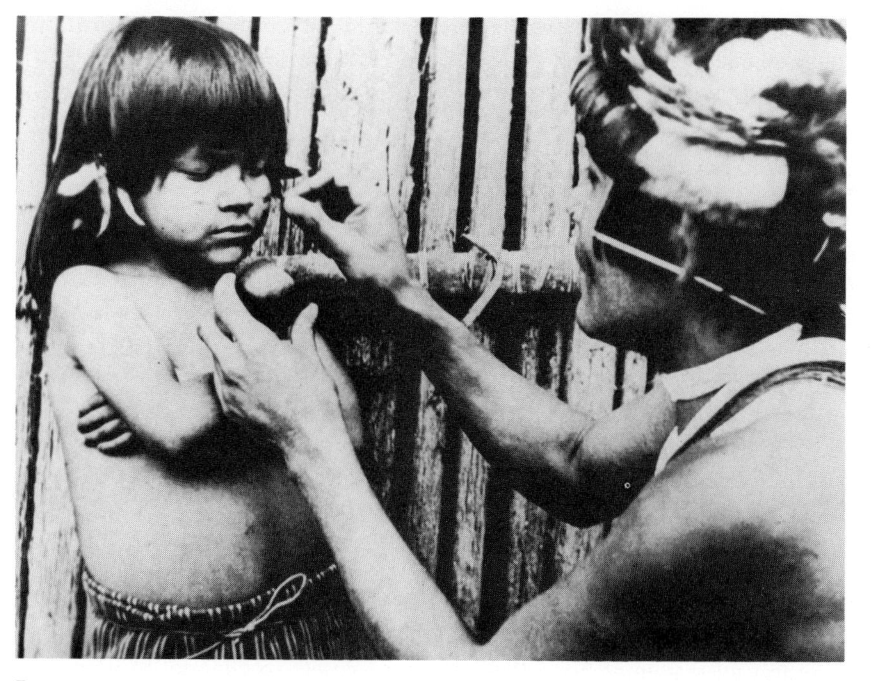

Figure 12-3. In this child's culture, headhunting is an accepted form of behavior.

behavior patterns but a tremendous number of acquired ones. Culture becomes possible because of man's great capacity for learning.

Culture refers to the pattern of behaving, perceiving, thinking, and feeling of a given nation or group of people. The matrix of a culture contains both conscious and unconscious components. Some cultural elements are codified as legal, religious, ethical, and moral principles or mandates. But culture also includes a pattern of unverbalized and largely unconscious assumptions, premises, and values that are considered to be self-evident and inherent. Culture involves shared beliefs and practices, as well as shared anticipations of rewards and punishments contingent on certain types of behavior. It includes not only how one is expected to behave but also how one expects others to behave toward him (role relationships).

Culture entails a kind of social inheritance from previous generations that is almost as inevitable as is biological inheritance. Culture imposes on its members a pattern of life that is learned early and is invested with considerable emotion. Deviations from cultural patterns usually incur either socially or self-induced suffering in terms of comfort, status, safety, or modifications of one's self-concept.

The socialization of a child consists largely in learning the pattern of his culture. Man makes tools, rules, and habits of living; he accumulates knowledge, develops attitudes and values, and transmits them to succeeding generations as a cultural pattern within which the individual is socialized.

A culture is never homogeneous. Within any given culture various subcultures can be distinguished. The stratification of society into classes or castes is almost universal. In a *caste system* the stratification is dominantly closed, with little or no movement in or out of the various castes. Caste differences are often enhanced by physical distinctions, such as skin color, caste marks, or dress. In some cases caste boundaries are maintained by religious or legal sanctions. Membership in a caste is usually hereditary.

A *social class* is a group of people who are roughly similar in terms of wealth, education, occupation, or general prestige. Social classes are relatively open, and people can move from one to another. The more complex and differentiated a society, the greater the number of class distinctions recognized within it. All culture and all systems of stratification are subject to change. In general, the more rapid the social change, the more open the system of stratification becomes, and the greater the class or caste mobility.

The individual's initial placement in the class system is determined by his parents' position. The child typically learns quite early in life about relative social status, and, although he may not know the names of the social classes, he is aware that certain other people are above and below him. The child not only becomes aware of his social status, but he is trained in the behaviors appropriate to that position. He consciously and unconsciously acquires aspirations, expectations, attitudes, beliefs, tastes, and skills appropriate to the status of his family. Because of residential proximity, school location, family friendships, and parental pressures, like-classed children tend to constitute peer groups. The child's peer group normally reinforces the social-class characteristics of the family. Members of different social classes behave differently in a wide variety of rather fundamental and pervasive ways.

Social class in the United States has been shown to be significantly related to such diverse factors as life expectancy, incidence and type of mental illness, fertility rates, child-rearing practices, family stability, marital relations, values placed on education, and style of life. Social classes are often correlated with ethnic and religious groupings, which tend to accentuate each other. Hostile attitudes and abrasive behavior perpetuate and reinforce social-class differences, as the result of both legal and social discrimination and prejudicial stereotyping.

In stereotyping, people are perceived on the basis of group membership rather than in terms of their own unique characteristics. Prejudicial perception carries with it a constellation of expectations and judgments, and each individual member is characterized by the category in which he is placed. National and ethnic stereotypes may seem to be useful in making rapid categorical decisions with a minimum of deliberation.

ROLES

A great deal of social behavior is role dictated. Roles, which are socially prescribed ways of acting in particular situations, are culturally defined and depend on the shared beliefs and expectancies of others and of ourselves. Like other cultural components, role enactment contributes to the consistency and uniformity that characterize most social processes. A role exists independently of the person enacting it: a role in a play exists independently of any particular actor, and a social role, such as parent, student, teacher, policeman, or college president, consists of a pattern of behavior and mutual expectancies apart from the particular individuals who enact them. Every role assumes its complement. That is, one person can fulfill the role of teacher only if others will play the role of student.

Roles and the personalities enacting them interact. No two actors portray the role of Hamlet in exactly the same way. The tones of voice, the inflections, and the varying emphases constitute the individual's interpretation of the role. An actor may even delete some lines and substitute modern terms for Elizabethan ones, but the essential features of the part must be retained or Hamlet is no longer Hamlet, and the role is changed. The important roles that one plays over long periods of time leave their residue in the personality. The person who sets out to play the role of a musician because someone else expects him to do so may begin by playing the part but end up a competent musician with music permeating every aspect of his being. The young physician who grows a mustache and wears conservative suits, only because he considers his new role to require it may end up as the conservative, knowledgeable doctor of his original role enactment.

Certain occupational roles are partially prescribed by law. Doctors, lawyers, and teachers have legally defined procedures for licensing and practice. Professional organizations further codify ethical and professional conduct. Less formally, the education of these professions inculcates, and the expectancies of the general public reinforces, proper role behavior.

Sex Roles

The biological distinction of sex is genetic, but the sex roles that society dictates are acquired. Proper sex roles are defined in terms of dress, play, interests, speech, and occupations. A boy is active, aggressive, noisy, and dirty; he plays football and may become an engineer. A girl is quiet, submissive, and neat; she plays house, sews for dolls, likes music, and is dressed in pink rather than blue. The boy who acts like a girl is a sissy; the girl who acts like a boy is a tomboy. However, the sex-typing for males is more rigid than it is for females. It is worse to be a sissy than to be a tomboy. Girls can and do wear male apparel with impunity, but males wear female dress at considerable risk.

Male and female life-styles are quite arbitrary. In the United States today, part of the masculine sex role is to be less interested than women in personal adornment. However, in the eighteenth century, European noblemen took a lively interest in curled wigs, silks and satins. Recently there has been a resurgence of male interest in personal adornment among certain subcultures in the United States and Europe.

Conformity and Nonconformity

The average child learns about conformity and nonconformity rather early in life. He discovers that to talk, think, believe, and act as others do are conducive to social acceptance and continued group membership. Conversely, he discovers that being different can result in social isolation and ostracism. To be like the majority of one's peers is to be safe, to be too different is risky. To enjoy the advantages of one's culture, one must submit to the cultural dictates of others and conform to their expectancies. Each person learns that he can avoid endless trial and error by observing the patterns of behavior of the prestigious members of his society and imitating them. Since the culture provides many ready-made solutions to life's problems, it is much easier to follow cultural dictates than to work out one's own unique solutions. Cultural dictates acquire the force of moral imperatives and become resistant to critical appraisal because of their self-evident nature.

Nevertheless, there are forces within most cultures that encourage nonconformity. Children discover that certain affiliative and affectional rewards accrue to the individual who conforms to social norms, but they also observe that an additional increment of affection and prestige is bestowed on those people who exceed the norm in socially approved directions. Mother loves her boy when he is a "good sport" and plays according to the rules of the game. However, she loves him still more when he also wins. A child does not obtain prestige by being like the hundred other individuals in his set. To gain the attention and esteem accorded exceptional individuals, he must be different. He must run the risk of being a nonconformist.

Sometimes nonconformity to the dictates of the general culture takes the form of extreme conformity to the behavior patterns and values of a subculture, clique, or gang. The adolescent may rebel against the dominant culture in order to be acceptable to a peer group whose approval is more important to him. Defiance of the broader social conventions may be the price of admittance to the inner circles that demand rigid conformity to their code. This conformity and nonconformity must be judged within their appropriate contexts.

Some conditions of conformity. A series of studies carried out over a period of nearly 50 years has documented a tendency toward consensus and agreement in judgments made in groups, as compared with similar judgments made when a person is alone. In general, there seems to be an almost ineradicable tendency for members of a group to move toward agreement. There is a convergence of individual judgments toward a central value even when the members of the group are strangers and have no knowledge of one another's performances. The tendency toward consensus is greater when the individual judgments are known to the other members of the group. It is greater still after discussion of the problem. The consensus is further increased when a unanimous group judgment must be rendered. The shifts of opinion involved and the increasing concensus in group situations are augmented when the persons holding contrary opinions are friends, are numerous, and are prestigious. We shall describe a series of representative experiments that support these propositions.

Allport (1924) had subjects judge the degree of pleasantness of a series of odors and the heaviness of a series of weights. The subjects made fewer judgments toward the extreme ends of a scale when they were working side by side in a group than when they were working alone. In the "together" condition the individuals worked in one another's presence with no communication; it was simply a co-working group. These subjects seemed to be trying to avoid extreme deviations from the *presumed* norm of the group.

Judgmental shifts toward an emerging group norm. The classic study on this topic was made by Sherif (1936). His study made use of the autokinetic illusion, which consists of the apparent movement of a small, stationary light in a completely dark room. A light under these circumstances cannot be localized accurately because of the absence of any reference points. Although it is perfectly stationary, the light seems to move in various directions and to varying extents. There are great individual differences among subjects as to the direction and extent of the apparent movement, but in the course of 100 judgments each subject settles down to a consistent mean value from day to day.

After individual values had stabilized in private sessions, subjects were combined into groups of two or three and asked to report their judgments aloud. Under these circumstances their judgments rapidly converged toward a central value for the group. In these groups there were no discussion, no request for unanimity, and no sanction for agreement or disagreement. Nevertheless, the individuals were in much closer agreement after they had made their judgments in groups than before.

Judgmental shifts toward a contrived norm. Asch (1952) went one step farther and made use of a contrived and erroneous group norm to influence individual judgments. The purpose of his experiment was disguised. Naive participants were requested to serve in an experiment on visual perception. The subjects were shown two cards, one containing three lines and the other one line. The task was to select the line on the first card that was of the same length as the line on the second card. The judgments were to be called aloud. The naive subject was seated in line with a group of other subjects—really stooges—next to the far left. The order of reporting was from right to left, so the naive subject was always next to the last. The judgments were easy, and, on the first two matches, all the people in the line were unanimous. The judgments on the third set of lines were equally easy, but each of the people to the naive subject's right called out the same erroneous number. On subsequent trials a unanimous majority frequently reported an incorrect answer. Since all the subjects except one were really confederates of the experimenter, they were reporting falsely according to a prearranged schedule.

The judgments required were not difficult: subjects working alone made practically no errors in judging the lines. However, even when the equivalence between the standard line and one of the set of three was clearly evident, about one-third of the judgments made by normal college students in this experiment were incorrect but in accordance with the group judgment. Subjects differed widely in their susceptibilities to the group influence, but a large number succumbed to a marked degee. Asch was able to characterize *some of his subjects* as either largely independent or largely conforming, although the majority of subjects conformed on some trials and were independent on others.

Conformity and nonconformity as personality characteristics. Although we have not stressed the fact, all studies find large individual differences in the extent to which subjects conform. The amount of conforming behavior shown by a particular individual also shows some inconsistency across different kinds of task. In the Asch experiments about one-third of the judgments conformed to the group response; two-thirds of the judgments did not. These percentages were not particularly meaningful, since they could be shifted by varying the objective discrepancy between the standard line and the line the majority called equal to the standard. As the discrepancy increased, the number of subjects who yielded to the majority edict grew smaller.

Additional situational factors that have been found to influence the degree of conformity induced by group influences are the size of the group and the attractiveness of the group to the individual. Asch used groups ranging from 2 to 15 but found that the group effect increased only slightly when the number was increased beyond 30. Propaganda techniques and advertising programs assume that the creation of an impression of universality contributes to the acceptance of a proposition. It has been shown experimentally that increasing the attractiveness of a group in the eyes of the subject increases the tendency of the individual to conform (Jackson & Saltzstein, 1958). When all the members of a group were competing against other groups for a prize that was to be shared equally, the degree of conforming behavior was increased (Krech, Crutchfield, & Ballachey, 1962).

However, despite the many situational variables that influence the conformity-nonconformity dimension of social behavior, some consistent personality characteristics are found to be influential determinants. The distinction made by Witkin (1964) between field-dependent and field-independent people is relevant to the personal variables in conformity. Although Witkin did not relate this variable to conformity-nonconformity, his field-independent people would probably be more resistant to group pressures to conform than would his field-dependent people.

Studies have shown that feelings of personal inadequacy and inferiority are associated with a strong conformity bent (Krech et al., 1962). Conversely, people who were led to believe that they were very good at making perceptual judgments conformed less in an Asch-type situation than did subjects who were convinced that they were poor at this kind of task (Gerard, 1961). In the conformity-nonconformity dimension of behavior there is a dynamic interplay between such internal factors as personality traits, motivational trends, and the need for consistency and such external ones as power and prestige of the people making up the group, size of the group, and the ease of the task or judgment.

GROUP FUNCTIONS

Social groups perform many functions in the life of the individual. They serve as a principal agent for his socialization. They first establish, and then serve as a means of satisfying, his affiliative and prestige motives. Groups assist the individual in achieving his life's goals. They are the major determinants of his attitudes and ideals, his value systems, and his conscience. They are also a major reference point in his self-evaluations and in the development of his self-control.

In a stable, well-integrated, and relatively homogeneous society, the various groups and subgroups provide fairly consistent answers to many of life's problems. In simpler societies, a person's group memberships and identifications are relatively few and comparatively stable. However, modern Western man is often caught up in the race for upward social mobility, in the dilemmas and contradictions of status striving, and in the perplexities of marginal membership resulting from the demands and expectancies of diverse social groups. He finds himself in conflict as he tries to live the different roles required by diverse groups, which frequently demand contradictory adjustment on his part. Through face-to-face contacts, through the mass media, and through the formal educational processes, young people are subject to various pressures, demands, and ideologies.

As a person passes from one group situation to another and reacts to the ever-increasing demands, pressures, and appeals of new group situations, it becomes increasingly difficult for him to establish and maintain consistent role relationships and ties of belonging. The individual's *reference groups* are those to which he relates himself or to which he aspires to relate himself. When one feels himself rejected or functioning marginally within the larger culture, he is often caught by the positive attractions of a subgroup, which then becomes his primary reference group and whose values and norms become important determinants of his behavior. A person can have both positive and negative reference groups. A positive reference group is one in which the individual strives to be accepted and treated as a member. A negative reference group is one that the individual opposes and does not want to be considered a member of.

When an individual becomes estranged from a group in which he formerly held membership, the estrangement is perceived by his former associates as repudiation of both the group and the individuals comprising it, and this action ordinarily evokes a hostile response from them. As the social relations between the individual and the group deteriorate, the norms of the group become less imperative and binding for him. As he progressively withdraws from the group and is penalized by the group members, he receives progressively fewer rewards for adherence to their norms. Once started, the process generally moves forward with his ever-increasing detachment from the group, in terms of attitudes and values as well as social contacts.

After a person detaches himself from his former primary groups, his social needs may lead to his affiliation with a minority "outgroup." His orientation toward the divergent outgroup values and practices, and his affirmation of them, widen the gap and reinforce the hostility between himself and his former ingroup associates. Through the mutual negative reinforcement incident to his dissociation and alienation from the dominant group's values, the person becomes doubly motivated to orient himself toward the values of another group and to affiliate with it. When estrangement from the dominant culture is not accompanied by affiliation with another reference group, the person becomes alienated and socially rootless and may retreat into social isolation and privacy.

ALIENATION 5 elements

The concept of alienation has come down to us from the German idealistic philosophy of Georg Hegel, the political philosophy of Karl Marx, and the sociological theory of Emile Durkheim (Coser & Rosenberg, 1964). Recently it has been used to refer to a wide variety of discontents and disrupting influences in modern society. A term closely related to alienation is *anomie*—a condition of normlessness, a moral vacuum, an absence of rules or guides to conduct, a state sometimes referred to as "de-regulation." Anomie, like alienation, presupposes a prior condition in which behavior was normatively regulated. Social change destroys the norms, attentuates the regulative power of tradition, cuts people free from their anchors, and produces anomie. At the present time alienation and its various synonyms have an important place in most discussions of unattached, marginal individuals—the normless, the isolated, the "hippies." These terms are used today largely within a social-psychological framework.

One element of alienation is *powerlessness*. In this context, powerlessness refers to the individual's belief that his own behavior cannot significantly determine the outcomes of his life or the realization of his goals. He feels that his behavior is predominantly controlled by external rather than internal forces. Powerlessness in a broader sense also refers to the individual's sense of his lack of influence over socioeconomic and political events.

A second component of alienation is *meaninglessness*. This term refers to the individual's sense of a lack of understanding of the events in which he is engaged. The alienated individual is uncertain as to what he can believe. He feels that he lacks the minimum requirements for making rational decisions. He has a low expectancy that any meaningful predictions about the future consequences of any given line of conduct can be made. This aspect of alienation may range from the belief that the individual himself cannot make sense out of his world to the belief that the universe is inherently unintelligible.

A third component of alienation is *normlessness*, or the absence of social norms for the regulation and evaluation of individual conduct. The theme underlying the concept of normlessness is that social and moral values have been submerged in the welter of self-seeking private and corporate interests striving for the superficial symbols of success by any means that are effective. The alienated person perceives himself as caught up in a highly competitive, industrialized, and manipulative society in which individuals live in a climate of mutual distrust. An alienated person may believe that morally questionable behavior is required to achieve the goals that are highly valued in his society.

The fourth aspect of alienation is *isolation*. In its current context this term most often refers to an intellectual isolation from popular cultural standards. The alienated individual assigns a low value to goals and beliefs that are highly valued in the dominant culture. Isolation involves an apartness from society that is more intellectual than social.

The fifth and final component of alienation is *self-estrangement*, which was emphasized by Erich Fromm (1955) in *The Sane Society*. Fromm describes a person's "experiencing himself as an alien" and becoming "estranged from himself." These phrases suggest a duality of self that is probably nothing more than a metaphor. One may become alienated from one's culture, but how can one become estranged from himself? Fromm implicitly assumes some ideal human condition, and to be self-estranged is to be something less than one might be if the circumstances of one's life were different. To be insincere, to live in terms of "what other people will think," to live in rigid conformity—these are characteristics of the self-estranged person. Reisman's "other-directed" individual is in this sense self-estranged. Erikson (1964) has called self-estrangement a "loss of one's sense of personal identity" and has interpreted many of the social-action movements of the 1960s as actions of estranged youth in search of identity.

THE SOCIAL-ACTION MOVEMENT AS A SEARCH FOR IDENTITY

There is much in the social-action movements of young people that can be interpreted as a search for identity. Young people are learning that values and knowledge are becoming increasingly relative. They are told that factual data, which used to double in millennia or centuries, are now doubling every decade. Old conceptions are being replaced by newer ones at an ever-faster rate. Students are reminded that much of what they are now learning will be out of date virtually by the time they are ready to use it. Many of the occupations in which they will find employment do not now exist. Rapid social and economic change always contributes to a sense of uncertainty and discontinuity. The social-action movements suggest a restless seeking for a sense of continuity between past, present, and future—a sense of continuity that is considered to be a crucial ingredient of a healthy personality (Gelinean & Kantor, 1964).

A dominant theme in the social-action movements of the 1960s was a search for old or "lost" values. These movements attempted to overcome the uncertainties and diffusion of ideals of the present by a return to earlier values and simpler ways of life. The tremendous appeal of folk music, the return to nature, the revived interest in Thoreau and Rousseau, the glorification of the "noble savage," and a turning to the more contemplative philosophies of the East—all suggest a nostalgia for simpler cultural roots, traditions, and philosophies.

Figure 12-4. A peace march in Washington, D. C.

Many persons engaged in these movements advance an oversimplified, even childlike, view of good and evil. Their magical and omnipotent slogans not only represent oversimplified solutions to social problems but also increase personal commitment, create an exaggerated sense of rightness and invulnerability, and rationalize many forms of behavior that would otherwise be shunned. Public demonstrations, picketing, rituals, and distinctive garb—whether formal uniforms, leather jackets, or hippie attire—all can contribute to the participant's feeling of identity and power. Public pronouncements, press conferences, and TV coverage also can contribute to the individual's feeling of importance. For the individual who has failed to achieve an adequate sense of autonomy, social movements can constitute vehicles for accelerating the breakaway from childhood dependencies with the help of a dedicated peer group.

Many individuals rationalize their search for identity and autonomy by perceiving themselves as acting in the interest of personal ideals, the social good, and the general well-being of mankind. Illegal activities are sometimes justified in terms of a "higher law" or a "greater good." Sincerity of purpose and feeling is contrasted with the social, political, and personal hypocrisy of the adult world. Righteousness may produce a feeling of invulnerability and an assurance of ultimate success. Physical discomforts, self-sacrifice, dramatic renunciation, and even burning oneself to death in public may be perceived as evidence of the intensity of commitment. Such acts may be reminiscent of the asceticism of certain religious orders. The heroic deed may somehow be perceived as imbuing the doer with the power to change the course of world events. Lesser sacrificial deeds may seem to show up the banality and mediocrity of middle-class existence and to be in contrast to the hypocrisies and inconsistencies of the world.

The appeal to sincerity of belief and depth of conviction as an index of "rightness" may represent a return to a belief in an infallible conscience as the proper guide to conduct. One youth group of the 1960s dedicated to social action called itself "Conscience." The ethic of social relativism does not provide a firm basis for adolescents in search of certainties in an unstable and constantly changing world. A return to the belief in an infallible conscience provides this certainty and makes it possible for the individual to sustain and validate his own unique identity and enhance his feeling of individuality and autonomy. However, if each person's conscience is unique, then validating deviant behavior strictly in terms of sincerity of motive and feeling makes each person a law unto himself.

Thus we are presented with the paradox of youth in search of autonomy and individual identity joining up with kindred souls to form groups within which there is great pressure for conformity. Although they reject conformity to values and patterns of the larger society, protest groups often become relentlessly intolerant of unaffiliated youths and of members who lack dedicated commitment or doctrinal purity.

The social-action movements may at times become destructive, but there is evidence that they may have at least short-term effects in reducing crime and mental illness (Solomon & Fishman, 1964; Fishman & Solomon, 1964). Social action perceived as consonant with one's beliefs and social action that provides a redress of grievances may reduce the motivation to act out one's motives in more personally and socially destructive ways. For individuals participating in such movements, the issues of ideological commitment, leadership, and self-certainty and the anticipation of achievement may be at least temporarily solved. Feelings of alienation and exile that result from failure to develop an adequate sense of identity and that at times may lead to delinquency and crime or at other times, to introspection, moodiness, or a kind of existential pessimism, may be alleviated to some degree by the intellectual rationalizations, the personal commitments, impulsive actions, risk taking, and suffering characteristic of certain social action movements.

SUMMARY

Adjustment involves the responses one makes to or the way in which he learns to cope with his feelings, emotions, motives, and environmental circumstances. Adjustment, as such, need not be conceived of as either evaluative or conformative. Thus socially unacceptable behavior—or any other means of coping with the total situation of one's emotions, motives, and circumstances—may be considered adjustive in this broad sense.

Frustration and conflict are part of everyone's life. They can be viewed as responses of an emotional or motivational nature. Means of coping with frustration and conflict, and with the resultant emotional arousal, are acquired through the course of experience. When habits of responding in these situations become well established, they can be termed *behavior mechanisms.*

Personality refers to an individual's unique organization of relatively permanent reaction patterns and characteristics, which influence the way others respond to him. Personality has a primary social reference. It also gives particular weight to the unique characteristics of the individual. Personality has both a stimulus aspect and a response aspect and emphasizes their dynamic interaction.

The determinants of personality are both genetic and environmental, organic and social. The effects of physique on personality are more indirect than direct. The variables determining the effects of infantile deprivation on the later personality structure of humans have still to be worked out. No regular relationships between most specific child-rearing practices and personality development in the offspring have been established. There does seem to be some general relationship between ratings of parental characteristics, such as character structure, maternal role, and maternal conduct toward child, and the child's adjustment.

A person cannot be understood apart from his social history and the nature of the social environment in which he lives. From the moment of birth other people are the most significant segment of the child's environment. Although fairly complex forms of social organization and communication are found in the lower animals, only man has developed a true culture.

Culture refers to the total way of life of a society. It has a particular reference to the accumulated social learnings that are shared and transmitted from one generation to another. Culture provides a number of ready-made solutions to many of life's problems and allows the individual to learn a great deal without endless trial and error. Cultural dictates acquire the force of moral imperatives and become resistant to critical appraisal.

Within any broad culture, there are subcultures, castes, and social classes. Much social behavior is also role dictated. Roles depend on the shared expectancies of ourselves and others. Roles and personality interact, each influencing the other. Conformity-nonconformity to cultural expectancy is an important dimension of social behavior.

Group membership serves important positive functions for the individual, and many forms of personal and social pathology are currently ascribed to social alienation. The five elements, or components, of alienation are feelings of powerlessness, meaninglessness, normlessness, isolation, and self-estrangement. Many of the social-action movements of the 1960s have been interpreted as manifestations of alienated youth in search of a sense of personal identity.

SUGGESTED READINGS

Blum, G. S. *Psychodynamics: The science of unconscious mental forces.* Belmont, Calif.: Brooks/Cole, 1966. This volume focuses on unconscious determinants of behavior, mechanisms of defense, and influence on perception, thought, and action (paperback).

Lawson, R. *Frustration.* New York: Macmillan, 1965. Theories and research on frustration are presented in an interesting fashion in this paperback book.

Sawrey, J. M., & Telford, C. W. *Psychology of adjustment.* (3rd ed.) Boston: Allyn and Bacon, 1971. This introductory text on adjustment presents a comprehensive coverage of the general nature and problems of adjustive behavior. The roles of motivation and learning are emphasized.

Sears, P. S. *In pursuit of self-esteem: Case studies of eight elementary school children.* Belmont, Calif.: Wadsworth, 1964. This paperback is an in-depth study of two teachers and eight children over a two-year period.

Southwell, E. A., & Merbaum, M. (Eds.) *Personality: Readings in theory and research.* (2nd ed.) Belmont, Calif.: Brooks/Cole, 1971. This selection of original articles makes an excellent supplement to this chapter.

Walker, E. L., & Heynes, R. W. *An anatomy for conformity.* Belmont, Calif.: Brooks/Cole, 1967. This book is an account of interdisciplinary research on the problems of conformity and nonconformity.

Zajonc, R. B. *Social psychology: An experimental approach.* Belmont, Calif.: Brooks/Cole, 1966. This book's systematic but interesting account of social psychology keeps close to the available research data. The book is a good supplement to this chapter (paperback).

Appendix: Statistics

This Appendix is designed to present some of the major ideas and processes involved in measurement and statistics. Students of introductory psychology cannot reasonably be expected to master complex statistical processes or inferences involved in using statistics. However, some elementary understanding is imperative in dealing adequately with psychological studies.

DESCRIPTIVE STATISTICS

When extensive data must be dealt with, one must classify or code them in such a way as to make their meaning more readily comprehensible. Simplifying and summarizing statements about groups of data are termed *descriptive statistics.*

Frequency Distributions and their Representations

Raw data may be made more understandable by grouping them in a *frequency distribution.* The raw data supplied in Table A-1 represent scores obtained by individuals taking an achievement test in social studies. The raw scores represent the number of questions answered correctly by each student.

Table A-1. Raw scores.

Student	*Number correct*	*Student*	*Number correct*
A	45	N	44
B	51	O	53
C	23	P	36
D	69	Q	46
E	39	R	32
F	47	S	64
G	42	T	27
H	35	U	46
I	58	V	33
J	43	W	54
K	44	X	47
L	53	Y	41
M	47	Z	56

Some information can be obtained from inspecting the data in Table A-1. For the meaning of these data to stand out a little more clearly, they can be arranged in rank order from highest to lowest, as shown in Table A-2.

Table A-2. Scores in rank order.

69	45
64	44
58	44
56	43
54	42
53	41
53	39
51	36
47	35
47	33
47	32
46	27
46	23

When one inspects Table A-2, one can observe more readily that the highest score obtained was 69 and the lowest score was 23. The student in the middle of the distribution received a score of about 45, and quite a few students scored in the 40s. This table could be made to reflect the nature of the scores more simply by grouping the scores that were fairly close together. With little injustice, the scores can be grouped into intervals of threes, and a tally of the number of persons scoring in that interval can be made, as in Table A-3.

Table A-3. Scores grouped and tallied.

Score interval	*Number of persons in the interval*
68-70	1
65-67	0
62-64	1
59-61	0
56-58	2
53-55	3
50-52	1
47-49	3
44-46	5
41-43	3
38-40	1
35-37	2
32-34	2
29-31	0
26-28	1
23-25	1

The number of intervals into which a distribution of raw scores is grouped depends on the problem being investigated and the amount of consolidation of scores necessary to make the meaning stand out more clearly.

Sometimes a frequency distribution can be made more understandable if it is presented graphically. Using the same data as were used in Table A-3, a *frequency histogram* can be constructed, as in Figure A-1. Histograms are constructed by drawing rectangles whose bases are given by the class interval and whose heights are determined by the number of cases scoring in that interval. Such data also may be presented in the form of a *frequency polygon,* as in Figure A-2. By plotting the number of cases scoring in a class interval as if all cases in the interval scored at the center, and by connecting the points thus obtained, a frequency polygon can be constructed. If one extra class interval is added to each end of the distribution, both ends of the plotted line

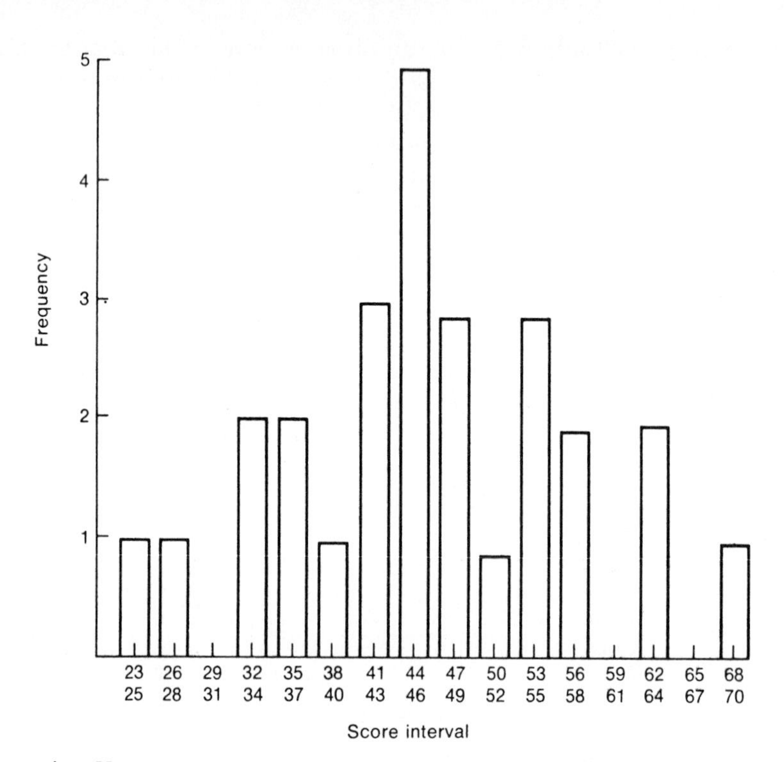

Figure A-1. Histogram showing test-score frequencies.

will come back to the base line to make the polygon complete (since no one obtained scores for either the lowest or highest interval employed, the plotted line will drop to zero). Whether one uses a table, a frequency histogram, or a frequency polygon to depict data is a matter of which form will present the data most understandably. Figures A-1 and A-2 presumably would be more symmetrical and less variable if there were more cases in the distribution; however, they are probably illustrative of many distributions of limited numbers of measures, and the distribution does approach "normalcy."

The various measures of central tendency are indicators of the middle of the distribution around which other scores tend to cluster. In a perfectly normal or symmetrical distribution of scores, the mode, median, and mean will be identical. In such distributions the most frequently occurring score (*mode*), the place in the distribution above which and below which 50 percent of the cases fall (*median*), and the average (*mean*) are all represented by the same number (see Figure A-3).

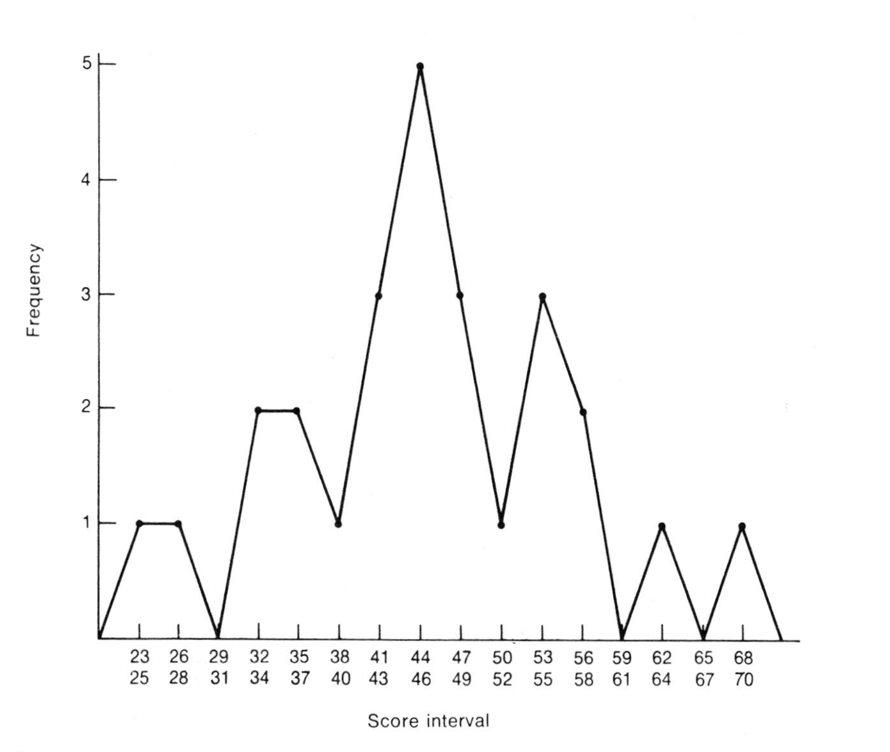

Figure A-2. Polygon showing test-score frequencies.

Many distributions are not perfectly symmetrical. Asymmetrical distributions obtained by psychologists often, but not always, indicate unrepresentative samples. An asymmetrical distribution of scores is said to be *skewed*. That is, more individuals tend to score closer to one end of the distribution than to the other. In this case, the various measures of central tendency will not be identical (see Figure A-3). For example, if a distribution of the grades obtained on a

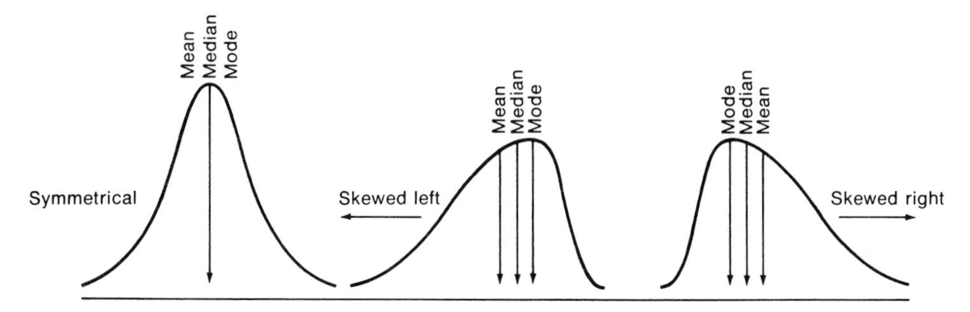

Figure A-3. Normal and skewed distributions.

series of tests taken by a class of less than average ability were to be plotted, the most frequently occurring grades would be those at the lower end of the distribution, with a few *B*s and very few *A*s. These data would tend to be skewed to the right, or *negatively* skewed. If the scores obtained on the same tests taken by a class of superior students were to be plotted, there would be a preponderance of *B*s and *A*s, with a lesser number of individuals scoring in the lower part of the distribution. This distribution would be skewed left, or *positively* skewed. The direction of skewness is designated by the direction in which the longest tail of the distribution curve is found. When distribtuions are skewed, differences will exist among the measures of central tendency. Since statistical procedures are employed to make the meaning of the data stand out more clearly, the selection of the measure of central tendency to be used with skewed distributions may cause certain interpretations of data to be more likely than others.

Suppose that management and labor are attempting to agree on a wage raise. If the industry has a small number of unskilled laborers, few skilled workers, and a number of highly paid specialists and executives, the distribution of income will be skewed to the left, and the *modal* income will be higher than either the *median* or *mean*. In such an instance the meaning of the data that management and labor want reflected by the measure of central tendency is likely to differ, and each group may choose to use the one that is the more favorable to its position.

An important consideration in choosing a measure of central tendency has to do with whether or not one wants the measure to reflect the influence of extreme scores. In computing the median, the absolute difference between the scores of individuals is ignored. An extremely high score or an extremely low score in a distribution is simply counted as a single score and does not affect the median. Thus, if one is dealing with a relatively small number of scores, and there are scores that are much larger or smaller than the majority of scores, the most appropriate measure is probably the median. However, if one wishes for the extreme score values to be reflected in the size of the measure employed, the mean should be selected because it will reflect this influence. The mean should be chosen as a measure of central tendency when the distribution contains a large number of fairly evenly distributed scores or when it is desirable to have extreme values reflected in the measure taken.

Measures of Variation

In describing or summarizing data, their meaning can be made clearer if, in addition to knowing what the mean, median, or mode is, we have some knowledge of how the data are distributed around the measures of central tendency. Measures of variability reflect the distribution of scores.

A very simple measure of variability (one that has no reference to central tendency) is known as the *range*. The range is simply the score distance between the lowest and highest measures. In the case of the students' test scores, the highest score obtained was 69 and the lowest 23. If the lower is subtracted from the higher score, the difference is 46. The range is then 46 + 1, or 47, because both the lower and higher scores were obtained by someone in the sample. This simple measure gives us the distance between the lowest and highest scores obtained and adds to our understanding of the data.

Other descriptions and summarizations of a simple sort can yield information relative to distributions of scores. *Percentile scores* can be assigned to different values in a distribution. The point in a distribution below which a given percent of the cases fall can be determined fairly readily. We recall that we calculated the median by counting up into a ranked distribution of scores until we reached 50 percent of the cases. We could count up into the distribution any given percent of the cases and determine the score value for it in the same way. In our distribution of scores in Table A-3, the 50th percentile score was 45.3. This is the point below which 50 percent of the cases fall. The 75th percentile in that distribution is 53, and the 25th percentile is 39. By using these latter two percentile scores, we can compute a measure of variation known as *quartile deviation*. If we subtract the 25th percentile score from the 75th percentile score (55 − 39 = 14) and divide by 2, we obtain the quartile deviation (Q = 7). This figure tells us that 50 percent of the cases fall between the median minus seven and the median plus seven, or between 38.3 and 52.3. This measure of variation around the *median* of the distribution gives us a better understanding of the distribution of scores than we could obtain from just a knowledge of the median and range.

Measures of variation are necessary because it is quite possible for two sets of data to have the same mean or median but to be quite different in terms of the way the scores are distributed around that measure. For example, the mean of the three scores 40, 50, and 60 is 50; it is the same as the mean of the three

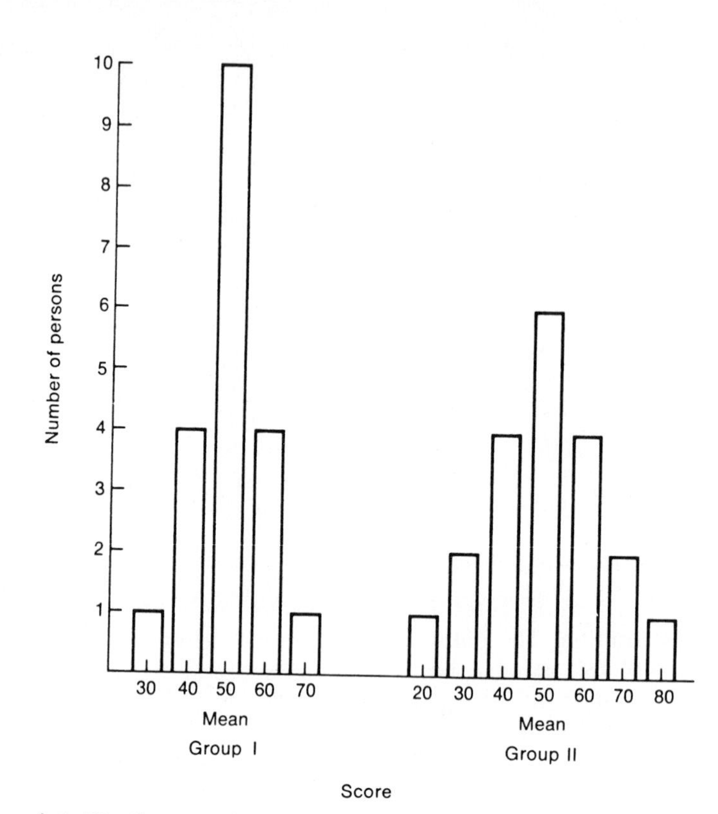

Figure A-4. Distributions of scores with near but differing variability.

scores, 49, 50, and 51, but the variability of scores around that mean is much greater in the first instance, and the shapes of the distributions are different. Figure A-4 contains two distributions with identical means but differing variations. The most widely used measure of variability, indicating how scores are distributed around the mean of the scores, is called the *standard deviation,* the symbol for which is the lowercase Greek letter sigma (σ). The standard deviation represents the distance on either side of the mean that will include approximately 68 percent of the cases in a normal distribution. In calculating σ, one must determine the deviation (D) of each score from the mean and square it. The average of these squares is then obtained. The standard deviation is the square root of this sum of the squares divided by the number of scores. In formula form,

$$\sigma = \sqrt{\frac{\text{sum of } D^2}{N}}.$$

The standard deviation of the distribution of the students' scores (Table A-3) is 10.3. When the mean is 45.36, approximately 68 percent of the scores will fall between $45.36 - 10.3$ and $45.36 + 10.3$. The standard deviation is employed as a part of other statistical processes, such as correlation, and can be used in scaling data. It is a preferred measure of variability because of its stability when measures are taken of comparable groups and because of the equal intervals between scores assigned to deviation from the mean.

Standard deviation may be used as a basis for assigning values to raw scores. Any score based on some multiple of the standard deviation is known as a *standard score.* Many scores used in psychological measurement are based on distance from the mean in terms of standard deviation. Using standard deviation as a base, one can assign the mean some arbitrary value such as 500, 100, or 50, and the standard deviation is given corresponding values of 100, 20, and 10. This procedure does away with negative signs and decimals. If the value of 50 is assigned to the mean, a score 1σ above the mean is 60 $(50 + 10)$, 2σ above the mean is 70, 1σ below the mean 40, 2σ below the mean 30, and so forth. Fractions of σ value are assigned the appropriate proportions of ten. Such scores are called *T scores.*

Distributions of scores are so frequently near enough to normal that a table based on a perfectly normal distribution can be used to indicate the equivalence of certain scores. Table A-4 provides a basis for interpreting one score in terms of another for normal distributions. For example, a score of 39 on our students' test is $.62\sigma$ below the mean. The *T*-score value of this raw score would be 44 and the percentile score (the percent of scores exceeded) 27.

Standard scores, like percentile scores, are assigned to a given raw score in relationship to the set of scores from which it is drawn. Percentile scores give the percentage of the group that is exceeded by a given individual, and standard scores designate the distance, in standard deviations and portions thereof, a given score is from the mean.

Correlation

It is often desirable to know what relationship exists between two sets of scores. Suppose that the students who took the test that was represented in Table A-1 had each taken a test of reading ability and their scores were available. Let us say further that Table A-1 shows the results of a test in a course

Table A-4.

Standard-deviation value	*T score*	*Percentile scores*
3.0	80	99.9
2.5	75	99.4
2.0	70	97.7
1.5	65	93.3
1.0	60	84.1
0.5	55	69.1
0.0	50	50.0
−0.5	45	30.9
−1.0	40	15.9
−1.5	35	6.7
−2.0	30	2.3
−2.5	25	0.6
−3.0	20	0.1

on social studies. It would be interesting to know the relationship between a student's score on a test of reading and his achievement on a social studies test. Do students who score high on the test of reading also tend to score high on the social studies test? Is there no relationship between how one scores on the two tests? Do students who score high on one test tend to score low on the other? Statistical information can be brought to bear on these problems. Indices of how one set of measures varies in relationship to another can be computed. Such procedures are termed correlational procedures. They yield a number termed the *coefficient of correlation*. This correlation coefficient indicates the *degree* of relationship between the variables of concern. Coefficients of correlation may vary from a value of −1 through 0 to +1. If the relationship between the scores is a perfect one (either −1 or +1), we would be able to predict exactly what the score on one test was from knowledge of how a student scored on the other. If the relationship between the scores is perfectly negative (−1), we would predict from a high score on one test an equally low score on the other; if it is perfectly positive (+1), we would predict from a high score on one test an equally high one on the other. If there were no relationship between the two variables (0), we could make no prediction as to a person's score on one test from knowledge of how he scored on the other. Such perfect relationships are seldom found in psychological investigations. Usually some degree of relationship less than perfection (+1.0 or −1.0) is to be found. Therefore, correlations are expressed in proportions of the number 1 expressed as a decimal, with the positive or negative sign attached to indicate the direction of the obtained relationship. The most commonly used method of computing a correlation is the Pearson *product-moment method.* A correlation so obtained is designated r.

Negative coefficients are obtained when correlating age in grade with achievement, or with amount retained with time elapsed since learning or memorization. Positive coefficients are obtained when correlating height and weight, grade in school with achievement, intelligence of parents and children, and a great number of other measures of human attributes and performances. The general tendency is for human abilities to correlate positively with one another.

Because correlation coefficients vary from -1 through 0 to $+1$, there is a temptation to interpret a correlation coefficient as indicating the percent of relationship between the two variables. This interpretation would imply that an r of .50 is twice as large as one of .25, but it is wrong. Actually, an estimate of the percentage of variance that is common to the two variables can be made by squaring the obtained correlation and multiplying it by 100. It can then be seen that an r of .50 accounts for 25 percent of the variance.

The tendency to assume a causal relationship between two variables when they are positively correlated should be avoided. A high correlation between two variables is not sufficient to prove that one thing causes the other. A third or fourth factor might be operative, or the correlation might be attributed to chance. For example, if one were learning to type at the same time that the cost-of-living index was going up, the daily increase in typing speed might be positively correlated with the cost-of-living index! No one would be naive enough to suppose that one factor here was the cause of the other. The correlation would be attributed to chance. As the apparent dependency of the two variables increases, the temptation to assume causality becomes greater. In growing children, weight and school achievement are positively correlated. But when weight and school achievement are correlated for children of the *same age,* the correlation then is reduced to near 0. Thus school achievement is not the cause of weight; neither is weight the cause of school achievement. A third factor, that of age, is operative.

When two sets of data are found to correlate highly, it is *possible* that one factor may be causing the other. The search for causes of relationship is a legitimate psychological concern, and correlation can help. But, alone, it does not tell us the cause of a relationship.

STATISTICAL INFERENCE

Psychologists and other scientists take measures of various kinds and manipulate these measures mathematically to make the possible meaning of the collected data stand out more clearly. Measures of central tendency and measures of variability are calculated to describe the data better. Once these descriptive data are in hand, they can be used in the interpretation of the data. Data are also used in making inferences.

Let us assume that the psychologist wants to determine which of two kinds of problems can be solved more quickly by 12-year-old boys in the public schools. He has limited resources and cannot possibly use *all* the boys who are 12 years old at any given time in seeking the answer to the problem. A reasonable way to proceed is to take a sample of 12-year-old boys and determine if this sample group can solve one problem more readily than the other. When he gets through with his investigation, he will be able to say something about how his sample of boys performed relative to the two problems. He wants to be able to generalize from his data by making inferences about how all 12-year-old boys in the public schools would perform. His inferences relative to how 12-year-old boys in the public schools (*the population*) would perform is based on the performance of the boys whose performance he studied (*the sample*). Let us assume that he had a sample of 200 boys. If he were to take successive samples of 200 boys, we would not expect that the *mean* time used to solve each of the problems would be identical for each successive group. We would expect slightly different results to be obtained for each of several samples of 200 boys. These obtained differences could be attributable to *errors of sampling*. We would not expect that a perfectly representative sample (representative of the entire population of 12-year-old boys in the public schools) would be obtained by drawing one sample of 200 boys from the population of 12-year-olds in the public schools.

Statistical inference deals with the problem of making an inference about some feature of a population based solely on information obtained from a sample of that population. To make statistical inferences from data, we must examine carefully the relationships revealed by the data taken from the sample we have investigated. Inferences must always be made under conditions in which there is an element of uncertainty because of the existence of sampling errors.

Let us assume that the first sample of 200 boys was able to solve the first problem in the mean time of 4 minutes. If successive samples of 200 boys were drawn, we would expect that they would have differing means. What size difference between the first sample and the second sample mean could be expected by chance? An estimate can be made by calculating the *standard error of the mean* (σm). In this calculation the standard deviation and the size of the sample are both given consideration in the formula

$$\sigma M = \frac{\sigma}{\sqrt{N}},$$

where σ is the standard deviation of the distribution of scores and N is the number of cases from which the sample mean is computed. The larger the number of cases in our sample, and the smaller the standard deviation of the sample, the less the uncertainty about the representativeness of the sample we have drawn. The standard error is interpreted as a proportion of the standard deviation of the sample within which the mean of the population is likely to be found. It tells us how representative of the population mean our sample mean may be.

Many psychological experiments are conducted that employ differences or lack of differences obtained as measurements under two different conditions. The question that arises in such situations has to do with whether the obtained difference represents a true difference or if it is simply the result of sampling errors.

The significance of obtained differences can be put to statistical test so that the probability that the obtained difference might have occurred by chance can be stated with some confidence. The computation is dependent on how precise the sample means themselves are (σ_M) and how great the obtained difference is between them. If the scores in the samples are highly variable and the difference between the sample means is small, we have little reason to expect that the population means differ. However, if the scores in each sample show little variability and the difference between the means is large, we may have greater confidence that the population means truly differ.

From the standard error of the means of two samples, we can compute a *standard error of the difference between two means* (σD_M). The obtained difference can then be evaluated by using the *critical ratio,* or ratio of the obtained difference between the means to the standard error of the difference between means. Critical ratio is interpreted in terms of the probability that a ratio this high or higher could have been obtained by chance. A statement—that thus-and-such a difference could have been obtained by chance so many out of 100 times if the population means were identical—is what is obtained. Usually, if it can be said that this difference would occur by chance less than .05 times in 100, the difference is looked on as being representative, and we have confidence in our results. Thus, if statistically significant differences were obtained between the times required for the sample of 200 boys to solve the two different problems, we might assume that the obtained differences represented real differences.

Using variations of the procedures for determining the standard error of the mean or the significance of the difference between means, statements about the reliability of the other statistics can be made. Thus the significance of a correlation, the significance of the difference between percentages, and the significance of the differences between correlations may be stated in terms of probability.

References

CHAPTER 1 THE SUBJECT MATTER OF PSYCHOLOGY

Ammons, C. H., Worchel, P., & Dallenbach, K. M. "Facial vision," the perception of obstacles out-of-doors by blindfolded and blindfolded-deafened subjects. *American Journal of Psychology,* 1953, **66,** 519–553.

Bachrach, A. J. *Psychological research.* New York: Random House, 1962.

Boring, E. G. *A history of experimental psychology.* (2nd ed.) New York: Appleton-Century-Crofts, 1950.

Butler, J. M., & Rice, L. N. *Quantitative naturalistic research.* Englewood Cliffs, N. J.: Prentice-Hall, 1963.

Cochran, W. G., & Cox, G. M. *Experimental designs.* (2nd ed.) New York: Wiley, 1957.

Cotzin, M., & Dallenbach, K. M. "Facial vision": The role of pitch and loudness in the perception of obstacles by the blind. *American Journal of Psychology,* 1950, **63,** 485–515.

Darwin, C. P. *The life and letters of Charles Darwin.* New York: Appleton-Century-Crofts, 1896.

Griffin, D. R., & Galambos, R. Obstacle avoidance by flying bats: The cry of bats. *Journal of Experimental Zoology,* 1942, **89,** 475–490.

Hallowell, A. I. Ojibwa ontology, behavior, and world view. In S. Diamond (Ed.), *Primitive views of the world.* New York: Columbia University Press, 1964.

Hippocrates, *The genuine works of Hippocrates,* Vol. 11. Translated from the Greek by Francis Adams. London: The Sydenham Society, 1869.

Huff, D. *How to lie with statistics.* New York: Norton, 1954.

Hume, D. *Hume's moral and political philosophy* (reprinted from the 1777 ed.). New York: Hafner, 1948.

Madden, E. H. *The structure of scientific thought.* Boston: Houghton Mifflin, 1960.

Minium, E. W. *Statistical reasoning in psychology and education.* New York: Wiley, 1970.

Moser, C. A. *Survey methods in social investigation.* London: Heinemann, 1958.

Myrdal, G. *An American dilemma: The Negro problem and modern democracy.* New York: Harper & Brothers, 1944.

Nagel, E. *The structure of science: Problems in the logic of scientific explanation.* New York: Harcourt, Brace, and World, 1961.

Pearson, K. *Grammar of science.* London: Macmillan, 1911.

Piaget, J. *The child's conception of physical causality.* London: Kegan Paul, 1930.

Silberman, C. E. *Crisis in black and white.* New York: Random House, 1964.

Simpson, D. The dimensions of world poverty. *Scientific American,* 1968, **219,** (5), 27–35.

Supa, M., Cotzin, M., & Dallenbach, K. M. Facial vision: The perception of obstacles by the blind. *American Journal of Experimental Psychology,* 1944, **57,** 133–183.

Telford, C. W., & Sawrey, J. M. *The exceptional individual.* (Rev. Ed.) Englewood Cliffs, N. J.: Prentice-Hall, 1971.

Tocqueville, A. de. *Democracy in America.* New York: Knopf, 1945 ed.

Warren, H. C. *A history of the association psychology.* New York: Scribner's, 1921.

Worchel, P., & Dallenbach, K. M. Facial vision: Perception of obstacles by the deaf-blind. *American Journal of Psychology,* 1947, **60,** 502–553.

Worchel, P., Mauney, J., & Andrews, J. G. The perception of obstacles by the blind. *Journal of Experimental Psychology,* 1950, **40,** 746–751.

Worchel, P., & Mauney, J. The effects of practice on the perception of obstacles by the blind. *Journal of Experimental Psychology,* 1951, **41,** 170–176.

CHAPTER 2 THE BIOLOGICAL BASIS OF HUMAN BEHAVIOR

Begleiter, H., & Platz, A. Evoked potentials: Modifications by classical conditioning. *Science,* 1969, **166,** 769–771.

Ewert, P. H. A study of the effect of inverted stimulation upon spatially coordinated behavior. *Genetic Psychological Monographs,* 1930, **7,** 177–363.

Fetz, E. E. Operant conditioning of cortical unit activity. *Science,* 1969, **163,** 555–557.

Fox, S. S., & Rudell, A. P. Operant controlled neural event: Formal and systematic approach to electrical coding of behavior in the brain. *Science,* 1968, **162,** 1299–1302.

Furshpan, E. J., & Potter, D. D. Transmission at the giant synapses of the crayfish. *Journal of Physiology,* 1959, **145,** 289–325.

Glaser, G. H. (Ed.), *EEG and behavior.* New York: Basic Books, 1963.

Gouras, P. Trichromatic mechanisms in single cortical neurons. *Science,* 1970, **168,** 489–492.

Harlow, F., & Harlow, M. K. Learning to love. *American Scientist,* 1966, **54,** 244–272.

Held, J., & Bossom, J. Neonatal deprivation and adult rearrangement. *Journal of Comparative and Physiological Psychology,* 1961, **54,** 33–37.

Held, R., & Freedman, S. J. Plasticity in human sensorimotor control. *Science,* 1963, **142,** 455–462.

Hyvärinen, J., Sakata, H., Talbot, W. H., & Mountcastle, V. B. Neuronal coding by cortical cells of the frequency of oscillating peripheral stimuli. *Science,* 1968, **162,** 1130.

Jacobson, M. Development of specific neuronal connections. *Science,* 1969, **163,** 543–547.

James, W. *Psychology: The briefer course.* New York: Holt, 1892.

Jasper, H. Reticular-cortical systems and theories of the integrative action of the brain. In H. F. Harlow & C. N. Woolsey (Eds.), *Biological and biochemical bases of behavior.* Madison: University of Wisconsin Press, 1958.

John, E. R., Shimakochi, M., & Bartlett, F. Neural readout from memory during generalization. *Science,* 1969, **164,** 1534–1536.

Kennedy, D., Selverston, A. I., & Remler, M. P. Analysis of restricted neuronal networks. *Science,* 1969, **164,** 1488–1496.

Komisaruk, B. R., & Olds, J. Neuronal correlates of behavior in freely moving rats. *Science,* 1968, **161,** 811–812.

Konishi, M. Hearing, single-unit analysis and vocalization in songbirds. *Science,* 1969, **166,** 1178–1180.

Lassek, A. M. *The human brain: From primitive to modern.* Springfield, Ill.: Thomas, 1957.

Levine, M. Human discrimination learning: The subset-sampling assumption. *Psychological Bulletin,* 1970, **74,** 397–404.

Lindsley, D. B. Attention, consciousness, sleep, and wakefulness. In J. Field (Ed.), *Handbook of physiology,* Section I, Neurophysiology. Vol. III. Baltimore: Williams and Wilkins, 1960. 1553–1593.

MacRae, A. W. Channel capacity in absolute judgment tasks. *Psychological Bulletin,* 1970, **73,** 112–121.

Morgan, C. T. *Physiological psychology.* (3rd ed.) New York: McGraw-Hill, 1965.

Munn, N. L. *Psychology.* (5th ed.) Boston: Houghton Mifflin, 1966.

Penfield, W. *The excitable cortex in conscious man.* Springfield, Ill.: Thomas, 1958.

Penfield, W., & Jasper, H. H. *Epilepsy and the functional anatomy of the human brain.* Boston: Little, Brown, 1954.

Penfield, W., & Roberts, L. *Speech and brain-mechanisms.* Princeton, N. J.: Princeton University Press, 1959.

Phillips, M. I., & Olds, J. Unit activities: Motivation—dependent responses from midbrain neurons. *Science,* 1969, **165,** 1269–1291.

Pomeranz, B., & Chung, S. H. Dendritic-tree anatomy codes form vision physiology in tadpole retina. *Science,* 1970, **170,** 983–984.

Quastler, H. (Ed.) *Information-theory in psychology: Problems and methods.* Glencoe, Ill.: Free Press, 1955.

Robinson, D. A. Eye movement control in primates. *Science,* 1968, **161,** 1219–1224.

Scott, J. P. *Early experience and the organization of behavior.* Belmont, Calif.: Brooks/Cole, 1968.

Smith, N. S., & Coons, E. E. Temporal summation and refractoriness in hypothalamic reward neurons as measured by self-stimulation behavior. *Science,* 1970, **169,** 782–784.

Sperry, R. W. Mechanisms of neural maturation. In S. S. Stevens (Ed.), *Handbook of experimental psychology.* New York: Wiley, 1951.

Sperry, R. W. Physiological plasticity and brain circuit theory. In H. F. Harlow & C. N. Woolsey (Eds.), *Biological and biochemical bases of behavior.* Madison: University of Wisconsin Press, 1958.

Sperry, R. W. Cerebral organization and behavior. *Science,* 1961, **33,** 1749–1757.

Stevens, S. S. Neural events and the psychophysical law. *Science,* 1970, **170,** 1043–1050.

Stratton, G. M. Vision without inversion of the retinal image. *Psychological Review*, 1897, **4**, 341–360, 463–481.

Wehmer, F. Effects of prior experience with objects on maternal behaviors in the rat. *Journal of Comparative and Physiological Psychology*, 1965, **60**, 294–296.

CHAPTER 3 PERCEPTUAL PROCESSES: I. GENERAL ASPECTS

Abrahamson, I. G., & Levitt, H. Statistical analysis of data from experiments in human signal detection. *Journal of Mathematical Psychology*, 1969, **6**, 391–417.

Adrian, E. D. *The basis of sensation*. London: Christophers, 1928.

Ashley, W. R., Harper, R. S., & Runyon, D. L. The perceived size of coins in normal and hypnotically induced economic states. *American Journal of Psychology*, 1951, **64**, 564–572.

Bruner, J. S., & Goodman, C. C. Value and need as organizing factors in perception. *Journal of Abnormal and Social Psychology*, 1947, **13**, 33–44.

Burtt, H. E. *Psychology of advertising*. Boston: Houghton Mifflin, 1938.

Chapanis, A. *Man-machine engineering*. Belmont, Calif.: Wadsworth, 1965.

Chomsky, N. *Aspects of the theory of syntax*. Cambridge Mass.: MIT Press, 1965.

Djupesland, G. Electromyography of the tympanic muscles in man. *International Audiology*, 1965, **4**, 34–41.

Edwards, W., Lindman, H., & Savage, J. J. Bayesian statistical inference for psychological research. *Psychological Review*, 1963, **70**, 193–242.

Estes, W. K. Probability learning. In A. W. Melton (Ed.), *Categories of human learning*. New York: Academic Press, 1964.

Fieandt, K. von. *The world of perception*. Homewood, Ill.: Dorsey Press, 1966.

Fitts, P. M., & Posner, M. I. *Human performance*. Belmont, Calif.: Brooks/Cole, 1967.

Freeman, R. B. Perspective determinants of visual size-constancy in binocular and monocular cats. *American Journal of Psychology*, 1968, **81**, 67–73.

Fuster, J. M. Subcortical effects of stimulation of brain stem on tachistoscopic perception. *Science*, 1958, **127**, 150.

Gibson, E. J. *Principles of perceptual learning development*. New York: Appleton-Century-Croft, 1969.

Gibson, E. J. The development of perception as an adaptive process. *American Scientist*, 1970, **58**, 98–108.

Gibson, E. J., & Walk, D. R. The "visual cliff." *Scientific American*, 1960, **202,** 64–71.

Gregory, R. L. Visual illusions. *Scientific American*, 1968, **219,** 66–76.

Hernandez-Péon, R., Scherrer, H., & Jauvet, M. Modification of electrical activity in cochlear nucleus during "attention" in unanesthetized cats. *Science*, 1956, **123,** 331–332.

Holway, A. N., & Boring, E. G. Determinants of apparent visual size with distance variant. *American Journal of Psychology*, 1941, **54,** 21–37.

Hubel, D. H., Henson, C. O., Rupert, A., & Galambos, G. Attention units in the auditory cortex. *Science*, 1959, **129,** 1279–1280.

Ittelson, W. H. *Visual space perception.* New York: Springer, 1960.

Kintsch, W. *Memory, learning, and conceptual processes.* New York: Wiley, 1970.

Lashley, K. S., and Russell, J. T. The mechanisms of vision. XI. A preliminary test of innate organization. *Journal of Genetic Psychology*, 1934, **45,** 136–144.

Leibowitz, H., Brislin, R., Perlmutter, L., & Hennessy, R. Ponzo perspective illusion as a manifestation of space perception. *Science*, 1969, **166,** 1174–1176.

Lenneberg, E. H. On explaining language. *Science*, 1969, **164,** 635–643.

Müller, J. The doctrine of the specific energies of nerves. In W. Dennis, (Ed.), *Readings in the history of psychology.* New York: Appleton, 1948. Originally published in Germany in 1838.

Munn, N. L. *Psychology.* (5th ed.) Boston: Houghton Mifflin, 1966.

Pecan, E. V., & Schvaneveldt, R. W. Probability learning as a function of age, sex, and type of constraint. *Developmental Psychology*, 1970, **2,** 384–388.

Scott, J. P. *Early experience and the organization of behavior.* Belmont, Calif.: Brooks/Cole, 1968.

Skinner, B. F. *Verbal behavior.* New York: Appleton-Century-Crofts, 1957.

Stacey, B., & Pike, R. Apparent size, apparent depth, and the Müller-Lyer illusion. *Perception and Psychophysics*, 1970, **7,** 125–128.

Strong, E. K. *Research Bulletin.* New York: Association of National Advertisers, 1915.

Thompson, R. F., Mayers, K. S., Robertson, R. T., & Patterson, C. J. Number coding in association cortex in the cat. *Science*, 1970, **168,** 271–273.

Walk, R. D. The study of visual depth and distance perception in animals. In D. S. Lehrman, R. A. Hinde, & E. Shaw (Eds.), *Advances in the study of behavior*, Vol. I. New York: Academic Press, 1965. Pp. 99–154.

Wheeler, R. H. *The science of psychology.* New York: Crowell, 1940.

White, B. L. Child development research: An edifice without a foundation. *Merrill-Palmer Quarterly*, 1969, **15**, 49–70.

Wispe, L. G., & Drambarean, N. C. Physiological needs, word frequency, and visual deviation thresholds. *Journal of Experimental Psychology*, 1953, **46**, 25–31.

Witkin, H. A. Origins of cognitive style. In C. Sheerer (Ed.), *Cognition: Theory, research, promise.* New York: Harper & Row, 1964.

Young, P. T. Auditory localization with acoustical transposition of the ears. *Journal of Experimental Psychology*, 1928, **11**, 399–429.

CHAPTER 4 PERCEPTUAL PROCESSES: II. A MORE ANALYTICAL VIEW

Békésy, G. von. *Experiments in hearing.* New York: McGraw-Hill, 1960.

Békésy, G. von. The ear. In S. Coopersmith (Ed.), *Frontiers of psychological research.* San Francisco: Freeman, 1966.

Best, C. H., & Taylor, N. B. *The physiological basis of medical practice.* Baltimore: Williams and Wilkins, 1955.

Bredberg, G., Lindeman, H. H., Ader, H. W., & West, R. Scanning electron microscopy of the organ of Corti. *Science*, 1970, **170**, 861–863.

Clark, B., & Graybiel, A. Factors contributing to the delay in the perception of the oculogyral illusion. *American Journal of Psychology*, 1966, **79**, 377–388.

DeValois, R. L., & Jacobs, G. H. Primate color vision. *Science*, 1968, **166**, 533–540.

Frank, M., & Pfaffmann, C. Taste nerve fibers: A random distribution of sensitivities to four tastes. *Science*, 1969, **164**, 1183–1185.

Geldard, F. A. *The human senses.* New York: Wiley, 1953.

Gouras, P. Trichromatic mechanisms in single cortical neurons. *Science*, 1970, **168**, 489–491.

Granit, R. *Receptors and sensory perception.* New Haven, Conn.: Yale University Press, 1955.

Granit, R. Neural activity in the retina. In *Handbook of physiology.* Vol. 1. Washington, D. C.: American Physiological Society, 1959.

Hartley, S. H. *Principles of perception.* New York: Harper & Row, 1969.

Hirsch, H. V. B., and D. N. Spinelli. Visual experience modifies distribution of horizontally and vertically oriented receptive fields in cats. *Science,* 1970, **168,** 869–871.

Ittelson, W. H. *Visual Space perception.* New York: Springer, 1960.

Kimble, G. A., & Garmezy, N. *Principles of general psychology.* (2nd ed.) New York: Ronald Press, 1963.

Marler, P. Animal communication signals. *Science,* 1967, **157,** 769–774.

Marsh, J. T., Worden, F. G., & Smith, J. C. Auditory frequency-following response: Neural or artifact. *Science,* 1970, **169,** 1222–1223.

McDermott, W. P. Size perception in the presence of individual cues for distance. *Journal of General Psychology,* 1969, **81,** 189–202.

Morgan, C. T. *Physiological psychology.* (3rd ed.) New York: McGraw-Hill, 1965.

Pantle, A., & Sekuler, R. Size-detecting mechanisms in human vision. *Science,* 1968, **102,** 1146–1148.

Pearlman, A. L., & Daw, N. W. Opponent color cells in the cat lateral geniculate nucleus. *Science,* 1970, **167,** 84–86.

Pfaffmann, C. The sense of taste. In J. Field, H. W. Magoun, & V. E. Hall (Eds.), *Handbook of physiology,* Vol. I. Washington, D. C.: American Physiological Society, 1959.

Rose, J. E., Greenwood, D. D., Goldberg, J. M., & Hind, J. E. Some discharge characteristics of single neurons in the inferior colliculus of the cat. *Journal of Neurophysiology,* 1963, **26,** 294–320.

Rushton, W. A. H. Visual pigments in man. *Scientific American,* 1962, **207,** 120–132.

Sternbach, R. A. Congenital insensitivity to pain, a critique. *Psychological Bulletin,* 1963, **60,** 183–192.

Thompson, R. F. *Foundations of psychological psychology.* New York: Harper & Row, 1967.

Thompson, R. F., Mayers, K. S., Robertson, R. T., & Patterson, C. J. Number coding in the association cortex in the cat. *Science,* 1970, **168,** 271–273.

Tiorentini, A., & Maffei, L. Electrophysiological evidence for disparity detectors in human visual system. *Science,* 1970, **169,** 208–209.

Walk, R. D. Monocular compared to binocular depth perceptions in human infants. *Science,* 1968, **162,** 473–475.

Wall, P. D. Cord cells responding to touch, damage, and temperature of skin. *Journal of Neurophysiology,* 1960, **23,** 197–210.

Young, P. T. Auditory localization with acoustical transposition of the ears. *Journal of Experimental Psychology,* 1928, **11,** 399–429.

CHAPTER 5 ELEMENTARY LEARNING

Azrin, N. H., Holz, W. C., & Hake, D. F. Fixed-ratio punishment. *Journal of the Experimental Analysis of Behavior,* 1963, **6,** 141–148.

Bass, B. Gradients in response percentages as indices of non-spatial generalization. *Journal of Experimental Psychology,* 1958, **56,** 278–281.

Boe, E. E. Extinction as a function of intensity of punishment, amount of training, and reinforcement of a competing response. *Canadian Journal of Psychology,* 1964, **18,** 328–342.

Boe, E. E., & Church, R. M. Permanent effects of punishment during extinction. *Journal of Comparative and Physiological Psychology,* 1967, **63,** 486–492.

Boe, E. E., & Church, R. M. *Punishment: Issues and experiments.* New York: Appleton-Century-Crofts, 1968.

Byrne, W. F., et al. Memory transfer. *Science,* 1966, **153,** 658.

Corning, W. C., & John, E. R. Effects of ribonuclease on retention of conditioned planarians. *Science,* 1961, **134,** 1363–1365.

Cowles, J. T. Food-tokens as incentives for learning by chimpanzees. *Comparative Psychology Monographs,* 1937, **14,** 1–96.

D'Amato, M. R. Transfer of secondary reinforcement across the hunger and thirst drives. *Journal of Experimental Psychology,* 1955, **49,** 352–356.

Day, L. M., & Bentley, M. A note on learning in the paramecium. *Journal of Animal Behavior,* 1911, **1,** 167.

Eriksen, S. C. The relative effect of a cerebral lesion upon learning, retention, and transfer. *Journal of Comparative Psychology,* 1939, **27,** 373–391.

Estes, W. K. An experimental study of punishment. *Psychological Monographs,* 1944, **57** (3, Whole No. 263).

Ferster, C. B., & Skinner, B. F. *Schedules of reinforcement.* New York: Appleton-Century-Crofts, 1957.

Finch, G., & Culler, E. Higher order conditioning with constant motivation. *American Journal of Psychology,* 1934, **46,** 596–602.

Gaito, J. DNA and RNA as memory molecules. *Psychological Review,* 1963, **70,** 471–480.

Greenspoon, J., & Foreman, S. Effect of delay of knowledge of results on learning a motor task. *Journal of Experimental Psychology,* 1956, **51,** 226–228.

Grice, G. R. The relation of secondary reinforcement to delayed reward in visual discrimination learning. *Journal of Experimental Psychology,* 1948, **38,** 1–16.

Grice, G. R., & Saltz, E. The generalization of an instrumental response to stimuli varying in the size dimension. *Journal of Experimental Psychology,* 1950, **40,** 702–708.

Halas, E. S., James, R. T., & Knutson, C. L. An attempt at classical conditioning in the planarian. *Journal of Comparative and Physiological Psychology,* 1962, **55,** 969–971.

Hatry, A. L., Keith-Lee, P., & Morton, W. J. Planaria: Memory transfer through cannibalism reexamined. *Science,* 1964, **146,** 274–275.

Hilgard, E. R., & Campbell, A. A. The course of acquisition and retention of conditioned eyelid responses in man. *Journal of Experimental Psychology,* 1936, **19,** 227–247.

Hilgard, E. R., & Marquis, D. H. *Conditioning and learning.* New York: Appleton-Century-Crofts, 1940.

Hovland, C. I. The generalization of conditioned responses: I. The sensory generalization of conditioned responses with varying frequencies of tone. *Journal of General Psychology,* 1937, **17,** 125–148.

Hudgins, C. V. Conditioning and the voluntary control of the pupillary light reflex. *Journal of Genetic Psychology,* 1933, **8,** 3–51.

Hutt, P. J. Rate of bar-pressing as a function of quality and quantity of food reward. *Journal of Comparative and Physiological Psychology,* 1954, **47,** 235–239.

Jacobson, A. L. Learning in flatworms and annelids. *Psychological Bulletin,* 1963, **60,** 74–94.

Kamin, L. J. The delay of punishment gradient. *Journal of Comparative and Physiological Psychology,* 1959, **52,** 434–437.

Kanfer, F. H. The effect of partial reinforcement on acquisition and extinction of a class of verbal responses. *Journal of Experimental Psychology,* 1954, **48,** 424–432.

Karsh, E. B. Effects of number of rewarded trials and intensity of punishment on running speed. *Journal of Comparative and Physiological Psychology,* 1962, **55,** 44–51.

Kimble, G. A. *Hilgard and Marquis' conditioning and learning.* (2nd ed.) New York: Appleton-Century-Crofts, 1961.

Kitai, S. T. Generalization between photic and electrical stimulation to the visual system. *Journal of Comparative and Physiological Psychology,* 1966, **61,** 319–324.

Krech, D. The chemistry of learning. *Saturday Review,* Jan. 20, 1968, pp. 48–68.

Lashley, K. S. Brain mechanisms and intelligence. Chicago: University of Chicago Press, 1929.

Long, E. R., Hammack, J. T., & Campbell, B. J. Intermittent reinforcement of operant behavior in children. *Journal of Experimental Analysis of Behavior*, 1959, **1**, 315–339.

Luttges, M., Johnson, T., Buck, C., Holand, J., & McGaugh, J. An examination of "transfer of training" of nucleic acid. *Science*, 1966, **151**, 834–837.

Marquis, D. P. Can conditioned responses be established in the newborn infant? *Journal of Genetic Psychology*, 1930, **39**, 479–492.

McConnell, J. V., Jacobson, A. L., & Kimble, D. P. The effects of regeneration upon retention of a conditioned response in the planarian. *Journal of Comparative and Physiological Psychology*, 1959, **52**, 1–5.

Mednick, S. A., & Freedman, J. L. Stimulus generalization. *Psychological Bulletin*, 1960, **57**, 169–200.

Miller, W. C., & Greene, J. E. Generalization of an avoidance response to varying intensities of sound. *Journal of Comparative and Physiological Psychology*, 1954, **47**, 136–139.

Morgan, C. T. *Physiological psychology. (3rd ed.) New York: McGraw-Hill*, 1965.

Myers, W. A., & Trapold, M. A. Two failures to demonstrate superiority of a generalized secondary reinforcer. *Psychonomic Science*, 1966, **5**, 321–322.

Nielsen, H. C., Knight, J. M., & Porter, P. B. Subcortical conditioning, generalization, and transfer. *Journal of Comparative and Physiological Psychology*, 1962, **55**, 168–173.

Pavlov, I. P. *Conditioned reflexes*. London: Oxford University Press, 1927.

Prokasy, W. F. (Ed.) *Classical conditioning: A symposium*. New York: Appleton-Century-Crofts, 1965.

Pryor, G. T., Otis, L. S., & Uyeno, E. Chronic electroshock effects on brain weight, brain chemistry and behavior. *Psychonomic Science*, 1966, **4**, 85–86.

Rachman, S., & Eysenck, H. J. Reply to a "critique and reformulation" of behavior therapy. *Psychological Bulletin*, 1966, **65**, 165–169.

Razran, G. The observable unconscious and the inferable conscious in current Soviet psychophysiology: Interoceptive conditioning, semantic conditioning, and the orienting reflex. *Psychological Review*, 1961, **68**, 81–147.

Razran, G. Russian physiologists' psychology and American experimental psychology: A historical and a systematic collation and a look into the future. *Psychological Bulletin*, 1965, **63**, 42–64.

Rock, R. T., Jr. The influence upon learning of the quantitative variation of aftereffects. *Teachers College, Columbia: Contributions to Education*, 1935, No. 650.

Rosenzweig, M. R., Bennett, E. L., & Krech, D. Cerebral effects of environmental complexity and training among adult rats. *Journal of Comparative and Physiological Psychology*, 1964, **57**, 438–439.

Saltzman, J. J. Maze learning in the absence of primary reinforcement: A study of secondary reinforcement. *Journal of Comparative and Physiological Psychology,* 1949, **42,** 161–172.

Sanford, F. H. *Psychology: A scientific study of man.* (2nd ed.) Belmont, Calif.: Brooks/Cole, 1965.

Sawrey, W. L., Conger, J. J., & Turrell, R. B. An experimental investigation of the role of psychological factors in the production of gastric ulcers in rats. *Journal of Comparative and Physiological Psychology,* 1956, **49,** 457–461.

Sawrey, W. L., & Sawrey, J. M. UCS effects on ulceration following fear conditioning. *Psychonomic Science,* 1968, **10,** 85–86.

Sawrey, J. M., & Telford, C. W. *Educational psychology.* (3rd ed.) Boston: Allyn and Bacon, 1968.

Skinner, B. F. *The behavior of organisms.* New York: Appleton-Century-Crofts, 1938.

Skinner, B. F. Are theories of learning necessary? *Psychological Review,* 1950, **57,** 193–216.

Smith, K. V. Visual discrimination in the cat: The postoperative effects of removal of the striate cortex upon intensity discrimination. *Journal of Genetic Psychology,* 1937, **51,** 329–369.

Spence, K. W. The role of secondary reinforcement in delayed reward learning. *Psychological Review,* 1947, **54,** 1–8.

Thompson, R. F. *Foundations of physiological psychology.* New York: Harper & Row, 1967.

Thompson, R., & Malin, C. F. The effect of neocortical lesions on retention of a successive brightness discrimination in rats. *Journal of Comparative and Physiological Psychology,* 1961, **54,** 326–328.

Thompson, R., & McConnell, J. V. Classical conditioning in the planarian, *Dugesia dorotocephala. Journal of Comparative and Physiological Psychology,* 1955, **48,** 65–68.

Thorndike, E. L. *Animal intelligence: Experimental studies.* New York: Macmillan, 1911.

Walters, R. H., & Demkow, L. Timing of punishment as a determinant of response inhibition. *Child Development,* 1963, **34,** 207–214.

Walters, R. W., Parks, R. D., & Cane, V. Timing of punishment and the observation of consequences to others as determinants of response inhibition. *Journal of Experimental Child Psychology,* 1965, **2,** 10–30.

Watson, J. B., & Raynor, R. Conditioned emotional reactions. *Journal of Experimental Psychology,* 1920, **3,** 1–14.

Weinberger, N. M. Effect of detainment on extinction of avoidance responses. *Journal of Comparative and Physiological Psychology,* 1965, **60,** 135–138.

Wike, E. L., & Barrientos, G. Secondary reinforcement and multiple drive reduction. *Journal of Comparative and Physiological Psychology,* 1958, **51,** 640–643.

Wolfe, J. B. Effectiveness of token rewards for chimpanzees. *Comparative Psychology Monographs,* 1936, **60,** 1–72.

CHAPTER 6 LEARNING: THEORY AND PROCESS

Baer, D. M., & Sherman, J. A. Reinforcement control of generalized imitation in young children. *Journal of Experimental Child Psychology,* 1964, **1,** 37–49.

Bandura, A. Social learning through imitation. In M. R. Jones (Ed.), *Nebraska symposium on motivation.* Lincoln: University of Nebraska Press, 1962. Pp. 211–269.

Bandura, A. Influence of models' reinforcement contiguous on the acquisition of imitative responses. *Journal of Personality and Social Psychology,* 1965, **1,** 589–595.

Birch, H. G. The relation of previous experience to insightful problem solving. *Journal of Comparative Psychology,* 1945, **38,** 367–383.

Bruner, J. S. Structures in learning. *NEA Journal,* 1963, **52,** 26–27.

Church, R. M. Transmission of learned behavior between rats. *Journal of Abnormal and Social Psychology,* 1957, **54,** 163–165.

Creelman, M. B. *The experimental investigation of meaning.* New York: Springer, 1966.

Duncan, C. P. Transfer after training with single versus multiple tasks. *Journal of Experimental Psychology,* 1958, **55,** 63–72.

Ellis, H. C. *The transfer of learning.* New York: Macmillan, 1965.

Erickson, S. C. Variability of attack in massed and distributed practice. *Journal of Experimental Psychology,* 1942, **31,** 339–345.

Gagné, R. M. The acquisition of knowledge. *Psychological Review,* 1962, **69,** 355–365.

Gates, A. I. Recitation as a factor in memorizing. *Archives of Psychology,* 1917, **6** (35).

Glaze, J. A. The association value of nonsense syllables. *Journal of Genetic Psychology,* 1928, **35,** 255–269.

Harlow, H. F. The formation of learning sets. *Psychological Review,* 1949, **56,** 51–65.

Harlow, H. F., & Harlow, M. K. Learning to think. *Scientific American,* 1949, **181,** 36–39.

Hull, C. L. The meaningfulness of 320 selected nonsense syllables. American Journal of Psychology, 1933, **45,** 730–734.

Hull, C. L. *Essentials of behavior.* New Haven, Conn.: Yale University Press, 1951.

James, W. *Principles of psychology,* Vol. I. New York: Holt, 1890.

Kendler, H. H., Greenberg, A., & Richman, H. The influence of massed and distributed practice on the development of mental set. *Journal of Experimental Psychology,* 1952, **43,** 21–25.

Kimble, G. A. Performance and reminiscence in motor learning as a function of the degree of distribution of practice. *Journal of Experimental Psychology,* 1949, **39,** 500–510.

Köhler, W. *The mentality of apes.* New York: Harcourt, 1925.

Köhler, W. *Gestalt psychology.* New York: Liveright, 1929.

Lanzetta, J. T., & Kanareff, V. T. The effects of congruent and conflicting social and task feedback on the acquisition of an imitative response. *Journal of Experimental Psychology,* 1961, **62,** 322–328.

Lyon, D. O. The relation of length of material to time taken for learning and optimum distribution of time. *Journal of Educational Psychology,* 1914, **5,** 1–9, 85–91, 155–163.

MacDougal, W., & Smith, W. Some experiments in learning and retention. *British Journal of Psychology,* 1919, **10,** 199.

Madsen, M. C. Distribution of practice and level of intelligence. *Psychological Reports* 1963, **13,** 39–42.

Maltzman, I. On the training of originality. *Psychological Review,* 1960, **67,** 229–242.

McGaugh, J. L., Jennings, R. D., & Thomson, C. W. Effect of distribution of practice on the maze learning of descendants of the Tryon maze bright and maze dull rats. *Psychological Reports,* 1962, **10,** 147–150.

McGeoch, J. A., & Irion, A. L. *The psychology of human learning.* (2nd ed.) New York: McKay 1953.

Miller, N. E., & Dollard, J. *Social learning and imitation.* New Haven, Conn.: Yale University Press, 1941.

Noble, C. E. Emotionality (*e*) and meaningfulness (*m*). *Psychological Reports, 1958,* **4,** 16–17.

Noble, C. E., Stockwell, F. E., & Pryer, M. W. Meaningfulness (*m*) and association value (*a*) in paired associate syllable learning. *Psychological Reports,* 1957, **3,** 441–452.

Osgood, C. E., & Suci, G. J. Factor analysis of meaning. *Journal of Experimental Psychology,* 1955, **50,** 325–338.

Riley, D. A. Rote learning as a function of distribution of practice and the complexity of the situation. *Journal of Experimental Psychology*, 1952, **43,** 88–95.

Sahakian, W. S. *Psychology of learning: Systems, models, and theories.* Chicago: Markham, 1970.

Sanford, E. C. A letter to Dr. Tichener. *Studies on psychology: Tichener commemorative volume*, 1917, **9,** 5–10.

Sawrey, J. M., & Telford, C. W. *Educational psychology.* (3rd ed.) Boston: Allyn and Bacon, 1968.

Skaggs, E. B., & Grossman, S. The optimum number of readings before introducing prompting in verbatim learning. *Archives of Psychology*, 1930, **18,** 5–14.

Skinner, B. F. Reinforcement today. *American Psychologist*, 1958, **13,** 94–99.

Spence, K. W. The differential response in animals to stimuli varying within a single dimension. *Psychological Review*, 1937, **44,** 430–444.

Stimbert, V. E., Schaffer, R. W., & Grimsley, D. L. Acquisition of imitative responses in rats. *Psychonomic Science*, 1966, **5,** 339–340.

Thorndike, E. L. *Educational psychology.* New York: Lemcke and Buechner, 1903.

Thorndike, E. L. *Human learning.* New York: Century, 1931.

Thorndike, E. L., & Woodworth, R. S. The influence of improvement in one mental function upon the efficiency of other functions. *Psychological Review*, 1901, **8,** 247–261, 384–395, 553–564.

Tolman, E. C. *Purposive behavior in animals and men.* New York: Appleton-Century-Crofts, 1932.

Ulrich, J. L. The distribution of effort in learning in the white rat. *Behavioral Monographs*, 1915, **2** (10).

Underwood, B. J., & Schulz, R. *Meaningfulness and verbal learning.* Philadelphia: Lippincott, 1960.

Warden, C. J. The distribution of practice in animal learning. *Comparative Psychology Monographs*, 1923, **1** (3).

Woodrow, H. The effect of type of training upon transference. *Journal of Educational Psychology*, 1927, **18,** 159--172.

CHAPTER 7 RETENTION AND FORGETTING

Adams, H. E., & Lewis, D. J. Electroconvulsive shock, retrograde amnesia, and competing responses. *Journal of Comparative and Psysiological Psychology*, 1962, **55,** 299–301.

Alper T. G. The interrupted task method in studies of selected recall. *Psychological Review*, 1952, **59**, 71–88.

Ammons, R. B., Farr, R. G., Block, E., Newmann E., Dey, M., Marion, R., & Ammons, C. H. Long term retention of perceptual motor skills. *Journal of Experimental Psychology*, 1958, **55**, 318–328.

Atkinson, J. W. The achievement motive and recall of interrupted and completed tasks. *Journal of Experimental Psychology*, 1953, **46**, 381–390.

Bennett, E. L., & Calvin, M. Failure to train planarians reliably. *Neuroscience Research Program Bulletin*, 1964, **2** (4), 3–24.

Broadbent, D. E. A mechanical model for human attention and immediate memory. *Psychological Review*, 1957, **64**, 205–215.

Brown, R. W., & McNeill, D. The "tip-of-the-tongue" phonomenon. *Journal of Verbal Learning and Verbal Behavior*, 1966, **5**, 325–327.

Bugelski, B. R. An attempt to reconcile unlearning and reproductive inhibition. *Journal of Experimental Psychology*, 1948, **38**, 670–682.

Bugelski, B. R., & Cadwallader, T. A. A reappraisal of the transfer and retroaction surface. *Journal of Experimental Psychology*, 1956, **52**, 360–366.

Burtt, H. E. An experimental study of early childhood memory: Final report. *Journal of Genetic Psychology*, 1941, **58**, 435–439.

Buschke, H. Input-output, short-term storage. *Journal of Verbal Learning and Verbal Behavior*, 1968, **7**, 900–903.

Clemes, S. R. Repression and hypnotic amnesia. *Journal of Abnormal and Social Psychology*, 1964, **69**, 62–69.

Coons, E. E., & Miller, N. E. Conflict versus consolidation of memory traces to explain "retrograde amnesia" produced by ECS. *Journal of Comparative and Physiological Psychology*, 1960, **53**, 524–631.

Cranor, K. T. The use of the problem method in college clothing classes. *Journal of Home Economics*, 1931, **23**, 438–441.

Davis, R. A. *Psychology of learning*. New York: McGraw-Hill, 1935.

Duncan, C. P. The retroactive effect of electroshock on learning. *Journal of Comparative and Physiological Psychology*, 1949, **42**, 32–44.

Ebbinghaus, H. *Memory: A contribution to experimental psychology* (1885). Trans. by H. A. Ruger & C. E. Bussenius. New York: Teachers College, Columbia University, 1913.

Edwards, A. L. The retention of affective experiences: A criticism and restatement of the problem. *Psychological Review*, 1942, **49**, 43–53.

Forlano, G. School learning with various methods of practice and rewards. *Teachers College, Columbia, Contributions to Education*, 1936, No. 688.

Gates, A. I. Recitation as a factor in memorizing. *Archives of Psychology,* 1917, **6,** (35).

Geyer, M. T. Influence of changing the expected time of recall. *Journal of Experimental Psychology,* 1930, **13,** 290–292.

Harlow, H. F., Uhling, H., & Maslow, A. H. Comparative behavior of primates: I. Delayed reaction tests on primates from the lemur to the orangutan. *Journal of Comparative Psychology* 1932, **13,** 313–344.

Hebb, D. O. *The organization of behavior.* New York: Wiley, 1949.

Hebb, D. O., & Foord, E. N. Errors of visual recognition and the nature of the trace. *Journal of Experimental Psychology,* 1945, **35,** 335–348.

Hilgard, E. R., Irvine, R. P., & Whipple, J. E. Rote memorization, understanding and transfer: An extension of Katona's card trick experiments. *Journal of Experimental Psychology,* 1953, **46,** 288–292.

Hudspeth, W. J., McGaugh, J. L., & Thomson, C. W. Aversive and amnesic effects of electroconvulsive shock. *Journal of Comparative and Physiological Psychology,* 1964, **57,** 61–64.

Hunter, W. S. The delayed reaction in animals and children. *Behavioral Monographs,* 1913, **2** (1).

Hydén, H. Biochemical changes in glial cells and nerve cells at varying activity. In *Biochemistry of the central nervous system: Proceedings of the Fourth International Congress of Biochemistry,* Vol. III. London: Pergamon, 1959. Pp. 64–89.

Hydén, H., & Egyhâzi, E. Glial RNA changes during a learning experiment in rats. *Proceedings of the National Academy of Science of the United States,* 1963, **49,** 618–624.

Jacobson, A. L., Babich, F. R., Bribash, S., & Jacobson, A. Differential approach tendencies produced by injection of ribonucleic acid from trained rats. *Science,* 1965, **150,** 636–637.

Jenkins, J. G., & Dallenbach, K. M. Oblivescence during sleep and waking. *American Journal of Psychology,* 1924, **35,** 605–612.

Katona, G. *Organizing and memorizing* New York: Hafner, 1940.

Kintsch, W. *Learning, memory and conceptual processes.* New York: Wiley, 1970.

Krueger, W. C. F. The effect of overlearning on retention. *Journal of Experimental Psychology,* 1929, **12,** 71–78.

Krueger, W. C. F. Further studies in overlearning. *Journal of Experimental Psychology,* 1930, **13,** 152–163.

Leavitt, H. F., & Schlosberg, H. The retention of verbal and motor skills. *Journal of Experimental Psychology,* 1944, **34,** 404–417.

Lewis, D. J., & Maher, B. A. Neural consolidation and electroconvulsive shock. *Psychological Review,* 1965, **72,** 225–239.

Lewis, D. J., & Maher, B. A. Electroconvulsive shock and inhibition: Some problems reconsidered. *Psychological Review*, 1966, **73**, 388–392.

Luh, C. W. The conditions of retention. *Psychological Monographs*, 1922, **31** (142).

Madsen, M. C., & McGaugh, J. L. The effect of ECS on one-trial avoidance learning. *Journal of Comparative and Physiological Psychology*, 1961, **54**, 522–523.

McConnell, J. V. Comparative physiology: Learning in invertebrates. *Annual Review of Physiology*, 1966, **28**, 107–136.

McDougall, W. P. Differential retention of course outcomes in educational psychology. *Journal of Educational Psychology*, 1958, **49**, 53–60.

McGaugh, J. L., & Petrinovich, L. F. Neural consolidation and electroconvulsive shock reexamined. *Psychological Review*, 1966, **73**, 382–387.

McGeoch, J. A. The influence of associative value upon the difficulty of nonsense-syllable lists. *Journal of Genetic Psychology*, 1930, **37**, 421–426.

McGeoch, J. A. *The psychology of human learning.* New York: McKay, 1942.

McGeoch, J. A., & Irion, A. L. *The psychology of human learning.* (2nd ed.) New York: McKay, 1952.

McGeoch, J. A., & Melton, A. W. The comparative retention values of maze habits and nonsense syllables. *Journal of Experimental Psychology*, 1929, **12**, 392–414.

Melton, A. W. Implication of short-term memory for a general theory of memory. *Journal of Verbal Learning and Verbal Behavior*, 1963, **2**, 1–21.

Minami, H., & Dallenbach, K. M. The effect upon learning and retention in the cockroach. *American Journal of Psychology* 1946, **59**, 2–58.

Müller, G. E., & Pilzecker, A. Sperimentelle Beitrage zur Lehre vom Gedachtniss. *Zeitschrift für Psychologische Ergebnisse*, 1900, **1**, 1–288.

Munn, N. L. *Handbook of psychological research on the rat.* Boston: Houghton Mifflin, 1950. Pp. 272–278.

Newman, E. B. Forgetting of meaningful material during sleep and waking. *American Journal of Psychology*, 1939, **52**, 65–71.

Osgood, C. E. *Method and theory in experimental psychology.* New York: Oxford University Press, 1956.

Pan, S. Influence of context upon learning and recall. *Journal of Experimental Psychology*, 1926, **9**, 468–491.

Peterson, J. The effect of attitude on immediate and delayed reproduction: A class experiment. *Journal of Educational Psychology*, 1916, **7**, 523–532.

Peterson, L. R. Short-term verbal memory and learning. *Psychological Review*, 1966, **73**, 193–207.

Peterson, L. R., & Peterson, M. J. Short-term retention of individual verbal items. *Journal of Experimental Psychology,* 1959, **58,** 193–198.

Postman, L. The temporal course of proactive inhibition for serial lists. *Journal of Experimental Psychology,* 1962, **63,** 361–369.

Postman, L., & Alper, T. F. Retroactive inhibition as a function of the time of interpolation of the inhibitor between learning and recall. *American Journal of Psychology,* 1946, **59,** 439–449.

Riley, D. A. Memory for form. In L. Postman (Ed.), *Psychology in the making.* New York: Knopf, 162. Pp. 402–465.

Robinson, E. S. The similarity factor in retroaction. *American Journal of Psychology,* 1927, **39,** 297–312.

Seibert, L. C. A series of experiments on the learning of French vocabulary. *Johns Hopkins University Studies in Education,* 1932, No. 18.

Sharp, A. A. An experimental test of Freud's doctrine of the relation of hedonic tone to memory revival. *Journal of Experimental Psychology,* 1938, **22,** 395–418.

Skinner, B. F. Are theories of learning necessary? *Psychological Review,* 1950, **57,** 193–216.

Slamecka, N. J., & Ceraso, J. Retroactive and proactive inhibition of verbal learning. *Psychological Bulletin* 1960, **57,** 449-475.

Spitzer, H. F. Studies in retention. *Journal of Educational Psychology,* 1939, **30,** 641–656.

Swift, E. J. Memory of skillful movements. *Psychological Bulletin,* 1906, **3,** 181–187.

Thisted, M. N., & Remmers, H. H. The effect of temporal set on learning. *Journal of Applied Psychology,* 1932, **16,** 257–268.

Thompson, R., & Dean, W. A. A further study on the retroactive effect of ECS. *Journal of Comparative and Physiological Psychology,* 1955, **48,** 488–491.

Thomson, C. W., McGaugh, J. L., Smith, C. E., Hudspeth, W. J., & Westbrook, W. H. Strain differences in the retroactive effects of electroconvulsive shock on maze learning. *Canadian Journal of Psychology* 1961, **15,** 69–74.

Tinklepaugh, O. L. An experimental study of representative factors in monkeys. *Journal of Comparative Psychology,* 1928, **8,** 197–236.

Titchener, E. B. Relearning after 46 years. *American Journal of Psychology,* 1923, **34,** 468–469.

Towne, B. M. An individual curve of learning: A study in typewriting. *Journal of Experimental Psychology,* 1922, **5,** 79–92.

Tsai, C. A. Comparative study of retention curves for motor habits. *Comparative Psychology Monographs,* 1924, **2** (11).

Tyler, R. Some findings in the field of college biology, *Scientific Education*, 1943, **18**, 133–142.

Tyler, R. W. *Constructing achievement tests.* Columbus: Ohio State University Press, 1934.

Underwood, B. J. *Experimental psychology: An introduction.* New York: Appleton-Century-Crofts, 1949.

Underwood, B. J. Interference and forgetting. *Psychological Review*, 1957, **64**, 49–60.

Ward, A. H., & Davis, R. W. Individual differences in retention of general subject matter in the case of three measurable objectives. *Journal of Experimental Education*, 1938, **7**, 24–30.

Weiss, W., & Margolius, G. The effect of content stimuli on learning and retention. *Journal of Experimental Psychology, 1954,* **48**, 318–322.

Williams, M. Memory studies in electric convulsive therapy. *Journal of Neurology, Neurosurgery, and Psychiatry*, 1950, **13**, 30–35.

Worcester, D. A. Retention after long periods. *Journal of Educational Psychology*, 1923, **14**, 113–114.

Zellar, A. F. Experimental analogue of repression III. *Journal of Experimental Psychology*, 1951, **42**, 32–38.

Zelman, A., Kabot, L., Jacobson, R., & McConnell, J. V. Transfer of training through injection of "conditioned" RNA into untrained worms. *Worm Runner's Digest*, 1963, **5**, 14–21.

Zubin, J., & Barrera, S. E. Effect of electric convulsive therapy on memory. *Proceedings of the Society of Experimental Biology and Medicine*, 1941, **48**, 596–597.

CHAPTER 8 IDEATIONAL PROCESSES

Baum, M. H. Single concept learning as a function of intralist generalization. *Journal of Experimental Psychology*, 1954, **47**, 89–94.

Beck, E. C., & Doty, R. W. Conditioned flexion reflexes acquired during combined catalepsy and de-efferentation. *Journal of Comparative and Physiological Psychology*, 1957, **50**, 211–216.

Bourne, L. E., Jr. *Human conceptual learning*. Boston: Allyn and Bacon, 1966.

Covington, M. V., & Crutchfield, R. S. Experiments in the use of programmed instruction for the facilitation of creative problem solving. *Programmed Instruction* (January 1965). Pamphlet.

Dement, W. The effects of dream deprivation. *Science,* 1960, **131,** 1705–1707.

Dewey, J. *How we think.* Boston: Heath 1933.

Duncker, K. On problem-solving. *Psychological Monographs, 1945,* **55,** 111–113.

Ewert, P. H. Eye movements during reading and recall. *Journal of General Psychology,* 1933, **8,** 65–84.

Flavell, J. H. *The developmental psychology of Jean Piaget.* New York: Van Nostrand, 1963.

Foulkes, D. *The psychology of sleep.* New York: Scribner's, 1966.

Gagné, R. M., & Smith, E. C., Jr. A study of the effects of verbalization on problem solving. *Journal of Experimental Psychology,* 1962, **63,** 12–18.

Getzels, J. W., & Jackson, P. W. *Creativity and intelligence.* New York: Wiley, 1962.

Guilford, J. P. Intellectual factors in productive thinking. In M. J. Aschner & C. E. Bish (Eds.), *Productive thinking in education.* Washington, D. C.: National Education Association, 1965.

Heidbreder, E. The attainment of concepts. *Journal of Psychology,* 1949, **27,** 263–309.

Hull, C. L. Quantitative aspects of the evolution of concepts. *Psychological Monographs,* 1920, **28** (Whole No. 123).

Inhelder, B., & Piaget, J. *The growth of logical thinking from childhood to adolescence.* New York: Basic Books, 1958.

Jacobson, E. Electrophysiology of mental activities. *American Journal of Psychology,* 1932, **44,** 677–694.

Kales, A. Dream deprivation: An experimental reappraisal. *Nature,* 1964, **204,** 1337–1338.

Kintsch, W. *Learning, memory and conceptual processes.* New York: Wiley, 1970.

MacKinnon, D. W. The nature and nurture of creative talent. *American Psychologist,* 1962, **17,** 484–495.

Maltzman, I. On the training of originality. *Psychological Review,* 1960, **67,** 229–242.

Max, L. W. Experimental study of the motor theory of consciousness. IV. Action current responses in the deaf during awakening, kinesthetic imagery and abstract thinking. *Journal of Comparative Psychology,* 1937, **24,** 301–344.

Mearns, H. *Creative power: The education of youth in the creative arts.* New York: Dover, 1958.

Mednick, S. The associative basis of the creative process. *Psychological Review,* 1962, **69,** 220–232.

Miller, G. A. Some psychological studies of grammar. *American Psychologist*, 1962, **17**, 748–762.

Morton, J. T. *The distortion of syllogistic reasoning produced by personal connections.* Unpublished doctoral dissertation, Northwestern University, 1942.

Phelan, J. G. Inhibiting effects of attempts to verbalize on attainment and use of complex conjunctive concepts. *Psychological Reports*, 1968, **22**, 785–793.

Piaget, J. The general problems of the psychobiological development of the child. In J. M. Tanner & B. Inhelder (Eds.), *Discussions on child development*, Vol. IV. New York: International Universities Press, 1960.

Piaget, J. Quantification, conservation, and nativism. *Science*, 1968, **162**, 976–979.

Rogers, C. R. Toward a theory of creativity. In H. H. Anderson (Ed.), *Creativity and its cultivation. New York: Harper*, 1959.

Rogers, C. R. Learning to be free. *NEA Journal*, 1963, **52**, 28–31.

Rossman, J. *The psychology of the inventor.* Washington, D. C.: Inventor's Publishing Company, 1931.

Shepp, B. E., Zeaman, D. Discrimination learning of size and brightness by retardates. *Journal of Comparative and Physiological Psychology*, 1966, **62**, 55–59.

Smith, S. M., Brown, H. O., Toman, J. E. P., & Goodman, L. S. The lack of cerebral effects of d. Tubocurarine. *Anesthesiology*, 1947, **8**, 1–14.

Torrance, E. P. *Guiding creative talent.* Englewood Cliffs, N. J.: Prentice-Hall, 1962.

Totten, E. Eye movements during visual imagery. *Comparative Psychology Monographs*, 1935, **11** (3).

Wallas, G. *The art of thought.* New York: Harcourt, 1926.

CHAPTER 9 MEASUREMENT OF ABILITIES

Alper, T. G., & Boring, E. G. Intelligence tests scores of northern and southern white and Negro recruits in 1918. *Journal of Abnormal and Social Psychology*, 1944, **39**, 471–474.

Asher, E. J. The inadequacy of current intelligence tests for testing Kentucky mountain children. *Journal of Genetic Psychology*, 1935, **46**, 480–486.

Barron, F. Originality in relation to personality and intellect. *Journal of Personality*, 1957, **25**, 730–742.

Barron, F. The dream of art and poetry. *Psychology Today*, 1968, **2** (7), 18–23, 66.

Bayley, N. Mental growth in young children. *Yearbook of the National Society for the Study of Education*, 1940, **39**, (II), 11–47.

Bayley, N. Mental development. In C. W. Harris (Ed.), *Encyclopedia of educational research. New York: Macmillan,* 1960. Pp. 817–823.

Bloom, B. S. *Stability and change in human characteristics.* New York: Wiley, 1964.

Boas, F. *Changes in bodily form of descendants of immigrants.* Washington, D. C.: U. S. Senate Document No. 208, 1911.

Bodmer, W. F., & Cavalli-Sforza, L. L. Intelligence and race. *Scientific American,* 1970, **223** (4), 19–29.

Bonsall, M., & Stefflre, R. The temperament of gifted children. *California Journal of Educational Research,* 1955, **6,** 195–199.

Brigham, C. C. *A study of American intelligence.* Princeton, N. J.: Princeton University Press, 1923.

Burks, B. S. The relative influence of nature and nurture upon mental development: A comparative study of foster parent-child resemblance. *Yearbook of the National Society for the Study of Education,* 1928, **27** (I), 219–316.

Burks, B. S., Jensen D. W., & Terman, L. M. *The promises of youth: Follow-up studies of a thousand gifted children (Genetic studies of genius,* Vol. III). Stanford, Calif.: Stanford University Press, 1930.

Conrad, H. S., & Jones, H. E. A second study of familial resemblance in intelligence. *Yearbook of the National Society for the Study of Education,* 1940, **39,** 97–141.

Cooper, R. N., & Zubek, J. P. Effects of enriched and restricted environments on the learning ability of bright and dull rats. *Canadian Journal of Psychology,* 1958, **12,** 159–164.

Dreger, R. M., Miller, K. S. Comparative psychological studies of Negroes and whites in the United States. *Psychological Bulletin,* 1960, **57,** 361–402.

Dreger, R. M., & Miller, K. S. Comparative psychological studies of Negroes and whites in the United States: 1959–65. *Psychological Bulletin, Monograph Supplement,* 1968, **70** (3), part 2.

Garrett, H. E. The SPSSI and racial differences. *American Psychologist,* 1962, **17,** 260–263.

Getzels, J. W., & Jackson, P. W. *Creativity and intelligence.* New York: Wiley, 1962.

Gordon, H. Mental and scholastic tests among retarded children: An inquiry into the effects of schooling on the various tests. *Educational Pamphlets,* 1923, No. 44.

Guilford, J. P. Traits of creativity. In H. H. Anderson (Ed.), *Creativity and its cultivation.* New York: Harper, 1959.

Guilford, J. P., & Merrifield, P. R. *The structure of intellect model: Its uses and implications (Reports from the Psychology Laboratory, No. 24).* Los Angeles: University of Southern California, 1960.

Harvey, O. J., Hoffmeister, J. K., Coates, C., & White, B. J. A partial evaluation of Torrance's test of creativity. *American Educational Research Journal,* 1970, **7,** 359–372.

Hilgard, E. R., & Atkinson, R. C. *Introduction to psychology.* (4th ed.) New York: Harcourt Brace Jovanovich, 1967.

Hobson, J. R. Sex differences in primary mental abilities. *Journal of Educational Research,* 1947, **41,** 126–132.

Honzik, M. P., MacFarlane, J. W., & Allen, C. The stability of mental tests performance between two and eighteen years. *Journal of Experimental Education,* 1948, **17,** 309–324.

Howard, J. L., & Plant, W. T. Psychometric evaluation of an Operation Headstart Program. *Journal of Genetic Psychology,* 1967, **111,** 281–288.

Jensen, A. R. Social class, race, and genetics: Implications for education. *American Educational Research Journal,* 1968, **5,** 1–42.

Jensen, A. R. How much can we boost IQ and scholastic achievement? *Harvard Educational Review,* 1969, **39,** 1–123.

Jones, A. M. An analytical study of one hundred and twenty superior children. *Psychology Clinic,* 1925, **16,** 19–76.

Kelley, T. L. *Interpretation of educational measures, Yonkers, N. Y.: World,* 1927. Pp. 28–29.

Kidd, J. W. Toward a more precise definition of mental retardation. *Mental Retardation,* 1964, **2,** 209–212.

Klineberg, O. *Negro intelligence and selective migration.* New York: Columbia University Press, 1935.

Kuder, G. F., & Richardson, M. W. The theory of the estimation of test reliability. *Psychometrika,* 1937, **2,** 151–160.

Leahy, A. M. Nature-nurture and intelligence. *Genetic Psychology Monographs,* 1935, **17,** 235–308.

Lee, E. S. Negro intelligence and selective migration: A Philadelphia test of the Klineberg hypothesis. *American Sociological Review,* 1951, **16,** 227–233.

MacKinnon, D. W. What do we mean by talent and how do we test for it? *The search for talent.* New York: College Entrance Examination Board, 1960. Pp. 20–29.

McCord, W. M., & Demerath, N. J. Negro versus white intelligence: A continuing controversy. *Harvard Educational Review,* 1968, **38,** 120–135.

McNemar, Q. Lost: Our intelligence? Why? *American Psychologist,* 1964, **19,** 871–882.

Meyer, W. J., & Bendig, A. W. A longitudinal study of primary mental abilities. *Journal of Educational Psychology,* 1961, **52,** 50–60.

Monahan, J. E., & Hollingworth, L. S. Neuromuscular capacity of children who test above 135 IQ (Stanford-Binet). *Journal of Educational Psychology,* 1927, **18,** 88–96.

Newman, H. H., Freeman, F. H., & Holinger, K. J. *Twins: A study of heredity and environment.* Chicago: University of Chicago Press, 1937.

Plant, W. T., Herold, P. L., & Southern, M. L. *Technical progress report #6.* Washington, D. C.: U. S. Office of Education, Cooperative Research Branch, Project 3102, 1967.

Riessman, F. *The culturally deprived child.* New York: Harper, 1962.

Shaycroft, M. F., et al. *Project talent: Studies of a complete age group age 15.* Pittsburgh: University of Pittsburgh, 1963. Mimeographed.

Shuey, A. M. *The testing of Negro intelligence* (2nd ed.) New York: Social Science Press, 1966.

Skodak, M., & Skeels, H. M. A final follow-up of one hundred adopted children. *Journal of Genetic Psychology,* 1944, **75,** 3–19.

Smith, S. Language and non-verbal test performance of racial groups in Honolulu before and after a 14-year interval. *Journal of Genetic Psychology,* 1942, **26,** 51–93.

Sontag, L., Baker, C., & Nelson, V. Mental growth and personality: A longitudinal study. *Monographs of Social Research in Child Development,* 1958, **23** (2) 1–143.

Stewart, N. A.G.C.T. scores of Army personnel grouped by occupation. *Occupations,* 1947, **26,** 5–41.

Tanner, J. M. *Growth at adolescence.* Springfield, Ill.: Thomas, 1955.

Telford, C. W. Comparative studies of full- and mixed-blood North Dakota Indians. *Psychological Monographs,* 1938, **50,** 116–129.

Terman, L. M., & Merrill, M. A. *Measuring intelligence.* Boston: Houghton Mifflin, 1937.

Terman, L. M., & Merrill, M. A. *Stanford-Binet intelligence scale.* Boston: Houghton Mifflin, 1960.

Terman, L. M., & Oden, M. H. *The gifted group at mid-life.* Stanford, Calif.: Stanford University Press, 1959.

Thoday, J. M., & Gibson, J. B. Environmental and genetical contributions to class differences: A model experiment. *Science,* 1970, **167,** 990–992.

Torrance, E. P. *Guiding creative talent.* Englewood Cliffs, N. J.: Prentice-Hall, 1962.

Torrance, E. P., *Torrance tests of creativity.* Princeton, N. J.: Personnel Press, 1966.

Tulkin, S. R. Race, class, family, and school achievement. *Journal of Personality and Social Psychology,* 1968, **9,** 31–37.

Wechsler, D. *The measurement of adult intelligence.* Baltimore: Williams and Wilkins 1939.

Wechsler, D. *Wechsler intelligence scale for children.* New York: The Psychological Corporation, 1949.

Wechsler, D. *Manual for the Wechsler adult intelligence scale.* New York: The Psychological Corporation, 1955.

Witty, P. A. *A study of one hundred gifted children.* University of Kansas Bulletin on Education, State Teachers College Studies Educ., 1. No. 13, 1930.

Witty, P. A. A genetic study of fifty gifted children. *Yearbook of the National Society for the Study of Education,* 1940, **39,** 401–408.

Yerkes, R. N. (Ed.) Psychological examining in the United States Army. *Memoirs, National Academy of Science,* 1921, XV, 890.

CHAPTER 10 MOTIVATION: BASIC PROCESSES

Bass, B. The effect of drive variations within and between subjects on conditioning performance. Unpublished doctoral dissertation, State University of Iowa, 1958.

Beach, F. A. Relative effects of androgen upon the mating behavior of male rats subjected to pre-brain injury or castration. *Journal of Experimental Zoology,* 1944, **97,** 249–285.

Beach, F. A. Instinctive behavior: Reproductive activities. In S. Stevens (Ed.), *Handbook of experimental psychology.* New York: Wiley, 1951.

Beach, F. A. The descent of instinct. *Psychological Review,* 1955, **62,** 401–410.

Beach, F. A. Characteristics of masculine sex drive. In M. R. Jones (Ed.), *Nebraska symposium on motivation.* Lincoln: University of Nebraska Press, 1956.

Berlyne, D. E. *Conflict, arousal, and curiosity.* New York: McGraw-Hill, 1960.

Berlyne, D. E. Curiosity and exploration. *Science,* 1966, **153,** 25–33.

Berlyne, D. E. Arousal and reinforcement. In D. Levine (Ed.), *Nebraska symposium on motivation, 1967.* Lincoln: University of Nebraska Press, 1967.

Birch, D., & Veroff, J. *Motivation: A study of action.* Belmont, Calif.: Brooks/Cole, 1966.

Bolles, R. C. *Theory of motivation.* New York: Harper & Row, 1967.

Bolles, R., & Petrinovich, L. A. technique for obtaining rapid drive discrimination in the rat. *Journal of Comparative and Physiological Psychology,* 1954, **47,** 378–380.

Broadhurst, P. L. Emotionality and the Yerkes-Dodson law. *Journal of Experimental Psychology,* 1957, **54,** 345–352.

Brown, J. S. *The motivation of behavior.* New York: McGraw-Hill, 1961.

Bursten, B., & Delgado, J. M. R. Positive reinforcement induced by intracerebral stimulation in the monkey. *Journal of Comparative and Physiological Psychology,* 1958, **51,** 6–10.

Butler, J. M., & Rice, L. N. Adience, self-actualization, and drive theory. In J. P. Wepman & R. W. Heine (Eds.), *Concepts of personality.* Chicago: Aldine, 1963.

Butler, R. A. Discrimination learning by Rhesus monkeys to visual-exploration motivation. *Journal of Comparative and Physiological Psychology,* 1953, **46,** 95–98.

Butler, R. A., & Harlow, H. F. Persistence of visual exploration in monkeys. *Journal of Comparative and Physiological Psychology,* 1954, **47,** 258–263.

Campbell, B. A., & Kraeling, D. Response strength as a function of drive level and amount of drive reduction. *Journal of Experimental Psychology,* 1953, **45,** 97–101.

Cannon ,W. B. *Bodily changes in pain hunger, fear, and rage.* (2nd ed.) New York: Appleton-Century-Crofts, 1929.

Cofer, C. N., & Appley, M. H. *Motivation: Theory and research.* New York: Wiley, 1964.

Darwin, C. *The expression of emotion in man and animals.* New York: Appleton-Century-Crofts, 1873.

Dewey, J. The need for social psychology. *Psychological Review,* 1917, **24,** 266–277.

Dunlap, K. Are there any instincts? *Journal of Abnormal Psychology,* 1919–1920, **14,** 307–311.

Easterbrook, J. A. The effect of emotion on cue utilization and the organization of behavior. *Psychological Review,* 1959, **66,** 183–201.

Farber, I. E. Response fixation under anxiety and nonanxiety conditions. *Journal of Experimental Psychology,* 1948, **38,** 111–131.

Finger, F. W., & Reid, L. S. The effect of water deprivation and subsequent satiation upon general activity in the rat. *Journal of Comparative and Physiological Psychology, 1952,* **45,** 368–372.

Fiske, P. W., & Maddi, S. R. *Functions of varied experience.* Homewood, Ill.: Dorsey Press, 1961.

Fowler, H. *Curiosity and exploratory behavior.* New York: Macmillan, 1965.

Fredenburg, N. C. Response strength as a function of alley length and time of deprivation. Unpublished master's thesis, State University of Iowa, 1956.

Glickman, S. E., & Schiff, B. B. A biological theory of reinforcement. *Psychological Review,* 1967, **74,** 81–109.

Grossman, M. I. Integration of current views on the regulation of hunger and appetite. In R. W. Miner (Ed.), The regulation of hunger and appetite. *Annals of the New York Academy of Sciences,* **63,** Art. 1. New York: New York Academy of Sciences, 1955.

Hall, J. F. *Psychology of motivation.* Philadelphia: Lippincott, 1961.

Hall, J. F., Smith, K., Schmitze, S. B., & Hanford, P. V. Elevation of activity level in the rat, following transition from ad libitum to restricted feeding. *Journal of Comparative and Physiological Psychology,* 1953, **46,** 429–433.

Harlow, H. F. Motivation as a factor in the acquisition of new responses. In M. R. Jones (Ed.), *Current theory and research in motivation: A symposium.* Lincoln: University of Nebraska, 1953.

Harlow, H. F. The nature of love. *American Psychologist,* 1958, **13,** 673–685.

Harlow, H. F., Harlow, M. K., & Meyer, D. B. Learning motivated by a manipulation drive. *Journal of Experimental Psychology,* 1950, **40,** 228–234.

Hebb, D. O. *The organization of behavior.* New York: Wiley, 1949.

Hebb, D. O. Drives and the C.N.S. (conceptual nervous system). *Psychological Review,* 1955, **62,** 243–254.

Horenstein, B. R. Performance of conditioned responses as a function of strength of hunger drive. *Journal of Comparative and Physiological Psychology,* 1951, **44,** 210–224.

Hull, C. L. *Principles of behavior.* New York. Appleton-Century-Crofts, 1943.

Hunt, J. McV., & Quay, H. C. Early vibratory experience and the question of innate reinforcement value of vibration and other stimuli. *Psychological Review,* 1961, **68,** 149–156.

Jenkins, J. J., & Hanratty, J. A. Drive intensity discrimination in the albino rat. *Journal of Comparative and Physiological Psychology,* 1949, **42,** 228–232.

Kling, J. W., & Matsumiya, Y. Relative reinforcement values of food and intracranial stimulation. *Science,* 1962, **135,** 668–670.

Lindsley, D. B. Emotion. In S. Stevens (Ed.), *Handbook of experimental psychology.* New York: Wiley, 1951.

Lindsley, D. B. Psychophysiology and motivation. In M. R. Jones (Ed.), *Nebraska symposium on motivation.* Lincoln: University of Nebraska Press, 1957.

Lorenz, K. The comparative method in studying innate behavior patterns. *Symposium on Social and Experimental Biology,* 1950, **4,** 221–268.

Masserman, J. H. *Principles of dynamic psychiatry.* Philadelphia: Saunders, 1946.

McDougall, W. *An introduction to social psychology. London: Methuen,* 1908.

McDougall, W. *Outline of psychology.* New York: Scribner's, 1923.

Meier, G. W., Foshee, D. P., Wittrig, J. J., Peeler, D. F., & Huff, F. W. Helson's residual factor versus innate S.R. relations. *Psychological Review,* 1960, **6,** 61–62.

Miller, N. E. Central stimulation and other new approaches to motivation and reward. *American Psychologist,* 1958, **13,** 100–108.

Miller, N. E., Sampliner, R. I., & Woodrow, P. Thirst reducing effects of water by stomach fistula vs. water by mouth measured by both a consummatory and an instrumental response. *Journal of Comparative and Physiological Psychology,* 1957, **50,** 1–5.

Mogenson, G. J. Avoidance responses to rewarding brain stimulation: Replication and extension. *Journal of Comparative and Physiological Psychology,* 1964, **58,** 465–467.

Montgomery, K. C. The role of exploratory drive in learning. *Journal of Comparative and Physiological Psychology,* 1954, **47,** 60–64.

Morgan, C. T. *Physiological psychology.* New York: McGraw-Hill, 1943.

Morgan, C. T., & Stellar, E. *Physiological psychology.* (2nd ed.) New York: McGraw-Hill, 1950.

Moruzzi, G., & Magoun, H. W. Brain stem reticular formation and activation of the EEG. *Electroencephalography and Clinical Neurophysiology,* 1949, **1,** 455–473.

Olds, J. Satiation effects in self-stimulation of the brain. *Journal of Comparative and Physiological Psychology,* 1958, **51,** 675–678.

Olds, J., & Milner, P. Positive reinforcement produced by electrical stimulation of septal area and other regions of the rat brain. *Journal of Comparative and Physiological Psychology,* 1954, **47,** 419–427.

Passey, G. E. The influence of intensity of unconditioned stimulus upon acquisition of a conditioned response. *Journal of Experimental Psychology,* 1948, **38,** 420–428.

Piaget, J. *The origins of intelligence in children.* New York: International Universities Press, 1952.

Richter, C. P. Animal behavior and internal drives. *Quarterly Review of Biology,* 1927, **2** (3), 307–343.

Roberts, W. W. Both rewarding and punishing effects from stimulation of posterior hypothalamus of cat with same electrode at same intensity. *Journal of Comparative and Physiological Psychology,* 1958, **51,** 400–407.

Routtenberg, A. The two-arousal hypothesis: Reticular formation and limbic system. *Psychological Review,* 1968, **75,** 51–80.

Siegel, P. S. The relationship between voluntary water intake, body weight loss, and number of hours of water deprivation in the rat. *Journal of Comparative Physiological Psychology,* 1947, **40,** 231–238.

Smith, O. A. Stimulation of lateral and medial hypothalamus and food intake in the rat. *Anatomical Review*, 1956, **124**, 363–364.

Sokolov, E. N. Higher nervous functions: The orienting reflex. *Annual Review of Physiology*, 1963, **25**, 545–586.

Spence, K. W. A theory of emotionally based drive (*D*), and its relation to performance in simple learning situations. *American Psychologist*, 1958, **13**, 131–141.

Spence, K. W., & Platt J. R. UCS intensity and performance in eyelid conditioning. *Psychological Bulletin*, 1966, **65**, 1–10.

Thorndike, E. L. *Educational psychology*, Vol. II. *The original nature of man*. New York: Teachers College, Columbia University, 1913.

Thorpe, W. H. *Learning and instinct in animals*. (2nd ed.) London: Methusen, 1963.

Tinbergen, N. *The herring gull's world*. New York: Basic Books, 1961.

Tolman, E. C., Hall, C. S., & Bretnall, E. P. A disproof of the laws of effect and substitution of the laws of emphasis, motivation, and disruption. *Journal of Experimental Psychology*, 1932, **15**, 601–614.

Walker, E. L. Psychological complexity as a basis for a theory of motivation and choice. In D. Levine (Ed.), *Nebraska symposium on motivation*. Lincoln: University of Nebraska Press, 1964. Pp. 47–98.

Watson, J. B. *Behavior: An introduction to comparative psychology*. New York: Holt, 1914.

Watson, J. B. *Behaviorism*. New York: Norton, 1925.

Whalen, R. E. Sexual motivation. *Psychological Review*, 1966, **73**, 151–163.

Woodworth, R. S. *Dynamic psychology*. New York: Columbia University Press, 1918.

Yerkes, R. M., & Dodson, J. D. The relation of strength of stimulus to rapidity of habit formation. *Journal of Comparative Neurology*, 1908, **18**, 458–482.

CHAPTER 11 MOTIVATION: COMPLEX PROCESSES

Amsel, A. The effect upon level of consummatory response of the addition of anxiety to a motivational complex. *Journal of Experimental Psychology*, 1950, **40**, 709–715.

Atkinson, J. W. *An introduction to motivation*. Princeton, N.J.: Van Nostrand, 1964.

Brown, J. S. Problems presented by the concept of acquired drives. In *Current theory and research in motivation: A symposium*. Lincoln: University of Nebraska Press, 1953.

Brown, J. S. *The motivation of behavior.* New York: McGraw-Hill, 1961.

Brown, J. S., & Jacobs, A. The role of fear in the motivation and acquisition of responses. *Journal of Experimental Psychology,* 1949, **39,** 747–759.

Brown, J. S., Kalish, H. I., & Farber, I. E. Conditioned fear as revealed by magnitude of startle response to an auditory stimulus. *Journal of Experimental Psychology,* 1951, **41,** 317–328.

Cannon, W. B. *Bodily changes in pain, hunger, fear, and rage.* (2nd ed.) New York: Appleton-Century-Crofts, 1929.

Cowles, J. T. Food tokens as incentives for learning by chimpanzees. *Comparative Psychology Monographs,* 1937, **14** (5).

Dollard, J., & Miller, N. E. *Personality and psychotherapy.* New York: McGraw-Hill, 1950.

Estes, W. K., & Skinner, B. F. Some quantitative properties of anxiety. *Journal of Experimental Psychology,* 1941, **29,** 390–400.

Festinger, L. Wish, expectation, and group standards as affecting level of aspiration. *Journal of Abnormal and Social Psychology,* 1942, **37,** 184–200.

Freud, S. *The problem of anxiety.* New York: Norton, 1936.

Goldstein, K. *Human nature in the light of psychopathology.* Cambridge, Mass.: Harvard University Press, 1940.

Gordon, W. M., & Berlyne, D. E. Drive level and flexibility in paired associate nonsense-syllable learning. *Quarterly Journal of Experimental Psychology,* 1954, **6,** 181–185.

Gwinn, G. T. Resistance to extinction of learned fear drives. *Journal of Experimental Psychology,* 1951, **42,** 6–12.

Hebb, D. O. Drives and the C.N.S. (conceptual nervous system). *Psychological Review,* 1955, **62,** 243–254.

Hilgard, E. R., Sait, E. M., & Margaret, G. A. Level of aspiration as affected by relative standing in an experimental social group. *Journal of Experimental Psychology,* 1940, **27,** 411–421.

Hoppe, F. Erfolg und Misserfolg. *Psychologische Forschung,* 1930, **14,** 1–62.

Jersild, S. T. Emotional development. In L. Carmichael (Ed.), *Manual of child psychology.* New York: Wiley, 1954.

Jucknat, M. Accomplishment level of aspiration and self-consciousness. *Psychologische Forschung,* 1937, **22,** 99.

Kalish, H. I. Strength of fear as a function of the number of acquisition and extinction trials. *Journal of Experimental Psychology,* 1954, **47,** 1–9.

Kostansek, D. J., & Sawrey, J.M. Acquisition and extinction of shuttle box avoidance with complex stimuli. *Psychonomic Science,* 1965, **3,** 369–370.

Lantz, B. Some dynamic aspects of success and failure. *Psychological Monographs,* 1945, **271,** 140.

Masserman, J. H. The neurotic cat. *Psychology Today,* 1967, **6,** 37–57.

Matarazzo, J. D., Ulett, G. A., & Saslow, G. Human maze performance as a function of increasing levels of anxiety. *Journal of Genetic Psychology,* 1965, **53,** 79–96.

McClelland, D. C., Atkinson, J. W., Clark, R. A., & Lowell, E. L. *The achievement motive.* New York: Appleton-Century-Crofts, 1953.

Meryman, J. J. Magnitude of startle response as a function of hunger and fear. Unpublished master's thesis, State University of Iowa, 1952.

Meryman, J. J. The magnitude of an unconditioned G.S.R. as a function of fear conditioned at a long C.S.-U.C.S. interval. Unpublished doctoral dissertation, State University of Iowa, 1953.

Miller, N. E. Studies of fear as an acquirable drive: I. Fear as motivation and fear reduction as reinforcement in the learning of new responses. *Journal of Experimental Psychology,* 1948, **38,** 89–101.

Miller, N. E. Learnable drives and rewards. In S. S. Stevens (Ed.), *Handbook of experimental psychology,* New York: Wiley, 1951.

Montague, E. K. The role of anxiety in serial rote learning. *Journal of Experimental Psychology,* 1953, **45,** 91–96.

Mowrer, O. H. A stimulus-response analysis of anxiety and its role as a reinforcing agent. *Psychological Review,* 1939, **46,** 553–565.

Mowrer, O. H., & Lamoreaux, R. R. Avoidance conditioning and signal duration: A study of secondary motivation and reward. *Psychological Monographs,* 1942, **54** (5).

Sawrey, W. L., & Sawrey, J. M. Conditioned fear and restraint in ulceration. *Journal of Comparative and Physiological Psychology,* 1964, **57,** 150–151.

Solomon, R. L., & Wynne, L. C. Traumatic avoidance learning: The principle of anxiety conservation and partial irreversibility. *Psychological Review,* 1954, **61,** 353–385.

Spence, K. W. Current interpretations of learning data and some recent developments in stimulus-response theory. In *Learning theory, personality theory, and clinical research: The Kentucky symposium.* New York: Wiley, 1953.

Spence, K. W. Anxiety (drive) level and performance in eyelid conditioning. *Psychological Bulletin,* 1964, **61,** 129–139.

Spence, K. W., Taylor, E., & Farber, I. E. The relation of electric shock and anxiety to level of performance in eyelid conditioning. *Journal of Experimental Psychology,* 1954, **48,** 404–408.

Spielberger, C. D. The effects of manifest anxiety on the academic achievement of college students. *Mental Hygiene,* 1962, **42,** 420–426.

Taylor, J. A. The relationship of anxiety to the conditioned eyelid response. *Journal of Experimental Psychology*, 1951, **41**, 81–92.

Taylor, J. A. Drive theory and manifest anxiety. *Psychological Bulletin*, 1956, **53**, 303–320.

Taylor, J. A., & Chapman, J. Paired-associate learning as related to anxiety. *American Journal of Psychology*, 1955, **68**, 671.

Taylor, J. A., & Spence, K. W. The relationship of anxiety level to performance in serial learning. *Journal of Experimental Psychology*, 1952, **44**, 61–64.

Wenar, C. Reaction time as a function of manifest anxiety and stimulus intensity. *Journal of Abnormal and Social Psychology*, 1954, **49**, 335–340.

Wolfe, J. B. Effectiveness of token rewards for chimpanzees. *Comparative Psychology Monographs*, 1936, **12** (5).

CHAPTER 12 PERSONAL AND SOCIAL BEHAVIOR

Adler, A. *The practice and theory of individual psychology.* New York: Harcourt, 1929.

Allport, F. H. *Social psychology.* Boston: Houghton Mifflin, 1924.

Amsel, A. The role of frustrative nonreward in noncontinuous reward situations. *Psychological Bulletin*, 1958, **55**, 102–119.

Amsel, A. Frustrative nonreward in partial reinforcement and discrimination learning: Some recent history and theoretical extension. *Psychological Review*, 1962, **69**, 306–328.

Amsel, A., & Ward, R. W. Motivational properties of frustration: II. Frustration drive stimulus and frustration reduction in selective learning. *Journal of Experimental Psychology*, 1954, **48**, 37–47.

Asch, S. *Social psychology.* New York: Prentice-Hall, 1952.

Behrens, M. L. Child rearing and the character structure of the mother. *Child Development*, 1954, **25**, 225–238.

Brown, J. S. Gradients of approach and avoidance responses and their relation to level of motivation. *Journal of Comparative and Physiological Psychology*, 1948, **41**, 450–465.

Brown, J. S. *The motivation of behavior.* New York: McGraw-Hill, 1961.

Brown, R. *Social psychology.* New York: Free Press, 1965.

Brown, W. L., & Gentry, G. The effects of intra-maze delay. II. Various intervals of delay. *Journal of Comparative Psysiology*, 1948, **41**, 403–407.

Coser, L. A., & Rosenberg, B. (Eds.) *Sociological theory.* (2nd ed.) New York: Macmillan, 1964.

Dimock, H. S. *Rediscovering the adolescent.* New York: Associative Press, 1937.

Erikson, E. H. A memorandum on identity and Negro youth. *Journal of Social issues,* 1964, **20,** 29–42.

Fishman, J. R., & Solomon, F. Youth and social action. *Journal of Social Issues,* 1964, **20,** 1–29.

Fries, M. E., & Levi, D. Interrelated factors in development. *American Journal of Orthopsychiatry,* 1938, **8,** 726–752.

Fries, M. E., & Woolf, P. J. Some hypotheses on the role of congenital activity type in personality development. *Psychoanalytical Studies of the Child,* 1953, **8,** 48–62.

Fromm, E. *The sane society.* New York: Holt, 1955.

Gelinean, V. A., & Kantor, D. Pro-social commitment among college students. *Journal of Social Issues,* 1964, **40,** 112–130.

Gerard, H. B. Inconsistency of beliefs and their implications. Paper read at American Psychological Association Convention, New York, September 1961.

Goldfarb, W. Variations in adolescent adjustment of institutionally reared children. *American Journal of Orthopsychiatry,* 1947, **17,** 449–457.

Harlow, H. F. The heterosexual affectional system in monkeys. *American Psychologist,* 1962, **17,** 1–9.

Hilgard, E. R., & Marquis, D. G. Acquisition, extinction, and retention of conditioned lid responses to light in dogs. *Journal of Comparative Psychology,* 1935, **19,** 29–58.

Hovland, C. I. Inhibition of reinforcement and phenomena of experimental extinction. *Proceedings of the National Academy of Sciences of the United States,* 1936, **22,** 430–433.

Hovland, C. I., & Sears, R. R. Experiments on motor conflict: I. Types of conflict and their modes of resolution. *Journal of Experimental Psychology,* 1938, **23,** 477–493.

Irwin, O. C. The amount and nature of activity in newborn infants under constant external stimulating conditions during the first ten days of life. *Genetic Psychological Monographs,* 1930, **8,** 1–92.

Jackson, J. M., & Saltzstein, H. D. The effect of person-group relationships on conformity processes. *Journal of Abnormal and Social Psychology,* 1958, **57,** 17–24.

Jost, H. Some physiological changes during frustration. *Child Development,* 1941, **12,** 9–15.

Krech, D., Crutchfield, R. S., & Ballachey, E. L. *Individual in society.* New York: McGraw-Hill 1962.

Lewin, K. *A dynamic theory of personality.* New York: McGraw-Hill 1935.

Maas, H. S. *The young adult adjustment of twenty wartime residential nursery children.* New York: Child Welfare League of America, 1963.

Melzack, R., & Scott, T. H. The effects of early experience on the response to pain. *Journal of Comparative and Physiological Psychology,* 1957, **50,** 155–161.

Mirsky, I. A. Physiologic, psychologic, and social determinants in the etiology of duodenal ulcers. *American Journal of Digestive Disorders,* 1958, **3,** 285–314.

Montague, M. F. A. Constitutional and prenatal factors in infant and child health. In M. J. E. Sonn (Ed.), *Symposium on the healthy personality.* New York: Josiah Macy, Jr., Foundation, 1950.

Newton, N. R., & Newton, M. Relationship of ability to breast feed and maternal attitudes toward breast feeding. *Pediatrics,* 1950, **5,** 869–875.

Rheingold, H. L. The modification of social responsiveness in institutional babies. *Social Research in Child Development Monographs,* 1956, **21** (63).

Rheingold, H. L. The effect of environmental stimulation upon social and exploratory behavior in the human infant. In M. B. Foss (Ed.), *Determinants of infant behavior.* London: Methuen, 1961.

Rogers, P. V., & Richter, C. P. Anatomical comparison between the adrenal glands of wild Norway, wild Alexandrine, and domestic Norway rats. *Endocrinology,* 1948, **42,** 46–55.

Sawrey, J. M., & Telford, C. W. *Dynamics of mental health.* Boston: Allyn and Bacon, 1963.

Sawrey, J. M., & Telford, C. W. *The psychology of adjustment.* (3rd ed.) Boston: Allyn and Bacon, 1971.

Sewell, W. H. Infant training and the personality of the child. *American Journal of Sociology,* 1952, **58,** 150–159.

Sherif, M. *The psychology of social norms.* New York: Harper, 1936.

Silverman, S. S. Clothes and appearance: Their psychological implications for teenage girls. *Teachers College, Columbia, Contributions to Education,* 1945, No. 912.

Skinner, B. F. Drive and reflex strength. *Journal of General Psychology,* 1932, **6,** 22–37.

Solomon, F., & Fishman, J. R. Youth and peace: A psychosocial study of student peace demonstrators in Washington D. C. *Journal of Social Issues,* 1964, **20,** 54–73.

Spitz, R. A. The psychogenic diseases of infancy: An attempt at their etiological classification. In R. S. Eissler et al. (Eds.), *The psychoanalytic study of the child,* Vol. 6. New York: International Universities Press, 1951.

Stockard, C. R., Anderson, O. D., & James, W. T. *Genetic and endocrine basis for differences in form and behavior.* Philadelphia: Wistar Institute of Anatomy and Biology, 1941.

Thomas, W. I. *Primitive behavior.* New York: McGraw-Hill, 1937.

Wenar, C. The effects of a motor handicap on personality: I. The effects on level of aspiration. *Child Development,* 1953, **24,** 123–130.

Wenar, C. The effects of a motor handicap on personality: II. The effects on integrative ability. *Child Development,* 1954, **25,** 287–294.

Witkin, H. A. Origins of cognitive style. In C. Scheerer (Ed.), *Cognition: Theory, research, promise.* New York: Harper & Row 1964.

Wood, J. A. *The uncivilized races of man.* Hartford, Conn.: J. B. Burr and Hyde, 1872.

Author Index

Abrahamson, I.G., 90, 413
Adams, H.E., 245, 423
Ader, H.W., 135, 415
Adler, A., 370, 441
Adrian, E.E., 82, 413
Allen, C., 304, 432
Allport, F.H., 383, 441
Alper, T.G., 239, 241, 299, 424, 427, 430
Alpern, M., 155
Ammons, C.H., 28, 29, 229, 409, 424
Ammons, R.B., 229, 424
Amsel, A., 347, 360, 438, 441
Anderson, B.F., 33
Anderson, O.D., 369
Anderson, R.C., 279
Andrews, J.G., 26, 410
Appley, M.H., 324, 335, 435
Aristotle, 2, 3
Asch, S., 384, 441
Asher, E.J., 308, 430
Ashley, W.R., 93, 413
Atkinson, J.W., 244, 357, 358, 424, 440
Atkinson, R.C., 286, 432
Ausubel, D.P., 279
Azrin, N.H., 173, 417

Babich, F.P., 240, 425
Bachrach, A.J., 29, 33, 409
Baer, D.M., 198, 421
Baker, C., 300, 433
Ballachey, E.L., 385, 386, 442
Ban, T., 193
Bandura, A., 198, 199, 219, 421
Barrera, S.E., 244, 428
Barrientos, G., 182, 421
Barron, F., 294, 430
Bartlett, F.C., 56, 247, 411
Bass, B., 171, 337, 417, 434
Baum, M.H., 362, 428
Bayley, N., 304, 430, 431
Beach, F.A., 315, 316, 323, 329, 330, 434
Beck, E.C., 265, 438
Begleiter, H., 56, 411
Békésy, G. von, 129, 131, 156, 415
Bell, Charles, 4
Bendig, A.W., 297, 432
Bennett, E.L., 189, 240, 419, 424
Bentley, M., 160, 417
Berger, H., 57
Berlyne, D.E., 319, 331, 332, 348, 434, 439
Best, C.H., 154, 415
Birch, D., 327, 334, 434
Bloom, B.S., 300, 431
Blum, G.S., 393
Boas, F., 301, 431
Bodmer, W.F., 299, 431
Boe, E.E., 173, 417
Bolles, R.C., 318, 319, 334, 434
Bonsall, M., 294, 431
Boring, E.G., 3-6, 33, 96, 299, 409, 414, 430
Bossom, J., 62, 411
Bourne, L.E., Jr., 262, 438
Bredberg, C., 135, 415
Bretnall, E.P., 329, 438
Bribash, S., 240, 425
Brigham, C.C., 302, 431
Brislin, R., 99, 414
Broadbent, D.E., 245, 424
Broadhurst, P.L., 329
Broca, 5
Brown, H.O., 266, 430
Brown, J.S., 319, 325, 327, 335, 339, 341, 342, 350, 352, 361, 364, 376, 435, 439, 441
Brown, R.W., 236, 239, 424
Bruner, J.S., 93, 209, 413, 421
Buck, C., 49, 192
Bugelski, B.R., 212, 240, 424
Burks, B.S., 293, 305, 306, 431
Bursten, B., 325, 435
Burtt, H.E., 86, 223, 413, 424
Buschke, H., 245, 424
Butler, J.M., 23, 331, 409, 435
Butler, R.A., 331, 435
Butter, C.M., 71, 156
Byrne, W.F., 191, 417

Cadwallader, T.A., 242, 424
Calvin, M., 240, 424
Campbell, A.A., 174, 418
Campbell, B.A., 329, 435
Campbell, B.J., 179, 419
Cane, V., 180, 420
Cannon, W.B., 327, 338, 435, 439
Capaldi, E.J., 34
Cavalli-Sforza, L.L., 299, 431
Ceraso, J., 242, 427
Chapanis, A., 108, 413
Chapman, J., 347, 441
Chomsky, N., 91, 413
Chung, S.H., 56, 412
Church, R.M., 173, 198, 417, 421
Clark, B., 148, 415
Clark, R.A., 357, 440
Clemes, S.R., 244, 424
Coates, C., 295, 432
Cochran, W.G., 19, 29, 409
Cofer, C.N., 324, 335, 435
Conger, J.J., 174, 420
Conrad, H.S., 304, 431
Coons, E.E., 56, 245, 412, 424
Cooper, R.N., 300, 431
Corning, W.C., 191, 417
Coser, L.A., 387, 442
Cotzin, M., 26, 28, 409
Covington, M.V., 271, 428
Cowles, J.T., 81, 352, 417, 439
Cox, G.M., 19, 39, 409
Cranor, K.T., 238, 424
Creelman, M.B., 209, 421
Cruickshank, W.M., 312
Crutchfield, R.S., 271, 385, 386, 428, 442
Culler, E., 175, 417

Dallenback, K.M., 26, 28, 209, 242, 243, 410, 425, 426
D'Amato, R.M., 182, 417
Darwin, C., 6, 15, 315, 416, 435
Davis, R.A., 239, 424
Davis, R.W., 232, 424, 428
Daw, N.W., 117, 119, 416
Day, L.M., 160, 417
Dean, W.A., 244, 437
Delgado, J.M.R., 325, 435
Dember, W.N., 109
Dement, W., 274, 429
Demerath, N.J., 299, 302, 432
Demkow, L., 180, 420
Descartes, R., 2, 3, 32, 315
DeValois, R.L., 119, 415
Dewey, J., 250, 316, 429, 435
Dimock, H.S., 373, 442
Djupesland, G., 83, 413
Dodson, J.D., 329, 438
Dollard, J., 198, 354, 422, 439
Doty, R.W., 265, 428
Drambarean, N.C., 93, 415
Dreger, R.M., 302, 431
Duncan, C.P., 215, 244, 421, 424
Duncker, K., 258, 429
Dunlap, K., 316, 435
Durkheim, E., 387

Easterbrook, J.A., 329, 435
Ebbinghaus, H., 223, 227, 230, 248, 424
Edwards, A.L., 237, 424
Edwards, W., 90, 413
Egyhâzi, E., 240, 425
Ellis, H.C., 219
English, A.C., 33
English, H.B., 33
Eriksen, S.C., 186, 206, 417, 421
Erikson, E.H., 389, 442
Estes, W.K., 90, 173, 346, 413, 417, 439
Ewert, P.H., 62, 266, 411, 429
Eysenck, H.J., 183, 419

Farber, I.E., 325, 339, 347, 435, 439, 440
Farr, R.G., 229, 424
Fashee, D.P., 331, 437
Fechner, G., 5, 32
Ferster, C.B., 177, 178, 417
Festinger, L., 357, 439
Fetz, E.E., 56, 411
Fieandt, K. von, 78, 97
Finch, G., 175, 417
Finger, F.W., 326, 435
Fishman, J.R., 391, 442, 443
Fiske, D.W., 358
Fiske, P.W., 331, 435
Fitts, P.M., 108, 413
Flavell, J.H., 260, 429
Foord, E.N., 237, 425
Foreman, S., 181, 417
Forgus, R.H., 109
Forlano, G., 234, 424
Foulkes, D., 272, 273, 275, 429
Fowler, H., 331, 358, 435
Fox, S.S., 56, 411
Frank, M., 151, 415
Fredenburg, N.C., 327, 435
Freedman, J.L., 170, 419
Freedman, S.J., 62, 411
Freeman, F.H., 300, 433
Freeman, R.B., 105, 413
Freud, S., 338, 439
Fries, M.E., 370, 442
Fritsch, G., 5
Fromm, E., 389, 442
Furshpan, E.J., 56, 411

Gagné, R.M., 215, 267, 421, 429
Gaito, J., 191, 417
Galambos, R., 28, 85, 410, 414
Galen, 4
Garmezy, N., 148, 416
Garrett, H.E., 302, 431
Gates, A.J., 211, 234, 421, 425
Geldard, F.A., 142, 415
Gelinean, V.A., 389, 442
Gentry, G., 361, 441
Gerard, H.B., 386, 442
Getzels, J.W., 268, 269, 294, 296, 312, 429, 431
Geyer, M.T., 234, 425
Gibson, E.J., 102, 105, 413, 414
Gibson, J.B., 299, 433
Glaser, G.H., 59, 411
Glaze, J.A., 207, 421
Glickman, S.E., 325, 435
Goldberg, J.M., 137, 416
Goldfarb, W., 374, 442
Goldstein, K., 343, 439
Goodman, C.C., 93, 413
Goodman, L.S., 266, 430
Gordon, H., 308, 431
Gordon, W.M., 348, 439
Gouras, P., 44, 56, 119, 411, 415
Granit, R., 141, 415
Graybill, A., 148, 415
Greenberg, A., 206, 422
Greene, J.E., 171, 419
Greenspoon, J., 181, 417
Greenwood, D.D., 137, 416
Gregory, R.L., 99, 100, 101, 414
Gregory, R.W., 156
Grice, G.R., 171, 180, 417, 418
Griffin, D.R., 28, 410
Grimsley, D.L., 198, 423
Grossman, M.I., 327, 328, 436
Grossman, S., 210, 423
Guilford, J.P., 253, 268, 295, 429, 431
Gwinn, G.T., 342, 439

Hake, D.F., 173, 417

Halas, E.S., 160, 418
Hall, C.S., 328, 438
Hall, J.F., 326, 329, 436
Hallowell, A.J., 1, 410
Hammack, J.T., 179, 419
Hanford, P.W., 326, 436
Hanratty, J.A., 318, 436
Harlow, H.F., 69, 215, 224, 331, 332, 335, 374, 411, 421, 425, 435, 436, 442
Harlow, M.K., 69, 215, 332, 411, 421, 436
Harper, R.S., 93, 413
Hartley, S.H., 141, 415
Harvey, O.J., 295, 432
Hatry, A.L., 191, 418
Hebb, D.O., 237, 245, 319, 330, 348, 425, 436, 439
Hegel, Georg, 387
Heidbreder, E., 362, 429
Held, J., 62, 411
Helmholtz, H.L.F., 5, 32
Hennessy, R., 99, 414
Henson, C.O., 85, 414
Hernandez-Peón, R., 85, 414
Herold, P.L., 308, 433
Heynes, R.W., 394
Hilgard, E.R., 163, 174, 233, 286, 357, 361, 418, 425, 432, 439, 442
Hind, J.E., 137, 416
Hippocrates, 4, 410
Hirsch, H.V.B., 117, 416
Hitzig, E., 5
Hobson, J.R., 297, 432
Hoffmeister, J.K., 295, 432
Holand, J., 192, 419
Hollingworth, L.S., 293, 433
Holway, A.N., 96, 414
Holz, W.C., 173, 417
Holzinger, K.J., 300, 433
Honzig, M.P., 304, 432
Horenstein, B.R., 327, 436
Hovland, C.I., 171, 364, 418, 442
Howard, J.L., 308, 432
Hubel, D.H., 85, 414
Hudgins, C.V., 164, 418
Hudspeth, W.J., 245, 425
Huff, D., 31, 410
Huff, F.W., 331, 437
Hull, C.L., 208, 217, 262, 319, 422, 429, 436
Hume, D., 20, 410
Hunt, J.M.V., 331, 436
Hunter, W.S., 224, 425
Hutt, P.J., 150, 418
Hydén, H., 240, 425
Hyvärinen, J., 56, 411

Inhelder, B., 260, 279, 429
Irion, A.L., 210, 228, 229, 422, 426
Irvine, R.P., 233, 425
Irwin, O.C., 370, 442
Ittelson, W.H., 99, 126, 414, 416

Jackson, J.M., 385, 422
Jackson, P.W., 268, 269, 294, 296, 312, 429, 431
Jacobs, A., 342, 439
Jacobs, G.H., 119, 415
Jacobson, E., 266, 429
Jacobson, M., 38, 56, 411
Jacobson, R., 240, 428
James, R.T., 160, 418
James, W., 35, 36, 213, 411, 422
James, W.T., 369, 444
Jasper, H., 55, 411
Jauvet, M., 85, 414
Jenkins, J.G., 242, 425
Jenkins, J.J., 318, 436
Jennings, R.D., 206, 422
Jensen, A.R., 299, 300, 303, 432
Jensen, D.W., 293, 431
Jersild, S.T., 343, 439
John, E.R., 56, 191, 411, 417
Johnson, T., 192, 419
Jones, A.M., 293, 304, 431, 432
Jucknat, M., 356, 439

Kabat, L., 240, 428
Kales, A., 274, 429
Kalish, H.I., 342, 359, 439
Kanareff, V.T., 199, 422
Kanfer, F.H., 179, 418
Kantor, D., 389, 442
Karsh, E.B., 173, 418
Katona, G., 233, 425
Keith, L.P., 191, 418
Kelley, T.L., 285, 432
Kendler, H.H., 206, 422
Kennedy, D., 57, 411
Kidd, J.W., 291, 432
Kimble, G.A., 148, 160, 163, 180, 193, 206, 416, 418, 422
Kintsch, W., 91, 229, 263, 414, 425, 429
Kitai, S.T., 188, 418
Klein, G.S., 248
Klineberg, O., 302, 432
Kling, J.W., 325, 436
Knight, J.M., 188, 419
Knutson, C.L., 160, 418
Köhler, W., 201, 213, 422
Komisaruk, B.R., 56, 411
Konishi, M., 56, 412
Kostansek, D.J., 345, 439
Kraeling, D., 329, 435
Krech, D., 189, 190, 385, 386, 418, 419, 442
Krueger, W.C.F., 230, 231, 425
Kuder, G.F., 285, 432

Lamareaux, R.R., 342, 440
Lantz, B., 357, 440
Lanzetta, J.T., 199, 422
Lashley, K.S., 104, 185, 414, 418
Lassek, A.M., 48, 412
Lawrence, M., 155
Lawson, R., 393
Leahy, A.M., 306, 432
Leavitt, H.F., 235, 425
Lee, E.S., 302, 432
Leibowitz, H.W., 99, 110, 414
Lenneberg, E.H., 91, 414
Levi, D., 370, 442
Levine, D., 358
Levine, M., 44, 412
Levitt, H., 90, 413
Lewin, K., 239, 363, 424, 443
Lewis, D.J., 245, 423, 425, 426
Lindeman, H.H., 135, 415
Lindman, H., 90, 413
Lindsley, D., 319, 323, 424, 436
Locke, J., 2, 3, 32
Logan, F.A., 219
Long, E.R., 179, 419
Lorenz, K., 317, 436
Louttit, R.T., 71
Lowell, E.L., 357, 440
Luk, C.W., 226, 230
Luttges, M., 191, 419
Lyon, D.O., 209, 422

Maas, H.S., 375, 443
MacDougal, W., 209, 316, 422, 436
MacFarlane, J.W., 304, 432
MacRae, A.W., 44, 412
Madden, E.H., 19, 410
Maddi, S.R., 331, 358, 435
Madsen, M.C., 206, 245, 422, 426

Maffei, L., 117, 416
Magendie, F., 4
Magenson, G.J., 325, 437
Magoun, H.W., 324, 437
Maher, B.A., 245, 425, 426
Malin, C.F., 187, 420
Maltzman, I., 215, 271, 422, 429
Manis, B., 279
Margaret, G.A., 357, 439
Margolius, G., 238, 428
Marion, R., 229, 424
Marler, P., 131, 416
Marquis, D.P., 163, 164, 361, 419, 442
Marsh, J.T., 136, 416
Marx, Karl, 387
Maslow, A.H., 224, 425
Masserman, J.H., 325, 346, 436, 440
Matarazzo, J.D., 347, 440
Matsumiya, Y., 325, 436
Mauney, J., 26, 28, 410
Max, L.W., 267, 429
Mayers, K.S., 78, 118, 414, 416
McClelland, D.C., 357, 358, 440
McConnell, J.V., 160, 240, 419, 420, 428
McCord, W.M., 299, 302, 432
McDermott, W.P., 128, 416
McDougall, W.P., 232, 426
McGaugh, J., 192, 206, 419, 422
McGeoch, J.A., 210, 228, 229, 233, 235, 240, 422, 426
McKinnon, D.W., 269, 295, 296, 429, 432
McNeill, D., 236, 239, 424
Mearns, H., 271, 429
Mednick, S.A., 170, 271, 419, 429
Meier, G.W., 331, 437
Melton, A.W., 235, 246, 426
Melzack, R., 374, 443
Merbaum, M., 393
Merrifield, P.R., 295, 431
Merrill, M.A., 288, 304, 433
Meryman, J.J., 340, 440
Meyer, D.B., 332, 436
Miller, G.A., 263, 430
Miller, K.S., 302, 431
Miller, N.E., 198, 245, 327, 328, 338, 354, 422, 437, 439, 440
Miller, W.C., 171, 419
Milner, P., 325, 437
Minami, H., 242, 426
Minium, E.W., 29, 31, 410
Mirsky, I.A., 370, 443
Monahan, J.E., 293, 433
Montague, E.K., 347, 440
Montague, M.F., 374, 443
Montgomery, K.S., 331, 437
Moore, J.W., 193
Morgan, C.T., 137, 147, 149, 153, 186–188, 316, 416, 419, 437
Morton, J.T., 258, 430
Morton, W.J., 191, 418
Moruzzi, G., 324, 437
Moser, C.A., 24, 410
Mountcastle, V.B., 56, 411
Mowrer, O.H., 335, 342, 440
Mueller, C.G., 156
Müller, G.E., 244, 436
Muller, J., 4, 75, 414
Munn, H.L., 48, 85, 224, 412, 414, 426
Myers, W.A., 182, 419

Nagel, E., 19, 410
Nelson, V., 300, 433
Newcomb, T.M., 335
Newman, E.B., 229, 232, 424, 426
Newman, H.H., 300, 433
Newton, M., 376, 443
Newton, N.R., 376, 443
Nielsen, H.C., 188, 419
Noble, C.E., 208, 422
Nowlis, V., 335

Oden, M.H., 293, 295, 312, 433
Olds, J., 44, 56, 325, 411, 412, 437
Osgood, C.E., 208, 241, 422, 426
Otis, L.S., 190, 419

Pan, S., 238, 426
Pantle, A., 116, 416
Parks, D.R., 180, 420
Passey, G.E., 328, 437
Patterson, C.J., 78, 118, 414, 416
Paul, I.H., 248
Pavlov, I.P., 162, 165, 175, 419
Pearlman, A.L., 117, 119, 416
Pearson, K., 20, 410
Pecan, E.V., 90, 414
Peeler, D.F., 331, 437
Penfield, W., 49, 53, 54, 55, 64, 412
Perlmutter, L., 99, 414
Peterson, J., 234, 245, 426
Peterson, L.R., 245, 427
Peterson, M.J., 245, 427
Petrinovich, L.A., 318, 434
Pfaffmann, C., 151, 416
Phelan, J.G., 262, 430
Phillips, M.I., 44, 56, 412
Piaget, J., 11, 260, 279, 332, 410, 429, 430, 437
Pike, R., 100, 414
Pilzecker, A., 244, 426
Plant, W.T., 308, 432, 433
Plato, 2
Platt, J.R., 328, 438
Platz, A., 56, 411
Pomeranz, B., 56, 412
Porter, P.B., 188, 419
Posner, M.I., 108, 413
Postman, L., 231, 241, 335, 427
Potter, D.D., 56, 411
Prokasy, W.F., 164, 419
Pryer, M.W., 208, 422
Pryor, G.T., 190, 419

Quastler, H., 44, 412
Quay, H.C., 331, 436

Rachman, S., 183, 419
Raynor, R., 170, 183, 420
Razran, G., 170, 171, 419
Reid, L.S., 326, 435
Remler, M.P., 57, 411
Remmers, H.H., 234, 427
Rheingold, H.L., 374, 375, 443
Rice, I.N., 331, 435
Rice, L.N., 23, 409
Richardson, M.W., 285, 432
Richman, H., 206, 422
Richter, C.P., 327, 364, 437, 443
Riessman, F., 303, 433
Riley, D.A., 206, 237, 423, 427
Roberts, L., 53, 54, 55, 64, 412
Roberts, W.W., 325, 437
Robertson, R.T., 78, 118, 414, 416
Robinson, D., 44, 412
Robinson, E.S., 241, 427
Rock, R.T., Jr., 180, 419
Rogers, C.R., 270, 430
Rogers, P.V., 364, 443
Rose, J.E., 137, 416
Rosenberg, B., 387, 442
Rosenzweig, M.R., 189, 419
Rossman, J., 251, 430

Routtenberg, A., 325, 437
Rudell, A.P., 56, 411
Runyon, D.L., 93, 413
Rupert, A., 85, 414
Rushton, W.A.H., 119, 416
Russell, J.T., 104, 414

Sahakian, W.S., 216, 423
Sait, E.M., 357, 439
Sakata, H., 56, 411
Saltz, E., 171, 418
Saltzman, I.J., 182, 420
Saltzstein, H.D., 385, 442
Sampliner, R.I., 327, 437
Sanford, E.C., 209, 423
Sanford, F.H., 34
Saslow, G., 347, 440
Savage, J.J., 90, 413
Sawrey, J.M., 18, 172, 174, 199, 312, 342, 345, 369, 372, 410, 420, 423, 433, 439, 441, 443
Sawrey, W.L., 174, 342, 420, 440
Schaffer, R.W., 198, 423
Scherrer, H., 85, 414
Schiff, B.B., 325, 435
Schlasberg, H., 235, 425
Schmitze, S.B., 326, 436
Schulz, R., 208, 423
Schvaneveldt, R.W., 90, 414
Scott, J.P., 105, 414
Scott, T.H., 374, 443
Sears, P.S., 393
Sears, R.R., 364, 442
Seibert, L.C., 234, 427
Sekuler, R., 116, 416
Selverston, A.I., 57, 411
Sewell, W.H., 375, 443
Sharp, A.A., 237, 244, 427
Shaycroft, M.F., 294, 433
Sheer, D., 71
Shepp, B.E., 262, 430
Sherif, M., 384, 443
Sherman, J.A., 198, 421
Shimakochi, M., 56, 411
Shuey, A.M., 302, 433
Siegel, P.S., 327, 437
Silverman, S.S., 372, 443
Skaggs, E.B., 210, 423
Skeels, H.M., 306, 433
Skinner, B.F., 99, 167, 174, 177, 178, 199, 346, 361, 414, 420, 423, 443
Skodak, M., 306, 433
Slamecka, N.J., 242, 248, 427
Smith, B.D., 335
Smith, E.C., Jr., 267, 429
Smith, J.C., 136, 416
Smith, J.L., 245, 427
Smith, K., 329, 436
Smith, K.V., 186, 420
Smith, N.S., 56, 412
Smith, O.A., 328, 438
Smith, S., 308, 433
Smith, S.M., 266, 430
Smith, W., 209, 422
Smith, W.I., 193
Socrates, 2
Sokolov, E.N., 331, 438
Solomon, F., 391, 442, 443
Solomon, R.L., 345, 440
Sontag, L., 300, 433
Southern, M.L., 308, 433
Southwell, E.A., 393
Spence, K.W., 180, 214, 328, 347, 420, 423, 438, 440
Sperry, R.W., 56, 61, 412
Spinelli, D.N., 117, 416
Spitz, R.A., 374, 443
Spitzer, H.F., 231, 427
Staats, A.W., 193, 219
Staats, C.K., 219
Stacey, B., 100, 414
Stefflre, R., 294, 431
Stellar, E., 326, 437
Sternback, R.A., 137, 416
Stevens, C.F., 71
Stevens, S.S., 44, 412
Stewart, N., 307, 308, 433
Stimbert, V.E., 198, 423
Stockard, C.R., 369, 444
Stockwell, F.E., 208, 422
Stratton, G.M., 62, 413
Strong, E.K., 86, 414
Suci, G.J., 208, 422
Supa, M., 26, 410
Surzuki, S., 200
Swift, E.J., 235, 427

Talbot, W.H., 56, 411
Tanner, J.M., 301, 433
Taylor, J.A., 345–347, 441
Taylor, N.B., 154, 415
Teevan, R.C., 335
Telford, C.W., 18, 172, 199, 302, 312, 369, 372, 410, 420, 423, 433, 443
Terman, L.M., 288, 293, 295, 304, 312, 433
Thisted, M.N., 234, 427
Thoday, J.M., 299, 433
Thomas, W.I., 372, 444
Thompson, R., 160, 187, 188, 244, 419, 420, 427
Thompson, R.F., 71, 78, 118, 151, 414, 416
Thomson, C.W., 206, 422
Thorndike, E.L., 177, 212, 213, 214, 316, 420, 423, 438
Thorpe, W.H., 317, 438
Tinbergen, N., 317, 438
Tinkelpaugh, O.L., 224, 427
Tiorentini, A., 117, 416
Titchener, E.B., 223, 427
Tocqueville, A., 410
Tolman, E.C., 217, 328, 423, 438
Toman, J.E.P., 266, 430
Torrance, E.P., 269, 271, 279, 294, 296, 430, 433
Totten, E., 266, 430
Towne, B.M., 235, 427
Trapold, M.A., 182, 419
Tsai, C.A., 223, 427
Tulkin, S.R., 302, 433
Turrell, R.B., 174, 420
Tyler, R.W., 232, 428

Uhling, H., 224, 425
Ulett, G.A., 347, 440
Ulrich, J.L., 206, 423
Underwood, B.F., 208, 243, 423, 428
Uyeno, E., 190, 419

Veroff, J., 327, 334, 434

Wagner, A.R., 219
Walk, R.D., 104, 105, 128, 414, 416
Walker, E.L., 34, 110, 193, 331, 394, 438
Wall, P.D., 141, 416
Wallas, G., 250, 430
Walters, R.H., 180, 219, 420
Ward, A.H., 232, 428
Ward, R.W., 360, 441
Warden, C.J., 206, 423
Warren, H.C., 2, 3, 410
Watson, J.B., 170, 183, 316, 420, 438
Weber, E., 5, 32, 79
Wechsler, D., 290, 434
Wehmer, F., 69, 413
Weintraub, D.J., 110
Weiss, W., 238, 428

Wenar, C., 347, 372, 441, 444
West, R., 135, 415
Westbrook, W.H., 245, 427
Whalen, R.E., 330, 438
Wheeler, R.H., 79, 414
Whipple, J.E., 233, 425
White, B.L., 105, 295, 415, 432
Wike, E.L., 182, 421
Williams, M., 244, 428
Wispe, L.G., 93, 415
Witkin, H.A., 106, 385, 415, 444
Wittrig, J.J., 331, 437
Witty, P.A., 293, 434
Wolfe, J.B., 181, 352, 421, 441
Wolsk, D., 155
Wood, J.A., 372, 444
Woodrow, H., 214, 423
Woodrow, P., 327
Woodworth, R.S., 213, 316, 423, 438
Woolf, P.J., 370, 442
Worcester, D.A., 223, 428
Worchel, P., 26, 27, 28, 409, 410
Worden, F.G., 136, 416
Wundt, W., 6
Wynne, L.C., 345, 440

Yerkes, R.N., 301, 329, 434, 438
Young, P.T., 102, 138, 415, 416

Zajonc, R.B., 394
Zeaman, D., 262, 430
Zellar, A.F., 244, 428
Zelman, A., 240, 428
Zubek, J.P., 300, 431
Zubin, J., 244, 428

Subject Index

Acetylcholinesterase, 189
Adaptation:
  neurophysiology of, 80–81
  sensory, 80
Adjustment, patterns of, 366–367
Adrenal glands, 64, 66
Aerial perspective, 125
Affection, 353–354
After-images:
  color-mixing by, 123
  negative, 122–123
  positive, 123
  types of, 122
Alienation, elements of, 388–389
Amnesia, 184
Anecdotal data, limitations of, 14–15
"Animal spirits," 4
Animism:
  children's belief in, 1
  primitive belief in, 1
Anosmia, 152
Anxiety:
  "free-floating," 345
  measure of, 345–346
  performance level and, 368
Aphasia, forms of, 53–54
Arousal, 314, 324–325
Artistic ability, tests of, 311
Association, English school, 3
Association areas, electrical stimulation of, 55
Associationism, 3
Association value, 207
Associative meaning, dimensions of, 208
Associative strength, 322
Attention:
  acquired determinants, 87–88
  behavioral components of, 82–83
  central nervous system activities, 84–85
  determinants of, 85–89
  EEG changes in, 84
  limited channel characteristics, 81
  muscular tension, 84
  objective determinants, 86–87
  postural adjustments, 83
  sense-organ adjustments, 82–83
  unitary nature, 89
  visceral changes, 84
Audition:
  adequate stimuli, 129–130
  directional perceptions, 138
  distance perception, 137–138
  frequency theory, 130
  neural processing, 137
Audition (continued)
  place-frequency theory, 136
  sensory range, 131
  theories, 134–137
Auditory beats, 132
Autonomic nervous system, subdivisions, 44–45
Axon, 41

Behavior:
  covert, 9
  overt, 9
Binet-type tests, development of, 287
Brain, localization of functions, 5
Brain ventricles, 37
Brain waves, 57-59
Brightness, stimulus determinants, 113

Case study:
  components, 25
  source of psychological data, 24–25
Causality, conceptions of, 20
Central tendency, 400–401
Cerebral cortex:
  association functions, 53
  auditory areas, 51
  electrical stimulation, 51
  motor areas, 52

Cerebral cortex (continued)
  sensory functions, 49–52
  speech areas, 53–55
  visual areas, 50
Cerebrum, 47
Cholinesterase, 189
Circumstantiality, 277
Classical conditioning:
  description, 162
  example, 163–164
Clinical methods, 24–25
Cochlea, 129–133
Color-blindness:
  causes, 120–121
  forms of, 120
  nature, 120
Color mixture:
  additive, 121
  laws, 122
  subtractive, 121
Color vision:
  cones, 118
  "opponent" and "nonopponent" cones, 119
  photoreceptors, 118–119
Concept(s):
  acquisition, 259, 261–263
  language and, 263–264
Concept acquisition:
  experimental studies, 261–262
  hypothesis testing, 262
  language as mediator, 264
  rule learning, 262–263
Concept development, Piaget's stages, 260–261
Conditioned fear, 344
Conditioned response (C.R.):
  extinction, 172–173
  spontaneous recovery, 172–173
Conditioned stimulus (C.S.), cortical stimulation, 188
Conditioning:
  breadth of, 183–184
  classical, 162–164
  cortical stimulation and, 188
  differential, 176–177
  discrimination in, 176–177
  higher order, 175–176
  imitation and, 197–198
  instrumental, 164–169
  interstimulus interval variable, 182–183
  stimulus duration variables, 183
Conditioning (continued)
  stimulus intensity variables, 183
Cones, differential distribution, 120
Conflict:
  approach-approach, 364
  approach-avoidance, 365
  avoidance-avoidance, 365
  double approach-avoidance, 366
  varieties, 364–367
Conformity:
  conditions of, 383
  group norms and, 384
Conscience, 391
Consciousness, nature of, 13–14
Convergent thinking, 295
Correlation:
  coefficient, 404
  meaning of, 30
  negative coefficient, 405
  product-moment, 405
Counterconditioning, 173
Creative children:
  characteristics of parents, 270
  personal characteristics of, 296
Creative people, adult characteristics, 269
Creativity:
  conditions conducive to, 270
  definitions, 268
  development of, 271
  divergent thinking, 295
  individual originality, 268
  IQ and, 294
  "psychological freedom" and, 270
  "psychological safety" and, 270
  tests, 268, 295
  utilitarian, 268
Critical ratio, 407
Culture:
  components, 380
  nature, 378
Curiosity, 331–332
Cutaneous senses, number, 139

Data, frequency distribution, 396
Decision making, 259
Delayed reaction:
  extent of delay, 224
Delayed reaction (continued)
  symbolic processes in, 224
Dementia, 4
Dendrite, 41
Deprivation, sleep, 274
Deviation:
  quartile, 401
  standard, 402
Difference tones, 132
Distance:
  psychological, 363
  visual perception, 124–128
Distance perception:
  aerial perspective in, 125
  apparent rate of movement, 127
  color saturation in, 126
  distinctness of lights and shadows in, 126
  gradients of texture, 126
  integration of cues, 128–129
  interposition of objects, 125
  linear perspective, 124–125
  strains of accommodation in, 128
  strains of convergence in, 127
Distortions in recall:
  assimilation as cause, 237
  disintegration as cause, 237
Distribution:
  frequency, 396
  normal, 398
  skewed, 399
  symmetrical, 399
Divergent thinking, 295
DNA, 39, 190–192
Dreaming, time spent in, 273
Dreams:
  characteristics, 271
  hallucinatory nature of, 271
  illusory components, 271
  latent content, 274
  manifest content, 274–275
  objective evidence, 272
  recall of, 272
Drive:
  primary sources, 319
  sources, 317
  theory, 318
  unitary concept of, 318–319
Dualism, primitive belief in, 1

Ear, anatomy, 133–134
Eardrum, 133
Ectoderm, 36

EEG (electroencephalogram), nature, 57–59
Effector, types, 39–40
Ego involvement, learning and, 238
Emotion:
  meanings, 332–333
  motivation and, 332–333
Endocrine system, 64–68
"Engram," 184
Entoderm, 36
Environment:
  enriched, 189
  impoverished, 189
Escape training, 165–166
Experimentation, as source of data, 26
Exploration, 331
Extinction:
  punishment and, 173–174
  schedules of reinforcement and, 178–179

Fear:
  conditioning, 338
  drive effects, 338–339
  early experience and, 343
  energizing effects, 338–339
  innateness, 343–344
  overt manifestation, 346–347
  persistence, 344–345
  reduction, 341–342
Field dependence, 123
Field independence, 123
Field observation:
  participant-observer, 23
  research method, 23
Fixed idea, 277
Forgetting:
  course of, 227–228
  interference theory, 240–243
  motivation and, 243–244
  organic causes, 239–240
  perseveration-consolidation hypothesis, 244
  proactive interference and, 243
  repression and, 243
  retroactive interference, 240–241
  theories, 239–246
Form discrimination, cortical localization, 189
Frustration:
  conflicts as source, 363
Frustration (continued)
  response delay as, 360–361
  thwarting and, 361–362

Ganglia, 44
Generalization, stimulus, 170–171
Goal, 314
Gradients of texture, 126
Gregariousness, 354
Group:
  norms, 384
  reference, 386–387

Higher-order conditioning, 175–176
Histogram, 397
Homeostasis:
  definition of, 321
  motivation and, 321–322
Hot, elementary sensory components, 141
Hue, stimulus determinants of, 113
Hunger, physiological correlates, 327–328
Hydrocephalus, 48
Hypnotism, 5

Ideation:
  as a neural process, 265
  overt response and, 265
Identity, search for, 389
Illumination, problem solving and, 255
Illusions:
  definition, 99
  distorted-room, 98
  examples of, 99–102
  explanations of, 100–101
  idiosyncratic, 103
Imagination:
  productive, 278
  reproductive, 278
Imitation:
  conditioning in, 197–198
  descriptive nature of, 196
  explanatory value of, 195–196
  reinforcement in, 199–201
Incubation, problem solving and, 254
Incus (anvil), 133
Insight:
  descriptive nature of, 201–202
Insight (continued)
  prior experience and, 202
  trial-and-error and, 201–202
Instinct, current status of concept, 317
Instrumental conditioning:
  classical conditioning and, 164–165
  escape training as, 165–166
  positive-reward training as, 166–167
  reinforcement in, 177–182
  reinforcing successive approximations in, 168
  trial-and-error learning as, 169–170
  varieties of, 164
Intellectually superior children:
  academic achievements of, 293
  adult status of, 294
  personality characteristics, 294
  physical characteristics of, 293
  social traits of, 294
  Terman's study of, 293
Intelligence:
  distribution of, 291–297
  hereditability values, 299
  measurement of, 286
  nature-nurture variables in, 299
  race and, 298–302
  sex and, 299
  tests of, 286–288
Intelligence quotient (IQ):
  calculation of, 289
  changes in, 308
  constancy of, 303–304
  foster-children status, 306
  sources of variability, 303–304
  twin variability, 305
  uses of, 305
  variability and age, 304
Intelligence tests:
  Binet's contribution, 286
  group, 291
  as measures of current performance, 289
  Stanford-Binet, 288
Interposition, 125
Intervening variables, 158
Isolation, 388

Just noticeable difference (JND), 5, 176

Kinesthetic sense:
adequate stimuli for, 145
importance of, 144
location of receptors, 145

Labyrinthine sense:
adequate stimuli for, 145–149
receptors for, 146
Language:
acquisition of, 90
motivation by, 349–350
rules of, 90–91
Language acquisition, rule learning in, 263
Lateral geniculate, 116
Learning:
attempting recall and, 210–211
attitude and, 201
cortical functions in, 185–187
cortical localization in, 185
criteria of, 203–204
definition of, 158–159
distribution of practice and, 205–207
DNA and, 190–191
imitation as a form of, 195–200
importance of, 160
inferential evidences for, 158
knowledge of results and, 207
measuring progress in, 203–205
neural growth in, 189
neural locus of, 187–188
physiological bases of, 184–192
RNA and, 190–192
role of repetition in, 212
size of units and, 209–210
strain differences in, 186
synaptic resistance in, 189
theories of, 215–217
transfer of, 212–215
universality of, 160
vicarious functioning in, 186
Learning sets, 215
Learning theory:
cognitive, 216–217
current trends, 217–218
omnibus vs. miniature forms of, 217–218
Learning theory (continued)
stimulus-response type, 216–217
Linear perspective, 124–125
"Looming," 104–105
Loudness, stimulus determinants of, 130

Malleus (hammer), 133
Manifest anxiety scale, 345–346
Manipulation, 331
Massed practice, 205–206
Maze learning, cortical localization for, 185–186
Mean:
definition of, 30
standard error of, 407
Meaningfulness, learning and, 207–208
Mechanical ability, measures of, 309
Mechanism, behavior, 367
Mechanistic behavioral conceptions, 3
Median, 30, 398
Medulla oblongata, 45
Memory:
definition of, 224–225
learning and, 221
long-term, 245–246
RNA and, 240
short-term, 245–246
two-process theory of, 245–246
Memory trace, 222
Mental age, meaning of, 287
Mental retardation:
causes, 292
differing degrees, 293
endogenous causes, 292
exogenous causes, 292
incidence of, 292
variability of, 292
Mental set:
inflexibility and, 257
reasoning and, 257–258
Mesencephalon, 45
Mesoderm, 36
Mind, conceptions of, 14
Mode, 400
Motivation:
achievement, 356–357
acquired sources, 337
affectional tendencies and, 353
Motivation (continued)
animistic conception, 314–315
anxiety and, 338
arousal and, 324
components, 313-314
drive and, 314
emotion and, 332-333
fear and, 338
historical conceptions, 314–317
hunger as a source, 325–327
instincts and, 315–317
language and, 349–350
noxious stimuli and, 328–329
prestige-oriented, 355–356
reasoning and, 251–252
role of stimulation in, 322–324
sexual, 329–330
stimulus characteristics and, 330–331
thirst as a source, 325–327
Motive:
classes of, 352
function of cues, 351–352
money seeking as, 352–353
Motor cortical areas, overlap with sensory, 63
Musical abilities, tests of, 310
Myelin sheath, 42

Need, 314, 320–321
Nerve impulse:
electrical nature of, 5
nature of, 42–43
rate of transmission, 5
Nerves:
cranial, 44
spinal, 44
Nervous system:
coding of nerve impulses in, 55–57
growth of, 59–60
spontaneous activity of, 57–58
subdivisions of, 44
Neural coding, 77
Neural crest, 37
Neural discharges, binary nature of, 44
Neural groove, 37
Neural plate, 37
Neurilemma, 42
Neuron:
nature of, 41
parts of, 41–42

Neuron (continued)
types of, 42
Nonconformity, 382–383
Normlessness, 388
Norms:
contrived, 384
group, 384
Noxious stimulation, 328

Objectivity:
definition, 285
how obtained, 285
Obsessions, 277
"Obstacle sense," 26–29
Olfaction:
adequate stimuli for, 152
elementary qualities, 152
Optic nerve, regeneration, 60
Organic sense:
adequate stimuli for, 153–154
components, 153
location, 153
Organism, irritability of, 75
Out-group, 387
Ovaries, 66
Overlearning, massed practice and, 231

Pain, adequate stimuli for, 143–144
Pancreas, 67
Paradoxical cold, 141
Paradoxical warmth, 141
Parathyroid, 66
Percentile score, 401
Perception:
closure, 94–95
constancy, 95–98
determinants, 91–93
field dependence, 107
field independence, 107
hypothesis selection in, 89
innate discriminations in, 104–105
meaning components, 91
motivational states and, 93
organizational principles, 94–95
organized nature, 94–95
personality variables, 106–108
reduced cues, 91–92
sensory components, 91
"sets" in, 91
shape constancy, 95–96
Perception (continued)
size constancy, 95–96
social, 106
stimulus-detection theory, 89
Perceptual constancy, 95–98
Perseveration-consolidation hypothesis, 244
"Personal equation," 5
Personality:
abnormal, 376–377
child-rearing practices and, 375–376
constitutional factors, 369
definition, 367–368
determinants, 369–371
early experiences and, 374
environmental influences, 373–376
genetic factors, 369–370
physique and, 370
response aspect, 368
social-interaction aspect, 368
stimulus-value component, 368
Philosophy, psychological roots in, 2–3
Phi-phenomenon, 102–103
Physiological limit, 205
Physiological zero, 140
Physiology, psychology's roots in, 4
Physique:
cultural ideals, 372
social evaluations, 371
Pitch, stimulus determinant, 130
Pituitary, 67
Placenta, 67
Plateau, 204
Polygon, 397
Pons, 45
Positive-reward training, 166-167
Powerlessness, 388
Proactive interference, 243
Processes, social, 378
Prosencephalon, 45
Psychological data, sources, 14–19
Psychological distance, 363
Psychological processes, reification, 12–13
"Psychological safety," 270
Psychology:
biosocial nature, 10
definitions, 7–9
Psychology (continued)
relation to other sciences, 9–10
terminology, 11
Punishment, 173–174

Questionnaire:
limitations, 24
source of data, 24

Range, 30
Reaction, delayed, 224
Reasoning:
autonomous motivation, 252
decisions made without, 259
definition, 250
Dewey's description, 250–251
divergent thinking in, 253
emotional bias and, 258–259
factors influencing, 256–259
hypotheses in, 253–254
illumination in, 255
incubation in, 254
"mental set" and, 279–280
motivation for, 251–252
preparation in, 253
recognition of problem, 252–253
relevant information and, 256
sensitivity to problems in, 253
steps, 255–256
utilitarian motivation, 252
verification in, 255
Wallas' stages, 250
Recall:
distortions in, 236–237
stimulus situations and, 237–238
Receptors, nature, 39
Refractory period, 43
Reinforcement:
amount, 179–180
delay, 180–181
fear reduction as, 341–342
fixed-interval schedules, 177–178
imitation and, 199–201
partial, 177–178
schedules, 177–180
secondary, 181–182
variable-ratio schedules, 178–179
Reliability:
coefficient, 284

Reliability (continued)
definition, 284
minimal requirements, 285
split-half, 284
test-retest, 284
Repression, 243
Retention:
delayed reaction as evidence, 224–225
dynamic factors in, 235–236
ego involvement and, 238–239
evidences of, 222-223
factors affecting, 228–237
general concepts and, 232
"intention" and, 233–234
level of original learning and, 229–230
meaningfulness and, 231–233
measurement, 225–227
motor vs. ideational materials, 235
overlearning and, 229–230
periodic recall and, 234–235
rate of original learning and, 228–229
recall as measure, 225
recognition as index, 225
relearning as measure of, 226–227
"savings" method of measurement, 223
specific details and, 232
Retina:
functional layers, 116
receptor cells, 116
rods and cones, 116
Retinal disparity, 127
Retinal image, distortions, 62
Retroactive interference, similarity and, 241
Rhombencephalon, 45
RNA, 39, 190–192, 240
Rods, differential distributions, 120
Roles:
sex, 382
social, 381

Sampling, errors, 406
Saturation, stimulus determinants, 114
Science, role of measurement, 29
Scientific method, characteristics, 15–19
Scientific methodology:
nature, 21–23
philosophical assumptions, 19–21
Score:
standard, 403
t, 403
Senility, RNA and, 191
Sensory cortical areas, overlap with motor, 63
Sex:
drive function, 354
roles, 382
Sex glands, 66
Size constancy, innateness, 105
Skew, negative, 400
Skill, acquisition, 202–212
Skinner box, 167, 201
Sleep:
EEG activity and, 272
ideational activity in, 272
Sleep deprivation, effects of, 274
Social:
action, 389
conformity, 382
nonconformity, 382
roles, 381
Social class, importance, 380–381
Socialization, 378
Spaced practice, 205–209
Special abilities, 309–311
Specific nerve energies, 4
Spontaneous recovery, 172–173
Stabilimeter, 339
Standard deviation, 402–403
Standard error, critical ratio and, 407
Stanford-Binet test:
administration, 289
description, 288
Stapes (stirrup), 133
Statistical significance, 31
Statistics:
descriptive, 393
inferential, 406
Stimulus:
definition, 76
encoding, 77
exteroceptive, 76
noxious, 328
proprioceptive, 76
transduction of, 77
Stimulus generalization, examples of, 171–172
Summation tones, 132
Symbolic processes, delayed reactions as evidence, 224
Synapse, 43

Tabula rasa concept of mind, 3
Taste:
adequate stimuli, 148–149
elementary experiences, 149
receptors, 148–149
"Taste blindness," 151
Technology, scientific investigation and, 22
Testes, 66
Thalamus, 116
Thermal sense, adequate stimuli, 140–141
Thinking:
neuromuscular activity in, 264–266
paranoid forms, 276
pathological forms, 276–277
physiological processes in, 264–266
psychotic, 277
Thirst, physiological correlates, 327–328
Threshold:
absolute, 78
differential, 79
sensory, 78–79
Thwarting:
personal characteristics and, 361
social sources, 362
Thyroid, 66
Timbre, stimulus determinants, 130
"Tip-of-the-tongue" (TOT) phenomenon, 236
Touch:
adequate stimuli, 142–143
differential sensitivity, 123
Transfer of learning:
enhancement of, 214–215
identical-element theory of, 213–214
"learning to learn" in, 215
mental discipline and, 212
transposition and, 214
Transposition, 214
Trial-and-error learning, components, 169–170

T-scores, 403
Tympanic membrane, 133

Unconditioned response (UR), 162
Unconditioned stimulus (US), cortical stimulation as, 188
Understanding:
  feeling level, 17
  levels of, 17–18

Valence:
  negative, 363
  positive, 363
Validity:
  coefficient, 282
Validity (continued)
  definition, 281
  examples, 282
  specificity of, 284
  statistical measures of, 282
Verifiability, in scientific research, 22
Verification, problem solving and, 255
Vicarious functioning, 186
Vision:
  adequate stimuli, 112
  color, 118–120
  cortical areas, 117
  neural coding in, 117
  stimulus variables, 112
Visual accommodation, 128
"Visual cliff," 104
Visual convergence, 127
Visual distortions, adjustment to, 61–62
Visual field, 115
Visual perception, retinal disparity in, 127
Visual stimuli, dimensions, 113–115

Weber's law, 79
Wechsler Adult Intelligence Scale (WAIS), characteristics, 289–290
Wechsler-Bellevue Intelligence Scale (WISC), characteristics, 290